TURNING POINTS IN
American Educational History

A BLAISDELL BOOK IN EDUCATION

CONSULTING EDITOR

John I. Goodlad, University of California at Los Angeles

Turning Points in

AMERICAN EDUCATIONAL HISTORY

EDITED AND WITH INTRODUCTIONS
by *David B. Tyack*

BLAISDELL PUBLISHING COMPANY

A DIVISION OF GINN AND COMPANY

Waltham, Massachusetts · Toronto · London

For Peter and Daniel

FOREWORD

Professor Tyack's *Turning Points in American Educational History* will be welcomed by tired readers of treatises (or readers of tired treatises) on educational history. Certainly, there has not been a plethora of stimulating texts to aid inquiry in this field.

Three of the many features stand out. First, the turning points which Professor Tyack has so discerningly selected are placed within the larger context of their times. They *are* educational turning points simply because this country was at turning points in its own swift transition from epoch to epoch. Education is seen as larger than schools and schools, in turn, are seen as reflecting people, conventional wisdom, and events in the emerging society. This is how to treat history meaningfully, but the author is one of only a few educational historians who have so favored us.

Second, Professor Tyack has dusted off for our reading pleasure a fascinating array of primary documents: letters, diaries, memoirs, pages from schoolbooks of the time. As one who majored in history at college, I speak feelingly on this point. Only one course brought me into the real stuff of history and close to the method of historians. All the rest drew upon secondary and tertiary source materials, too often dry summaries and trite generalizations. Some readers of this volume may well experience for the first time, then, the fun of identifying with and speculating about other times and other places.

Third, Professor Tyack has achieved a masterful balance between his introduction to each cluster of selections and the selections themselves. Through the former, he provides a perspective by means of which the latter take on a fullness which otherwise might be lacking, at least for the neophyte in this field. But even the specialist will profit from these essays, if only to sharpen his own disagreements. In his choice of readings, the author shoots with a rifle: not using second-hand generalizations but, instead, the letter of an immigrant, newly arrived; the proposals of a schoolman-politician; or the papers of a then-President of the United States.

There is plenty to discuss: Professor Tyack's interpretations, the extent to which his selections are properly representative, and, of course, the times that the combination of these two are designed to reveal. Classes in the history of American education are certain to be enlivened and enlightened by Professor Tyack's book.

JOHN I. GOODLAD

CONTENTS

INTRODUCTION

The mapping of the terrain of American educational history has been transformed in recent years. Historians have become newly aware of the crucial role of education in shaping American society; educators have sought new perspectives on the past as they attempt to chart their way into the uncertain future. This book of primary sources and interpretive essays is an exploration of the fascinating and complex topography of our educational history.

In 1954 a group of distinguished American historians met "to discuss the need of studying the role of education, not in its institutional forms alone but in terms of all the influences that have helped to shape the rising generation." This meeting, and the subsequent formation of a Committee on the Role of Education in American History, marked a new and fruitful interest of general American historians in the impact of education on American society. As the Committee members observed, education "may be approached from two different directions. The historian may ask how it has come to take the shape it has. The end product of research in this case is an explanation of the character education has acquired as a creation of society. Or the historian may—and we trust he will—approach education, saying: Here is a constellation of institutions—what difference have they made in the life of the society around them?"

Historians have interpreted the history of education to include far more than schooling and its impact. In its most inclusive terms, educational history has been defined by Bernard Bailyn as the study of "the entire process by which a culture transmits itself across the generations." Thus construed, the field sweeps beyond formal instruction to include family and church, library and youth groups, and all the other varied means of shaping intellect and character. Whether the historian of education adopts the larger cultural definition or restricts himself to the role of schools, clearly the study of education will assume an increasingly important place in general historical research and teaching. It will help to answer puzzling questions in social history: the assimilation of millions of immigrants of dozens of nations; the cultural flowering of cities in the wilderness; the development of our patterns of political belief and action.

To intellectual history the study of education will give clues concerning the conceptual equipment of each generation.

This new view of the role of education in American society locates educational history as a legitimate part of liberal education, comparable to the study of political institutions, beliefs, and processes. As an enterprise which occupies one out of four Americans, education obviously warrants careful analysis by any thoughtful citizen.

The new interest in education among general historians encourages those who see educational history as a neglected cultural study, but it raises questions about the field as part of the professional preparation of teachers. If one may claim that educational history is a valid part of anyone's liberal education, does it have any particular importance for teachers? I believe that it does.

As *general* education for teachers, educational history can rarely be useful or functional in a narrow sense. Instead it should be a kind of knowledge which is interesting and valuable in its own right, though it also can give educators lasting insights and habits of analysis which will benefit them professionally. Inquiry into educational history can assist teachers to interpret and generalize their experience and to free themselves from unexamined routine.

Perhaps no institution in our society is more constricted by unexamined tradition and unconscious ritual than the school. In order either to attack or defend tradition intelligently, one first needs to understand it. Consider the countless cases in which we assume that the educational practices of the present stem from some inscrutable and ineluctable past: the Carnegie unit, for example, seems not to be the outworn reform of an earlier era, now become a tribal ceremony, but a sacred convention—that is, until it is examined in the light of its time and our own. One reason why education is subject to monotonous cycles of reform and reaction is that few recognize that today's headache is the result of last night's binge. As the Committee on the Role of Education in American History observed, a faulty knowledge of our educational history has "affected adversely the planning of curricula, the formulation of policy, and the administration of educational agencies in the continuing crisis of American education." All thoughtful citizens have a stake in education; teachers have a vested interest.

In studying institutional traditions and alternative options, teachers need to understand the social role and context of education conceived both as schooling and, more broadly, as cultural transmission. What tasks has society assigned to various social agencies in different periods and why? How have educational innovators operated both within and without the educational system? How has the actual change matched

the intent of the reformers? What have been the unintended consequences or unperceived results of reforms? What have been the various
models for the transaction of school and society? Ours is an educational
system peculiarly responsive to the community. What effect has this
responsiveness, or vulnerability, had at different times in our history?
Who made educational decisions? On what grounds? What alternate decisions might have been made, and what might their consequences have
been? What have been the lost causes and permanent innovations? By
examining our educational history in this open-ended manner, by investigating the options, the individual and group decisions, the social conditions that restricted or expanded choices, teachers may become aware of
actual opportunities and the necessity for wise decisions in the present.
Otherwise they may be perpetuating an unexamined relation of school
and society by default or indulging in utopian daydreaming. History as
embodied in institutions and attitudes has a momentum which deflects
naive attempts at reform, but history perceptively grasped can assist
needed innovation and conservation.

To understand educational history one needs to become a historian
himself. The best way to do this is to encounter the primary sources
from which historians construct interpretations. These sources are legion:
laws and letters, autobiographies and demographic data, speeches and
eyewitness accounts, philosophical writings and children's textbooks.
What criteria can guide a significant selection of sources and topics from
such a plethora of materials? In the present state of investigation into
the role of education in American history, no selection can pretend to be
comprehensive or authoritative.

Although I have attempted to indicate the wealth and variety of our
educational traditions in the primary sources included in this book, I have
aimed at depth rather than breadth. While not neglecting the broader
definition of education as cultural transmission, I have selected sources
which deal largely with formal schooling (and have concentrated mostly
on elementary and secondary schools since Richard Hofstadter and Wilson Smith have edited an excellent two-volume set of sources on higher
education *). I have chosen topics which illustrate conflicts of value and
turning points in our educational heritage and have not hesitated to state
my own views on the ideological issues expressed in the readings. At the
same time, I have sought not to provide set answers but rather to disclose
issues worthy of further exploration and discussion. I am much indebted to colleagues and students who have helped me to collect and
interpret these sources.

---

* *American Higher Education: A Documentary History* (Chicago: University of
Chicago Press, 1961).

Often in times of acute change men become deeply concerned about familiar institutions. So it has been with schools. Grave challenges prompted Americans sometimes to cling to the old with new vigor and awareness, sometimes to seek new means to preserve old values, sometimes to alter or retain attitudes and institutions with blind disregard for causes and consequences. While recognizing ways in which impersonal forces have circumscribed individual decisions, I have focused on the privilege and burden of choice in past and present. Roads not taken as well as roads taken have shaped our history and our options today.

TURNING POINTS IN
American Educational History

A City upon a Hill: 1

Education in the Massachusetts Bay Colony

To the Puritans the world, seen and unseen, was intensely dramatic.
All history, all knowledge, all everyday experience constituted God's
education of man. Ardently the Puritans sought to interpret the meaning of this education, for thereby God disclosed the means of salvation
and the path of righteous conduct. Their quest was an anxious one, for
God could not be expected to conform to human standards of reason,
justice, or mercy. Insofar as God had revealed his will in the Bible and
in His covenant with His chosen people, the Puritans had a guide; and in
the Biblical Commonwealth of Massachusetts Bay they meant to establish a city upon a hill, a home for saints and a model for the regeneration
of Christendom.

In contrast to their copious works on theology, the Puritans wrote
little explicitly about formal education. This hardly reveals indifference, for the Puritans desired literacy and learning so zealously that
they quickly established schools in the wilderness of New England. So
deeply rooted in their total pattern of thought and feeling were Puritan
assumptions about education that it is misleading to concentrate solely
on the external features of Puritan education—the types of schools, the
nature of support and control, and the details of the curriculum. By
focusing on these external features a pioneer educational historian, Ellwood P. Cubberley, came to the conclusion that the Puritan educational
laws of 1642 and 1647 were "the very foundation-stones upon which our
American public school systems have been founded." But when seen in
the context of the times by imaginative projection into their world, the
educational achievement of the Puritans emerges more as an anxious attempt to conserve old traditions amid the threat of new conditions than

1

as a new and daring venture which led to our present public educational system.

The chief teacher in the Massachusetts Bay Colony was the preacher, often called "master."

> After God had carried us safe to *New-England*, and wee had builded our houses, provided necessaries for our liveli-hood, rear'd convenient places for Gods worship, and setled the Civill Government: One of the next things we longed for, and looked after was to advance *Learning* and perpetuate it to Posterity; dreading to leave an illiterate Ministery to the Churches, when our present Ministers shall lie in the Dust.

So said the author of *New Englands First Fruits* in describing the motives for founding Harvard College in 1636. The Puritans needed skilled leaders, clerical and lay, to guide the Biblical Commonwealth. For hours in the icy cold of winter and the soggy heat of summer congregations listened to intricate sermons in bare meeting houses. All the institutions of society—school, church, family, civil government—had a common ultimate purpose: the salvation of the individual. Convinced that man was fallen and could be saved from endless damnation only by the infusion of God's grace—a gift he vouchsafed only to the elect—the Puritans sought a knowledge inseparable from faith and a faith inseparable from regeneration and saintly conduct.

"It's with an ignorant sinner in the midst of all means," said Thomas Hooker, "as with a sick man in an Apothecaries shop, full of the choicest medicines in the darkest night: though there be the choicest of all receipts at hand, and he may take what he needs, yet because he cannot see what he takes, and how to use them, he may kill himself, or increase his distempers, but never cure any disease." The humblest Puritan had to be able to read the word of God. His ministers needed the sharpest tools of scholarship—logic and Biblical languages especially—in order to interpret that word correctly, for the task was for more than mortal stakes.

In a time of high infant mortality Puritans wasted little time in instructing their children. As one of the verses in the *New England Primer* said,

> I in the burying place may see
> Graves shorter there than I;
> From Death's arrest no age is free,
> Young children too may die.
> My God, may such an awful sight,
> Awakening be to me!
> Oh! that by early grace I might
> For Death prepared be.

Through the diaries of many Puritan parents runs a common note of concern for their children's spiritual health, of worry at times that their children might be too cheerful and carefree. A child was not only ignorant but sinful in nature. His parents and teachers had a sacred obligation to instill proper beliefs and habits in him, since truth and virtue had to be imposed from the outside on the inherently wayward child. The child was warned that he stood on the edge of an abyss: "You are all naturally in a miserable state and condition," said Jonathan Edwards, the great eighteenth-century theologian. "In a little while you will be in eternity, some sooner and some later. . . . God is angry with you every day. How dreadful to have God angry with you. How dreadful it will be to be in Hell among the devils and to know that you must be there to all eternity. Consider how it will be when you come to die and are unconverted." Today such sermons and the dreary pages of the *New England Primer* seem morbid at best and sadistic at worst, but the abyss was a fact to the Puritans and hence their concern. Fear might hasten repentance, and repentance might precede God's pardoning of sin and act of regeneration. The Puritans did not believe that correct belief and upright behavior alone would save a child, but as Edmund Morgan has observed, they thought "it was unlikely that he would be saved without them."

The Puritans were "moral athletes." After crossing an angry sea and enduring the trials of the wilderness to create a model society, they were of no mind to tolerate sloth and disorder. When parents slighted the Christian education of their children, the leaders of the colony did not stand idly by. The acts of the General Court in 1642 and 1648 reveal indignation at the "great neglect in many parents and masters in training up their children in learning, and labor." In England the family played a crucial role in the transfer of culture across the generations, and Puritan social thought placed heavy burdens of religious socialization upon the family. The two acts of the 1640's, together with other evidence, indicate widespread concern about the weakening of the family's role and worry over juvenile delinquency in the city upon a hill. If parents neglected their duty to teach their children to read, to catechize them, and to teach them some useful employment, then the state had to intervene by taking the children from their parents or masters. The Commonwealth could not permit children to grow up "rude, stubborn and unruly." In 1646 the General Court passed a law stating that "if a man have a stubborn or rebellious son of sufficient years of understanding, viz. 16 who will not obey the voice of his father or the voice of his mother, and when they have chastened him will not harken to them, then shall his father and mother being his natural parents, lay hold on him, and bring him to the magistrates assembled in Court, and testify to them by sufficient evidence that this their son is stubborn and rebellious, and will not obey their voice and chastizement, but lives in sundry notorious crimes, *such a son will be put to death.*" (emphasis added)   The magistrates expressed concern again and again about "the dissolute lives and practices of such as doe live from under family government."

Clearly, citizens of a Biblical Commonwealth could not allow "sin and prophanes to increase."   The laws of 1642 and 1648 sought to buttress traditional family structure and the system of apprenticeship by requiring compulsory literacy and job training, not, it should be noted, by compulsory *schooling*.   These laws expressed, as Bernard Bailyn has written, "a sudden awareness, a heightened consciousness of what the family had meant in education, of how much of the burden of imparting civilization to the young it had borne, and of what its loss might mean. . . ." Now certain tasks of socialization which had been done unconsciously in a more static social order needed to be explicitly defined.   A new self-consciousness about education emerged.   The experience of life in the wilderness altered familiar patterns of authority: often the children adapted to the new environment more easily than their elders.   The abundance of land made it possible for young men to become independent and for the large patrilineal families to subdivide into nuclear units.   The older hierarchical order of society lost some of its force and some of its sanctions.

When the Puritans created schools, they sought to reproduce what they remembered of education in England.   Neither schooling nor architecture did the settlers innovate; nostalgia and fear of barbarism prompted them to imitate.   Harvard was based on its model Emmanuel College, Cambridge, where many of the leading colonists had been educated.   The classical curriculum and customs of the Latin grammar schools followed English precedent.   And the dame schools—in which housewives taught children to read in their homes—resembled those in countless villages in England.

Few external constraints inhibited departures from educational tradition. The American Puritans had free rein for innovation within the limitations of their modest financial resources.   They were relatively immune from control from the mother country and not embroiled in the terrible civil war which devastated England.   They were creating institutions anew and had no established old guard to unseat.   New conceptions of schooling abounded in England.   John Milton had sketched a bold plan of humanistic education in his tractate *Of Education;* the Commonwealth educators John Durie, Samuel Hartlib, and William Petty advocated reforms designed to make elementary schooling more utilitarian.

But struggling against cultural decline on the frontier, the American Puritans had little inclination to experiment, little desire to abandon familiar educational traditions.

In one respect, however, the Massachusetts General Court did make a new departure: educational finance. This departure was not so much a reasoned and deliberate policy as it was a desperate expedient. Typically in England schools had been supported by a variety of means: royal grants, benefactions of wealthy men, or guilds which created schools for the sons of members. Similarly, in the Massachusetts Bay Colony grammar schools in nine towns were founded by private benefactions. Lack of disposable wealth and reliable outlets for investment in the colony, however, led to difficulty. The Puritans found it necessary to supplement income from investments and tuition fees by various types of aid from the towns, including taxes levied on all householders. Schools had been plentiful in the old country, and the act of 1647 indicates that the General Court wished to uphold familiar standards by new means. The act offered alternative means of paying the teachers—"either by the parents or masters of such children, or by the inhabitants in genrall"—but made it clear that there was no debating *whether* a town should have a school. Taking advantage of local rivalries, the Court stimulated the establishment of grammar schools by forcing towns to "pay 5 pounds to the [nearest town school] till they shall performe this order." A new act passed in 1648 suggests that the two previous laws needed reinforcement. The language of this act of 1648 indicates that the Puritans were concerned less about the means of education than about the results: they wanted a rising generation which would be literate, pious, and industrious. The fact that the Court chose, among other devices, public support of schools was in a sense incidental to their intent.

The Puritans' new self-consciousness about the importance of schooling, their cautious new departure in "public" financing and control of schools, prefigured changes to come in American education. But the Puritan achievement in education is inseparable from their religious world view and from the trials they encountered in establishing a city upon a hill; it is misleading to read present views of public education into the Puritan experiment. The founding of public education as it is known today would stem from a new world view and new trials in the nineteenth century.

1.1   Professor Bernard Bailyn Discusses the English Inheritance of Puritan Society.

The forms of education assumed by the first generation of settlers in America were a direct inheritance from the medieval past. Serving the needs of a homogeneous, slowly changing rural society, they were largely instinctive and traditional, little articulated and little formalized. The most important agency in the transfer of culture was not formal institutions of instruction or public instruments of communication, but the family; and the character of family life in late sixteenth- and early seventeenth-century England is critical for understanding the history of education in colonial America.

The family familiar to the early colonists was a patrilineal group of extended kinship gathered into a single household. By modern standards it was large. Besides children, who often remained in the home well into maturity, it included a wide range of other dependents: nieces and nephews, cousins, and, except for families at the lowest rung of society, servants in filial discipline. In the Elizabethan family the conjugal unit was only the nucleus of a broad kinship community whose outer edges merged almost imperceptibly into the society at large.

The organization of this group reflected and reinforced the general structure of social authority. Control rested with the male head to whom all others were subordinate. His sanctions were powerful; they were rooted deep in the cultural soil. They rested upon tradition that went back beyond the memory of man; on the instinctive sense of order as hierarchy, whether in the cosmic chain of being or in human society; on the processes of law that reduced the female to perpetual dependency and calibrated a detailed scale of male subordination and servitude; and, above all, on the restrictions of the economy, which made the establishment of independent households a difficult enterprise.

It was these patriarchal kinship communities that shouldered most of the burden of education. They were, in the first place, the primary agencies in the socialization of the child. Not only did the family introduce him to the basic forms of civilized living, but it shaped his attitudes, formed his patterns of behavior, endowed him with manners and morals. It introduced him to the world; and in so doing reinforced the structure of its authority. For the world to the child was an intricate, mysterious contrivance in controlling which untutored skills, raw nature, mere vigor counted for less than knowledge and experience. The child's de-

Bernard Bailyn, *Education in the Forming of American Society: Needs and Opportunities for Study* (Chapel Hill: University of North Carolina Press, 1960), pp. 15–21. Reprinted by permission of the University of North Carolina Press.

pendence on his elders was not an arbitrary decree of fate; it was not only biologically but socially functional.

But the family's educational role was not restricted to elementary socialization. Within these kinship groupings, skills that provided at least the first step in vocational training were taught and practiced. In a great many cases, as among the agricultural laboring population and small tradesmen who together comprised the overwhelming majority of the population, all the vocational instruction necessary for mature life was provided by the family.

The family's role in vocational training was extended and formalized in a most important institution of education, apprenticeship. Apprenticeship was the contractual exchange of vocational training in an atmosphere of family nurture for absolute personal service over a stated period of years. Like other forms of bonded servitude, it was a condition of dependency, a childlike state of legal incompetence, in which the master's role, and responsibilities, was indistinguishable from the father's, and the servant's obligations were as total, as moral, and as personal as the son's. Servants of almost every degree were included within the family, and it was the family's discipline that most directly enforced the condition of bondage. The master's parental concern for his servants, and especially for apprentices, included care for their moral welfare as well as for their material condition. He was expected and required by law to bring them up in good Christian cultivation, and to see to their proper deportment.

What the family left undone by way of informal education the local community most often completed. It did so in entirely natural ways, for so elaborate was the architecture of family organization and so deeply founded was it in the soil of stable, slowly changing village and town communities in which intermarriage among the same groups had taken place generation after generation, that it was at times difficult for the child to know where the family left off and the greater society began. The external community, comprising with the family a continuous world, naturally extended instruction and discipline in work and in the conduct of life. And it introduced the youth in a most significant way to a further discipline, that of government and the state. So extensive and intricate were the community's involvements with the family and yet so important was its function as a public agency that the youth moved naturally and gradually across the border-line that separates the personal from the impersonal world of authority.

More explicit in its educational function than either family or community was the church. Aside from its role as formal educator exercised through institutions of pedagogy which it supported and staffed, in its primary purpose of serving the spiritual welfare and guarding the morals of the community it performed other less obvious but not less important educational functions. It furthered the introduction of the child to society by instructing him in the system of thought and imagery which underlay the culture's values and aims. It provided the highest sanctions for the accepted forms of behavior, and brought the child into close relationship with the intangible loyalties, the ethos and highest principles, of the society in which he lived. In this educational role, organized religion had a powerfully unifying influence. Indistinguishable at the parish level from the local community, agent and ward of the state, it served as a mechanism of social integration. In all its functions, and especially in those that may be called educational, its force was centripetal.

Family, community, and church together accounted for the greater part of the mechanism by which English culture transferred itself across the generations. The instruments of deliberate pedagogy, of explicit, literate education, accounted for a smaller, though indispensable, portion of the process. For all the interest in formal instruction shown in the century after the Reformation in England, and for all the extension of explicitly educational agencies, the span of pedagogy in the entire spectrum of education remained small. The cultural burdens it bore were relatively slight. Formal instruction in elementary and grammar schools, and in the university, was highly utilitarian. Its avowed purpose was the training of the individual for specific social roles. Of the love of letters, knowledge, and science for their own sakes in Elizabethan and Stuart England there was, needless to say, no lack; but the justification for formal education was not phrased in terms of the enrichment of the personality and the satisfactions of knowledge. Literacy had its uses required for the daily tasks of an increasing part of the population. Latin grammar and classical literature, far from being then the cultural ornaments they have since become, were practical subjects of instruction: as necessary for the physician as for the architect, as useful to the local functionary as to the statesman. Even the middle classes, for whom classical education had acquired a special meaning as a symbol of social ascent, justified their interest in grammar school training by reference to its moral and social utility. And the universities' function as professional schools had not been transformed by the influx of sons of gentle and noble families; it had merely been broadened to include training for public responsibility.

The sense of utility that dominated formal education was related in a significant way to the occupational structure of the society. Despite a considerable amount of occupational mobility, the normal expectation was that the child would develop along familiar lines, that the divergence of his career from that of his parents' and grandparents' would be limited, and that he could proceed with confidence and security along a well-worn path whose turnings and inclines had long been known and could be dealt with by measures specified by tradition.

Whatever their limitations by modern standards, formal institutions of instruction occupied a strategic place in English life, and they therefore fell within the concern of the state. But the role of the state in formal education, though forceful, was indirect. It was exhortatory, empowering, supervisory, regulatory; it was, with rare exceptions, neither initiating nor sustaining. Support for schools and universities was almost universally from private benefaction, usually in the form of land endowments; public taxation was rare and where it existed, local and temporary. The reliable support from endowment funds gave educational institutions above the elementary level a measure of autonomy, an independence from passing influences which allowed them to function conservatively, retarding rather than furthering change in their freedom from all but the most urgent pressures.

Of these characteristics of education as it existed in late sixteenth- and early seventeenth-century England prospective emigrants to America would hardly have been aware, and not simply because they were not habituated to think in such terms. They had little cause to probe the assumptions and circumstances that underlay their culture's self-perpetuation. The rapid expansion of instructional facilities of which they were witness had not sprung from dissatisfaction with the traditional modes of education, but from the opposite, from confidence, from satisfaction, and from the desire and the capacity to deal more fully, in familiar ways, with familiar social needs. The basis of education lay secure within the continuing traditions of an integrated, unified culture. The future might be uncertain, but the uncertainties were limited. Nothing disturbed the confident expectation that the world of the child's maturity would be the same as that of the parents' youth, and that the past would continue to be an effective guide to the future.

1.2   Governor John Winthrop Preaches a Sermon in 1630 on Board the Arbella en route to the Massachusetts Bay Colony: "A Modell of Christian Charity."

God Almightie in his most holy and wise providence hath soe disposed of the Condicion of mankined, as in all times some must be rich some

John Winthrop, "A Modell of Christian Charity," *The Winthrop Papers* (Boston: Massachusetts Historical Society, 1931), II, pp. 282–284, 292–295. Reprinted by permission of the Massachusetts Historical Society.

poore, some highe and eminent in power and dignite; others meane and in subieccion.

The Reason Hereof

1. Reas: *First*, to hold conformity with the rest of his workes, being delighted to shewe forthe the glory of his wisdome in the variety and differance of the Creatures and the glory of his power, in ordering all these differences for the preservacion and good of the whole, and the glory of his greatnes that as it is the glory of princes to haue many officers, soe this great King will haue many Stewards counting himselfe more honoured in dispenceing his guifts to man by man, then if hee did it by his owne immediate hand.

2. Reas: *Secondly*, That he might haue the more occasion to manifest the worke of his Spirit: first, vpon the wicked in moderateing and restraineing them: soe that the riche and mighty should not eate vpp the poore, nor the poore, and dispised rise vpp against theire superiours, and shake off theire yoake; 2ly in the regenerate in exerciseing his graces in them, as in the greate ones, theire loue mercy, gentlenes, temperance etc., in the poore and inferiour sorte, theire faithe, patience, obedience etc:

3. Reas: *Thirdly*, That every man might haue need of other, and from hence they might be all knitt more nearly together in the Bond of brotherly affeccion: from hence it appeares plainely that noe man is made more honourable then another or more wealthy etc., out of any perticuler and singuler respect to himselfe but for the glory of his Creator and the Common good of the Creature, Man; Therefore God still reserues the property of these guifts to himselfe as Ezek: 16. 17. he there calls wealthe his gold and his silver etc. Prov: 3. 9. he claimes theire seruice as his due honour the Lord with thy riches etc. All men being thus (by divine providence) rancked into two sortes, riche and poore; vnder the first, are comprehended all such as are able to liue comfortably by theire owne meanes duely improued; and all others are poore according to the former distribution. There are two rules whereby wee are to walke one towards another: JUSTICE and MERCY. These are allwayes distinguished in theire Act and in theire obiect, yet may they both concurre in the same Subiect in eache respect; as sometimes there may be an occasion of shewing mercy to a rich man, in some sudden danger of distresse, and allsoe doeing of meere Justice to a poor man in regard of some perticuler contract etc. There is likewise a double Lawe by which wee are regulated in our conversacion one towardes another: in both the former respects, the lawe of nature and the lawe of grace, or the morrall lawe or the lawe of the gospell, to omitt the rule of Justice as not propperly belonging to this purpose

otherwise then it may fall into consideracion in some perticuler Cases: By the first of these lawes man as he was enabled soe withall [is] commaunded to loue his neighbour as himselfe vpon this ground stands all the precepts of the morrall lawe, which concernes our dealings with men.   To apply this to the works of mercy this lawe requires two things first that every man afford his help to another in every want or distresse Secondly, That hee performe this out of the same affeccion, which makes him carefull of his owne good according to that of our Saviour Math: [7.12] Whatsoever ye would that men should doe to you.   This was practised by Abraham and Lott in entertaineing the Angells and the old man of Gibea.

The Lawe of Grace or the Gospell hath some differance from the former as in these respectes first the lawe of nature was giuen to man in the estate of innocency; this of the gospell in the estate of regeneracy: 2ly, the former propounds one man to another, as the same fleshe and Image of god, this is a brother in Christ allsoe, and in the Communion of the same spirit and soe teacheth vs to put a difference betweene Christians and others. Doe good to all especially to the household of faith; vpon this ground the Israelites were to putt a difference betweene the brethren of such as were strangers though not of the Canaanites.   3ly. The Lawe of nature could giue noe rules for dealeing with enemies for all are to be considered as freinds in the estate of innocency, but the Gospell commaunds loue to an enemy. proofe.   If thine Enemie hunger feede him; Loue your Enemies doe good to them that hate you Math: 5. 44. . . . .

From the former Consideracions ariseth these Conclusions.

1. First, This loue among Christians is a reall thing not Imaginarie.

2ly. This loue is as absolutely necessary to the being of the body of Christ, as the sinewes and other ligaments of a naturall body are to the being of that body.

3ly. This loue is a divine spirituall nature free, actiue strong Couragious permanent vnder valueing all things beneathe its propper obiect, and of all the graces this makes vs nearer to resemble the virtues of our heavenly father.

4ly, It restes in the loue and wellfare of its beloued, for the full and certaine knowledge of these truthes concerning the nature vse, [and] excellency of this grace, that which the holy ghost hath left recorded 1. Cor. 13. may giue full satisfaccion which is needfull for every true member of this louely body of the Lord Jesus, to worke vpon theire heartes, by prayer meditacion continuall exercise at least of the speciall [power] of this grace till Christ be formed in them and they in him all in eache other knitt together by this bond of loue.

It rests now to make some applicacion of this discourse by the present designe which gaue the occasion of writeing of it.   Herein are 4 things to be propounded: first the persons, 2ly, the worke, 3ly, the end, 4ly the meanes.

1. For the persons, wee are a Company professing our selues fellow members of Christ, In which respect only though wee were absent from eache other many miles, and had our imploymentes as farre distant, yet wee ought to account our selues knitt together by this bond of loue, and liue in the exercise of it, if wee would haue comforte of our being in Christ, this was notorious in the practise of the Christians in former times, as is testified of the Waldenses from the mouth of one of the adversaries Aeneas Syluius, mutuo [solent amare] penè antequam norint, they vse to loue any of theire owne religion even before they were acquainted with them.

2ly. for the worke wee haue in hand, it is by a mutuall consent through a speciall overruleing providence, and a more then an ordinary approbation of the Churches of Christ to seeke out a place of Cohabitation and Consorteshipp vnder a due forme of Government both ciuill and ecclesiasticall. In such cases as this the care of the publique must oversway all private respects, by which not onely conscience, but meare Ciuill pollicy doth binde vs; for it is a true rule that perticuler estates cannott subsist in the ruine of the publique.

3ly. The end is to improue our liues to doe more seruice to the Lord the comforte and encrease of the body of christe whereof wee are members that our selues and posterity may be the better preserued from the Common corrupcions of this euill world to serue the Lord and worke out our Salvacion vnder the power and purity of his holy Ordinances.

4ly. for the meanes whereby this must bee effected, they are 2fold, a Conformity with the worke and end wee aime at, these wee see are extraordinary, therefore wee must not content our selues with vsuall ordinary means whatsoever wee did or ought to haue done when wee liued in England, the same must wee doe and more allsoe where wee goe: That which the most in theire Churches maineteine as a truthe in profession onely, wee must bring into familiar and constant practise, as in this duty of loue wee must loue brotherly without dissimulation, wee must loue one another with a pure hearte feruently wee must beare one anothers burthens, wee must not looke onely on our owne things, but allsoe on the things of our brethren, neither must wee think that the lord will beare with such faileings at our hands as hee dothe from those among whome wee haue liued, and that for 3 Reasons.

1. In regard of the more neare bond of mariage, betweene him and vs, wherein he hath taken vs to be his after a most strickt and peculiar manner which will make him the more Jealous of our loue and obedience soe he tells the people of Israell, you onely haue I knowne of all the families of the Earthe therefore will I punishe you for your Transgressions.

2ly. because the lord will be sanctified in them that come neare him. Wee know that there were many that corrupted the seruice of the Lord some setting vpp Alters before his owne, others offering both strange fire and strange Sacrifices allsoe; yet there came noe fire from heaven, or other sudden Judgement vpon them as did vpon Nadab and Abihu whoe yet wee may thinke did not sinne presumptuously.

3ly. When God giues a speciall Commission he lookes to haue it stricktly obserued in every Article, when hee gaue Saule a Commission to destroy Amaleck hee indented with him vpon certaine Articles and because hee failed in one of the least, and that vpon a faire pretence it lost him the kingdome, which should haue beene his reward, if hee had obserued his Commission: Thus stands the cause betweene God and vs, wee are entered into Covenant with him for this worke, wee haue taken out a Commission, the Lord hath giuen vs leaue to drawe our owne Articles wee haue professed to enterprise these Accions vpon these and these ends, wee haue herevpon besought him of favour and blessing: Now if the Lord shall please to heare vs, and bring vs in peace to the place wee desire, then hath hee ratified this Covenant and sealed our Commission, [and] will expect a strickt performance of the Articles contained in it, but if wee shall neglect the observacion of these Articles which are the ends wee haue propounded, and dissembling with our God, shall fall to embrace this present world and prosecute our carnall intencions, seekeing great things for our selues and our posterity, the Lord will surely breake out in wrathe against vs be revenged of such a periured people and make vs knowe the price of the breache of such a Covenant.

Now the onely way to avoyde this shipwracke and to provide for our posterity is to followe the Counsell of Micah, to doe Justly, to loue mercy, to walke humbly with our God, for this end, wee must be knitt together in this worke as one man, wee must entertaine each other in brotherly Affeccion, wee must be willing to abridge our selues of our superfluities, for the supply of others necessities, wee must vphold a familiar Commerce together in all meekenes, gentlenes, patience and liberallity, wee must delight in eache other, make others Condicions our owne reioyce together, mourne together, labour, and suffer together, allwayes haueing before our eyes our Commission and Community in the worke, our Community as members of the same body, soe shall wee keepe the vnitie of the spirit in the bond of peace, the Lord will be our God and delight to dwell among vs, as his owne people and will commaund a blessing vpon vs in all our wayes, soe that wee shall see much more of his wisdome power goodnes and truthe then formerly wee haue beene acquainted with, wee shall finde that the God of Israell is among vs, when tenn of vs shall be able to resist a thousand of our enemies, when hee shall make vs a prayse and glory, that men shall say of succeeding plantacions: the lord make it like that of New England: for wee must Consider that wee shall be as a Citty vpon a Hill, the eies of all people are vppon vs; soe that if wee shall deale falsely with our god in this worke wee haue vndertaken and soe cause him to withdrawe his present help from vs, wee shall be made a story and a by-word through the world, wee shall open the mouthes of enemies to speake euill of the wayes of god and all professours for Gods sake; wee shall shame the faces of many of gods worthy seruants, and cause theire prayers to be turned into Cursses vpon vs till wee be consumed out of the good land whether wee are goeing: And to shutt vpp this discourse with that exhortacion of Moses that faithfull seruant of the Lord in his last farewell to Israell Deut. 30. Beloued there is now sett before vs life, and good, deathe and euill in that wee are Commaunded this day to loue the Lord our God, and to loue one another to walke in his wayes and to keepe his Commaundements and his Ordinance, and his lawes, and the Articles of our Covenant with him that wee may liue and be multiplyed, and that the Lord our God may blesse vs in the land whether wee goe to possesse it: But if our heartes shall turne away soe that wee will not obey, but shall be seduced and worshipp [serue *cancelled*] other Gods our pleasures, and proffitts, and serue them; it is propounded vnto vs this day, wee shall surely perishe out of the good Land whether wee passe over this vast Sea to possesse it.

> Therefore lett vs choose life,
> that wee, and our Seede,
> may liue; by obeyeing his
> voyce, and cleaueing to him,
> for hee is our life, and
> our prosperity.

1.3 Massachusetts Educational Laws of 1642, 1647, and 1648.

Law of 1642

This court, taking into consideration the great neglect of many parents and masters in training up their children in learning, and labor, and other implyments which may be proffitable to the common wealth, do hereupon order and decree, that in euery towne the chosen men ap-

Laws of 1642 and 1647 reproduced, with expansions of contracted words, from Nathaniel B. Shurtleff (ed.), *Records of the Governor and Company of Massachusetts Bay in New England* (Boston: William White, 1853), II, pp. 6–7, 203. The Law of 1648 is reproduced in a footnote in Marcus W. Jernegan, "Compulsory Education in the American Colonies," *School Review*, XXVI (November 1918), footnote 1, pp. 740–741. Reprinted by permission of the *School Review*.

pointed for managing the prudentiall affajres of the same shall hence-
forth stand charged with the care of the redresse of this evill, so as they
shalbee sufficiently punished by fines for the neglect thereof, upon pre-
sentment of the grand iury, or other information or complaint in any
Court within this iurisdiction; and for this end they, or the greater number of them, shall have power to take account from time to time of all
parents and masters, and of their children, concerning their calling and
implyment of their children, especially of their ability to read and understand the principles of religion and the capitall lawes of this country, and
to impose fines upon such as shall refuse to render such accounts to them
when they shall be required; and they shall have power, with consent of
any Court or the magistrate, to put forth apprentices the children of such
as they shall [find] not to be able and fitt to imploy and bring up . . .
and they are to take care of such as are sett to keep cattle be set to some
other imployment withall; as spinning upon the rock, knitting, weaving
tape, etc. and that boyes and girles be not sufferd to converse together,
so as may occasion any wanton, dishonest, or immodest behavior; and
for their better performance of this trust committed to them, they may
divide the towne amongst them, appointing to every of the said townes-
men a certaine number of families to have special oversight of. They
are also to provide that a sufficient quantity of materialls, as hemp, flaxe,
etc., may be raised in their severall townes, and tooles and implements
provided for working out the same; and for their assistance in this so
needful and beneficiall imployment, if they meete with any difficulty or
opposition which they cannot well master by their own power, they may
have recourse to some of the magistrates, who shall take such course for
their help and incuragment as the occasion shall require according to
iustice; and the said townsmen, at the next Court in those limits, after the
end of their year, shall give a breife account in writing of their proceedings herein, provided that they have bene so required by some Court or
magistrate a month at least before; and this order to continew for two
yeares, and till the Court shall take further order.

Law of 1647

It being one chiefe project of that ould deluder, Satan, to keepe men
from the knowledge of the Scriptures, as in former times by keeping them
in an unknowne tongue, so in these latter times by perswading from the
used of tongues, that so at least the true sence and meaning of the originall
might be clouded by false glosses of saint seeming deceivers, that learning may not be buried in the grave of our fathers in the church and commonwealth, the Lord assisting our endeavors,—

It is therefore ordered, that every towneship in this iurisdiction, after the Lord hath increased them to the number of 50 housholders, shall then forthwith appoint one within their towne to teach all such children as shall resort to him to write and reade, whose wages shall be paid either by the parents or masters of such children, or by the inhabitants in generall, by way of supply, as the maior part of those that order the prudentials of the towne shall appoint; provided, those that send their children be not oppressed by paying much more than they can have them taught for in other townes; and it is further ordered, that where any towne shall increase to the number of 100 families or householders, they shall set up a grammer schoole, the master thereof being able to instruct youth so farr as they may be fited for the university, provided, that if any towne neglect the performance hereof above one yeare, that every such towne shall pay £5 to the next schoole till they shall performe this order.

Law of 1648

Forasmuch as the good education of children is of singular behoof and benefit to any Common-wealth; and whereas many parents and masters are too indulgent and negligent of their duty in that kinde. It is therefore ordered that the Select men of everie town, in the severall precincts and quarters where they dwell, shall have a vigilant eye over their brethren and neighbours, to see, first that none of them shall suffer so much barbarism in any of their families as not to indeavour to teach by themselves or others, their children and apprentices so much learning as may inable them perfectly to read the english tongue, and knowledge of the Capital lawes; upon penaltie of twentie shillings for each neglect therin. Also that all masters of families doe once a week (at the least) catechize their children and servants in the grounds and principles of Religion, and if any be unable to doe so much: that then at least they procure such children or apprentices to learn some short orthodox catechism without book, that they may be able to answer unto the questions that shall be propounded to them out of such catechism by their parents or masters or any of the Select men when they shall call them to a tryall of what they have learned in this kinde. And further that all parents and masters do breed and bring up their children and apprentices in some honest lawfull calling, labour or imployment, either in husbandry, or some other trade profitable for themselves, and the Common-wealth if they will not or can not train them up in learning to fit them for higher imployments. And if any of the Select men after admonition by them given to such masters of families shal finde them still negligent of their dutie in the particulars aforementioned, wherby children and servants become rude, stubborn and unruly; the said Select men with the help of two Magistrates, or the next County court for the Shire, shall take such children or apprentices from them and place them with some masters for years (boyes till they come to twenty one, and girls eighteen years of age compleat) which will more strictly look into and force them to submit unto government according to the rules of this order, if by fair means and former instructions they will not be drawn unto it.

1.4   A Court Attempts to Enforce the Law of 1648: A Warrant to the Constable of Topsfield, March 2, 1668.

Whereas the law published by the Honered Generall Court lib. I, pag 76, doe require all Townes from time to time to dispose of all single persons and inmates within their Towns to service or otherwise and in pag. 16, tit. children & youth, It is required of the selectmen that they see that all youth under family Government be taught to read perfectly the english tongue, have knowledge in the capital laws, and be taught some orthodox catechism, and that they be brought up to some honest employment, profitable to themselves and to the commonwealth, and in case of neglect, on the part of famaly Governours, after admonition given them, the sayd selectmen are required, with the helpe of two magistrates, or next court of that shire to take such children or apprentices from them, and place them forth with such as will looke more straitly to them. The neglect whereof, as by sad experience from court to court abundantly appears, doth occasion much sin and prophanes to increase among us, to the dishonor of God, and the ensueing of many children and servants, by the dissolute lives and practices of such as doe live from under family Government and is a great discouragement to most family governours, who consciently indeavour to bring up their youth in all christian nurture, as the laws of God and this commonwealth doth require . . . the court doth expect and will require that the sayd laws be accordingly attended, the prevalency of the former neglect notwithstanding, and you are also required to take a list of the names of those young persons within the bounds of your Town, and all adjacent farmes though out of all Towne bounds, who do live from under family government viz. doe not serve their parents or masters, as children apprentices, hired servants, or journeymen ought to do and usually did in our native country, being subject to there commands & discipline and the same you are to returne to the next court to be held at Ipswich the 30 day of this month, etc. . . .

Records and Files of the Quarterly Courts of Essex County, Massachusetts, 1636–1671 (Salem, 1911–14), IV, p. 212.

1.5   A Description of the Curriculum and Methods of a Grammar School in England, 1637–1660, by Charles Hoole, a Schoolmaster.

A New Discovery of the Old Art of Teaching Schoole, in Four Small Treatises

1		A Petty-Schoole	In a
2	concerning	The Usher's Duty	Grammar
3		The Master's Method	Schoole
4		Scholastick Discipline	

Showing how Children in their playing years may
grammatically attain to a
firm groundedness and exercise of the Latine, Greek
and Hebrew Tongues.

Written about Twenty-three yeares ago, for the benefit of *Rotherham* School, where it was first used; and after 14 years' trial by diligent practise in London in many particulars enlarged, and now at last published for the general profit, especially of young Schoole-Masters. By *Charles Hoole*, Master of Arts, and Teacher of a Private Grammar School in Lothbury Gardens, London.

London: Printed by *J. T.*, for Andrew Crook, at the *Green Dragon*, in Paul's Churchyard 1660.

The Usher's Duty, or a Plat-forme of Teaching Lilie's Grammar, by C. H.

. . . .

But because their wits are now ripened for the better understanding of Grammar, and it is necessary for them to be made wholly acquainted with it before they proceed to the exact reading of Authors, and making School-exercises, I would have them spend one quarter of a yeare chiefly in getting *Figurae* and *Prosodia* and making daily repetition of the whole Accidents and Common-Grammars, so that this third year will be well bestowed in teaching children of between nine and ten years of age the whole *Grammar*, and the right use of it, in a method answerable to their capacities, and not much differing from the common mode of teaching.

The Master's Method, or the Exercising of Scholars in Grammars, Authour, and Exercises; Greek, Latine, and Hebrew.

Arthur F. Leach (ed.), *Educational Charters and Documents, 598 to 1909* (Cambridge, England: Cambridge University Press, 1911), pp. 530–534.

Chapter I.

p. 129. *How to make the Scholars of the fourth Form very perfect in the* Art *of Grammar and* Elements *of Rhetorick; and how to enter them upon Greek in an easy way. How to practise them (as they read* Terence *and* Ovid de Tristibus *and his* Metamorphosis, *and* Janua Latinae linguae *and* Sturmius, *and* Textor's Epistles) *in getting* Copy *of words, and learning their* Derivations *and* Differences *and in* varying phrases. *How to show them the right way of* double translating *and* writing a most pure Latine style. *How to acquaint them with all sorts of* English *and* Latine verses *and to make them to write* familiar *and* elegant Epistles, *either in English or Latine,* upon all occasions.

Chapter II.

p. 167. *How to teach Scholars in the fifth form to keep and improve the Latine and Greek Grammars, and Rhetorick, and how to acquaint them with an Oratory, stile and pronunciation. How to help them to translate Latine into Greek, and to make Greek verses as they read* Isocrates *and* Theognis. *How they may profit well in reading* Virgil, *and easily learn to make good Theams and elegant Verses with delight and certainty. And what Catechismes they may learn in Greek.*

V Form.

I have experienced it to be a most effectual mean to draw on my Scholars to emulate one another, who could make the best exercises of their own in the most Rhetoricall style, and have often seen the most bashfull and least promising boyes to outstrip their fellowes in pronouncing with a courage and comely gesture; and for bringing up this use first in my School I must here thank that modest and ingenious gentleman, Mr Edward Perkins, who was then my Usher, for advising me to set upon it. For I found nothing that I did formerly to put such a spirit into my Scholars, and make them like so many Nightingales, to contend who could most melodiously tune his voice and frame style to pronounce and imitate the the prementioned orations. . . .

On Tuesdaies and Thursdaies in the afternoons, after other tasks ended to collect Short Histories out of Plutarch, &c.; Apologues out of Æsop, Hieroglyphicks out of Pierius and Causinus, Emblems and Symbols out of Alciat, Bega, Quarles, &c.; Ancient Laws and Customs out of Diodorus Siculus, &c. Witty Sentences out of Golden Grove, Moral Philosophie, &c. Rhetorical exornations out of Vossius, Farnabie, Butler, &c. Topical pieces out of Caussinus, &c. Descriptions of things natural and artificial out of Orbis Pictus, &c., which, together with all that can be got of this nature, should be laid up in the Schoole Library for Scholars to pick what they can . . . out of these they are to write on a Theme set.

Chapter III.

How to enter Scholars of the Sixth Forme in Hebrew; How to employ them in reading the best and most difficult Authours in Latine and Greeke, and how to acquaint them with all manner of Schoole Exercises, Latine, Greek or Hebrew.

p. 193. Though it be found a thing very rare, and is by some adjudged to be of little use for School boyes to make exercises in Hebrew; yet it is no small ornament and commendation to a Schoole (as Westminster Schoole at present can evidence) that Scholars are able to make orations and verses in Hebrew, Arabick or other Oriental Tongues, to the amazement of most of their hearers, who are angry at their own ignorance, because they know not well what is then said or written.

p. 202. The constant employment of this Sixth Form is:—

1. To read twelve verses out of the Greek Testament every morning before Parts.
2. To repeat Latine and Greek Grammar Parts and Elementa Rhetorices every Thursday morning.
3. To learn the Hebrew Tongue on Mondaies, Tuesdaies and Wednesdaies for morning Parts.
4. To read Hesiod, Homer, Pindar and Lycophron for forenoon lessons on Mondaies and Wednesdaies.
5. Zenophon, Sophocles, Euripides and Aristophanes on Tuesdaies and Thursdaies.
6. Laubegeois Breviarium Graecae linguae for afternoon Parts on Mondaies and Wednesdaies.
7. Lucian's Select Dialogues and Pontani Progymnasmata Latinitatis on Tuesday afternoons; and
8. Tullie's orations, Plinie's Panegyricos, Quintilian's Declamations on Thursdaye afternoons, and Goodwin's Antiquities at leisure times.
9. Their exercises for oratory should be to make Themes, Orations and Declamations, Latine, Greek and Hebrew; and for Poetry to make Verses upon such Themes as are appointed them every week.
10. And to exercise themselves in Anagrams, Epigrams, Epitaph, Epithalamias, Eclogues and Acrosticks, English, Latine, Greek and Hebrew.
11. Their Catechismes are Nowell and Birket in Greek and the Church Catechisme in Hebrew.

So that in six, or at the most seven, yeares time (which children commonly squander away, if they be not continued at the Schoole after they can read English and write well) they may easily attaine to such knowledge in the Latine, Greek and Hebrew Tongues as is requisite to furnish them for future studies in the Universities, or to enable them for any ingenuous profession or employments which their friends shall think fit to put them upon in other places.

1.6   Rules and Regulations of the Hopkins Grammar School in New Haven, Connecticut, in 1648.

1. The Erection of the said Schoole being principally for the Institucion of hopeful youth in the Latin tongue, and other learned Languages soe far as to prepare such youths for the Colledge and publique service of the Country in Church, & Commonwealth.   The Chiefe work of the Schoole Master is to Instruct all such youth as are or may be by theire parents or Friends sent, or Committed unto him to that end with all diligence faithfulness and Constancy out of any of the townes of this County of New haven upon his sallary accompt only, otherwise Gratis.   And if any Boyes are sent to the Master of the said Schoole from any other part of the Colony, or Country, Each such boy or youth to pay ten shillings to the Master at or upon his entrance into the said Schoole.

2. That noe Boyes be admitted into the said Schoole for the learning of English Books, but such as have been before taught to spell the letters well & begin to Read, thereby to perfect theire right Spelling, & Reading, or to learne to write, & Cypher for numeracion, & addicion, & noe further, & that all others either too young & not instructed in letters & spelling, & all Girles be excluded as Improper & inconsistent with such a Grammar Schoole as the law injoines, as is the Designe of this Settlement, And that noe Boyes be admitted from other townes for the learning of English, without liberty & specially licence from the Comitte.

3. That the Master & Schollars duly attend the Schoole Houres viz. from 6 in the morning to 11 o Clock in the forenoone, And from 1 a Clock in the afternone to 5 a Clock in the afternoone in Summer and 4 in Winter.

4. That the Master shall make a list or Catalogue of his Schollars names And appoint a Monitor in his turne fore one week or longer tyme as the Master shall see Cause, who shall every morning & noone at least once a day at the set tyme Call over the names of the Schollars and Note down the Late Commers, or Absent, And in fit season Call such to an accompt That the faulty, & truants may be Corrected or reproved, as their fault shall desearve.

American Journal of Education, IV (March, 1858), p. 710.   (Contractions of words have been expanded.)

5. That the Schollars being called together the Master shall every morning begin his work with a short Prayer for a blessing on his Laboures & theire Learning.

6. That the prayer being ended the Master shall Assigne to every of his Schollars theire places of Sitting according to theire degrees of learning. And that (having theire Parts, or Lessons appointed them) they keep theire Seates, & stir not out of Doors, with [out] Leave of the Master, and not above two at one tyme, & soe successively: unless in Cases of necessity.

7. That the Schollars behave themselves at all tymes, especially in Schoole tyme with due Reverence to their Master, & with Sobriety & quietnes among themselves, without fighting, Quarrelling or calling one anothr or any others, bad names, or useing bad words in Cursing, taking the name of God in vaine, or other prophane, obscene, or Corrupt speeches which if any doe, That the Master Forthwith give them due Correcion. And if any prove incorrigible in such bad manners & wicked Corrupting language & speeches, notwithstanding formr warnings, admonishions & Correcion that such be expelled the Schoole as pernicious & dangerous examples to the Rest.

8. That if any of the Schoole Boyes be observed to play, sleep, or behave themselves rudely, or irreverently, or be any way disorderly at meeting on the Saboath Days or any other tyme of the Publique worships of God that upon informacion or Complaint thereof to the due Conviccion of the offender or offenders, The Master shall give them due Correccions to the degree of the Offence. And that All Correccions be with Moderacion.

9. That noe Lattine Boyes be allowed upon any pretence (sickness, and disability excepted) to withdraw, or absent themselvs from the Schoole, without liberty graunted by the Master, and that noe such liberty be granted but upon ticket from the Parents or frends, & on grounds sufficient as in Cases extraordinary or absolute necessity.

10. That all the Lattin Schollars, & all other of the Boyes of Competent age and Capacity give the Master an accompt of one passage or sentence at least of the sermons the foregoing Saboth on the 2d day morning. And that from 1 to 3 in the afternoone of every last day of the week be Improved by the Master in Catechizing of his Schollars that are Capeable.

1.7   Excerpts from "The New England Primer."

Time cuts down all,
Both great and small.

Uriah's beauteous Wife
made David seek his life.

Whales in the Sea,
GOD's Voice obey.

Youth forward slips
Death soonest nips

Zaccheus he
Did climb the Tree
His Lord to see.

An Alphabet of Lessons for Youth

A wise Son makes a glad Father, but a foolish Son is the heaviness of his Mother.

Better is a little with the Fear of the Lord, than great Treasure and Trouble therewith.

Come unto Christ all ye that labour and are heavy laden, and he will give you Rest.

Do not the abominable Thing which I hate, saith the Lord.

Except a man be born again he cannot see the Kingdom of God.

Foolishness is bound up in the Heart of a Child, but the Rod of Correction shall drive it from him.

Grieve not the Holy Spirit, lest it depart from thee.

Holiness becomes God's House forever.

It is good for me to draw near unto God.

Reproduction of *The New England Primer* of ca. 1785–1790 printed in Boston by E. Draper: in Twentieth Century Reprint by Ginn and Company. Reprinted by permission of Ginn and Company.

Verses for Little Children

Though I am young, a little one
If I can speak and go alone,
Then I must learn to know the Lord
And learn to read his holy word.
'Tis time to seek to God and pray
For what I want for ev'ry day:
I have a precious soul to save
And I a mortal body have.
Tho' I am young, yet I may die,
And hasten to eternity:
There is a dreadful fiery Hell,
Where wicked ones must always dwell;
There is a heaven full of joy,
Where godly ones must always stay;
To one of these my soul must fly,
As in a moment when I die:
When God that made me calls me home,
I must not stay, I must be gone.
He gave me life, and gives me breath.
And he can save my soul from death.
By Jesus Christ my only Lord,
According to his holy word.
He cloathes my back and makes me warm;
He saves my flesh and bones from harm;
He gives me bread and milk and meat,
And all I have that's good to eat.
When I am sick, he if he please,
Can make me well, and give me ease:
He gives me sleep and quiet rest,
Whereby my body is refresh'd,
The Lord is good and kind to me,
And very thankful I must be:
I must not sin as others do,
Lest I lay down in sorrow too:
For God is angry ev'ry day,
With wicked ones that go astray,
All sinful words I must refrain:
I must not take God's name in vain.
I must not work, I must not play,
Upon God's holy Sabbath-day

And if my parents speak the word,
I must obey them in the Lord,
Nor steal, nor lie, nor spend my days,
In idle tales and foolish plays.
I must obey my Lord's commands,
Do something with my little hands:
Remember my Creator now,
In youth which time will it allow
Young Samuel that little child,
He served the Lord, lived undefiled;
Him in his service God employed,
While Eli's wicked children dyed.
When wicked children mocking said,
To an old man, "*Go up bald Head:*"
God was displeased with them, and sent
Two bears which them in pieces rent.

1.8   The Statutes of Harvard College, 1642–1646.

1. When any scholar is able to read fully, or such like classical Latin author *extempore*, and make and speak true Latin in verse and prose *suo (ut aiunt) Marte*, and decline perfectly the paradigms of nouns and verbs in the Greek tongue, then may he be admitted into the College, nor shall any claim admission before such qualifications.

2. Every one shall consider the main end of his life and studies, to know God and Jesus Christ, which is eternal life; John xvii. 3.

3. Seeing the Lord giveth wisdom, every one shall seriously, by prayer in secret, seek wisdom of Him; Proverbs ii. 2, 3, &c.

4. Every one shall so exercise himself in reading the Scriptures twice a day, that they be ready to give an account of their proficiency therein, both in theoretical observations of language and logic, and in practical and spiritual truths, as their Tutor shall require, according to their several abilities respectively, seeing the entrance of the word giveth light, &c.; Psalm cxix. 130.

5. In the public church assembly, they shall carefully shun all gestures that show any contempt or neglect of God's ordinances, and be ready to give an account to their Tutors of their profiting, and to use the helps of storing themselves with knowledge, as their Tutors shall direct them.

As quoted by Josiah Quincy, *The History of Harvard University* (Cambridge: John Owen, 1840), I, pp. 515–517.

And all Sophisters and Bachelors (until themselves make common place) shall publicly repeat sermons in the Hall, whenever they are called forth.

6. They shall eschew all profanation of God's holy name, attributes, word, ordinances, and times of worship; and study, with reverence and love, carefully to retain God and his truth in their minds.

7. They shall honor as their parents, magistrates, elders, tutors, and aged persons, by being silent in their presence (except they be called on to answer), not gainsaying; showing all those laudable expressions of honor and reverence in their presence that are in use, as bowing before them, standing uncovered, or the like.

8. They shall be slow to speak, and eschew not only oaths, lies, and uncertain rumors, but likewise all idle, foolish, bitter scoffing, frothy, wanton words, and offensive gestures.

9. None shall pragmatically intrude or intermeddle in other men's affairs.

10. During their residence they shall studiously redeem their time, observe the general hours appointed for all the scholars, and the special hour for their own lecture, and then diligently attend the lectures, without any disturbance by word or gesture; and, if of anything they doubt, they shall inquire of their fellows, or in case of non-resolution, modestly of their Tutors.

11. None shall, under any pretence whatsoever, frequent the company and society of such men as lead an ungirt and dissolute life. Neither shall any, without license of the Overseers of the College, be of the artillery or trainband. Nor shall any, without the license of the Overseers of the College, his Tutor's leave, or, in his absence, the call of parents or guardians, go out to another town.

12. No scholar shall buy, sell, or exchange any thing, to the value of sixpence, without the allowance of his parents, guardians, or Tutors; and whosoever is found to have sold or bought any such things without acquainting their tutors or parents, shall forfeit the value of the commodity, or the restoring of it, according to the discretion of the President.

13. The scholars shall never use their mother tongue, except that in public exercises of oratory, or such like, they be called to make them in English.

14. If any scholar, being in health, shall be absent from prayers or lectures, except in case of urgent necessity, or by the leave of his Tutor, he shall be liable to admonition (or such punishment as the President shall think meet), if he offend above once a week.

15. Every scholar shall be called by his surname only, till he be invested with his first degree, except he be a fellow commoner, or knight's eldest son, or of superior nobility.

16. No scholar shall, under any pretence of recreation or other cause whatever (unless foreshowed and allowed by the President or his Tutor), be absent from his studies or appointed exercises, above an hour at morning bever, half an hour at afternoon bever, an hour and a half at dinner, and so long at supper.

17. If any scholar shall transgress any of the laws of God, or the House, out of perverseness, or apparent negligence, after twice admonition, he shall be liable, if not *adultus*, to correction; if *adultus*, his name shall be given up to the Overseers of the College, that he may be publicly dealt with after the desert of his fault; but in greater offences such gradual proceeding shall not be exercised.

18. Every scholar, that on proof is found able to read the original of the Old and New Testament into the Latin tongue, and to resolve them logically, withal being of honest life and conversation, and at any public act hath the approbation of the Overseers and Master of the College, may be invested with his first degree.

19. Every scholar, that giveth up in writing a synopsis or summary of Logic, Natural and Moral Philosophy, Arithmetic, Geometry, and Astronomy, and is ready to defend his theses or positions, withal skilled in the originals as aforesaid, and still continues honest and studious, at any public act after trial he shall be capable of the second degree, of Master of Arts.

The Making of a Gentleman: 2
Education and Social Class in Virginia

Early settlers of Virginia shared many attitudes characteristic of the builders of the Bay Colony, but by mid-eighteenth century Virginia sharply diverged from Massachusetts in educational thought and practice. The Puritans sought universal literacy, but the education of the "vulgar Herd" was only a casual and haphazard concern of the leaders in Virginia. In moving from seventeenth-century Massachusetts to eighteenth-century Virginia one senses a marked decompression in religious climate; in place of "sin and profanes" the Virginia teacher's foes become the awkward and uncouth. Leaders in both colonies feared a lapse into barbarism, but New Englanders decried a decline from Puritan religious and moral standards, while in Virginia the planters feared Dogpatch. The Virginia planter's desire to reproduce the life of the English gentry shaped his educational ideal: education should fit the gentleman to play his social role. Formal *schooling* played a minor part in this *education*, the family and association with social equals the major part.

The popular legend of the Virginia planter, like that of the Puritan, has partially obscured his reality. In a defense of the South written shortly after the Civil War, a Virginian gave classic expression to the dualism of the legends:

> In the ante-revolutionary period, the differences between the populations of the Northern and Southern colonies had already been strongly developed. The early colonists did not bear with them from the mother-country to the shores of the New World any greater degree of congeniality than existed among them at home. They had come not only from different stocks of population, but from different feuds in religion and politics. There could be no congeniality between the Puritan exiles who established themselves upon the cold and rugged and cheerless soil of New England,

and the Cavaliers who sought the brighter climate of the South, and drank in their baronial halls in Virginia confusion to roundheads and regicides.

In the early history of the Northern colonists we find no slight traces of the modern *Yankee;* although it remained for those subsequent influences which educate nations as well as individuals to complete that character, to add new vices to it, and to give it its full development. But the intolerance of the Puritan, the painful thrift of the Northern colonists, their external forms of piety, their jaundiced legislation, their convenient morals, their lack of the sentimentalism which makes up the half of modern civilization, and their unremitting hunt after selfish aggrandizement are traits of character which are yet visible in their descendants. On the other hand, the colonists of Virginia and the Carolinas were from the first distinguished for their polite manners, their fine sentiments, their attachment to a sort of feudal life, their landed gentry, their love of field-sports and dangerous adventure, and the prodigal and improvident aristocracy that dispensed its stores in constant rounds of hospitality and gaiety.

The picture is, of course, a familiar one. The nasty Puritan was the fellow who opposed bear baiting not because it hurt the bear but because it pleased the spectators; who wore dark clothes and lectured children on predestination; who peddled wooden nutmeg and cheated as a matter of principle; who was out to make over the world in his own craven image. The cartoon Puritan of the 1920's with his wagging finger and constant command THOU SHALT NOT completed the unlovely portrait.

By contrast the Cavalier of the legend—illuminated by Wilbur Cash in *The Mind of the South*—was as attractive in his vices as in his virtues. His ancestors fled from the persecution of Cromwell and stepped off the boat in Virginia with jeweled sword in one hand and a family coat of arms in the other, dressed in a silken doublet and quoting Horace. The Cavalier's mansion had white pillars and clipped lawns and hedges. He hunted fox in the morning, sipped mint juleps in the afternoon, and danced all night with beautiful women—that is, when he wasn't betting the family fortune at the gambling table. His slaves were too numerous to count and his fields too vast to survey.

To some extent this legend of the Cavalier was based on the aspirations of the planters, aspirations which shaped their conception of education. Education became a way of creating—and defining—the gentleman.

In the original blueprint of the colony of Virginia the founders anticipated that the new settlement would be in most respects a microcosm of old England. In the first migrations to Jamestown the upper as well as the middle and lower ranks of British society were well represented. But being uprooted from a traditional social structure produced a new self-consciousness in the colonists. In the struggle with the frontier, the traditional leaders did less well than the tough, horny-handed sons and daughters of toil, many of whom came over as indentured servants and convicts during the first half-century of settlement.

In tobacco the colonists found a staple crop with a ready market in the mother country. Exports jumped from 20,000 pounds in 1617 to one-half million pounds in 1627. From the start geography favored the development of scattered plantations. Deep rivers—the James, the Potomac, the Rappahannock, and the York—indented the fertile tidelands and provided a cheap and convenient means of transport. Running west to east, they became the highways of the colony and linked the plantations more to England and to the merchants of London than to the other colonies on the Atlantic seaboard. As plantations grew, farmers erected docks and warehouses at the river's edge where transatlantic ships loaded casks of tobacco. On the return trip they carried colonists and finished goods.

In the seventeenth century, the typical plantation in the Virginia tidewater was a small family farm, not the grand plantation of the Cavalier legend. Land was abundant and labor scarce, and the indentured servant had ample opportunity to become an independent yeoman. It is estimated that one third to one half of the white immigrants to Virginia in the seventeenth century were bondsmen. After serving four or five years they were free to acquire their own farms. Seldom had it been easier for migrants to subsist—wild game was abundant, the soil was rich, the climate mild. But as the century wore on, tobacco mined the soil and the navigation acts made it more difficult to compete in the world market. The crowning blow to the independent yeoman in the tidewater, however, was the spread of Negro slavery.

From the 1680's on, the more prosperous planters began to import Negro slaves in increasing numbers. Labor had always been a problem in the colony, and the Africans met the demand for labor cheap enough to produce tobacco at a profitable price. By the first decade of the eighteenth century white immigration to Virginia trickled to a thin stream, and many of these migrants simply used Virginia as a port of entry to the backwoods. The large established planters bought land and slaves in ever greater amounts and the age of consolidation began.

Who were these large planters, and by what means did they consolidate their wealth, social position, and political power? As Bernard Bailyn has observed, the ancestors of the First Families of Virginia (F.F.V.) were for the most part middle-class Englishmen who came to the colony in the middle of the seventeenth century. The Blands, the Digges, the Carters, the Burwells, the Byrds, the Ludwells, the Masons—the founders of these families came to Virginia within ten years on either side of 1655 and were mostly younger sons of London businessmen with claims to Virginia land and influence in the government. They came to America to exploit the family investment and had funds to buy lands and establish themselves in the new world. Usually they were able to settle on lands already under cultivation. Their aims were not only financial: as younger sons of prosperous but socially and politically undistinguished families, they were socially marginal but ambitious to be accepted as gentlemen. America offered them an opportunity to fulfill the dream of the London tradesman: to join the landed gentry.

Since they had capital to buy land and slaves and influence with governmental circles in London and Williamsburg, they could satisfy their ambitions with striking speed and success. Within a generation they had secure positions as gentlemen planters. Their children formed a clique of gentlemen and ladies united by intermarriage, wealth, social position, and political power.

A major legacy of the planter oligarchy, and the tradition which clearly shaped their educational theory and practice, was the planters' social ideal: reproducing the life of the English country gentleman. This ideal of gentility naturally depended in large part upon the consolidation of economic and social position. Yet the ideal had a kind of magnetism and independent force, too. Many of the actions of the planters, such as their retaining classical training for their sons, can be explained adequately only by reference to this social goal.

Some Virginia grandees aspired to higher things than the life of the rural gentry, to the life of the upper aristocracy, but most were content to emulate the squire: to acquire a manor house, to sit on the local vestry, to oversee the poor, to run a plantation and sit in fine patriarchal fashion at the head of the family table. Well might they be content with this status, for in most of the F.F.V. there was a tradesman lurking in the near ancestry. Many of the planters themselves engaged in commerce and finance. Was it possible to *become* a gentleman at all?

In theory a man was educated to be a gentleman one hundred years before he was born; social position was ascribed, not achieved. When King James' nurse asked him to make her son a gentleman, the King replied, "A gentleman I never could make him, though I could make him a lord." Yet in point of fact there was considerable social mobility in England, though less than in the American colonies. It was often possible, despite the sort of snobbery Jane Austen described, for a wealthy tradesman in England to move to the country, marry an impoverished gentlewoman, and bequeath a higher social status to his children. A secure financial standing, a country estate, discharge of religious and political duties—these were normally associated with the country gentleman in England as in Virginia. But education and manners—using the term in its broadest sense to include grace, breeding, polish—were also crucial.

Books on the conduct and training of a gentleman, eagerly read both in England and in the colonies, give interesting clues about how the gentleman should act.   Paradoxically, he should not be bound by the rule book, but should be spontaneously graceful.   He should be an amateur in all things to erase the curse of doing things for money.   He should dance well, but not be so expertly fussy as the dancing master; he should understand Latin puns and be able to read inscriptions but not have the scholar's squint; he should be graceful in conversation, in sports, in all the arts of pleasing—but never too expert, lest he lose the air of the debonair amateur.   In his moral code honor was the key: he must never lie, steal, betray a friend, or be cowardly.   Towards the sins of the flesh the gentleman might be a bit more tolerant than on points of honor; if one drank a bit too much sherry, or had a discreet amorous affair, one's friends would understand.   The education of the gentleman was well fixed by tradition—he normally attended a grammar school and Oxford or Cambridge where he had a suitably mandarin course of studies, often completed by a trip to the continent to acquire a final polish.

The Virginia planters tried to copy not only the houses, furniture, hospitality, music, and education, but also the inner spirit of aristocracy of the English country gentleman.   For a long time the struggle against barbarism on the frontier was an uphill battle for the socially ambitious. William Fitzhugh, the son of a London woolen draper with pretensions to gentility, bitterly complained in 1687 that "Society that is good and ingenious is very scarce and seldom to be come at except in books.   Good education of children is almost impossible and better never to be born than be ill-bred."   From the metropolis of London Dr. Johnson scoffed at the provincials:

> To a man of mere animal life, you can urge no argument against going to America, but that it will be some time before he can get the earth to produce.   But a man of any intellectual enjoyment will not easily go and immerse himself and his posterity for ages in barbarism.

The danger of succumbing to a slothful and barbaric life was ever present.   Some of William Byrd's descriptions of poor whites on the North Carolina frontier, which he called Lubberland, make Li'l Abner's friends a cultural elite and Dogpatch a beehive of activity.

In one respect Virginia proved barren soil for a class of gentlemen common in England: highly trained professional men.   James Maury, Jefferson's grammar school teacher, commented bitterly on the low estate of professional training in the colony and on the popular scorn for the learned man.   Maury concluded not that something should be done about the prestige or the standards of the learned professions, even though he was himself a minister, but rather he observed sadly that as things were, few self-respecting planters would want their sons to become lawyers, doctors, or ministers.

As planters in the vast wilderness that was America, the Virginians knew that they did not have a self-contained civilization: they were stolid provincials. William Byrd's diary describes his hard work to maintain this standard of cultivation—how different from the properly casual and amateur spirit appropriate to the aristocrat!

13. I rose about 6, read Hebrew and Greek. I prayed and had tea. I danced. The weather was cold and clear, the wind northwest. I wrote several things and walked till dinner, when I ate tripe. After dinner put things in order and walked. All well at the Falls, thank God. I talked with my people, sat an hour with my children, retired, read English, and prayed . . .
19. I rose about 6, read Hebrew and Greek. I prayed and had hominy. The weather continued very cold and clear, the wind northwest. However, Mr. Randolph went away and I wrote several things till dinner when I ate rice milk. After dinner it grew cloudy and threatened snow but it came not. I danced because I could not walk. At night talked with my people and prayed.
20. I rose about 6, read Hebrew and Greek. I prayed and had tea. I danced. The weather was cold and clear, the wind west and thawed a little. I wrote English and walked in the gallery till dinner when I ate sparerib. After dinner put several things in order. We lost one of the flats. At night came Mr. Ward. I talked with my people and prayed. Dreamed my wife was drowned . . .

The planters often felt isolated on their lonely plantations. One visitor reported one of the longest visits on record: a couple visited a planter who was so pleased to have company "that their stay was prolonged until two children were born to the visiting couple." Some of their attempts to reproduce the customary activities of the English gentry amounted to parody. Just as the strictures against deer poaching were obsolete in a wilderness full of game, so their fox hunts led to incongruities. This is a contemporary description of a fox hunt:

Hunting in Virginia is a far different thing from its English original. . . . A local peculiarity—the abundance of game—upsets all system. The practise seems to be for the company to enter a wood, beat up the quarters for anything from a hog to a snake, and take their chance for a chase. If the game went off well, and it was possible to follow it through the thickets and morasses, ten to one that at every hundred yards up sprung so many rivals that horses and hunters were puzzled which to select, and every buck, if he chose could have a deer to himself—an arrangement that I was told proved generally satisfactory, since it enabled the worst rider, when all was over, to talk about as many difficulties surmounted as the best.

The presence of a laboring class of African slaves modified the transplantation of the social ideal of the English country gentleman. The

Negro slave was not the English peasant, nor was the planter-master in this role comparable to the squire. As the largest single element in the population, the slaves subtly and powerfully affected the speech, legal codes, work routines, and many other activities of whites. The need to supervise the slaves restricted the freedom of action of the planter and cut into his leisure time. Diaries of even the wealthier planters indicate that their days were filled with overseeing plowing and planting, with keeping commercial records, and with supervising endless details of administering the plantation.

This very lack of leisure time for the average large planter helps to explain why the Virginia gentleman, like his successor the Southern planter of the nineteenth century, mostly had an imitative rather than a creative culture. Although a few of the planters had large libraries and wrote books, although a few might be called intellectuals, by and large the planters got their learning by ear and spent their free time in active sports outdoors or in indoor sports like dancing and gambling. The main exception to this lack of creative accomplishment and intellectual achievement was the great practical skill and theoretical acumen of Virginians in government, for Virginians won great distinction in political thought and statesmanship.

Formal instruction was relatively unimportant in Virginia. Customarily an individual planter or a group of neighbors hired a tutor like Philip Fithian to teach their children and to prepare the boys for college (normally William and Mary but sometimes European schools). William and Mary was chartered in 1693 but probably did not begin to offer instruction at the collegiate level until about 1729. In a few settlements there were regular grammar schools comparable to those in New England. With the exception of a few charity schools, the poor had few opportunities for education and the rate of illiteracy was much higher in Virginia than in New England. The great dispersal of population in the tidewater made schooling costly and difficult. Even after the Revolution when Jefferson argued that universal education was essential to the preservation of republican government, the planters did little to provide educational opportunity for the common people.

In the middle of the eighteenth century the total pattern of education in the colony reflected the social aspirations of the dominant planter class. Although Maury made a persuasive case for a more utilitarian curriculum in schools, his argument carried little weight with the provincial gentry. To them classical training was a traditional badge of the gentleman, an argument sufficient to refute mere logic. And the planter's chief education was his socialization in his family and in association with his peers, his performance in the political, social, and economic roles assigned to his class as the ruling elite in tidewater Virginia.

2.1 Parson James Maury, Thomas Jefferson's Teacher, Writes Another Teacher in 1762 about the Education Appropriate for a Virginia Gentleman.

An Acquaintance with the Languages, antiently spoken in Greece & Italy, is necessary, absolutely necesary, for those, who wish to make any reputable Figure in Divinity, Medicine or Law.

It is also delightful, ornamental & useful, nay even necessary to such, as, in some other Parts of the World, turn in the more exalted Spheres of Life.

For Instance, it is so to the English Gentleman of the upper Class, whose Opulence places him far above the perplexing Pursuits and sordid Cares, in which Persons of inferior Fortunes are usually engaged.

It is likewise most eminently to the British Nobleman, whose vast annual Revenues rank him with, nay set him above, many, who, in other Countries, claim the royal Stile & Title; & warrant his indulging himself in the Enjoyment of that calm Retreat from the Bustle of the World, of that studious Leisure and Philosophic Repose, which furnish him with the happiest Opportunities, not barely of making transient Visits to, but even fixing his Residence within, those sacred Recesses, sequestered Seats & classic Grounds, which are the Muses' favourite Haunts; a Repose, a Leisure, a Retreat, which nought, but his Countries pressing Calls, on some great Emergencies, has a Right to break in upon or interrupt.

To such as are included in the two last Instances, Studies of this Sort, besides being useful Embellishments, which indeed they are to all who are at Liberty to pursue them, are also, in the highest Degree, necessary. For, Sir, so active a Principle is the human Mind, that tho' Fortune exempt a Man from the Necessity of what we call Business, yet it can by no Means be reconciled to a torpid & dronish State of Inaction. Now a Taste & Relish for the liberal Sciences and politer Arts, by furnishing the Mind with Materials to work upon, rescue such from Pursuits, which are either trivial or unworthy of Man, especially Men of this elevated Rank, or else criminal, destructive & flagitious. . . .

It long has been, & still is, Matter of Doubt with me whether the Study of the Grecian & Roman Tongues be (I do not say necessary, for it seems quite obvious it is not, but even) proper for all our Youth, who are sent to a Grammar-school, who have Genius equal to the Task, & the Circum-

Helen Bulloc (ed.), "A Dissertation on Education in the Form of a Letter from James Maury to Robert Jackson, July 17, 1762," *Papers of the Albemarle County Historical Society*, II (April, 1942), pp. 39–60. Reprinted by permission of the Albemarle County Historical Society.

stances of whose Parents bid fair for placing them above manual Labor & servile Employments, after their Attainment to Manhood. In the Instances above-mentioned, indeed, the Propriety, & even Necessity, of these Studies, are undeniable: but in this Case, which involves almost all our Youth above the lower Ranks in this Quarter of the World, I am far from convinced, that they are necessary or proper.

In Education it can be no irrational Maxim, that the Part, which, either the Circumstances, the natural Turn, the inclination, or the Talents of the Learner may either require or incline or capacitate him to act in the World, be ever in his Teacher's View; & that even his puerile Studies & earlier Exercises always converge & centre in that one Point.

What his future Circumstances may be in Reference to Fortune, may with Probability be conjectured from those of his Parents; which, if they be but a Remove or two from the Vulgar, are generally nearly guessed at in this country.

Whether he may have a natural Turn or Genius for either of the learned Professions, is what cannot usually be discovered very early in Life. However, as I cannot at present recollect that the Son of any one Parent of a larger Fortune has, of late Years, been brought up to either of the three; since the Profits of neither are adequate to the Expence of a proper Education for, or to the Fatigue of a diligent Discharge of, the Duties of either of them; a Tutor, methinks, may hence conclude, that such Parents will not judge it eligible to train up their Sons for either of them.

With the Reasons of this Mr. B—(oucher) as he has not long been resident here, may, possibly, be yet unacquainted; but, in time, they will, doubtless, be quite obvious to him. So undistinguishing are the Generality of our Countrymen, that he will see a Quack or Empyric get Bread & Fame, where Esculapius himself would starve:—see a frontless Pleader, well practiced in every petty Artifice of Quibble & Chicane, acquire Reputation, where a Hortentius, a Cicero, or a Pliny, would be considered as his inferiors; & see, to his Astonishment & Mortification, an empty & vociferous Pulpit-declaimer, especially if deeply read in Hoyle, extolled & caressed by the Vulgar, both small & great, above an Atterbury, a Tillotson, or a Sherlock. In short, he will see Gentlemen of the two former of these Professions galloping away their Time & Constitutions to very little Purpose, before superior & glaring Merit shall establish here & there one, in the Decline of Life, in Reputation & Competence. And, as to the other, he will likewise observe, that they resemble those in leading the Life of Post-boys, but differ from them in a very essential Respect; towit, that, be their Merit great or small, they cannot be discriminated, but are jumbled together into one general & undistinguished Mass, under the common Denomination of Parsons, &, as such, treated, as if they were the only Members of the Community, who are divested of all Title to those Rights & Privileges, the Preservation whereof seems to have first tempted Mankind to quit a State of Nature for the social & Civil Life.

Things standing thus among us, few Men of Fortune will expend on their Son's Education the Sums requisite to carry them thro' a regular Course of Studies, proper to qualify them for shining in either of these Professions. If therefore the Parents possess considerable Estates, a Preceptor may well in general conclude, their Sons are not destined for either of these.

It is then to be considered, what Kind of Education may be most suited for such, who, when they shall settle in the World, are to be masters of competent Fortunes, which they are to improve, either by the Culture of our Staple, by Merchandise, or by some other Method, than either of the Learned Professions. And such are most of those among us, who class with the Gentry.

Now, Sir, the Business, which these are usually obliged to pursue;—the variety of Cares, insep[ar]able from their Situation & Way of Life; render it quite obvious, they can have but little Opportunity or Leisure, after they launch out into the busy World, to apply to the Study of the Languages.—Moreover, few, very few of them prosecute their Studies, either in private or public Schools, so long as their twentieth Year. Besides, they commonly marry very Young, & are thence in the early Stages of Life encumbered with Families. And, tho' you suppose them born to the greatest Fortunes, yet the prudent Management of a large Virginia Estate requires so frequent & close an Inspection, in Order, not only to improve, but preserve it, that the Possessor, when once he comes to be charged with the Care of it, can expect but little of that Leisure & Repose, which are requisite for a pleasurable or successful Engagement in such Parts of Literature, as the Languages, Criticism, & curious & deep Researches into Antiquity.

And yet, Sir, Parts of Literature there evidently are, with which even a Virginia Gentleman ought to have some Acquaintance; destitute of which, he must inevitably make but a ridiculous & awkward Figure in Life. And the Rudiments of these must be acquired in Childhood & Youth, or not at all.

For, if he have not some general Acquaintance with History, he can give or receive but very little Satisfaction or Benefit in private Conversation; nor can acquit himself with any tolerable Measure of Honor & Dexterity in any of those public Stations, which are generally filled by Persons of his Rank. Some of his Time then must be spent this Way.

Again, without a Smattering at least in Geography & Chronology, his Progress in historical Knowledge will be extremely slow; & a Study, which, with those Helps, would have been pleasant & delightful, as well as instructive, without them, will be fruitless & distasteful. These then also come in for Part of his Attention.

But further, if he have not, at least a general knowledge of the Laws, Constitution, Interests & religion of his Country; when called by Authority to the Distribution of Justice, or by his Country to bear a Part in the weighty Business of Legislation, he must ever be at a Loss how to Act. He may as often both act & judge wrong, as right; & so will but illy answer the just Expectations, either of *him*, who nominates to the one, or of *those*, who elect to the other of those momentous Trusts. These Branches of [*sic*] together with the customary Vacations & the needless Interruptions, which are here given to the Studies of Youth thro' the indiscreet Fondness of Parents, will allow but a small Pittance of Time for gaining an Insight into these most useful Departments of Literature. So that to me it seems quite plain, one or other must be neglected. In which Case, I deem it no Matter of intricate Discussion to determine where the Preference is due.

For, Sir, tho' the Knowledge of these ancient Tongues be valuable; may it not yet be bought too dear? And, if the Acquisition of it, or rather laying a Foundation for acquiring it (more than which is not usually done at School) be a Business, which our Gentlemen cannot afterwards take Time to Pursue; & if the Pursuit of it, while at School, must divert them from that of those other Studies just now mentioned, which are to be of daily Use to them as long as they live; surely, the Time, devoted to the Study of these Languages, is, in this Case, but illy spent. For, in the first Place, it is a Study, which they cannot master, while at School, nor, in the next, perfect themselves in afterwards. . . .

But, Sir, let us change the Prospect. From viewing a Virginia Gentleman, born to an affluent Fortune, of which we have but very few (if no Fortunes are properly affluent, but such, as leave the Possessors an Overplus of Income, after all their Wants, whether real or imaginary, have been supplied) let us contemplate another, who will be obliged to call in the Assistance of some lucrative Business to help out his little Patrimony to support himself & his family, when he shall have one, in such Manner, as to prevent his mingling with & being lost among the vulgar Herd. And here, I trust, the Reasonableness of what has been said, will be still more evident & conspicuous.

Here then is a Person, to be educated, who, when come to a state of Manhood, besides the necessary Cares of Economy & good Husbandry, must recur to some profitable Vocation to preserve & improve his patrimonial Estate.

It will not, I believe, be denied, that about his 14 or 15th Year he should be put under some Person, eminent in the Business he chooses, in Order to gain an Insight into all its Modes, Forms & Mysteries, without which it is not to be carried on with Reputation or Success. The earlier then he lays a Foundation for the general Knowledge, mentioned above, as necessary for every Gentleman, the sooner he will be at Liberty to engage in Exercises, peculiarly adapted to qualify him for the Part he is to act. And the sooner this can be done, so much the better.

Gentlemen of this Sort are frequently called to the highest Posts of Honor and Trust in this Country. It is therefore reasonable to crowd as much of this most useful Knowledge as possible into that short Paren-thesis of Time (if the Expression may be allowed) which stands between these two Periods, his beginning to learn the first Elements, & his quitting his scholastic Studies, to apply himself principally to acquire a Skill in the destined Business, whatever it be. But, if that short Space be filled with Latin & Greek; I doubt, his Pains & Time cannot justly be said to have been laid out to Advantage. For it is not possible for him to acquire a tolerable Stock of classical Knowledge, at the same Time have Leisure for such useful & necessary Studies, as English Grammar, reading, writ-ing, arithmetic, History, Geography, Chronology, the more practical Parts of the Mathematics, Rhetoric, Eloquence & other Species of polite & useful Learning; nor for gaining an Acquaintance with, & taste for, some of the most instructive, entertaining & finished Productions of Genius in his own Language. And yet as much general Knowledge of these Kinds ought to be acquired while under a Tutor, as possible; since afterwards but little can be done that Way. For his Application to the Business he makes Choice of, after he is removed from School, which is usually early in Life, both during his Apprenticeship, and when he shall be at Liberty to act for himself, will find him so much Employment, in the first Period to qualify himself for it, & in the next to prosecute it with Advantage, as will soon convince him, that the Study of those Languages, which were once the great Object of his Attention, must now be either wholly laid aside, or else resumed only by way of Amusement, in some of those va-cant Intervals, which, I believe, you, Sir, have been taught by Experi-ence, Gentlemen of Business, incumbered also with the Cares of an Estate, in such a Country as ours, but rarely enjoy.

But if our Gentleman of Business proposes to conduct it with Prudence, Dexterity & Success; if he proposes to give or receive Pleasure & Delight in any of those short Snatches of Leisure, which his Affairs may allow him for social Enjoyment; if he would not lose his Share in Conversation, that turns upon Topics of higher Import, than the Chances of a Card or a Dye, the Pedigree & Virtues of some renowned Stud, or the important & manly Science of breeding, keeping & fighting Cocks; if he aspires to store his Mind with such Knowledge & Wisdom, as may render him a Comfort to himself, & useful, if not ornamental, to Society; if he wish to be Master of the Art of communicating what he knows, either by writing, or orally, amidst a Groupe of Friends of Taste, or in public Assemblies, with a tolerable Degree of Propriety, Energy and Elegance:—if, I say, he would reap such an Harvest as this, the Seeds must be sown in the proper Season. . . .

The Truth of it is, where there is a Strong Presumption, that a Youth, when he shall have attained unto Manhood, will become a Man of Business; it is but reasonable he should, while under his Tutor, be chiefly employed in Studies, that will be useful to him in the approaching active Scenes of Life. Others, however valuable, curious, or entertaining in themselves, yet, if they tend not this Way, are not to him worth the Time & Paines, that must be bestowed on them. Such a Pupil, it is evident, & such are most of our Gentlemen's Sons in this Country, ought to be instructed as soon as possible in the most necessar[y] Branches of useful, practical Knowledge. And, if, at the same Time, he be regularly conducted thro' a Course of English Grammar, if due care be taken to acquaint him with his Mother Tongue by reading such Authors, as have written in it, & as, if a judicious Choice be made, will refine his Taste, strengthen his Judgment, enrich & entertain his Fancy, augment his Knowledge, better his Heart & raise his Piety, & so be of Service to him thro' every Period of his Existence; depend upon it, he will be extremely well equipped for acting his Part with signal Credit & Applause. Nay, without the Aid of foreign Languages, I can almost venture to affirm, he will be able to convey what he knows or thinks on any Subject, either on Paper or viva voce, in a neater, more elegant & better adjusted Dress, than the Thoughts & Sentiments of most of those amongst our Gentry, who have spent many Years in the Study of those Languages, are generally observed to come abroad in.

And this will answer all the Ends, which a Person, who is to fill such a Station in Life, can expect or wish from this part of Education. To which, I believe, we may further add, that this is much more than can (I do not say be expected, because Men's Expectations may be too sanguine, but than can) be, or than is usually effected by the present Mode of educating our Youth: of which, perhaps, no favourable Opinion will be formed, if we are to judge from the Proficiency in Literature, that has been made by the Generality, either of those, who have received their Education here, or of others, who have been sent to Great Britain for that Purpose. As to the former, the Causes of their Miscarriage are too obvious to escape our Notice. And, as to the Plan, on which the latter have been educated, it would be surprising indeed, were the success of it generally such, as to prove it proper for *our Youth*.—For our Youth, I repeat it again; because the Genius of our People, their Way of Life, their Circumstances in Point of Fortune, the Customs & Manners & Humors of the Country, difference us in so many important Respects from Europeans, that a Plan of Education, however judiciously adapted to these last, would no more fit us, than an Almanac, calculated for the Latitude of London, would that of Williamsburg.

2.2 A Letter from a Young Princeton Graduate, Philip Fithian, Written in 1774 to His Successor as Tutor in the Robert Carter Family in Virginia.

I never reflect, but with secret, and peculiar pleasure, on the time when I studied in *Deerfield* with you, & several other pleasant Companions, under our common, & much respected instructor, Mr *Green*. And I acknowledge now, with a thankful heart, the many favours, which I received from your family while I was a member of it. This sense of obligation to your Family, And personal friendship for you, have excited me, when it was in my power, to introduce you to the business which I now occupy; into a family, where, if you be prudent and industrious, I am confident you will speedily acquire to yourself both Honour & Profit—But inasmuch as you are wholly a stranger to this Province; & have had little or no Experience in the business which you ar shortly to enter upon; & lest, from common Fame, which is often erroneous, you shall have entertained other notions of the manners of the People here, & of your business as a Tutor, than you will find, when you come, to be actually true; I hope you will not think it *vain* or *untimely*, if I venture to lay before you some Rules for your direction which I have collected from a year's observation. I shall class what I have to say in the following order. First. I shall attempt to give you some direction for the plan of your Conduct among your neighbours, & the People in General here, so long as you sustain the character of a Tutor. Then I shall advise you concerning the rules which I think will be most profitable & convenient in the management of your little lovely charge, the School. Last of all. I shall mention several Rules for your personal conduct. I choose to proceed in the order I have laid down, as well that you may more fully & speedily recieve my mind, as

Hunter Dickinson Farish (ed.), *Journal and Letters of Philip Vickers Fithian, 1773–1774: A Plantation Tutor of the Old Dominion* (Williamsburg: Colonial Williamsburg, Inc., 1945), pp. 208–222. Reprinted by permission of Colonial Williamsburg, Inc.

that you may also the more readily select out and apply what you shall find to be most necessary.

1. When you have thought of removinging, for a Time, out of the Colony in which you was born, & in which you have hitherto constantly resided, I make no doubt but you have at the same time expected to find a very considerable alteration of manners, among your new acquaintances, & some peculiarities toto Caelo different, from any you have before been accustomed to. Such a thought is natural; And you will if you come into Virginia, in much shorter time than a year, be convinced that it is just. In New-Jersey Government throughout, but especially in the Counties where you have any personal acquaintance, Gentlemen in the first rank of Dignity & Quality, of the Council, general Assembly, inferior Magistrates, Clergy-men, or independent Gentlemen, without the smallest fear of bringing any manner of reproach either on their office, or their high-born, long recorded Families associate freely & commonly with Farmers & Mechanicks tho' they be poor & industrious. Ingenuity & industry are the Strongest, & most approved recommendations to a Man in that Colony. The manners of the People seem to me, (probably I am overborn by the force of prejudice in favour of my native Soil), to bear some considerable resemblance of the manners in the ancient Spartan Common-Wealth—The Valour of its Inhabitants—was the best, & only security of that State against the enemy; & the wise laws of its renowned Legislator were the powerful Cement which kept them firm & invincible—In our Government, the laborious part of Men, who are commonly ranked in the midling or lower Class, are accounted the strenth & Honour of the Colony; & the encouragement they receive from Gentlemen in the highest stations is the spring of Industry, next to their private advantage. The Level which is admired in New-Jersey Government, among People of every rank, arises, no doubt, from the very great division of the lands in that Province, & consequently from the near approach to an equality of Wealth amongst the Inhabitants, since it is not famous for trade. You know very well that the Lands in a small township are divided, & then again subdivided into two & three Hundred Separate, proper, creditable estates; for example *Deerfield & Fairfield* two Townships, or Precincts, in which you & I are tolerably well acquainted, in the former of which, are the Seats of two Judges of the Sessions; & in the latter resides one of the representatives in General Assembly for the County; But if 16,000 £ would purchase the whole landed estates of these three Gentlemen, who are supposed to be the most wealthy in the County, if we rate their Land at the Low Consideration of 4 £ p acre, with all conveniences, each would have 4000 Acres. Now you may suppose how small a quantity many must have when two or three hundred Landholders reside in each of these

small Precincts; Hence we see Gentlemen, when they are not actually engaged in the publick Service, on their farms, setting a laborious example
to their Domesticks, & on the other hand we see labourers at the Tables &
in the Parlours of their Betters enjoying the advantage, & honour of their
society and Conversation—I do not call it an objection to this, that some
few, who have no substance but work like Slaves as necssity drives them
for a few Months in the year; with the price of this Labour they visit
Philadelphia; & having there acquired a fashionable Coat, & a Stock of
Impudence, return home to spend the remainder of the year, in idleness &
disgrace!—But you will find the tables turned the moment you enter this
Colony.   The very Slaves, in some families here, could not be bought
under 30,000 £. Such amazing property, no matter how deep it is involved, blows up the owners to an imagination, which is visible in all, but
in various degrees according to their respective virtue, that they are exalted as much above other Men in worth & precedency, as blind stupid
fortune has made a difference in their property; excepting always the
value they put upon posts of honour, & mental acquirements—For example,
if you should travel through this Colony, with a well-confirmed testi-
monial of your having finished with Credit a Course of studies at Nassau-
Hall; you would be rated, without any more questions asked, either about
your family, your Estate, your business, or your intention, at 10,000 £;
and you might come, & go, & converse, & keep company, according to this
value; & you would be dispised & slighted if yo[u] rated yourself a far-
thing cheaper. But when I am giving directions to you, from an expectation that you will be shortly a resident here, altho you have gone
through a College Course, & for any thing I know, have never written a
Libel, nor stolen a Turkey, yet I think myself in duty bound to advise
you, lest some powdered Coxcomb should reproach your education, to
cheapen your price about 5000 £; because any young Gentleman travelling
through the Colony, as I said before, is presum'd to be acquainted with
Dancing, Boxing, playing the Fiddle, & Small-Sword, & Cards. Several
of which you was only entering upon, when I left New-Jersey; towards
the Close of last year; and if you stay here any time your Barrenness in
these must be detected. I will however allow, that in the Family where
you act as tutor you place yourself, according to your most accute Calculation, at a perfect equidistance between the father & the eldest Son. Or
let the same distance be observed in every article of behaviour between
you & the eldest Son, as there ought to be, by the latest & most approved
precepts of Moral-Philosophy, between the eldest Son, & his next youngest Brother. But whenever you go from Home, where you are to act on
your own footing, either to a Ball; or to a *Horse-Race*, or to a *Cock-Fight*,
or to a *Fish-Feast*, I advise that you rate yourself very low, & if you bett

at all, remember that 10,000 £ in Reputation & learning does not amount to a handful of Shillings in ready Cash!—One considerable advantage which you promise yourself by coming to this Colony is to extend the Limits of your acquaintance; this is laudable, & if you have enough of prudence & firmness, it will be of singular advantage—Yet attempt slowly & with the most Jealous Circumspection—If you fix your familiarity wrong in a single instance, you are in danger of total, if not immediate ruin—You come here, it is true, with an intention to teach, but you ought likewise to have an inclination to learn. At any rate I solemnly injoin it upon you, that you never suffer the spirit of a Pedagogue to attend you without the walls of your little Seminary. In all promiscuous Company be as silent & attentive as Decency will allow you, for you have nothing to communicate, which such company, will hear with pleasure, but you may learn many things which, in after life, will do you singular service.— In regard to Company in general, if you think it worth the while to attend to my example, I can easily instruct you in the manner of my Conduct in this respect. I commonly attend Church; and often, at the request of Gentlemen, after Service according to the custom, dine abroad on Sunday—I seldom fail, when invited by Mr or Mrs *Carter*, of going out with them; but I make it a point, however strongly solicited to the contrary, to return home with them too—Except in one of these cases, I seldom go out, but with a valuable variety of books I live according to Horace's direction, & love "Secretum Iter et fallentis Semita Vitae." Close retirement and a life by Stealth. The last direction I shall venture to mention on this head, is, that you abstain totally from Women. What I would have you understand from this, is, that by a train of faultless conduct in the whole course of your tutorship, you make every Lady within the Sphere of your acquaintance, who is between twelve & forty years of age, so much pleased with your person, & so fully satisfied as to your abilities in the capacity of—a Teacher; & in short, fully convinced, that, from a principle of Duty, you have, both by night & by day endeavoured to acquit yourself honourably, in the Character of a Tutor; & that, on this account, you have their free & hearty consent, without making any manner of demand upon you, either to stay longer in the County with them, which they would choose, or whenever your business calls you away, that they may not have it in their Power either by charms or Justice to detain you, & when you must leave them, have their sincere wishes & constant prayrs for Length of days & much prosperity, I therefore beg that you will attend litterally to this advice, & abstain totally from Women. But this last precaution, which I have been at some pains to dress in the plainest language, I am much inclined to think, will be wholly useless in regard to you, notwithstanding it is founded in that *Honour* and *Equity* which is on all hands allow'd to be due from one Sex to the other, & to many of your *age*, & *Standing* no doubt would be entirely salutary. Because the necessary connections which you have had with the Fair, from your Puberty upwards have been so unfavourable & ill-fated, that instead of apprehending any danger on the score of over fondness, I am fearful your rancour has grown so inveterate at length, as, not only to preserve you, in thought & practice, pure of every Fleshly foible, but has carried you so far towards the other extream, as that you will need many persuasions, when your circumstances shall seem to require it, to bring you back to a rational & manly habit of thinking & acting with respect to the Sex; which yet, after all (& eternally will continue to be, tho it is so much courted & whined after) if considered in the fullest manner, & set forth to the best advantage, never rises above its divine definition Viz "The weaker Vessel." But without detaining you any longer with a matter merely depending on accident or Circumstance I pass on to the second General Head; in which "Ludis atque Jocis amotis" I shall offer to your consideration & recommend for your practice several Rules concerning the management of the School.

2. You will act wisely, if, from the beginning, you convince all your Scholars which you may easily do, of your abilities in the several branches, which you shall profess to teach; you are not to tell them, totidem Verbis, "that you understand, perhaps as well as any man on the Continent both the Latin & Greek Classicks"; "& have gone through the usual Course in the noted College of New-Jersey, under Dr Witherspoon, so universally known & admired, where you have studied Criticism, Oratory, History, not to mention Mathematical & philosophical Studies, & dipt a good way into the French-Language, & that you have learn'd a smattering of Dancing, Cards &c. &c. &c." For Dun-p or Hack—n or the most profound dunce in your College or School would have too much sense to pass such impudence by, & not despise and reproach it; but you may speedily & certainly make them think you a "Clever Fellow" (which is a phrase in use here for a good Scholar) if you never mention any thing before them, only what you seem to be wholly master of—This will teach them never to dispute your determination, & always to rely upon your Judgment; two things which are most essential for your peace, & their advantage. That you may avoid yourself of this with certainty I shall recommend for your practice the following method, as useful at least, if not intirely necessary. Read over carefully, the lessons in Latin & Greek, in your leisure hours, that the story & Language be fresh in your memory, when you are hearing the respective lessons; for your memory is treacherous, & I am pretty certain it would confound you if you should be accosted by a pert School-Boy, in the midst of a blunder, with "Physician heal thy-

self"!—You ought likewise to do this with those who are working Figures; probably you may think that because the highest Cypherer is only in decimal arithmetic, it is not there fore worth your critical attention to be looking previously into the several Sums.   But you are to consider that a sum in the Square-Root, or even in the Single Rule of three direct, is to your Pupils of as great importance, as the most abstruse problem in the Mathematicks to an able artist; & you may lay this down for a Maxim, that they will reckon upon your abilities, according as they find you acquainted & expert in what they themselves are studying.   If therefore you have resolution (as I do not question your ability) to carry this plan which I have laid down into execution; you will thereby convince them of the propriety of their Subordination to you, & obedience to your instructions, so that you may lead them, without any resistance, and fix them to the Study of whatever Science you think proper, in which they will rise according to their respective Capacities.   I have said that you ought to strive "from the beginning" in fixing this very material article in the minds of your Scholars, Viz a Sense of your authority; for one error of Judgment, or false determination will diminish your Ability with them more than doing forty things with truth would increase your authority— They act in this case as you would do in the company of a number of Strangers—A whole evenings conversation, if it was tolerable good Sense, would perhaps make little or no impression on you; But if through hast in speaking, or inattention, any one should let fall a sentence either remarkably foolish, or grossly wicked, it would be difficult if not impossible to persuade you presently that the author was not either a *thick-Scull*, or a *Villain!*—The education of children requires constant unremitting attention.   The meanest qualification you can mention in a useful teacher is *diligence* And without diligence no possible abilities or qualifications can bring children on either with speed or profit.   There must be a Combination of qualifications which must all operate strongly & uniformly. In short, give this said Pedagogizing the softest name you will, it is still a "difficult Task."   You will meet with numberless difficulties, in your new imployment, which you never dreamt had yet existence.   All these you must endeavour to resist & Subdue.   This I have seen compared to a Man swimming against a current of Water.   But I am mistaken if you will agree, after having six months practice, that the comparison be strong as the truth: You will add to the figure, I am certain, & throw into the Current sharp fragments of *Ice*, & *Blocks*, which would make swimming not only difficult but dangerous!   I am not urging these things to discourage you; they are hints for your direction, which, if you will attend to, tho' at first the practice seem rough & unpleasant, shall yet make the remainder of your task pleasing, & the whole of it useful, I will mention several of these Obstacles that you may the more easily guard against them. You will, in the first place, be often solicited, probably oftner than you would wish, to ride abroad; this, however, if you do it moderately, & in seasonable time, & go to proper company, I recommend as conducive to health to one in your sedentary manner of living. But if you go much into company, you will find it extremely difficulty to break away with any manner of credit till very late at night or in most cases for several days, & if you are wanting to your School, you do manifest injury to your Imployer. In this case, I advise you to copy Mr *Carter*. Whenever he invites you, ride. You may *stay*, and talk, & drink, & ride to as great excess as he; & may with safety associate yourself with those whom you find to be his intimates. In all other Cases, except when you ride to Church, at least till you are very intimate in the Colony, you had better ride to a certain Stump, or to some noted plantation, or pretty landscape; you will have in this every advantage of exercise, the additional advantage of undisturbed Meditation, & you will be under no Jealous apprehension in point of behaviour, nor any restraint as to the time of your return.

Another current difficulty will be petitions for holidays. You must have good deal of steadiness if you are able to evade cleverly this practice which has grown so habitual to your little charge from a false method in their early education that they absolutely claim it as a necessary right. You must also as much as you can, avoid visible partiality. At least you must never suffer your fondness for one Scholar to grow so manifest, as that all your School shall see you look over a fault in him or her which same fault, if committed by another, you severely chastise. This will certainly produce in the others hatred & contempt. A fourth difficulty, and the last I shall mention, consists in knowing when, & in what measure to give the Boys Liberty to go from Home. The two younger Boys are wholly under your inspection; so that not only the progress they make in learning, but their moral Conduct (for both of these are critically observed & examined) either justifies or condemns your management to the World. If you keep them much at home, & close to business, they themselves will call you unfeeling and cruel; & refuse to be industrious; if you suffer them to go much abroad they are certainly out of the way of improvement by Study, probably, by discovering their gross Ignorance, they will expose to ridicule both themselves & all their former instructors, & possibly they may commit actual Crimes so as very much to injure themselves; & scandalize their family; but in each of these you will have a large share of blame, perhaps more than the parents, or even the Boys themselves—It will be said that the parents gave them no licence relying wholly on your Judgment & prudence, this will in good measure Justify them to the world. And as to the Boys they are full of youthful impetuosity &

vigour, & these compel them, when they are free of restraint, to commit actions which with proper management they had surely avoided. I say, when you lay these things together, & view them on every side you will find so many perplexities arising in your mind, from a sense of ignorance of your duty, that you will proceed with caution & moderation, & will be carefull to examine with some precision into the circumstances of *time, company,* & *Business* when you license them to go out entirely at the risk of your Reputation—But the practice of three or four Weeks will give you a more full notion of these & many other incidents than I am able now either to recollect or express; I shall have gained my End if these hints prevent you from setting off wrong, & doing inadvertantly at first what your Scholars will assert to be precedents for your after conduct. I go on, therefore, in the third place as I proposed,

3. To mention several Rules for your personal conduct. The happy Education which you have had in point of religion, you ought to consider as an important and distinguishing Blessing of Heaven. That train of useful *Instruction, Advice* & *Example* to which you have been accustomed from your infancy is a more perfect, & will be a safer guide in your future walk, than any directions I am able to give you. You have taken notice of a method for Assistance in Composition, which Longinus recommends.

Place, says he, in imagination, several eminent ancient Authors before your Eyes, & suppose that they inspect your Work, a Sense of inferiority would make you diligent, & your composition accurate. Perhaps the same advice when transferr'd to Morality, would be equally salutary. Unless it be objected that a Belief of Gods presence at all times in every place is the strongest possible restraint against commiting Sin. This I constantly admit; but when I consider how easily our minds are put in motion, & how strongly they are sometimes agitated merely by the senses, & that the senses are affected most by things which fall under their immediate notice, I am fully convinced that if some such plan as I have just mentioned should be fallen upon, & practised, it would make a visible and useful change in our behaviour—In this place I think it needful to caution you against hasty & ill founded prejudices. When you enter among a people, & find that their manner of living, their *Eating, Drinking, Diversions, Exercise* &c, are in many respects different from any thing you have been accustomed to, you will be apt to fix your opinion in an instant, & (as some divines deal with poor Sinners) you will condemn all before you without any meaning or distinction what seems in your Judgment disagreeable at first view, when you are smitten with the novelty. You will be making ten thousand Comparisons. The face of the Country, The *Soil,* the *Buildings,* the *Slaves,* the *Tobacco,* the method of spending *Sunday* among Christians; *Ditto* among the Negroes; the three grand divisions of time at the Church on Sundays, Viz. before Service giving & receiving letters of business, reading Advertisements, consulting about the price of Tobacco, Grain &c, & settling either the lineage, Age, or qualities of favourite Horses 2. In the Church at Service, prayrs read over in haste, a Sermon seldom under & never over twenty minutes, but always made up of sound morality, or deep studied Metaphysicks. 3. After Service is over three quarters of an hour spent in strolling round the Church among the Crowd, in which time you will be invited by several different Gentlemen home with them to dinner. The Balls, the Fish-Feasts, the Dancing-Schools, the Christnings the Cock fights, the Horse-Races, the Chariots, the Ladies Masked, for it is a custom among the Westmorland Ladies whenever they go from home, to muffle up their heads, & Necks, leaving only a narrow passage for the Eyes, in Cotton or silk handkerchiefs; I was in distress for them when I first came into the Colony, for every Woman that I saw abroad, I looked upon as ill either with the *Mumps* or Tooth-Ach!—I say, you will be often observing & comparing these things which I have enumerated, & many more that now escape me, with the manner of spending Money time & credit at Cohansie: You are young, &, (you will allow me the Expression) in the morning of Life. But I hope you have plann'd off, and entered upon the work which is necessary to be performed in the course of your Day; if not, I think it my duty to acquaint you, that a combination of the amusements which I have just now mentioned, being always before your Eyes, & inviting your Compliance will have a strong tendency to keep you doubtful & unsetled, in your notions of Morality & Religion, or else will fix you in a false & dangerous habit of *thinking* & *acting*, which must terminate at length in Sorrow & despair. You are therefore, if you count any thing upon the value of my advice, to fix the plan in which you would spend your life; let this be done with deliberation, Candour, & precission, looking to him for direction, by fervent Prayr, who is the "Wonderful Counsellor"; & when you have done this, let no importunity of whatever kind prevail over you, & cause you to transgress your own Limitations. I have already exceeded the usual bounds of an Epistle. But you will easily pardon a little prolixity, when I assure you it flows from a heart deeply impressed with a sense of the many difficulties which you must encounter, & the dangers which will surround you when you come first out from the peaceful recess of Contemplation, & enter, young and unexperienced, into the tumultuous undiscerning World. I submit these hints to your consideration, & have nothing more than sincere & ardent wishes for your present & perpetual Felicity.

Education as Artifact: Benjamin Franklin and the Instruction of "A Rising People"

"All that has happened to you," an English friend wrote Benjamin Franklin, "is also connected with the detail of the manners and situation of a *rising* people; and in this respect I do not think that the writings of Caesar and Tacitus can be more interesting to a true judge of human nature and society." Indeed the story of Franklin's life has mythical sweep and significance. The son of a soap boiler who stood before kings, a runaway apprentice printer who became minister plenipotentiary, Franklin had a career of constant change and discontinuity. His mobility—intellectual, geographical, social—would have staggered a less resilient man.

This mobility has often been interpreted simply as a protean success story, posing few puzzles either to Franklin or to the historian. But in his educational writings Franklin reveals, consciously and unconsciously, the novel challenges, stresses, and ambiguities of his "open-ended universe." Like Henry Adams, Bernard Bailyn has noted, Franklin fought to locate himself "in an unfamiliar world, a world . . . which by early training and normal expectations" he was not equipped to meet.

With apparent casualness Franklin cast aside two traditional guides in education—academic custom and religious orthodoxy—though he knew that thereby he invited reprisal. More ambiguous were his attempts to find new ways to relate education and social roles, for here he dealt not with pedagogues or theologues but with the whole power structure of the community and with the vexing question of social mobility through schooling. His own social ascent created stresses in his life which he managed to reconcile only partially in his educational proposals. Academic custom, religion, and the established social structure—these were forces with which Franklin contended when he sought to design schools as efficient artifacts for the instruction of "a *rising* people."

50

Magnificently self-educated, regarding every encounter with the world as an opportunity to learn, Franklin by no means confused education with schooling. He exploited the many ways in which society could transmit culture to the next generation by example, by precept, and by a host of agencies of socialization. In his *Autobiography*, in *The Way to Wealth* and the other sayings of Poor Richard, in the Junto, in his projected work on *The Art of Virtue*, and in a number of other enterprises he displayed a conscious pedagogical intent. Still, he feared that self-education or informal education was haphazard and inefficient. Consequently he planned a school as an ingenious artifact, a conscious construction like the Franklin stove which precedes the Academy in his recital of projects in the *Autobiography*.

Unlike European higher education, which arose originally from groups of teachers and students assembled together, gradually knit by religious tradition and academic custom, Franklin's Academy was self-consciously constructed and presented in full and novel detail to meet new needs as he saw them. In his *Proposals Relating to the Education of Youth in Pennsylvania* (1749) and the subsequent *Idea of the English School, Sketch'd Out for the Consideration of the Trustees of the Philadelphia Academy* (1751), he left little to the imagination; like the stove, his schools were new-modeled and ready to use. He described not only a curriculum but also an entire process of education. "Thus instructed," Franklin concluded confidently in his *Idea of the English School*, "youth will come out of this school fitted for learning any business, calling, or profession."

Franklin's canny common sense and intellectual curiosity and enthusiasm led him to reforms not obvious to the formally educated whose "trained incapacity" blinded them to alternatives. In the inner circle of the educational establishment, however, his lack of formal schooling was a liability. Consider the way in which Franklin presented his views. Although the *Proposals* were highly explicit and detailed, he called them mere "Hints toward forming a Plan." He had already learned the value of self-depreciation, for in his project for the public subscription library he had discovered "the Impropriety of presenting one's self as the Proposer of any useful Project that might be suppos'd to raise one's Reputation in the smallest degree above that of one's Neighbor's, when one has need of their Assistance to accomplish that Project."

The Academy was trickier still, for how could an upstart printer without formal schooling tell the liberally educated first men of Philadelphia—some of whom had attended universities in Europe—what the curriculum should be? His assault on academic tradition had to be disguised. In a letter to the learned Dr. Samuel Johnson of New York, requesting his reactions to the plan for the English school, Franklin protested that "I am very unfit for designing a school, having never been educated myself (except as a tradesman) nor ever concerned in educating others." Johnson made the comforting reply that "Nobody would imagine that the draught you had made . . . was done by a Tradesman."

Franklin, ever ingenious, ever humble, a consummate deadpan, may well have perpetrated a hoax: to sanctify his *Proposals* he swamped his own prose in interminable footnotes from the writings of "the famous Milton," "the great Mr. Locke," "the ingenious Mr. Hutcheson," "the learned Mr. Obadiah Walker," "the much admired Mons. Rollin," and "the learned and ingenious Dr. George Turnbull." So often did Franklin have tongue in cheek that it was hard to tell when he was serious—legend has it that he was not asked to write the Declaration of Independence for fear he might insert a joke.

Legitimacy he lacked, but not ideas. A comparison of the *Autobiography* with the *Proposals* alone—excluding his letters and other writings—reveals the extent to which Franklin was systematizing his self-education. In stressing the importance of "MORALITY, by descanting . . . on the Causes of the Rise or Fall of any Man's Character, Fortune, Power . . . the Advantages of Temperance, Order, Frugality, Industry, Perseverance, &c." he reiterated a common practice of the Junto, and his own "Project for arriving at moral Perfection." Franklin prized skillful writing. The *Autobiography* recounts the same practice he recommends for students in the Academy: they "should be put on Writing Letters to each other, making Abstracts of what they read; or writing the same things in their own Words; telling or writing Stories lately read, in their own Expressions." Science widened his acquaintance, giving him social opportunities available in no other way; hence he justified natural history as a subject which would "furnish [students] with matter for their letters. . . . The Conversation of all will be improved by it, as Occasions frequently occur of making Natural Observations, which are instructive, agreeable, and entertaining in almost all Companies." A zealous debater in his youth, Franklin naturally assumed that students would eagerly discuss "Questions of Right and Wrong" and would "ardently desire Victory." Then would be the time to introduce logic. Impressed by the power of oratory, and distressed by what he regarded as his own inarticulateness, Franklin insisted that students study public speaking, though he added, as his own experience had taught him, that "Modern Political Oratory being chiefly performed by the Pen and Press, its Advantages over the Ancient in some Respects are to be shown; as that its effects are more extensive, more lasting, &c." His persistent keynote of utility, his advocacy of English over the classics, his stress on history and science—these clearly stem from his own experience.

Skillfully, Franklin chose only those statements of his learned authors which supported his opinions, eliminating their arguments for the classics and conventional justifications of education on aesthetic or genteel grounds. He turned to them chiefly to buttress his argument for instruction in the vernacular, and in history, science, agriculture, and physical education. Franklin the swimmer found it necessary to defend his proposal that students "be frequently exercis'd in . . . Swimming" by footnote references from Locke, Hutcheson, Charlemagne, and Henry the Great of France. Franklin the Deist quoted Milton's declaration that "The *End* of Learning is to repair the Ruins of our first Parents by regaining to *know God aright*. . . ." With such an array of authorities there was nothing original or presumptuous, after all, about the self-educated printer telling Philadelphian gentlemen how to build a school: "As some Things here propos'd may be found to differ a little from the Forms of Education in common Use, [Franklin said] the . . . Quotations are to shew the Opinions of several learned Men, who have carefully considered and wrote expresly on the Subject. . . ."

In point of fact, as he had shown much earlier in his satire on Harvard in the fourth "Dogood Paper," Franklin had little regard for "the Forms of Education in common Use." They were as inefficient as an open fireplace. Many years later he would return to this familiar theme in attacking "an unaccountable Prejudice in favour of ancient customs and Habitudes" in education, calling the teaching of Latin and Greek a useless fetish.

In writing his *Proposals* and his *Idea of the English School* Franklin took no tradition for granted. For the most part, American secondary and higher education had been extremely conservative, for men liberally educated in England had tried to reproduce what they remembered of old patterns. Franklin, by contrast, had no vested interest in tradition. Everything studied had to be justified on its own merits and carefully organized in a sequence which would make sense to the students and prepare them for active lives.

Franklin made the heretical assumption that students would enjoy school. Again and again words like "delightful," "agreeable," "entertaining," and "pleasure" appear along with the omnipresent "useful." Franklin was no narrow pragmatist. The man who had devoted his leisure to learning assumed that education should be pleasant. He painstakingly planned instruction so that one subject would lead naturally to the next. History was the central discipline. From it students moved to geography, chronology, ancient customs, oratory, "*Publick Religion*," government, logic, and languages and literature. Franklin believed that "almost all Kinds of useful Knowledge" might thus be "introduc'd to Advantage, and with Pleasure to the Students."

History would open a door to the classics for those who chose to enter. Students should learn of "the Pleasure found in Reading the Originals" and realize that knowledge of Latin and Greek was "a distinguishing Ornament." Franklin knew that Latin was a badge of status, and thus had social if not practical value. But the classics had to hold their own in the academic market place.

Here in Franklin's *Proposals* was a tremendous and quite deliberate shift of the burden of proof in educational decisions. With all knowledge competing for a place in the curriculum, mere tradition was no justification at all.

Like academic custom, religion shaped most education during the colonial period. The desire to propagate the faith inspired the founding of many a school and college; sectarian spirit permeated American education. By contrast, Franklin cared no more about religion than he did about educational tradition: neither should determine the purpose and character of schooling. To be sure, he did observe in passing—perhaps for strategic reasons, considering his audience—that history would "also afford frequent opportunities of showing the Necessity of a *Publick Religion*, from its Usefulness to the Publick; the Advantages of a Religious Character among private Persons; the Mischiefs of Superstition, &c. and the Excellency of the CHRISTIAN RELIGION above all others antient or modern." But this comment resembled his prudent advice to his daughter Sally to go to church while he preferred to stay at home on the Sabbath. Franklin cared about moral behavior, not theology; and behavior, not doctrine, was the proper concern of the teacher. Franklin's nonchalance about religion in the *Proposals* bothered the evangelist George Whitefield: "There wants *aliquid Christi* in it," he complained. Franklin's reference to "publick Religion," Whitefield said, was "mentioned too late, and too soon passed over."

To Franklin the child was inherently neither sinful nor good: he was impressionable. It was the teacher's duty to imprint useful information and moral habits. Franklin speaks not of his "sins" but of his "errata," mistakes inscribed on the blank pages of experience which could be corrected in a new edition. In his "bold and arduous Project of arriving at moral Perfection"—programed instruction in virtue for himself and the rising generation—it is Franklin, not God, who places the black spots on the lined white sheets of his moral account book. This is an open universe indeed, in which Franklin is defendant and prosecutor, judge and jury. In his educational scheme emulation and pleasure replace fear, and worldly prosperity and recognition replace divine sanctions.

Although he rejected academic and religious tradition as guides, Franklin could not so easily ignore colonial social structure. In the American colonies secondary and higher education had been closely interwoven not only with academic custom and religion but also with traditionally defined social roles. Colonial education was predominantly a two-track system, with elementary education at most for the laboring classes and secondary and higher education required for the learned. Collegiate education was intended for the rich and wellborn and for men who intended to enter the learned professions.

In his *Proposals* for the Academy Franklin urged the trustees to "look upon the Students as in some Sort their Children, treat them with Familiarity and Affection, and when they have behav'd well, and gone through their Studies, and are about to enter the World, zealously unite, and make all the Interest that can be made to establish them, whether in Business, Offices, Marriages, or any other Thing for their Advantage, *preferably to all other Persons whatsoever even of equal Merit*" [italics added]. So important was the principle of preferential treatment of alumni that Franklin repeated it almost word for word in the constitution of the Academy.

What did Franklin have in mind in proposing such a tightly knit in-group of influential trustees and favored Academy graduates? The trustees represented the Philadelphia establishment, "the principal Gentlemen of the Province." Of the twenty-four, fifteen had the title "Esquire," suggesting that they had high social standing; eight were wealthy merchants; several were prominent doctors, judges, and lawyers; almost all occupied important positions of political leadership in the Provincial Assembly or City Council. From the beginning, and increasingly as time went on, membership on the Board of Trustees signified social, political, and economic eminence in the colony. Many of the trustees' families became linked through marriage, further consolidating their leadership.

In such a group of eminent and liberally educated men Franklin, the self-educated and self-made man, was an anomaly. He was useful as publicist and promoter, but the trustees seemed little disposed to honor his opinions. After a political disagreement in 1756, they displaced him as president of the Board, though he continued to serve as trustee until his death. "The Trustees have reap'd the full Advantage of my Head, Hands, Heart and Purse, in getting through the first Difficulties of the Design," Franklin wrote bitterly to his friend Professor Ebenezer Kinnersley in 1759, "and when they thought they could do without me, they laid me aside." Never on easy terms with Philadelphia's patrician group, Franklin alienated the conservative elite politically by his opposition to the Pennsylvania proprietors and educationally by his assault on classical tradition. He had solicited the support of the patricians in establishing

the Academy, but he lived to regret their sabotage of his utilitarian curriculum.

Knowing as he did the power of the establishment, why did Franklin
wish the trustees to adopt the Academy graduates as their favorites? He
knew that such "splendid Promises dazzled the Eyes of the Publick." But
such preferment might lead to less, not more, social mobility and might
make the way to wealth more difficult for future Ben Franklins. Might
not the Academy become a high road for snobbery? This might attract
students and patrons, but was it in keeping with Franklin's intent?

A simple explanation of Franklin's plan of preferment might be his desire to embody in the Academy the plan of mutual aid which had worked
so well in the Junto. The members of the club regularly shared news of
how their fellow citizens were making money, discussed whether the
Junto could help "any deserving stranger," and asked, "In what manner
can the Junto . . . assist you in any of your honorable designs?" Franklin himself had received help from a number of influential citizens. And
he observed that the system of European patronage often gave opportunities to poor scholars unavailable in the colonies:

> Something seems wanting in America to incite and stimulate Youth to
> study. In Europe the Encouragements to Learning are of themselves much
> greater than can be given here. Whoever distinguishes himself there, in
> either of the three learned Professions, gains Fame, and often Wealth and
> Power: a poor Man's Son has a Chance, if he studies hard, to rise, either in
> the Law or the Church, to gainful Offices or Benefices; to an extraordinary
> Pitch of Grandeur; to have a voice in Parliament, a seat among the Peers;
> as a Statesman or first Minister to govern Nations, and even to mix his
> Blood with Princes.

Franklin owed not a particle of his reputation to formal education, yet
in this daydream of grandeur he seemed to be hinting of a new and fantastic mobility for the poor through schooling. It contrasts bluntly, however, with an account of the progress of the Academy and English School
he published shortly thereafter in a newspaper. In this article he said
that the trustees were planning to open a "Charity School [the English
School] within two Years for the Instruction of Poor Children gratis,
in Reading, Writing and Arithmetick, and the first Principles of Virtue
and Piety." This was to be the school from which, as he would write
the next year, the students would emerge "fitted for learning any Business, Calling or Profession." As for the Academy, though he did not
write explicitly about any plan of scholarships for the indigent, he anticipated that "a Number of the poorer Sort will hereby be qualified to act as
Schoolmasters in the Country. . . ."

This was a far cry from being a "first Minister" or gloriously mixing

with the blood of princes. It seems clear that Franklin's plan of preferment was something more complicated than simply inserting the policy
of the Junto into the plan for the Academy. The Junto was also called
the "Leather Apron Club," and was composed largely of artisans, clerks,
and tradesmen. The trustees of the Academy were a different group
again, far more prestigious and powerful.

Perhaps part of the clue to Franklin's plan of preferment lies in the
stresses and ambiguities of his own ascent. Already in 1749 there were
signs of that curious forking of aspiration which led Franklin later at
Passy to try to marry one of his grandsons to Madame Brillon's daughter,
and, when rebuffed, to train another grandson as a printer. Franklin had
committed the cardinal artisan's sin—which he later admitted as one of
his "errata"—of breaking his apprenticeship to his brother. This act further cut him off from his family, whose religious teachings he had already discarded. Adopting one of his many roles, he then passed himself off to a ship captain as a young man "that had got a naughty girl with
child," and boarded the ship for New York.

Robert Sayre has observed that the first part of the *Autobiography* re-
sembles a picaresque novel, with the hero encountering a succession of
villains and friends as he tests provisional identities: "clergyman, seaman,
tallow chandler and soap boiler, printer, poet, swimming instructor, and
merchant." As time went on Franklin added to these the roles of politician, soldier, scientist, and diplomat. Uninhibited by dogmatic religion,
unimpaired by formal education, aided by social and economic opportunities, he was free to experiment, to test himself and his environment
by intellect and industry and humor.

Skilled through early practice in adapting to an abruptly changing and
discontinuous world, he would later respond flexibly to the incongruous
expectations of others: in Philadelphia, he wore the clothes of a prosperous burgher; in London, as colonial agent, the silver buckles and sword
of the court; in Paris, the fur cap and shining white clothes of the simple
philosopher from Pennsylvania. But the discontinuities were sometimes
painful. His son William, raised as a gentleman, took the English side
as Royal Governor of New Jersey during the Revolution: "Nothing has
ever hurt me so much and affected me with such keen sensations as to
find myself deserted in my old age by my only son," Franklin wrote William, "and not only deserted, but to find him taking up arms against me
in a cause wherein my good fame, fortune, and life were all at stake."
Poignantly, from his own broken apprenticeship to his son's apostasy,
Franklin knew the pain of dissolving family ties. With self-conscious
dramatization, aware of the mythic dimensions of his career, he signed
his will as "Benjamin Franklin, of Philadelphia, printer, late Minister

Plenipotentiary From the United States of America to the Court of France, now President of the State of Pennsylvania."

In 1749 much of this lay ahead, but Franklin had already had enough experience as one of the preeminent self-made men of his generation to know the ambiguity of mobility. As guide of a rising generation he had discarded the certainties of sectarian dogma and academic custom. His ironic detachment and playful adaptation to diverse roles enabled him to make his way adroitly through an ever-changing and sometimes threatening environment. Yet possibly in his plan of preferment for the graduates of the Academy and in his desire to systematize for others his self-education, he was attempting to smooth the steepness of ascent and create through schooling a more comfortable path into occupational and social roles which were becoming discontinuous between the generations.

3.1   Selections from Franklin's "Autobiography"

My elder brothers were all put apprentices to different trades. I was put to the grammar-school at eight years of age, my father intending to devote me, as the tithe of his sons, to the service of the Church. My early readiness in learning to read (which must have been very early, as I do not remember when I could not read), and the opinion of all his friends, that I should certainly make a good scholar, encouraged him in this purpose of his. My uncle Benjamin, too, approved of it, and proposed to give me all his short-hand volumes of sermons, I suppose as a stock to set up with, if I would learn his character. I continued, however, at the grammar-school not quite one year, though in that time I had risen gradually from the middle of the class of that year to be the head of it, and farther was removed into the next class above it, in order to go with that into the third at the end of the year. But my father, in the meantime, from a view of the expense of a college education, which having so large a family he could not well afford, and the mean living many so educated were afterwards able to obtain—reasons that he gave to his friends in my hearing—altered his first intention, took me from the grammar-school, and sent me to a school for writing and arithmetic, kept by a then famous man, Mr. George Brownell, very successful in his profession generally, and that by mild, encouraging methods. Under him I acquired fair writing pretty soon, but I failed in the arithmetic, and made no progress in it. At ten years old I was taken home to assist my father in his business, which was that of a tallow-chandler and sope-boiler; a business he was not bred

Benjamin Franklin, *Autobiography* (New York: P. F. Collier and Sons, 1909), I, pp. 10–11, 14–19, 56–61, 80–86, 117–119.

to, but had assumed on his arrival in New England, and on finding his dying trade would not maintain his family, being in little request. Accordingly, I was employed in cutting wick for the candles, filling the dipping mold and the molds for cast candles, attending the shop, going of errands, etc.

I disliked the trade, and had a strong inclination for the sea, but my father declared against it; however, living near the water, I was much in and about it, learnt early to swim well, and to manage boats; and when in a boat or canoe with other boys, I was commonly allowed to govern, especially in any case of difficulty; and upon other occasions I was generally a leader among the boys, and sometimes led them into scrapes, of which I will mention one instance, as it shows an early projecting public spirit, tho' not then justly conducted.

There was a salt-marsh that bounded part of the mill-pond, on the edge of which, at high water, we used to stand to fish for minnows. By much trampling, we had made it a mere quagmire. My proposal was to build a wharff there fit for us to stand upon, and I showed my comrades a large heap of stones, which were intended for a new house near the marsh, and which would very well suit our purpose. Accordingly, in the evening, when the workmen were gone, I assembled a number of my play-fellows, and working with them diligently like so many emmets, sometimes two or three to a stone, we brought them all away and built our little wharff. The next morning the workmen were surprised at missing the stones, which were found in our wharff. Inquiry was made after the removers; we were discovered and complained of; several of us were corrected by our fathers; and though I pleaded the usefulness of the work, mine convinced me that nothing was useful which was not honest. . . .

From a child I was fond of reading, and all the little money that came into my hands was ever laid out in books. Pleased with the Pilgrim's Progress, my first collection was of John Bunyan's works in separate little volumes. I afterward sold them to enable me to buy R. Burton's Historical Collections; they were small chapmen's books, and cheap, 40 or 50 in all. My father's little library consisted chiefly of books in polemic divinity, most of which I read, and have since often regretted that, at a time when I had such a thirst for knowledge, more proper books had not fallen in my way, since it was now resolved I should not be a clergyman. Plutarch's Lives there was in which I read abundantly, and I still think that time spent to great advantage. There was also a book of De Foe's, called an Essay on Projects, and another of Dr. Mather's, called Essays to do Good, which perhaps gave me a turn of thinking that had an influence on some of the principal future events of my life.

This bookish inclination at length determined my father to make me a printer, though he had already one son (James) of that profession.   In 1717 my brother James returned from England with a press and letters to set up his business in Boston.   I liked it much better than that of my father, but still had a hankering for the sea.   To prevent the apprehended effect of such an inclination, my father was impatient to have me bound to my brother.   I stood out some time, but at last was persuaded, and signed the indentures when I was yet but twelve years old.   I was to serve as an apprentice till I was twenty-one years of age, only I was to be allowed journeyman's wages during the last year.   In a little time I made great proficiency in the business, and became a useful hand to my brother. I now had access to better books.   An acquaintance with the apprentices of booksellers enabled me sometimes to borrow a small one, which I was careful to return soon and clean.   Often I sat up in my room reading the greatest part of the night, when the book was borrowed in the evening and to be returned early in the morning, lest it should be missed or wanted.

And after some time an ingenious tradesman, Mr. Matthew Adams, who had a pretty collection of books, and who frequented our printing-house, took notice of me, invited me to his library, and very kindly lent me such books as I chose to read.   I now took a fancy to poetry, and made some little pieces, my brother, thinking it might turn to account, encouraged me, and put me on composing occasional ballads.   One was called *The Lighthouse Tragedy*, and contained an account of the drowning of Captain Worthilake, with his two daughters: the other was a sailor's song, on the taking of *Teach* (or Blackbeard) the pirate.   They were wretched stuff, in the Grub-street-ballad style; and when they were printed he sent me about the town to sell them.   The first sold wonderfully, the event being recent, having made a great noise.   This flattered my vanity; but my father discouraged me by ridiculing my performances, and telling me verse-makers were generally beggars.   So I escaped being a poet, most probably a very bad one; but as prose writing had been of great use to me in the course of my life, and was a principal means of my advancement, I shall tell you how, in such a situation, I acquired what little ability I have in that way.

There was another bookish lad in the town, John Collins by name, with whom I was intimately acquainted.   We sometimes disputed, and very fond we were of argument, and very desirous of confuting one another, which disputatious turn, by the way, is apt to become a very bad habit, making people often extremely disagreeable in company by the contradiction that is necessary to bring it into practice; and thence, besides souring and spoiling the conversation, is productive of disgusts and, perhaps enmities where you may have occasion for friendship.   I had caught it by reading my father's books of dispute about religion.   Persons of good sense, I have since observed, seldom fall into it, except lawyers, university men, and men of all sorts that have been bred at Edinborough.

A question was once, somehow or other, started between Collins and me, of the propriety of educating the female sex in learning, and their abilities for study. He was of opinion that it was improper, and that they were naturally unequal to it. I took the contrary side, perhaps a little for dispute's sake. He was naturally more eloquent, had a ready plenty of words; and sometimes, as I thought, bore me down more by his fluency than by the strength of his reasons. As we parted without settling the point, and were not to see one another again for some time, I sat down to put my arguments in writing, which I copied fair and sent to him. He answered, and I replied. Three or four letters of a side had passed, when my father happened to find my papers and read them. Without entering into the discussion, he took occasion to talk to me about the manner of my writing; observed that, though I had the advantage of my antagonist in correct spelling and pointing (which I ow'd to the printing-house), I fell far short in elegance of expression, in method and in perspicuity, of which he convinced me by several instances. I saw the justice of his remark, and thence grew more attentive to the manner in writing, and determined to endeavor at improvement.

About this time I met with an odd volume of the *Spectator*. It was the third. I had never before seen any of them. I bought it, read it over and over, and was much delighted with it. I thought the writing excellent, and wished, if possible, to imitate it. With this view I took some of the papers, and, making short hints of the sentiment in each sentence, laid them by a few days, and then, without looking at the book, try'd to compleat the papers again, by expressing each hinted sentiment at length, and as fully as it had been expressed before, in any suitable words that should come to hand. Then I compared my *Spectator* with the original, discovered some of my faults, and corrected them. But I found I wanted a stock of words, or a readiness in recollecting and using them, which I thought I should have acquired before that time if I had gone on making verses; since the continual occasion for words of the same import, but of different length, to suit the measure, or of different sound for the rhyme, would have laid me under a constant necessity of searching for variety, and also have tended to fix that variety in my mind, and make me master of it. Therefore I took some of the tales and turned them into verse; and, after a time, when I had pretty well forgotten the prose, turned them back again. I also sometimes jumbled my collections of hints into confusion, and after some weeks endeavored to reduce them into the best order, before I began to form the full sentences and compleat the paper. This was to teach me method in the arrangement of thoughts. By comparing my work afterwards with the original, I discovered many faults and amended them; but I sometimes had the pleasure of fancying that, in certain particulars of small import, I had been lucky enough to improve the method or the language, and this encouraged me to think I might possibly in time come to be a tolerable English writer, of which I was extremely ambitious. My time for these exercises and for reading was at night, after work or before it began in the morning, or on Sundays, when I contrived to be in the printing-house alone, evading as much as I could the common attendance on public worship which my father used to exact on me when I was under his care, and which indeed I still thought a duty, though I could not, as it seemed to me, afford time to practise it.

When about 16 years of age I happened to meet with a book, written by one Tryon, recommending a vegetable diet. I determined to go into it. My brother, being yet unmarried, did not keep house, but boarded himself and his apprentices in another family. My refusing to eat flesh occasioned an inconveniency, and I was frequently chid for my singularity. I made myself acquainted with Tryon's manner of preparing some of his dishes, such as boiling potatoes or rice, making hasty pudding, and a few others, and then proposed to my brother, that if he would give me, weekly, half the money he paid for my board, I would board myself. He instantly agreed to it, and I presently found that I could save half what he paid me. This was an additional fund for buying books. But I had another advantage in it. My brother and the rest going from the printing-house to their meals, I remained there alone, and, despatching presently my light repast, which often was no more than a bisket or a slice of bread, a handful of raisins or a tart from the pastrycook's, and a glass of water, had the rest of the time till their return for study, in which I made the greater progress, from that greater clearness of head and quicker apprehension which usually attend temperance in eating and drinking.

And now it was that, being on some occasion made asham'd of my ignorance in figures, which I had twice failed in learning when at school, I took Cocker's book of Arithmetick, and went through the whole by myself with great ease. I also read Seller's and Shermy's books of Navigation, and became acquainted with the little geometry they contain; but never proceeded far in that science. And I read about this time Locke *On Human Understanding*, and the *Art of Thinking*, by Messrs. du Port Royal.

While I was intent on improving my language, I met with an English grammar (I think it was Greenwood's), at the end of which there were two little sketches of the arts of rhetoric and logic, the latter finishing with a specimen of a dispute in the Socratic method; and soon after I procur'd Xenophon's Memorable Things of Socrates, wherein there are many instances of the same method. I was charm'd with it, adopted it, dropt my abrupt contradiction and positive argumentation, and put on the humble inquirer and doubter. And being then, from reading Shaftesbury and Collins, become a real doubter in many points of our religious doctrine, I found this method safest for myself and very embarrassing to those against whom I used it; therefore I took a delight in it, practis'd it continually, and grew very artful and expert in drawing people, even of superior knowledge, into concessions, the consequences of which they did not foresee, entangling them in difficulties out of which they could not extricate themselves, and so obtaining victories that neither myself nor my cause always deserved. I continu'd this method some few years, but gradually left it, retaining only the habit of expressing myself in terms of modest diffidence; never using, when I advanced any thing that may possibly be disputed, the words *certainly, undoubtedly,* or any others that give the air of positiveness to an opinion; but rather say, I conceive or apprehend a thing to be so and so; it appears to me, or *I should think it so or so,* for such and such reasons; or *I imagine it to be so;* or *it is so, if I am not mistaken.* This habit, I believe, has been of great advantage to me when I have had occasion to inculcate my opinions, and persuade men into measures that I have been from time to time engag'd in promoting; and, as the chief ends of conversation are to *inform* or to be *informed,* to *please* or to *persuade,* I wish well-meaning, sensible men would not lessen their power of doing good by a positive, assuming manner, that seldom fails to disgust, tends to create opposition, and to defeat every one of those purposes for which speech was given to us, to wit, giving or receiving information or pleasure. For, if you would inform, a positive and dogmatical manner in advancing your sentiments may provoke contradiction and prevent a candid attention. If you wish information and improvement from the knowledge of others, and yet at the same time express yourself as firmly fix'd in your present opinions, modest, sensible men, who do not love disputation, will probably leave you undisturbed in the possession of your error. And by such a manner, you can seldom hope to recommend yourself in *pleasing* your hearers, or to persuade those whose concurrence you desire. Pope says, judiciously:

> *Men should be taught as if you taught them not,*
> *And things unknown propos'd as things forgot;* . . .

I should have mentioned before, that, in the autumn of the preceding year, I had form'd most of my ingenious acquaintance into a club of mutual improvement, which we called the Junto; we met on Friday evenings. The rules that I drew up required that every member, in his turn, should produce one or more queries on any point of Morals, Politics, or Natural Philosophy, to be discuss'd by the company; and once in three months produce and read an essay of his own writing, on any subject he pleased.   Our debates were to be under the direction of a president, and to be conducted in the sincere spirit of inquiry after truth, without fondness for dispute, or desire of victory; and, to prevent warmth, all expressions of positiveness in opinions, or direction contradiction, were after some time made contraband, and prohibited under small pecuniary penalties.

The first members were Joseph Breintnal, a copyer of deeds for the scriveners, a good-natur'd, friendly, middleag'd man, a great lover of poetry, reading all he could meet with, and writing some that was tolerable; very ingenious in many little Nicknackeries, and of sensible conversation.

Thomas Godfrey, a self-taught mathematician, great in his way, and afterward inventor of what is now called Hadley's Quadrant. But he knew little out of his way, and was not a pleasing companion; as, like most great mathematicians I have met with, he expected universal precision in everything said, or was for ever denying or distinguishing upon trifles, to the disturbance of all conversation. He soon left us.

Nicholas Scull, a surveyor, afterwards surveyor-general, who lov'd books, and sometimes made a few verses.

William Parsons, bred a shoemaker, but loving reading, had acquir'd a considerable share of mathematics, which he first studied with a view to astrology, that he afterwards laught at it.   He also became surveyor-general.

William Maugridge, a joiner, a most exquisite mechanic, and a solid, sensible man.

Hugh Meredith, Stephen Potts, and George Webb I have characteriz'd before.

Robert Grace, a young gentleman of some fortune, generous, lively, and witty; a lover of punning and of his friends.

And William Coleman, then a merchant's clerk, about my age, who had the coolest, clearest head, the best heart, and the exactest morals of almost any man I ever met with.   He became afterwards a merchant of great note, and one of our provincial judges.   Our friendship continued without interruption to his death, upward of forty years; and the club continued almost as long, and was the best school of philosophy, morality, and politics that then existed in the province; for our queries, which were read the week preceding their discussion, put us upon reading with attention upon the several subjects, that we might speak more to the purpose; and here, too, we acquired better habits of conversation, every thing being studied in our rules which might prevent our disgusting each other. From hence the long continuance of the club, which I shall have frequent occasion to speak further of hereafter. . . .

I had been religiously educated as a Presbyterian; and tho' some of the dogmas of that persuasion, such as *the eternal decrees of God, election, reprobation, etc.,* appeared to me unintelligible, others doubtful, and I early absented myself from the public assemblies of the sect, Sunday being my studying day, I never was without some religious principles. I never doubted, for instance, the existence of the Deity; that he made the world, and govern'd it by his Providence; that the most acceptable service of God was the doing good to man; that our souls are immortal; and that all crime will be punished, and virtue rewarded, either here or hereafter. These I esteem'd the essentials of every religion; and, being to be found in all the religions we had in our country, I respected them all, tho' with different degrees of respect, as I found them more or less mix'd with other articles, which, without any tendency to inspire, promote, or confirm morality, serv'd principally to divide us, and make us unfriendly to one another. This respect to all, with an opinion that the worst had some good effects, induc'd me to avoid all discourse that might tend to lessen the good opinion another might have of his own religion; and as our province increas'd in people, and new places of worship were continually wanted, and generally erected by voluntary contributions, my mite for such purpose, whatever might be the sect, was never refused.

Tho' I seldom attended any public worship, I had still an opinion of its propriety, and of its utility when rightly conducted, and I regularly paid my annual subscription for the support of the only Presbyterian minister or meeting we had in Philadelphia. He us'd to visit me sometimes as a friend, and admonish me to attend his administrations, and I was now and then prevail'd on to do so, once for five Sundays successively. Had he been in my opinion a good preacher, perhaps I might have continued, notwithstanding the occasion I had for the Sunday's leisure in my course of study; but his discourses were chiefly either polemic arguments, or explications of the peculiar doctrines of our sect, and were all to me very dry, uninteresting, and unedifying, since not a single moral principle was inculcated or enforc'd, their aim seeming to be rather to make us Presbyterians than good citizens.

At length he took for his text that verse of the fourth chapter of Philippians, "*Finally, brethren, whatsoever things are true, honest, just, pure, lovely, or of good report, if there be any virtue, or any praise, think on these things.*" And I imagin'd, in a sermon on such a text, we could not miss of having some morality. But he confin'd himself to five points only, as meant by the apostle, viz.: 1. Keeping holy the Sabbath day. 2. Being diligent in reading the holy Scriptures. 3. Attending duly the publick worship. 4. Partaking of the Sacrament. 5. Paying a due respect to God's ministers. These might be all good things; but, as they were not the kind of good things that I expected from that text, I despaired of ever meeting with them from any other, was disgusted, and attended his preaching no more. I had some years before compos'd a little Liturgy, or form of prayer, for my own private use (viz., in 1728), entitled, *Articles of Belief* and *Acts of Religion*. I return'd to the use of this, and went no more to the public assemblies. My conduct might be blameable, but I leave it, without attempting further to excuse it; my present purpose being to relate facts, and not to make apologies for them.

It was about this time I conceiv'd the bold and arduous project of arriving at moral perfection. I wish'd to live without committing any fault at any time; I would conquer all that either natural inclination, custom, or company might lead me into. As I knew, or thought I knew, what was right and wrong, I did not see why I might not always do the one and avoid the other. But I soon found I had undertaken a task of more difficulty than I had imagined. While my care was employ'd in guarding against one fault, I was often surprised by another; habit took the advantage of inattention; inclination was sometimes too strong for reason. I concluded, at length, that the mere speculative conviction that it was our interest to be completely virtuous, was not sufficient to prevent our slipping; and that the contrary habits must be broken, and good ones acquired and established, before we can have any dependence on a steady, uniform rectitude of conduct. For this purpose I therefore contrived the following method.

In the various enumerations of the moral virtues I had met with in my reading, I found the catalogue more or less numerous, as different writers included more or fewer ideas under the same name. Temperance, for example, was by some confined to eating and drinking, while by others it was extended to mean the moderating every other pleasure, appetite, inclination, or passion, bodily or mental, even to our avarice and ambition. I propos'd to myself, for the sake of clearness, to use rather more names, with fewer ideas annex'd to each, than a few names with more ideas; and I included under thirteen names of virtues all that at that time occurr'd to me as necessary or desirable, and annexed to each a short precept, which fully express'd the extent I gave to its meaning.

These names of virtues, with their precepts, were:

1. TEMPERANCE.

Eat not to dullness; drink not to elevation.

2. SILENCE.

Speak not but what may benefit others or yourself; avoid trifling conversation.

3. ORDER.

Let all your things have their places; let each part of your business have its time.

4. RESOLUTION.

Resolve to perform what you ought; perform without fail what you resolve.

5. FRUGALITY.

Make no expense but to do good to others or yourself; *i.e.*, waste nothing.

6. INDUSTRY.

Lose no time; be always employ'd in something useful; cut off all unnecessary actions.

7. SINCERITY.

Use no hurtful deceit; think innocently and justly, and, if you speak, speak accordingly.

8. JUSTICE.

Wrong none by doing injuries, or omitting the benefits that are your duty.

9. MODERATION.

Avoid extreams; forbear resenting injuries so much as you think they deserve.

10. CLEANLINESS.

Tolerate no uncleanliness in body, cloaths, or habitation.

11. TRANQUILLITY.

Be not disturbed at trifles, or at accidents common or unavoidable.

12. CHASTITY.

Rarely use venery but for health or offspring, never to dulness, weakness, or the injury of your own or another's peace or reputation.

13. HUMILITY.

Imitate Jesus and Socrates.

My intention being to acquire the *habitude* of all these virtues, I judg'd it would be well not to distract my attention by attempting the whole at once, but to fix it on one of them at a time; and, when I should have gone of that, then to proceed to another, and so on, till I should have gone thro' the thirteen; and, as the previous acquisition of some might facilitate the acquisition of certain others, I arrang'd them with that view, as they stand above.   Temperance first, as it tends to procure that coolness and clearness of head, which is so necessary where constant vigilance was to be kept up, and guard maintained against the unremitting attraction of ancient habits, and the force of perpetual temptations.   This being acquir'd and establish'd, Silence would be more easy; and my desire being to gain knowledge at the same time that I improv'd in virtue, and considering that in conversation it was obtain'd rather by the use of the ears than of the tongue, and therefore wishing to break a habit I was getting into of prattling, punning, and joking, which only made me acceptable to trifling company, I gave *Silence* the second place.   This and the next, *Order*, I expected would allow me more time for attending to my project and my studies.   *Resolution*, once become habitual, would keep me firm in my endeavors to obtain all the subsequent virtues; *Frugality* and Industry freeing me from my remaining debt, and producing affluence and independence, would make more easy the practice of Sincerity and Justice, etc., etc.   Conceiving then, that, agreeably to the advice of Pythagoras in his Golden Verses, daily examination would be necessary, I contrived the following method for conducting that examination.

I made a little book, in which I allotted a page for each of the virtues. I rul'd each page with red ink, so as to have seven columns, one for each day of the week, marking each column with a letter for the day.   I cross'd these columns with thirteen red lines, marking the beginning of each line with the first letter of one of the virtues, on which line, and in its proper column, I might mark, by a little black spot, every fault I found upon examination to have been committed respecting that virtue upon that day. I determined to give a week's strict attention to each of the virtues successively. Thus, in the first week, my great guard was to avoid every the least offence against *Temperance*, leaving the other virtues to their ordinary chance, only marking every evening the faults of the day.   Thus, if in the first week I could keep my first line, marked T, clear of spots, I suppos'd the habit of that virtue so much strengthen'd, and its opposite weaken'd, that I might venture extending my attention to include the next, and for the following week keep both lines clear of spots.   Proceeding thus to the last, I could go thro' a course compleat in thirteen weeks, and four courses in a year.   And like him who, having a garden to weed, does not attempt to eradicate all the bad herbs at once, which would exceed his reach and his strength, but works on one of the beds at a time, and, having accomplish'd the first, proceeds to a second, so I should have, I hoped, the encouraging pleasure of seeing on my pages the progress I made in virtue, by clearing successively my lines of their spots, till in the end, by a number of courses, I should be happy in viewing a clean book, after a thirteen weeks' daily examination. . . .

Form of the pages.

TEMPERANCE.						
EAT NOT TO DULNESS; DRINK NOT TO ELEVATION.						
S.	M.	T.	W.	T.	F.	S.
T.						
S.	*	*		*		*
O.	* *	*	*		*	*	*
R.			*			*	
F.		*		*			
I.			*				
S.							
J.							
M.							
C.							
T.							
C.							
H.							

Peace being concluded, and the association business therefore at an end, I turn'd my thoughts again to the affair of establishing an academy. The first step I took was to associate in the design a number of active friends, of whom the Junto furnished a good part; the next was to write and publish a pamphlet, entitled *Proposals Relating to the Education of Youth in Pennsylvania.* This I distributed among the principal inhabitants gratis; and as soon as I could suppose their minds a little prepared by the perusal of it, I set on foot a subscription for opening and supporting an academy; it was to be paid in quotas yearly for five years; by so dividing it, I judg'd the subscription might be larger, and I believe it was so, amounting to no less, if I remember right, than five thousand pounds.

In the introduction to these proposals, I stated their publication, not as an act of mine, but of some *publick-spirited gentlemen,* avoiding as much as I could, according to my usual rule, the presenting myself to the publick as the author of any scheme for their benefit.

The subscribers, to carry the project into immediate execution, chose out of their number twenty-four trustees, and appointed Mr. Francis, then attorney-general, and myself to draw up constitutions for the government of the academy; which being done and signed, a house was hired, masters engag'd, and the schools opened, I think, in the same year, 1749.

The scholars increasing fast, the house was soon found too small, and we were looking out for a piece of ground, properly situated, with intention to build, when Providence threw into our way a large house ready built, which, with a few alterations, might well serve our purpose. This was the building before mentioned, erected by the hearers of Mr. Whitefield, and was obtained for us in the following manner.

It is to be noted that the contributions to this building being made by people of different sects, care was taken in the nomination of trustees, in whom the building and ground was to be vested, that a predominancy should not be given to any sect, lest in time that predominancy might be a means of appropriating the whole to the use of such sect, contrary to the original intention. It was therefore that one of each sect was appointed, viz., one Church-of-England man, one Presbyterian, one Baptist, one Moravian, etc., those, in case of vacancy by death, were to fill it by election from among the contributors. The Moravian happen'd not to please his colleagues, and on his death they resolved to have no other of that sect. The difficulty then was, how to avoid having two of some other sect, by means of the new choice.

Several persons were named, and for that reason not agreed to. At length one mention'd me, with the observation that I was merely an honest man, and of no sect at all, which prevail'd with them to chuse me. The enthusiasm which existed when the house was built had long since abated, and its trustees had not been able to procure fresh contributions for paying the ground-rent, and discharging some other debts the building had occasion'd, which embarrass'd them greatly. Being now a member of both setts of trustees, that for the building and that for the Academy, I had a good opportunity of negotiating with both, and brought them finally to an agreement, by which the trustees for the building were to cede it to those of the academy, the latter undertaking to discharge the debt, to keep for ever open in the building a large hall for occasional preachers, according to the original intention, and maintain a free-school for the instruction of poor children. Writings were accordingly drawn, and on paying the debts the trustees of the academy were put in possession of the premises; and by dividing the great and lofty hall into stories, and different rooms above and below for the several schools, and purchasing some additional ground, the whole was soon made fit for our purpose, and the scholars remov'd into the building. The care and trouble of agreeing with the workmen, purchasing materials, and superintending the work, fell upon me; and I went thro' it the more cheerfully, as it did not then interfere with my private business, having the year before taken a very able, industrious, and honest partner, Mr. David Hall, with whose character I was well acquainted, as he had work'd for me four years. He took off my hands all care of the printing-office, paying me punctually my share of the profits. This partnership continued eighteen years, successfully for us both.

The trustees of the academy, after a while, were incorporated by a charter from the governor; their funds were increas'd by contributions in Britain and grants of land from the proprietaries, to which the Assembly has since made considerable addition; and thus was established the present University of Philadelphia. I have been continued one of its trustees from the beginning, now near forty years, and have had the very great pleasure of seeing a number of the youth who have receiv'd their education in it, distinguish'd by their improv'd abilities, serviceable in public stations, and ornaments to their country.

3.2 Franklin Proposes His Academy in 1749.

It has long been regretted as a Misfortune to the Youth of this Province, that we have no ACADEMY, in which they might receive the Accomplishments of a regular Education.

The following Paper of *Hints* towards forming a Plan for that Purpose, is so far approv'd by some publick-spirited Gentlemen, to whom it has been privately communicated, that they have directed a Number of Copies to be made by the Press, and properly distributed, in order to obtain the Sentiments and Advice of Men of Learning, Understanding, and Experience in these Matters; and have determin'd to use their Interest and best Endeavours, to have the Scheme, when compleated, carried gradually into Execution; in which they have Reason to believe they shall have the hearty Concurrence and Assistance of many who are Wellwishers to their Country.

Those who incline to favour the Design with their Advice, either as to the Parts of Learning to be taught, the Order of Study, the Method of Teaching, the Oeconomy of the School, or any other Matter of Importance to the Success of the Undertaking, are desired to communicate their

Benjamin Franklin, "Proposals Relating to the Education of Youth in Pennsylvania," in Leonard Labaree *et al.* (eds.), *The Papers of Benjamin Franklin* (New Haven: Yale University Press, 1961), III, pp. 397–419. Reprinted by permission of the Yale University Press.

Sentiments as soon as may be, by Letter directed to B. Franklin, Printer, in Philadelphia.

Authors Quoted in this Paper

1. The famous Milton, whose Learning and Abilities are well known and who had practised some Time the Education of Youth, so could speak from Experience.
2. The great Mr. Locke, who wrote a Treatise on Education, well known, and much esteem'd, being translated into most of the modern Languages of Europe.
3. *Dialogues on Education*, 2 Vols. Octavo, that are much esteem'd, having had two Editions in 3 Years. Suppos'd to be wrote by the ingenious Mr. Hutcheson (Author of *A Treatise on the Passions*, and another on the *Ideas of Beauty and Virtue*) who has had much Experience in Educating of Youth, being a Professor in the College at Glasgow, &c.
4. The learned Mr. Obadiah Walker, who had been many Years a Tutor to young Noblemen, and wrote a Treatise *on the Education of a young Gentleman;* of which the Fifth Edition was printed 1687.
5. The much admired Mons. Rollin, whose whole Life was spent in a College; and wrote 4 Vols. on Education, under the Title of, *The Method of Teaching and Studying the Belles Lettres;* which are translated into English, Italian, and most of the modern Languages.
6. The learned and ingenious Dr. George Turnbull, Chaplain to the present Prince of Wales; who has had much Experience in the Educating of Youth, and publish'd a Book, Octavo, intituled, *Observations on Liberal Education, in all its Branches,* 1742.
   With some others.

Proposals, etc.

The good Education of Youth has been esteemed by wise Men in all Ages, as the surest Foundation of the Happiness both of private Families and of Common-wealths. Almost all Governments have therefore made it a principal Object of their Attention, to establish and endow with proper Revenues, such Seminaries of Learning, as might supply the succeeding Age with Men qualified to serve the Publick with Honour to themselves, and to their Country.

Many of the first Settlers of these Provinces, were Men who had received a good Education in Europe, and to their Wisdom and good management we owe much of our present Prosperity. But their Hands were full, and they could not do all Things. The present Race are not thought to be generally of equal Ability: For though the American Youth are allow'd not to want Capacity; yet the best Capacities require Cultivation, it being truly with them, as with the best Ground, which unless well tilled and sowed with profitable Seed, produces only ranker Weeds.

That we may obtain the Advantages arising from an Increase of Knowledge, and prevent as much as may be the mischievous Consequences that would attend a general Ignorance among us, the following *Hints* are offered towards forming a Plan for the Education of the Youth of Pennsylvania, viz.

It is propos'd,

That some Persons of Leisure and publick Spirit, apply for a Charter, by which they may be incorporated, with Power to erect an Academy for the Education of Youth, to govern the same, provide Masters, make Rules, receive Donations, purchase Lands, &c. and to add to their Number, from Time to Time such other Persons as they shall judge suitable.

That the Members of the Corporation make it their Pleasure, and in some Degree their Business, to visit the Academy often, encourage and countenance the Youth, countenance and assist the Masters, and by all Means in their Power advance the Usefulness and Reputation of the Design; that they look on the Students as in some Sort their Children, treat them with Familiarity and Affection, and when they have behav'd well, and gone through their Studies, and are to enter the World, zealously unite and make all the Interest that can be made to establish them, whether in Business, Offices, Marriages, or any other Thing for their Advantage, preferably to all other Persons whatsoever even of equal Merit.

And if Men may, and frequently do, catch a Taste for cultivating Flowers, for Planting, Grafting, Inoculating, and the like, as to despise all other Amusements for their Sake, why may not we expect they should acquire a Relish for that *more useful* Culture of young Minds. Thompson says,

> 'Tis Joy to see the human Blossoms blow,
> When infant Reason grows apace, and calls
> For the kind Hand of an assiduous Care;
> Delightful Task! to rear the tender Thought,
> To teach the young Idea how to shoot,
> To pour the fresh Instruction o'er the Mind,
> To breathe th' enliv'ning Spirit, and to fix
> The generous Purpose in the glowing Breast.

That a House be provided for the Academy, if not in the Town, not many Miles from it; the Situation high and dry, and if it may be, not far from a River, having a Garden, Orchard, Meadow, and a Field or two.

That the House be furnished with a Library (if in the Country, if in the Town, the Town Libraries may serve) with Maps of all Countries, Globes, some mathematical Instruments, an Apparatus for Experiments in Natural Philosophy, and for Mechanics; Prints, of all Kinds, Prospects, Buildings, Machines, &c.

That the Rector be a Man of good Understanding, good Morals, diligent and patient, learn'd in the Languages and Sciences, and a correct pure Speaker and Writer of the English Tongue; to have such Tutors under him as shall be necessary.

That the boarding Scholars diet together, plainly, temperately, and frugally.

That to keep them in Health, and to strengthen and render active their Bodies, they be frequently exercis'd in Running, Leaping, Wrestling, and Swimming, &c.

That they have peculiar Habits to distinguish them from other Youth, if the Academy be in or near the Town; for this, among other Reasons, that their Behaviour may be the better observed.

As to their Studies, it would be well if they could be taught *every Thing* that is useful, and *every Thing* that is ornamental: But Art is long, and their Time is short. It is therefore propos'd that they learn those Things that are likely to be *most useful* and *most ornamental*, Regard being had to the several Professions for which they are intended.

All should be taught to write a *fair Hand*, and swift, as that is useful to All. And with it may be learnt something of *Drawing*, by imitation of Prints, and some of the first Principles of Perspective.

Arithmetick, Accounts, and some of the first Principles of *Geometry* and *Astronomy*.

The English Language might be taught by Grammar; in which some of our best Writers, as Tillotson, Addison, Pope, Algernon Sidney, Cato's Letters, &c. should be Classicks: The *Stiles* principally to be cultivated, being the *clear* and the *concise*. Reading should also be taught, and pronouncing, properly, distinctly, emphatically; not with an even Tone, which *under-does*, nor a theatrical, which *over-does* Nature.

To form their Stile, they should be put on Writing Letters to each other, making Abstracts of what they read; or writing the same Things in their own Words; telling or writing Stories lately read, in their own Expressions. All to be revis'd and corrected by the Tutor, who should give his Reasons, explain the Force and Import of Words, &c.

To form their Pronunciation, they may be put on making Declamations, repeating Speeches, delivering Orations, &c. The Tutor assisting at the Rehearsals, teaching, advising, correcting their Accent, &c.

But if History be made a constant Part of their Reading, such as the

Translations of the Greek and Roman Historians, and the modern Histories of antient Greece and Rome, &c. may not almost all Kinds of useful Knowledge be that Way introduc'd to Advantage, and with Pleasure to the Student? As

Geography, by reading with Maps, and being required to point out the Places *where* the greatest Actions were done, to give their old and new Names, with the Bounds, Situation, Extent of the Countries concern'd, &c.

Chronology, by the Help of Helvicus or some other Writer of the Kind, who will enable them to tell *when* those Events happened; what Princes were Cotemporaries, what States or famous Men flourish'd about that Time, &c. The several principal Epochas to be first well fix'd in their Memories.

Antient Customs, religious and civil, being frequently mentioned in History, will give Occasion for explaining them; in which the Prints of Medals, Basso Relievo's, and antient Monuments will greatly assist.

Morality, by descanting and making continual Observations on the Causes of the Rise or Fall of any Man's Character, Fortune, Power, &c. mention'd in History; the Advantages of Temperance, Order, Frugality, Industry, Perseverance, &c. &c. Indeed the general natural Tendency of Reading good History, must be, to fix in the Minds of Youth deep Impressions of the Beauty and Usefulness of Virtue of all Kinds, Publick Spirit, Fortitude, &c.

History will show the wonderful Effects of Oratory, in governing, turning and leading great Bodies of Mankind, Armies, Cities, Nations. When the Minds of Youth are struck with Admiration at this, then is the Time to give them the Principles of that Art, which they will study with Taste and Application. Then they may be made acquainted with the best Models among the Antients, their Beauties being particularly pointed out to them. Modern Political Oratory being chiefly performed by the Pen and Press, its Advantages over the Antients in some Respects are to be shown; as that its Effects are more extensive, more lasting, &c.

History will also afford frequent Opportunities of showing the Necessity of a *Publick Religion*, from its Usefulness to the Publick; the Advantage of a Religious Character among private Persons; the Mischiefs of Superstition, &c. and the Excellency of the Christian Religion above all others antient or modern.

History will also give Occasion to expatiate on the Advantage of Civil Orders and Constitutions, how Men and their Properties are protected by joining in Societies and establishing Government; their Industry encouraged and rewarded, Arts invented, and Life made more comfortable: The Advantages of *Liberty*, Mischiefs of *Licentiousness*, Benefits arising from good Laws and a due Execution of Justice, &c. Thus may the first Principles of sound *Politicks* be fix'd in the Minds of Youth.

On *Historical* Occasions, Questions of Right and Wrong, Justice and Injustice, will naturally arise, and may be put to Youth, which they may debate in Conversation and in Writing. When they ardently desire Victory, for the Sake of the Praise attending it, they will begin to feel the Want, and be sensible of the Use of *Logic*, or the Art of Reasoning to *discover* Truth, and of Arguing to *defend* it, and *convince* Adversaries. This would be the Time to acquaint them with the Principles of that Art. Grotius, Puffendorff, and some other Writers of the same Kind, may be used on these Occasions to decide their Disputes. Publick Disputes warm the Imagination, whet the Industry, and strengthen the natural Abilities.

When Youth are told, that the Great Men whose Lives and Actions they read in History, spoke two of the best Languages that ever were, the most expressive, copious, beautiful; and that the finest Writings, the most correct Compositions, the most perfect Productions of human Wit and Wisdom, are in those Languages, which have endured Ages, and will endure while there are Men; that no Translation can do them Justice, or give the Pleasure found in Reading the Originals; that those Languages contain all Science; that one of them is become almost universal, being the Language of Learned Men in all Countries; that to understand them is a distinguishing Ornament, &c. they may be thereby made desirous of learning those Languages, and their Industry sharpen'd in the Acquisition of them. All intended for Divinity should be taught the Latin and Greek; for Physick, the Latin, Greek and French; for Law, the Latin and French; Merchants, the French, German, and Spanish: And though all should not be compell'd to learn Latin, Greek, or the modern foreign Languages; yet none that have an ardent Desire to learn them should be refused; their English, Arithmetick, and other Studies absolutely necessary, being at the same Time not neglected.

If the new *Universal History* were also read, it would give a *connected* Idea of human Affairs, so far as it goes, which should be follow'd by the best modern Histories, particularly of our Mother Country; then of these Colonies; which should be accompanied with Observations on their Rise, Encrease, Use to Great-Britain, Encouragements, Discouragements, &c. the Means to make them flourish, secure their Liberties, &c.

With the History of Men, Times and Nations, should be read at proper Hours or Days, some of the best *Histories of Nature*, which would not only be delightful to Youth, and furnish them with Matter for their Letters, &c. as well as other History; but afterwards of great Use to them, whether they are Merchants, Handicrafts, or Divines; enabling the first the better to understand many Commodities, Drugs, &c. the second to improve his Trade or Handicraft by new Mixtures, Materials, &c. and the last to adorn his Discourses by beautiful Comparisons, and strengthen them by new Proofs of Divine Providence. The Conversation of all will be improved by it, as Occasions frequently occur of making Natural Observations, which are instructive, agreeable, and entertaining in almost all Companies. *Natural History* will also afford Opportunities of introducing many Observations, relating to the Preservation of Health, which may be afterwards of great Use. Arbuthnot on Air and Aliment, Sanctorius on Perspiration, Lemery on Foods, and some others, may now be read, and a very little Explanation will make them sufficiently intelligible to Youth.

While they are reading Natural History, might not a little *Gardening, Planting, Grafting, Inoculating,* &c. be taught and practised; and now and then Excursions made to the neighbouring Plantations of the best Farmers, their Methods observ'd and reason'd upon for the Information of Youth. The Improvement of Agriculture being useful to all, and Skill in it no Disparagement to any.

The History of *Commerce*, of the Invention of Arts, Rise of Manufactures, Progress of Trade, Change of its Seats, with the Reasons, Causes, &c. may also be made entertaining to Youth, and will be useful to all. And this, with the Accounts in other History of the prodigious Force and Effect of Engines and Machines used in War, will naturally introduce a Desire to be instructed in *Mechanicks*, and to be inform'd of the Principles of that Art by which weak Men perform such Wonders, Labour is sav'd, Manufactures expedited, &c. &c. This will be the Time to show them Prints of antient and modern Machines, to explain them, to let them be copied, and to give Lectures in Mechanical Philosophy.

With the whole should be constantly inculcated and cultivated, that *Benignity of Mind,* which shows itself in *searching for* and *seizing* every Opportunity *to serve* and *to oblige;* and is the Foundation of what is called Good Breeding; highly useful to the Possessor, and most agreeable to all.

The Idea of what is *true Merit*, should also be often presented to Youth, explain'd and impress'd on their Minds, as consisting in an *Inclination* join'd with an *Ability* to serve Mankind, one's Country, Friends and Family; which *Ability* is (with the Blessing of God) to be acquir'd or greatly encreas'd by *true Learning;* and should indeed be the great *Aim* and *End* of all Learning.

3.3   Franklin Outlines an English School in 1751.

It is expected that every Scholar to be admitted into this School, be at least able to pronounce and divide the Syllables in Reading, and to write a legible Hand.   None to be receiv'd that are under [   ] Years of Age. [Left blank in the original; Franklin later suggested that the boys should be from eight to sixteen years of age.]

First or Lowest Class

Let the first Class learn the *English Grammar* Rules, and at the same time let particular Care be taken to improve them in *Orthography*.   Perhaps the latter is best done by *Pairing* the Scholars, two of those nearest equal in their Spelling to be put together; let these strive for Victory, each propounding Ten Words every Day to the other to be spelt.   He that spells truly most of the other's Words, is Victor for that Day; he that is Victor most Days in a Month, to obtain a Prize, a pretty neat Book of some Kind useful in their future Studies.   This Method fixes the Attention of Children extreamly to the Orthography of Words, and makes them good Spellers very early.   'Tis a Shame for a Man to be so ignorant of this little Art, in his own Language, as to be perpetually confounding Words of like Sound and different Significations; the Consciousness of which Defect, makes some Men, otherwise of good Learning and Understanding, averse to Writing even a common Letter.

Let the Pieces read by the Scholars in this Class be short, such as Croxall's Fables, and little Stories.   In giving the Lesson, let it be read to them; let the Meaning of the difficult Words in it be explained to them, and let them con it over by themselves before they are called to read to the Master, or Usher; who is to take particular Care that they do not read too fast, and that they duly observe the Stops and Pauses.   A Vocabulary of the most usual difficult Words might be formed for their Use, with Explanations; and they might daily get a few of those Words and Explanations by Heart, which would a little exercise their Memories; or at least they might write a Number of them in a small Book for the Purpose, which would help to fix the Meaning of those Words in their Minds, and at the same Time furnish every one with a little Dictionary for his future Use.

Benjamin Franklin, "Idea of the English School, Sketch'd out for the Consideration of the Trustees of the Philadelphia Academy," in Leonard Labaree *et al.* (eds.), *The Papers of Benjamin Franklin* (New Haven: Yale University Press, 1961), IV, pp. 102–108.   Reprinted by permission of the Yale University Press.

The Second Class to be Taught

Reading with Attention, and with proper Modulations of the Voice according to the Sentiments and Subject.

Some short Pieces, not exceeding the Length of a *Spectator*, to be given this Class as Lessons (and some of the easier *Spectators* would be very suitable for the Purpose.) These Lessons might be given over Night as Tasks, the Scholars to study them against the Morning. Let it then be required of them to give an Account, first of the Parts of Speech, and Construction of one or two Sentences; this will oblige them to recur frequently to their Grammar, and fix its principal Rules in their Memory. Next of the *Intention* of the Writer, or the *Scope* of the Piece; the Meaning of each Sentence, and of every uncommon Word. This would early acquaint them with the Meaning and Force of Words, and give them that most necessary Habit, of Reading with Attention.

The Master then to read the Piece with the proper Modulations of Voice, due Emphasis, and suitable Action, where Action is required; and put the Youth on imitating his Manner.

Where the Author has us'd an Expression not the best, let it be pointed out; and let his Beauties be particularly remarked to the Youth.

Let the Lessons for Reading be varied, that the Youth may be made acquainted with good Stiles of all Kinds in Prose and Verse, and the proper Manner of reading each Kind. Sometimes a well-told Story, a Piece of a Sermon, a General's Speech to his Soldiers, a Speech in a Tragedy, some Part of a Comedy, an Ode, a Satyr, a Letter, Blank Verse, Hudibrastick, Heroic, &c. But let such Lessons for Reading be chosen, as contain some useful Instruction, whereby the Understandings or Morals of the Youth, may at the same Time be improv'd.

It is requir'd that they should first study and understand the Lessons, before they are put upon reading them properly, to which End each Boy should have an English Dictionary to help him over Difficulties. When our Boys read English to us, we are apt to imagine *they* understand what *they* read because *we* do, and because 'tis their Mother Tongue. But they often read as Parrots speak, knowing little or nothing of the Meaning. And it is impossible a Reader should give the due Modulation to his Voice, and pronounce properly, unless his Understanding goes before his Tongue, and makes him Master of the Sentiment. Accustoming Boys to read aloud what they do not first understand, is the Cause of those even set Tones so common among Readers, which when they have once got a Habit of using, they find so difficult to correct: By which Means, among Fifty Readers we scarcely find a good One. For want of good Reading, Pieces publish'd with a View to influence the Minds of Men for their own or the publick Benefit, lose Half their Force.   Were there but one good Reader in a Neighbourhood, a publick Orator might be heard throughout a Nation with the same Advantages, and have the same Effect on his Audience, as if they stood within the Reach of his Voice.

The Third Class to be Taught

Speaking properly and gracefully, which is near of Kin to good Reading, and naturally follows it in the Studies of Youth.   Let the Scholars of this Class begin with learning the Elements of Rhetoric from some short System, so as to be able to give an Account of the most usual Tropes and Figures.   Let all their bad Habits of Speaking, all Offences against good Grammar, all corrupt or foreign Accents, and all improper Phrases, be pointed out to them.   Short Speeches from the Roman or other History, or from our *Parliamentary Debates*, might be got by heart, and deliver'd with the proper Action, &c.   Speeches and Scenes in our best Tragedies and Comedies (avoiding every Thing that could injure the Morals of Youth) might likewise be got by Rote, and the Boys exercis'd in delivering or acting them; great Care being taken to form their Manner after the truest Models.

For their farther Improvement, and a little to vary their Studies, let them now begin to read *History*, after having got by Heart a short Table of the principal Epochas in Chronology.   They may begin with Rollin's *Antient and Roman Histories*, and proceed at proper Hours as they go thro' the subsequent Classes, with the best Histories of our own Nation and Colonies.   Let Emulation be excited among the Boys by giving, Weekly, little Prizes, or other small Encouragements to those who are able to give the best Account of what they have read, as to Times, Places, Names of Persons, &c.   This will make them read with Attention, and imprint the History well in their Memories.   In remarking on the History, the Master will have fine Opportunities of instilling Instruction of various Kinds, and improving the Morals as well as the Understandings of Youth.

The Natural and Mechanic History contain'd in *Spectacle de la Nature*, might also be begun in this Class, and continued thro' the subsequent Classes by other Books of the same Kind: For next to the Knowledge of *Duty*, this Kind of Knowledge is certainly the most useful, as well as the most entertaining.   The Merchant may thereby be enabled better to understand many Commodities in Trade; the Handicraftsman to improve his Business by new Instruments, Mixtures and Materials; and frequently Hints are given of new Manufactures, or new Methods of improving Land, that may be set on foot greatly to the Advantage of a Country.

The Fourth Class to be Taught

Composition. Writing one's own Language well, is the next necessary Accomplishment after good Speaking. 'Tis the Writing-Master's Business to take Care that the Boys make fair Characters, and place them straight and even in the Lines: But to *form their Stile*, and even to take Care that the Stops and Capitals are properly disposed, is the Part of the English Master. The Boys should be put on Writing Letters to each other on any common Occurrences, and on various Subjects, imaginary Business, &c. containing little Stories, Accounts of their late Reading, what Parts of Authors please them, and why. Letters of Congratulation, of Compliment, of Request, of Thanks, of Recommendation, of Admonition, of Consolation, of Expostulation, Excuse, &c. In these they should be taught to express themselves clearly, concisely, and naturally, without affected Words, or high-flown Phrases. All their Letters to pass through the Master's Hand, who is to point out the Faults, advise the Corrections, and commend what he finds right. Some of the best Letters published in our own Language, as Sir William Temple's, those of Pope, and his Friends, and some others, might be set before the Youth as Models, their Beauties pointed out and explained by the Master, the Letters themselves transcrib'd by the Scholar.

Dr. Johnson's *Ethices Elementa*, or first Principles of Morality, may now be read by the Scholars, and explain'd by the Master, to lay a solid Foundation of Virtue and Piety in their Minds. And as this Class continues the Reading of History, let them now at proper Hours receive some farther Instructions in Chronology, and in that Part of Geography (from the Mathematical Master) which is necessary to understand the Maps and Globes. They should also be acquainted with the modern Names of the Places they find mention'd in antient Writers. The Exercises of good Reading and proper Speaking still continued at suitable Times.

Fifth Class

To improve the Youth in *Composition*, they may now, besides continuing to write Letters, begin to write little Essays in Prose; and sometimes in Verse, not to make them Poets, but for this Reason, that nothing acquaints a Lad so speedily with Variety of Expression, as the Necessity of finding such Words and Phrases as will suit with the Measure, Sound and Rhime of Verse, and at the same Time well express the Sentiment. These Essays should all pass under the Master's Eye, who will point out their Faults, and put the Writer on correcting them. Where the Judgment is not ripe enough for forming new Essays, let the Sentiments of a

Spectator be given, and requir'd to be cloath'd in a Scholar's own Words; or the Circumstances of some good Story, the Scholar to find Expression. Let them be put sometimes on abridging a Paragraph of a diffuse Author, sometimes on dilating or amplifying what is wrote more closely. And now let Dr. Johnson's *Noetica*, or first Principles of human Knowledge, containing a Logic, or Art of Reasoning, &c. be read by the Youth, and the Difficulties that may occur to them be explained by the Master. The Reading of History, and the Exercises of good Reading and just Speaking still continued.

Sixth Class

In this Class, besides continuing the Studies of the preceding, in History, Rhetoric, Logic, Moral and Natural Philosophy, the best English Authors may be read and explain'd; as Tillotson, Milton, Locke, Addison, Pope, Swift, the higher Papers in the *Spectator* and *Guardian*, the best Translations of Homer, Virgil and Horace, of *Telemachus*, *Travels of Cyrus*, &c.

Once a Year, let there be publick Exercises in the Hall, the Trustees and Citizens present. Then let fine gilt Books be given as Prizes to such Boys as distinguish themselves, and excel the others in any Branch of Learning; making three Degrees of Comparison; giving the best Prize to him that performs best; a less valuable One to him that comes up next to the best; and another to the third. Commendations, Encouragement and Advice to the rest; keeping up their Hopes that by Industry they may excel another Time. The Names of those that obtain the Prizes, to be yearly printed in a List.

The Hours of each Day are to be divided and dispos'd in such a Manner, as that some Classes may be with the Writing-Master, improving their Hands, others with the Mathematical Master, learning Arithmetick, Accompts, Geography, Use of the Globes, Drawing, Mechanicks, &c. while the rest are in the English School, under the English Master's Care.

Thus instructed, Youth will come out of this School fitted for learning any Business, Calling or Profession, except such wherein Languages are required; and tho' unacquainted with any antient or foreign Tongue, they will be Masters of their own, which is of more immediate and general Use; and withal will have attain'd many other valuable Accomplishments; the Time usually spent in acquiring those Languages, often without Success, being here employ'd in laying such a Foundation of Knowledge and Ability, as, properly improv'd, may qualify them to pass thro' and execute the several Offices of civil Life, with Advantage and Reputation to themselves and Country.

Forming the National Character: 4
Paradox in the Educational Thought
of the Revolutionary Generation

"Most of the *distresses* of our country, and of the *mistakes* which Europeans have formed of us," Benjamin Rush wrote in 1786, "have arisen from a belief that the American Revolution is *over*. This is so far from being the case that we have only finished the first act of the great drama. We have changed our forms of government, but it remains yet to effect a revolution in our principles, opinions, and manners so as to accomodate them to the forms of government we have adopted. This is the most difficult part of the business of the patriots and legislators of our country." In much the same spirit Noah Webster called for an "ASSOCIATION OF AMERICAN PATRIOTS for the purpose of forming a NATIONAL CHARACTER." Self-consciously, many Americans of the revolutionary generation sought to construct the artifact of American nationality.

As successful revolutionaries, Americans tried to conserve and consolidate their gains. Just as the Puritans had feared failure in their errand into the wilderness, so many leaders in the early Republic, charged with a deep sense of destiny, masked a dark vein of anxiety by assertive nationalism. A number of them believed that history demonstrated that republics were as evanescent as fireflies on a summer evening, that Europe was conspiring to wreck the new nation, that internal disorders and factions were threatening to shatter the republican community.

The age-old problem of balancing order and liberty haunted intellectuals of the revolutionary generation. Was it possible to stabilize freedom and preserve republican principles? Where along the spectrum from tyranny to anarchy would Americans find the proper synthesis of ordered liberty? "We daily see matter of a perishable nature rendered durable by certain chemical operations," observed Rush. "In like manner, I conceive, that it is possible to analyze and combine power in such a way as not only to increase the happiness, but to promote the duration of republican forms of government far beyond the terms limited for them by history, or the common opinions of mankind." One means of doing this was schooling.

Educational theorists of the period were concerned mainly with constructing institutions, not tearing them down. They stood at an opposite pole from Rousseau, who sought to extricate Émile from a corrupting society. Three writers expressing a common concern for education but representing different shades of opinion on the function of schooling were Thomas Jefferson, Noah Webster, and Benjamin Rush. As a devout libertarian, Jefferson feared a new absolutism. In his "Bill for the More General Diffusion of Knowledge" he warned that "experience hath shewn, that even under the best forms [of government], those entrusted with power have, in time, and by slow operations, perverted it into tyranny. . . ." The Federalist Webster, conservative compared to Jefferson, worried that republican government might prove anarchical. "The United States are in no danger of monarchy or the aristocracy of hereditary estates and offices," he said. "But these states will always be exposed to *anarchy* and *faction*, because these evils approach under the delusive but specious guise of *patriotism*." Rush, more concerned about preserving freedom than Webster, but alarmed at centrifugal forces in American society, wrote that Americans "understood perfectly the principles of liberty, yet most of us were ignorant of the forms and combinations of power in republics."

Thus from the educational theories of Jefferson, Rush, and Webster emerged definitions of the republican American. Not content with unconscious and haphazard socialization provided by family, political meeting, press, and informal associations, not trusting in the "givenness" of political beliefs and institutions, these men sought to instruct Americans deliberately in schools. Having fought a war to free the United States from one centralized authority, they attempted to create a new unity, a common citizenship and culture, and an appeal to a common future. In this quest for a balance between order and liberty, for the proper transaction between the individual and society, Jefferson, Rush, and Webster encountered a conflict still inherent in the education of the citizen and still expressed in the injunction to teachers to train students to think critically but to be patriotic above all. Hence proceeded a paradox from their search for ordered liberty: the free American was to be, in political convictions, the uniform American. In Jefferson's case the paradox became sharpest in his insistence on a type of political sectarianism at the University of Virginia. It emerged in Rush's demand that children should be made "republican machines" despite his opinion that government was a "progressive" science. And Webster not only desired political orthodoxy but grew alarmed at any deviation of free Americans from a common cultural standard. As a result, in differing degrees, they saw conformity as the price of liberty.

Negatively, they defined Americanism as the rejection of European ideas and institutions. Even while Jefferson enjoyed the sophisticated life of Paris, he praised American innocence, just as Franklin had posed in France in his fur cap as nature's own philosopher. America had no feudal tradition, no encrustation of illiberal institutions, no corrupt and gothic history to live down. America's newness was its greatest asset. To the extent that monarchical customs lingered in the United States, its citizenry had to cultivate the art of forgetting.

A pervasive fear of European contamination persuaded the Georgia legislature to pass a law in 1785 disbarring its residents from civic office for as many years as they had studied abroad (if sent overseas under the age of sixteen). George Washington advocated a federal university so that American youth would not need to go abroad for higher education and run the danger of "contracting principles unfavorable to republican government." He believed that such an institution would assimilate "the principles, opinions, and manners" of Americans: "The more homogeneous our citizens can be made in these particulars, the greater will be our prospect of permanent union. . . ." Jefferson argued all his life against the policy of educating Americans abroad:

> Cast your eye over America: who are the men of most learning, of most eloquence, most beloved by their country and most trusted and promoted by them? They are those who have been educated among them, and whose manners, morals and habits are perfectly homogeneous with those of the country . . . the consequences of foreign education are alarming to me as an American.

The "perfectly homogeneous" American, then, must be educated at home. Further, he must study American textbooks. For America to use the textbooks of the Old World, Noah Webster wrote in the preface of his spelling book, "would be to stamp the wrinkles of decrepit age upon the bloom of youth and to plant the seeds of decay in a vigorous constitution." Instead, he urged, America must "prevent the introduction of foreign vices and corruptions . . . promote virtue and patriotism [and] . . . diffuse an uniformity and purity of language. . . ." The same impulse which drove Joel Barlow to write his patriotic epic the *Columbiad* and Philip Freneau his republican poems, and Charles Wilson Peale to paint American themes, impelled textbook writers like Noah Webster and Jedediah Morse to exalt American language, geography, and history. Students should study America first and last. Education must be a republican *paideia*, an all-out effort to Americanize through the schools, the press, the pulpit, the work of the artist, the courtroom, the political assembly— by all the means of shaping character and intellect.

Noah Webster wished to inculcate uniformity in spelling, pronunciation, and political and economic principles. "However detestable personal pride may be," he declared, "yet there is a national pride and a provincial, that are the noblest passions of the republican patriot. . . . For my own part, I frankly acknowledge, I have too much pride not to wish to see America assume a national character." His textbooks were the chief weapon of his campaign for nationalism; in them he sought to homogenize the language "by demolishing those odious distinctions of provincial dialects which are the subject of reciprocal ridicule in different States," to instruct in patriotic principles by a judicious selection of speeches of representative leaders, and to hasten the flowering of American literature. In his essay "On the Education of Youth in America" Webster observed that

> our national character is not yet formed; and it is an object of vast magnitude that systems of Education should be adopted and pursued, which may not only diffuse a knowledge of the sciences, but may implant, in the minds of American youth, the principles of virtue and of liberty; and inspire them with just and liberal ideas of government, and with an inviolable attachment to their own country.

Only American teachers should be employed, skilled in "prepossessing the mind with good principles." As soon as the American child "opens his lips, he should rehearse the history of his own country; he should lisp the praise of liberty, and of those illustrious heroes and statesmen who have wrought a revolution in her favor." Benjamin Rush agreed with Webster's policy of transforming American statesmen into demi-gods. Though he had not admired Washington's leadership during the war, he concurred with a friend who thought it wise to tell less than the full truth about the founding fathers: "Let the world admire our patriots and heroes. Their supposed talents and virtues by commanding attention will serve the cause of patriotism and of our country."

Rush stated in its most unequivocal form the paradox that the *free* American was the *uniform* republican. Whereas heterogeneous colonial education largely perpetuated existing differences in society, Rush proposed "one general, and uniform system of education" which would "render the mass of the people more homogeneous, and thereby fit them more easily for uniform and peaceable government." Webster, Rush, and Jefferson believed that education must be systematic, useful, and uniformly republican in aim. The only social agency capable of creating such an educational system was the government, whether state or national. "I consider it as possible to convert men into republican machines," declared Rush.

> This must be done, if we expect them to perform their parts properly, in the great machine of the government of the state. That republic is sophisticated with monarchy or aristocracy that does not revolve upon the wills of the people, and these must be fitted to each other by means of education before they can be made to produce regularity and unison in government.

Rush was far more explicit about republican behavior than about republican beliefs. When he turned to the principles which must be impressed upon the pupil, he simply declared, "He must be taught that there can be no durable liberty but in a republic, and that government, like all other sciences, is of a progressive nature. The chains which have bound this science in Europe are happily unloosened in America." This grandiose trust in the "progressive nature" of political science, coupled with a desire to use the schools to homogenize the citizenry, created an illusion of consensus which sometimes obscured actual political bias. The result could be indoctrination disguised by the sense of "givenness" of American political ideas and institutions.

Rush, Jefferson, and Webster shared a common eighteenth-century faith in the diffusion of knowledge, a trust expressed in almost all the early American state constitutions. In *Sketches of American Policy* Webster contended that "a general diffusion of science is our best guard against the approaches of corruption, the prevalence of religious error, the intrigues of ambition and against the open assaults of external foes." "Enlighten the people generally, and tyranny and oppression of body and mind will vanish like evil spirits at the dawn of day," wrote Jefferson, arguing that "the diffusion of knowledge among the people is to be the instrument" of vast progress. All three agreed in theory that elementary instruction of all classes was more important than higher education of an elite. Jefferson and Rush believed that it was wise to disenfranchise the illiterate. None of them, however, wrote in detail about what kind of political knowledge should be diffused.

In his bill for education in Virginia, Jefferson wrote that every teacher should "give assurance of fidelity to the commonwealth," but he did not specify the curriculum for the common people beyond the three R's and history. In *Notes on the State of Virginia*, he commented that young children, too immature for religious inquiries, should have their minds "stored with the most useful facts from Grecian, Roman, European, and American history." Later he indicated what sort of history was most "useful" when he tried to have an expurgated and liberalized version of Hume's history taught at the University of Virginia. He feared that if

Americans read the Tory Hume, they would slide into Federalist doctrine. Thus he approved the policy of the editor who "gives you the text of Hume, purely and verbally, till he comes to some misrepresentation or omission . . . he then alters the text silently, makes it say what truth and candor say it should be, and resumes the original text again, as soon as it becomes innocent, without having warned you of your rescue from misguidance." Like Rush, who wanted a romanticized view of the founding fathers taught to instill a uniform patriotism, Jefferson preferred to diffuse knowledge which would produce homogeneous—and Whig—political views. Dialectic, the clash of factions, the battle of opinions in the "progressive science" of government had no place in the schoolroom.

Both Webster and Rush believed that the teacher should be an absolute monarch. "The government of schools . . . should be *arbitrary*," wrote Rush. "By this mode of education we prepare our youth for the subordination of laws, and thereby qualify them for becoming good citizens of the republic. I am satisfied that the most useful citizens have been formed from those youth who have never known or felt their own wills till they were one and twenty years of age. . . ." Instruction in the principles of government became indoctrination: witness the "Federal Catechism" which Webster appended to the 1798 edition of his *American Spelling Book* in which he told children of the advantages of republicanism and the defects of monarchy, aristocracy, and democracy.

There were, indeed, ambiguities in this notion of diffusing knowledge. Webster wrote in 1796 that public information would correct the evil of faction, maintaining that when the people *"understand* public affairs, they *will not do wrong."* But in his conservative old age he lost this trust:

> . . . the opinion that intelligence in the people of a country will preserve a republican government must depend for its accuracy on the fact of an intimate or necessary connection between *knowledge* and *principle.* It must suppose that men who *know* what is right will *do* what is right; for if this is not the general fact, then intelligence will not preserve a just administration nor maintain the Constitution and laws. But from what evidence can we infer that men who *know* what is right will *do* what is right? In what history of mankind, political or ecclesiastical, are the facts recorded which authorize the presumption, much less the belief, that correct action will proceed from correct knowledge?

Webster, Rush, and Jefferson believed that republican leaders required a special education. Their conception of the training of leaders emerges notably in the case of Jefferson, who founded the University of Virginia in his old age, fulfilling a lifelong ambition. While he advocated primary education on abstract principles, higher education was an intensely personal matter; in effect he was trying to institutionalize his own varied education.

All of the first six Presidents of the United States urged the creation of a national university to prepare an elite. Benjamin Rush even suggested that Congress pass a law "to prevent any person [thirty years after the founding of the university] being chosen or appointed into power or office who has not taken his degree in the federal university." Rush believed that such an institution could be a place "where the youth of all the states may be melted (as it were) together into one mass of citizens. . . ."

In his bill of 1779 "For the More General Diffusion of Knowledge," Jefferson had sketched a plan for the selection and education of a natural aristocracy which would supplement but not supplant the aristocracy of birth and wealth. He designed a rigorous system to select these natural aristocrats for scholarships—"raking a few geniuses from the rubbish" he called it. The majority of students in the grammar schools and at William and Mary would continue to be the sons of planters and professional men who had long enjoyed a near monopoly of formal education.

Jefferson believed that the people could be divided into two major groups, the "laboring and the learned." Consequently, the educational system had two tracks. The laboring class needed but the three years of elementary schooling in which the basic precepts of republicanism were to be inculcated along with the three R's. The learned class was composed of those destined for the professions and the wealthy, who "may aspire to share in conducting the affairs of the nation. . . ." His scholarship boys, the few students of talent and virtue raked from the rubbish, constituted the natural aristocracy. One of Jefferson's remarkable assumptions was that the electorate would select his natural aristocrats for office, as their expected prerogative in colonial times. Such an assumption would soon be outmoded in the shifting style of political leadership to come in the Jacksonian period. It was a normal carry-over, however, from the patrician pattern of political power in pre-war Virginia. Although his proposal to reform William and Mary did not succeed, Jefferson returned in later years to his earlier desire to found a true university in Virginia.

In common with most of the educational theorists of the revolutionary generation, Jefferson did not operate on egalitarian principles of leadership. Like Rush, who proposed the remarkable plan of an interlocking directorate of the federal university and the federal government, he believed that the education of the guardians was of consummate importance. They must think and act correctly, for the fate of the state was in their hands. Thus it is revealing to examine Jefferson's practical role in his one successful educational reform, the founding of the University of Virginia, a role in which he appears as the high priest of political sectarianism.

Religious sectarianism in higher education was, of course, no new phenomenon. Harvard, William and Mary, and most of the other colonial colleges had been founded to prepare orthodox ecclesiastical and political leaders. It was precisely this sectarian cast of William and Mary which had most disturbed Jefferson about his alma mater and had impelled him to attempt unsuccessfully to render it a secular institution in 1779.

Passionately anti-clerical, Jefferson declared a lifelong war against religious bigotry. Like many other eighteenth-century liberals, he acquired a profound distaste for theology and what he called "metaphysics," choosing instead to interpret Christianity as a humanistic moral code. He edited the Gospels in a new and improved Jeffersonian Bible, culling the genuine sayings of Christ from the spurious "as easily distinguishable as diamonds in a dunghill." A zealous advocate of tolerance, he prided himself on Virginia's Bill for Establishing Religious Freedom. He opposed the establishment of any church, contending "that to compel a man to furnish contributions of money for the propagation of opinions which he disbelieves and abhors is sinful and tyrannical . . . truth is great and will prevail if left to herself. . . ." To the end he remained consistent and forceful in his defense of religious liberty, and claimed that he "never attempted to make a convert, nor wished to change another's creed."

About theology Jefferson cared little, but political ideology was another matter. It is here that Jefferson's rigid liberalism became apparent, and nowhere more so than in his work as founder of the University of Virginia. To Jefferson, political principles separated people into camps almost as distinct as the split between the regenerate and the unregenerate for the Puritan. "The Division into Whig and Tory is founded in the nature of men," he wrote; "the weakly and nerveless, the rich and corrupt seeing more safety and accessibility in a strong executive; the healthy, firm and virtuous, feeling confidence in their physical and moral resources, and willing to part with only so much power as is necessary for their government. . . ." Obviously, American leaders must be Whigs.

Religious or philosophical heresies did not matter, but political heresy did. In 1811 Jefferson wrote that "the eyes of the virtuous all over the earth are turned with anxiety on us, as the only depositories of the sacred fire of liberty, and . . . our falling into anarchy would decide forever the destinies of mankind, and seal the political heresy that man is incapable of self-government." In his study of *Jefferson and Civil Liberties: the Darker Side*, Leonard Levy contends that Jefferson was convinced that "the great American experiment in self-government and liberty was in nearly constant danger. He completely identified with that experiment, to the point that an attack on him or on the wisdom of his policies quickly became transmuted in his mind as a threat to the security of the tender democratic plant." Just as the revolutionary generation had earlier feared the taint of European monarchical maxims, so the liberal Jefferson came to fear that future leaders would be contaminated by Federalist doctrine.

Jefferson had given a libertarian charter to the University of Virginia, proclaiming that it "will be based on the illimitable freedom of the human mind. For here we are not afraid to follow the truth wherever it may lead, nor to tolerate any error as long as reason is left free to combat it." But when the time came to hire the faculty, he wrote to James Madison, "In the selection of our Law Professor we must be rigorously attentive to his political principles." He insisted on the importance of finding an orthodox advocate of states-rights republicanism, for

> It is in our seminary that the vestal flame is to be kept alive; from thence it is to spread anew over our own and the sister States. If we are true and vigilant in our trust, within a dozen or twenty years a majority of our own legislature will be from one school, and many disciples will have carried its doctrine home with them to their several states, and will have leavened thus the whole mass.

"Seminary," "vestal flame," "disciples," "doctrine," "leavened thus the whole mass"—what are these terms if not the vocabulary of the sectarian? In a letter to an ally in the legislature, Jefferson spoke of "the political holy charge" which the university would transmit to the students.

Jefferson also insisted that the lay Board of Visitors prescribe the textbooks:

> There is one branch in which we are the best judges, in which heresies may be taught, of so interesting a character to our own State, and to the United States, as to make it a duty in us to lay down the principles which are to be taught. It is that of government. . . . It is our duty to guard against the dissemination of such [Federalist] principles among our youth, and the diffusion of that poison, by a previous prescription of the texts to be followed in their discourses.

Jefferson's prescription of texts meant to a Federalist Virginian such as Chief Justice Marshall, who favored a strong central government, that he was being compelled by the state to contribute money for the propagation of opinions which he disbelieved and abhorred. If the true test of tolerance is to permit heresies about which one cares deeply, then the Virginian Federalists might appear greater libertarians than the man who "swore eternal hostility to tyranny over the minds of men." Perhaps no one saw more clearly than Benjamin Rush that a new field of sectarian battle was emerging after the Revolution. "We only change the names of our vices and follies in different periods of time," he wrote. "Religious bigotry has yielded to political intolerance. The man who used to hate his neighbor for being a Churchman or a Quaker now hates him with equal cordiality for being a Tory." Indeed, as Rush himself demonstrated in his own comments on "republican machines," it was difficult to be a consistent libertarian in a nation striving to articulate and inculcate liberal republican principles.

The United States was a great experiment. Earnestly, Jefferson, Rush, and Webster worked to make it succeed. Experience could give no guarantee that citizens would be loyal to the principles and institutions which made them free; yet, at the same time, only if individuals could dissent with impunity from the most fundamental convictions of society would they know that they were indeed free. From this clash of necessary consensus and of freedom to dissent stemmed the paradoxical nature of the educational theories of the three intellectuals. Determined to preserve the heritage of the Revolution, to unify the nation, and to inculcate proper principles of government, they advocated a kind of republican indoctrination, hoping that the ensuing enlightenment would bring a salutary uniformity.

During the period from the Revolution to Jefferson's death in 1826 the educational theories of Webster, Rush, and Jefferson had little influence on educational institutions. Webster did reach the rising generation through his textbooks (it is estimated that over 20,000,000 copies of his speller alone were sold). Schools were heterogeneous rather than uniform, serving to perpetuate religious, sectional, social, and economic groupings. The patterns of colonial educational support, control, and ideology persisted, while institutional innovations like the monitorial system, the Sunday school, and the infant school were imported from England. The sectarian splintering which had begun before the Revolution continued unabated, and religious motivation remained a prime mover in the founding of schools. "In education, as in so many other spheres of social action," Bernard Bailyn has noted, the effects of the Revolution "were to free the trends of the colonial period from legal and institutional incumbrances and to confirm them, to formalize them, to give them the sanction of law in a framework of enlightened political thought." The population was too scattered, too varied, too lacking in surplus and taxable wealth to create the types of systematic public education envisaged by the theorists; and community support for schools took the more familiar channels of denominational, local, and class allegiance. But the concept of uniform, systematic education serving republican purposes did not disappear. Later, when new challenges confronted society during the period of the common school crusade, the ideas would emerge again, fortified by added sanctions and new anxieties.

4.1   Noah Webster "On the Education of Youth in America."

The Education of youth is, in all governments, an object of the first consequence. The impressions received in early life, usually form the characters
of individuals; a union of which forms the general character of a nation. . . .

Education is a subject which has been exhausted by the ablest writers,
both among the ancients and moderns. I am not vain enough to suppose I
can suggest any new ideas upon so trite a theme as Education in general;
but perhaps the manner of conducting the youth in America may be capable of some improvement. Our constitutions of civil government are
not yet firmly established; our national character is not yet formed; and
it is an object of vast magnitude that systems of Education should be
adopted and pursued, which may not only diffuse a knowledge of the sciences, but may implant, in the minds of the American youth, the principles
of virtue and of liberty; and inspire them with just and liberal ideas of
government, and with an inviolable attachment to their own country. It
now becomes every American to examin the modes of Education in Europe, to see how far they are applicable in this country, and whether it
is not possible to make some valuable alterations, adapted to our local and
political circumstances. Let us examin the subject in two views. First,
as it respects arts and sciences. Secondly, as it is connected with morals
and government. In each of these articles, let us see what errors may be
found, and what improvements suggested, in our present practice.

The first error that I would mention, is, a too general attention to the
dead languages, with a neglect of our own. . . .

But the high estimation in which the learned languages have been held,
has discouraged a due attention to our own. People find themselves able
without much study to write and speak the English intelligibly, and thus
have been led to think rules of no utility. This opinion has produced various and arbitrary practices, in the use of the language, even among men of
the most information and accuracy; and this diversity has produced another opinion, both false and injurious to the language, that there are no
rules or principles on which the pronunciation and construction can be
settled.

This neglect is so general, that there is scarcely an institution to be found
in the country, where the English tongue is taught regularly, from its elements to its true and elegant construction, in prose and verse. Perhaps in

Noah Webster, *A Collection of Essays and Fugitiv Writings. On Moral, Historical,
Political and Literary Subjects* (Boston: I. Thomas and E. E. Andrews, 1790), pp.
1, 3, 6, 15–19, 22–26, 30–31, 36.

most schools, boys are taught the definition of the parts of speech, and a few hard names which they do not understand, and which the teacher seldom attempts to explain; this is called *learning grammar*. This practice of learning questions and answers without acquiring any ideas, has given rise to a common remark, *that grammar is a dry study;* and so is every other study which is prosecuted without improving the head or the heart. The study of geography is equally dry, when the subject is not understood. But when grammar is taught by the help of visible objects; when children perceive that differences of words arise from differences in things, which they may learn at a very early period of life, the study becomes entertaining, as well as improving. In general, when a study of any kind is tiresome to a person, it is a presumptive evidence that he does not make any proficiency in knowlege, and this is almost always the fault of the instructor. . . .

But the principal defect in our plan of Education in America, is, the want of good teachers in the academies and common schools. By good teachers I mean, men of unblemished reputation, and possessed of abilities, competent to their stations. That a man should be master of what he undertakes to teach, is a point that will not be disputed; and yet it is certain that abilities are often dispensed with, either thro inattention or fear of expense.

To those who employ ignorant men to instruct their children, permit me to suggest one important idea: That it is better for youth to have *no* Education, than to have a bad one; for it is more difficult to eradicate habits, than to impress new ideas. The tender shrub is easily bent to any figure; but the tree, which has acquired its full growth, resists all impressions.

Yet abilities are not the sole requisites. The instructors of youth ought, of all men, to be the most prudent, accomplished, agreeable and respectable. What avail a man's part, if, while he is the "wisest and brightest," he is the "meanest of mankind?" The pernicious effects of bad example on the *minds* of youth will probably be acknowledged; but with a view to *improvement*, it is indispensably necessary that the teachers should possess good breeding and agreeable manners. In order to give full effect to instructions, it is requisite that they should proceed from a man who is loved and respected. But a low bred clown, or morose tyrant, can command neither love nor respect; and that pupil who has no motive for application to books, but the fear of a rod, will not make a scholar.

The rod is often necessary in school; especially after the children have been accustomed to disobedience and a licentious behavior at home. All government originates in families, and if neglected there, it will hardly exist in society; but the want of it must be supplied by the rod in school, the penal laws of the state, and the terrors of divine wrath from the pulpit. The government both of families and schools should be absolute. There should, in families, be no appeal from one parent to another, with the prospect of pardon for offences. The one should always vindicate, at least apparently, the conduct of the other. In schools the master should be absolute in command; for it is utterly impossible for any man to support order and discipline among children, who are indulged with an appeal to their parents. A proper subordination in families would generally supersede the necessity of severity in schools; and a strict discipline in both is the best foundation of good order in political society.

If parents should say, "we cannot give the instructors of our children unlimited authority over them, for it may be abused and our children injured;" I would answer, they must not place them under the direction of any man, in whose temper, judgement and abilities, they do not repose perfect confidence. The teacher should be, if such can be found, as judicious and reasonable a man as the parent.

There can be little improvement in schools, without strict subordination; there can be no subordination, without principles of esteem and respect in the pupils; and the pupils cannot esteem and respect a man who is not in himself respectable, and who is not treated with respect by their parents. It may be laid down as an invariable maxim, that a person is not fit to superintend the Education of children, who has not the qualifications which will command the esteem and respect of his pupils. This maxim is founded on a truth which every person may have observed; that children always *love* an *amiable* man, and always *esteem* a *respectable* one. Men and women have their passions, which often rule their judgement and their conduct. They have their caprices, their interests and their prejudices, which at times incline them to treat the most meritorious characters with disrespect. But children, artless and unsuspecting, resign their hearts to any person whose manners are agreeable, and whose conduct is respectable. Whenever, therefore, pupils cease to respect their teacher, he should be instantly dismissed.

Respect for an instructor will often supply the place of a rod of correction. The pupil's attachment will lead him to close attention to his studies; he fears not the *rod* so much as the *displeasure* of his teacher; he waits for a smile, or dreads a frown; he receives his instructions and copies his manners. This generous principle, the fear of offending will prompt youth to exertion; and instead of severity on the one hand, and of slavish fear, with reluctant obedience on the other, mutual esteem, respect and confidence strew flowers in the road to knowledge.

With respect to morals and civil society, the other view in which I proposed to treat this subject, the effects of Education are so certain and extensive, that it behooves every parent and guardian to be particularly attentive to the characters of the men, whose province it is to form the minds of youth.

From a strange inversion of the order of nature, the cause of which it is not necessary to unfold, the most important business in civil society, is, in many parts of America, committed to the most worthless characters. The Education of youth, an employment of more consequence than making laws and preaching the gospel, because it lays the foundation on which both law and gospel rest for success; this Education is sunk to a level with the most menial services. In most instances we find the higher seminaries of learning intrusted to men of good characters, and possessed of the moral virtues and social affections. But many of our inferior schools, which, so far as the heart is concerned, are as important as colleges, are kept by men of no breeding, and many of them, by men infamous for the most detestable vices. Will this be denied? will it be denied, that before the war, it was a frequent practice for gentlemen to purchase convicts, who had been transported for their crimes, and employ them as private tutors in their families?

Gracious Heavens! Must the wretches, who have forfeited their lives, and been pronounced unworthy to be inhabitants of a *foreign* country, be entrusted with the Education, the morals, the character of *American* youth? . . .

Our legislators frame laws for the suppression of vice and immorality; our divines thunder, from the pulpit, the terrors of infinite wrath, against the vices that stain the characters of men. And do laws and preaching effect a reformation of manners? Experience would not give a very favorable answer to this inquiry. The reason is obvious; the attempts are directed to the wrong objects. Laws can only check the public effects of vicious principles; but can never reach the principles themselves; and preaching is not very intelligible to people, till they arrive at an age when their principles are rooted, or their habits firmly established. An attempt to eradicate old habits, is as absurd, as to lop off the branches of a huge oak, in order to root it out of a rich soil. The most that such clipping will effect, is to prevent a further growth.

The only practicable method to reform mankind, is to begin with children; to banish, if possible, from their company, every low bred, drunken, immoral character. Virtue and vice will not grow together in a great degree, but they will grow where they are planted, and when one has taken root, it is not easily supplanted by the other. The great art of correcting mankind therefore, consists in prepossessing the mind with good principles.

For this reason society requires that the Education of youth should be watched with the most scrupulous attention. Education, in a great measure, forms the moral characters of men, and morals are the basis of government. Education should therefore be the first care of a Legislature; not merely the institution of schools, but the furnishing of them with the best men for teachers. A good system of Education should be the first article in the code of political regulations; for it is much easier to introduce and establish an effectual system for preserving morals, than to correct, by penal statutes, the ill effects of a bad system. I am so fully persuaded of this, that I shall almost adore that great man who shall change our practice and opinions and make it respectable for the first and best men to superintend the Education of youth.

Another defect in our schools, which, since the revolution, is become inexcuseable, is the want of proper books. The collections which are now used consist of essays that respect foreign and ancient nations. The minds of youth are perpetually led to the history of Greece and Rome or to Great Britain; boys are constantly repeating the declamations of Demosthenes and Cicero, or debates upon some political question in the British Parliament. These are excellent specimens of good sense, polished style and perfect oratory; but they are not interesting to children. They cannot be very useful except to young gentlemen who want them as models of reasoning and eloquence, in the pulpit or at the bar.

But every child in America should be acquainted with his own country. He should read books that furnish him with ideas that will be useful to him in life and practice. As soon as he opens his lips, he should rehearse the history of his own country; he should lisp the praise of liberty, and of those illustrious heroes and statesmen, who have wrought a revolution in her favor.

A selection of essays, respecting the settlement and geography of America; the history of the late revolution and of the most remarkable characters and events that distinguished it, and a compendium of the principles of the federal and provincial governments, should be the principal school book in the United States. These are interesting objects to every man; they call home the minds of youth and fix them upon the interests of their own country, and they assist in forming attachments to it, as well as in enlarging the understanding. . . .

In despotic governments, the people should have little or no education, except what tends to inspire them with a servile fear. Information is fatal to despotism.

In monarchies, education should be partial, and adapted to the rank of each class of citizens. But "in a republican government," says the same writer, "the whole power of education is required." Here every class of people should *know* and *love* the laws. This knowledge should be diffused by means of schools and newspapers; and an attachment to the laws may be formed by early impressions upon the mind.

Two regulations are essential to the continuance of republican governments: 1. Such a distribution of lands and such principles of descent and alienation, as shall give every citizen a power of acquiring what his industry merits. 2. Such a system of education as gives every citizen an opportunity of acquiring knowlege and fitting himself for places of trust. These are fundamental articles; the *sine qua non* of the existence of the American republics.

Hence the absurdity of our copying the manners and adopting the institutions of Monarchies.

In several States, we find laws passed, establishing provision for colleges and academies, where people of property may educate their sons; but no provision is made for instructing the poorer rank of people, even in reading and writing. Yet in these same States, every citizen who is worth a few shillings annually, is entitled to vote for legislators. This appears to me a most glaring solecism in government. The constitutions are *republican*, and the laws of education are *monarchical*. The *former* extend civil rights to every honest industrious man; the *latter* deprive a large proportion of the citizens of a most valuable privilege.

In our American republics, where governments is in the hands of the people, knowledge should be fully diffused by means of public schools. Of such consequence is it to society, that the people who make laws, should be well informed, that I conceive no Legislature can be justified in neglecting proper establishments for this purpose.

When I speak of a diffusion of knowlege, I do not mean merely a knowlege of spelling books, and the New Testament. An acquaintance with ethics, and with the general principles of law, commerce, money and government, is necessary for the yeomanry of a republican state. This acquaintance they might obtain by means of books calculated for schools, and read by the children, during the winter months, and by the circulation of public papers.

"In Rome it was the common exercise of boys at school, to learn the laws of the twelve tables by heart, as they did their poets and classic authors." What an excellent practice this in a free government!

It is said, indeed by many, that our common people are already too well informed. Strange paradox! The truth is, they have too much knowlege and spirit to resign their share in government, and are not sufficiently informed to govern themselves in all cases of difficulty.

There are some acts of the American legislatures which astonish men of information; and blunders in legislation are frequently ascribed to bad intentions. But if we examin the men who compose these legislatures, we shall find that wrong measures generally proceed from ignorance either in the men themselves, or in their constituents. They often mistake their own interest, because they do not foresee the remote consequences of a measure.

It may be true that all men cannot be legislators; but the more generally knowlege is diffused among the substantial yeomanry, the more perfect will be the laws of a republican state.

Every small district should be furnished with a school, at least four months in a year; when boys are not otherwise employed. This school should be kept by the most reputable and well informed man in the district. Here children should be taught the usual branches of learning; submission to superiors and to laws; the moral or social duties; the history and transactions of their own country; the principles of liberty and government. Here the rough manners of the wilderness should be softened, and the principles of virtue and good behaviour inculcated. The *virtues* of men are of more consequence to society than their *abilities;* and for this reason, the *heart* should be cultivated with more assiduity than the *head*.

Such a general system of education is neither impracticable nor difficult; and excepting the formation of a federal government that shall be efficient and permanent, it demands the first attention of American patriots. Until such a system shall be adopted and pursued; until the Statesman and Divine shall unite their efforts in *forming* the human mind, rather than in loping its excrescences, after it has been neglected; until Legislators discover that the only way to make good citizens and subjects, is to nourish them from infancy; and until parents shall be convinced that the *worst* of men are not the proper teachers to make the *best;* mankind cannot know to what a degree of perfection society and government may be carried. America affords the fairest opportunities for making the experiment, and opens the most encouraging prospect of success. . . .

Before I quit this subject, I beg leave to make some remarks on a practice which appears to be attended with important consequences; I mean that of sending boys to Europe for an education, or sending to Europe for teachers. This was right before the revolution; at least so far as national attachments where concerned; but the propriety of it ceased with our political relation to Great Britain.

In the first place, our honor as an independent nation is concerned in the establishment of literary institutions, adequate to all our own purposes; without sending our youth abroad, or depending on other nations for books and instructors. It is very little to the reputation of America to have it said abroad, that after the heroic atchievements of the late war, these independent people are obliged to send to Europe for men and books to teach their children A B C.

But in another point of view, a foreign education is directly opposite to our political interests, and ought to be discountenanced, if not prohibited.

Every person of common observation will grant, that most men prefer the manners and the government of that country where they are educated. Let ten American youths be sent, each to a different European kingdom, and live there from the age of twelve to twenty, and each will give the preference to the country where he has resided. . . .

Americans, unshackle your minds, and act like independent beings. You have been children long enough, subject to the control, and subservient to the interest of a haughty parent. You have now an interest of your own to augment and defend: You have an empire to raise and support by your exertions, and a national character to establish and extend by your wisdom and virtues. To effect these great objects, it is necessary to frame a liberal plan of policy, and build it on a broad system of education. Before this system can be formed and embraced, the Americans must *believe*, and *act* from the belief, that it is dishonorable to waste life in mimicking the follies of other nations and basking in the sunshine of foreign glory.

4.2   Benjamin Rush Outlines a Plan for Public Schools in Pennsylvania.

For the purpose of diffusing knowledge through every part of the state, I beg leave to propose the following simple plan.

  I. Let there be one university in the state, and let this be established in the capital. Let law, physic divinity, the law of nature and nations, œconomy, &c. be taught in it by public lectures in the winter season, after the manner of the European universities, and let the professors receive such salaries from the state as will enable them to deliver their lectures at a moderate price.

 II. Let there be four colleges. One in Philadelphia,—one at Carlisle—a third, for the benefit of our German fellow citizens, at Manheim, —and a fourth, some years hence, at Pittsburgh. In these colleges, let young men be instructed in mathematics and in the higher branches of science, in the same manner that they are now taught in our American colleges. After they have taken a degree in one of these colleges, let them, if they can afford it, complete their studies by spending a season or two in attending the lectures in the university. I prefer four colleges in the state to one or two, for there is a certain size of colleges as there is of towns and armies,

Benjamin Rush, *A Plan for the Establishment of Public Schools* . . . (Philadelphia: Thomas Dobson, 1786), pp. 4–6, 7–10.

that is most favourable to morals and good government. Oxford and Cambridge in England are the seats of dissipation, while the more numerous, and less crouded universities and colleges in Scotland, are remarkable for the order, diligence, and decent behaviour of their students.

III. Let there be an academy established in each county, for the purpose of instructing youth in the learned languages, and thereby preparing them to enter college.

IV. Let there be free schools established in every township, or in districts consisting of one hundred families. In these schools, let children be taught to read and write the English and German languages, and the use of figures. Such of them as have parents that can afford to send them from home, and are disposed to extend their educations, may remove their children from the free school to the county academy.

By this plan, the whole state will be tied together by one system of education. The university will in time furnish masters for the colleges, and the colleges will furnish masters for the academies and free schools, while the free Schools, in their turns, will supply the academies—the colleges, and the university, with scholars—students, and pupils. The same systems of grammar, oratory and philosophy will be taught in every part of the state, and the literary features of Pennsylvania will thus designate one great, and equally enlightned family. . . .

But, how shall we bear the expence of these literary institutions under the present weight of our taxes?—I answer—These institutions are designed to *lessen* our taxes. They will enlighten us in the great business of finance —they will teach us to encrease the ability of the state to support government, by encreasing the profits of agriculture, and by promoting manufactures. They will teach us all the modern improvements and advantages of inland navigation. They will defend us from hasty and expensive experiments in government, by unfolding to us the experience and folly of past ages, and thus, instead of adding to our taxes and debts, they will furnish us with the true secret of lessening and discharging both of them.

But, shall the estates of orphans, batchelors and persons who have no children be taxed to pay for the support of schools from which they can derive no benefit? I answer in the affirmative, to the first part of the objection, and I deny the truth of the latter part of it. Every member of the community is interested in the propagation of virtue and knowledge in the state. But I will go further, and add, it will be true œconomy in individuals to support public schools. The batchelor will in time save his tax for this purpose, by being able to sleep with fewer bolts and locks to his doors,—the estates of orphans will in time be benefited, by being protected from the ravages of unprincipled and idle boys, and the children of wealthy parents will be less tempted, by bad company, to extravagance. Fewer pillories and whipping posts, and smaller jails, with their usual expences and taxes, will be necessary when our youth are properly educated, than at present. I believe it could be proved, that the expences of confining, trying and executing criminals amount every year, in most of the counties, to more money than would be sufficient to maintain all the schools that would be necessary in each county. The confessions of these criminals generally show us, that their vices and punishments are the fatal consequences of the want of a proper education in early life.

I submit these detatched hints to the consideration of the legislature and of the citizens of Pennsylvania. The plan for the free schools is taken chiefly from the plans which have long been used with success in Scotland, and in the Eastern states of America, where the influence of learning in promoting religion, morals, manners, government, &c. has never been exceeded in any country.

4.3 Rush's "Thoughts upon the Mode of Education, Proper in a Republic."

The business of education has acquired a new complexion by the independence of our country. The form of government we have assumed, has created a new class of duties to every American. It becomes us, therefore, to examine our former habits upon this subject, and in laying the foundations for nurseries of wise and good men, to adapt our modes of teaching to the peculiar form of our government.

The first remark that I shall make upon this subject is, that an education in our own, is to be preferred to an education in a foreign country. The principle of patriotism stands in need of the reinforcement of *prejudice*, and it is well known that our strongest prejudices in favour of our country are formed in the first one and twenty years of our lives. The policy of the Lacedamonians is well worthy of our imitation. When Antipater demanded fifty of their children as hostages for the fulfilment of a distant engagement, those wise republicans refused to comply with his demand, but readily offered him double the number of their adult citizens, whose habits and prejudices could not be shaken by residing in a foreign country. Passing by, in this place, the advantages to the community from the early attachment of youth to the laws and constitution of their country, I shall only remark, that young men who have trodden the paths of science

Benjamin Rush, *ibid.*, pp. 13–23.

together, or have joined in the same sports, whether of swimming, scat-
ing, fishing, or hunting, generally feel, thro' life, such ties to each other, as
add greatly to the obligations of mutual benevolence.

I conceive the education of our youth in this country to be peculiarly
necessary in Pennsylvania, while our citizens are composed of the natives
of so many different kingdoms in Europe. Our Schools of learning, by
producing one general, and uniform system of education, will render the
mass of the people more homogeneous, and thereby fit them more easily
for uniform and peaceable government.

I proceed, in the next place, to enquire, what mode of education we
shall adopt so as to secure to the state all the advantages that are to be derived from the proper instruction of youth; and here I beg leave to remark
that the only foundation for a useful education in a republic is to be laid
in Religion. Without this, there can be no virtue, and without virtue
there can be no liberty, and liberty is the object and life of all republican
governments.

Such is my veneration for every religion that reveals the attributes of
the Deity, or a future state of rewards and punishments, that I had rather
see the opinions of Confucius or Mahomed inculcated upon our youth,
than see them grow up wholly devoid of a system of religious principles.
But the religion I mean to recommend in this place, is the religion of Jesus
Christ.

It is foreign to my purpose to hint at the arguments which establish the
truth of the Christian revelation. My only business is to declare, that all
its doctrines and precepts are calculated to promote the happiness of society, and the safety and well being of civil government. A Christian cannot fail of being a republican. The history of the creation of man, and of
the relation of our species to each other by birth, which is recorded in
the Old Testament, is the best refutation that can be given to the divine
right of kings, and the strongest argument that can be used in favour of
the original and natural equality of all mankind. A Christian, I say again,
cannot fail of being a republican, for every precept of the Gospel incul-
cates those degrees of humility, self-denial, and brotherly kindness, which
are directly opposed to the pride of monarchy and the pageantry of a
court. A Christian cannot fail of being useful to the republic, for his religion teacheth him that no man "liveth to himself." And lastly, a Christian cannot fail of being wholly inoffensive, for his religion teacheth him,
in all things to do to others what he would wish, in like circumstances,
they should do to him.

I am aware that I dissent from one of those paradoxical opinions with
which modern times abound; that it is improper to fill the minds of youth
with religious prejudices of any kind, and that they should be left to

choose their own principles, after they have arrived at an age in which they are capable of judging for themselves. Could we preserve the mind in childhood and youth a perfect blank, this plan of education would have more to recommend it; but this we know to be impossible. The human mind runs as naturally into principles as it does after facts. It submits with difficulty, to those restraints or partial discoveries which are imposed upon it in the infancy of reason. Hence the impatience of children to be informed upon all subjects that relate to the invisible world. But I beg leave to ask, Why should we pursue a different plan of education with respect to religion from that which we pursue in teaching the arts and sciences? Do we leave our youth to acquire systems of geography, philosophy, or politics, till they have arrived at an age in which they are capable of judgeing for themselves? We do not. I claim no more then for religion, than for the other sciences, and I add further, that if our youth are disposed after they are of age to think for themselves, a knowledge of *one* system will be the best means of conducting them in a free enquiry into other systems of religion, just as an acquaintance with one system of philosophy is the best introduction to the study of all the other systems in the world.

I must beg leave upon this subject to go one step further. In order more effectually to secure to our youth the advantages of a religious education, it is necessary to impose upon them the doctrines and discipline of a particular church. Man is naturally an ungovernable animal, and observations on particular societies and countries will teach us, that when we add the restraints of eclesiastical, to those of domestic and civil government, we produce, in him, the highest degrees of order and virtue. That fashionable liberality which refuses to associate with any one sect of Christians is seldom useful to itself, or to society, and may fitly be compared to the unprofitable bravery of a soldier, who wastes his valour in solitary enterprizes, without the aid or effect of military associations. Far be it from me to recommend the doctrines or modes of worship of any one denomination of Christians. I only recommend to the persons entrusted with the education of youth, to inculcate upon them a strict conformity to that mode of worship which is most agreeable to their consciences, or the inclinations of their parents.

Under this head, I must be excused in not agreeing with those modern writers who have opposed the use of the Bible as a school book. The only objection I know to it is, its division into chapters and verses, and its improper punctuation, which render it a more difficult book to read *well*, than many others; but these defects may easily be corrected; and the disadvantages of them are not to be mentioned with the immense advantages of making children early, and intimately acquainted with the means of acquiring happiness both here and hereafter. How great is the difference between making young people acquainted with the interesting and entertaining truths contained in the Bible, and the fables of Moore and Croxall, or the doubtful histories of antiquity! I maintain that there is no book of its size in the whole world, that contains half so much useful knowledge for the government of states, or the direction of the affairs of individuals as the bible. To object to the practice of having it read in schools, because it tends to destroy our veneration for it, is an argument that applies with equal force, against the frequency of public worship, and all other religious exercises. The first impressions upon the mind are the most durable. They survive the wreck of the memory, and exist in old age after the ideas acquired in middle life have been obliterated. Of how much consequence then must it be to the human mind in the evening of life, to be able to recal those ideas which are most essential to its happiness; and these are to be found chiefly in the Bible. The great delight which old people take in reading the Bible, I am persuaded is derived chiefly from its histories and precepts being *associated* with the events of childhood and youth, the recollection of which forms a material part of their pleasures.

I do not mean to exclude books of history, poetry or even fables from our schools. They may, and should be read frequently by our young people, but if the Bible is made to give way to them altogether, I foresee that it will be read, in a short time, only in churches, and in a few years will probably be found only in the offices of magistrates, and in courts of justice.

NEXT to the duty which young men owe to their Creator, I wish to see a SUPREME REGARD TO THEIR COUNTRY, inculcated upon them. When the Duke of Sully became prime minister to Henry the IVth of France, the first thing he did, he tells us, "Was to subdue and forget his own heart." The same duty is incumbent upon every citizen of a republic. Our country includes family, friends and property, and should be preferred to them all. Let our pupil be taught that he does not belong to himself, but that he is public property. Let him be taught to love his family, but let him be taught, at the same time, that he must forsake and even forgive them, when the welfare of his country requires it. He must watch for the state as if its liberties depended upon his vigilance alone, but he must do this in such a manner as not to defraud his creditors, or neglect his family. He must love private life, but he must decline no station, however public or responsable it may be, when called to it by the suffrages of his fellow-citizens. He must love popularity, but he must despise it when set in competition with the dictates of his judgement, or the real interest of his country. He must love character, and have a due sense of injuries, but he must be taught to appeal only to the laws of the state, to defend the one, and punish the other. He must love family honour, but he must be taught that neither the rank nor antiquity of his ancestors can command respect, without personal merit. He must avoid neutrality in all questions that divide the state, but he must shun the rage, and acrimony of party spirit. He must be taught to love his fellow creatures in every part of the world, but he must cherish with a more intense and peculiar affection, the citizens of Pennsylvania and of the United States. I do not wish to see our youth educated with a single prejudice against any nation or country; but we impose a task upon human nature, repugnant alike to reason, revelation and the ordinary dimensions of the human heart, when we require him to embrace, with equal affection, the whole family of mankind. He must be taught to amass wealth, but it must be only to encrease his power of contributing to the wants and demands of the state. He must be indulged occasionally in amusements, but he must be taught that study and business should be his principal pursuits in life. Above all he must love life, and endeavour to acquire as many of its conveniences as possible by industry and œconomy, but he must be taught that this life "Is not his own," when the safety of his country requires it. These are practicable lessons, and the history of the commonwealths of Greece and Rome show, that human nature, without the aids of Christianity, has attained these degrees of perfection.

While we inculcate these republican duties upon our pupil, we must not neglect, at the same time, to inspire him with republican principles. He must be taught that there can be no durable liberty but in a republic, and that government, like all other sciences, is of a progressive nature. The chains which have bound this science in Europe are happily unloosed in America. *Here* it is open to investigation and improvement. While philosophy has protected us by its discoveries from a thousand natural evils, government has unhappily followed with an unequal pace. It would be to dishonour human genius only to name the many defects which still exist in the best systems of legislation. We daily see matter of a perishable nature rendered durable by certain chemical operations. In like manner, I conceive, that it is possible to analyze and combine power in such a manner as not only to encrease the happiness, but to promote the duration of republican forms of government far beyond the terms limited for them by history, or the common opinions of mankind.

4.4 Thomas Jefferson's "Bill for Establishing Religious Freedom."

Section I

Well aware that the opinions and belief of men depend not on their own will, but follow involuntarily the evidence proposed to their minds; that Almighty God hath created the mind free, and manifested his supreme will that free it shall remain by making it altogether insusceptible of restraint; that all attempts to influence it by temporal punishments, or burthens, or by civil incapacitations, tend only to beget habits of hypocrisy and meanness, and are a departure from the plan of the holy author of our religion, who being lord both of body and mind, yet choose not to propagate it by coercions on either, as was in his Almighty power to do, but to exalt it by its influence on reason alone; that the impious presumption of legislature and ruler, civil as well as ecclesiastical, who, being themselves but fallible and uninspired men, have assumed dominion over the faith of others, setting up their own opinions and modes of thinking as the only true and infallible, and as such endeavoring to impose them on others, hath established and maintained false religions over the greatest part of the world and through all time: That to compel a man to furnish contributions of money for the propagation of opinions which he disbelieves and abhors, is sinful and tyrannical; that even the forcing him to support this or that teacher of his own religious persuasion, is depriving him of the comfortable liberty of giving his contributions to the particular pastor whose morals he would make his pattern, and whose powers he feels most persuasive to righteousness; and is withdrawing from the ministry those temporary rewards, which proceeding from an approbation of their personal conduct, are an additional incitement to earnest and unremitting labours for the instruction of mankind; that our civil rights have no dependence on our religious opinions, any more than our opinions in physics or geometry; and therefore the proscribing any citizen as unworthy the public confidence by laying upon him an incapacity of being called to offices of trust or emolument, unless he profess or renounce this or that religious opinion, is depriving him injudiciously of those privileges and advantages to which, in common with his fellow-citizens, he has a natural right; that it tends also to corrupt the principles of that very religion it is meant to encourage, by bribing with a monopoly of worldly honours and emoluments, those who will externally profess and conform to it; that though indeed these are criminals who do not withstand such temptation,

Paul L. Ford, ed., *The Works of Thomas Jefferson* (New York: G. P. Putnam's Sons, 1904) II, pp. 438–441.

yet neither are those innocent who lay the bait in their way; that the opinions of men are not the object of civil government, nor under its jurisdiction; that to suffer the civil magistrate to intrude his powers into the field of opinion and to restrain the profession or propagation of principles on supposition of their ill tendency is a dangerous falacy, which at once destroys all religious liberty, because he being of course judge of that tendency will make his opinions the rule of judgment, and approve or condemn the sentiments of others only as they shall square with or differ from his own; that it is time enough for the rightful purposes of civil government for its officers to interfere when principles break out into overt acts against peace and good order; and finally, that truth is great and will prevail if left to herself; that she is the proper and sufficient antagonist to error, and has nothing to fear from the conflict unless by human interposition disarmed of her natural weapons, free argument and debate; errors ceasing to be dangerous when it is permitted freely to contradict them.

Section II

We the General Assembly of Virginia do enact that no man shall be compelled to frequent or support any religious worship, place, or ministry whatsoever, nor shall be enforced, restrained, molested, or burthened in his body or goods, or shall otherwise suffer, on account of his religious opinions or belief; but that all men shall be free to profess, and by argument to maintain, their opinions in matters of religion, and that the same shall in no wise diminish, enlarge, or affect their civil capacities.

Section III

And though we well know that this Assembly, elected by the people for their ordinary purposes of legislation only, have no power to restrain the acts of succeeding Assemblies, constituted with powers equal to our own, and that therefore to declare this act to be irrevocable would be of no effect in law; yet we are free to declare, and do declare, that the rights hereby asserted are of the natural rights of mankind, and that if any act shall be hereafter passed to repeal the present or to narrow its operations, such act will be an infringement of natural right.

4.5 Jefferson's "Bill for the More General Diffusion of Knowledge."

Section I

Whereas it appeareth that however certain forms of government are better calculated than others to protect individuals in the free exercise of their natural rights, and are at the same time themselves better guarded against degeneracy, yet experience hath shewn, that even under the best forms, those entrusted with power have, in time, and by slow operations, perverted it into tyranny; and it is believed that the most effectual means of preventing this would be, to illuminate, as far as practicable, the minds of the people at large, and more especially to give them knowledge of those facts, which history exhibiteth, that, possessed thereby of the experience of other ages and countries, they may be enabled to know ambition under all its shapes, and prompt to exert their natural powers to defeat its purposes; And whereas it is generally true that that people will be happiest whose laws are best, and are best administered, and that laws will be wisely formed, and honestly administered, in proportion as those who form and administer them are wise and honest; whence it becomes expedient for promoting the publick happiness that those persons, whom nature hath endowed with genius and virtue, should be rendered by liberal education worthy to receive, and able to guard the sacred deposit of the rights and liberties of their fellow citizens, and that they should be called to that charge without regard to wealth, birth or other accidental condition or circumstance; but the indigence of the greater number disabling them from so educating, at their own expence, those of their children whom nature hath fitly formed and disposed to become useful instruments for the public, it is better that such should be sought for and educated at the common expence of all, than that the happiness of all should be confined to the weak or wicked:

Section II

Be it therefore enacted by the General Assembly, that in every county within this commonwealth, there shall be chosen annually, by the electors qualified to vote for Delegates, three of the most honest and able men of their country, to be called the Alderman of the county; and that the election of the said Aldermen shall be held at the same time and place, before the same persons, and notified and conducted in the same manner as by law is directed, for the annual election of Delegates for the county.

Paul L. Ford, ed., *ibid.*, II, pp. 414–426.

Section III

The person before whom such election is holden shall certify to the court of the said county the names of the Aldermen chosen, in order that the same may be entered of record, and shall give notice of their election to the said Aldermen within a fortnight after such election.

Section IV

The said Aldermen on the first Monday in October, if it be fair, and if not, then on the next fair day, excluding Sunday, shall meet at the court-house of their county, and proceed to divide their said county into hundreds, bounding the same by water courses, mountains, or limits, to be run and marked, if they think necessary, by the county surveyor, and at the county expence, regulating the size of the said hundreds, according to the best of their discretion, so as that they may contain a convenient number of children to make up a school, and be of such convenient size that all the children within each hundred may daily attend the school to be established therein, and distinguishing each hundred by a particular name; which division, with the names of the several hundreds, shall be returned to the court of the county and be entered of record, and shall remain unaltered until the increase or decrease of inhabitants shall render an alteration necessary, in the opinion of any succeeding Alderman, and also in the opinion of the court of the county.

Section V

The electors aforesaid residing within every hundred shall meet on the third Monday in October after the first election of Aldermen, at such place, within their hundred, as the said Aldermen shall direct, notice thereof being previously given to them by such person residing within the hundred as the said Aldermen shall require who is hereby enjoined to obey such requisition, on pain of being punished by amercement and imprisonment. The electors being so assembled shall choose the most convenient place within their hundred for building a school-house. If two or more places, having a greater number of votes than any others, shall yet be equal between themselves, the Aldermen, or such of them as are not of the same hundred, on information thereof, shall decide between them. The said Aldermen shall forthwith proceed to have a school-house built at the said place, and shall see that the same shall be kept in repair, and, when necessary, that it be rebuilt; but whenever they shall think necessary that it be rebuilt, they shall give notice as before directed, to the electors of the hundred to meet at the said school-house on such a day as they shall appoint, to determine by vote, in the manner before directed, whether it shall be rebuilt at the same, or what other place in the hundred.

Section VI

At every of those schools shall be taught reading, writing, and common arithmetick, and the books which shall be used therein for instructing the children to read shall be such as will at the same time make them acquainted with Græcian, Roman, English, and American history. At these schools all the free children, male and female, resident within the respective hundred, shall be intitled to receive tuition gratis, for the term of three years, and as much longer, at their private expence, as their parents, guardians, or friends shall think proper.

Section VII

Over every ten of these schools (or such other number nearest thereto, as the number of hundreds in the county will admit, without fractional divisions) an overseer shall be appointed annually by the aldermen at their first meeting, eminent for his learning, integrity, and fidelity to the commonwealth, whose business and duty it shall be, from time to time, to appoint a teacher to each school, who shall give assurance of fidelity to the commonwealth, and to remove him as he shall see cause; to visit every school once in every half year at the least; to examine the scholars; see that any general plan of reading and instruction recommended by the visitors of William and Mary College shall be observed; and to superintend the conduct of the teacher in everything relative to his school.

Section VIII

Every teacher shall receive a salary of ———— by the year, which, with the expences of building and repairing the school-houses, shall be provided in such manner as other county expences are by law directed to be provided and shall also have his diet, lodging, and washing found him, to be levied in like manner, save only that such levy shall be on the inhabitants of each hundred for the board of their own teacher only.

Section IX

And in order that grammer schools may be rendered convenient to the youth in every part of the commonwealth, be it therefore enacted, that on the first Monday in November, after the first appointment of overseers for the hundred schools, if fair, and if not, then on the next fair day, excluding Sunday, after the hour of one in the afternoon, the said overseers appointed for the schools in the counties of Princess Ann, Norfolk, Nansemond and Isle-of-Wight, shall meet at Nansemond court-house; those for the counties of Southampton, Sussex, Surry and Prince George, shall meet at Sussex court-house; those for the counties of Brunswick, Mecklenburg and Lunenburg, shall meet at Lunenburg court-house; those for the counties of Dinwiddie, Amelia and Chesterfield, shall meet at Chesterfield court-house; those for the counties of Powhatan, Cumberland, Goochland, Henrico and Hanover, shall meet at Henrico court-house; those for the counties of Prince Edward, Charlotte and Halifax, shall meet at Charlotte court-house; those for the counties of Henry, Pittsylvania and Bedford shall meet at Pittsylvania court-house; those for the counties of Buckingham, Amherst, Albemarle and Fluvanna, shall meet at Albemarle court-house; those for the counties of Botetourt, Rockbridge, Montgomery, Washington and Kentucky, shall meet at Botetourt court-house; those for the counties of Augusta, Rockingham and Greenbriar, shall meet at Augusta court-house; those for the counties of Accomack and Northampton, shall meet at Accomack court-house; those for the counties of Elizabeth City, Warwick, York, Gloucester, James City, Charles City and New-Kent, shall meet at James City court-house; those for the counties of Middlesex, Essex, King and Queen, King William and Caroline, shall meet at King and Queen court-house; those for the counties of Lancaster, Northumberland, Richmond and Westmoreland, shall meet at Richmond court-house; those for the counties of King George, Stafford, Spotsylvania, Prince William and Fairfax, shall meet at Spotsylvania court-house; those for the counties of Loudoun and Fauquier, shall meet at Loudoun court-house; those for the counties of Culpeper, Orange and Louisa, shall meet at Orange court-house; those for the county of Shenandoah and Frederick, shall meet at Frederick court-house; those for the counties of Hampshire and Berkeley, shall meet at Berkeley court-house; and those for the counties of Yohogania, Monongalia, and Ohio, shall meet at the Monongalia court-house; and shall fix on such place in some one of the counties in their district as shall be most proper for situating a grammer school-house, endeavoring that the situation be as central as may be to the inhabitants of the said counties, that it be furnished with good water, convenient to plentiful supplies of provision and fuel, and more than all things that it be healthy. And if a majority of the overseers present should not concur in their choice of any one place proposed, the method of determining shall be as follows: If two places only were proposed, and the votes be divided, they shall decide between them by fair and equal lot; if more than two places were proposed, the question shall be put on those two which on the first division had the greater number of votes; or if no two places had a greater number of votes than the others, then it shall be decided by fair and equal lot (unless it can be agreed by a majority of votes) which of the places having equal numbers shall be thrown out of the competition, so that the question shall be put on the remaining two, and if on this ultimate question the votes shall be equally divided, it shall then be decided finally by lot.

Section X

The said overseers having determined the place at which the grammer school for their district shall be built, shall forthwith (unless they can otherwise agree with the proprietors of the circumjacent lands as to location and price) make application to the clerk of the county in which the said house is to be situated, who shall thereupon issue a writ, in the nature of a writ of ad quod damnum, directed to the sheriff of the said county commanding him to summon and impannel twelve fit persons to meet at the place so destined for the grammer school-house, on a certain day, to be named in the said writ, not less than five, nor more than ten, days from the date thereof; and also to give notice of the same to the proprietors and tenants of the lands to be viewed if they be found within the county, and if not, then to their agents therein if any they have. Which freeholders shall be charged by the said sheriff impartially, and to the best of their skill and judgment to view the lands round about the said place and to locate and circumscribe, by certain meets and bounds, one hundred acres thereof, having regard therein principally to the benefit and convenience of the said school, but respecting in some measure also the convenience of the said proprietors, and to value and appraise the same in so many several and distinct parcels as shall be owned or held by several and distinct owners or tenants, and according to their respective interests and estates therein. And after such location and appraisement so made, the said sheriff shall forthwith return the same under the hands and seals of the said jurors, together with the writ, to the clerk's office of the said county and the right and property of the said proprietors and tenants in the said lands so circumscribed shall be immediately devested and be transferred to the commonwealth for the use of the said grammer school, in full and absolute dominion, any want of consent or disability to consent in the said owners or tenants notwithstanding. But it shall not be lawful for the said overseers so to situate the grammer school-house, nor to the said jurors so to locate the said lands, as to include the mansion-house of the proprietor of the lands, nor the offices, curtilage, or garden, thereunto immediately belonging.

Section XI

The said overseers shall forthwith proceed to have a house of brick or stone, for the said grammer school, with necessary offices, built on the said lands, which grammer school-house shall contain a room for the school, a hall to dine in, four rooms for a master and usher, and ten or twelve lodging rooms for the scholars.

Section XII

To each of the said grammer schools shall be allowed out of the public treasury, the sum of ————— pounds, out of which shall be paid by the Treasurer, on warrant from the Auditors, to the proprietors or tenants of the lands located, the value of their several interests as fixed by the jury, and the balance thereof shall be delivered to the said overseers to defray the expense of the said buildings.

Section XIII

In either of these grammer schools shall be taught the Latin and Greek languages, English Grammer, geography, and the higher part of numerical arithmetick, to wit, vulgar and decimal fractions, and the extrication of the square and cube roots.

Section XIV

A visiter from each county constituting the district shall be appointed, by the overseers, for the county, in the month of October annually, either from their own body or from their county at large, which visiters, or the greater part of them, meeting together at the said grammer school on the first Monday in November, if fair, and if not, then on the next fair day, excluding Sunday, shall have power to choose their own Rector, who shall call and preside at future meetings, to employ from time to time a master, and if necessary, an usher, for the said school, to remove them at their will, and to settle the price of tuition to be paid by the scholars. They shall also visit the school twice in every year at the least, either together or separately at their discretion, examine the scholars, and see that any general plan of instruction recommended by the visiters, of William and Mary College shall be observed. The said masters and ushers, before they enter on the execution of their office, shall give assurance of fidelity to the commonwealth.

Section XV

A steward shall be employed, and removed at will by the master, on such wages as the visiters shall direct; which steward shall see to the procuring provisions, fuel, servants for cooking, waiting, house cleaning, washing, mending, and gardening on the most reasonable terms; the expence of which, together with the steward's wages, shall be divided equally among all the scholars boarding either on the public or private expence. And the part of those who are on private expence, and also the price of their tuitions due to the master or usher, shall be paid quarterly by the respective scholars, their parents, or guardians, and shall be recoverable, if withheld, together with costs, on motion in any Court of Record, ten days notice thereof being previously given to the party, and a jury impannelled to try the issue joined, or enquire of the damages. The said steward shall also, under the direction of the visiters, see that the houses be kept in repair, and necessary enclosures be made and repaired, the accounts for which, shall, from time to time, be submitted to the Auditors, and on their warrant paid by the Treasurer.

Section XVI

Every overseer of the hundred schools shall, in the month of September annually, after the most diligent and impartial examination and inquiry, appoint from among the boys who shall have been two years at the least at some one of the schools under his superintendance, and whose parents are too poor to give them farther education, some one of the best and most promising genius and disposition, to proceed to the grammer school of his district; which appointment shall be made in the court-house of the county and on the court day for that month if fair, and if not, then on the next fair day, excluding Sunday, in the presence of the Aldermen, or two of them at the least, assembled on the bench for that purpose, the said overseer being previously sworn by them to make such appointment, without favor or affection, according to the best of his skill and judgment, and being interrogated by the said Aldermen, either on their own motion, or on suggestions from their parents, guardians, friends, or teachers of the children, competitors for such appointment; which teachers the parents shall attend for the information of the Aldermen. On which interrogatories the said Aldermen, if they be not satisfied with the appointment proposed, shall have right to negative it; whereupon the said visiter may proceed to make a new appointment, and the said Aldermen again to interrogate and negative, and so toties quoties until an appointment be approved.

Section XVII

Every boy so appointed shall be authorized to proceed to the grammer school of his district, there to be educated and boarded during such time as is hereafter limited; and his quota of the expences of the house together with a compensation to the master or usher for his tuition, at the rate of twenty dollars by the year, shall be paid by the Treasurer quarterly on warrant from the Auditors.

Section XVIII

A visitation shall be held, for the purpose of probation, annually at the said grammer school on the last Monday in September, if fair, and if not, then on the next fair day, excluding Sunday, at which one third of the boys sent thither by appointment of the said overseers, and who shall have been there one year only, shall be discontinued as public foundationers, being those who, on the most diligent examination and enquiry, shall be thought to be the least promising genius and disposition; and of those who shall have been there two years, all shall be discontinued save one only the best in genius and disposition, who shall be at liberty to continue there four years longer on the public foundation, and shall thence forward be deemed a senior.

Section XIX

The visiters for the districts which, or any part of which, be southward and westward of James river, as known by that name, or by the names of Fluvanna and Jackson's river, in every other year, to wit, at the probation meetings held in the years, distinguished in the Christian computation by odd numbers, and the visiters for all the other districts at their said meetings to be held in those years, distinguished by even numbers, after diligent examination and enquiry as before directed, shall chuse one among the said seniors, of the best learning and most hopeful genius and disposition, who shall be authorized by them to proceed to William and Mary College; there to be educated, boarded, and clothed, three years; the expence of which annually shall be paid by the Treasurer on warrant from the Auditors.

4.6   Jefferson Urges His Friend George Wythe to "Preach . . . A Crusade against Ignorance."

If all the sovereigns of Europe were to set themselves to work to emancipate the minds of their subjects from their present ignorance & prejudices, & that as zealously as they now endeavor the contrary, a thousand years would not place them on that high ground on which our common people are now setting out.   Ours could not have been so fairly put into the hands of their own common sense had they not been separated from their parent stock & kept from contamination, either from them, or the other people of the old world, by the intervention of so wide an ocean.   To know the worth of this, one must see the want of it here.   I think by far the most important bill in our whole code is that for the diffusion of knowledge among the people.   No other sure foundation can be devised, for the preservation of freedom and happiness.   If anybody thinks that kings, nobles, or priests are good conservators of the public happiness send them here.   It is the best school in the universe to cure them of that folly.   They will see here with their own eyes that these descriptions of men are an abandoned confederacy against the happiness of the mass of the people.   The omnipotence of their effect cannot be better proved than in this country particularly, where notwithstanding the finest soil upon earth, the finest climate under heaven, and a people of the most benevolent, the most gay and amiable character of which the human form is susceptible, where such a people I say, surrounded by so many blessings from nature, are yet loaded with misery by kings, nobles and priests, and by them alone.   Preach, my dear Sir, a crusade against ignorance; establish & improve the law for educating the common people.   Let our countrymen know that the people alone can protect us against these evils, and that the tax which will be paid for this purpose is not more than the thousandth part of what will be paid to kings, priests & nobles who will rise up among us if we leave the people in ignorance.

Paul L. Ford, ed., *ibid.*, V, pp. 153–154.

4.7   Jefferson Discusses the Fate of His Proposed Education Bill.

We thought, that on this subject a systematical plan of general education should be proposed, and I was requested to undertake it.   I accordingly prepared three bills for the Revisal, proposing three distinct grades of ed-

Autobiography, in *ibid.*, I, pp. 75–76.

ucation, reaching all classes. 1. Elementary schools for all children generally, rich and poor. 2. Colleges for a middle degree of instruction, calculated for the common purposes of life, and such as would be desirable for all who were in easy circumstances. And 3d. an ultimate grade for teaching the sciences generally, & in their highest degree. The first bill proposed to lay off every county into Hundreds or Wards, of a proper size and population for a school, in which reading, writing, and common arithmetic should be taught; and that the whole state should be divided into 24 districts, in each of which should be a school for classical learning, grammar, geography, and the higher branches of numerical arithmetic. The second bill proposed to amend the constitution of Wm. & Mary College, to enlarge it's sphere of science, and to make it in fact an University. The third was for the establishment of a library. These bills were not acted on until the same year '96. and then only so much of the first as provided for elementary schools. The College of Wm. & Mary was an establishment purely of the Church of England, the Visitors were required to be all of that Church; the Professors to subscribe it's 39 Articles, it's Students to learn it's Catechism, and one of its fundamental objects was declared to be to raise up Ministers for that church. The religious jealousies therefore of all the dissenters took alarm lest this might give an ascendancy to the Anglican sect and refused acting on that bill. Its local eccentricity too and unhealthy autumnal climate lessened the general inclination towards it. And in the Elementary bill they inserted a provision which completely defeated it, for they left it to the court of each county to determine for itself when this act should be carried into execution, within their county. One provision of the bill was that the expenses of these schools should be borne by the inhabitants of the county, every one in proportion to his general tax-rate. This would throw on wealth the education of the poor; and the justices, being generally of the more wealthy class, were unwilling to incur that burthen, and I believe it was not suffered to commence in a single county.

The Common School Crusade   *5*

During the first half of the nineteenth century European visitors to the United States noted great esteem for education—education through school-room, jury, lyceum, library, caucus, newspaper. The republic's health re-lied on enlightenment, Massachusetts had declared in its Constitution of 1780: "Wisdom and knowledge, as well as virtue, diffused generally among the people. . . . [are] necessary for the preservation of their rights and liberties." And politics, said the astute French observer, Alexis de Tocqueville, "are the end and aim of education . . . . the jury is intro-duced into the games of schoolboys, and parliamentary forms are observed in the order of a feast." Governors and presidents, selectmen and senators proclaimed this traditional faith in education, and none more characteris-tically than Abraham Lincoln in declaring himself a candidate for the state assembly in 1832:

> Upon the subject of education, not presuming to dictate any plan or system respecting it, I can only say that I view it as the most important subject which we as a people can be engaged in. That every man may receive at least a moderate education, and thereby be enabled to read the histories of his own and other countries, by which he may duly appreciate the value of our free institutions, appears to be an object of vital importance, even on this account alone, to say nothing of the advantages and satisfaction to be derived from being able to read the Scriptures and other works, both of a religious and moral nature, for themselves. For my part, I desire to see the time when education, and by its means, morality, sobriety, enterprise, and industry, shall become much more general than at present, and should be gratified to have it in my power to contribute something to the advance-ment of any measure which might have a tendency to accelerate the happy period.

Lincoln's letter to the voters represented a common attitude: he was com-mitted, in general, to education as productive of all good, but vague, even nonchalant, about means. "Not presuming to dictate any plan or sys-tem," he would happily support "any measure" for public enlightenment.

In the next few decades Americans would become much more specific about means as they translated their generalized esteem for education into the institution known as the common school.   In the early nineteenth century there were few sharp lines between "public" and "private" education. States liberally subsidized "private" academies and colleges while towns and cities helped to support " private" charity schools.   In granting charters to educational institutions, states assumed that institutions sponsored by individuals or sects would serve the public interest, and that the state stood to benefit if students attended the school of their choice.   Neither were there clear lines between "sectarian" and " non-sectarian" schools. Many publicly supported schools taught a Protestant consensus and many sectarian schools were free for poor children regardless of faith.

During the colonial period, most schools had perpetuated differences of religion, occupation, national origin, and social class.   During the early national period, despite the desire of the revolutionary educational reformers for a homogeneous citizenry, education continued to be heterogeneous, maintaining much of its sectarian energy and social diversity.   Philanthropists brought to the United States the English invention of the Sunday school.   The Sunday school gave secular instruction to children who worked in factories, but rapidly it changed into a tool of the evangelical Protestant churches.   In the growing cities of the East coast, humanitarians founded "free school societies" to educate poor children.   These societies often employed Joseph Lancaster's plan of cheap mass instruction by means of " monitors " (or children who served as teachers' aides). All over the countryside academies sprang up, reaching a total of over 6,000 in 1850, when they enrolled about 263,000 pupils.   Chartered as quasi-public ventures, like banks or canals, these academies were generally controlled by private boards of trustees.   But they often received public funds and eagerly accepted all students who would attend and could pay the fees.   They filled a vacuum in secondary education, particularly in rural areas.   With entrepreneurial zeal Americans also founded colleges until the number of institutions far outran the demand.

Except in the South and a few rural areas, then, America did not lack schools, public and private, sectarian and non-denominational, utilitarian and ornamental, high and low.   Still the institutions were a hodgepodge, founded for profit or charity, for propagating the faith or selling town lots in a new village on the frontier, for advancing learning or keeping children off the streets.   Beginning in the 1820's a number of Americans began to wonder if American schools were good enough or systematic enough to carry the burden placed on them.   Out of decades of criticism and reform—the ferment called the common school crusade—emerged a basic democratic institution.   From the clash of new social conditions and old articles of faith, interpreted by eloquent and determined reformers, came the American common school. So clear were the outlines of this institution after the Civil War that European visitors like Francis Adams could talk confidently about "the free school *system* of the United States."

The crusade began in the settled older regions of the East, where new social conditions—urbanization, industrialism, immigration, and the democratization of politics—were most visible and painful. These new forces unleashed social, political, and economic conflicts, and educational historians have traditionally seen the common school crusade as itself a series of "battles." It is true that many citizens did oppose the common school: taxpayers—urban landlords and dirt farmers alike—who could see no reason to educate the children of others; sectarian groups who attacked public schools as godless or covertly Protestant; patrons and proprietors of private schools; laborers who opposed education beyond the three R's as a subsidy of the wealthy; and patricians who clung to an elitism which was going out of style in Jacksonian America. But the remarkable characteristic of the common school crusade was its universality. All types of people—merchant and union organizer, Whig and Democrat, Calvinist and Unitarian, easterner and westerner—joined the cause, often with quite different motives. The movement was more remarkable for the consensus it secured than for the conflict it aroused.

On the right wing of the movement stood Daniel Webster. Although born the son of a poor farmer on the New Hampshire frontier, Webster became spokesman for the patrician class of Boston, as Federalist, then Whig, Senator from Massachusetts. Like many other conservatives, he saw the common school as a means of purifying "the whole moral atmosphere." "We hope for a security, beyond the law, and above the law," he asserted in the Massachusetts Constitutional Convention of 1820–21, "in the prevalence of enlightened and well-principled moral sentiment." Only universal education could assure this security, especially in a time when all men were gaining the vote. Many another Whig agreed. In a land where the people was king, it was essential to educate the sovereign. "It is vain to seek in the positive structure of society for those securities, which must depend in the main upon its spirit," said a Whig from Maine: "Who shall take care of the keepers?" The Federalist Judge Joseph Story, alarmed at the views and actions of the Jacksonian Democrats, counseled teachers in 1834 to "repress the inordinate love of innovation of the young, the ignorant, and the restless." Amid the earthquakes of partisan politics, the schoolhouse must stand firm. The schoolmaster must inculcate correct doctrine in the rising generation lest demagogues outwit an ignorant and unruly people.

Edward Everett, another conservative, was also a champion of the free school. During his term as Whig Governor of Massachusetts the State Board of Education was formed and its first secretary, Horace Mann, chosen. Everett's zeal for the common school stemmed as much from fear as from hope. In his speech on "The Importance of Education in a Republic" he pointed out that the democratization of politics had created duties which would be a menace if performed by an ignorant citizenry: voting, jury duty, militia service, and serving in public office. No longer, as in the halcyon days of Federalism, could office be limited substantially to a select class. In 1839, in the midst of the age of the common man, Everett said, there were only three options: "We must have officers unqualified for their duties;—or we must educate a privileged class to monopolize the honors and emoluments of place;—or we must establish such a system of general education, as will furnish a supply of well-informed, intelligent, and respectable citizens, in every part of the country, and in every walk of life, capable of discharging the trusts which the people may devolve upon them. It is superfluous to say, which of the three courses is most congenial with the spirit of republicanism." With the changing style of political leadership in the Jacksonian period, with increased popular participation in the political process, Jefferson's idea of training a natural aristocracy to guide the nation would no longer work. When everyman might be his own politician, the patrician decided that everyman must be educated.

The workingmen's associations also wanted good public education, but for different reasons. The workingmen rejoiced in growing political equality, yet they feared that industrialization and concentration of wealth —the hated "monopolies"—were restricting their equality of economic opportunity. Many of the union leaders were skilled craftsmen who saw their trades invaded by machines. Some feared that they and their children would become mere cogs in a factory and saw ahead "generation on generation, reared up in profound ignorance, and the final prostration of their liberties at the shrine of a powerful aristocracy." Anxious about slipping downwards in economic and social status and appealing to traditional republican values, they turned to public education for rescue.

In Pennsylvania, where free schools were sparse and designed only for the poor, the workingmen argued that common schools should be established, open to all without taint of pauperism and so good that the rich, who could afford private education for their children, could find no better. Monopolistic access to education must be broken, for when workingmen see "the glaring inequality of society, they are constrained to believe, that until the means of equal instruction shall be equally secured to all, liberty is but an unmeaning word, and equality an empty shadow. . . ."

To insure this republican education the managers of the schools must be placed "under the control and suffrage of the people."

For the most part the workingmen did not seek to pull down the rich; rather they sought equality of opportunity for their children, an equal chance at the main chance. Indeed, in their arguments they appealed, as did the conservatives, to the past: they were only trying to realize "those cardinal principles of republican liberty which were declared in '76, and which can only be sustained by the adoption of an ample system of public instruction, calculated to impart equality as well as mental culture. . . ." When Robert Owen and his followers in New York suggested that all children be taken from their parents and educated in boarding schools where they should have the same food, clothes, and instruction, the workingmen rebelled. They did not want a classless society, nor did they wish to disrupt the basic social institution, the family. Disadvantaged they might be, but they were proud and hoped to better their lot within society as it was.

In 1832 the labor journals described conditions of child labor which distressed not only workingmen but also sensitive citizens from all walks of life. They found that 1,600 children between seven and sixteen years were working in the mills, most of them between thirteen and fourteen hours a day, with no opportunity for schooling save after eight thirty in the evening and on Sunday. The report applauded the practice of the Lowell mills, which did not employ children under twelve, and the few factories which allowed children to spend a small portion of the year in school. Hardly radical, the committee called not for the abolition of child labor, but for the regulation of the hours of child labor. Even a little education might prevent "the sacrifice of the dearest interests of thousands of the rising generation of our country, to the cupidity and avarice of their employers."

The democratization of politics and the advent of industrialism posed problems which Americans hoped education could solve. So, too, did immigration. Only a trickle in the two generations following the Revolutionary War, immigration increased sharply in the 1830's and 1840's, especially when Irish potato famines and the unrest in Germany brought waves of settlers. Nervous about their own "Americanism," natives grew alarmed about assimilating the newcomers. When the teachers of Cincinnati discussed the immigrant problem, Calvin Stowe and William McGuffey argued that public schools held out the best hope of turning foreign children into Americans. No random education would do; it must be uniform and systematic. Americans must define what it meant to be American and must find ways of inculcating patriotism in the young. In the textbooks of McGuffey and his contemporaries children would find the national pattern.

Patricians, workingmen, nativists, average citizens—Americans found in their traditional belief in education a way to reconcile their articles of faith with new social conditions. Most Americans at the time believed in progress, in a benevolent God, in equality of opportunity, in the mission of the United States to serve as a model of republican virtue to the world. Yet social evils—intemperance, crime, slums, ignorance—were all the more visible and ominous because of the rapid growth of cities. It was a period of great humanitarian ferment, when philanthropists tried to eliminate drunkenness, aid the poor and blind and insane, free slaves, and assure women their rights. Many of those who attacked these evils, like Horace Mann, were humanitarians who regarded education as the starting point for universal reform.

The chief contribution of the common school reformers was to articulate and focus the generalized American belief in education and to make it relevant to the aspirations and anxieties of the age. In so doing, gradually, partly consciously, partly unintentionally, they gave form and content and purpose to the public school. The schools did not arise from spontaneous generation. Mann wrote sadly in his journal after one of his unsuccessful evangelical tours that "when I am about to present my gospel of education in some new place, I feel as if I were standing in bad weather before the door of a house and vainly pulling the bell, with no one at home, or all too busy to see me."

The best known crusaders for common schools served stints as state superintendents of education. In comparison with European ministers of education they had little power. Mann, for example, had a legislative mandate only to collect statistics, diffuse information about educational innovations, "suggest" improvements in schooling to the Board and legislature, collect such textbooks and apparatus "as can be obtained without expense to the commonwealth," and to help organize meetings of teachers, school board members, and "friends of education generally." The heart of his task, buried in a list of other duties, was "arousing and guiding public sentiment in relation to the practical interests of education." "Let the next generation, then, be my client," said lawyer Mann. In such a cause, he wrote, "I must be a fluid sort of man, adapting myself to tastes, opinions, habits, manners, as far as this can be done without hypocrisy or insincerity, or a compromise of principle." Appealing to the profit motive of manufacturers, the status anxieties of workers, the sympathies of humanitarians, the pride of patriots, he realized that "many men I shall meet . . . are accessible only through a single motive or . . . are encased in prejudice and jealousy, and need, not to be subdued, but to be re-modelled."

Lacking formal power, the reformer needed the eloquence and craft of a trial lawyer, the sophistication of a politician, the zeal and supernatural sanctions of a preacher, the sharp pen of a journalist, and the learning of a professor. Taken as a group the chief reformers had all these skills. Mann was lawyer, politician, writer, and college president. The others had careers similar to his: Henry Barnard, Robert Breckinridge, James Carter, Isaac Crary, Ninian Edwards, Samuel Galloway, Samuel Lewis, Charles Mercer, Caleb Mills, John Pierce, Calvin Stowe, John Swett, and Calvin Wiley. In the pattern of multiple careers common at the time, eleven of the fourteen were elected to political office; nine were lawyers; ten edited journals; six were college presidents or professors; and four were ministers (almost all were deeply religious men). Nine of the fourteen were born in New England, where they early came to know the public district school. With the exception of Swett, none were career teachers in public schools. The reformers emulated each others' articles in the journals, regarding work in other states as social laboratories for reform ideas. Though ranging from Massachusetts to California, the crusaders came to similar conclusions about the purpose and institutional character of the common school. Out of the diversity of American education in the early nineteenth century had come, by mid-century, a remarkable degree of consensus.

These reformers agreed that the common school was to be public—not a "private" school affected with the public interest, not a "public" school supported in part by private charity—a school controlled by publicly elected or appointed officials, financed from the public treasury. The common school was to be free, paid for by the taxpayers at large, not by tuition charged the parents. It was, ideally, so fine a school that no one would wish to send children to private schools: *"The Common School is common, not as inferior* [said one reformer], *not as the school for poor men's children, but as the light and air are common. It ought to be the best school because it is the first school; and in all good works the beginning is one half."* It would teach children the three R's, but knowledge alone was not enough: it also had to promote a non-sectarian Christian morality and a non-partisan republicanism. Only a school which was public, free, of the highest quality, and which inculcated individual and civic virtue could vindicate American faith in education. With this educational creed the American people agreed—not everywhere, not everyone, not at the same time, but gradually and with increasing conviction. An institution was born.

5.1   Senator Daniel Webster States the Conservative Case for Public Education, 1821.

I must yet advert to another most interesting topic,—the Free Schools. In this particular, New England may be allowed to claim, I think, a merit of a peculiar character. She early adopted, and has constantly maintained the principle, that it is the undoubted right and the bounden duty of government to provide for the instruction of all youth. That which is elsewhere left to chance or to charity, we secure by law. For the purpose of public instruction, we hold every man subject to taxation in proportion to his property, and we look not to the question, whether he himself have, or have not, children to be benefited by the education for which he pays. We regard it as a wise and liberal system of police, by which property, and life, and the peace of society are secured. We seek to prevent in some measure the extension of the penal code, by inspiring a salutary and conservative principle of virtue and of knowledge in an early age. We strive to excite a feeling of respectability, and a sense of character, by enlarging the capacity and increasing the sphere of intellectual enjoyment. By general instruction, we seek, as far as possible, to purify the whole moral atmosphere; to keep good sentiments uppermost, and to turn the strong current of feeling and opinion, as well as the censures of the law and the denunciations of religion, against immorality and crime. We hope for a security beyond the law, and above the law, in the prevalence of an enlightened and well-principled moral sentiment. We hope to continue and prolong the time, when, in the villages and farm-houses of New England, there may be undisturbed sleep within unbarred doors. And knowing that our government rests directly on the public will, in order that we may preserve it we endeavor to give a safe and proper direction to that public will. We do not, indeed, expect all men to be philosophers or statesmen; but we confidently trust, and our expectation of the duration of our system of government rests on that trust, that, by the diffusion of general knowledge and good and virtuous sentiments, the political fabric may be secure, as well against open violence and overthrow, as against the slow, but sure, undermining of licentiousness.

Daniel Webster, *Works* (Boston: Little, Brown, and Company, 1854), I, pp. 41–42.

5.2 Whig Governor Edward Everett of Massachusetts Discusses "The Importance of Education in a Republic," 1839.

But on the system established in the United States, where the people are not only in theory the source of power, but in practice are actually called upon, constantly, to take an efficient part in constituting and administering the government, it is plain that education is universally and indispensably necessary, to enable them to exercise their rights and perform their duties. This will be put beyond question by considering a few particulars.

I. The first duty, in a popular government, is that which is attached to the elective franchise; though I fear it is too little regarded in this light. It is not merely the right, but it is the duty, of the citizen, by the exercise of the right of suffrage, to take a part, at periods recurring after short intervals, in organizing the government. This duty cannot be discharged with rectitude, unless it be discharged with intelligence; and it becomes the duty of the citizen to make up his own mind on all the great questions which arise in administering the government. How numerous and important these questions are, I need not say. Since you and I, Mr President, have been of years to observe the march of affairs, the people of the United States have been called to make up a practical judgment on the following, among other great questions,—the *protective policy*, that is, on the legislation necessary to introduce and establish an infant branch of manufactures; a question, however easily disposed of by theorists, on both sides, of infinite practical difficulty; on *internal improvement*, that is, the construction of public works of communication between the various parts of the country, at the expense of the general government; on the *circulating medium*, and how far the currency, which is the representative of value, must have intrinsic value itself; on the *different families of the human race* existing in the country and the rights and duties which result from their relation to each other; on the *relations* of the country with *foreign* powers, in reference to colonial trade, disputed boundaries, and indemnification for wrongs and spoliations; on the disposal of the *public domain*, and its bearings on the progress of population and of republican government in the mighty west; on the nature of our political system, as consisting in the harmonious *adjustment of the federal and state governments*. I have named only a part of the questions which, within the last twenty years, have been, some of them constantly, before the community —the turning-points of municipal, state, and national elections. The good citizen, who is not willing to be the slave of a party because he is a member

Edward Everett, *Orations and Speeches on Various Occasions* (Boston: Little, Brown and Company, 1878), II, pp. 316–321, 323.

of it, must make up his mind for himself on all those great questions, or he cannot exercise the right of suffrage with intelligence and independence. As the majority of the people are well or ill informed on these subjects, the public policy of the country will be guided by wisdom and truth, or the reverse.

I do not mean that it is necesary that every citizen should receive an education which would enable him to argue all these questions, at length, in a deliberative or popular assembly; but, while it is his right and his duty to give effect to his judgment at the polls, and while the constitution necessarily gives as much weight to the vote of the uninformed and ignorant as to that of the well-instructed and intelligent citizen, it is plain that the avenues to information should be as wide and numerous as possible; and that the utmost practicable extension should be given to a system of education which will confer on every citizen the capacity of deriving knowledge, with readiness and accuracy, from books and documents. The whole energy of the state should be directed to multiply the numbers of those capable of forming an independent and rational judgment of their own, and to diminish as much as possible the numbers of the opposite class, who, being blinded by ignorance, are at the mercy of any one who has an interest and the skill to delude them.

II. But the exercise of the elective franchise is only the beginning of the duties of the citizen. The constitution makes it the right, the laws make it the duty, of all citizens, within certain ages to bear arms. It may sound strangely to connect this duty with the subject of education. I hope no practical demonstration of the connection of the topics will ever arise among us. But this right and this duty, lightly esteemed in quiet times, may become of fearful import. Arms are placed in the hands of the citizen for the most important purposes; not for parade and holiday display, but to defend his country against violence from abroad; to maintain the supremacy of the laws; to preserve the peace of the community. Heaven grant that the day may be far distant when our citizens shall be called to wield them for either purpose. But if the experience of the past warrant an anticipation of the future, the time may come when this duty, also, is to be performed. It will not then be a matter of indifference whether the honor and peace of the community are committed to an ignorant and benighted multitude, like those which swell the ranks of the mercenary standing armies of Europe, or to an educated and intelligent population, whose powers of reflection have been strengthened by exercise, and who are able to discriminate between constitutional liberty and arbitrary power on the one hand, and anarchy on the other.

III. There are other civil duties to be performed, for which education furnishes a still more direct and appropriate preparation. The law of the land calls the citizen to take a part in the administration of justice. Twelve men are placed in the jury-box, to decide on the numberless questions which arise in the community—questions of character, of property, and of life. The jury passes on your fortune and your reputation; pronounces whether you live or die. Go into the courts; are they light matters which those twelve men are to decide? Look in the anxious faces of those whose estates, whose good name, whose all, is at stake, hanging on the intelligence of those twelve men, or any one of them. What assurance is there, but that which comes from our schools, that these men will understand and do their duty? Those little boys, now sporting in the streets, or conning their tasks in our town schools, in a few short years will be summoned, in their turns, to discharge this important trust. Can we deem it a matter of indifference whether or not their minds have been early accustomed to follow a train of thoughts or a statement of facts? Did not the secretary give us, this morning, from his own experience, the instance of a witness who, in a case of slander, where every thing turned on his testimony, first swore that what he saw, he saw through one window, and then through another, and then through a door? Woe to the community, where the degree of stolidity and ignorance, necessary to constitute such a witness, abound; and where it must appear, not only on the stand, but in the jury-box. It appears to me a most imperative duty, on the part of a state which calls its citizens to discharge this momentous office, to do all in its power to qualify them for it by a general system of education. Is it said, there is learned counsel to argue and explain the cause to a jury, however ignorant? But there is counsel on both sides; the jury must decide after hearing them both. But the court will instruct the jury. No doubt, as far as the law is concerned; but the court's instructions are addressed to minds supposed to be capable of following out an argument, estimating evidence, and making up an independent opinion. I do not say, that there are not some minds to whom the best opportunities of education would not impart the requisite qualifications of an intelligent juror. But I may appeal to every professional character and magistrate in this convention, that, in an important case, if he were to be called on to select a jury on which he could place full reliance, he would select men of good common sense, who had received a good common education.

IV. But I have not yet named all the civil duties for which education is needed, as the preparatory discipline. The various official trusts in society are to be filled, from a commission of the peace to the place of chief justice; from a constable up to the president of the United States. The sphere of duty of some of these functionaries is narrow; of others, large and inexpressibly responsible; of none, insignificant. Taken together, they make up the administration of free government—the greatest merely temporal interest of civilized man.   There are three courses, between which we must choose.   We must have officers unqualified for their duties; or we must educate a privileged class, to monopolize the honors and emoluments of place; or we must establish such a system of general education, as will furnish a supply of well-informed, intelligent, and respectable citizens, in every part of the country and in every walk of life, capable of discharging the trusts which the people may devolve upon them.   The topic is of great compass, but I cannot dwell upon it.   It is superfluous to say which of the three courses is most congenial with the spirit of republicanism.

V. I have thus far spoken of those reasons for promoting common school education, which spring from the nature of our government. There are others, derived from the condition of our country.   Individual enterprise is every where stimulated; the paths of adventure are opened; the boundless west prevents the older settlements from being overstocked, and gives scope for an unexampled development of energy.   Education is wanted, to enlighten and direct those active, moving powers.   Without it, much wild vigor will be exerted in vain.   Energy alone is not enough; it must be turned to feasible objects, and work by sound principles.

Again, this spirit of enterprise runs naturally towards the acquisition of wealth.   In this I find no matter of reproach; only let it not be a merely Carthaginian prosperity.   Let a taste for reading and reflection be cultivated, as well as property acquired.   Let us give our children the keys of knowledge, as well as an establishment in business.   Let them, in youth, form habits and tastes which will remain with them in after-life, in old age, and furnish rational entertainment at all times.   When we collect the little circle, at the family board and at the fireside, in our long winter evenings, let us be able to talk of subjects of interest and importance,—the productions and institutions of our own and foreign countries; the history of our venerated fathers; the wonders of the material universe; the experience of our race; great moral interests and duties;—subjects surely as important as dollars and cents.   Let us, from early years, teach our children to rise above the dust beneath their feet, to the consideration of the great spiritual concerns of immortal natures.   A mere bookworm is a worthless character; but a mere money-getter is no better.

It is a great mistake, to suppose that it is necesary to be a professional man, in order to have leisure to indulge a taste for reading.   Far otherwise. I believe the mechanic, the engineer, the husbandman, the trader, have quite as much leisure as the average of men in the learned professions.   I know some men, busily engaged in these different callings of active life, whose minds are well stored with various useful knowledge acquired from books. There would be more such men, if education in our common schools were, as it well might be, of a higher order; and if common school libraries, well furnished, were introduced into every district, as I trust, in due time, they will be. . . .

No leisure, Mr President, for reading? Is there a man in the community, of an intelligent mind, and with any, the least tincture of improvement, derived from education, who, when coming, at nightfall, from his labor, (I care not how hard or humble,) if told that, beneath his roof, he would find Shakespeare, or Milton, or Scott, or Irving, or Channing, seated in actual presence by his fireside, and waiting to converse with him, would talk of wanting leisure or of fatigue?

5.3 Horace Mann Speaks in 1842 on the Perils of Popular Government.

Fellow-Citizens, we have sterner duties to perform than to assemble here, annually, to listen to glorifications of our great country and our great people, of our super-Ciceronian and super-Demosthenean orators, and to praise poetry and art and genius that are to be, *at sometime;* and then, after refreshing ourselves with feast and jovial song, to close the day with some gairish show, and forthwith to vote ourselves upon the pension list for the residue of the year, in consideration of such meritorious services. The quiet seat of an honorary member in our community, is not so easily won. Trusts, responsibilities, interests, vaster in amount, more sacred in character, than ever before in the providence of God were committed to any people have been committed to us. The great experiment of Republicanism,—of the capacity of man for self-government,—is to be tried anew, which wherever it has been tried,—in Greece, in Rome, in Italy,—has failed, through an incapacity in the people to enjoy liberty without abusing it. Another trial is to be made whether mankind will enjoy more and suffer less, under the ambition and rapacity of an irresponsible parliament, or of irresponsible parties;—under an hereditary sovereign who must, at least, prove his right to destroy, by showing his birth, or under mobs, which are like wild beasts, that prove their right to devour by showing their teeth. A vacant continent is here to be filled up with innumerable millions of human beings who may be happy through our wisdom, but must be miserable through our folly. Religion,—the ark of God,—which, of old times, was closed that it might not be profaned,—is here thrown open to all, whether Christian, Jew, or Pagan; and yet is to be guarded

Horace Mann, *Life and Works* (Boston: Walker, Fuller and Company, 1865–1868), IV, pp. 345, 354, 355, 364–365.

from desecration and sacrilege lest we perish with a deeper perdition than ever befel any other people. . . .

Two dangers then, equally fatal, impend over us;—the danger of ignorance which does not know its duty, and the danger of vice which, knowing, contemns it. To ensure prosperity, the mass of the people must be both well informed, and upright; but it is obvious that one portion of them may be honest but ignorant, while the residue are educated but fraudful.

When, therefore, we say that our government must be administered by adequate knowledge, and according to the unchangeable principles of rectitude, we mean that it must be administered by men who have acquired this knowledge, and whose conduct is guided by these principles. The knowledge and virtue we need are not abstractions, idealities, bodiless conceptions;—they must be incarnated in human form, imbodied in the living head and heart; they must glow with such fervid vitality as to burst forth spontaneously into action. Instead of our talking so much of those qualities, they must be such a matter of course as not to be talked of. . . .

I believe in the capability of man for self-government,—my whole soul thereto most joyously consenting. Nay, if there be any heresy among men, or blasphemy against God, at which the philosopher might be allowed to forget his equanimity, and the Christian his charity,—it is the heresy and the blasphemy of believing and avowing, that the infinitely good and all-wise Author of the universe persists in creating and sustaining a race of beings, who, by a law of their nature, are forever doomed to suffer all the atrocities and agonies of misgovernment, either from the hands of others, or from their own. The doctrine of the inherent and necessary disability of mankind for self-government should be regarded not simply with denial, but with abhorrence;—not with disproof only, but with execration. To sweep so foul a creed from the precincts of truth, and utterly to consume it, rhetoric should become a whirlwind, and logic fire. Indeed, I have never known a man who desired the establishment of monarchical and aristocratical institutions amongst us, who had not a mental reservation, that, in such case, he and his family should belong to the privileged orders.

Still, if asked the broad question, whether man is capable of self-government, I must answer it conditionally. If by man, in the inquiry, is meant the Feejee Islanders; or the convicts at Botany Bay; or the people of Mexico and of some of the South American Republics (so called); or those as a class, in our own country, who can neither read nor write; or those who can read and write, and who possess talents and an education by force of which they get treasury, or post-office, or bank appointments, and then abscond with all the money they can steal; I answer unhesitatingly that *man*, or rather *such men*, are not fit for self-government. . . .

The great truth should every where have been inculcated, by example as well as by precept, that for the dependant to vote from malice, or envy, or wantonness, involves substantially the moral guilt of treason; and for the superior to compel the dependant, through fear or bribery, to vote against his judgment, involves the baseness as well as the guilt of subornation of treason. Had this been done, our days of election would never have been, as they now so often are, days of turbulence, and bacchanalian riot, of insulting triumph or revengeful defeat; but they would have been days of thoughtfulness and of solemnity, such as befit a day whose setting sun will witness the ruin or the rescue of so much of human welfare.

Had this been done, our pioneer settlers would not have abandoned their homes, for the western wilderness, until they could have carried all the blessed influences,—the power and the spirit of education,—with them. No prospect of wealth would have tempted them to leave a land of moral culture for a moral desert. Then our civilization, as it expanded, would have been laden with blessings. We might, indeed, have subjugated less territory by the arts of industry and enterprise; but as a thousand-fold requital for this, we should have subjugated fewer aborigines by fraud and violence. Instead of the unenviable power which belongs to the sword, we should have enjoyed the godlike power which resides in beneficence.

And until all this work of improvement is done,—until this indifference of the wealthy and the educated towards the masses shall cease, and legislative bounty shall atone for past penuriousness, there can be no security for any class or description of men, nor for any interest, human or divine. With additional thousands of voters, every year crossing the line of manhood to decree the destiny of the nation, without additional knowledge and morality, things must accelerate from worse to worse. Amid increasing darkness and degeneracy, every man's rights may be invaded through legislation,—through the annulment of charters or the abrogation of remedies;—and through the corruption of jurors, or even of one juror on the panel of twelve, every man's right of redress may be denied for the grossest aggressions. As parties alternate, the rich may now be plundered of a life of gains; and now, through vindictive legislation, the arms of the laboring man struck dead by his side. And if, amid these scenes, even Washington should arise, and from the battlements of the capitol, should utter a warning voice, the mad populace would hurl him from the Tarpeian.

5.4   Mrs. Horace Mann on Childhood in the Cities and the Fatherhood of God.

And as I see the poor and neglected children in the streets, or in their own wretched houses, and how they live and grovel in low practices, gradually losing the sweet innocence of infantile expression, and becoming coarse and violent, even brutal, I wonder still more at the torpidity of society upon this subject. Nothing is such a proof of its selfishness as this neglect. Nothing makes me feel so keenly the need of a new organization of things. I do not like the thought of merging the sacred family relation in communities where all live together in public as it were, but it seems as if something might be done for the children of the needy that is not yet done. These poor city children are sequestered even from the influences of Nature. How strange that the more favored individuals should not seek every means to give them what culture they can have amid these brick walls. So much might be done by the help of the salient imagination of childhood, that we should be helped more than half way by blessed Nature herself. I often take an unfashionable walk inside the Mall on Sunday afternoon, when the Irish people bring their babes to play upon the green. I think it is the best institution in the city, and it would be a good idea to appoint a Commissioner in each ward to bring all the street children there every day and watch them while they play, and see that all have fair play. If school committees were formed of women, I think such an office might be created.

What faith we need to forgive heaven for the things that are! "How much that is, is *not* right!," I am sometimes tempted to exclaim. I have no idea, however, that Pope meant anything but the eternal ɪs, when he wrote "Whatever is, is right." It would have been better for superficial thinkers, if he had never said it however, for I often hear it quoted to defend what I consider the marring, not the making of God's plans. I have no doubt there is a remedy for every individual case of misery in this world, if eyes were only open to see it, but this couching process is the needful thing, and *that* God has left us to think out for ourselves. We know that there are millions who live and die in ignorance of all that makes God *God*, or a Father. To these he is only the being that created them, and they may well ask, "Why did he make us? to suffer? to sin?"—for they are conscious only of the irregularities of that creation by which they are tortured. They never see the wonderful adaptation of things to each other;—they know nothing of the harmonies of their being with the being of others,

Mary Peabody Mann and Elizabeth Peabody, *Moral Culture of Infancy and Kindergarten Guide* (Boston: T. O. H. P. Burnham, 1863), pp. 107–108.

or with Nature. The sort of education they get in cities, where life is stirring briskly around them, and each one seems scrambling to get the best morsel for himself, only makes them worse, unless something is done to evoke order for them out of this chaos. . . .

5.5 A Report on Child Labor.

The Committee appointed to take into consideration the subject of the education of children in manufacturing districts, have attended to that duty, and beg leave to report:

That from statements of facts, made to your committee, by delegates to this body, the number of youth and children of both sexes, under sixteen years of age, employed in Manufactories, constitute about two fifths of the whole number of persons employed. From the returns from a number of manufactories, your committee have made up the following summary, which, with some few exceptions and slight variations, they are fully persuaded will serve as a fair specimen of the general state of things. The regular returns made, include establishments in Massachusetts, New Hampshire, and Rhode Island; which employ altogether, something more than four thousand hands. Of these, sixteen hundred are between the ages of seven and sixteen years. In the return from Hope Factory, Rhode Island, it is stated that the practice is, to ring the first bell in the morning, at ten minutes after the break of day, the second bell at ten minutes after the first, in five minutes after which, or in twenty five minutes after the break of day, all hands are to be at their labor. The time for shutting the gates at night, as the signal for labor to cease, is eight o'clock by the factory time, which is from twenty to twenty five minutes behind the true time. And the only respite from labor during the day, is twenty five minutes at breakfast, and the same number at dinner. From the village of Nashua, in the town of Dunstable, N.H., we learn that the time of labor is from the break of day, in the morning, until eight o'clock in the evening; and that the factory time is twenty five minutes behind the true solar time. From the Arkwright and Harris Mills in Coventry, R.I., it is stated that the last bell in the morning rings and the wheel starts, as early as the help can see to work; and that a great part of the year, as early as four o'clock. Labor ceases at eight o'clock at night, factory time, and one hour in the day is allowed for meals. From the Rock-land Factory in Scituate, R.I., the Richmond Factory, in the same town, the various establishments at Fall River, Mass., and those at Somerworth, N.H. we

John R. Commons *et al*, eds., *A Documentary History of American Industrial Society* (Cleveland: Arthur H. Clark Company, 1910), V, pp. 195–199.

collect similar details.   At the numerous establishments in the village of Pawtucket, the state of things is very similar, with the exception of the fact that within a few weeks, public opinion has had the effect to reduce the factory time to the true solar standard.   And in fact, we believe these details to serve very nearly, to illustrate the general practice.

From these facts, your committee gather the following conclusions—

1. That on a general average the youth and children that are employed in the Cotton Mills, are compelled to labor at least thirteen and a half, perhaps fourteen hours per day, factory time.   And

2. That in addition to this, there are about twenty or twenty five minutes added, by reason of that time being so much, slower than the true solar time—thus making a day of labor to consist of at least fourteen hours, winter and summer, out of which, is allowed, on an average not to exceed one hour, for rest and refreshment.   Your committee also learn, that in general, no child can be taken from a Cotton Mill, to be placed at school, for any length of time, however short, without certain loss of employ; as, with very few exceptions, no provision is made by manufacturers, to obtain temporary help of this description, in order that one class may enjoy the advantages of the school, while the other class is employed in the mill.   Nor are parents, having a number of children in a mill, allowed to withdraw one or more, without withdrawing the whole; and for which reason, as such children are generally the offspring of parents, whose poverty has made them entirely dependent on the will of their employers, and are very seldom taken from the mills to be placed in school.

From all the facts in the case it is with regret, that your Committee are absolutely forced to the conclusion, that the only opportunities allowed to children generally, employed in manufactories, to obtain an education are on the Sabbath, and after half past 8 o'clock of the evening of other days. To these facts however, your Committee take pleasure in adding two or three others of a more honorable character.   It is believed that in the town of Lowell, no children are admitted to the labors of the mills, under twelve years of age; and that the various corporations provide and support a sufficient number of good schools, for the education of those that have not attained that age.   In the Chicopee Factory Village, Springfield, Mass., and also in the town of New Market, N.H., we also learn that schools are provided, and the children actually employed in mills, allowed the privilege of attending school, during a portion, say about one quarter of the year.   Your Committee mention these facts as honorable exceptions to the general rule, with a desire to do justice to all concerned, and the hope that others may be inspired by their example, to go much farther still, in their efforts to remove the existing evils.   A few more instances of the above character may exist; but if so, they have not come to the knowledge of your committee, and they have every reason to believe them to be extremely rare.

Your committee cannot therefore, without the violation of a solemn trust, withhold their unanimous opinion, that the opportunities allowed to children and youth employed in manufactories, to obtain an education suitable to the character of American freemen, and the wives and mothers of such, are altogether inadequate to the purpose; that the evils complained of are unjust and cruel; and are no less than the sacrifice of the dearest interests of thousands of the rising generation of our country, to the cupidity and avarice of their employers. And they can see no other result in prospect, as likely to eventuate from such practices than generation on generation, reared up in profound ignorance, and the final prostration of their liberties at the shrine of a powerful aristocracy. Deeply deploring the existing evils, and deprecating the dreadful abuses that may be hereafter practiced, your committee respectfully recommend the adoption of the following resolutions:

Resolved, that a committee of vigilance be appointed in each state represented in this convention, whose duty it shall be to collect and publish facts respecting the condition of laboring men, women, and children, and abuses practised on them by their employers: that it shall also be the duty of said committee, as soon as may be, to get up memorials to the Legislatures of their respective states, praying for the regulation of the hours of labor, according to the standard adopted by this Association, and for some wholesome regulations with regard to the education of children and youth employed in manufactures; and to make report of their doings at the meeting of this body, on the first Thursday of September next. . . .

5.6   Report on Education by the Working Men's Committee, 1830.

Report of the Joint Committees of the City and County of Philadelphia, appointed September, 1829, to ascertain the state of public instruction in Pennsylvania, and to digest and propose such improvements in education as may be deemed essential to the intellectual and moral prosperity of the people.

It is now nearly five months since the committees were appointed to cooperate on this arduous duty. But the importance of the subject; the time expended in research and enquiry, in order to procure information relative to it; and the multiplied discussions and deliberations necessary to recon-

John R. Commons *et al*, eds., *ibid.*, pp. 94–103.

cile and correct their own different and sometimes conflicting views, will, they believe, constitute a reasonable apology for this long delay.

After devoting all the attention to the subject, and making every enquiry which their little leisure and ability would permit, they are forced into the conviction, that there is great defect in the educational system of Pennsylvania; and that much remains to be accomplished before it will have reached that point of improvement which the resources of the state would justify, and which the intellectual condition of the people and the preservation of our republican institutions demand.

With the exception of this city and county, the city and incorporated borough of Lancaster, and the city of Pittsburgh, erected into "school districts" since 1818, it appears that the entire state is destitute of any provisions for public instruction, except those furnished by the enactment of 1809. This law requires the assessors of the several counties to ascertain and return the number of children whose parents are unable, through poverty, to educate them; and such children are permitted to be instructed at the most convenient schools at the expense of their respective counties.

The provisions of this act, however, are incomplete and frequently inoperative. They are, in some instances, but partially executed; in others, perverted and abused—and in many cases entirely and culpably neglected. The funds appropriated by the act, have, in some instances, been embezzled by fraudulent agents; and in others, partial returns of the children have been made, and some have been illegally and intentionally excluded from participating in the provisions of the law. From a parsimonious desire of saving the county funds, the cheapest, and consequently the most inefficient schools have been usually selected by the commisioners of the several counties.

The elementary schools throughout the state are irresponsible institutions, established by individuals, from mere motives of private speculation or gain, who are sometimes destitute of character, and frequently, of the requisite attainments and abilities. From the circumstance of the schools being the absolute property of individuals, no supervision or effectual control can be exercised over them; hence, ignorance, inattention, and even immorality, prevail to a lamentable extent among their teachers.

In some districts, no schools whatever exist! No means whatever of acquiring education are resorted to; while ignorance, and its never failing consequence, crime, are found to prevail in these neglected sports, to a greater extent than in other more favored portions of the state.

The "three school districts," however, which have been alluded to, are not liable to these objections. Much good, in particular, has resulted from the establishment of the first of these, comprising this city and county, and which owes its establishment to the persevering efforts of a few individuals, who, in order to succeed, even so far, were compelled to combat the ignorance, the prejudices, and the pecuniary interests of many active and hostile opponents.

But the principles on which these "school districts" are founded, are yet, in the opinion of the committees, extremely defective and inefficient. Their leading feature is pauperism! They are confined exclusively to the children of the poor, while there are, perhaps, thousands of children whose parents are unable to afford for them, a good private education, yet whose standing, professions or connexions in society effectually exclude them from taking the benefit of a poor law. There are great numbers, even of the poorest parents, who hold a dependence on the public bounty to be incompatible with the rights and liberties of an American citizen, and whose deep and cherished consciousness of independence determines them rather to starve the intellect of their offspring, than submit to become the objects of public charity.

There are, also, many poor families, who are totally unable to maintain and clothe their children, while at the schools; and who are compelled to place them, at a very early age, at some kind of labor that may assist in supporting them, or to bind them out as apprentices to relieve themselves entirely of the burthen of their maintenance and education, while the practice formerly universal, of schooling apprentices, has, of late years, greatly diminished and is still diminishing.

Another radical and glaring defect in the existing public school system is the very limited amount of instruction it affords, even to the comparatively small number of youth, who enjoy its benefits. It extends, in no case, further than a tolerable proficiency in reading, writing, and arithmetic, and sometimes to a slight acquaintance with geography. Besides these, the girls are taught a few simple branches of industry. A great proportion of scholars, however, from the causes already enumerated, acquire but a very slight and partial knowledge of these branches.

The present public school system, limited as it is to three solitary school districts, makes no provision for the care and instruction of children under five years old. This class of children is numerous, especially among the poor, and it frequently happens that the parents, or parent, (perhaps a widow) whose only resource for a livelihood is her needle or wash tub, is compelled to keep her elder children from the school to take charge of the younger ones, while her own hands are industriously employed in procuring a subsistence for them. Such instances are far from being rare, and form a very prominent and lamentable drawback on the utility of the schools in these districts. The care thus bestowed on infants, is insufficient and very partial. They are frequently exposed to the most pernicious influences and impressions. The seeds of vice, thus early scattered over the infant soil, are too often permitted to ripen, as life advances, till they fill society with violence and outrage, and yield an abundant harvest for magdalens and penitentiaries.

An opinion is entertained by many good and wise persons, and supported to a considerable extent, by actual experiment, that proper schools for supplying a judicious infant training, would effectually prevent much of that vicious depravity of character which penal codes and punishments are vainly intended to counteract. Such schools would, at least, relieve, in a great measure, many indigent parents, from the care of children, which in many cases occupies as much of their times as would be necessary to earn the children a subsistence. They would also afford many youth an opportunity of participating in the benefits of the public schools, who otherwise must, of necessity, be detained from them.

From this view of the public instruction in Pennsylvania, it is manifest that, even in "the school districts," to say nothing of the remainder of the state, a very large proportion of youth are either partially or entirely destitute of education.

It is true the state is not without its colleges and universities, several of which have been fostered with liberal supplies from the public purse. Let it be observed, however, that the funds so applied, have been appropriated exclusively for the benefit of the wealthy, who are thereby enabled to procure a liberal education for their children, upon lower terms than it could otherwise be afforded them. Funds thus expended, may serve to engender an aristocracy of talent, and place knowledge, the chief element of power, in the hands of the privileged few; but can never secure the common prosperity of a nation nor confer intellectual as well as political equality on a people.

The original element of despotism is a monopoly of talent, which consigns the multitude to comparative ignorance, and secures the balance of knowledge on the side of the rich and the rulers. If then the healthy existence of a free government be, as the committee believe, rooted in the will of the American people, it follows as a necessary consequence, of a government based upon that will, that this monopoly should be broken up, and that the means of equal knowledge, (the only security for equal liberty) should be rendered, by legal provision, the common property of all classes.

In a republic, the people constitute the government, and by wielding its powers in accordance with the dictates, either of their intelligence or their ignorance; of their judgment or their caprices, are the makers and the rulers of their own good or evil destiny. They frame the laws and create the institutions, that promote their happiness or produce their destruction. If they be wise and intelligent, no laws but what are just and equal will receive their approbation, or be sustained by their suffrages. If they be ignorant and capricious, they will be deceived by mistaken or designing rulers, into the support of laws that are unequal and unjust.

It appears, therefore, to the committees that there can be no real liberty without a wide diffusion of real intelligence; that the members of a republic, should all be alike instructed in the nature and character of their equal rights and duties, as human beings, and as citizens; and that education, instead of being limited as in our public poor schools, to a simple acquaintance with words and cyphers, should tend, as far as possible, to the production of a just disposition, virtuous habits, and rational self governing character.

When the committees contemplate their own condition, and that of the great mass of their fellow laborers; when they look around on the glaring inequality of society, they are constrained to believe, that until the means of equal instruction shall be equally secured to all, liberty is but an unmeaning word, and equality an empty shadow, whose substance to be realized must first be planted by an equal education and proper training in the minds, in the habits, in the manners, and in the feelings of the community.

While, however, the committees believe it their duty to exhibit, fully and openly, the main features and principles of a system of education which can alone comport with the spirit of American liberty, and the equal prosperity and happiness of the people, they are not prepared to assert, that the establishment of such a system in its fullness and purity, throughout the state, is by any means attainable at a single step. While they maintain that each human being has an equal right to a full development of all his powers, moral, physical and intellectual; that the common good of society can never be promoted in its fullness till all shall be equally secured and protected in the enjoyment of this right, and that it is the first great duty of the states, to secure the same to all its members; yet, such is now the degraded state of education in Pennsylvania compared with what, in the opinion of the committees, education for a free people should be, that they despair of so great a change as must be involved in passing from one to the other, being accomplished suddenly throughout the state. No new system of education could probably be devised with consequences so manifestly beneficial, as to awaken at once in the public mind, a general conviction and concurrence in the necessity of its universal adoption.

The committees are aware, also, that it is their duty to consult the views, the feelings, and the prejudices, not of a single district or county merely, but of the state in general. The measure which it is their business to propose, is one designed to be of universal extent and influence, and must, to be successful, be based upon the manifest wishes of nearly the whole commonwealth. It is not, therefore, to what would constitute a perfect education only, but also, to what may be rendered practicable—it is not with a view, exclusively, to the kind of education every child of Pennsylvania ought to have, but likewise to what it is possible, under existing circumstances, views, and prejudices, every child of Pennsylvania may and can have, that they have drawn up a bill or outline of what they deem a system of public education, adapted to the present condition and necessities of the state in general.

The principal points in which the bill for establishing common schools, accompanying this report, differs from the existing system of free schools, are as follows:

1. Its provisions, instead of being limited to three single districts, are designed to extend throughout the commonwealth.
2d. It places the managers of the public schools, immediately under the control and suffrage of the people.
3d. Its benefits and privileges will not, as at present, be limited as an act of charity to the poor alone, but will extend equally and of right to all classes, and be supported at the expense of all.
4th. It lays a foundation for infantile, as well as juvenile instruction. And lastly, it leaves the door open to every possible improvement which human benevolence and ingenuity may be able to introduce.

While, however, the committees would urge the establishment of common elementary schools throughout the state, as comprising, perhaps, the best general system of education which is at present attainable, it is but just to exhibit, also, some of the defects as well as the advantages of such schools; and to suggest such further measures as appear calculated to obviate such defects.

The instruction afforded by common schools, such as are contemplated in the bill for a general system of education, being only elementary, must, of necessity, produce but a very limited development of the human faculties. It would indeed diminish, but could not destroy, the present, injurious monopoly of talent. While the higher branches of literature and science remain accessible only to the children of the wealthy, there must still be a balance of knowledge, and with it a "balance of power," in the hands of the privileged few, the rich and the rulers.

Another radical defect in the best system of common schools yet established will be found in its not being adapted to meet the wants and necessities of those who stand most in need of it. Very many of the poorest parents are totally unable to clothe and maintain their children while at school, and are compelled to employ their time, while yet very young, in aiding to procure a subsistence. In the city of New York, a much more efficient system of education exists than in this city, and common schools have been in successful operation for the last ten or twelve years; yet there are at the present time upwards of 24,000 children between the ages of 5 and 15 years, who attend no schools whatever, and this apparently criminal neglect of attending the schools is traced, chiefly, to the circumstance just mentioned. It is evidently therefore, of no avail, how free the schools may be, while those children who stand most in need of them, are, through the necessity of their parents, either retained from them altogether, or withdrawn at an improper age, to assist in procuring a subsistence.

The constitution of this state declares that "the legislature shall provide schools in which the poor may be taught gratis." If this signifies that the poor shall have an opportunity afforded for instruction, it must involve means equal to the end. The poverty of the poor must be no obstruction, otherwise the constitution is a dead letter—nay, worse, an insult on their unfortunate condition and feelings.

The committees, therefore, believe, that one school, at least, should be established in each county, in which some principle should be adopted, calculated to obviate the defects that have been alluded to, and by which the children of all who desire it, may be enabled to procure, at their own expense, a liberal and scientific education. They are of the opinion that a principle fully calculated to secure this object, will be found in a union of agricultural and mechanical with literary and scientific instruction; and they have therefore, in addition to a plan of common elementary schools, drawn up and appended to this report, the substance of a bill providing for the establishment of high schools, or model schools, based upon this principle, which they also present for public deliberation.

5.7 The Workingmen of Pennsylvania Call for "An Equal and Republican System of Mental Instruction."

Fellow-Citizens: In offering to your consideration a subject of such importance, we shall state the ground which has led us to a separation from the two great political parties which have heretofore misruled and misrepresented the people, and the reasons for dissenting from existing laws, which we consider unreasonable and unjust, operating like an incubus upon the equitable energies of those who constitute the true wealth and strength of our country, thereby nullifying in practice the glorious principle and vivifying declaration that "all men are born equal." Too long have the operatives of this country, as in all others, been left without a suitable representation in the local, state and national councils to guard their in-

John R. Commons *et al*, eds., *ibid.*, pp. 114–117.

terests and crush a power in its origin that ultimately deadens and paralyses their efforts to sustain their rank and privileges as freemen; a power which while it holds them amenable, yet, through the influence of the powers that be, passes by the malversations of the great, the rich, and the powerful.

In assuming a title, our object is not to draw another useless line of distinction between our fellow-citizens for mere electioneering purposes—it is that all thinking as we do may rally under one banner, and by a unity in action produce the desired end.

The main pillar of our system is general education; for it is an axiom no longer controverted, that the stability of a republic depends mainly upon the intelligence of its citizens—that in proportion as they become wise they become virtuous and happy—that the period for forming a good and useful citizen is in youth, ere ignorance and crime have deluded the mind by a lengthened dominion over it, and therefore that an early and suitable education for each child is of primary importance in maintaining the public weal.

It is now forty years since the adoption of the constitution of Pennsylvania, and although that instrument strongly recommends that provision be made for the education of our youth at the public expense, yet during that long period, has the salutary and patriotic obligation been disregarded by our legislative authority, and thousands are now suffering the consequences of this disregard to the public welfare on the part of our rulers.

It is true, that some attempts have been made to remedy the omission in two or three districts of the state, but they have proved ineffectual. The very spirit in which these provisions have been made not only defeats the object intended, but tends also to draw still broader the line of distinction between the rich and the poor. All who receive the limited knowledge imparted by the present system of public education are looked upon as paupers, drawing from a fount which they have in no wise contributed towards creating. The spirit of independence and of feeling in which all participate, cause the honest and industrious poor to reject a proffered bounty that connects with its reception a seeming disgrace. This honest pride in relation to charity schools, however injurious its effects may be on the poor man's offspring, is nevertheless commendable, inasmuch as it is in accordance with the spirit of our free institutions, with our elevated national character—and such a narrow policy is less than they have a right to demand at the hands of our representatives.

It is in vain for the opponents of equal education to assert that the poor, if left to themselves, will use their exertions to educate their children, and that the expenses saved them by its being accomplished by public means, will be expended by the parent on less important subjects; for it is a lamentable fact, that persons destitute of education are ignorant of the loss they sustain, and hence, fail to avert the evil from their offspring. The ignorance of the parent generally extends to his children's children, while the blessings of a liberal education are handed down from father to son as as legacy which poverty cannot impoverish.

We confidently anticipate the cordial co-operation of our brethren throughout the state in favour of this great object, so essential to our happiness as freemen. All must be aware of the necessity of the prompt interference of the people in behalf of those cardinal principles of republican liberty which were declared in '76, and which can only be sustained by the adoption of an ample system of public instruction, calculated to impart equality as well as mental culture—the establishment of institutions where the children of the poor and the rich may meet at that period of life, when the pomp and circumstance of wealth have not engendered pride; when the only distinction known, will be the celebrity each may acquire by their acts of good fellowship; when the best opportunity is afforded for forming associations that will endure through life, and where the obloquy attending the present system will not attach. The objection that the children of the wealthy will not be sent to these schools, is one of minor importance. Our main object is to secure the benefits of education for those who would otherwise be destitute, and to place them mentally on a level with the most favored in the world's gifts. As poverty is not a crime, neither is wealth a virtue. Why then so much anxiety to be associated with a particular portion of our citizens merely on account of their wealth? They form but a small portion of the entire population of our country, and as its safety must depend upon the majority, 'tis there our duty and our exertions should be directed.

It has been remarked, and with much plausibility, that if common schools were established, and provided with suitable instructors in the various departments of a thorough education, the numbers attending "colleges" would be much diminished. This position we admit and cheerfully assent to. Our object is not to raise the hue and cry against colleges—it is not to drag down and chain the intellect of others to the common extent of learning by endeavoring to enlist the public voice against them, but it is to make each avenue of learning the certain pathway to the entire field of science.

Let us unite then, fellow citizens, on a measure fraught with such momentous consequences—a measure involving the happiness or misery of posterity. We are all equally interested in preventing crime by contributing to the means of knowledge and virtue. Consider the responsibility which rests upon us as parents and citizens of a free state. We should constantly bear in mind that the prosperity and happiness of our beloved country essentially depend on the speedy adoption of an equal and republican system of mental instruction.

5.8 Conservative Opposition to Free Public Education.

"Education and general information—these must indeed constitute our only true National Bulwark. May the day soon come when in point of literary acquirements the poorest peasant shall stand on a level with his more wealthy neighbours."

It is our strong inclination and our obvious interest that literary acquirements should be universal; but we should be guilty of imposture, if we professed to believe in the possibility of that consummation. Literature cannot be acquired without leisure, and wealth gives leisure. Universal opulence, or even competency, is a chimera, as man and society are constituted. There will ever be distinctions of condition, of capacity, of knowledge and ignorance, in spite of all the fond conceits which may be indulged, or the wild projects which may be tried, to the contrary. The "peasant" must labor during those hours of the day, which his wealthy neighbor can give to the abstract culture of his mind; otherwise, the earth would not yield enough for the subsistence of all: the mechanic cannot abandon the operations of his trade, for general studies; if he should, most of the conveniences of life and objects of exchange would be wanting; languor, decay, poverty, discontent would soon be visible among all classes. No government, no statesman, no philanthropist, can furnish what is incompatible with the very organization and being of civil society. *Education, the most comprehensive, should be, and is, open to the whole community; but it must cost to every one, time and money; and those are means which every one cannot possess simultaneously.* Doubtless, more of education and of information is attainable for all in this republic, than can be had any where else by the poor or the operatives, so called. . . .

We can readily pardon the editor of the United States *Gazette* for not perceiving that the scheme of Universal Equal Education at the expense of the State, is virtually "Agrarianism." It would be a compulsory application of the means of the richer, for the direct use of the poorer classes; and so far an arbitrary division of property among them. The declared object is, to procure the opportunity of instruction for the child or children of every citizen; to elevate the standard of the education of the working classes, or equalize the standard for all classes; which would, doubtless, be to lower or narrow that which the rich may now compass. But the most sensible and reflecting possessors of property sufficient to enable

John R. Commons *et al*, eds., *ibid.*, pp. 107–108, 110–112.

them to educate their children in the most liberal and efficacious way, and upon the broadest scale, would prefer to share their means for any other purpose, or in any other mode, than such as would injuriously affect or circumscribe the proficiency of their offspring. A public meeting of "the Mechanics and other Working Men of the City and County of New York," was held in the city, on the 17 inst., and among the principles for which they have "resolved" to contend, we find the following:

"In Education—The adoption of a general system of instruction, at the expense of the State, which shall afford to children, however rich or poor, equal means to obtain useful learning. To effect this, it is believed that a system of direct taxation will not be necessary, as the surplus revenue of the State and United States Governments will, in a very few years, afford ample means—but even if it were necessary to resort to direct taxation to accomplish this all-important object, and the amount paid by the wealthy should be far greater than that paid by our less eligibly situated fellow-citizens, an equivalent to them would be found in the increased ability and usefulness of the educated citizen to serve and to promote the best interests of the State; in the increased permanency of our institutions—and in the superior protection of liberty, person and property."

Thus, a direct tax for "the equal means of obtaining useful learning" is not deemed improbable, and it is admitted that the amount which would be paid by the wealthy would be "far greater" than that paid by their "less eligibly situated fellow citizens." Here, we contend, would be the action, if not the name, of the Agrarian system. Authority—that is, the State—is to force the more eligibly situated citizens to contribute a part (which might be very considerable) of their means, for the accommodation of the rest; and this is equivalent to the idea of an actual, compulsory partition of their substance. The more thriving members of the "mechanical and other working classes" would themselves feel the evil of the direct taxation; they would find that they had toiled for the benefit of other families than their own. One of the chief excitements to industry, among those classes, is the hope of earning the means of educating their children respectably or liberally: that incentive would be removed, and the scheme of State and equal education be thus a premium for comparative idleness, to be taken out of the pockets of the laborious and conscientious. . . .

We have no confidence in any compulsory equalizations; it has been well observed that they pull down what is above, but never much raise what is below, and often "depress high and low together beneath the level of what was originally the lowest." By no possibility could a perfect equality be procured. A scheme of universal equal education, attempted in reality, would be an unexampled bed of Procrustes, for the understandings of our youth, and in fact, could not be used with any degree of equality of profit, unless the dispositions and circumstances of parents and children were nearly the same; to accomplish which phenomenon, in a nation of many millions, engaged in a great variety of pursuits, would be beyond human power. . . .

5.9 Calvin Stowe Talks About the Americanization of Immigrants and Dr. Daniel Drake Responds to His Address.

Calvin Stowe

It is a work of the highest benevolence to receive the wandering stranger, to provide for the wants of his mind, and prepare him for usefulness, elevation, and happiness as a citizen of our own happy country. None but he who has felt it, can know all the loneliness and heart-sickness, of the poor immigrant when he first finds himself in a foreign land, surrounded by people of strange habits and an unknown tongue. How sweet in such circumstances is the voice of unexpected sympathy, especially from the lips of the intelligent teacher, inquiring after the moral welfare of himself and his children? . . .

But if neither the feelings of benevolence nor the precepts of the Bible have power to compel us to extend our fostering hand to the stranger; it would seem that an enlightened regard to our own interests might induce us to do it. A nation's strength is in the number and moral worth of its inhabitants; and the vast extent of our still uncultivated territory demands the hands of millions of cultivators. Of the fifteen hundred millions of acres in the United States, but nine hundred millions are now under cultivation, and even these are as yet imperfectly improved and might be rendered immensely more productive. On the largest calculation, our cultivated soil is to the uncultivated only as five to ten. Let us then invite cultivators who are now starving in overpeopled districts; and let us see to it, that as fast as they arrive they be made intelligent, virtuous, religious, or at least have the means of becoming so. This vast ocean of mind which is already rolling in upon us—how glorious to make it all available for good! What an empire would this be! How unspeakably superior to the glories of all the empires of the ancient world, founded in conquest and sustained by oppression! planted in blood and watered by the tears of captive millions! Empires on which the Prince of Darkness only could look with complacency! But here we would have one, that would be an object of joyful contemplation to the Almighty Prince of Peace!

Transactions of the Fifth Annual Meeting of the Western Literary Institute and College of Professional Teachers (Cincinnati: Executive Committee, 1836), pp. 65–66, 68–71, 75, 81–82.

Let us now be reminded, that unless we educate our immigrants, they will be our ruin. It is no longer a mere question of benevolence, of duty, or of enlightened self-interest, but the intellectual and religious training of our foreign population has become essential to our own safety; we are prompted to it by the instinct of self-preservation. The wave of immigration has begun to roll from the old world to the new, and no human power can stop it; our civil constitution affords perilous facilities for foreign naturalization, and it is probably too late to think of amending it. Perhaps it is not desirable; perhaps a wise Providence intended that we should have this spur in our sides to stimulate us to the requisite efforts in behalf of the moral welfare of the oppressed millions who are taking refuge among us. . . .

Now, we have no choice left. These people are in our midst; they are coming among us more and more: and we must labor, we must labor incessantly and perseveringly to prevent the evils, and to secure the good which may arise from their association with us.

It is not merely from the ignorant and vicious foreigner that danger is to be apprehended. To sustain an extended republic like our own, there must be a *national* feeling, a national assimilation; and nothing could be more fatal to our prospects of future national prosperity, than to have our population become a congeries of clans, congregating without coalescing, and condemned to contiguity without sympathy. The graphic imagery which the genius of oriental prophecy applied to the unwieldy and loose-jointed Roman empire, would in this case be still more fatally applicable to our own widely spread republic. . . .

It is altogether essential to our national strength and peace, if not even to our national existence, that the foreigners who settle on our soil, should cease to be Europeans and become Americans; and as our national language is English, and as our literature, our manners, and our institutions are of English origin, and the whole foundation of our society English, it is necessary that they become substantially Anglo-Americans. Let them be like grafts which become branches of the parent stock; improve its fruit, and add to its beauty and its vigor; and not like the parasitical missletoe, which never incorporates itself with the trunk from which it derives its nourishment, but exhausts its sap, withers its foliage, despoils it of its strength, and sooner or later by destroying its support, involves itself in ruin. It is ungrateful as well as dangerous for the foreigners who are among us, to make for themselves interests that are different from the interests of the whole nation, and to sustain candidates for public office on the ground that they belong to their people; and partizans who tamper with feelings like these, are sowing seeds which will produce harvests of dissension and blood. What is their nation? and who are their people? Their nation is the American nation, and their people are the American people; or they have no business on the American soil. We must become one nation; and it must be our great endeavor to effect this object so desirable and so necessary to our national welfare.

The most effectual, and indeed the only effectual way, to produce this individuality and harmony of national feeling and character, is to bring our children into the same schools and have them educated together. The children of immigrants must be taught English and prepared for the common English schools; and the safety of the republic requires that destitute children should be sought out and made to attend the public schools. The public schools should be our best schools, and possess a character sufficiently elevated to secure the patronage of the influential and the wealthy, that all the children of our republic may be educated together. This would be our strongest national ægis, the surest palladium of our country. . . .

National character is often greatly improved by the commingling of different ingredients. The peculiar excellencies of the English character, which have given it its vigor and preponderating influence, and made the English almost the universal language, and those who speak it, masters of nearly half the globe, originated in the mingling of the Norman French with the Saxon German; and that too under all the disadvantages of haughty conquest on the one hand, and hated subjection on the other. Our present circumstances are infinitely more favorable. We can unite under all the sweet influences of affection, of gratitude, and of reciprocal advantage. Let us, then, make the most of the German mind that is among us; and from the mixture produce a compound, which, like the Corinthian brass, shall be more precious than the purest gold. . . .

Dr. Daniel Drake

But, of these and of all other emigrants, it must also be said, that many of their social peculiarities and national prejudices, do, of necessity, cling to them, and may impart to our society a diversified character. Such a community is not a compound, but an unconsolidated mass; and to acquire uniformity, it must be subjected to the crucible of social amalgamation. The school-house is that crucible, and the schoolmaster is the only alchemist who can bring fine gold out of the crude and discordant materials. It is only, sir, on the children and youth of our emigrant population, that we can act with effect. The feelings, modes of thinking, and customs of the parents, are so fixed, that they can, at most, be but slightly modified; and if their vernacular tongue is different from our own, they will prefer to use it still. As native Americans it is our duty to prevent an entailment of these upon their children; and the hereditary establishment among us of a distinct caste of foreigners. Pennsylvania, by not attending to this in due time, is compelled to cherish in her bosom an exotic population; which, it is true, possesses many valuable qualities, but still remains to this hour unimbued with the principles of her institutions—uninspired by the spirit of that social and political improvement, which every where else, is active. The Emigrant Friend's Society is directed against this conservative tendency; and if properly encouraged by the present and future efforts of the general community, cannot fail to be successful. I am convinced sir, that there is a strong disposition in the younger portion of our German population, to adopt the fashions and language which belong to this country; and, as professor McGuffy remarked last evening, on a different occasion, the children will re-act on the parents, and the young become the teachers of the old.

To have evidence of this, one need but stand, on a Sabbath morning, near any of the German churches of our city, and observe the costume of the families, either Papist or Protestant, which are about to enter. The parents will be dressed according to the fashions of Germany, but the children, to a great degree, in that of the United States; the mothers will appear in caps, only, or even with naked hair, the daughters in bonnets, made according to the prevailing fashions of the city. Let us then persevere, and we may hope to shape the rising generation to our own model, and give such activity to the work of social amalgation, as will, at last, secure uniformity of character; and may raise that which left to itself would be a foreign and inferior mass, into an element of social strength and beauty—in harmony with the other elements of Western Society.

5.10 James G. Carter Discusses the Defects of the Common Schools of Massachusetts.

Before we attempt, however, to take a single step towards reform let us see what we have to amend. Unless faults can be shown to exist in the organization of our system of popular education, and great ones; it will do but little good to recommend improvements. For it is with communities as with individuals; and "no one," says Fisher Ames, "is less likely to improve, than the coxcomb, who fancies he has already learned out." The pride, which we of New England have been accustomed to feel and, perhaps, to manifest, in our free schools, as the best in the country, and in the world, has not improved their condition. But, on the contrary, the

James G. Carter, *Essays on Popular Education* . . . (Boston: Dutton and Wentworth, 1826), pp. 34–37, 40–41.

great complacency with which we contemplate this institution is a most effectual bar to all improvements in it. The time has come, when we owe it to our country and ourselves to speak the whole truth in this matter, even though it disturb our self-satisfaction a little.

It will be convenient to point out the faults of the public provisions for popular education under the two following heads; first, the "Summer Free Schools," which are, generally, taught in the country towns for a few months in the warm season of the year by females; and second, the "Winter Free Schools," which are taught by men, commonly, for a shorter period, during the cold season. Children of both sexes of from four to ten or twelve years, usually attend these primary summer schools, and females often to a much later age. This is a very interesting period of human life. No one, who has reflected much upon the subject of early discipline; no one, I trust, who has even followed me through the preceding essays, can doubt, that it is one of the most important parts, if not the very most important part of our lives, as it regards the influence of education in its widest sense. It is important as it regards the development of the powers of the body, or physical education. Because the parts of the body, the limbs, the muscles, the organs, or whatever are the technical names for them, now assume a firmness and consistency in discharging their proper functions, or they become distorted and enfeebled; and these habits, thus early contracted, became a part of ourselves and are as abiding as our lives. Yet what has been done in this branch of education? Nothing at all, absolutely nothing at all, even in our best schools. This period is vitally important as it regards the cultivation of the heart and its affections. What has been done here? Chance and ill-directed efforts make up all the education, which we have received or are giving to our children in the schools in this department. Finally, it is important to us, as it regards the discipline of the head, the developement of the understanding and its faculties. What have we done in this department? We have done something, indeed, and think that we have done much. We have done, and we continue to do, *more* than we do *well*. We resort to many expedients and apply many means, without distinctly understanding, either what we wish to attain, whether it be possible to attain it, or if so, the adaptation of our means to its attainment. Success here, therefore, if the best possible results have ever been gained in any instance, has been more the result of chance than of skill.

To whom do we assign the business of governing and instructing our children from four to twelve years of age? Who take upon themselves the trust of forming those principles and habits, which are to be strengthened and confirmed in manhood, and make our innocent little ones through life, happy or miserable in themselves, and the blessings or the curses of society? To analyze, in detail, the habits, which are formed and confirmed in these first schools, to trace the abiding influence of good ones, or to describe the inveteracy of bad ones, would lead me from my present purpose. But are these interesting years of life and these important branches of education committed to those, who understand their importance or their influence upon the future character? Are they committed to those, who would know what to do, to discharge their high trust successfully if they did, indeed, understand their importance? I think not. And I am persuaded, that all, who have reflected but for a moment upon the age, the acquirements, and the experience of those who assume to conduct this branch of education, must have come to the same conclusion.

The teachers of the primary summer schools have rarely had any education beyond what they have acquired in the very schools where they begin to teach. Their attainments, therefore, to say the least, are usually *very moderate.* But this is not the worst of it. They are often very young, they are constantly changing their employment, and consequently can have but little experience; and what is worse than all, they never have had any direct preparation for their profession. This is the only service, in which we venture to employ young, and often, ignorant persons, without some previous instruction in their appropriate duties. We require experience in all those, whom we employ to perform the slightest mechanical labour for us. We would not buy a coat or a hat of one, who should undertake to make them without a previous apprenticeship. Nor would any one have the hardihood to offer to us the result of his first essay in manufacturing either of these articles. We do not even send an old shoe to be mended, except it be to a workman of whose skill we have had ample proof. Yet we commit our children to be educated to those, who know nothing, absolutely nothing, of the complicated and difficult duties assigned to them. Shall we trust the developement of the delicate bodies, the susceptible hearts, and the tender minds of our little children to those who have no knowledge of their nature? Can they, can these rude hands finish the workmanship of the Almighty? No language can express the astonishment, which a moments reflection on this subject excites in me.

But I must return to the examination of the qualifications of the female teachers of the primary summer schools, from which purpose I have unconsciously a little departed to indulge in a general remark. They are a class of teachers unknown in our laws regulating the schools unless it be by some latitude of construction. No standard of attainments is fixed, at which they must arrive before they assume the business of instruction. So that any one *keeps school*, which is a very different thing from *teaching school*, who wishes to do it, and can persuade, by herself, or her friends, a small district to employ her. And this is not a very difficult matter, especially when the remuneration for the employment is so very trifling. The farce of an examination and a certificate from the minister of the town, for it is a perfect farce, amounts to no efficient check upon the obtrusions of ignorance and inexperience. As no standard is fixed by law, each minister makes a standard for himself, and alters it as often as the peculiar circumstances of the case require. And there will always be enough of peculiar circumstances to render a refusal inexpedient.

Let those, who are conversant with the manner in which these schools are managed, say, whether this description of them undervalues their character and efficacy. Let those, who conduct them, pause and consider whether all is well, and whether there are not abuses and perversions in them, which call loudly for attention and reformation. Compare the acquirements, the experience, the knowledge of teaching possessed by these instructers, not one with another, for the standard is much too low; but with what they might be, under more favourable circumstances and with proper preparation. Compare the improvement made in these little nurseries of piety and religion, of knowledge and rational liberty, not one with another, for the progress in all of them is much too slow; but with what the infant mind and heart are capable of, at this early age, under the most favourable auspices. And there can be no doubt, that all will arrive at the same conclusions; a dissatisfaction with the condition of these schools; and an astonishment, that the public have been so long contented with so small results from means, which all will acknowledge capable of doing so much. . . .

The young man, who lays down his axe and aspires to take up the "rod" and rule in a village school, has, usually, in common with other young men, a degree of dignity and self-complacency, which it is dangerous to the extent of his power to disturb. And when he comes to his minister, sustained by his own influence in the parish, and that of a respectable father and perhaps a large family of friends, and asks of him the legal approbation for a teacher, it is a pretty delicate matter to refuse it. A firm and conscientious refusal of approbation to a school-master, has led, in more instances than one, to a firm and conscientious refusal to hear the minister preach. And, by the parish difficulties growing out of so small an affair, he has found himself at last "unsettled" and thrown with his family, perhaps in his old age, upon the world to seek and gain his subsistence as he may. This is truly martyrdom. And martyrs in ordinary times are rare. Even good men can make peace with their consciences on better terms. So much for the literary qualifications of instructers.

It is the intention of the school-law to secure good, moral characters in the public instructers by requiring the approbation, as to this qualification, of the selectmen of the town, where the school is to be taught. No doubt selectmen are as good judges of morality as any body of men, which could readily be appealed to. But either we are a very moral people, or they are not very discriminating; for instances are rare, indeed, of refusal of their approbation on this ground. If a young man be moral enough to keep out of the State-Prison, he will find no difficulty in getting approbation for a school-master. These things ought not to be so. Both the moral and the intellectual character of the rising generation are influenced more by their instructers, during the period of from four to twelve years of age, than by any cause so entirely within our control. It becomes then of momentous concern to the community, in a moral and religious, as well as in political point of view, that this influence should be the greatest and the best possible. That it is not now so, every one, I trust, who has followed me through my preceding essays, is convinced. And if something be not done, and that speedily, to improve the condition of the free schools, and especially the primary *summer schools*, they will not only fail of their happiest influence, but in a short time of all influence which will be worth estimating.

If the policy of the legislature, in regard to free schools, for the last twenty years be not changed, the institution, which has been the glory of New England will, in twenty years more, be extinct. If the State continue to relieve themselves of the trouble of providing for the instruction of the whole people, and to shift the responsibility upon the towns, and the towns upon the districts, and the districts upon individuals, each will take care of himself and his own family as he is able, and as he appreciates the blessing of a good education. The rich will, as a class, have much better instruction than they now have, while the poor will have much worse or none at all. The academies and private schools will be carried to much greater perfection than they have been, while the public free schools will become stationary or retrograde; till at length, they will be thrown for support upon the gratuitous, and of course capricious and uncertain efforts of individuals; and then, like the lower schools of the crowded cities of Europe, they will soon degenerate into mere mechanical establishments, such as the famous *seminaries* of London, Birmingham, and Manchester of which we hear so much lately, not for rational moral and intellectual instruction of human beings, but for training young animals to march, sing, and draw figures in sand,—establishments, in which the power of one man is so prodigiously multiplied, that he can overlook, direct and control the intellectual exercises of a thousand! And this wretched mockery of education, they must be right glad to accept as a charity, instead of inheriting as their birthright as good instruction as the country affords.

5.11 Two Teachers Reminisce About Their Days in a District School in New England.

First Teacher

Ten years ago I was called to superintend a district school in the village of B———, in Connecticut, for one year. The school had usually been under the care of a male instructer four or five months in the winter, and a female as many months of summer; with a vacation in the spring, and another in the fall, of from one to two months each. The instructers had been changed often; few of them ever taught two seasons in succession. The school was large, and the pupils rather ungovernable; though perhaps not more so than is usually the case with large schools in our thickly settled villages. Some of the teachers had been comparatively excellent, but no one remaining in the school more than four or five months, little could be done, except assisting the pupils in recalling what they had forgotten during the previous long vacation, inculcating new laws and ways of instruction, and perhaps introducing some new school-book. In this school I remainèd almost constantly two years, with the exception of five months, when the vacancy was supplied by an excellent instructress. Since my connexion with the school was dissolved, I have watched its progress with intense interest, and, in compliance with your request, I proceed to give you a brief history of it.

When I took charge of the school the pupils were not all collected until an hour after it was opened in the morning. My first object was to establish the habit of punctuality by my own example, and by preparing every comfort and inducement in my power. I prepared a fire, when fires were necessary, every morning, at least an hour before the time of opening the school; and if in any instance it was found impossible to be present myself for the purpose, some person was employed, in whom the most complete confidence could be placed.

School was commenced precisely at 9 A.M., and 1 P.M., throughout the year. Not aware of the necessity of the strictest adherence to my *hours*, the parents at first, in some instances, prepared dinner so late, that in order to be at the school-room precisely at *one*, I sometimes went away fasting. It is but justice to say, however, that no family in the district ever permitted such a thing to occur more than once.

As might very naturally be inferred, this course was followed by *punctuality* on the part of parents and children; especially the former. If the children sometimes loitered on the road, the fault should be attributed chiefly to the failure of the instructer to adopt such plans, and introduce

American Annals of Instruction, II (August and October, 1831), pp. 380–383, 468–472.

such modes of instruction, as were best calculated to make them regard school as a pleasant place, rather than a gloomy prison. Still the pupils were nearly all present when the school was opened. A few were from a quarter to half an hour later. Seldom, however, were they an hour or an hour and a half too late, as is common in many schools. Perhaps the fact that I made it a practice to tell stories, and instruct those who came in early, before nine o'clock, was not without its influence.

There was another excellent feature preserved in the school. The scholars attended *steadily*. The greatest number I ever had on my catalogue was but about sixty, and this only during a very short period of the winter; yet the school averaged fortyfour throughout the year. I do not believe another instance of the kind could at that time have been found in the state—I say *of the kind;* for many pupils had a mile to walk, and some nearly two; and the winter was very severe.

It is a fact highly creditable to the parents and visiters of the school, and which contributed not a little to its prosperity, that nearly every child was provided with all the books and implements which he needed, and of course a vast amount of time and trouble in borrowing was saved. In summer the house, to render the room more pleasant, and furnish amusement for the children, was adorned with evergreens, pictures, &c. Perhaps it should be added, that every child came to school clad in clean, wholesome apparel; but I cannot say they returned so; for the school, instead of being surrounded with grass, was placed in a sand bank, and I found it next to impossible to preserve the pupils from carrying away the evidences of it.

When I entered the school, there were fifteen scholars under five years of age. The greater part were under four, and several only about three. The plan of sending children to school so young was at that time generally unpopular; and much complaint was made by the parents of others, and by myself. I stoutly maintained, that no child ought to be sent to school under five years of age. But the parents insisted on sending them, and I was obliged to submit. To meet the exigency, means were provided at the schoolhouse for allowing them to sleep occasionally during the hot weather. Eleven of the number alluded to, had received no previous instruction.

In spite of my prejudices, however, the youngest pupils made the best progress. At the end of one year many of them were able to spell and read better than children ordinarily are, who have been instructed two winters and two summers.

Since I left the school, a lady who had taught during the five months of my absence already mentioned, has superintended it nearly every summer, and a part of the time in the winter. Her methods of instruction and government have been uniform and of an improved character. Several able instructers have been employed in the winter; one or two of whom are among the best qualified instructers in this country. The vacations have been very short; the school, in fact, is continued nearly throughout the year. The wages of instructers have, in some instances, been nearly twice as great as those of other instructers, in that vicinity, in schools of similar size. Females receive from one dollar and a half to two dollars a week besides their board. One gentleman was paid twentythree dollars a month, besides being furnished with board and an excellent room; while in the adjoining town, no teacher has ever, so far as I can learn, received more than twelve dollars a month; and females rarely more than seventy-five cents a week and their board. I have even known near twenty instances of instructers being employed at ten, eleven, and twelve dollars a month, and females at one dollar a week, and furnish their own board. Two or three of the best receive twelve dollars and board themselves; and walk about two miles to school daily!

In the school district of B——— the inhabitants tax themselves to an amount nearly as great as they receive from the school fund. There are few districts in Connecticut that do this.

The result of all this effort on the part of this district has been most happy. For ten years the school has flourished beyond any example in that region. Those children who began at three to four years of age and made rapid progress, having been almost constantly under the best of instruction ever since, with little change of instructers, or books (except reading books), have maintained their superior rank in comparison with other children, notwithstanding the general opinion which prevails that their progress must necessarily be interrupted, and that there always is, in such cases, a falling off.

It should be added that nearly all the instructers have had a *School Library*. This has exerted a good influence. I have recently been informed, that the district has purchased a permanent library.

What has contributed to raise the character of the schools at B——— generally, and this among others, is the fact, that every teacher is obliged to undergo a thorough and extensive examination. I have seen teachers rejected who had taught the best schools in some of the adjoining towns. Even if a teacher has been examined in the town several times, he is not permitted to teach until he has undergone another examination. I have taught there *seven seasons*, and have been regularly examined in every instance but one.

Nor have *visiters* and *parents* been entirely unmindful of the schools. During some seasons, not a week passes, sometimes not a day, but some parent calls to witness the progress of his children. Public exhibitions are, I believe, chiefly dispensed with. The visiters or parents see the school in its usual dress.

In the school to which these remarks have been generally applied, the Pestalozzian system of instruction has been adopted by the greater part of the teachers. The pupils have not been studying mere words, without receiving any ideas—nor have they been merely *receiving* those ideas in a passive manner. Nor has the memory alone been cultivated, to the neglect of the other faculties. They have been taught to teach themselves, rather than sit still and receive knowledge, as a vessel receives whatever liquid we choose to pour into it. They have been taught to use their judgment, and indeed all their other faculties, as well as the memory. . . .

Second Teacher

The school house stood near the centre of the district, at the junction of four roads, so near the usual track of carriages, that a large stone was set up at the end of the building to defend it from injury. Except in the dry season the ground is wet, permitting small collections of water on the surface, and the soil by no means firm. The spot is peculiarly exposed to the bleak winds of winter; nor are there at present any shade trees near, to shelter the children from the scorching rays of the summer's sun during their recreations. There were a few formerly; but they were cut down many years ago. Neither is there any such thing as an outhouse of *any kind*, not even a wood shed.

The size of the building was twenty two feet long, by twenty broad. From the floor to the ceiling, it was seven feet. The chimney and entry took up about four feet at one end, leaving the school room itself, twenty feet by eighteen. Around three sides of the room, were connected desks, arranged so that when the pupils were sitting at them, their faces were towards the instructor and their backs towards the wall. Attached to the sides of the desks nearest to the instructor, were benches for small pupils. The instructor's desk and chair occupied the centre. On this desk were stationed a rod or ferule; sometimes both. These, with books, writings, inkstands, rules, and plummets, with a fire shovel, and a pair of tongs, (often broken,) were the principal furniture.

The windows were five in number, of twelve panes each. They were situated so low in the walls, as to give full opportunity to the pupils, to see every traveller as he passed, and to be easily broken. The places of the broken panes, were usually supplied with hats, during the school hours. The entry was four feet square. A depression in the chimney on one side of the entry, furnished a place of deposit for about half of the hats, and spare clothes of the boys; and the rest were left on the floor, often to be trampled upon. The girls generally carried their bonnets, &c. into the school room. The floor and ceiling were level, and the walls were plastered.

The room was warmed by a large and deep fire place. So large was it, and so little efficacious in warming the room otherwise, that I have seen about *one eighth of a cord of good wood*, burning in it at a time. In severe weather, it was estimated that the amount usually consumed, was not far from a cord, or one hundred and twenty eight feet, a week.

The new building erected about five years since, has many improvements upon the former. It is of brick; the room is larger and higher; it is better lighted, and has an improved fire place. The writing desks for the pupils are attached to the walls, and the seats for the smaller pupils have backs. Besides, the local situation of the house is changed. It stands two or three rods from the road side, on a firm soil; but there are no shade trees near, nor any out houses. Like the former house, it has a cold bleak situation in winter. With regard to an entry, however, there now is none. The whole building forms but one room.

The school was not unfrequently broken up for a day or two for want of wood in former years; but since they have used a smaller fire place, this occurrence has been more rare. The instructor or pupils were, however, sometimes compelled to cut or saw it, to prevent the closing of the school. The wood was left in the road near the house, so that it was often buried in the snow or wet with the rain. At the best, it was usually burnt green. The fires were to be kindled, about half an hour before the time of beginning the school. Often, the scholar, whose lot it was, neglected to build it. In consequence of this, the house was frequently cold and uncomfortable about half the forenoon, when the fire being very large, the excess of heat became equally distressing. Frequently too, we were annoyed by smoke. The greatest amount of suffering, however, arose from excessive heat, particularly at the close of the day. The pupils being in a free perspiration when they retired, were very liable to take cold.

The ventilation of the school room, was as much neglected as its temperature; and its cleanliness, more perhaps than either. Situated as the house was, the latter might seem to be in a measure unavoidable. There were, however, no arrangements made for cleaning feet at the door, or for washing floors, windows, &c. In the summer the floor was washed, perhaps once in two or three weeks.

The winter school has usually been opened about the first of December, and continued from twelve to sixteen weeks. The summer school is commenced about the first of May. Formerly this was also continued about three or four months; but within ten years the term has been lengthened usually to twenty weeks. Males have been uniformly employed in winter, and females in summer.

The instructors have usually been changed every season, but sometimes they have been continued two successive summers or winters. A strong prejudice has always existed against employing the same instructor more than once or twice in the same district. This prejudice has yielded in one instance, so far that an instructor who had taught two successive winters, twenty five years before, was employed another season. I have not been able to ascertain the exact number of different instructors who have been engaged in the school during the last thirty years; but I can distinctly recollect *thirtyseven*. Many of them, both males and females, were from sixteen to eighteen years of age, and a few, over twentyone.

Good moral character, and a thorough knowledge of the common branches, were formerly considered as indispensable qualifications in an instructor. The instructors were chiefly selected from the most respectable families in town. But for fifteen or twenty years, these things have not been so much regarded. They have indeed been deemed desirable; but the most common method now seems to be, to ascertain as near as possible the dividend for that season from the public treasury, and then, fix upon a teacher who will take charge of the school three to four months, for this money. He must indeed be able to obtain a license from the Board of Visitors; but this has become nearly a matter of course, provided he can spell, read, and write. In general, the candidate is some favorite or relative of the District Committee. It gives me great pleasure, however, to say that the *moral* character of almost every instructor, so far as I know, has been unexceptionable.

Instructors have usually boarded in the families of the pupils. Their compensation has varied from seven to eleven dollars a month for males; and from sixtytwo and a half cents to one dollar a week for females. Within the last ten years, however, the price of instruction has rarely been less than nine dollars in the former case, and seventy five cents in the latter. In the few instances in which the instructors have furnished their own board, the compensation has been about the same; it being supposed that they could work at some employment of their own, enough to pay their board, especially females. The only exceptions which I can recollect are two; both within five years. In one of these instances the instructor received twelve dollars, and in the other, eleven dollars and fifty cents a month.

It often happens that no family of the district is prepared to receive the Instructor. In such cases it is expected he will repair to the house of the District Committee. Some, however, from delicacy, or other causes, choose to go to their own homes, when near, until a place is provided.

Two of the Board of Visitors usually visit the winter schools twice during the term. In the summer, their visits are often omitted. These visits usually occupy from one hour to an hour and a half. They are spent in merely hearing a few hurried lessons, and in making some remarks, general in their character. Formerly, it was customary to examine the pupils in some approved catechism; but this practice has been omitted for twenty years.

The parents seldom visit the school, except by special invitation. The greater number pay very little attention to it at all. There are, however, a few who are gradually awaking to the importance of good instruction; but there are also a few, who oppose every thing which is suggested, as at the least, useless; and are scarcely willing their children should be governed in the school.

The school books have been about the same for thirty years. Webster's Spelling Book, the American Preceptor, and the New Testament, have been the principal books used. Before the appearance of the American Preceptor, Dwight's Geography was used as a reading book. A few of the Introduction to the American Orator were introduced about twelve years since, and more recently, Jack Halyard.

Until within a few years, no studies have been permitted in the day school, but spelling, reading and writing. Arithmetic was taught by a few instructors, one or two evenings in a week. But in spite of a most determined opposition, arithmetic is now permitted in the day school, and a few pupils study geography.

5.12   A Teacher Describes His Philosophy of Discipline in 1831.

Much advantage will sometimes result from appealing to the pupils themselves in various matters of the *police*, if I may so term it, of the school, and showing them that what is done results from a desire to promote their own comfort and convenience.

'You leave the doors open a great deal, boys,' says one teacher. 'You must put a stop to this practice. I cannot suffer it any longer.'

Perhaps a threat is added; the boys look with an expression of half sullenness, half defiance at the master, and resolve to forget to shut the doors as often as they can. He who first is guilty of the neglect and receives for it a reprimand or a punishment, is regarded as suffering for noble resistance to tyranny.

Another teacher manages in a different way.

'How many of you have suffered any inconvenience from the cold to-

Ibid., II (January, 1831), pp. 30–33.

day?' inquires he with a pleasant look. A great many hands are raised in reply.

'I have thought,' continues he, 'that the cold is increased by having the doors left open. It is some trouble to take care always to shut them, but I suppose you are willing to take this trouble for the sake of keeping yourselves warm. How many are willing to try to shut the doors, on condition that all the rest will?'

The hands are generally raised.

'Nearly all. But is it not probable that you will forget. What shall I do if any forget?'

A pause.

'How many are willing to be sent back if they forget?'

Many hands are up, and the teacher promises to do the best he can to help them keep themselves warm, by noticing who leaves the doors open, and sending them back. The boys will, if the business is kindly and gently managed in some such way as above described, even appoint a committee to notice and report the names of those who neglect to shut the doors. This last measure may perhaps be carried into effect in some such way as the following.

'I am not certain that I can notice carefully enough to accomplish your object. You know that I am very busy, and sometimes so occupied that I do not observe that the door is open until some of the scholars have become quite cold from it. Whenever *men* undertake to remedy any evil, they always like to adopt efficient measures if they try any. Will you do anything more effectual than to ask me to notice and speak to any person who leaves open the door.'

A pause.

'I do not know what you can do unless you appoint a committee to notice, who can do it more effectually than I. But I do not know that the boys would be willing to have a committee notice them and report their names to me. Perhaps, however, most of them would, as this is a matter of common interest. How many would be willing?'

In every school where the master habitually treats the scholars with the kindness and frankness which they deserve, nearly every hand will be raised.

'Nearly all are willing. Then I have no objection to your appointing a committee. How many shall there be?'

Boys. 'Three.' 'Five.' 'Two.'

'Several numbers are mentioned. How many are in favour of five? Of three? Of two? The majority are in favour of three?'

With the same spirit and in substantially the same manner the other arrangements may be made. In all such references of minor business to the boys themselves, however, great care should be taken to prevent their supposing that they hold the reins of government. No principles but those of *implicit submission* will answer at all in a school or a family. The teacher must be an *absolute monarch*. He may, however, like other absolute monarchs, delegate power.

Take another instance of the manner in which the pupils of a school may be led to take an interest in carrying its arrangements into effect.

'I observed today that several of the boys did not come in immediately after the recess. It was five minutes after the bell rang before all were in. Now I think I should do wrong to take more than fifteen minutes recess, though I should like more myself, and therefore if it takes you five minutes to come in, I ought to ring the bell at the end of ten. How many are in favour of having the bell rung after ten minutes, so as to allow you five minutes to come in.'

No votes.

"Perhaps then you think that it is not necessary to have so much as ten minutes. I do not know but that you would like to try today, and see how much time is necessary. And certainly if you find that it will not take more than one minute, I shall be glad to let you have the whole time. How many are in favour of being allowed today to try.'

The hands will in such a case generally be raised.

'I am willing that you should try today, and will regulate the ringing of the bell hereafter according to your own decision.'

The boys will, after such remarks, nearly all be punctual, and will look with uneasiness and impatience upon the loiterers who come in late. The master says, on the next day—

'I noticed, yesterday, that nearly all were in their seats in a very short time after the bell rang; but a few were quite tardy. Would it be right for me to ring the bell earlier, and thus shorten the recesses of the whole school, on account of these few loiterers?'

Boys. 'No Sir.'

'Would it be right for me to allow these few to be tardy, and come in when they pleased?'

Boys. 'No Sir.'

'What shall I do?'

A pause.

'I will wait until tomorrow; perhaps all will be punctual. I think every generous boy will be, especially when he reflects that by prolonging his play a little for one day, he is doing all in his power to shorten permanently the pleasures of his companions.'

Such a course will, if carried into all the plans and management of a school, soon produce a strong public sentiment in favour of what is right.

5.13 Walt Whitman Describes "The Whip in Schools" and Other Defects of Public Education.

The Whip in Schools

We wish our Brooklyn teachers could have had the pleasure, as we had, of hearing Horace Mann's address on Education the other night, at the Tabernacle in New York. It embodied nearly all the philosophy which modern thinkers and writers have settled to be philosophy on the subject —and treated with great clearness and no little severity the old fallacies that unfortunately are by no means yet completely routed from among us. "They who expel wrong doing by means of physical chastisement," said Mr. Mann, "cast out devils, through Beelzebub, the prince of devils!" Are not some of our Brooklyn teachers a little too profuse of this satanic power?

It is with no unkind spirit that we affirm—and call all good and sound modern reasoners on the subject to back us—that the instructor who uses the lash in his school at all, is unworthy to hold the power he does hold. That he has found no other means—that he ever brings himself into a predicament where the honor of his *authority* demands the use of the rod— that he has not been forearmed with some escape which, in emergency, will enable him to avoid such a use—that he can bethink him of no better and easier, and gentle and more humane plan to ensure obedience than thrashing, proves him fit perhaps for dog-whipper, or menagerie-tamer, but not for the holy office of fashioning an immortal human soul.

Do we speak strongly on this subject! Ah, we know how much need there is of it! Of the thousands of bright hearted, and red-cheeked young creatures who are gathered together in this country in schools, and drilled by the sound of whistles, the tinkle of bells, and the dread of ratans, to go through certain evolutions with the limbs, and speak by rote certain lessons with the voice—we feel how much more could be made of them under a milder and truer system. How many noble spirited boys are beaten into sullen and spiteful endurance of what there is no earthly need—sharp taunts, blows, and frowning looks! Awake! parent and teacher, to higher ideas for your kind, in the young freshness wherewith God has formed them, than to suppose there are not a hundred better ways of drawing out what is good, and repelling what is bad, in them, than the ferrule and the rod!

As a general thing the faults of our public schools system are—crowding

Walt Whitman, *Brooklyn Evening Star*, October 22, 1845; *Brooklyn Daily Eagle*, February 4, 1847.

too many students together, insufficiency of books, and their cost being taxed directly on the pupil—and the flogging system, which in a portion of the schools still holds its wretched sway. With pride we unite in the numerous commendations of the grand free school system of this State—with its twelve thousand seminaries, and its twenty thousand teachers, to whom each child, rich or poor, can come without money and without price! But we are none the less aware that the prodigious sum—hundreds of thousands of dollars—annually expended on these schools, might be expended to more profit. We have by no means ascended to the height of the great argument of education. The monotonous *old* still resists the fresh philosophical *new*. Form and precedent often are more thought of than reality. What are mere "order" or "learning lessons," or all the routine of the simple *outside* of school-keeping?—Absolutely nothing, in themselves; and only valuable, as far as they help the higher objects of educating the child. To teach the child *book grammar* is nothing; to teach him by example, by practice, by thoroughly clarifying the principles of correct syntax, *how to talk and write harmoniously*, is every thing. To put him through the arithmetic is not much; to make him able to compare, calculate, and quickly seize the bearings of a practical figure-question such as occurs in business every hour, is a good deal. Mere atlas geography is a sham, too, unless the learner have the position of places in his mind, and *know* the direction, distances, bearings, etc., of the countries, seas, cities, rivers and mountains, whose names (as our miserable school geographies give them,) he runs over so glibly. We care very little indeed for—what is the pride of many teachers' hearts—the military discipline of their schools, and the slavish obedience of their pupils to the imperial nod or waved hand of the master. As to the flogging plan, it is the most wretched item yet left of the ignorance and inefficiency of school-keeping. It has surrounded the office, (properly one of the noblest on earth,) with a character of contemptibleness and petty malignance, that will stick to it as long as whipping sticks among teachers' habits. What nobleness can reside in a man who catches boys by the collar and cuffs their ears? What elevation or dignity of character can even a child's elastic thoughts connect with one who cuts him over the back with a ratan or makes him hold out his hand to receive the whack of a ferule? For teachers' own sakes—for the true height and majesty of their office, hardly second to the priesthood—they should one and all unite in precluding this petty and foolish punishment—this degrader and bringerdown of their high standing. As things are, the word school-teacher is identified with a dozen unpleasant and ridiculous associations—a sour face, a whip, hard knuckles snapped on tender heads, no gentle, fatherly kindness, no inciting of young ambition in its noble phases, none of the beautifiers of author-

ity, but all that is small, ludicrous, and in after life productive of indignation. We have reason to think that the flogging system still prevails in
several of our Brooklyn schools to quite a wretched extent. In the school
in Baltic st. under a former management, forty children in the boys' department were thrashed in the course of one morning! and in the female
department a little girl was so cut and marked with the ratan over back,
neck and shoulders, for some trifling offence, that the livid marks remained there for several days! This is a pretty fact for the character of
our public seminaries! Justice to the mass of the teachers, however, demands that they should not be confounded with these ultra and repulsive
cases. In general, doubtless, they whip with moderation—if that word
may be applied to such a punishment at all. Nor do we mean to impugn
the motives altogether. *They* think they are doing right. So did the
Spanish torturers in Peru—inquisitors in Spain—and the learned doctors
who denounced Jenner.

5.14   A Recollection of Schooling at Prairie View, Kansas, in the 1870's.

Prairie View was the official name, so far as it had any, of a country school
district in southeastern Kansas. Its capital was a small white-painted building which was not only the schoolhouse, but the center—educational, social, dramatic, political, and religious—of a pioneer community of the
prairie region of the West. I describe it as it was in the 1870's and early
1880's when I was a youthful member of that community. . . .

Our schoolhouse was the one-room-and-hall kind common in that region. Inside, most of the space was occupied by the schoolroom with
well-windowed sides but with the rear wall blank. There were two doors
leading into the narrow windowless hall but only one from the hall to the
exterior of the building. The schoolroom had a low platform in front
and on it a desk or table for the teacher. Facing him sat the pupils of all
sizes, the smaller ones in front—presumably because they were a restless
lot and needed the most watching. Behind them sat the larger pupils, the
largest ones occupying the coveted seat against the blank wall. The boys
sat on one side of the room and the girls on the other; sometimes a brother
and a sister were allowed to share the same seat, probably to allow them
to look over some of the books together and thus spare the expense of
two sets. In the kindergarten latitude sat the big iron stove. On very
cold days we could drag up benches and all sit near its red-hot flanks. It

Marshall A. Barber, *The Schoolhouse at Prairie View* (Lawrence, Kansas: University
of Kansas Press, 1953), pp. 1, 11–13, 27–29. Reprinted by permission of the University
of Kansas Press.

was a smelly kind. We once had a school stove which burned clean logs like our home fires, but it was early displaced by one addicted to a dirty soft coal.

Our desks were of different sizes and probably designed to fit different sizes of pupil, but there was a greater variety in stature among the children than among the desks. At one time we had plain wooden desks which did not fold up to protect the books. We just stuck them into a sort of shelf under the top. Later we got a patent collapsing kind whose top folded down and shut the books, slates, and sometimes less lawful articles into a compact, rectangular, vertical mass. This kind of furniture was especially prone to get out of order and need replacement—maybe the crafty salesman counted on that. The desks had a well for ink, and only the boldest boys ventured to carve names or figures on their shiny tops.

One felt much freer with the old kind of desk which was sometimes elaborately sculptured. They were not only rich in initials and names but were sometimes carved to represent whole biographies. The top of a desk might represent the farm of a mythical "S" (maybe of Mr. Schnaik the bachelor). Here he had built his house and here his barn. Here was a path which led to his well; here he had dug his well. This scheme was not so elaborate as that of a certain Buddhist temple in Java, where the illiterate can follow every detail of the life of his saint, but perhaps it contained the germ of the same idea—the transmission of knowledge without the tedious process of reading. As I remember, these wooden histories were favorites with some of the German children, who sometimes found reading English a bit difficult.

When the new furniture came in, some of the old longer benches were retained. I am sure we had none so primitive as those consisting of a half-log with the flat side smoothed to make a seat and the legs stuck into the rounded belly, reminiscent of those stiff-legged quadrupeds whose pictures used to stray into the margins of children's copy-books. We had a smooth hard kind, made entirely of boards with a broad support over which the seat board projected, the whole end effect suggesting to me the teacher's frown overhanging the rest of his face.

We also had a much longer bench, often put into the corners of the room and used for recitations. I associate reading and history with a long bench placed in the northwest corner of the room. For arithmetic when one stood at the blackboard or for oral spelling we did not need recitation benches, but I have a vague association of these benches with mental arithmetic; maybe the hardness of the bench was associated in my mind with the hardness of the problem—I was not good at arithmetic.

The rest of the furniture of the room was mostly attached to the front wall. There was a broad blackboard in front with a trough below it for pointers, erasers, chalk, and such chalk-dust as was not absorbed by our lungs. That trough was a good place for switches too, but maybe I imagine the switches through the association of chalk and the punishment of sin. Chalk, especially the longer pieces, was a commodity not to be taken from the schoolroom; it was public property and not replaceable without paying out school money. On the broad blackboard all writing was erasable, but just above it we had a narrower sort where the letters of the alphabet were permanently written. And it was so beautifully done, almost (I thought) as if Mr. Spencer himself had deigned to visit our school and write those letters as an everlasting model. I used to gaze at those wavy, shaded capitals for hours, I think. It was my first clear impression of the unattainable.

Much of the remainder of the front wall was covered with maps. I presume many countries were hung there, but, curiously, all I can clearly remember was one impressive word, "Mediterranean.". . .

The first day of school was an important event because then we met the new teacher. At the winter term, which ran from November to March, we were likely to get a man teacher, usually one in his twenties or over. He was generally a Kansan but now and then we got one from another state; Mr. Early Carder, I remember, came from Ohio and had an impressive exotic air about him and probably received forty dollars a month for his services. Sometimes we had the same teacher year after year, perhaps a man who intended to make a profession of teaching; but often it was someone who later went into business or took up a profession.

At the spring term we were more likely to have a lady teacher, occasionally one who came from our neighborhood and was only a few years older than the biggest girls. Perhaps she had obtained a second-grade certificate at the teachers' summer school and wanted to earn a few dollars before getting married. Once or twice we got an excellent lady teacher who was well qualified to teach and remained with us summer and winter for a period of years.

Teachers' salaries were low; but, it was thought, teachers ought not to demand much when they could get board and room for two dollars per week. We never descended as low as to "board teachers around"—that is, to house them inexpensively among several members of the community, two or three weeks with one host and a week or two with another. That was a capital way to get acquainted but must have been terribly hard on the teacher, who might get an unpleasant host. We had never heard of a formal parent-teacher organization. Of course, any parent could practice the ancient rule of giving a second whipping to a child who had been punished at school and complained of it at home.

The first day of school was the time when some teachers announced their code of discipline. Our school was not a bad one. I never heard of any organized opposition to the teacher's rule, such as shutting the teacher out on the first day; that sort of mutiny would not have been considered smart. Possibly our behavior was affected by the presence of the German children, who naturally had a respect for discipline. Whippings were rather uncommon. I remember one case where a teacher employed trial by jury for some serious infraction of rules. The jurors were some older boys of the school, and I remember well seeing the jury file outdoors to the south side of the school to deliberate. I think the accused was found guilty and punished by whipping.

Of course, we had many minor sins and minor punishments. We had to stand on the floor now and then without dunce cap, a punishment we did not mind very much. Lee Dugan, however, once fainted away when undergoing this punishment. First he dropped his book; then Lee himself fell to the floor, to the consternation of all beholders! I was a member of a gang who had to stay in during recess. We had waged warfare with spears of long, hard weed-stems, and our battle would probably have gone unnoticed had not one stem hit a boy's face and caused real blood to flow.

One teacher announced at the beginning of the term that he had but one simple rule for us to follow, "Be good." I am sorry that I do not remember how this rule worked—I think quite as well as a long list of crimes and punishments. We had a Mr. Findlay one term who had a peculiar way of punishing whispering. He had handy at his desk a long wooden ruler which he hurled at the guilty pupil. Now a common characteristic of this offense is that two whispering heads are often held close together, and I cannot too much admire the skill of Mr. Findlay in that he rarely hit the wrong pupil. Then the poor culprit had to retrieve the ruler and carry it back to the teacher, who never had to leave his comfortable chair. The trembling lad walked slowly and cautiously to the teacher's desk, holding out the ruler so as to keep as much space as possible between him and the teacher. This teacher was not long employed; he soon went into the hardware business in a neighboring town. I wonder if the trembling customer ever dared to return an unwanted piece of hardware to Mr. Findlay.

We had to stay in at recess sometimes, but I think we were never punished by being deprived of a holiday. That would never do, because a boy's father might have picked out a job for him to do on a Saturday, and sometimes the teacher did farm-work too. And very wisely we were never punished by being made to learn extra verses (we never called them "lines"). Wisely, I think, for the child's dislike of discipline may extend to the means used for inflicting it, and some bits of noble verse may be long flavored by bitter punishment. The punishment may be salutary, but the association remains. I lost a taste for apple compote almost permanently because my mother used it as a vehicle for certain distasteful pills.

At the beginning of the term the teacher had to arrange the pupils in classes, for we had no formal grades. A new teacher sometimes asked each pupil what reader he was in the last term and classified him temporarily in that way, subject to promotion or demotion at some later time.

5.15   An Englishman, Francis Adams, Describes "The Free School System of the United States" to His Countrymen in 1875.

To sum up, it is not pretended by Americans—it never has been advanced by the section of Englishmen who are attracted by American institutions, and especially by the common school—that their system is even theoretically perfect, much less that it produces in practice the utmost measure of success. It is the habit of American educationists, ungrudgingly, and with sincere admiration, to give the palm to Germany. Nor is this a mere complimentary recognition of excellence. It is shown to be genuine by the manner in which they are accepting from Germany, not only lessons in the details of educational science, but vital principles like compulsion.

But while the German system is mature, and has probably reached, or nearly reached, the highest point of excellence, that of the United States is still in its infancy. Therefore, the most important consideration for Americans is whether they have started upon the right lines. The process of undoing, as we find in England, is sometimes more difficult and laborious than that of constructing.

That which impresses us most in regard to America is the grasp which the schools have upon the sympathy and intelligence of the people. Those of the cities are the lions of America. The intelligent foreigner, and also, as it would appear from some recent criticisms, the unintelligent foreigner who visits the States, into whatever town he goes, is taken to the schools as the first objects of interest. Amongst public questions education occupies the foremost place, and of all topics it is that upon which the American speaker is most ready and most willing to enlarge. Public intelligence has recognised the fact that the highest and best interests of the nation are indissolubly bound up with the question. Thus every American feels not only a personal but a patriotic interest in the welfare of the schools. Ow-

Francis Adams, *The Free School System of the United States* (London: Chapman and Hall, 1875), pp. 239–248.

ing to this popular feeling their organisation possesses a spring and force and energy which are in strong contrast with the sluggish instincts of the parochial system.

This widespread popular regard which constitutes the propelling power, appears to be chiefly due to two features—government by the people, and ownership by the people. It is a vast proprietary scheme, in which every citizen has a share. While it is undoubtedly true that all do not set the same value on school rights, it is also certain that their existence immensely stimulates public interest and diffuses a sense of responsibility through the entire community.

For no reason is the principle of local government more dearly prized, than because of the control which it gives the people over the schools. They would be as ready to surrender all municipal powers and privileges as to transfer their management to a sect or to any other private organisation. This recognition of responsibility is the mainspring of the system, and the cause of its best results. In another generation the same feeling will prevail in England. It would undoubtedly create surprise and opposition if, in this country, an unrepresentative body were to claim the right to control the municipal government of a town. Yet such a city as Gloucester still acquiesces in the important work of education being transacted by voluntary societies. It might with equal or even greater discretion, transfer to the Dean and Chapter the functions of the Corporation.

That the decentralisation of the American system is excessive, and leads to inefficiency in certain cases, has already been explained. That any radical change will be made is highly improbable. The advocates of a federal law under which large powers would be vested in the National Bureau of Education, are at present in a hopeless minority. The principle of State sovereignty is too firmly rooted in the public mind, and has worked too well, to be easily shaken. Of late years, however, a disposition has been manifested to increase the powers of State Superintendents and State Boards of Education; and, in the view of Englishmen, this is a movement in the right direction. The principle of local government should be supplemented by adequate power in the Executive of the State to meet those cases in which, from public apathy or other causes, the local authorities fail to perform their duties. It is also worthy of the consideration of American educationists whether the State taxes, which now provide a very considerable portion of the school income, could not be administered by a State department under some such scheme as our English plan of "payment by results." Under such an arrangement a minimum standard might be fixed for each State, which would ensure the performance of certain definite work in a year. The danger that School Boards would limit their efforts to earning the State grant would not be great in a country where public emulation is so general. New York would still compete with Boston, and Chicago with Cincinnati, in the development of the best methods and the attainment of the highest results; and the example of all the great cities would still have its due effect upon the country towns and districts. The powers of the State Executive would then, as now, be subject to the will of the people, whose voice would determine the general policy of education. It appears to be extremely improbable that, in a country where the best intelligence circulates so commonly through all ranks of society, the schools would fall into a narrow groove, or lose the energy and independence which now characterise them. While such a scheme would incalculably benefit the backward districts, it need not, in any appreciable degree, hamper the more advanced and energetic localities.

A Ministerial department at the head of the school system in each State need not be inconsistent with the most ample exercise of local discretion; and there would be no reason to fear that in America such a department would be permitted to usurp the functions of School Boards. It is difficult to see how compulsion can be effectively carried out otherwise.

The advantages of the establishment of the National Bureau of Education cannot be over-estimated. By bringing together the results in each State educational thought and enterprise have been greatly quickened. Even with its present limited powers, the action of the Bureau is full of promise for the future.

The means provided for local inspection or supervision are very ample, the rule, subject to a few exceptions, being an inspector or superintendent for each county. The benefits of the plan are apparent from the State reports. The duties of the County Superintendent are largely consultative; he is more the friend and adviser of the local school managers than their superior officer. In some respects he possesses advantages over English inspectors. The latter is an officer whose visits are generally looked forward to with apprehension, and back upon with relief. The unexpressed but well-understood rule is, that he is not to be afforded too much insight into the exact condition of the schools. The most popular inspector is the one whose duties sit most easily upon his shoulders, and who is content with the most brief and cursory inspection.

In some of the States it is the duty of the County Superintendents to examine the scholars. The State Reports give very little information respecting the examinations in the country districts, but in the towns they appear to be of the most thorough and searching description.

The popularity of the schools is attested by the large aggregate attendance. It is evident from the number of scholars enrolled annually, that, practically, all American children, and a large percentage of the children of foreign parentage, attend school at some period. In the cities a large number attend with great regularity, but a very considerable percentage are also very irregular in their attendance. In the country districts irregular attendance is the greatest bane of the schools. For this there is but one remedy—compulsion.

It cannot be denied that compulsion of any kind is repugnant to American ideas of government. In a country where individual freedom is a passion, to force children into school, even for their own good, appears at first sight to be an arbitrary proceeding, and opposed to popular government. Nevertheless, so strong is the determination to have efficient schools, that Americans have, to a large extent, overcome their natural repugnance to compulsory school laws, and in every State the question is being urged upon the consideration of the several Legislatures.

Indirect compulsion, in various forms, has been tried, and has failed under circumstances which afforded the most favourable conditions for the experiment. The co-operation of employers in Connecticut and Rhode Island, and other States to carry out the law, afforded an excellent opportunity for testing its value. The result of the experiment has proved that there is a class of parents who cannot be reached except by direct compulsion. The experience of England and the United States on this subject points to exactly the same conclusion.

The laws providing for direct compulsion which have been passed in seven or eight States are regarded as tentative. The evidence as to their operation is at present incomplete. In Michigan, it must be admitted that the result has not been satisfactory. That is owing, however, not to any strenuous opposition to the law, but to the want of proper means of administration. It only indicates the necessity of a vigorous State department to superintend the action of the local authorities.

The period of school attendance is being gradually lengthened throughout the Union. In this respect the laws are behind the spirit of the people. The school terms in many of the States are considerably longer than the periods required by law. The present compulsory laws only aim at securing from 200 to 140 attendances during the year, half of which must be consecutive. With the gradual increase of the school term, and as the idea of compulsion becomes familiar, it will no doubt be possible to increase the number of compulsory attendances.

Hitherto the work of American educationists has not, except in some of the large cities, been greatly obstructed by a "religious difficulty." The first aim of the schools has been to provide a good secular education, leaving religious instruction mainly to the Churches and the Sunday schools. The schools have generally been opened by some short religious exercise —the reading of the Bible, prayer, or singing of a hymn. A very large measure of success has attended this practice. With it the great majority of Americans are well content, and were it not for the Catholic element in the population the custom would probably continue unchallenged, at any rate for the present. As it is, however, there are indications that the peace which has hitherto so generally prevailed is about to be disturbed. The conflicts which have already taken place in New York, Cincinnati, and other cities, afford sufficient evidence that the common school will not be permitted to continue on its present basis without a contest. Either it must be abandoned, and the parochial school substituted for it, or the teaching given in it must be purely secular. Of these alternatives, there can be little doubt that the overwhelming majority of Americans would prefer the latter. The parochial or denominational system is opposed to the whole current of American feeling. The sentiment of the country must undergo the most radical change before it will be possible for it to obtain national recognition. No such revolution is probable. The Roman Catholic element consists chiefly of the Irish population. The American is not readily inoculated with Irish ideas. On the contrary, the Irishman who seeks a home in the United States becomes an American. The conversion of the Roman Catholics to the common school, as a national institution, is more likely than the conversion of Americans to a denominational system.

But it does appear probable that the common school will, in time, be made purely secular. Larger numbers of schools, including all those of such cities as Cincinnati and St. Louis, are wholly secular already. And the same movement has commenced in Chicago. The idea that the secular school is godless or infidel does not exist outside the Roman Catholic communion. There is nothing horrifying to the Protestant American in teaching secular subjects at one time and place, and leaving religion to be taught at another time and place. The fact that these secular schools do exist and find favour with the American people is noteworthy, especially when it is remembered that religious feeling is much more general, and has taken a far stronger hold upon the masses, than in this country.

It has been seen that the profession of teaching in America labours under some serious disadvantages. The want of a sufficient number of normal training schools to supply the requisite staff of trained teachers is the most marked deficiency. How to surmount this obstacle is one of the most important problems of discussion at the present time. The energy and resources of American educationists will be severely tasked in providing adequate means of training, and it must necessarily be a work of considerable time. In the interval, the deficiency of training is much less observable than in other countries, on account of the great natural aptitude of Americans, and especially of American women, for the work of teaching.

The shortness of the school term and the low rate of salaries also combine to keep the profession of the teacher below its proper level. In both these particulars considerable progress has been made within the last few years, and the improvement still continues.

As a set-off to the disadvantages which have been noted, the standing of the teachers is socially high. In this respect the contrast with England is remarkable.

The extensive employment of women as teachers has been due partly to natural causes, but more to the conviction, which experience has confirmed, that women are better qualified for the work of elementary teaching than men.

In all the discussions upon the means of supplying trained teachers, the English method of employing pupil teachers finds no support. The universal opinion is that the age when teaching may begin must be raised rather than lowered. The example of Germany in regard to this point is accepted as of higher authority than that of England.

The reports issued by the School Boards of the great cities—Boston, New York, Philadelphia, Cincinnati, St. Louis, Chicago, Cleveland, Washington, and many others—afford the fullest information respecting the studies of the schools, the ages of the scholars, and the results attained. A study of these reports, which American officials are always glad to supply, will satisfy any English reader how far the elementary schools of the cities of the United States are in advance of our own. If the elementary schools of England were free, and the course of study were raised above its present pauper level, a large proportion of the middle classes would be glad to send their children to them, in preference to inefficient private schools. There would then be no reason why the elementary schools of our large towns should not rival those of the great American cities, the results of which, in the absence of compulsion, must be regarded as very admirable.

Outside the larger cities it is not possible to ascertain the definite results of the schools. Much depends upon their size, much upon the public spirit of each locality, and much more upon the skill and energy of the teacher. There may be a great want of thoroughness, but there is sufficient evidence that these schools supply to the children generally, that invaluable and indispensable primary instruction which gives the start, and places the tools in the hand of every child, to be used afterwards as capacity or opportunity may determine. To use Mr. Morley's words, they are "not so absolutely illusory as to turn out the majority of their workers in the numb ignorance of an English boy to whom the Third Standard is an impassable bridge." This is faint praise. To those who have observed the working of hundreds of district schools in the small towns of Massachusetts, New York, Pennsylvania, and Ohio, it will seem to be absolute injustice.

The great popularity of the American system, which is manifest from the large enrolment and the amount of taxation contributed for its support, and which indeed no one disputes, is due mainly to one cause—that the schools are free. In sending a child to school no leave has to be asked, no patron has to be consulted, no charity has to be sued for or accepted. The schools belong to the people. They are proprietary schools.

The Conservative Persuasion: American Textbooks in the Nineteenth Century

The common school reforms firmly established the institutional structure and ideology of public education, but what did children actually learn in the classroom? Textbooks offer useful clues to the actual content of instruction in the nineteenth century. In the typical elementary school of that era the teacher was meagerly educated. Rote recitation was the commonest form of "teaching." Hence the textbook was in large degree the curriculum; children studied books rather than subjects (and the difference between the two was not clear even in some of the colleges of the day). In addition, graded textbook series aided the rural teacher in a one-room schoolhouse to adapt the work to her students, who varied widely in age and ability. Together with the Bible, textbooks were sometimes the only contact a schoolchild had with the broad world beyond his immediate community (in contrast with the many media available to children today).

The textbooks taught more than the three R's and facts about geography and history, for most Americans believed that the school should shape character as well as intellect. Thus textbook writers had a difficult task: to teach a moral and religious common denominator, a political and economic consensus. For commercial reasons, if for no other, they wished to avoid offending the patrons of the schools. The advertising blurb printed with *McGuffey's Eclectic Fourth Reader* in 1844, for example, announced that

> NO SECTARIAN matter has been admitted into this work. It has been submitted to the inspection of highly intelligent clergymen and teachers of the various Protestant and Catholic denominations, and nothing has been inserted, except with their united approbation. . . . NO SECTIONAL

matter, reflecting upon the local institutions, customs, or habits of any portion of the United States, is to be found among their contents, and hence they are extensively used at the South and at the North, in the East as well as the West.

Such grand impartiality did not imply a secular or apolitical tone, however: the publishers assured buyers that the books were *"decidedly moral and religious,"* and their pages resounded with praise of American heroes and institutions. Thus textbooks often revealed what their writers—and those who purchased the books—took to be a national consensus.

Textbooks also reflect changing conceptions of the child and models of character. Most social and behavioral scientists agree that the early years of childhood shape an individual's emotional and intellectual attitudes and behavior, yet few historians have paid much attention to childhood. Like the early parents' guides—the Dr. Spock's books of another time—primers indicated values which were consciously inculcated in the young. Religious orthodoxy and anxiety about salvation in early America spoke through the pages of the *New England Primer* (of which over 2,000,000 copies were sold). By the end of the eighteenth century, and continuing into the nineteenth century, schoolbooks became more denatured theologically, though still predominant was a common denominator of evangelical Protestantism. The older moral absolutism persisted. God became less the fearsome Judge than the Divine Underwriter who insured that the virtues of hard work, truthfulness, obedience, sobriety, and kindness would pay off both here and in the hereafter. The aphorisms of Poor Richard became a new kind of holy writ.

Though clothes and manners became less starched by 1800 than they had been previously, few Americans obeyed Rousseau's injunction: "Love childhood; look kindly on its play, its pleasures, its lovable instincts. . . ." Play was still suspect: "Unless care and labor are taken to keep down the evil propensities of little children to anger, idleness, *and too much play,* they will grow up in evil habits," warned one author. Noah Webster declared that "a wise child loves to learn his book; but the fool would choose to play with toys." In moderation, child labor was not a bad thing; one textbook noted that children still could learn even if they worked in a factory, for "they did not go to work in summer till 6 o'clock" and they might study before then.

Authors sometimes taught children by horrible example. The cardinal sin was disobedience, for the school reinforced parental authority. One cautionary tale for children bore the engaging title, the *Prodigal Daughter; or a strange and wonderful relation, shewing how a gentleman of vast estate in Bristol, had a proud and disobedient Daughter, who because her parents would not support her in all her extravagance, bargained with the*

Devil to poison them. How an Angel of the Lord informed her parents of her Design. How she lay in a trance for four days; and when she was put into the grave, she came to life again, etc. Stories of disobedience which found their way into the textbooks, however, generally displayed less imagination: usually disobedient children were simply drowned, run over by carriages, burned, or bitten by dogs.

God was the author of moral law; parents, ministers, and teachers the interpreters. On all sides temptations beset the child: lying, stealing, horseracing and gambling, bad spelling, idle games, and above all, drink. A hero of the *Analytical Spelling Book*, Jack Halyard, "got to a bottle of rum, very slily, and tasted a little; at first it made his mouth smart, and his nose tingle. He soon got over this, and thought it would be a pretty notion to take another dram. . . ." Tipsy Jack then proceeded to insult an old man and to abuse his own mother, but in the end all was right because he told the truth to his father. Jack was fortunate to escape the fate of a chronic tippler who exploded, a textbook said, when he tried to light his pipe. Morality was rarely boring: temptation, triumph or failure, win or lose, it was a dramatic affair. Sometimes, though, Americans tired of the treacle-coated world of the readers. Witness the bad boy as hero in the subversive literature of the day: Huck Finn, the lazy, lying, thieving renegade. Little wonder that Mark Twain warned a Brooklyn librarian that *The Adventures of Huckleberry Finn* was a book that would undermine the morals of the young.

So pervasive was the saccharine morality of the textbooks that a young newspaper reporter on the *Brooklyn Evening Star* wrote the following sermon on October 10, 1845:

> Boy, or young man, whose eyes hover over these lines! how much of your leisure time do you give to *loafing?* What vulgar habits of smoking cigars, chewing tobacco, or making frequent use of blasphemous or obscene language have you begun to form? What associations and appetites are you idly falling into, that future years will ripen in wickedness and shame? Consider these questions as addressed, not to everybody in general, but to *you*, in particular. . . .

The author was no budding parson, but Walt Whitman, who would later say in "Song of Myself":

> I loafe and invite my soul,
> I lean and loafe at my ease observing a spear of summer grass.

The authors of the schoolbooks were teachers, printers, journalists, lawyers, ministers, minor men of letters, and anyone else wishing to convey a message or supplement a meager income. A large proportion of the most popular authors—Noah Webster, Jedediah Morse, S. G. Goodrich,

William Woodbridge, Salem Town, C. A. Goodrich, Richard Parker, and George Hillard, for example—came from New England (and, incidentally, exalted their section in the schoolbooks). The notable exception was William Holmes McGuffey, born in Pennsylvania and raised in Ohio, the best-known American textbook writer. A college professor, McGuffey was no businessman; he signed a contract with his publisher, Truman and Smith, limiting his royalties to $1,000, a fact which must have proved painful when he saw about 50,000,000 copies of his *Readers* bought before his death in 1873. About 122,000,000 copies of his series were sold between 1836 and 1920, making them by far the most popular of all the textbooks.

At first the publishers were local printers serving nearby communities with pirated or locally commissioned works, but after the middle of the century with the advent of the railroad and large-scale production and distribution in the printing industry, textbooks became big business. Some publishers emulated competitive practices of entrepreneurs in other fields, indulging in arm-twisting and bribery to win state-wide or city-wide monopolies. Writers and publishers still needed to please the consumer by expressing a common denominator of thought and feeling, but their potential audience was no longer local but regional, and even national.

Most of the textbook writers were men of conservative persuasion. In their books the individual was on trial, but not the social order. The social hierarchy displayed the beneficent will of Providence. This accent on individual striving and social conservatism created a curious ambivalence in the schoolbooks: God would favor the hard-working and moral man with worldly success, yet it was sinful to be discontented with one's lot. The cult of the self-made man ran headlong into the problem of the deserving poor and the maldistribution of wealth. McGuffey's Honest George Ellet, who rose to riches through honesty and hard work, had countless counterparts in the children's books long before Horatio Alger (a somewhat degenerate member of the tribe since his heroes usually relied on luck). Providential payola came to those who practiced thrift, industry, and perseverance.

Still, all could see that some were poor but moral, some rich but greedy, and that there were great contrasts of wealth and poverty in America. Thus many of the texts romanticized poverty and pleaded for charity. Relying on the doctrine of the stewardship of wealth, they insisted that God created distinctions of condition so that the wealthy could exercise their benevolence and the poor could express their gratitude and dependence. To be dissatisfied with one's lot in life was sinful, an affront to God. "What better proof can we give of our wisdom," asked one schoolbook in 1815, "than to be content in the situation in which Providence has placed us?" Another asserted that "the poor disciplined into order, respect the rich." Public education would not make the lower classes restless: "is it at all rational to suppose, that a judicious education of the poor . . . will be liable to abuse in their hands, and lead them to forget their station and their duty. . . ." Resignation and ambition made strange partners, but together they sat in positions of honor in the text-books.

Understandably, one virtue much admired in the schoolbooks was attention to studies. McGuffey told the story of Idle George Jones as a warning:

> He would make such ludicrous blunders, that the whole class would burst out in a laugh. Such are the applauses an idler gets. He was wretched of course. He had been idle so long, that he hardly knew how to apply himself. All the good scholars avoided him. . . . He became discouraged and gradually grew dissipated.

The Child's Instructor gave a succinct definition of a BAD BOY, in which his academic failings had full play:

> A bad Boy is undutiful to his father and mother, disobedient and stubborn to his master, and ill-natured to all his play-fellows. He hates his book, and takes no pleasure in improving himself in any thing. He is sleepy and slothful in the morning, too idle to clean himself, and too wicked to say his prayers.

After a technicolor career of mischief, lying, swearing, fighting, and stealing, such a boy "generally dies a beggar."

Though scholarship was desirable, one might make too much of a good thing: the texts warned against reading and thinking too much and cautioned children about the vice of reading novels. A vein of anti-intellectualism lay close to the surface of the textbooks.

Inculcating a moral and religious common denominator was only one goal of the textbook writers. They wished to shape a national character as well as individual characters, and this required teaching an American political consensus. From the Revolution onward schoolbooks exalted patriotism and attempted to define Americanism. Avowedly non-partisan, textbook writers sought to avoid political controversy. This they did mainly by discussing—and creating—folk heroes, representative great men who in the texts generally stood ten feet tall above the petty bickerings and disputes of their time. To the conservative authors the foremost of these king-like heroes was George Washington, in whom clustered all the virtues of civic sainthood. "Immortal," "God-like," "Savior," Washington became a messiah: "We forget for a moment that he was a man. We regard him as some propitious divinity, sent from a better world than this, to take America by the hand, and lead her to independence, freedom, and happiness." Joining Washington in the pantheon of heroes—but on a lower pedestal—came Benjamin Franklin and Abraham Lincoln. Dead office holders became statesmen in the schoolbooks, with the more conservative men like Alexander Hamilton, John Marshall, John Adams, and Daniel Webster having an edge over the more liberal Thomas Jefferson and Andrew Jackson.

More concerned with national pride and cohesion—with a uniform national character—than with analytic thinking about public issues, the writers largely failed to deal with controversy, as Ruth Elson observes in her study of textbooks, *Guardians of Tradition*. A sharp sense of mission, of creating a republic upon a hill, lingered: "We stand under a fearful responsibility to our Creator and our fellow creatures," said one writer in 1845. "It has been His divine pleasure that we should be sent forth as the harbingers of free government on the earth, and in this attitude we are now before the world. The eyes of the world are upon us; and our example will probably be decisive of the cause of liberty." Consequently, in the apprehensive years before the Civil War texts stressed the need for unity.

As in Benjamin Rush's attempt to make "republican machines," American republicanism was usually defined in the textbooks not by belief, but by behavior and personal or group characteristics. Liberty was a mystical, revered, and unexamined concept. The American Revolution was not so much a rebellion as a reassertion of traditional values. Further dissent was clearly unnecessary. Early in the century, to be an American was to behave like an American—to be hard-working, moral, industrious, courageous, ingenious, and patriotic. But increasingly in the latter half-century—and usually unconsciously and by indirection—Americanism was defined in such a way that it could fit only the white, middle-class, Protestant, native-born citizen. Through uncomplimentary stereotypes, the Negro, the Catholic, the Jew, and foreigners of many nations were read out of the clan. Vicious racist assumptions—for example, "The White Race" is "Normal or Typical"—invaded the schoolbooks. "Race," defined incorrectly, rigidly classified people in a hierarchy of virtue. Pseudo-scientific evidence decreed that these hereditary barriers would prevent true assimilation and Americanization.

When matched against the realities of life in nineteenth-century America, the textbooks tended to present a never-never land for a large proportion of the population. Immigrant children in crowded slums read bucolic stories of blue-eyed tots on prosperous farms. Children growing up on the sod-house frontier read about castles and lords and noble Romans. Hamlin Garland wrote in *A Son of the Middle Border* about how the wonderful world of McGuffey's readers impressed a child on the gray and muddy plains:

> Our readers were almost the only counterchecks to the current of vulgarity and baseness which ran through the talk of the older boys, and I wish to acknowledge my deep obligation to Professor McGuffey, whoever he may have been, for the dignity and literary grace of his selections. From the pages of his readers I learned to know and love the pages of Scott, Byron, Southey, Wordsworth and a long line of the English masters. I got my first taste of Shakespeare from the selected scenes which I read in these books.

Many of the readers did include excellent literature; many gave children a common canon of allusion and reference which approximated an American mythology; many provided deprived students with a world of fantasy which enabled them to escape, briefly, the turmoil of their lives. And the picture of middle-class propriety and prosperity gave many children the goal of surmounting the poverty into which they had been born. Some fantasy is normal, even essential, in the growth of a child. But the textbooks so selected their themes as to disguise the real world, not to reveal it; to repress anxieties, not to confront them; to foster complacency among established groups rather than to include the dispossessed. In an urban and industrial society, whose agriculture was fast being mechanized and aimed at a world market, the schoolbooks painted a sentimental picture of rural bliss. In a period of great stress on the family, they drew a cloying picture of home sweet home. In times of industrial violence they ignored the condition of labor and described unions as the evil plots of foreigners, anarchists, and Communists. In the midst of unparalleled political corruption they portrayed statesmen of stainless steel. The Negro appeared infrequently in the texts, and then usually in the guise of Sambo. People of other nations often appeared as foils to illustrate the superior virtue of Americans. A pervasive Protestantism colored the readers and downgraded other religions either openly or by implication. A pluralistic, expansive society undergoing great intellectual, social, economic, and political change, was reduced in the textbooks, as Ruth Elson has observed, to a "fantasy made up by adults as a guide for their children, but inhabited by no one outside the pages of schoolbooks." Such was the conservative persuasion.

6.1   Noah Webster Writes a "Moral Catechism" for American Children.

A Moral Catechism: Or Lessons for Saturday

Question. WHAT is moral virtue?
Answer. It is an honest upright conduct in all our dealings with men.
Q. Can we always determine what is honest and just?
A. Perhaps not in every instance, but in general it is not difficult.
Q. What rules have we to direct us?
A. God's word contained in the Bible has furnished all necessary rules
to direct our conduct.
Q. In what part of the Bible are these rules to be found?
A. In almost every part; but the most important duties between men
are summed up in the beginning of Matthew, in Christ's Sermon on the
Mount.

Of Humility

Q. What is humility?
A. A lowly temper of mind.
Q. What are the advantages of humility?
A. The advantages of humility in this life are very numerous and great.
The humble man has few or no enemies. Every one loves him and is
ready to do him good. If he is rich and prosperous, people do not envy
him; if he is poor and unfortunate, every one pities him, and is disposed to
alleviate his distresses.
Q. What is pride?
A. A lofty high minded disposition.
Q. Is pride commendable?
A. By no means. A modest self-approving opinion of our own good
deeds is very right. It is natural; it is agreeable; and a spur to good actions. But we should not suffer our hearts to be blown up with pride,
whatever great and good deeds we have done; for pride brings upon us
the will of mankind, and displeasure of our Maker. . . .

Of Mercy

Q. What is mercy?
A. It is tenderness of heart.

Noah Webster, *The American Spelling Book* . . . (Boston: Isaiah Thomas and
Ebenezer Andrews, 1798), pp. 145–152.

Q. *What are the advantages of this virtue?*

A. The exercise of it tends to happify every one about us. Rulers of a merciful temper will make their *good* subjects happy; and will not torment the *bad*, with needless severity. Parents and masters will not abuse their children and servants with harsh treatment. More love, more confidence, more happiness, will subsist among men, and of course society will be happier. . . .

Of Peace Makers

Q. *Who are peace makers?*

A. All who endeavor to prevent quarrels and disputes among men; or to reconcile those who are separated by strife.

Q. *Is it unlawful to contend with others on any occasion?*

A. It is impossible to avoid some differences with men; but disputes should be always conducted with temper and moderation. The man who keeps his temper will not be rash, and do or say things which he will afterwards repent of. And though men should sometimes differ, still they should be friends. They should be ready to do kind offices for each other. . . .

Of Purity of Heart

Q. *What is a pure heart?*

A. A heart free from all bad desires and inclined to conform to the divine will in all things. . . .

Of Revenge

Q. *What is revenge?*

A. It is to injure a man because he has injured us.

Q. *Is this justifiable?*

A. Never, in any possible case. Revenge is perhaps the meanest as well as wickedest vice in society. Nothing but murder can equal it. . . .

Of Justice

Q. *What is justice?*

A. It is giving to every man his due.

Q. *Is it always easy to know what is just?*

A. It is generally easy; and where there is any difficulty in determining, let a man consult the golden rule—"To do to others, what he could reasonably wish they should do to him, in the same circumstances.". . .

Of Generosity

Q. *What is generosity?*

A. It is some act of kindness performed for another, which strict justice does not demand. . . .

Of Gratitude

Q. *What is gratitude?*

A. A thankfulness of heart for favors received. . . .

Of Truth

Q. *What is truth?*

A. It is speaking and acting agreeable to fact.

Q. *Is it a duty to speak truth at all times?*

A. If we speak at all, we should tell the truth. It is not always necessary to tell what we know. There are many things which concern ourselves and others, which we had better not publish to the world. . . .

Of Charity and Giving Alms

Q. *What is charity?*

A. It signifies giving to the poor, or it is a favorable opinion of men and their actions.

Q. *When and how far is it our duty to give to the poor?*

A. When others really want what we can spare without material injury to ourselves, it is our duty to give them something to relieve their wants.

Q. *When persons are reduced to want by their own laziness and vices, by drunkenness, gambling and the like, is it a duty to relieve them?*

A. In general it is not. The man who gives money and provisions to a lazy vicious man, becomes a partaker of his guilt. Perhaps it may be right, to give such a man a meal of victuals to keep him from starving, and it is certainly right to feed his wife and family, and make them comfortable. . . .

Of Avarice

Q. *What is avarice?*

A. An excessive desire of gaining wealth.

Q. *Is this commendable?*

A. It is not; but one of the meanest of vices. . . .

Of Frugality and Economy

Q. *What is the distinction between frugality and avarice?*

A. Frugality is a prudent saving of property from needless waste. Avarice gathers more and spends less than is wanted.

Q. *What is economy?*

A. It is frugality in expenses—it is a prudent management of one's estate. It disposes of property for useful purposes without waste.

Q. *How far does true economy extend?*

A. To the saving of every thing which it is not necessary to spend for comfort and convenience; and the keeping one's expenses within his income or earnings.

Q. *What is wastefulness?*

A. It is the spending of money for what is not wanted. If a man drinks a dram, which is not necessary for him, or buys a cane which he does not want, he wastes his money. He injures himself, as much as if he had thrown away his money. . . .

Of Industry

Q. *What is industry?*

A. It is a diligent attention to business in our several occupations.

Q. *Is labour a curse or a blessing?*

A. Hard labor or drudgery is often a curse by making life toilsome and painful. But constant moderate labor is the greatest blessing.

Q. *Why then do people complain of it?*

A. Because they do not know the evils of *not* labouring. Labor keeps the body in health, and makes men relish all their enjoyments. "The sleep of the laboring man is sweet," so is his food. He walks cheerfully and whistling about his fields or shop, and scarcely knows pain.

The rich and indolent first lose their health for want of action—They turn pale, their bodies are enfeebled, they lose their appetite for food and sleep, they yawn out a tasteless stupid life without pleasure, and often useless to the world. . . .

Of Cheerfulness

Q. *Is cheerfulness a virtue?*

A. It doubtless is, and a moral duty to practise it. . . .

6.2   Webster's "Federal Catechism."

A Federal Catechism (Containing a Short EXPLANATION of the CONSTITUTION of the UNITED STATES OF AMERICA, and the PRINCIPLES of GOVERNMENT).

For the Use of Schools

Q. *WHAT is a constitution of government?*

A. A constitution of government, or a political constitution, consists in certain standing rules or ordinances, agreed upon by a nation or state, determining the manner in which the supreme power shall be exercised over that nation or state, or rather how the legislative body shall be formed.

Q. *How many kinds of constitutions are there; or in how many ways may the sovereign power be exercised over a people?*

A. Constitutions are commonly divided into three kinds; *monarchy, aristocracy*, and *democracy*.

Q. *Explain the sorts of government.*

A. When the sovereign power is exercised by *one* person, the constitution is a *monarchy*. When a few rich men, or nobles, have the whole supreme power in their hands, the constitution is an *aristocracy*. When the supreme power is exercised by all the citizens, in a general meeting or assembly, the constitution is a *democracy*.

Q. *What are the faults of despotic governments?*

A. In a despotic government, a whole nation is at the disposal of one person. If this person, the prince, is of a cruel or tyrannical disposition, he may abuse his subjects, take away their lives, their property, or their liberty.

Q. *What objections are there to aristocracy?*

A. In an aristocracy, where a few rich men govern, the poor may be oppressed, the nobles may make laws to suit themselves and ruin the common people. Besides, the nobles, having equal power one with another, may quarrel and throw the state into confusion; in this case there is no person of superior power to settle the dispute.

Q. *What are the defects of democracy?*

A. In democracy, where the people all meet for the purpose of making laws, there are commonly tumults and disorders. A small city may sometimes be governed in this manner; but if the citizens are numerous, their assemblies make a crowd or mob, where debates cannot be carried on with coolness and candor, nor can arguments be heard: Therefore a pure democracy is generally a very bad government. It is often the most tyranni-

Noah Webster, *ibid.*, pp. 154–155.

cal government on earth; for a multitude is often rash, and will not hear reason.

Q. *Is there another and better form of government than any of these?*

A. There is. A *representative republic,* in which the people freely choose deputies to make laws for them, is much the best form of government hitherto invented.

Q. *What are the peculiar advantages of representative governments?*

A. When deputies or representatives are chosen to make laws, they will commonly consult the interest of the people who choose them, and if they do not, the people can choose others in their room. Besides, the deputies coming from all parts of a state, bring together all the knowledge and information necessary to show the true interest of the whole state; at the same time, being but few in number, they can hear arguments and debate peaceably on a subject. But the great security of such a government is, that the men who make laws, are to be governed by them; so that they are not apt to do wrong willfully. When men make laws for themselves, as well as for their neighbors, they are led by their own interest to make *good* laws.

Q. *Which of the forms or kinds of government is adopted by the American States?*

A. The states are all governed by constitutions that fall under the name of representative republics. The people choose deputies to act for them in making laws; and in general, the deputies, when assembled, have as full power to make and repeal laws, as the whole body of freemen would have, if they were collected for the same purpose. . . .

6.3   Noah Webster's Cynosure: "Character of a Young Lady."

1. Sophia is not a beauty, but in her presence beauties are discontented with themselves. At first, she scarcely appeared pretty; but the more she is beheld, the more agreeable she appears. She gains when others lose, and what she gains she never loses. She is equalled by none in a sweet expression of countenance; and without dazzling beholders she interests them.

2. She loves dress, and is a good judge of it; despises finery, but dresses with peculiar grace, mixing simplicity with elegance. Ignorant she is of what colors are in fashion; but knows well what suits her complexion. She covers her beauties; but so slightly, or rather artfully, as to give play to the imagination. She prepares herself for managing a family of her own by managing that of her father.

3. Cookery is familiar to her, with the price and quality of provisions;

Noah Webster, *An American Selection* . . . (Boston: Isaiah Thomas and Ebenezer T. Andrews, 1804), pp. 34–35.

and she is a ready accountant. Her chief view, however, is to serve her mother, and lighten her cares. She holds cleanness and neatness to be indispensable in a woman; and that a slattern is disgusting, especially if beautiful.

4. The attention given to externals, does not make her overlook her more material duties. Sophia's understanding is solid, without being profound. Her sensibility is too great for a perfect equality of temper; but her sweetness renders that inequality harmless. A harsh word does not make her angry; but her heart swells, and she retires to disburden it by weeping.

5. Recalled by her father and mother; she comes at the instant, wiping her eyes and appearing cheerful. She suffers with patience any wrong done her; but is impatient to repair any wrong she has done, and does it so cordially, as to make it appear meritorious. If she happen to disoblige a companion, her joy and her caresses, when restored to favor, shew the burthen that lay upon her good heart.

6. The love of virtue is Sophia's ruling passion. She loves it, because no other thing is so lovely: She loves it, because it is the glory of the female sex: She loves it as the only road to happiness, misery being the sure attendant of a woman without virtue: She loves it as dear to her respectable father and tender mother. These sentiments inspire her with a degree of enthusiasm, that elevates her soul and subdues every irregular appetite.

7. Of the absent she never talks but with circumspection, her female acquaintance especially. She has remarked, that what renders women prone to detraction, is talking of their own sex; and that they are more equitable with respect to the men. Sophia therefore never talks of women, but to express the good she knows of them: Of others she says nothing.

8. Without much knowledge of the world, she is attentive, obliging, and graceful in all she does. A good disposition does more for her than much art does for others. She possesses a degree of politeness which, void of ceremony, proceeds from a desire to please, and which consequently never fails to please.

6.4 A "Dialogue on the Choice of Business for Life."

Enter Edward, Charley, *and* Thomas

Edward. It appears to me high time for us to choose our business for life. Our academical studies will soon be completed; and I wish to look a little forward. What say you? am I right?

Caleb Bingham, *The Columbian Orator* . . . (Hartford: Lincoln and Gleason, 1807), pp. 150–153.

Charley. It may be well for *you:* poor men's sons must look out for themselves. My father is able to support me at my ease; and my mamma says she would rather see me laid in a coffin than shut up in a study, spoiling my eyes and racking my brains, plodding over your nonsensical minister, doctor, and lawyer books; and I am sure she would never have me confined behind a counter, or a merchant's desk. She intends I shall be brought up a gentleman. My mother is of noble blood, and she don't intend that I shall disgrace it.

Edw. Pray, master Charley, who was the father of your noble-blooded mother?

Char. A gentleman, I'd have you to know.

Edw. Yes, a gentleman cobler, to my knowledge.

Char. Aye, he followed that business, to be sure, sometimes, to stop the clamour of the vulgar. Then poor people could not bear to see a rich man living at his ease, or give a nobleman his title. But times are altering for the better, my mamma says: the rich begin to govern now. We shall soon live in style, and wear titles here as well as in England. She intends to send over and get my coat of arms, and she hopes to add a title to them.

Edw. High style! titles! and coats of arms! fine things in America, to be sure! Well, after all, I can't really disapprove of your mamma's plan. A lapstone, an awl, and shoe-hammer will make a fine picture, and may appear as well in your mother's parlour, as in her father's shop: and the title of cobler, or shoe-maker would well become her darling Charley.

Char. I will not be insulted on account of my grandfather's employment, I'll have you to know! I have heard my mother say, her father was grandson of an aunt of 'squire Thorn, who once had a horse that run a race with the famous horse of a cousin of the Duke of Bedford, of ———.

Edw. Quite enough! I am fully convinced of the justice of your claim to the title of Duke, or whatever you please. About as much merit in it, I perceive, as in your father's title to his estate. Ten thousand dollars drawn in a lottery! already two thirds spent. A title to nobility derived from the grandson of an aunt of 'quire Thorn, from 'squire Thorn's horse, or perhaps from some monkey, that has been a favorite playmate with the prince of Wales. These are to be the support of your ease and honor through life. Well, I believe there is no need of your troubling yourself about your future employment: that is already determined. Depend upon it, you will repent of your folly, or scratch a poor man's head as long as you live. I advise you to set about the former, in order to avoid the latter.

Char. I did not come to you for advice. I'll not bear your insults, or disgrace myself with your company any longer. My parents shall teach you better manners.

[*Exit Charley*]

Thomas. I pity the vanity and weakness of this poor lad. But reflection and experience will teach him the fallacy of his hopes.

Edw. Poor child; he does not know that his lottery money is almost gone; that his father's house is mortgaged for more than it is worth; and that the only care of his parents is to keep up the appearance of present grandeur, at the expense of future shame. Happy for us, that we are not deluded with such deceitful hopes.

Tho. My parents were poor; not proud. They experienced the want of learning; but were resolved their children should share the benefit of a good education. I am the fourth son, who owe the debt of filial gratitude. All but myself are well settled in business, and doing honor to themselves and their parents. If I fall short of their example, I shall be most ungrateful.

Edw. I have neither father nor mother to excite my gratitude, or stimulate my exertions. But I wish to behave in such a manner, that if my parents could look down and observe my actions, they might approve my conduct. Of my family, neither root nor branch remains: all have paid the debt of nature. They left a name for honesty; and I esteem that higher than a pretended title to greatness. They have left me a small farm, which, though not enough for my support, will with my own industry, be sufficient. For employment, to pass away the winter season, I have determined upon keeping a school for my neighbours' children.

Tho. I heartily approve of your determination. Our mother Earth rewards, with peace and plenty, those, who cultivate her face; but loads, with anxious cares, those, who dig her bowels for treasure. The life you contemplate is favorable to the enjoyment of social happiness, improvement of the mind, and security of virtue; and the task of training the tender mind is an employment, that ought to meet the encouragement, the gratitude of every parent, and the respect of every child.

Edw. I am pleased that you approve my choice. Will you frankly tell me your own?

Tho. I will: my intention is to follow the inclination of my kind parents. It is their desire that I should be a preacher. Their other sons have taken to other callings; and they wish to see one of their children in the desk. If their prayers are answered, I shall be fitted for the important task. To my youth, it appears formidable; but others, with less advantages, have succeeded, and been blessings to society, and an honor to their profession.

Edw. You have chosen the better part. Whatever the licentious may say to the contrary, the happiness of society must rest on the principles of virtue and religion; and the pulpit must be the nursery, where they are cultivated.

Tho. "————The pulpit;
And I name it, fill'd with solemn awe,
Must stand acknowledg'd, while the world shall stand,
The most important and effectual guard,
Support and ornament of virtue's cause.
There stands the messenger of truth.   There stands
The legate of the skies: his theme divine,
His office sacred, his credentials clear.
By him the violated law speaks out
Its thunders, and by him, in strains as sweet
As angels use, the gospel whispers peace."

My heart glows with the subject; and if my abilities could equal my zeal, I could at least hope to realize the sublime character so beautifully drawn by Cowper.

Edw. It is a laudable ambition to aim at eminence in religion, and excellence in virtue.

6.5   The Wonderful World of William Holmes McGuffey.

Eclectic First Reader

The Cool Shade

Come, let us go in-to the thick shade, for it is noon-day, and the summer sun beats hot upon our heads.

The shade is pleas-ant and cool; the branch-es meet a-bove our heads, and shut out the sun, as with a green cur-tain.

The grass is soft to our feet, and the clear brook wash-es the roots of the trees.

The sheep and cows can lie down to sleep in the cool shade, but we can do bet-ter; we can praise the great God who made us.

He made the warm sun, and the cool shade; the trees that grow up-ward, and the brooks that run a-long.

The plants and trees are made to give fruit to man.

All that live get life from God.   He made the poor man, as well as the rich man.

He made the dark man, as well as the fair man.   He made the fool, as well as the wise man.   All that move on the land are his; and so are all that fly in the air, and all that swim in the sea.

William Holmes McGuffey, *Eclectic First Reader* . . . (Cincinnati: Winthrop B. Smith & Co., 1853), pp. 28–31, 81, 94–96, 100–104.
————, *Eclectic Fourth Reader* . . . (Cincinnati: Winthrop B. Smith, 1844), pp. 39–41, 50–53, 72–73, 81–85, 89–91, 180–182, 317–320, 328–329.

The ox and the worm are both the work of his hand. In him they live and move. He it is that doth give food to them all, and when he speaks the word, they must all die.

The Poor Old Man

Jane, there is a poor old man at the door.

He asks for some-thing to eat. We will give him some bread and cheese.

He is cold. Will you give him some clothes too?

I will give him a suit of old clothes, which will be new to him.

Poor man! I wish he had a warm house to live in, and kind friends to live with him; then he would not have to beg from door to door.

We should be kind to the poor. We may be as poor as this old man, and need as much as he.

Shall I give him some cents to buy a pair of shoes?

No; you may give him a pair of shoes.

It is hard for the poor to have to beg from house to house.

Poor boys and girls some-times have to sleep out of doors all night. When it snows, they are ver-y cold, and when it rains, they get quite wet.

Who is it that gives us food to eat, and clothes to make us warm?

It is God, my child; he makes the sun to shine, and sends the rain up-on the earth, that we may have food.

God makes the wool grow up-on the lit-tle lambs, that we may have clothes to keep us warm. . . .

I once knew of a lit-tle girl who was told not to cross the street be-fore a car-riage. But she would not stop; and when the car-riage came up, it ran di-rect-ly o-ver her.

The Lit-tle Chim-ney Sweep

Some time a-go, there was a lit-tle chim-ney sweep, who had to sweep a chim-ney in the house of a ver-y rich la-dy. The lit-tle sweep went up at the kitch-en fire place, and came down in the cham-ber.

When he got in-to the cham-ber, he found him-self all a-lone. He stop-ped a mo-ment to look round up-on the rich things he saw there. As he look-ed on the top of the ta-ble, he saw a fine gold watch, with gold seals to it.

He had nev-er seen a-ny thing so beau-ti-ful be-fore, and he took it up in his hands. As he list-en-ed to hear it tick, it be-gan to play sweet mu-sic. He then thought, that if it was on-ly his own, how rich he would be; and then he thought he might hide it in his blank-et.

"Now," said he, "if I take it, I shall be a thief—and yet no bod-y sees me. No bod-y? Does not God see me? Could I ev-er a-gain be good? Could I then ev-er say my pray-ers a-gain to God? And what should I do when I come to die?

While the lit-tle sweep was think-ing a-bout tak-ing the la-dy's watch, he felt cold all o-ver, and trem-bled with fear.

"No," said he, "I can not take this watch. I would rath-er be a sweep and al-ways be poor, than steal." And down he laid the watch, and crept up the chim-ney.

Now the la-dy who own-ed the watch was just in the next room, and she could look through, and see and hear all that pass-ed. She did not say a-ny thing to the boy then, but let him go a-way.

The next day she sent for him, and when he came, she said to him, "Well, my lit-tle friend, why did you not take my watch yes-ter-day?" The lit-tle sweep then fell up-on his knees and told the la-dy all a-bout it.

Now, as the lit-tle sweep did not steal the gold watch, nor tell a-ny sto-ries a-bout it, the la-dy let him stay and live in her house. For ma-ny years she sent him to school, and when he grew up, he be-came a good man, and nev-er for-got the com-mand-ment which says, "Thou shalt not steal."

Had he ta-ken the la-dy's watch, he would have sto-len. Then he would have been sent to jail.

Let no lit-tle boy or girl ev-er take things with-out leave, for it is steal-ing; and they who steal are thieves.

You can not steal the small-est pin, with-out its be-ing a sin, nor with-out be-ing seen by that eye which nev-er sleeps.

The Bro-ken Win-dow

George El-let had a fine New Year's gift. What do you think it was? A bright sil-ver dol-lar! A mer-ry boy was George, when he thought of all the fine things he might buy with it. And as soon as the sun be-gan to make the air feel a lit-tle warm, he put on his cap and gloves, and ran in-to the street.

The ground was cov-er-ed with snow, but the sun shone out, and ev-er-y thing look-ed bright. As George went skipping a-long, he met some boys who were throw-ing snow-balls. This is fine sport, and George pull-ed off his gloves, and was soon as bu-sy as the rest. See, how he gath-ers up the snow, and press-es it be-tween his hands.

Now he has hit James Ma-son. But the ball was soft, and James is not hurt. Now he has made an-oth-er ball, and if James does not dodge, George will hit him a-gain. A-way goes the ball! But it miss-ed James,

and broke a win-dow on the oth-er side of the street. George was a-fraid
that some one would come out of the house and whip him; so he ran off,
as fast as he could.

As soon as he got round the next cor-ner, he stop-ped, be-cause he was
ver-y sor-ry for what he had done. Just then he saw a man car-ry-ing a
box with glass doors, full of pret-ty toys; and as George was on-ly eight
years old, he for-got the bro-ken win-dow, and ran aft-er the man.

As George was a-bout to buy a lit-tle house with doors and chim-neys,
and put his hand in his pock-et for the money, he thought of the bro-ken
win-dow. Then he said to him-self, "I have no right to spend this dol-lar
for a toy-house. I ought to go back, and pay for the glass I broke with
my snow-ball."

So he gave back the house to the toy-man, and turn-ed round. But he
was a-fraid of be-ing scold-ed or beat-en, and did not know what to do.
He went up and down the street, and felt ver-y bad-ly. He wish-ed to
buy some-thing nice with his mon-ey; and he al-so wished to pay for the
glass he had bro-ken.

At last he said to him-self, "It was wrong to break the win-dow, although I did not mean to do it. I will go and pay the man for it at once.
If it takes all my mon-ey, I will try not to be sor-ry; and I do not think
the man will hurt me, if I of-fer to pay for the mis-chief I have done."
He then start-ed off, and felt much hap-pi-er for hav-ing made up his
mind to do what was right.

He rang the door bell; and when the man came out, George said, "Sir,
I threw a snow-ball through your win-dow. But I did not in-tend to do
it, and am ver-y sor-ry, and I wish to pay you. Here is the dol-lar my
fa-ther gave me as a New Year's gift, this morn-ing."

The man took the dol-lar, and ask-ed George if he had a-ny more
mon-ey. George said he had not. "Well," said the man, "this will be
e-nough." So aft-er ask-ing George where he liv-ed, and what was his
name, he call-ed him an hon-est lad, and shut the door.

When George had paid the man, he ran a-way, and felt ver-y hap-py,
be-cause he had done what he knew to be right. He play-ed ver-y mer-
ri-ly all the fore-noon, al-though he had no mon-ey to spend; and went
home at din-ner time, with a face as ro-sy, and eyes as bright, as if nothing had gone wrong.

At din-ner, Mr. El-let ask-ed George what he had bought with his
mon-ey. George ver-y hon-est-ly told him all a-bout the bro-ken win-
dow, and said he felt ver-y well, with-out a-ny mon-ey to spend. When
din-ner was o-ver, Mr. El-let told George to go and look in his hat.

He did so, and found *two* sil-ver dol-lars. The man, whose win-dow
had been bro-ken, had been there, and told George's fa-ther a-bout it. He

al-so gave back the dol-lar which George had paid him, and *an-oth-er one* with it.

A few months aft-er that, the man came and told Mr. El-let that he want-ed a good boy to stay in his store, and would like to have George, as soon as he left school, for he was sure that George was an *hon-est boy*. George went to live with this man, who was a rich mer-chant. In a few years he be-came the mer-chant's part-ner, and is now rich. George oft-en thinks of the *bro-ken win-dow*.

Eclectic Fourth Reader

Respect for the Sabbath Rewarded—Edinburgh Paper

1. In the city of Bath, not many years since, lived a barber, who made a practice of following his ordinary occupation on the Lord's day. As he was pursuing his morning's employment, he happened to look into some place of worship, just as the minister was giving out his text, "Remember the Sabbath day, to keep it holy." He listened long enough to be con-vinced, that he was constantly breaking the laws of God and man, by shav-ing and dressing his customers on the Lord's day. He became uneasy, and went with a heavy heart to his Sabbath task.

2. At length he took courage, and opened his mind to his minister, who advised him to give up Sabbath dressing, and worship God. He replied that beggary would be the consequence. He had a flourishing trade, but it would almost all be lost. At length', after many a sleepless night spent in weeping and praying, he was determined to cast all his care upon God', as the more he reflected, the more his duty became apparent'.

3. He discontinued Sabbath dressing', went constantly and early to the public services of religion', and soon enjoyed that satisfaction of mind which is one of the rewards of doing our duty, and that peace of God which the world can neither give nor take away'. The consequences he foresaw, actually followed. His genteel customers left him, and he was nicknamed a Puritan' or Methodist'. He was obliged to give up his fash-ionable shop, and, in the course of years, became so reduced', as to take a cellar under the old market house, and shave the common people'.

4. One Saturday evening, between light and dark, a stranger from one of the coaches, asking for a barber, was directed by the ostler, to the cellar opposite. Coming in hastily, he requested to be shaved quickly, while they changed horses, *as he did not like to violate the Sabbath.* This was touching the barber on a tender chord. He burst into tears—asked the stranger to lend him a half-penny to buy a candle, as it was not light enough to shave him with safety. He did' so, revolving in his mind the extreme poverty' to which the poor man must be reduced'.

5. When shaved, he said, "There must be something extraordinary in your history, which I have not now time to hear. Here is half a crown for you. When I return, I will call and investigate your case. What is your name'?" "William Reed'," said the astonished barber. "William Reed'!" echoed the stranger: "William Reed'! by your dialect you are from the West'." "Yes, sir, from Kingston, near Taunton." "William Reed', from Kingston', near Taunton'! What was your father's' name?" "Thomas'." "Had he any brother?" "Yes, sir; one after whom I was named; but he went to the Indies', and, as we never heard from him', we supposed him to be dead'."

6. "Come along', follow me'," said the stranger, "I am going to see a person who says *his'* name is William Reed, of Kingston near Taunton. Come' and confront' him. If you prove to be indeed he who you say you are', I have glorious news for you. Your uncle is dead', and has left an immense fortune, which I will put you in possession of, when all legal debts are removed'."

7. They went by the coach'—saw the pretended William Reed', and proved him to be an impostor'. The stranger, who was a pious attorney', was soon legally satisfied of the barber's identity, and told him that he had advertised him in vain. Providence had now thrown him in his way', in a most extraordinary manner', and he had great pleasure in transferring a great many thousand pounds' to a worthy man'—the rightful heir of the property'. Thus was man's extremity', God's opportunity'. Had the poor barber possessed one *half-penny'*, or even had credit for a *candle'*, he might have remained unknown for years'; but he trusted God', who never said', "Seek ye my face" in vain'. . . .

True and False Philanthropy—Anonymous

Mr. Fantom. I despised a narrow' field. O for the reign of universal benevolence'! I want to make all *mankind* good and happy.

Mr. Goodman. Dear me'. Sure that must be a wholesale sort of a job: had you not better try your hand at a *town'* or *neighborhood'* first?

Mr. F. Sir, I have a plan in my head for relieving the miseries of the *whole world.* Every thing is bad as it now stands. I would alter all the the laws, and put an end to all the wars in the world. I would put an end to all punishments; I would not leave a single prisoner on the face of the globe. *This* is what I call doing things on a grand scale.

Mr. G. A scale with a vengeance! As to releasing the prisoners, however, I do not much like that, as it would be liberating a few rogues at the expense of all honest men; but as to the rest of your plan, if all countries would be so good as to turn *Christians*, it might be helped on a good deal.

There would be still misery enough left indeed'; because God intended this world should be earth and not heaven'. But, sir', among all your changes, you must destroy human corruption', before you can make the world quite as perfect as you pretend'.

Mr. F. *Your* project would *rivet* the chains which *mine* is designed to *break.*

Mr. G. Sir, I have no projects. Projects are, in general, the offspring of restlessness, vanity, and idleness. I am too busy' for projects', too contented' for theories', and, I hope, have too much honesty and humility' for a philosopher.' The utmost extent of my ambition at present is, to redress the wrongs of a poor apprentice, who has been cruelly used by his master: indeed, I have another little scheme, which is to prosecute a fellow, who has suffered a poor wretch in the poorhouse, of which he had the care, to perish through neglect, and you must assist me.

Mr. F. Let the town do that. You must not apply to me for the redress of such petty grievances. I own that the wrongs of the Poles and South Americans so fill my mind, as to leave me no time to attend to the petty sorrows of poorhouses, and apprentices. It is provinces', empires', continents', that the benevolence of the philosopher embraces; every one can do a little paltry good to his next neighbor.

Mr. G. Every one *can*', but I do not see that every one *does*'. If they would, indeed, your business would be ready done to your hands, and your grand ocean of benevolence would be filled with the drops, which private charity would throw into it. I am glad, however, you are such a friend to the prisoners', because I am just now getting a little subscription', to set free your poor old friend Tom Saunders', a very honest brother mechanic who first got into debt, and then into jail, through no fault of his own but merely through the pressure of the times'. A number of us have given a trifle every week towards maintaining his young family since he has been in prison; but we think we shall do much more service to Saunders, and indeed in the end, lighten our own expense, by paying down, at once, a little sum, to release him, and put him in the way of maintaining his family again. We have made up all the money except five dollars. I am already promised four, and you have nothing to do but to give me the fifth. And so, for a single dollar, without any of the trouble we have had in arranging the matter, you will, at once, have the pleasure of helping to save a worthy family from starving, of redeeming an old friend from jail, and of putting a little of your boasted benevolence into action. Realize! Mr. Fantom; there is nothing like realizing.

Mr. F. Why, hark' ye, Mr. Goodman', do not think I value a dollar'; no sir, I despise' money; it is trash', it is dirt', and beneath the regard of a wise man'. It is one of the unfeeling inventions of artificial society. Sir',

I could talk to you half a day on the abuse of riches', and my own contempt of money'.

Mr. G. O pray do not give yourself that trouble'. It will be a much easier way of proving your sincerity', just to put your hand in your pocket', and give' me a dollar without saying a word about' it: and then to you', who value *time'* so *much'*, and *money'* so *little'*, it will cut the matter short. But come now, (for I see you will give nothing), I should be mighty glad to know what is the sort of good you do yourselves, since you always object to what is done by others.

Mr. F. Sir, the object of a true philosopher is, to diffuse light and knowledge. I wish to see the whole world enlightened.

Mr. G. Well, Mr. Fantom, you are a wonderful man, to keep up such a stock of benevolence', at so small an expense'; to *love* mankind so dearly, and yet *avoid* all opportunities of doing them *good;* to have such a noble zeal for the *millions'*, and to feel so little compassion for the *units';*—to long to free *empires'* and enlighten *kingdoms'*, and deny instruction to your own *village'* and comfort to your own *family'*. Surely, none but a *philosopher'* could indulge so much *philanthropy'* and so much *frugality'* at the same time'. But come', do assist me in a partition I am making in our poorhouse, between the *old'*, whom I want to have better *fed'*, and the *young'*, whom I want to have more *worked'*.

Mr. F. Sir, my mind is so engrossed with the partition of Poland, that I cannot bring it down to an object of such insignificance. I despise the man, whose benevolence is swallowed up in the narrow concerns of his own family, or village, or country.

Mr. G. Well, now I have a notion, that it is as well to do one's *own'* duty, as the duty of *another'* man; and that to do good at *home'*, is as well as to do good *abroad'*. For *my* part', I had as lief help *Tom Saunders'* to freedom, as a *Pole'* or a *South American'*, though I should be very glad to help *them too.* But one must begin to love somewhere and to do good somewhere; and I think it is as natural to love one's own family, and to do good in one's own neighborhood as to any body else. And if every man in every family, village, and county did the same, why then all the schemes would meet, and the end of one village or town where I was doing good, would be the beginning of another village where somebody else was doing good; so my schemes would jut into my neighbor's; his projects would unite with those of some other local reformer; and all would fit with a sort of dovetail exactness.

Mr. F. Sir, a man of large views will be on the watch for great occasions to prove his benevolence.

Mr. G. Yes, sir; but if they are so distant that he cannot reach them, or so vast that he cannot grasp them, he may let a thousand little, snug, kind, good actions slip through his fingers in the meanwhile: and so, between the great things that he *cannot'* do, and the little ones that he *will'* not do, life passes, and *nothing'* will be done. . . .

*No Excellence without Labor—*Wirt

1. The education, moral and intellectual, of every individual, must be, chiefly, his own work. Rely upon it, that the ancients were right—both in morals and intellect—we give their final shape to our characters, and thus become, emphatically, the architects of our own fortune. How else could it happen, that young men, who have had precisely the some opportunities, should be continually presenting us with such different results, and rushing to such opposite destinies?

2. Difference of talent will not solve it, because that difference is very often in favor of the disappointed candidate. You will see issuing from the walls of the same college—nay, sometimes from the bosom of the same family—two young men, of whom one will be admitted to be a genius of high order, the other scarcely above the point of mediocrity; yet you will see the genius sinking and perishing in poverty, obscurity, and wretchedness: while on the other hand, you will observe the mediocre plodding his slow but sure way up the hill of life, gaining steadfast footing at every step, and mounting, at length, to eminence and distinction, an ornament to his family, a blessing to his country.

3. Now, whose work is this? Manifestly their own. They are the architects of their respective fortunes. The best seminary of learning that can open its portals to you, can do no more than to afford you the opportunity of instruction: but it must depend, at last, on yourselves, whether you will be instructed or not, or to what point you will push your instruction.

4. And of this be assured—I speak from observation a certain truth: THERE IS NO EXCELLENCE WITHOUT GREAT LABOR. It is the fiat of fate, from which no power of genius can absolve you.

*A Mother's Influence—*Ladies' Magazine

1. "I was a dull boy," said Judge B——, in answer to some remarks of Mrs. Wentworth, referring to the usual precocity of genius, and hinting at the display which the learned and celebrated Judge must have made in his juvenile studies—"I was a very dull boy. Till I was full nine years old, I dreaded the name of book and school.

2. "It is true, I had made some progress in the rudiments of English, and had begun the Latin Grammar; but this was wholly owing to the constant instruction and personal influence of my mother. It was only in obedience

to her, that I attended school. I would have preferred a severe whipping every day of my life, if by that means I might have been exempted from the task of study. I was the *drone* of the school.

3. "My mother began my education very early; I was her only child, and she a widow; you may easily imagine, therefore, how eager she must have been for my improvement. She tried every means that love, faith, and patience could suggest, to instruct me in my lessons and my duties. In the latter she was not disappointed. I may say, without boasting, that I was an obedient boy, for I loved my mother so well, that it was a pleasure to do her bidding.

4. "But I could not learn my book; the fountain of knowledge was, to my taste, bitter waters, and all the devices which ingenuity has invented to make learning easy, failed in my case. I had to wear the dunce cap at school, and so sluggish was my mind, that I did not care a straw for the disgrace, till I found it made my mother weep when she heard of it. Indeed I preferred to be at the foot of my class, for then I had no trouble about trying to keep my station; and even at the opening of the school, I always took my place at the foot; it seemed to fall naturally to me. I was as contented as Diogenes in his tub.

5. "Thus the time passed,' till the winter I entered my tenth year'. The school-master was preparing for a famous exhibition'; and as he knew how solicitous my mother was for my improvement, he called on her to ascertain if she thought it possible that *I* could take a part'. She *did'* think it possible—what *mother* would despair of her *only child?* She undertook to teach me the piece I was to speak.

6. "The teacher had selected that pithy little poem, so appropriate for the young tyro, beginning—

> "You'd scarce expect one of my age
> To speak in public on the stage,
> And if I chance to fall below
> Demosthenes or Cicero,
> Don't view me with a critic's eye,
> But pass my imperfections by, &c.

7. "These six lines were my first lesson; and after tea, my mother sat down to the task of teaching it, telling me that I must learn to recite those six lines, during that and the following evening. You smile', ladies', but it seemed an Herculean task to *me'*, and it was only my strong affection for my mother', that would have induced me to undertake' it.

8. "The teacher had promised me, that, if I spoke my piece well, he would give me a silver medal. I cared nothing for that, till my mother drew me to her, and, as she put back my hair and kissed my forehead in

her loving manner, said, "Oh, Robert! how happy I shall be to see you come home with the medal on!"—I thought then that I would try to obtain it. So I sat down cheerfully to my task.

9. "I recollect the scene as though it were but yesterday. My mother read the six lines to me a number of times over, and then she explained the meaning of the words. She told me of Demosthenes, and the efforts he made to overcome his natural defects. I remember asking her if I should get some pebbles to hold in *my'* mouth—whether it would do *me'* any good;—and how happy her laugh rang out at my witticism. Then she told me of Cicero, and of the great services he rendered his country, by his oratory and learning,—thus endeavoring to awaken my mind to some effort of imitation.

10. "I like to listen to stories, and it was in this manner that I had been taught what little I knew; for I could not comprehend words. I wanted images, and these, my mother, by her manner, and the comparisons she would draw from familiar things, could succeed in picturing to my imagination. In books, I found nothing but words, and those I could not remember. But I am growing tedious, I fear, as that evening was to my mother and myself.

11. "For two long hours she patiently taught' me. I read over the lines a hundred times; I recited them after her; sometimes, I would repeat two or three consecutive words'; and I could see her face brighten with hope'; but when she took the book for the last recitation', and after I had been studying most intently for some minutes', I could not repeat a *single-word'*. I can recollect now my sensation at that time. It seemed to me, that I knew all that my mother wished me to say; but a kind of wavering shadow would come between me and my lesson, and make all the words indistinct, and my will had no power to control these fancies.

12. "When my mother had vainly tried every possible method to make me recollect the two first lines, she was quite overcome. I believe her hope of my intellect was extinguished, and that she felt, for the first time, what all who knew me had predicted, that I would be a dunce. It must be a terrible trial for a sensible mother to think, that her only child is a fool. She burst into a passion of tears; covered her face with her hands, and sunk on her knees beside the sofa where we were sitting.

13. "I started up in amazement at her grief, for I had never before seen her so moved: she was habitually calm as a summer morning; but now her sobs and groans seemed bursting her heart. My knees trembled, and a burning heat rushed over my frame. At that moment, something seemed to open in my head, and a light—I can compare it to nothing else—seemed to be let into my brain.

14. "I saw, or felt,—*that* perhaps would be more proper,—every word of

the lesson I had been learning, as though it were graven with a pen of fire. I knew that I could repeat my lesson; and many *other* lessons that I had vainly tried to learn, now all were present to my memory in perfect arrangement. I stood in a state of entrancement, almost, as these new and clear ideas came thronging on my mind, till my dear mother arose from her kneeling posture, and stretched out her hand to draw me to her.

15. "Her face was deadly pale, but perfectly calm and resigned. I have her countenance now before me, mild and beautiful as an angel's. She had given up her hope of my mind, but her love was deeper and more tender, perhaps, because her pride in me had been utterly humbled. Oh, there is no earthly passion so disinterested as a mother's love! She thought, from my countenance, that I was frightened; and drawing me to her, she caressed me, and murmured, "my son', my dear son'."

16. " 'I can say my lesson, mother, I can say my lesson now'—I broke out and instantly repeated not only the six lines, but the whole poem which I had heard her read, but had never read myself. She was astonished; but when I went on to repeat hymns and poems which she had in vain tried to teach me for months and years, her joyful exclamations were raised in thanks to God; and her tears again flowed like rain.

17. "I do not think she retired' that night at all'; for she was kneeling by my bed-side when I went to sleep', and when I opened my eyes in the morning', she was bending over' me. Probably', she feared I might lose my memory', and watched my first awaking to confirm her hopes'. She was gratified. I recollected more clearly that morning than the previous evening. My whole being seemed changed. Every object looked brighter', and every word sounded with a new meaning'."

18. "Do you believe, that any new faculty of mind was given you?" asked Mrs. Wentworth.

"No'—surely not'—but my intellect was aroused and enlightened. How this was effected', I do not pretend to say'. I have never since found any difficulty in literary pursuits'; the exercise of my mind is my most pleasurable employment'. I gained the medal with great applause; and was sweetly rewarded by the praises and kisses of my mother.

19. "How happy she was'!—too happy for this world. I fear the alternations of grief and joy, had an injurious effect on her health. She passed away in a few months—and left me an orphan indeed. But her memory can never pass from me, while my reason remains. To her I am indebted, for all my enjoyment of intellect. I have no doubt, that, had a severe and chilling discipline been pursued with me at home, as it was at school, I should always have been a dull and ignorant being, perhaps an idiot. To a good, faithful, intelligent mother, what gratitude and respect do not her children owe?—I shall always vindicate the cause of woman." . . .

The Intemperate Husband—Mrs. Sigourney

1. There was one modification of her husband's persecutions, which the fullest measure of Jane Harwood's piety could not enable her to bear unmoved. This was unkindness to her feeble and suffering boy. It was at first commenced as the surest mode of distressing her. It opened a direct avenue to her heart.

2. What began in perverseness seemed to end in hatred, as evil habits sometimes create perverted principles. The wasted invalid shrunk from his father's glance and footstep, as from the approach of a foe. More than once had he taken him from the little bed which maternal care had provided for him, and forced him to go forth in the cold of the winter storm.

3. "I mean to harden him," said he. "All the neighbors know that you make such a fool of him, that he will never be able to get a living. For my part, I wish I had never been called to the trial of supporting a useless boy, who pretends to be sick only that he may be coaxed by a silly mother."

4. On such occasions, it was in vain that the mother attempted to protect her child. She might neither shelter him in her bosom, nor control the frantic violence of the father. Harshness, and the agitation of fear, deepened a disease which might else have yielded. The timid boy, in terror of his natural protector, withered away like a blighted flower. It was of no avail that friends remonstrated with the unfeeling parent, or that hoary-headed men warned him solemnly of his sins. *Intemperance* had destroyed his respect for man, and his fear of God.

5. Spring at length emerged from the shades of that heavy and bitter winter. But its smile brought no gladness to the declining child. Consumption fed upon his vitals, and his nights were full of pain.

6. "Mother, I wish I could smell the violets that grew upon the green bank by our old dear home." "It is too early for violets, my child. But the grass is beautifully green around us, and the birds sing sweetly, as if their hearts were full of praise."

7. "In my dreams last night, I saw the clear waters of the brook that ran by the bottom of my little garden. I wish I could taste them once more. And I heard such music, too, as used to come from that white church among the trees, where every Sunday the happy people meet to worship God."

8. The mother knew that the hectic fever had been long increasing, and saw there was such an unearthly brightness in his eye, that she feared his intellect wandered. She seated herself on his low bed, and bent over him to soothe and compose him. He lay silent for some time.

9. "Do you think my father will come?" Dreading the agonizing

agitation which in his paroxysms of coughing and pain, he evinced at the sound of his father's well-known footstep, she answered,—"I think not, love. You had better try to sleep."

10. "Mother, I wish he would come. I do not feel afraid now. Perhaps he would let me lay my cheek to his once more, as he used to do when I was a babe in my grand-mother's arms. I should be glad to say good bye to him, before I go to my Savior."

11. Gazing intently in his face, she saw the work of the destroyer, in lines too plain to be mistaken. "My son, my dear son—say, Lord Jesus, receive my spirit." "Mother," he replied, with a sweet smile upon his ghastly features, "he is ready. I desire to go to him. Hold the baby to me, that I may kiss her. That is all. Now sing to me, and oh! wrap me close in your arms, for I shiver with cold."

12. He clung, with a death grasp, to that bosom which had long been his sole earthly refuge. "Sing louder, dear mother,—a little louder,—I cannot hear you." A tremulous tone, as of a broken harp, rose above her grief, to comfort the dying child. One sigh of icy breath was upon her cheek, as she joined it to his—one shudder—and all was over.

13. She held the body long in her arms, as if fondly hoping to warm and restore it to life with her breath. Then she stretched it upon its bed, and kneeling beside it, hid her face in that grief which none but mothers feel. It was a deep and sacred solitude, alone with the dead. Nothing save the soft breathing of the sleeping babe fell upon that solemn pause.

14. Then the silence was broken by a wail of piercing sorrow. It ceased, and a voice arose—a voice of supplication for strength to endure, as "seeing Him who is invisible." Faith closed what was begun in weakness. It became a prayer of thanksgiving to Him who had released the dovelike spirit from the prison-house of pain, that it might taste the peace and mingle in the melody of heaven. . . .

The Righteous never Forsaken—Anonymous

1. It was Saturday night, and the widow of the Pine Cottage sat by her blazing fagots, with her five tattered children at her side, endeavoring by listening to the artlessness of their prattle, to dissipate the heavy gloom that pressed upon her mind. For a year, her own feeble hand had provided for her helpless family, for she had no supporter: she thought of no friend in all the wide, unfriendly world around.

2. But that mysterious Providence, the wisdom of whose ways is above human comprehension, had visited her with wasting sickness, and her little means had become exhausted. It was now, too, midwinter, and the snow lay heavy and deep through all the surrounding forests, while

storms still seemed gathering in the heavens, and the driving wind roared amidst the neighboring pines, and rocked her puny mansion.

3. The last herring smoked upon the coals before her; it was the only article of food she possessed, and no wonder her forlorn, desolate state brought up in her lone bosom all the anxieties of a mother, when she looked upon her children: and no wonder, forlorn as she was, if she suffered the heart swellings of despair to rise, even though she knew that he whose promise is to the widow and to the orphan, cannot forget his word.

4. Providence had, many years before, taken from her her eldest son, who went from his forest home to try his fortune on the high seas, since which she had heard no tidings of him; and in her latter time, had, by the hand of death, deprived her of the companion and staff of her earthly pilgrimage in the person of her husband. Yet to this hour she had been upborne; she had not only been able to provide for her little flock, but had never lost an opportunity of ministering to the wants of the miserable and destitute.

5. The indolent may well bear with poverty, while the ability to gain sustenance remains. The individual who has but his own wants to supply, may suffer with fortitude the winter of want; his affections are not wounded, his heart not wrung. The most desolate in populous cities may hope, for charity has not quite closed her hand and heart, and shut her eyes on misery.

6. But the industrious mother of helpless and depending children—far from the reach of human charity, has none of these to console her. And such a one was the widow of the Pine Cottage; but as she bent over the fire, and took up the last scanty remnant of food, to spread before her children, her spirits seemed to brighten up, as by some sudden and mysterious impulse, and Cowper's beautiful lines came uncalled across her mind—

> Judge not the Lord by feeble sense,
>   But trust him for his grace;
> Behind a frowning Providence
>   He hides a smiling face.

7. The smoked herring was scarcely laid upon the table when a gentle rap at the door, and loud barking of a dog, attracted the attention of the family. The children flew to open it, and a weary traveler, in tattered garments, and apparently indifferent health, entered and begged a lodging, and a mouthful of food; said he "it is now twenty-four hours since I tasted bread." The widow's heart bled anew as under a fresh complication of distresses; for her sympathies lingered not around her fireside. She hesitated not even now; rest and a share of all she had she proffered to the

stranger. "We shall not be forsaken," said she, "or suffer deeper for an act of charity."

8. The traveler drew near the board—but when he saw the scanty fare, he raised his eyes towards heaven with astonishment—"and is this *all* your store?" said he—"and a share of this do you offer to one you know not? then never saw I *charity* before! but madam," said he, continuing, "do you not wrong your *children* by giving a part of your last mouthful to a stranger?"

9. "Ah," said the poor widow, and the tear drops gushed into her eyes as she said it, "I have a *boy*, a darling *son*, somewhere on the face of the wide world, unless heaven has taken him away, and I only act towards you, as I would that others should act towards him. God, who sent manna from heaven, can provide for us as he did for Israel—and how should I this night offend him, if my son should be a wanderer, destitute as you, and he should have provided for him a home, even poor as this—were I to turn you unrelieved away."

10. The widow ended, and the stranger springing from his seat, clasped her in his arms,—"God indeed has provided your son a home—and has given him wealth to reward the goodness of his benefactress—my mother! oh my mother!" It was her long lost son; returned to her bosom from the Indies. He had chosen that disguise that he might the more completely surprise his family; and never was surprise more perfect, or followed by a sweeter cup of joy.

11. That humble residence in the forest was exchanged for one comfortable, and indeed beautiful, in the valley; and the widow lived long with her dutiful son, in the enjoyment of worldly plenty, and in the delightful employments of virtue: and at this day the passer-by is pointed to the willow that spreads its branches above her grave. . . .

The Patriotism of Western Literature—Dr. Drake

1. Our literature cannot fail to be patriotic, and its patriotism will be American—composed of a love of country, mingled with an admiration for our political institutions.

2. The slave, whose very mind has passed under the yoke, and the senseless ox, which he goads onward in the furrow, are attached to the spot of their animal companionship, and may even fight for the cabin and the field where they came into existence; but this affection, considered as an ingredient of patriotism, although the most universal, is the lowest; and to rise into a virtue, it must be discriminating and comprehensive, involving a varied association of ideas, and embracing the beautiful of the natural and moral world, as they appear around us.

3. To feel in his heart, and to infuse into his writings the spirit of such a patriotism, the scholar must feast his taste on the delicacies of our scenery, and dwell with enthusiasm on the genius of our constitution and laws. Thus sanctified in its character, this sentiment becomes a principle of moral and intellectual dignity—an element of fire, purifying and subliming the mass in which it glows.

4. As a guiding star to the will, its light is inferior only to that of Christianity. Heroic in its philanthropy, untiring in its enterprises, and sublime in the martyrdoms it willingly suffers, it justly occupies a high place among the virtues which ennoble the human character. A literature, animated with this patriotism, is a national blessing, and such will be the literature of the West.

5. The literature of the whole Union must be richly endowed with this spirit; but a double portion will be the lot of the interior, because the foreign influences, which dilute and vitiate this virtue in the extremities, cannot reach the heart of the continent, where all that lives and moves is American.

6. Hence a native of the West may be confided in as his country's hope. Compare him with the native of a great maritime city, on the verge of the nation,—his birth-place the fourth story of a house, hemmed in by surrounding edifices, his playground a pavement, the scene of his juvenile rambles an arcade of shops, his young eyes feasted on the flags of a hundred alien governments, the streets in which he wanders crowded with foreigners, and the ocean, common to all nations, forever expanding to his view.

7. Estimate *his* love of country, as far as it depends on local and early attachments, and then contrast him with the young backwoodsman, born and reared amidst objects, scenes and events, which you can all bring to mind;—the jutting rocks in the great road, half alive with organic remains, or sparkling with crystals; the quiet old walnut tree, dropping its nuts upon the yellow leaves, as the morning sun melts the October frost; the grape-vine swing; the chase after the cowardly black snake, till it creeps under the rotten log; the sitting down to rest upon the crumbling trunk, and an idle examination of the mushrooms and mosses which grow from its ruins.

8. Then, the wading in the shallow stream, and upturning of the flat stones, to find bait with which to fish in the deeper waters; next, the plunder of a bird's nest, to make necklaces of the speckled eggs, for her who has plundered him of his young heart; then, the beech-tree with its smooth body, on which he cuts the initials of her name interlocked with his own; finally, the great hollow stump, by the path that leads up the valley to the log school-house, its dry bark peeled off, and the stately poke-

weed growing from its center, and bending with crimson berries: which invite him to sit down and write upon its polished wood: how much pleasanter it is to extract ground squirrels from beneath its roots, than to extract the square root, under that labor-saving machine, the ferule of a teacher!

9. The affections of one who is blessed with such reminiscences, like the branches of our beautiful trumpet-flower, strike their roots into every surrounding object, and derive support from all which stand within their reach. The love of country is with him a constitutional and governing principle. If he be a mechanic, the wood and iron which he molds into form, are dear to his heart, because they remind him of his own hills and forests; if a husbandman, he holds companionship with growing corn, as the offspring of his native soil; if a legislator, his dreams are filled with sights of national prosperity, to flow from his beneficent enactments; if a scholar, devoted to the interests of literature, in his lone and excited hours of midnight study, while the winds are hushed, and all animated nature sleeps, the genius of his country hovers nigh, and sheds over its pages an essence of patriotism, sweeter than the honey-dew which the summer night distills upon the leaves of our forest trees. . . .

Duty of an American Orator—Grimke

1. One theme of duty still remains, and I have placed it alone: because of its peculiar dignity, sacredness, and importance.—Need I tell you that I speak of the union of the states? Let the American orator discharge all other duties but this, if indeed it be not impossible, with the energy and eloquence of John Rutledge, and the disinterested fidelity of Robert Morris, yet shall he be counted a traitor, if he attempt to dissolve the union.

2. His name, illustrious as it may have been, shall then be gibbeted on every hill-top throughout the land, a monument of his crime and punishment, and of the shame and grief of his country. If indeed he believe, (and doubtless there may be such,) that wisdom demands the dissolution of the union, that the south should be severed from the north, the west be independent of the east, let him cherish the sentiment, for his own sake, in the solitude of his breast, or breathe it only in the confidence of friendship.

3. Let him rest assured, that as his country tolerates the monarchist and aristocrat of the old world, she tolerates him; but should he plot the dismemberment of the union, the same trial, judgment, and execution await him as would await them, should they attempt to establish the aristocracy of Venice, or the monarchy of Austria, on the ruins of our confederacy.

To him as to them, she leaves freedom of speech; and the very licentious-ness of the press: and permits them to write, even in the spirit of scorn, and hatred, and unfairness.

4. She trembles not at such effort, reckless and hostile as they may be. She smiles at their impotence, while she mourns over their infatuation. But let them lift the hand of parricide, in the insolence of pride, or the madness of power, to strike their country, and her countenance, in all the severity and terrors of a parent's wrath shall smite them with amazement and horror. Let them strike, and the voices of millions of freemen from the city and hamlet, from the college and the farm-house, from the cabins amid the western wilds, and our ships scattered around the world, shall utter the stern irrevocable judgment, self banishment for life, or igno-minious death. . . .

Europe and America—Washington—Webster

[Extract from an address delivered at the celebration of the completion of the Bunker Hill Monument, June 17, 1843.]

1. Few topics are more inviting, or more fit for philosophical discussion, than the action and influence of the New World upon the Old; or the contributions of America to Europe.

2. Her obligations to Europe for science and art, laws, literature, and manners, America acknowledges as she ought, with respect and gratitude. And the people of the United States, descendants of the English stock, grateful for the treasures of knowledge derived from their English an-cestors, acknowledge, also, with thanks and filial regard, that among those ancestors, under the culture of Hambden and Sidney, and other assiduous friends, that seed of popular liberty first germinated, which, on our soil, has shot up to its full height, until its branches overshadow all the land.

3. But America has not failed to make returns. If she has not canceled the obligation, or equaled it by others of like weight, she has, at least, made respectable advances, and some approaches towards equality. And she admits, that, standing in the midst of civilized nations, and in a civilized age—a nation among nations—there is a high part which she is expected to act, for the general advance of human interests and human welfare.

4. American mines have filled the mints of Europe with the precious metals. The productions of the American soil and climate, have poured out their abundance of luxuries for the tables of the rich, and of necessaries for the sustenance of the poor. Birds and animals of beauty and value, have been added to the European stocks; and transplantations from the transcendent and unequaled riches of our forests, have mingled themselves profusely with the elms, and ashes, and druidical oaks of England.

5. America has made contributions far more vast. Who can estimate the amount, or the value, of the augmentation of the commerce of the world, that has resulted from America? Who can imagine to himself what would be the shock to the Eastern Continent, if the Atlantic were no longer traversable, or there were no longer American productions or American markets?

6. But America exercises influences, or holds out examples for the consideration of the Old World, of a much higher, because they are of a moral and political character. America has furnished to Europe, proof of the fact, that popular institutions, founded on equality and the principle of representation, are capable of maintaining governments—able to secure the rights of persons, property, and reputation.

7. America has proved that it is practicable to elevate the mass of mankind—that portion which, in Europe, is called the laboring, or lower class—to raise them to self-respect, to make them competent to act a part in the great right and great duty of self-government; and this, she has proved, may be done by the diffusion of knowledge. She holds out an example a thousand times more enchanting, than ever was presented before, to those nine-tenths of the human race, who are born without hereditary fortune or hereditary rank.

8. America has furnished to the world the character of Washington! And if our American institutions had done nothing else, that alone would have entitled them to the respect of mankind. Washington! "First in war, first in peace, and first in the hearts of his countrymen!" Washington is all our own!

9. The enthusiastic veneration and regard in which the people of the United States hold him, prove them to be worthy of such a countryman; while his reputation abroad reflects the highest honor on his country and its institutions. I would cheerfully put the question to any of the intelligence of Europe and the world, what character of the century, upon the whole, stands out on the relief of history, most pure, most respectable, most sublime; and I doubt not, that, by a suffrage approaching to unanimity, the answer would be—Washington!

6.6   More Cautionary Tales.

The Good Girl

1. There was once a little girl whose name was Fanny, who lived in that large white house which you may see at the corner.

Oliver Angell, *The Union No. 1; or Child's First Book* . . . (Philadelphia: E. H. Butler & Co, 1848), pp. 15, 55–57, 61–62, 64–65.

2. Fanny was a very good girl, and always did what she was told to do, without either pouting or grumbling, like some little girls whom I could name.

3. If her mamma was busy, and had not time to talk to her, Fanny never teased her; and if she was told to go into the nursery, she went immediately, without saying a word.

4. Yet Fanny liked very much to be with her mamma, and was always glad when she was told to come down again.

5. One day, as she was sitting by her mamma in the parlor, and playing with a pretty new box of letters which her papa had bought for her, a lady came into the room to speak with her mamma.

6. Fanny was sent out of the room, and as soon as she was told to go, she gathered up her letters in a moment, and placed them carefully in her box, and put it in its proper place.

7. She then left the room, as desired, without crying or ill humor, and amused herself with such playthings as she had there, until the lady was gone.

8. In a few days, the same lady called again, and brought with her a very pretty book, called "The Book of Games," containing a great many pictures. This book she gave to Fanny, "because," said she, "I saw, the other day, that you were a very good girl."

9. Fanny took the book, and thanked the lady for it. She thought to herself that she was twice paid for being good. She was paid by feeling very happy, and pleased with herself for being obedient and good humored, and now she was rewarded with a pretty new book. . . .

The Passionate Boy

1. I once knew a little boy who was very naughty, and used to get into a violent passion, and would strike and throw things at his brothers and sisters if they offended him.

2. One day he was playing with his little brother, who did something to vex him. He ran to the table to catch up an iron that the servant had been using, to throw at his brother.

3. It happened that the iron was very hot, so that when he caught hold of it, it burnt his hand so much, that all the skin came off, to his fingers' ends, and he suffered so much pain that he did not know what to do with himself.

4. Now this little boy did not like to feel pain himself, and yet he was just going to inflict pain upon his brother, by throwing the iron at him.

5. It almost always happens so; for when people get into a violent passion, they either do something, or say something, for which they are very

sorry afterwards.—Besides, violent anger makes a person feel very unhappy.

6. When you are at play, therefore, with your little companions, you should be very careful and not get angry with them, for if you get angry, you cannot enjoy the play any more, and there is great danger that you will hurt some one, for which you will be very sorry. . . .

Divine Providence

1. You know I have often told you that God made us all, and that it is He who gives us all the good things we enjoy. It is He who makes the corn to grow which we feed upon, and the fruits and the flowers which give us so much pleasure.

2. He causes the grass to spring up, which the horses, and cows, and sheep feed upon. He bids the sun to shine by day, to warm us, and make every thing look cheerful and pleasant; and He causes the moon and stars to give us light by night.

3. Without his care and goodness we could not live a single hour, and if he should bid us die, we should die in an instant.—Nothing in the world could keep us alive.

4. He is always kind and good. He comforts and supports us when nothing else can. In return for all this kindness, the only thing he requires of us is, to be grateful to him, to love him, and to obey him.

5. If we love him, we shall be good, for we shall then wish to please him; and we know that nothing can please him that is not good. He is the greatest, the wisest and the best of all beings, and it is our duty to love him with all our hearts, and to be good, because we know he wishes all his creatures to be happy; and, unless they are good, they can never be happy.

6.7   On Education and Early Rising.

Effects of Education upon individuals—Its importance to the publick—Wordsworth

> Alas! what differs more than man from man!
> And whence this difference?—whence but from himself?
> For, see the universal race, endowed
> With the same upright form!   The sun is fixed,
> And the infinite magnificence of heaven,

John Pierpont, *The American First Class Book* . . . (Boston: Hilliard, Gray, Little, and Wilkins, 1832), pp. 65, 333–335.

Within the reach of every human eye:
The sleepless ocean murmurs in all ears;
The vernal field infuses fresh delight
Into all hearts. Throughout the world of sense
Even as an object is sublime or fair,
That object is laid open to the view
Without reserve or veil; and as a power
Is salutary, or its influence sweet,
Are each and all enabled to perceive
That power, that influence, by impartial law.
  Gifts nobler are vouchsafed alike to all;—
Reason,—and, with that reason, smiles and tears;
Imagination, freedom of the will,
Conscience to guide and check; and death
To be foretasted,—immortality presumed.
Strange then, nor less than monstrous might be deemed
The failure, if the Almighty, to this point
Liberal and undistinguishing, should hide
The excellence of moral qualities
From common understanding; leaving truth
And virtue, difficult, abstruse and dark;
Hard to be won, and only by a few:—
Strange, should he deal herein with nice respects,
And frustrate all the rest! Believe it not:
The primal duties shine aloft—like stars;
The charities, that sooth, and heal, and bless,
Are scattered at the feet of man—like flowers.
The generous inclination, the just rule,
Kind wishes, and good actions, and pure thoughts—
No mystery is here; no special boon
For high and not for low,—for proudly graced
And not for meek in heart. The smoke ascends
To heaven as lightly from the cottage hearth,
As from the haughty palace. He whose soul
Ponders its true equality, may walk
The fields of earth with gratitude and hope;
Yet, in that meditation, will he find
Motive to sadder grief, when his thoughts turn
From nature's justice to the social wrongs
That make such difference betwixt man and man.
  Oh for the coming of that glorious time
When, prizing knowledge as her noblest wealth,

And best protection, this imperial realm
While she exacts allegiance, shall admit
An obligation on her part, to *teach*
Them who are born to serve her and obey;
Binding herself by statute to secure,
For all the children whom her soil maintains,
The rudiments of Letters, and to inform
The mind with moral and religious truth,
Both understood and practised—so that none
However destitute, be left to droop,
By timely culture unsustained, or run
Into a wild disorder; or be forced
To drudge through weary life without the aid
Of intellectual implements and tools;
A savage horde among the civilized,
A servile band among the lordly free!
 This right—as sacred, almost, as the right
To exist and be supplied with sustenance
And means of life,—the lisping babe proclaims
To be inherent in him, by Heaven's will,
For the protection of his innocence;
And the rude boy who knits his angry brow,
And lifts his wilful hand on mischief bent,
Or turns the sacred faculty of speech
To impious use—by process indirect,
Declares his due, while he makes known his need.
 This sacred right is fruitlessly announced,
This universal plea in vain addressed,
To eyes and ears of parents, who themselves
Did, in the time of their necessity,
Urge it in vain; and, therefore, like a prayer
That from the humblest floor ascends to heaven,
It mounts to reach the State's parental ear;
Who, if indeed she own a mother's heart,
And be not most unfeelingly devoid
Of gratitude to Providence, will grant
The unquestionable good.——
 The discipline of slavery is unknown
Amongst us,—hence the more do we require
The discipline of virtue:—order else
Cannot subsist, nor confidence, nor peace.
Thus, duties rising out of good possessed,

And prudent caution needful to avert
Impending evil, do alike require
That permanent provision should be made
For the whole people to be taught and trained:—
So shall licentiousness and black resolve
Be rooted out, and virtuous habits take
Their place; and genuine piety descend,
Like an inheritance, from age to age.

On early rising—Hurdis

Rise with the lark, and with the lark to bed.
The breath of night's destructive to the hue
Of every flower that blows. Go to the field,
And ask the humble daisy why it sleeps,
Soon as the sun departs: Why close the eyes
Of blossoms infinite, ere the still moon
Her oriental veil puts off? Think why,
Nor let the sweetest blossom be exposed
That nature boasts, to night's unkindly damp.
Well may it droop, and all its freshness lose,
Compelled to taste the rank and poisonous steam
Of midnight theatre, and morning ball.

6.8   On the Importance of Being Practical.

A pure, temperate atmosphere, and romantic scenery, are productive of clear intellects and brilliant imagination. America is far from being deficient in these advantages. The oratory, councils, and sagacity of its natives, prove that their conceptions are by no means cramped by physical causes.

This being granted, which cannot be denied, it will be extremely difficult to show a reason, why the mental powers of our ancestors, or their descendants, should suffer a decay in this country, so favourable by nature to sound judgment and brilliancy of thought.

Instead of forcing ourselves into such an absurd conclusion, we shall make an obvious distinction, which will lead to a conclusion, not derogatory to the American character; a distinction between natural genius, and its improvement by art. One depends on natural causes; the other, on the state of society.

Caleb Bingham, *Columbian Orator* . . . (Boston: J. H. A. Frost *et al.*, 1832), pp. 298–299.

With a well supported claim to the former, it is no dishonor to acknowledge ourselves inferiour to the elder nations of Europe in the latter. Considering the infant state of our country, and the nature of our government, we have more reason to boast, than be ashamed of our progress in the fine arts.

If not equal in this respect, to our mother country, we have made more rapid improvement than any other nation in the world. Our government and habits are republican; they cherish equal rights, and tend to an equal distribution of property. Our mode of education has the same tendency to promote an equal distribution of knowledge, and to make us emphatically a "republic of letters:" I would not be understood adepts in the fine arts, but participants of useful knowledge.

In the monarchical and aristocratic governments of Europe, the case is far different. A few privileged orders monopolize not only the wealth and honors, but the knowledge of their country. They produce a few profound scholars, who make study the business of their lives; we acquire a portion of science, as a necessary instrument of livelihood, and deem it absurd to devote our whole lives to the acquisition of implements, without having it in our power to make them useful to ourselves or others.

They have their thousands who are totally ignorant of letters; we have but very few, who are not instructed in the rudiments of science. They may boast a small number of masters in the fine arts; we are all scholars in the useful; and employed in improving the works of nature, rather than imitating them.

So strong is our propensity to useful employments, and so sure the reward of those who pursue them, that necessity, "the mother of invention," has reared but few professional poets, painters, or musicians among us. Those, who have occasionally pursued the imitative arts, from natural inclination, have given sufficient proof, that even in them, our capacity and genius are not inferiour to those of Europeans; but the encouragement they have met shows that the spirit of our habits and government tends rather to general improvement in the useful, than partial perfection in the amusing arts.

6.9 Arnold Guyot on the Family of Man.

Much has been said, much has been written, on this important question of the human races—one of the most difficult and most delicate the science of nature and history can propose to itself. I am not going to discuss it

Arnold Guyot, *Earth and Man* . . . (textbook translation by C. C. Felton; Boston: Gould, Kendall, and Lincoln, 1849), p. 244.

here; but what I desire is, to establish, in this province also, a great general fact, which, as it seems to me, has not been sufficiently insisted on, and to which has not been attributed the importance it deserves. This fact is the following:

While all the types of animals and of plants, about of equal rank along the same zone of latitude, go on decreasing in perfection, from the equatorial to the polar regions, in proportion to the temperatures, man presents to our view his purest, his most perfect type, at the very centre of the temperate continents, at the centre of Asia-Europe, in the regions of Iran, of Armenia, and of the Caucasus; and, departing from this geographical centre in the three grand directions of the lands, the types gradually lose the beauty of their forms in proportion to their distance, even to the extreme point of the southern continents, where we find the most deformed and degenerate races, and the lowest in the scale of humanity.

6.10   A Recollection of Textbooks and Lessons in a Pioneer Kansas School.

Arithmetic ranked high in our curriculum because it was considered so practical. That was why it was recited early in the day while the pupil's mind was fresh. We began arithmetic with the simplest sums in addition and subtraction and went up to the dizzy level where one extracted cube root. We had little nests of long and cubical blocks which were supposed to clarify the process of extraction, but I never understood the blocks. Arithmetic was a difficult subject for most of us, and we had one teacher who tried to make it more palatable by a simple game. Here were the rules: A problem was presented to two pupils who tried to "work" it and get the correct answer in the shortest possible time. The winner was pitted against a new problem and a new antagonist, whose privilege it was to select the kind of problem which was to be given out by the teacher. I had that choice one day and promptly chose "subtraction," a subject in which I then shone but dimly, but it was my best chance of beating Tommy Green, who was put against me. But that false teacher ignored my just choice and put in another sort of sum in which Tommy had been recently coached. She wanted to "show off" Tommy before the school and, of course, she had her way and Tommy won.

I felt much more kindly towards a teacher who explained common fractions by an apple neatly cut into segments in the presence of the class. I

Marshall A. Barber, *The Schoolhouse at Prairie View* (Lawrence, Kansas: University of Kansas Press, 1953), pp. 30–37. Reprinted by permission of the University of Kansas Press.

really understood fractions for the first time that day, and I was so interested that I forgot what became of the apple.

Reading was the subject next in importance, for it was thought the gateway to all knowledge. I had learned to read a little before I entered school and I soon got into the Third Reader. I wish I could remember the name of that reader. It fell into the post-McGuffey period or may have been McGuffey itself or strongly influenced by that famous writer. Maybe some reader can identify it by one poem on tobacco which it contained:

> Tobacco is a filthy weed,
> It was the Devil sowed the seed,
> It leaves a stench where'er it goes,
> It makes a chimney of the nose.

That poem was probably the precursor of the "required" instruction on the pernicious effect of tobacco and alcohol on the human system, a subject put in long after I left country school. I trust it had more influence than that third-reader rhyme did on me. What really influenced me was the admonition of our farm employees, who said sagely, "Tobacco's a bad habit; don't ever begin it," and who then would saw off a chunk of "Star" or light a smelly pipe and begin to "use" it with patent enjoyment. I also had a playmate, Vessie Toms, who told us that "Sweet Mary," a certain root we found in the woods and were fond of chewing, "was best mixed with terbaccer." My father did not indulge, but he had barrels of dried tobacco leaves which he used for concocting a sheep dip; and I think some of us got our first taste of tobacco from the stems of that useful "pharmaceutical," maybe when mixed with "Sweet Mary."

Writing perhaps came next in importance. It was largely an affair of copybooks and Mr. Spencer, and I hated it. We early affected a more level script which we called a "business hand"; why I do not know—maybe because we thought a business man had no time for Spencerian curlicues or shaded pothooks. Surely no business man would care for those Spencerian birds admired by all of us but attempted by only the more gifted pupils. These inky fowls had some very peculiar anatomical characteristics; but they were always singing and happy, so I supposed they did not mind. I wrote my first letter to my father, who was absent in Topeka on business. Since he never reproved me for that letter, I assume he never got around to reading it.

Spelling ranked high in our curriculum. There was perhaps more disgrace attached to misspelling in those times than at present; correct spelling was the mark of an educated person. And the subject was easy to study and easy to teach. It was largely a memory exercise for the pupil, and the teacher had only to call out the words from his spelling book and assign good or bad marks or other measure of standing to the pupil. The simplest way to conduct a recitation was to line the pupils along a board in the schoolroom floor. A word was called out and if the pupil missed it, it was repeated to the pupil next in line. If he got it right, he went above (to the right in our school) the misspeller, and in the course of the recitation might get to the head of the class—he did not need to be graded, his "standing" was evidence that he knew his lesson. There was a touch of the dramatic in standing up for oral recitation. I still have a picture in my mind of the correct speller marching head up to the top of the class and the misspellers shuffling downwards with eyes on their toes.

There were more formal "spelling-down" contests conducted by the teacher on Friday afternoons or at a night session with parents in attendance. The contenders were chosen by two leaders who formed their armies in two long lines along the schoolroom floor. A misspelling sent a contender to his seat, and the final result was plainly shown by the numbers surviving on each of the two sides. Sometimes one person "spelled down" all the rest. The "choosing up" was a wholesome exercise for us, whether for intellectual or athletic contests, for it gave one a clear idea of his standing in the estimation of his peers—there could be no favoritism shown by the leaders if they were going to win.

Sometimes we remained seated and the teacher pronounced words to the whole class. We wrote them down as best we could and handed in our papers at the close of the recitation. That was a sort of innovation, and even our immature judgments approved of the method—"you spell words as you have to write them," we reasoned.

I do not possess a copy of the spelling book we first used and I cannot identify it by name. It was the one which grouped on certain pages a lot of the most interesting sentences, ones which we read again and again just for the fun of it. They were designed to show how words of different meaning might have similar sounds; for example, "The guest guessed that the belle rang the bell." That sentence seemed to be sensible enough; but "Oh, John, did you owe for the ode?" did not somehow fit into our everyday life and economy. I wonder how many puns and punsters those sentences, read by so many generations of students, are responsible for.

This spelling book began with short words of two letters and at the end (on the right-hand side of the page) had rows of such stunners as "incomprehensibility" and "daguerreotype" which one gazed at worshipfully even if he never learned to spell them. Then there were innocent-looking rows of monosyllables like "sieve" and "seize" stickers which I have to look up even today. In later years, probably contemporary with the new desks, came a spelling book which arranged words by meaning rather than by number of syllables. I never wholly approved of the change. I missed those rows of snags which lay like knotty fence posts across the page.

History was largely taught from a single textbook. Our teachers did not stray far from the book; perhaps some of them feared to get into politics, which would hardly do for a public school. But the teacher ran little risk. It was generally assumed by our community that the Union and Republican party were right; the Prohibition and Populist parties had not come in prominence at that time, so that there was little of a political nature for us to quarrel about.

Our book was fair enough; there was little or no attempt at propaganda in it. It was full of pictures, chiefly of people notable in the history of the United States or of the colonies. I remember well a woodcut of a palisade used by the colonists during King Philip's War. A bold Indian, maybe King Philip himself, was shown wandering around outside the enclosure, reminding one of a boy seeking a knothole during a baseball game. We recited Presidents and some of the chief events of their administrations—there were not nearly so many ex-Presidents, living or dead, at that time.

The Civil War was a safe topic for the most timid teacher, for our neighborhood was almost unanimously Union. Many of the fathers of our pupils, perhaps a majority of them, were "Old Soldiers" who marched in procession on Memorial Day. Some of them were buried right by the schoolhouse, and the children used to put flags and flowers on their graves. One of our neighbors, the portly Mr. Foster, had been a prisoner in a Confederate camp, and his children told us how thin he was when he returned home after the War.

We hardly dreamed of war as a thing which could affect our lives, unless we joined the Army and fought Indians, who occasionally left their reservations and started some very lively skirmishes. The Civil War was only ten years past and the sky had not wholly cleared after that mighty storm. So there were some vague opinions that the South might "come back," talk probably revived by the Hayes-Tilden controversy in 1876. But for us children the war god was asleep and probably would never awaken again; the world had had enough of him. One morning some children, I think of German families, came to school with solemn news, "There is war again in the old country." I do not know what war that was; the Franco-German War was over and done. But how little this news impressed us children whether American or German. The children of tomorrow may be much more keenly interested by such tidings, for it may mean that they themselves may have to join huge armies and sail to the "old country."

Geography did not rank in importance with reading and arithmetic but was always taken seriously. We did a great deal of "bounding" countries, especially the States, and we learned capitals and their location. I remember well a ritual which began "Maine, Augusta, on the Kennebec River." I got that much of it from my sister, and I presume that in her more advanced class they continued this chant clear to California. We learned something about the material products of different countries but less about their spiritual output. I have quoted what we learned about the French, "a gay and polite people, fond of dancing and light wines." We bothered very little about the physical geography of countries except those characteristics which could be easily shown on maps, such as mountains, seas, and rivers. Map-making was a favorite part of geography for us; perhaps all children like to study with their hands. I was not good at maps, but I used to gaze by the hour at the wonderful accomplishments of my schoolmates as outlined on the blackboard. The continents were especially impressive, for they had a definite personality. Africa, a great head, negroid behind, held her sharp nose upturned at the lesser lands to the east. South America, smaller and decidedly more svelte, appeared to great advantage in maps. She had such an even coast which accommodated the wavy lines that delimited the oceans, and such big rivers, easily drawn in. And very convenient mountains—the Andes were just made for maps, one beautiful long range which contained volcanoes scattered almost from the top to bottom like buttons on a jacket.

We stuck closely to the surface of our planet, our teachers rarely mentioning anything related to geology or astronomy. One teacher did have us demonstrate the cause of the change of seasons. The stove was the sun, and a long pointer the axis of the earth. A pupil held the axis just so and walked around the stove from December to May.

Science formed no part of our regular curriculum. Now and then a teacher would introduce a bit of it informally. One teacher asked us what water is made of and told us to find out at home and report the next day. She got some very fantastic answers; none of them mentioned hydrogen or oxygen. She asked us one day what hops were used for. We did not know, since few if any of us had ever tasted beer in any form. Then she told us in one word, "bitters," an answer which left most of us still in the dark.

A teacher who, I am sure, had had some instruction in botany, tried to get us interested in leaves—not by showing us what a wonderful mechanical structure leaves have, nor by telling us something about the great part they play in the economy of nature, but by telling us about their classification, how some were "denticulate," some "obovate" or "narrow-lanceolate." He had us make collections of leaves and classify them according to their form. We were deeply impressed. We already knew a great deal about leaves and what they looked like, how this shape characterized oak and this willow and so on, but we had never associated simple leaves with those thundering polysyllables. We were intrigued as we were once by a little book we saw at home, which, we were told, actually enabled one to find out the name of a plant.

We knew a world of natural history, about all sorts of plants, especially those which bore edible fruits, about wild birds and mammals and those tame ones we saw daily on the farm. Farming itself was an important study in science. But that was learning which we were supposed to get at home, not in school. It should be acquired by experience or taught us by our elders, who probably knew much more about it than the teacher did, anyhow a lady teacher; she might be criticized if she took up school time for formal instruction on such things as animals or plants.

Probably the neighborhood sentiment was right—we needed instruction in things our parents could not or would not teach us, and we were getting about enough science on the farm.

6.11 Clarence Darrow Recalls His School Readers.

If we scholars did not grow up to be exemplary men and women, it surely was not the fault of our teachers or our parents,—or of the schoolbook publishers.

When I look back to those lessons that we learned, I marvel that I ever wandered from the straight path in the smallest possible degree. Whether we were learning to read or write, studying grammar or composition, in whatever book we chanced to take, there was the moral precept plain on every page. Our many transgressions could have come only from the fact that we really did not know what these lessons meant; and doubtless our teachers also never thought they had any sort of relation to our lives.

How these books were crammed with noble thoughts! In them every virtue was extolled and every vice condemned. I wonder now how the book publishers ever could have printed such tales, or how they reconciled themselves to the hypocrisy they must have felt when they sold the books.

This moral instruction concerned certain general themes. First of all, temperance was the great lesson taught. I well remember that we children believed that the first taste of liquor was the fatal one; and we believed that not one drop could be taken without leading us to everlasting

Reprinted with the permission of Charles Scribner's Sons from *Farmington*, by Clarence Darrow (New York: Charles Scribner's Sons, 1932), pp. 59–62 and 67–69.

ruin and despair. There were the almshouse, the jail, and the penitentiary square, in front of every child who even considered taking the first drink; while all the rewards of this world and the next were freely promised to the noble lad who should resist.

As I look back to-day, it seems as if every moral lesson in the universe must have grown into my being from those books. How could I have ever wandered from the narrow path? I look back to those little freckled, trifling boys and girls, and I hear them read their lessons in their books so long ago. The stories were all the same, from the beginning to the end. We began in the primer, and our instruction in reading and good conduct did not end until the covers of the last book were closed.

It seems to me to-day that I can hear those little urchins reading about the idle lazy boy who tried to get the bee and the cow and the horse to play with him,—though what he wanted of the bee I could never understand,—but they were all too busy with their work, and so he ran away from school and had a most miserable day alone. How could we children ever stay away from school after we had read this lesson? And yet, I cannot now recall that it made us love our books, or think one whit less of the free breeze, the waving grass and trees, or the alluring coaxing sun.

We were taught by our books that we must on all accounts speak the truth; that we must learn our lessons; that we must love our parents and our teachers; must enjoy work; must be generous and kind; must despise riches; must avoid ambition; and then, if we did all these things, some fairy godmother would come along at just the darkest hour and give us everything our hearts desired. Not one story in the book told how any good could ever come from wilfulness, or selfishness, or greed, or that any possible evil ever grew from thrift, or diligence, or generosity, or kindness. And yet, in spite of all these precepts, we were young savages, always grasping for the best, ever fighting and scheming to get the advantage of our playmates, our teachers, and our tasks.

A quarter of a century seems not to have wrought much change; we still believe in the old moral precepts, and teach them to others, but we still strive to get the best of everything for ourselves.

I wonder if the old school-readers have been changed since I was a boy at school. Are the same lessons there to-day? We were such striking examples of what the books would not do that one would almost think the publishers would drop the lessons out.

I try to recall the feelings of one child who read those stories in the little white school-house by the country road. What did they mean to me? Did I laugh at them, as I do to-day? Or did I really think that they were true, and try and try, and then fail in all I tried, as I do now? I presume the latter was the case; yet for my life I cannot recall the thoughts and feelings that these stories brought to me. But I can still recall the stories. . . .

One other story that has seemed particularly to impress itself upon my mind was about two boys, one named James and the other named John. I believe that these were their names, though possibly one was William and the other Henry. Anyhow, their uncle gave them each a parcel of books. James took out his pocketknife and cut the fine whipcord that bound his package, but John slowly and patiently untied his string and then rolled it into a nice little ball (the way a nice little boy would do) and carefully put it in his pocket. Some years after, there was a great shooting tournament, and James and John were both there with their bows and arrows; it was late in the game, and so far it was a tie. James seized his last arrow and bent his bow; the string broke and the prize was lost. The book does not tell us that in this emergency John offered his extra piece of whipcord to his brother; instead, the model prudent brother took up his last arrow, bent his bow, when, lo and behold! his string broke too; whereupon John reached into his pocket and pulled out the identical cord that he had untied so long ago, put it on the bow, and of course won the prize!

That miserable story must have cost me several years of valuable time, for ever since I first read it I have always tried to untie every knot that I could find; and although I have ever carefully tucked away all sorts of odd strings into my pockets, I never attended a shooting-match or won a prize in all my life.

One great beauty of the lessons which our school readers taught was the directness and certainty and promptness of the payment that came as a reward of good conduct. Then, too, the recompense was in no way uncertain or ethereal, but was always paid in cash, or something just as material and good. Neither was any combination of circumstances too remote or troublesome or impossible to be brought about. Everything in the universe seemed always ready to conspire to reward virtue and punish vice.

Becoming an American: 7

The Education of the Immigrant

The rolling waves of immigrants to the United States posed a sharp challenge to the common school. During the hundred years following 1815 over thirty-five million people came to this country in the greatest migration in history. Germany contributed the largest number, followed in order by Italy, Ireland, Great Britain, Austria-Hungary, Russia, and scores of other nations. Facing public education was the task of transforming these millions of newcomers—speaking dozens of languages, clinging to diverse folkways, owing multiple loyalties—into one people: *e pluribus unum.*

Although Americanization occurred in countless ways outside the classroom, a special burden rested upon the common school, for it was one institution which reached most of the young. In concert with other social agencies, formal and informal, schools accelerated the process of assimilation. German farmers who had retained their language and customs for centuries when transplanted to Russia became Americanized in one generation when they settled in Eureka, South Dakota. Children of parents who spoke a babel of tongues in the iron mines of the Mesabi range were taught meticulously correct English in the Minnesota grammar and high schools. Urban school systems prodded some young men and women to climb out of the ghettos to positions of affluence and influence.

Naturally, assimilation of ethnic groups proceeded at different paces in different environments, and immigrants adapted to American mores often only in a grudging and superficial manner. Americanization normally meant discarding old customs and values. Hence successful assimilation often disrupted families and sowed doubt and recrimination between the

228

generations. Some of these conflicts of cultures still reverberate in American society.

In order to Americanize, schoolmen first had to decide who was this new man, the American. In 1782 Crèvecoeur had asked this question and concluded that "this promiscuous breed, that race, now called Americans" had been the oppressed of Europe who had been regenerated in America by "new laws, a new mode of living, a new social system." These attitudes and institutions shaped the newcomer from the moment he stepped off the boat. Thus Crèvecoeur and DuPont de Nemours, Frenchmen, and Thomas Paine, Englishman, could become instant Americans. Although native Americans like Noah Webster might be self-conscious and nervous about the nature of "Americanism," Paine and Crèvecoeur could describe it confidently. As time passed, native citizens came increasingly to believe that American beliefs and folkways should be fixed not fluid, homogeneous not pluralistic. In 1835 the Ohio reformer Calvin Stowe warned teachers that "it is altogether essential to our national strength and peace, if not even to our national existence, that the foreigners who settle on our soil, should cease to be Europeans and become Americans. . . ." The schools must create a national feeling, a unity of thought and action, for "nothing could be more fatal to our prospects . . . than to have our population become a congeries of clans, congregating without coalescing, and condemned to contiguity without sympathy." Only deliberate effort "to shape the rising generation to our own model" in schools common to all could prevent this disaster. Though foreign adults might resist assimilation, their children might "re-act on the parents, and the young become the teachers of the old."

The process of uprooting and transplantation awoke immigrants to their own distinctiveness; for the first time they learned what it meant to be "Italian" or "Polish" by living in a land where their mores were not self-evident and unquestioned. And in turn, Americans were forced to define their own values more self-consciously in the process of teaching them to the newcomers. In the textbooks American heroes and history were glorified, often at the cost of other nations. The English language taught in the schools was largely prescriptive, its grammar artificial and usage canonical, as if to build barriers against foreign corruptions. And as Sara O'Brien demonstrated in her *English for Foreigners*, Americanization required clean hands, regular use of the tooth brush, a balanced diet, patient industry, neat dress, and an idyllic middle-class family life. The version of politics she taught was the Mugwump-Progressive ideal: immigrants should vote for the trained and disinterested public servant. If the strangers were dirty, ignorant of proper dress and food, linguistically barbaric, prone to elect corrupt bosses and to listen to demagogues, they must be taught otherwise. Often the most ardent American-izers in the schools were teachers who came from second or third genera-tion immigrant families.

In the middle of the nineteenth century hope ran high that the schools could unify the nation and that the hybrid people would be stronger than the native stock alone. "Let them be like grafts which become branches of the parent stock," said Stowe of the immigrants, "improve its fruit, and add to its beauty and its vigor; and not like the parasitical mistletoe, which never incorporates itself with the trunk from which it derives its nourish-ment, but exhausts its sap, withers its foliage, despoils it of its strength, and sooner or later, by destroying its supporter, involves itself in ruin."

Despite the usual reverence expressed toward the family in the text-books and in the official culture of the school, teachers were in effect tell-ing children that they must change their ways and not emulate their par-ents. The public schools became a wedge splitting immigrant children from their parents. When children entered the doors of the public school, they passed into a world unfamiliar to their elders, one which seemed to teach them to scorn inherited traditions. "Well, look what hap-pens when we send our children to school," one immigrant mother ex-claimed. "All they learn is to despise us. Look how they talk back to us!" Parents turned to their children for interpretation of the new soci-ety; their authority undermined, they lamented that the young were dis-respectful and unmanageable. One boy was haled into court for resist-ing his Italian father's discipline and retorted "Well, Judge, honest now, do you think an American ought to let himself be licked by a foreigner?" Although pained by the disintegration of the family and the frequent con-tempt of the children for foreign folkways, parents were ambivalent about the school. Like Mary Antin's father, many also hoped that edu-cation would open a door for their sons and daughters into the privileges of American society.

The child, caught in a conflict of cultures, could not often conform to the expectations of both the public school and the immigrant family. In a city ghetto the public school might simply be an unreal world whose rituals bore little meaning within the ethnic island. When the immigrant child was in a minority, adult pressures to conform to American customs were powerfully assisted by the child's peers. Ridicule was a rapid Ameri-canizer. The Chinese boy's pigtail, the Mexican girl's tortilla, the Italian child's baroque accent—these often disappeared as a result of belittling comments or schoolyard scuffles. And sometimes even kindness cut; Elizabeth Stern recalled that her schoolmates pitied her when she opened her lunch of gefüllte fish—thinking that she had squashed her lunch—and offered her their own sandwiches and dessert.

Now and then stalwarts stood up to the homogenizers. A teacher asked the Armenian Bagdasar Krekor Bagdigian what his name was. She replied in dismay "Oh, give that up and change your name to Smith, Jones, or a name like that and become Americanized. Give up everything you brought with you from the old country." Furious, Bagdigian refused, thinking to himself, "The Turkish sword did not succeed in making me a Turk and now this hare-brained woman is trying to make an American out of me." For some children the street gang became a means of identity apart from the orthodoxy of the home and the orthodoxy of the school. It was a group where adolescents might determine their own system of status and recognition.

Many immigrant groups supported, often at great sacrifice, their own private schools designed to perpetuate their religious and ethnic heritage. Norwegian Lutherans in Minnesota, Polish Catholics in Chicago, Russian Jews in Boston created their own educational systems, sometimes to supplement the public schools and sometimes to compete with them, but always to preserve their own culture. They juxtaposed their own ethnocentrism against American ethnocentrism, but by the second or third generation Americanism partially won: the children spoke English, preferred American folkways, blended with the general population at work, and retained ethnic peculiarities chiefly in their private lives and in their social circle (and sometimes in their religious and political associations as well).

The common school changed the immigrant, but the immigrant altered the school, too. The teacher in a ghetto classroom could not take familiar skills and attitudes for granted; now it was essential to take over a whole realm of duties formerly performed by the family. Teachers often gave children baths, taught them manners, proper dress, names for familiar objects. The teacher could no longer assume that a child knew how to speak English; in one school in New York, for example, there were twenty-five different nationalities. These difficulties staggered even the most dedicated and energetic teacher. In the large and heterogeneous classes—often containing fifty or more children of a half-dozen nationalities—strict routine reigned. Teachers were trained to believe that the school should start from scratch in implanting correct ideas and behavior; the children's background and environment were not to be trusted.

To the child the school might have meant bells clanging, seats bolted in long rows, silent marches in lines down dark corridors, books full of unfamiliar people and strange imperatives, an omniscient power structure represented by the Principal. But it was also one of the few places where there were no quarreling adults, roving gangs, or smells of leaking gas or rotting garbage; one of the few places where he could sit in a clean, warm, well-lighted room, secure in the routine, though probably a bit bored.

Often school was the main contact a ghetto child had with the wider society, and on the quality of this experience depended much of his desire to defy or to become a part of that society.

The community expected the school to be policeman as well as parent-surrogate. One principal, Angelo Patri, heard all sorts of complaints from people who thought the schools should *do* something about children's misbehavior: a candy peddlar whose beard was pulled by some boys; a sign painter who charged that rogues had stolen his ladder and left him perched high over the sidewalk; a delicatessen owner complaining that Rachel was in the habit of stealing dill pickles. Patri accepted the notion that the teacher was "responsible for what the child does out of school." How otherwise, he asked, "can the teacher ever know that her world counts in the life of the child?"

Anxiously, Americans turned to the common schools to solve problems larger than stolen pickles and yanked beards. A fear of ethnic diversity, of corruption, of class conflict led one superintendent of schools to conceive of public education as a para-military organization. "Its army of half a million teachers, sustained by popular devotion to the cause, must in times of peace and through peaceful measures fight this continuous battle for the perpetuity of national life," he declared. "This army stands to day holding the hands and hearts of tomorrow's nation. To make a citizenship whose intelligence, moral rectitude, and steadfast virtues will counteract . . . disintegrating forces and social disorders is the function and mission of our public schools."

In the late 1880's and 1890's, especially after panic over the Haymarket riot, schoolmen worried increasingly about teaching patriotism. They grew lyrical over flag rituals and patriotic badges. They held nationalistic ceremonies in the schools, inviting parents to attend. Teachers began to pay more and more attention to civics and United States history. In Frontenac, Kansas, a mining town where almost 88 per cent of the parents were foreign-born, pupils studied American history in the sixth, seventh, eighth, and ninth grades, in addition to learning about American heroes in the lower grades. The climax of patriotic instruction came in the years of World War I, when many citizens feared the "hyphenated Americans" as a domestic fifth column and sought to stamp out, in particular, the German language and vestiges of German culture. "What kind of American consciousness can grow in the atmosphere of sauerkraut and limburger cheese?" asked one super-patriot.

Although the schools reached most of the children of the foreign born —and thereby indirectly influenced the parents—little attention was paid to formal schooling of adult immigrants until the early twentieth century. Voluntary associations of native Americans, such as the Daughters of the

American Revolution, the Y.M.C.A., and employers' groups, as well as the immigrants' own mutual benefit associations and charities, did accomplish a good deal in introducing foreigners to American ideas and institutions, but haphazardly in comparison with the public schools.

By the second decade of the twentieth century, however, the federal, state, and local governments became interested in Americanizing the adult immigrant. The resulting adult education was not very successful. In Passaic, New Jersey workers explained that they were too tired to go to school after ten or more hours of labor and said that they had to work at night when the classes were held. Adults complained of the teaching methods and condescension of the instructors: "They treat you like a child because you don't know English." In time teachers became better trained and public funds flowed into the work more freely. But compulsion was lacking, and only a small percentage of the adult immigrants attended schools.

In the period of the common school crusade schoolmen had been hopeful that the hybrid but uniform American produced by public education and social assimilation would surpass both native and immigrant stock. Toward the end of the nineteenth century, however, racist myths about the inferiority of the "new immigrants" undermined faith in schooling as well as belief in the value of ethnic mixture. Bogus anthropologists divided the peoples of Europe into "races" and popularizers were quick to brand the "Teuton" or "Nordic" race superior to the "Alpine," "Mediterranean," and Jewish breeds. Immigration during the three decades before World War I consisted largely of people from southern and eastern Europe. These "new immigrants" were "illiterate, docile, lacking in self-reliance and initiative, and not possessing the Anglo-Saxon conceptions of law, order, and government," the educator Ellwood Cubberley complained in 1909. "Their coming has served to dilute tremendously our national stock, and to corrupt our national life." Cubberley believed that the only hope was to break up the ghettoes, for the nation was "afflicted with a serious case of racial indigestion."

While educated men began to doubt the possibility of Americanizing these new "racial" groups—with their inferior hereditary characteristics—red-neck nativists were unequivocal about the menace. "Ominous statistics proclaim the persistent development of a parasitic mass within our domain," said the Imperial Wizard of the Ku Klux Klan. "Our political system is clogged with foreign bodies which stubbornly refuse to be absorbed, and means must be found to meet the menace. We have taken unto ourselves a Trojan horse crowded with ignorance, illiteracy, and envy." Xenophobia in the postwar years, resurgence of strong nativist feeling, fear of economic competition from cheap foreign labor, and racist ideology combined to produce the climate of opinion in which Congress passed two immigration restriction bills in 1921 and 1924. The latter, especially, was based on the premise of the inferiority of the southern and eastern European immigrants. Not until 1965 was the quota system based on "racial" origins abolished. The restrictive laws represented, among other convictions, a decline of faith in assimilation through the common school, a fear that ethnic differences defied eradication through education.

Especially in the twentieth century a number of Americans questioned the wisdom of trying to eradicate ethnic differences. Diversity, said these pluralists, was a blessing, not a curse. What should the United States be, asked Horace Kallen, "—a unison, singing the old Anglo-Saxon theme 'America,' the America of the New England school, or a harmony, in which that theme shall be dominant, perhaps, among others, but one among many, not the only one?" The cultural pluralists quarreled with the social worker who reported "not yet Americanized; still eating Italian food." The children of immigrants should be taught to respect their parents' traditions, said a student of the *Social and Religious Life of Italians in America:* "When I discuss the matter with teachers in the public schools, I become aware that they possess a holy terror of teaching the language and history of Italy." Was it not the American nativist who was most guilty of clannishness?

From the time of the Revolution forward, substantial numbers of Americans supposed that the free citizen was the uniform man, that diversity somehow endangered the promise of American life since it threatened cohesiveness. Others saw a free society as a place where it was safe to be unpopular, comfortable to be different. The common school in successive decades expressed both points of view in differing degrees, seeking to strike the precarious balance of ordered liberty. The task of Americanizing the immigrant posed in all its complexity the problem of unity within diversity.

7.1   Experience of Mary Antin, a Russian Immigrant Girl.

The knowledge of such things as I am telling leaves marks upon the flesh and spirit. I remember little children in Polotzk with old, old faces and eyes glazed with secrets. I knew how to dodge and cringe and dissemble before I knew the names of the seasons. And I had plenty of time to ponder on these things, because I was so idle. If they had let me go to school, now—But of course they didn't.

Mary Antin, *The Promised Land* (Boston; Houghton Mifflin Company, 1912), pp. 26–27, 186, 198–200, 270–272. Reprinted by permission of the Houghton Mifflin Company.

There was no free school for girls, and even if your parents were rich enough to send you to a private school, you could not go very far. At the high school, which was under government control, Jewish children were admitted in limited numbers,—only ten to every hundred,—and even if you were among the lucky ones, you had your troubles. The tutor who prepared you talked all the time about the examinations you would have to pass, till you were scared. You heard on all sides that the brightest Jewish children were turned down if the examining officers did not like the turn of their noses. You went up to be examined with the other Jewish children, your heart heavy about that matter of your nose. There was a special examination for the Jewish candidates, of course; a nine-year-old Jewish child had to answer questions that a thirteen-year-old Gentile was hardly expected to understand. But that did not matter so much. You had been prepared for the thirteen-year-old test; you found the questions quite easy. You wrote your answers triumphantly—and you received a low rating, and there was no appeal.

I used to stand in the doorway of my father's store, munching an apple that did not taste good any more, and watch the pupils going home from school in twos and threes; the girls in neat brown dresses and black aprons and little stiff hats, the boys in trim uniforms with many buttons. They had ever so many books in the satchels on their backs. They would take them out at home, and read and write, and learn all sorts of interesting things. They looked to me like beings from another world than mine. But those whom I envied had their own troubles, as I often heard. Their school life was one struggle against injustice from instructors, spiteful treatment from fellow students, and insults from everybody. Those who, by heroic efforts and transcendent good luck, successfully finished the course, found themselves against a new wall, if they wished to go on. They were turned down at the universities, which admitted them in the ratio of three Jews to a hundred Gentiles, under the same debarring entrance conditions as at the high school,—especially rigorous examinations, dishonest marking, or arbitrary rulings without disguise. No, the Czar did not want us in the schools. . . .

In America, then, everything was free, as we had heard in Russia. Light was free; the streets were as bright as a synagogue on a holy day. Music was free; we had been serenaded, to our gaping delight, by a brass band of many pieces, soon after our installation on Union Place.

Education was free. That subject my father had written about repeatedly, as comprising his chief hope for us children, the essence of American opportunity, the treasure that no thief could touch, not even misfortune or poverty. It was the one thing that he was able to promise us when he sent for us; surer, safer than bread or shelter. On our second day I was thrilled with the realization of what this freedom of education meant. A little girl from across the alley came and offered to conduct us to school. My father was out, but we five between us had a few words of English by this time. We knew the word school. We understood. This child, who had never seen us till yesterday, who could not pronounce our names, who was not much better dressed than we, was able to offer us the freedom of the schools of Boston! No application made, no questions asked, no examinations, rulings, exclusions; no machinations, no fees. The doors stood open for every one of us. The smallest child could show us the way.

This incident impressed me more than anything I had heard in advance of the freedom of education in America. It was a concrete proof—almost the thing itself. One had to experience it to understand it. . . .

The apex of my civic pride and personal contentment was reached on the bright September morning when I entered the public school. That day I must always remember, even if I live to be so old that I cannot tell my name. To most people their first day at school is a memorable occasion. In my case the importance of the day was a hundred times magnified, on account of the years I had waited, the road I had come, and the conscious ambitions I entertained.

I am wearily aware that I am speaking in extreme figures, in superlatives. I wish I knew some other way to render the mental life of the immigrant child of reasoning age. I may have been ever so much an exception in acuteness of observation, powers of comparison, and abnormal self-consciousness; none the less were my thoughts and conduct typical of the attitude of the intelligent immigrant child toward American institutions. And what the child thinks and feels is a reflection of the hopes, desires, and purposes of the parents who brought him overseas, no matter how precocious and independent the child may be. Your immigrant inspectors will tell you what poverty the foreigner brings in his baggage, what want in his pockets. Let the overgrown boy of twelve, reverently drawing his letters in the baby class, testify to the noble dreams and high ideals that may be hidden beneath the greasy caftan of the immigrant. Speaking for the Jews, at least, I know I am safe in inviting such an investigation.

Who were my companions on my first day at school? Whose hand was in mine, as I stood, overcome with awe, by the teacher's desk, and whispered my name as my father prompted? Was it Frieda's steady, capable hand? Was it her loyal heart that throbbed, beat for beat with mine, as it had done through all our childish adventures? Frieda's heart did throb that day, but not with my emotions. My heart pulsed with joy and pride and ambition; in her heart longing fought with abnegation. For I was led to the schoolroom, with its sunshine and its singing and the teacher's cheery smile; while she was led to the workshop, with its foul air, care-lined faces, and the foreman's stern command. Our going to school was the fulfilment of my father's best promises to us, and Frieda's share in it was to fashion and fit the calico frocks in which the baby sister and I made our first appearance in a public schoolroom.

I remember to this day the gray pattern of the calico, so affectionately did I regard it as it hung upon the wall—my consecration robe awaiting the beatific day. And Frieda, I am sure, remembers it, too, so longingly did she regard it as the crisp, starchy breadths of it slid between her fingers. But whatever were her longings, she said nothing of them; she bent over the sewing-machine humming an Old-World melody. In every straight, smooth seam, perhaps, she tucked away some lingering impulse of childhood; but she matched the scrolls and flowers with the utmost care. If a sudden shock of rebellion made her straighten up for an instant, the next instant she was bending to adjust a ruffle to the best advantage. And when the momentous day arrived, and the little sister and I stood up to be arrayed, it was Frieda herself who patted and smoothed my stiff new calico; who made me turn round and round, to see that I was perfect; who stooped to pull out a disfiguring basting-thread. If there was anything in her heart besides sisterly love and pride and good-will, as we parted that morning, it was a sense of loss and a woman's acquiescence in her fate; for we had been close friends, and now our ways would lie apart. Longing she felt, but no envy. She did not grudge me what she was denied. . . .

If my head was not turned at this time it was because I was so busy from morning till night. My father did his best to make me vain and silly. He made much of me to every chance caller, boasting of my progress at school, and of my exalted friends, the teachers. For a schoolteacher was no ordinary mortal in his eyes; she was a superior being, set above the common run of men by her erudition and devotion to higher things. That a school-teacher could be shallow or petty, or greedy for pay, was a thing that he could not have been brought to believe, at this time. And he was right, if he could only have stuck to it in later years, when a new-born pessimism, fathered by his perception that in America, too, some things needed mending, threw him to the opposite extreme of opinion, crying that nothing in the American scheme of society or government was worth tinkering. . . .

In Polotzk we had been trained and watched, our days had been regulated, our conduct prescribed. In America, suddenly, we were let loose on the street. Why? Because my father having renounced his faith, and my mother being uncertain of hers, they had no particular creed to hold us to. The conception of a system of ethics independent of religion could not at once enter as an active principle in their life; so that they could give a child no reason why to be truthful or kind. And as with religion, so it fared with other branches of our domestic education. Chaos took the place of system; uncertainty, inconsistency undermined discipline. My parents knew only that they desired us to be like American children; and seeing how their neighbors gave their children boundless liberty, they turned us also loose, never doubting but that the American way was the best way. In public department, in etiquette, in all matters of social intercourse, they had no standards to go by, seeing that America was not Polotzk. In their bewilderment and uncertainty they needs must trust us children to learn from such models as the tenements afforded. More than this, they must step down from their throne of parental authority, and take the law from their children's mouths; for they had no other means of finding out what was good American form. The result was that laxity of domestic organization, that inversion of normal relations which makes for friction, and which sometimes ends in breaking up a family that was formerly united and happy.

This sad process of disintegration of home life may be observed in almost any immigrant family of our class and with our traditions and aspirations. It is part of the process of Americanization; an upheaval preceding the state of repose. It is the cross that the first and second generations must bear, an involuntary sacrifice for the sake of the future generations. These are the pains of adjustment, as racking as the pains of birth. And as the mother forgets her agonies in the bliss of clasping her babe to her breast, so the bent and heart-sore immigrant forgets exile and homesickness and ridicule and loss and estrangement, when he beholds his sons and daughters moving as Americans among Americans.

On Wheeler Street there were no real homes. There were miserable flats of three or four rooms, or fewer, in which families that did not practise race suicide cooked, washed, and ate; slept from two to four in a bed, in windowless bedrooms; quarrelled in the gray morning, and made up in the smoky evening; tormented each other, supported each other, saved each other, drove each other out of the house. But there was no common life in any form that means life. There was no room for it, for one thing. Beds and cribs took up most of the floor space, disorder packed the interspaces. The centre table in the "parlor" was not loaded with books. It held, invariably, a photograph album and an ornamental lamp with a paper shade; and the lamp was usually out of order. So there was as little motive for a common life as there was room. The yard was only big enough for the perennial rubbish heap. The narrow sidewalk was crowded. What were the people to do with themselves? There were the saloons, the missions, the libraries, the cheap amusement places, and the neighborhood houses. People selected their resorts according to their tastes. The children, let it be thankfully recorded, flocked mostly to the clubs; the little girls to sew, cook, dance, and play games; the little boys to hammer and paste, mend chairs, debate, and govern a toy republic. All these, of course, are forms of baptism by soap and water.

7.2 The Meaning of Americanization: "English for Foreigners" by Sara O'Brien, a Teacher in the Day and Evening Schools of Springfield, Massachusetts.

> The woman washes her hands.
> She washes them with warm water.
> She takes the brush in her hand.
> She washes her fingers.
> She washes her finger-nails.
> She wipes both hands dry.
> She wipes them on a towel.
> She cleans her finger-nails.
> She cuts her finger-nails.
> She files her finger-nails.
> She pushes back the skin from her nails.
> She has clean hands and nails. . . .
>
> This is a tooth-brush.
> It is my tooth-brush.
> I take it in my hand.
> I dip it in warm water.
> I shall brush my teeth.
> I brush my teeth.
> I brush my teeth with this tooth-brush.
> I brush all of my teeth.
> I brush them every day.
> I take this thread.
> I shall clean my teeth with it.
> I clean between my teeth with it.
> My teeth are clean and white.
> I take care of my teeth.
> I take good care of my teeth. . . .

Sara R. O'Brien, *English for Foreigners* (Boston: Houghton Mifflin Co., 1909), Book 1, pp. 16, 24, 34, 43, 55, 76–77, 82, 128–129, 140–141, 149.

See the men work!
They are working hard.
They work with shovels and pick-axes.
They dig into the ground.
They take up the dirt.
They take up the dirt with shovels.
They throw the dirt out.
They throw the stones out.
They are digging the cellar.
It is the cellar for a house. . . .

Do you eat good food?
Do you eat clean food?
Do you eat fresh meat?
Do you eat good meat?
Do you eat fresh fruit?
Do you eat fresh vegetables?
Keep the meat in the ice-chest.
Keep the doors of the ice-chest closed.
Keep all the food away from the dust and the flies. . . .

This is the family, in the sitting-room.
The family is made up of the father, the mother, and the children.
That is the father who is reading.
The father is the husband.
That is the mother who is sewing.
The mother is the wife.
The father and the mother are the parents.
The sister is playing the piano.
The brother is standing beside her.
The family makes the home.

Copy:—*There is no place like home.* . . .

How to Dress

A gentleman knows how to dress well. He doesn't buy clothes which he can't afford. He knows it is cheaper to pay cash for his clothes than to buy on credit.

A gentleman always wears clean clothes. He changes his clothes often. He airs the clothes which can't be washed. He knows that he must wear clean clothes to keep in good health. Unclean clothes bring disease to him, and may also bring disease into his home.

A gentleman is neat in his dress. He does not dress in loud colors. He likes better the kind of clothes which do not attract attention. It pays to dress neatly, for often a man is judged by his clothes.

The Workroom

Are you a tailor or a dressmaker? Perhaps you are a milliner. Do you work in a big shop making clothes? Is your workroom large, and does it have plenty of pure air coming in? Read Lesson XLVII again and then tell if your workroom is well aired. Is the air free from dust? It is not good to breathe air that has dust in it. Nothing will spread disease more quickly than dust. Of course no one should ever spit on the floor, because spit when dried soon rises as dust in the air.

How many people are in your workroom? If there are many people working in the same room with you, there should be more outside air coming in than if few people are there. In a small room the air becomes bad faster than in a large room. If gas-jets or lamps are burning in the workroom, they will use up the pure air very fast.

Be sure that you work in a warm, dry, and clean room. Never sit in a draft. Be sure that you have enough light to see your work easily. Do not work in a dim light.

Do you take a walk in the pure air in the lunch hour? This will help you to do your work better. . . .

A Coal-Mine

These men are miners and they are digging coal. They work very hard down in the mine. Do you see the little lamps on their caps? The sunlight never comes into the mine, because the mine is many feet below the surface of the earth.

One miner makes the blasts and other miners break the coal with drills and picks. The coal is loaded on to little cars. The mules haul the coal up to the top of the mine. How fast the mules go! They are glad to see the sunlight again. The coal will be sent down the roadway to be loaded on to cars and boats and carried to the cities and towns to be sold. Do you know the different kinds of coal? . . . .

The City Government

When many people live together in a city, there must be law and order. Without law and order, property and even life would be unsafe.

One man cannot make all the laws for a city, nor can one man keep order everywhere. Not all of the people in a city can come together to make the laws. So the people choose certain men to make the laws, and certain other men to carry out these laws. The city government is made up of men who make the laws for the city, and the men who see that these laws are obeyed.

Who is the head of the family in the home? There is a head to every factory, every shop, every store. In a city there must also be somebody at the head of the government. He is the mayor. Who is the mayor of this city? Where is his office? The mayor of the city is a very busy man. It is his duty to see that the city laws are obeyed, and to watch over all departments of the city government.

The mayor cannot himself do all this. He therefore has other men to help him.

The Board of Aldermen are the men who make the laws for the city. Is there a Common Council in the government of this city? What are the duties of the School Board? Name other departments of the city government.

These men who make and carry out the laws of the city are city officials, and are chosen by the people. The people should choose only honest and unselfish men for these offices. . . .

Citizenship

Are you a citizen of the United States? The United States takes care of all its citizens and gives them many rights. A citizen has the right to life, liberty, and happiness. He has the right to buy and sell, to have a home, and to help in making the government under which he lives a good government.

These rights of citizenship must be paid for by the men who enjoy them. A true citizen pays for his rights by obeying the laws, paying his taxes, and taking his part in protecting the government of the United States.

The law tells you what is best for you and for everybody else. You must obey the law, and you should help others to keep the law. A citizen obeys the laws because they are made by the people, for the good of all the people. A law-breaker not only hurts himself but others also. That is why the government must have courts of justice and jails. The only way to make good laws is by choosing the right men to make the laws. . . .

The American Flag

The American flag means liberty and justice for everybody. It is honored by all citizens on the land and on the sea. For it the soldiers of our army and the sailors of our navy are willing to fight and even to die.

The colors of the flag tell the story of the nation's freedom.   Red is for bravery, white is for purity, and blue is for justice.

The stripes tell the number of the original states of the United States, and the stars tell the number of states now in the Union.   How many stars has the flag now?

All Americans love the Stars and Stripes.   Let us all respect the flag and be true to it.

Copy:—*America is another word for opportunity.* . . .

7.3   A Principal's View of an Immigrant School in New York.

Now came my appointment as principal.   I stretched my arms and said, "Free at last, my own master!   I am limited only by my own vision."

I entered the new school, "My school," as I proudly called it.   There it was, a big, massive structure towering like a fortress above the elevated lines, fronting a large public park, the airy rooms full of sunshine.

It did not look out into the back-yards of tenements.   No smell of leaking gas stoves came in through the open windows.   In other days, if I gazed out of a school window I looked into the homes of the neighbours —squalid, noisy homes they were.   Whenever there was a quarrel, the loud shrieks and the bad language broke in upon the classroom recitation, and made the children blush and break into nervous laughter.   They were ashamed of their parents and their neighbourhood.

This new school of mine seemed altogether different.   I looked out of my office window at the trees on the hill beyond and watched them sway in the wind, like the restless backs of many elephants.   I saw the open spaces, the sunlight, the park, and I rejoiced.   These, I knew, were the teacher's best friends.

The day after my installation I went to my office ready to begin on "my school" and carry it up to the heights of power and efficiency.   "My school" should come into its own.   I do not remember now whether I intended to accomplish this in a day or a month, or a year, for as I sat thinking about it the half-past eight gong rang sharply, insistently.   It brought me up-standing in the office door.   I heard bell after bell beginning in the first room and follow in order from floor to floor, shrill out its call, cease, pass on its message to its neighbour in the next classroom to pass it along to the next, like a chain of energy linking up the classrooms for the day's work.   I had never heard anything quite like that before.

Angelo Patri, *A Schoolmaster of the Great City* (New York: Macmillan, 1921), pp. 24–32.

Then came the measured rhythm of many feet. From six entrances the children surged through the halls and into their classrooms. I had a blurred impression of sound, and colour and motion and many, many children and teachers all going swiftly by. I saw no individual faces, no distinct forms, just the great mass surging past. Stunned and bewildered I stood where I was until I realised that a great silence had settled over the building. The big school had begun its day's work and begun it without me.

I sat down at my desk because I didn't know what else to do. The clerk came in with the mail. The former principal who was still in the building with the fifteen hundred children he was to take to the new school came in to arrange some details of administration. With him I went over the number of classes in the school, the teachers who were to go and stay, the district lines and the number of children to be transferred in and out. This done he walked out of the office.

I was about to gather myself together and take hold of "my school," and then the gong rang again. I heard doors roll, bells trill, sharp commands, rhythmic footsteps, and the great surge of sound and colour and motion passed me again, children going in, children going out. They moved in classes, eyes front, hats off. A mass of children coming in to take the places of the mass that was going out. There was no time lost, just a tramp, tramp, a roll of a door, as it opened, a click as it shut and then silence as before.

The next day was the same—and the next! I had not taken hold. I left the office and walked through the school, corridors, classrooms and playgrounds listening and watching, trying to get an idea here and there.

I passed the open door of a classroom and saw a teacher smiling down at a little boy and all the other little boys smiling sympathetically at both. I was glad and walked towards the teacher. Instantly the smile disappeared, her body grew tense, the little boy sat down and all the other little boys sat up stiff and straight and put their hands behind them.

I tried to say something pleasant but I saw they were afraid of me and I went away.

I went into another room and the teacher was intent upon a little book, she was marking, and at the same time telling a boy that she hoped he'd learn something about grammar before he died, but she doubted it.

Without lifting her eyes and so missing seeing me, she said, "Walter, analyse, 'Come here.' "

A boy whose thoughts were a long way off jumped up and said—"Simple declarative, Come is the subject—here is the predicate verb," and sat down.

The class laughed heartily and the teacher said as she marked his failure, "Fine—But you forgot something— Come is the subject, here is the predicate, the period is the object."

Everyone laughed. Walter shook himself and analysed the sentence correctly. Then they realised my presence and froze over. The teacher apologised for not having noticed my entrance saying she thought it was one of the boys and asking me to be seated but I saw she was uncomfortable and I left.

A teacher brought me a disciplinary case. Before she could tell me the trouble she burst into tears. When I tried to tell her there was nothing to cry about she but cried the harder.

Was she afraid of the new principal? Why should she be afraid of him? Yet the scene was somewhat familiar. Oh, I remembered— "You are wasting your time. You are wasting the children's time. You are totally unfit for this work. If I had a son he should not be in your class."

Was that it?

This was bad. The teachers did not want me in the classrooms. They cried when they came to the office.

I'd make friends with the children. But I could not get at them. They were in classes in the rooms—in masses in the yards and corridors. Only the occasional bad one stood out as an individual with whom I could come in personal contact.

"My Dream School" was not so easy.

I thought a great deal about the situation. I know now that in those first days I interpreted the school through my finger tips and eyes and ears rather than through my intellect. I saw and heard the disorderly boy. I ached physically and mentally over the weak teacher, I saw every mistake she made, I heard every faulty intonation of her voice and felt a sense of personal injury. Why was she like that? Why couldn't she be big and fine? And the strong teacher! Why weren't they all like that? That was the way I wanted them. They must all measure up to the best. I rather felt than saw the peaks and hollows.

But in this restless, uncertain sea of motion, noise, colour and gongs; of constant going up-stairs and down-stairs, one learned to "go slow" and watch and wait for his opportunity.

In my discouragement I told an older principal about my efforts and failures.

"What do you mean?" he said in a puzzled fashion. "I don't understand you."

"I've tried to have the teachers and children feel that I'm their friend, that I'm eager to help them but I don't seem to be able to get them to speak or act freely in my presence. They are afraid of me!"

"Afraid of you? Of course they are and they ought to be. The teachers and children are all right. You'll find them well trained. Take my advice if you want any peace of mind and keep them under your thumb."

These were not the exact words that had disheartened me years before, but the idea was the same, and I remembered and understood. There was little danger of forgetting. I came upon this blind obedience repeatedly. Obedience, the loyal obedience that was school tradition.

"Let's try to have the children come to school fresh and clean," said I one day to a group of teachers. "Praise those who come in clean blouses and with well brushed hair."

Shortly after this a mother came in to see me. She laid a little package on my desk.

"Please, I bring you back this shirt."

Startled, I echoed, "Shirt? What shirt?"

"This shirt that the teacher gave my Jonas."

"Tell me about it," I said.

"The teacher said if they were good and sat up tall so that they got 'A' from the Lady Principal she would give them a blouse. Jonas told me and I told him he should try hard and get a blouse. So he did. He tried and tried and got one. But this blouse I don't like. Never I put a thin blouse on Jonas in February—only in April. I want you should take this back and give him a flannel one—a red one he likes."

Here she pulled the wrapping off a pretty little blue and white cotton blouse, and beamingly presented it to me.

Turning over her story in my mind I remembered she had said the "Lady Principal." I went in search of my assistant and handing her the blouse I said, "Do you know anything about that?"

"No, but maybe I would understand if you told me how you came by it."

I told her and she chuckled.

"Surely that's Miss North. You said to get the children to come in clean blouses so she talked to them daily and when I visited the room she showed me the boys I was to commend for neat appearance and encourage for their efforts to clean up."

"Let's go in and see the teacher," I suggested, still in the dark.

As we entered each little boy sat in the middle of his tiny bench, each held a primer carefully covered in brown paper with a red edged name-paster precisely fixed in the centre of the front cover; each wore a light coloured wash blouse—(I counted seven of the same sort as the one on my desk).

The sunshine came in through the windows and made little rainbows dance above the aquarium where the fishes looked as if they'd just been polished and put in their places.

"How fine you look," said the Lady Principal.

"Yes, we're all dressed for school. Do you think we can have A to-day?" asked the smiling teacher.

"I surely do. They're the cleanest boys in town."

"How do you manage about Jonas?" I asked.

"He came without his new blouse and I had an extra one, so I just slipped it over his other one so they'd all be alike. I'll take it off when he goes out and keep it for him."

The teacher had done her level best to carry out the principal's wishes. If the children would not wear clean blouses she would go out and buy them herself. If Jonas left his at home she would give him an extra one. At all events the principal must be obeyed and the class get an "A" rating.

"The teachers and children are all right. You'll find them well trained. They will do your bidding without question."

7.4 A Teacher's View of an Immigrant School in Boston.

I spent many years in the old Hancock School for girls on Parmenter Street. It was a shabby building with none of the architectural frills or happy conveniences of the modern school. Two ancient and feeble elms stood near it in those days and the sun bathed it from early morning to late afternoon. Inside was a traditional warmth and cheer. It was a famous school and was deluged with visitors from all walks of life. In the early years, there was a generous sprinkling of Jews, intelligent and pleasant people to teach. Soon, however, the Italians predominated and finally there were no Jews at all. The Italians, despite their Mussolinis and Caesars, are a modest people. The little folks are delightful, with an unusual courtesy. The adolescents, like those of any race, are of all sorts; heavy, dull, average: some lazy, some fairly intelligent, some extremely intelligent, a few of great talent, and a very few in the genius class. . . .

The odd thing about the first class is that while other classes may fade more or less from the memory, that first group given to the young green girl in a September of long ago, emerges strong and clear, with the distinction of a well cut cameo. I remember that first day of school, though it is more than forty years ago, better than I remember yesterday; I recall its events, its emotions, more vividly than this morning's. It was a pleasant time to be alive. The whole world though it may have been a smoldering volcano, was apparently at peace. There was positively not a

Marian A. Dogherty, *'Scusa Me Teacher* (Francestown, New Hampshire: Marshall Jones Company, 1943), pp. 14, 24–25, 34–39. Reprinted by permission of Miss Marian A. Dogherty.

thing to worry about except to acquit oneself with credit in a happily chosen profession. Of course the pay was small or so it seems today. But at that time it seemed to me ridiculously large: thirty-eight dollars a month was the handsome beginning, and one looked forward to an increase of four dollars each month after the first year. I wondered how I could spend it all! My happiness was complete and I felt such a feverish urge to start that I left home at half past seven though school began at nine and though it was a short half hour's ride. It was good to be in the open car, to breathe in the fresh September morning air, to ride through shaded quiet streets not yet awake, to see the gardens of petunias and asters, to feel the chill from the river as we went over the old bridge from Cambridge to Boston and finally to become a part of the turbulent city.

When I reached the master's office and told him it was hard to wait for the school term to begin, he shook with ill-suppressed laughter. That puzzled me. What was funny? Did he not feel that way, too?

Then he ushered me to the room that was to be mine. It had fifty-six desks besides extra movable ones, in case the class should be larger. School rooms were hospitable in those days. There was always room for one more. Fifty-six and sixty were average classes. There was a high platform where the teacher sat. This was her throne and helped to fix her above the rest of the world in the minds of the children. If they desired converse with her, they had to step *up;* when they returned to their own quarters, they must step *down.* Now, the platform is no more. As an institution, it is gone, and with it went a little of that reverence for the teacher, so wholesome for the child, so pleasant for her,—that reverence which like mercy is twice blessed, blessing him that gives as well as him that takes.

At quarter of nine on that first day, the children came eagerly in, stiffly starched, and shining from recent scrubbing. They were radiantly happy. It was the fourth grade and they had left forever the ignominy of a primary school. Report had it that they were to have "jographies" and "rithmetic" books. No longer would they be slightingly referred to as "in the third reader." Such insults were forever past. . . .

One day when the children were assembled in the hall, Cecilia recited Longfellow's "Children's Hour." The lines that run,

Do you think O blue eyed banditti, because you have scaled the wall,
Such an old moustache as I am is not a match for you all?

Cecilia spoke as follows:

Do you think, O blue eyed banditti, because yous have skated the wall,
Such an old moustache as I am is not a mash for yous all?

Funnier than Cecilia's mangling of the lines was the fact that no child in the audience suspected a joke, but applauded solemnly and generously. I am sure that the verse was as intelligible to them that way as any other. . . .

It was with that first class that I became aware that a teacher was subservient to a higher authority. I became increasingly aware of this subservience to an ever growing number of authorities with each succeeding year, until there is danger today of becoming aware of little else. A young teacher, however, eager to accomplish, forgets happily all the machinery of organization until it is forced upon her attention. It was unmistakably borne in upon me a few months after I had begun to teach. The genial principal came in one day to see how things were going with the new teacher. He took his seat on the platform beside me, thus temporarily sharing the throne, and announced that he would hear the little girls read.

The children were delighted to have any visitor, but especially a man, for the feminine influence preponderates in the public school. So, everything started pleasantly enough until one child, the first to read, failed to state the page on which the new chapter began. Our principal was a stickler for the proprieties, and the proper way to read in the public school in the year 1899 was to say, "Page 35, Chapter 4," and holding the book in the right hand, with the toes pointing at an angle of forty-five degrees, the head held straight and high, the eyes looking directly ahead, the pupil would lift up his voice and struggle in loud, unnatural tones. Now, I had attended to the position of the toes, the right arm, and the nose, but had failed to enforce the mentioning of page and chapter, for two reasons.

In the first place figures seemed to me a cold douche on the interest of a story and in the second place, I never could master Roman numerals myself and the chapters were always printed in those detestable x's and v's and l's. This grave omission at the very outset irritated the good man and he said in his most professional tone, "Perhaps, tomorrow, your teacher will tell you about Roman numerals." That was the first blow. I had failed to perform my duty and my superior officer had hinted as much with the additional suggestion that on the morrow I mend my ways. My heart sank. Would the children suspect? I watched them carefully. No, they were unconscious of everything excepting that they were having what in those days was termed a "perfectly bully" time.

Whenever the master would ask them a question, they would answer hastily, "Yes, ma'am."

"Say 'yes, *sir*' when you are talking to a gentleman," he said very sternly, and they replied cheerfully, "Yes, ma'am." This annoyed him doubly. Not only there was their lack of good taste, but what seemed like disobedience as well.

The word "spice" then occurring in the reading matter, the examiner propounded the question, "What is spice, who can tell me that?" Hands were raised everywhere. Cheerfully would they give of their store, be it knowledge, or be it darkest ignorance. "Carrots" exclaimed one. "No, ma'am, it ain't, it's bananas," said another. "No ma'am, teacher, spiders," ventured a third. When vegetables and fruits had failed, they tried bugs. Never had they seemed more pleased with themselves or with the world in general. An unnatural calm became apparent in the master's manner. "Put down your hands, children," he said quietly, "and tomorrow your teacher will tell you about spices." "Yes ma'am" they shouted joyously, as though he had made them a gift.

This was a signal for closing the visit. It had been painful to him and painful to me, but they had enjoyed it thoroughly. Mr. Dutton was a large man and he rose from the chair with all his natural dignity. Then, deciding to let bygones be bygones, he said kindly, "Good afternoon, little girls," and they spake as one voice, "Good afternoon, Mr. Dogherty."

The door closed with a bang!

As for me, only centuries of the civilization process kept me safe. Had I followed my primitive instincts—but it is no matter! Meanwhile, the wretches looked up pleasantly at me, as if wondering what entertainment came next on this diverting program. Determined that this sort of thing should never, never happen again, I made them say, "Good-night, Mr. Dutton" and "Good-morning, Dr. Dutton" over and over and over, until the walls reverberated with the name. Then I impersonated him, imitating his mode of approach, talking to them as he was wont, making it all as realistic as possible, letting them practice saying, "yes, sir," and "no, sir," and "thank you, sir." I finally dismissed them, long after the closing hour in the twilight of day and a midnight of interest. According to custom I said, "Good night, girls." In chastened but absent manner, they answered sleepily, "Good night, Mrs. Dutton."

7.5   A Report on "New Citizens for the Republic."

At the corner of Catherine and Henry Streets in New York is a large white building that overlooks and dominates its neighborhood. Placed in the middle of a region of tawdry flathouses and dirty streets, it stands out preeminent because of its solid cleanliness and unpretentiousness. It is the

A. R. Dugmore, "New Citizens for the Republic," *The World's Work*, April, 1903, pp. 3323–3326.

home of Public School No. 1.   In it are centered all the hopes of the miserably poor polyglot population of the surrounding district—for its pupils the scene of their greatest interest and endeavor, and for their parents an earnest of the freedom they have come far and worked hard to attain.

The child of American parentage is the exception in this school.   The pupils are of the different nationalities or races that have their separate quarters in the immediate neighborhood.   If they were to be divided according to their parental nationality, there would be twenty-five or more groups.   The majority of the pupils, however, are Swedes, Austrians, Greeks, Russians, English, Irish, Scotch, Welsh, Rumanians, Italians, Poles, Hungarians, Canadians, Armenians, Germans and Chinese.   The Germans, Russians and Polish predominate, for there are a very large number of Jewish pupils.

The most noticeable thing in the school is the perfectly friendly equality in which all these races mix; no prejudice is noticeable.   The different races are so scattered that there is no chance for organization and its attendant cliques and small school politics.   This is particularly interesting in the face of the fact that the one thing more than any other which binds the boys together is their intense common interest in party and city politics.   All political news is followed and every question is heatedly debated in and out of class.   This interest in politics and the training in argument and oratory it brings is probably due in large measure to the parents.   To them this opportunity for political discussion is an evidence of the freedom of the new country which has replaced the tyranny of the old.   The lack of organization and the lack of prejudice is shown by the fact that the "captain" or elected leader of a class composed with one exception of Jewish lads is the solitary exception—an Irish boy.   In another class the "captain" is Chinese.

The interest in politics is only one of the evidences of a great desire to "get along in the world."   Another is the fact that many of the boys are self-supporting.   The number of boys working their way through can only be guessed.   They are reluctant to tell anything about their home life or conditions.   It is known, however, that about one hundred and twenty of the six hundred odd boys in the grammar department are self-supporting.   A little Italian boy was late one morning and was asked for his excuse by the principal.   After much questioning he told his story: His mother was dead, and his father, who worked on the railways, and consequently was away from home most of the time, could send him only enough money to pay the rent of the two small rooms in which he and a smaller brother and sister lived.   To pay for their food and clothing he and his brother sold papers after school hours, making $4 a week.   The sister did the cooking and the housework.   This particular morning she had been ill and unable to leave her bed, and it had taken him so long to care for her and attend to her work that he had been late. This was told quietly and quite as a matter of course. The boy was fourteen years old. He had no idea that his story seemed extraordinary. He had never thought of trying to get help of any kind. This earnestness is carried into all the school work. The boys, because of the sacrifices their schooling brings, realize more keenly how valuable it is to them. . . .

It is a large task that schools of this kind are doing, taking the raw, low-class foreign boys of many nationalities and molding them into self-supporting, self-respecting citizens of the republic. The amount of this work done by the public schools in New York is indicated by the figures of the immigration bureau, for of the great body of foreigners who come into this country, more than two-thirds come through the port of New York, beyond which most of them rarely get. The results shown by the public schools seem little short of marvelous. There are many things in which, as a rule, the public consider that the public schools fail, but the one thing that cannot be denied—and it is the greatest—is that these boys and girls of foreign parentage catch readily the simple American ideas of independence and individual work and, with them, social progress.

7.6   A School Superintendent's Opinions on Americanization in Frontenac, Kansas.

The teacher gave a talk in school in one of the rooms where some children attended whose parents use liquor. He said: "How many of you ever saw any liquor?" Every hand went up. "How many ever tasted of liquor?" Most of the hands went up. "How many have ever seen a drunken man?" Every hand went up. "How many have ever seen a drunken woman?" A few hands went up.

One little boy said: "Lots of men come on the street cars and go to some houses and get liquor and carry it away in satchels." A little girl said that she had a jug that she took to the neighbors and they would give her some and she would take it home to her papa and mama, then when they would have some she would take the jug full back and give it to the neighbor.

Oh, the sincerity and simplicity of a child! How he opens his heart to his teacher and discloses all.

This was the opportunity of the teacher through these open hearted children to reach those parents. . . .

Loren Stiles Minckley, *Americanization through Education* (n.p., 1917), pp. 43, 63–64, 180–181, 185, 218–219, 228–230. Copyrighted 1917 by Loren Stiles Minckley.

How is the foreigner to be trained for citizenship? How are these men and women to become good citizens when they cannot speak or read except in their own language? How are they to know anything about this country and its laws? How are they to love it when it is strikes and contention most of the time, and they are out of employment one-third of the time and the other two-thirds receive a wage barely sufficient to keep the wolf from the door?

The Austrians, Germans and Italians each have their own hall where they assemble and have their social times in their own native tongue, so we see that they have no chance to learn patriotism in the social gatherings. Many of them never attend church so it is not here that they learn patriotism.

Where then are these foreign people to learn to love this great land of ours? Where and how are they to learn, "My country 'tis of thee, sweet land of liberty"?

This surely must be the task of the teacher of our public schools.

Shall we say the teacher must make good patriotic citizens, citizens who love the stars and stripes, citizens who will swear allegiance to the United States and especially against the land where father and mother have lived and died?

Must the teacher take a class of people who cannot understand one word of English and make them good loyal citizens? It must be done through the agency of our public schools.

We will endeavor to give a few steps by which this process is going on through the agency of the Frontenac Public Schools.

In the teaching of patriotism much emphasis is placed on history because of the foreign population. American history as a study is taken in the sixth, seventh, eighth, and first part of the ninth year. Together with the study of the text book, library books of a historic nature, including many of the biographies of our presidents are read by the pupils and the story related by them to the class. Much interest is awakened in this line of work.

During the final year some English, French, German, and Italian history is given in the way of supplementary work so that a better understanding of the American history may be had.

The pupils enjoy very much associating the events of their parents' native home with those of America and they become very much interested in history and are very patriotic.

Civics is taught in the seventh and eighth years. As much practical work as possible is given in the class. What they must do to become good citizens and vote. How foreigners are to become good citizens and just the steps that must be taken in getting out naturalization papers.

The local government of the city is taken up first. The mayor, council-men, justice and marshal with their various duties are discussed, then the government of county, state and nation.

Many of the boys and girls leave school in the seventh year. The boys, many of them, go to the mines and work to help support the family. Thus we see the importance of teaching these necessary subjects early in the course.

The children are led to discover for themselves through the study of history and civics the beauty of a free government and are taught all the way along from the primary through the twelve years that individual self-government is the fundamental principle.

This is done by placing them on their honor just as much as possible. They are never required to do things that are not reasonable. They are taught to know what is justice and never to submit to a thing that is wrong.

The principles of the foundation of our nation are thoroughly brought out.

The principles of government which caused our Pilgrim forefathers to leave their native land and seek a land where they are free to think and act as they choose so long as they infringe upon the rights of no other person are brought out. The terrible results and the stain that came upon the land when they chose to compel others to think as they thought is impressed upon the minds of the children.

They are taught individual self-government from the very start of American history. . . .

The greatest factor in teaching patriotism is personal liberty and indi-vidual self-government. All the way along through the school course this liberty and individual self-government must be taught.

The pupil must be taught to have decided opinions and not be afraid to assert them and to have fixed principles and to maintain them. They must be taught to respect the rights of others without yielding their own.

The entire school course should be liberty and personal rights. All fear must be removed to have true patriotic freedom. The very foundation of our government was personal freedom.

To teach patriotism in its broadest sense is to prepare the children for independent, self-governing, thinking citizens. . . .

Some may say that a boy is not worth much until he gets out away from his mother. That is a great mistake. If he can always be near his mother he will be a better man.

A certain young man was employed as principal of a high school. This high school was many miles from his home in another state. The boy had never been away from his parents for any great length of time.

He came to the school and began his work. Everything went well for about two weeks. He began to be sick. The superintendent told him that he must get better, for he did not know how he could get along without him. The principal said: "I believe that if I could see my mother I would be better. Do you know that this is the longest that I have ever been away from her? And she cried as hard as she could cry when I came away. I never saw her shed a tear before in my life. I can see her now just as she looked when she said good-bye."

The superintendent's mother had died when he was an infant and he knew nothing of a mother's love, but his feelings were touched and he said: "Send for your father and mother. You have a house ready for them as soon as they arrive and have them keep it for you." He did so at once. They arrived one day sooner than he expected. He found them at his boarding place when he went to dinner.

When he came back the first thing he said was:

"Whom do you think I found at the boarding house?"

It was not necessary for him to tell, for the superintendent knew.

This principal is now serving his third year in the same school and his mother has been keeping his house for him. He was only nineteen years old when he began his work as principal of the high school. His success is due in a great measure to the love shown to his mother. . . .

The next great problem is how are we to Americanize adults? Let us divide the adult foreigners into two classes. Those who have children in public schools and those who have no children in school.

We shall first consider those who have children in the schools. When these little tots of six summers first start to school many of their parents cannot speak English and the only English the children know has been learned on the street. As these children begin to learn the language they talk about it at home and their parents immediately become interested in their school work.

At this time the teacher must see to it that she makes the acquaintance of all the parents and gives them a cordial invitation to visit the school and see how the children are taught.

On one certain occasion invitations had been given to the parents to attend school from one o'clock P.M. to three-thirty and hear the children recite.

Each teacher had been particular to see that every pupil in her room had written an invitation. It is much better for the children to do the writing of the invitations, for the parent is more interested to see something that the child has done. And the pupil is very anxious to show papa and mama something that he has done himself.

At the appointed hour the parents began to make their appearance and at one-thirty every room was filled. There were about one hundred and fifty of the parents present, many of whom could not speak English, each anxious to hear his own boy and girl recite and to become acquainted with the teacher.

Many who had never met before came together and expressed their pleasure in various ways. A good feeling prevailed throughout the time and all went home feeling that it had been a very profitable half day.

These visiting days are held quite frequently and the parents of different nationalities are getting better acquainted with each other's ways; but the different nationalities do not mix only as it is done through the working of the public schools.

At these visiting day meetings the parents are invited to attend the night school and learn how to read English.

It is difficult to have a class composed of the different nationalities, for they do not care to mix. Great care and judgment has to be exercised on the part of the night school teacher, for they are quite sensitive and will do better if they can be taught in classes composed only of their own nationality. There is, however, an advantage gained socially in bringing the different nationalities together with the same object in view.

If they cannot read in their own language it is very hard work for them to learn to read English; but some of them do after they are quite advanced in years. If they never learn to read the effort made in trying is of much value.

If they cannot be persuaded to attend night school, visiting day meetings are of much value and especially so to the mothers, for they meet so many mothers whom they would not meet at any other gathering. Many have large families and their duties are such that it takes all of their time to care for the family and they do not attend any social functions as do our American women. The men are on the streets and mix far more than the women.

Another Americanizing agent is the public entertainments given by the school. It is surprising how everyone is interested in these gatherings. At least one child should be chosen from each family so that as many parents as possible will come out to the entertainment. The cantatas and drills should be carefully selected so that the patriotic spirit is felt. There should always be lessons of patriotism taught in all the entertainments.

7.7   J. R. Preston, Mississippi State Superintendent of Public Instruction, Discusses Patriotism.

Our republic was founded and is maintained upon the theory that the people through the representatives they choose, will make laws and manage the government for the highest good to the greatest number. Its best claim to superiority and its hope of perpetuity is that it is *for* the people.

Just now many thoughtful men who are true to its principles entertain grave doubts as to the accomplishment of its design. Here is a catalogue of conditions usually set up to justify their doubts: corrupt municipal administrations; public revenues inequitably collected through protective tariffs; a system of pensions costlier than a standing army, sapping the very manhood of its beneficiaries; an overflow of immigrants in the great North-west; three millions of paupers, living parasites on the body politic; eight millions of negroes producing political congestion in the Southern party politics in the hands of spoilsmen, who buy and sell the votes of freedmen; monopolies and vast combinations of capital sweeping the wealth into the coffers of the few; a brutal conflict between labor and capital; the tillers of the soil striking defiantly for relief from unjust discrimination against their interests; the poor glaring fiendishly at the rich because, through existing conditions, twenty-five thousand persons have been enabled to get possession of half the wealth of sixty-four millions.

Ours is a nation of busy people, each doing his level best to push his own enterprise to highest results. As a people they have never stopped to see which way the nation is drifting. When they had a war to fight they laid aside their daily pursuits and with mighty valor and businesslike activity fought it to a finish. They recognized a conflict which war alone could terminate, and in a terrible civil war they decided that a state could not secede and that slavery must go.

The grave political and social evils above mentioned, and many others resulting therefrom, are pressing to the front to-day for adjustment and correction. It must be conceded that they are of as vital import to the destiny of our nation and possibly more difficult to settle than the issues of the civil war.

The strongest cohesive forces of a nationality are common sympathies, identity of race and descent, the same language, the same religion, identity of political antecedents. Not one of these forces operates throughout our republic. Our congressmen, representing the wishes of their districts, strive for the interests of their sections with little care for the rest of the

National Education Association, *Journal of Proceedings and Addresses* (New York: National Education Association, 1891), pp. 102–105, 115.

country. One political policy does not suit the manufacturing East and the agricultural West. We have half the railways of the world to exchange our products for us and to facilitate the intermingling of our people. This is a strong mechanical bond, but it appeals to no higher motive than self-interest, and therefore cannot be relied upon to produce a true spirit of nationality. The press, except in rare cases, speaks only to the section in which it is printed. Sectional interests and prejudice once parted our nation in two; and there is danger ahead that this same spirit, if not counteracted, may sever us again. This time not the North and South; but the East, the West, the South, the Centre. We need the force of a dominant national patriotism to counterwork the perilous tendencies of this sectional spirit.

Sober, reflecting men—not alarmists, but true patriots—recognize these dangers, and are seeking to face them with candor and to lay the burden of averting them upon some efficient and responsible agency. Among these, I need hardly add, is not found the partisan politician. Felicity in dodging issues has marked his tribe since the days of Æschines. Many of the troubles above adverted to are directly traceable to the corrupt measures and methods instituted for party supremacy; and we may as well trust bacilli to cure us of yellow fever as to expect a politician to take a square stand against the wishes, interests, or prejudices of any considerable number of voters. Witness the contest last year, over the "little red schoolhouse."

With full confidence I assert that the public school is the agency we must rely upon. Its army of half a million teachers, sustained by popular devotion to the cause, must in times of peace and through peaceful measures fight this continuous battle for the perpetuity of national life. This army stands to-day holding the hands and hearts of to-morrow's nation. To make a citizenship whose intelligence, moral rectitude, and steadfast virtues will counteract these disintegrating forces and social disorders is the function and the mission of our public schools. Taxing property for education smacks of socialism, however much we may glorify it as an American idea. It won the sanction of common consent only because education, by producing counter currents, reacts on the worst tendencies of socialism.

Since true patriotism is to live for one's country, teaching patriotism resolves itself into making the best citizens. It is a step towards the evolution of a truer conception when the leading educational forces of a country are concentrated, as they are now, with practical unanimity, upon so vital a point.

The patriotism which can be developed by the schools is of two kinds: (1.) that which comes through exercise of the emotions; (2.) that which comes through a knowledge of the rights and duties of the citizen. Exercising patriotic emotions is but kindling the fire which is to fuse into a symmetrical whole and render stable the principles and convictions of rational patriotism.

As a foundation for teaching emotional patriotism we have the universal instinctive love of home, which draws its earliest breath from the caressing touch of a mother's hand, which is hallowed and strengthened by the sacred relations of the family, which throughout life is the anchor to upright conduct, nobility of character and good citizenship. The pertinent question is: How upon this basis can we best build up loyalty and love of country in the hearts and intellects of the millions who never enter college? Into the public schools they come from every kind of home—an incongruous collection, differing in capacity, hereditary proclivities, in passions, in tastes; similar in this, that they are integral units of the future state, that they bear a significant relation to each other, that they are susceptible to training. When they step over the door-sill of the public school they enter a sphere of equal rights and equal privileges, and out of these rights and privileges begin to germinate respect and love for the unseen agency which has provided such blessings.

The transition from love of home to love of country is easy, and should be made a fascinating and memorable experience. In his treatise on teaching patriotism, Col. Balch, of New York, has elaborated a plan for accomplishing this—by the use of flags and badges. With proper modifications to suit particular environments, this plan, if adopted and taught according to its spirit, would in a few years excite a patriotic enthusiasm glowing enough to win over the obdurate immigrant, and strong enough to uplift the children of all classes to that plane of recognized equality so dear to the human heart, so essential to the fibre of a true American citizen.

As a perpetual inspiration to patriotism every school should have a national and a state flag, and should teach their significance as symbols of law, justice, protection, liberty, government. Sentiments of reverence steadily develop as it dawns upon the mind of childhood, however vaguely, that through its flag the nation guarantees these inalienable rights. Moreover, child-mind needs something tangible, some emblem constantly in sight, around which it can cluster the virtues of citizenship and merge them into a feeling of patriotism. As form, color, size, are best taught by comparison of objects, noting agreements and differences, so may be instilled the clearest conception of all the qualities and duties of a true citizen.

When presented first as a mere object-lesson, the sensible properties of the flag will arouse curiosity and induce a strong desire to know its meaning. Here is the basis of its truly valuable use, viz: as an object-text, about which week after week can be grouped the most delightful and stimulating lessons of patriotic devotion. The occasions should be few or many as the character of the pupils demands. A rural school composed of the children of well-to-do, native-born farmers requires less instruction in patriotism than one in a colony of immigrants or in the pauper quarter of a city.

National holidays, memorial days, decoration days, and such other events as are pertinent and readily associated with the glory of our country should be freely used to give variety and vitality to lessons which may otherwise become monotonous and even dwarfing to the very sentiments they are intended to inspire. The willing spirits of children can be firmly biased by the exalted purposes formed by occasions like these.

One school day should be set apart every year as Patriot's Day. Planting trees and flowers to adorn school premises—an engaging practice now in vogue in most of the states—is undoubtedly a potent means of establishing attractive associations, and of endearing the school, and through it the state, to the hearts of future citizens. If this be a laudable practice, how much more worthy and significant to utilize a day to implant in their natures the seeds of genuine patriotism. Just as ground is prepared to nourish tree and flower so may hearts and intellects be quickened to cherish high resolve. . . .

7.8   A Critical Appraisal of the Education of the Adult Immigrant in Cleveland, Ohio, and in Passaic, New Jersey.

Cleveland

It appears that the educational officials of the Cleveland school system are highly satisfied with the quality of the work done in the evening elementary schools. In the printed report for 1914, and again in that for 1915, the city superintendent and the supervior of evening schools inform the public that "Our evening schools rank high as to quality and amount of work done, and are very much superior to nearly all of those in other cities in regularity of attendance and much lower in cost per capita."

It is impossible for the members of the Survey Staff to share the optimism of the superintendent and supervisor in this matter. During the course of the Survey 66 visits have been made by five members of the

Herbert Adolphus Miller, *The School and the Immigrant* (Cleveland: Survey Committee of the Cleveland Foundation, 1916), pp. 91–94.

United States Bureau of Education, *Bulletin No. 4* (Washington, D.C.: U.S. Printing Office, 1920), pp. 5–23.

Survey Staff to evening elementary classes. As a result the conclusion has been forced upon these observers that the work done in these classes is very far from ranking high in either quality or amount. While there are many enthusiastic teachers and hundreds of eagerly conscientious pupils, the classroom work exhibits an almost total lack of unified plan, matured method, and intelligent direction. The trouble is that the teaching methods have not been intelligently adapted to the needs and abilities of the pupils.

The typical characteristics of the work are well illustrated by that observed in five successive classrooms in one school visited in March, 1916. The pupils were almost entirely young foreign men of from 25 to 30 years of age. Many of them were employed in one of Cleveland's great steel manufacturing establishments. They were not illiterate, but they had almost no knowledge of English. They were all weary from their day's work and they kept awake only by the exercise of apparent effort.

In the first of the five classes a writing lesson was being conducted, and these husky laboring men were busily engaged in copying, "I am a yellow bird. I can sing. I can fly. I can sing to you."

In the second class the teacher was barely able to talk English and the work was almost entirely conducted by the translation method. The teacher made several fruitless attempts to get the pupils to speak English. He did this by telling them repeatedly, "Think the sentence in your own language and then try to translate it into English." After this had failed to produce satisfactory results, the teacher gave it up and had them read a selection about making pickles from cucumbers.

The third class was taught by a bright young foreigner who had apparently received a classical education. The work was conducted just as are many classes in Latin. The teacher spoke English almost perfectly, and although his pupils could neither speak nor understand it, he carefully explained to them about inflections, voices, moods, tenses, numbers, and persons. He then told them they that were to conjugate "to have" and "to be." After this was explained to them in their own language, the pupils all went to the board and began to write "I have, thou hast, he has." and "I am, thou art, he is," etc. The teacher explained that "art" was the second person singular, indicative mood, present tense, of the substantive verb "be." After this the class had a reading lesson from the third reader about a robin that said, "God loves the flowers and birds too much to send the cold to freeze them."

In the fourth room the pupils had a reading lesson about "Little drops of water, Little grains of sand." They then had a spelling lesson of the words in the reading selection. The teacher was interested, vivacious, and expended a great amount of nervous energy in talking very rapidly and almost incessantly. She took up most of the time with her own activity and most of the pupils could not understand what she was talking about.

In the fifth and last class the teacher was also most voluble and talked more than all the students combined. It was a reading lesson and the 14 men present were engaged in reading a selection beginning:

> Oh, baby, dear baby,
>   Whatever you do,
> You are king of the home
> And we all bend to you.

Similar examples might be multiplied from the written records of the work observed in the evening classes, and classes of the sort described may be seen by any one who will take the time to visit the evening schools of the city. Perhaps the most impressive characteristic of it all is that every teacher appears to be entirely free to teach whatever he pleases by any method that he wishes to use. The lessons assigned and the methods employed in the different rooms are astonishingly varied. There seems to be no effective supervision, no plan for improving the teachers in service, and no effort to find out which of the many methods used produces the best results.

Passaic

The Bureau of Education, in conducting the survey of adult education in Passaic, began with a survey of the general social and industrial conditions of the community, in order to determine the need for adult education. Obviously, since the public schools were created by the people for the use of all the people, it is necessary in making an estimate of any educational system to determine in the first place the needs and desires of the people. Important as this is in the matter of day-school education of children, it is doubly so in the study of adult education, for, while elementary-school education is compulsory, the attendance of adults at day or evening school is optional, and the very existence of the classes depends on the effectiveness of the schools in meeting the needs and desires of the people. Adult education is one of the few types of public education which has to meet the test of making good from day to day, or from night to night, with the people who come to the classes. . . .

In each of the interviews the people were asked if they would be more likely to come if they had teachers of their own nationality to teach them English. The response was immediate; their faces would light up as they replied, "Yes; that is different. Then we will not get discouraged in the beginning."

If these criticisms are carefully studied, it will be found that most of the fundamental reasons for the present failure in evening school instruction are touched upon in them. The criticisms are of three kinds—those that have to do with the method of instruction in the school; the attitude toward the foreign born, and conditions outside the school which make attendance difficult.

In the first place, investigation proved that it was true that the method of instruction did not sufficiently take into consideration the people who were being taught. . . .

With few exceptions there was no attempt at individual instruction. The pupils were taught as a class, instead of being divided into small groups and allowed to progress according to their ability. There was little use of the inductive method in determining the needs of each individual in the class and in developing his power of communication.

As it happens, the best teaching of English which was observed was in a class of workers taught by an organizer of one of the labor organizations. The enunciation was not always correct, but the spirit in the class was that of equals working out a problem together. There was the most thorough individual instruction, and an alertness on the part of the teacher in finding out the difficulties of each pupil and helping him to solve them. The men were working hard, even doing home work for each lesson, and there was an atmosphere of mutual helpfulness that was most inspiring.

But even if the instruction was of the best possible type, there is another reason for the present failure to secure large numbers in evening schools for which the school is not responsible in any way, and of which no amount of attraction on the part of the school can offset. We refer to the hours of work in the average industry and the prevalence of night work. Over and over again, as we have pointed out, when the workers were asked why they did not attend evening schools, the answer was a shrug and "How can I? I have night work," or "My wife works at night, I take care of the children." . . .

Growing Up Black:

The Education of the Negro

Shortly after the Civil War, General O. O. Howard visited a school for freedmen in South Carolina and asked the children what message he should take to their friends in the North. "Massa," said a little Negro boy, "tell 'em we is rising." Ex-slaves, young and old, men and women, flocked to study the alphabet and spelling book and Bible in old plantation sheds or at town streetcorners. The first generation of emancipated Negroes trusted that education would lead them to a promised land of opportunity, a hope soon shattered for a people disenfranchised, economically suppressed, socially barred by rigid rules of caste, and frequently subjected to humiliation or terror.

By contrast, first generation immigrants often feared the common school as a wedge between them and their children. But public education often led the second or third generation out of the ghetto into the mainstream of American life. Though often chauvinistic and intolerant in spirit, the common school did open opportunities to the children of the foreign born and helped to make one nation from many people. But with the Negro the tale was otherwise. The failure of Negro education is interwoven with the story of the larger failure of American society to make emancipation real.

Slavery was the "congenital defect" of the American republic. Slaves began their long journey in the dank jungles of Africa, wrenched from tribal folkways, chained to victims in front and in back, marched along trails where they saw skeletons of others who had fallen on the way. Perhaps a third of the victims died during the terrors of the Atlantic crossing. On small ships they were stacked like spoons, fed pulpy horsebeans, stifled and parched under the blasting sun, and seasick and cold in winter storms.

Systematically Africans were robbed of identity. Owners changed their names—a matter of great symbolic importance in many tribal cultures—and tried to eradicate their language and customs. When "broken in" and ready to be sold as plantation hands, they entered an institutional form of slavery which was harsher in its impact on personality and family structure than servitude in ancient times or in South America.

Slavery had not taken firm root in the English-speaking world prior to the importation of Negroes to the American colonies. Hence it lacked the legal and religious safeguards which cushioned its severities elsewhere. Alexis de Tocqueville observed that "the only means by which the ancients maintained slavery were fetters and death; the Americans of the South of the Union have discovered more intellectual securities for the duration of their power. They have employed their despotism and their violence against the human mind. In antiquity precautions were taken to prevent the slave from breaking his chains; at the present day measures are adopted to deprive him even of the desire for freedom." Once slavery had been regarded as a misfortune which could happen to anyone, but southern apologists argued that it was the only fit condition for an inferior and dependent race. In South America, Spanish and Portuguese legal and ecclesiastical tradition assured some checks on the power of masters: slaves had to be married in church; families could not be separated; and owners had to provide religious instruction.

But in the United States, as Stanley Elkins has pointed out, slavery was a closed system. Enjoying almost absolute power, the slaveowners took steps to fulfil their own prophecies: by trying to reduce the slave to a faceless and dependent child they created the shiftless, ignorant, amiable "Sambo" of the American stereotype. Marriage of slaves had no legal status; in many states it was against the law to teach a Negro to read; and a slave had no rights save those his master chose to give him. In short, the master owned the slave's mind as well as his labor. Legally the slave had no more identity than other forms of live property. Whether slaveowners treated slaves well or poorly—whether Negroes ate good food, had comfortable cabins, worked reasonable hours—is irrelevant to the issue Tocqueville raised: the institution of slavery was designed to liquidate independence and perpetuate dependence. Slaves sometimes openly rebelled; sometimes engaged in mild sabotage; but the role they were forced to play made deep inroads on their sense of identity and worth. "I've been a boy long enough," remarked a seventy-two year old man in Selma in 1964.

Slavery devastated family structure. The Negro father was not responsible for supporting his children nor could he protect his mate against miscegenation. At any time families might be broken up for sale. At auction slaves were described in terms normally reserved for brood mares and studs. The instability of the slave family and the childlike dependence enforced by masters proved exceedingly difficult to change after emancipation.

The experience of the emancipated slave, then, must be set against this dark background. Freedmen were puzzled as well as joyful; what did freedom mean? Certain changes had great symbolic value. Now they might move about, change their names, engage in politics, learn to read. The most available model of the free citizen was the white master, whose distinguishing characteristics seemed to be his aversion to manual labor, his classical education, and his political activism. "During the whole of the Reconstruction period," wrote the Negro leader Booker T. Washington, "two ideas were constantly agitating the minds of the coloured people, or, at least, the minds of a large part of the race. One of these was the craze for Greek and Latin learning, and the other was a desire to hold office. . . . There was a . . . feeling that a knowledge, however little, of the Greek and Latin languages would make one a very superior human being, something bordering almost on the supernatural."

Observers both friendly and hostile to the ex-slaves agreed that the emancipated Negroes passionately desired education. Sharing their hopes were a band of Yankee schoolteachers who came South from the old abolitionist strongholds to teach the Negro the meaning of freedom. Many of these teachers saw their work as the continuation of the war: "We might withdraw our swords, but we should send spelling books and Bibles to the front. The military might has been disbanded, but the missionaries should organize." They shared a sense of absolute righteousness, a belief that the South was the land of Satan, and Southerners sinners all—the whites, that is. "What a magnificent revenge Massachusetts has now . . . upon South Carolina," said one teacher. "Oh for an hour of the wizard's cunning, to evolve the spirit of Calhoun from the trance of death, and show him the thronging thousands of the people he despised as brutes, crowding around the school-house doors." One of the widely used readers was *The Freedmen's Book*, a selection edited by an abolitionist which included a speech by William Lloyd Garrison, a eulogy of the Haitian revolutionary Toussaint L'Ouverture, and other laudatory accounts of slave revolts. One excerpt declared that when southern whites want to sell goods to Negroes, "they will no longer call you Jack or Joe; they will begin to think that you are *Mr.* John Black and *Mr.* Joseph Brown."

The Southerners, their currency and banking ruined, their capital in slaves gone, their railroads destroyed, their wharves rotting, much of their land lying in swaths of devastation, their army defeated, had left "one inestimable privilege" which the Yankees couldn't take away: "to hate 'em. I git up at half-past four in the morning and sit up till twelve at night, to hate 'em." And hate them they did, making the life of the Yankee schoolteachers as miserable as possible. The teachers were of the martyr breed, willing to endure the slings of outraged Southerners, but many of them became discouraged because the Negroes did not live up to their exaggerated hopes. Still these missionaries did help to build anew the individuality of Negroes eroded by generations of slavery, and helped them to interpret and take advantage of their freedom.

Wilbur Cash, in his study of *The Mind of the South*, sketches the impact of the "Yankee schoolma'am" on the southern whites: "Generally horsefaced, bespectacled, and spare of frame, she was, of course, no proper intellectual, but . . . the South, with its vague standards in these matters, accepted her as such. It . . . read in the evils springing abundantly from her meddlesome stupidity categorical proof that Northern 'theory' was *in toto* altogether mad. And so she served as a distinct power in bringing Southern fear and hate to explicit focus in the purely ideological field—in setting up as definite a resistance to Yankee thought as to Yankee deeds."

After the first wave of northern interest in the ex-slave displayed by the Federal Freedmen's Bureau and various religious and charitable associations, a number of northern foundations continued to pour money into southern education. Following the precedent set by the Peabody Fund, northern philanthropists accepted the southern view that public education had to be segregated. Sometimes the agents of the foundations accepted without question the common view that Negro schools should be not only separate but also unequal; one agreed to pay less to teachers in Negro schools, explaining that "it did not cost so much to operate a Negro school as it did a white school." But in a time when the southern states were starving the Negro schools, the donations of the General Education Board, the Julius Rosenwald fund, and other large foundations raised the pitifully low level of preparation of teachers, paid for demonstration teachers and model schools, encouraged construction of decent schoolhouses by giving matching grants, and paid for agents who were educational circuit riders in the southern educational awakening.

During the nineteenth century and well into the twentieth, Negro education was primarily a branch of southern education, and subject to all the general handicaps of that region in addition to the special handicaps imposed by the racial caste system. Southern education generally trailed far behind the national average, reflecting the South's poor tax base, its thinly spread population, its high ratio of children to adults. Over 4,000,000 of the nation's 4,442,000 Negroes lived in the South in 1860; the proportion was about the same in 1890. Not until the large-scale northward migrations of the Negro in the twentieth century—especially as a result of the two world wars—did a substantial percentage of American Negroes come to live outside the South.

Public education in the South essentially began during the days of Reconstruction. Before the Civil War the common school took only meager root in a few southern states, but in the period from 1867 to 1877 state after state wrote extensive educational provisions into their constitutions. They voted generous support for schools, provided centralized supervision, and created schools for Negroes as well as whites. Two states — South Carolina and Louisiana—developed integrated school systems, but these lasted only a short while. Negro members of Reconstruction legislatures argued that integrated schools were their right under the Fourteenth Amendment and their guarantee that the schooling would in fact be equal. But in most southern states the public schools were segregated, even under Reconstruction legislatures.

Segregated schooling compounded the high cost of educating a rural population. When southern whites regained control of state affairs in 1877, conservatives cut back school expenditures sharply. By 1880, in comparison with 1871, the length of the school term dropped 20 per cent and outlays for schools fell 40 per cent. Opposition to Negro education grew virulent: why should whites pay for the education of Negroes, who paid few taxes, asked the retrenchers? Southern leaders devised a number of ways of disinheriting the Negro educationally, just as they displayed ingenuity in disenfranchising him. In 1874 the agent of the Peabody Fund told a group of South Carolina Negroes not to worry that separate schools would be unequal; but in 1932, after a long history of fiscal sabotage, one county in that state spent $8 on each Negro student in the public schools and $178 for each white.

Following the lead of the United States Congress in providing for Negro schools in the District of Columbia, some states allotted tax money to Negro schools only in proportion to receipts from Negro taxpayers. In the black belt counties of the deep South money from the public school funds was distributed on a per capita basis which included whites as well as Negroes, but in the apportionment of funds within the county the officials saw to it that the white schools received the lion's share. In one Mississippi county, to take an extreme example, each Negro child received $.18 to every $25 allotted to each white child (this in a county in which there were 974 white children and 4,016 Negro children enrolled). Poor whites from the "white" counties of Mississippi objected to the education of Negroes in general and the per capita distribution of the school fund in particular. Governor James Vardaman of Mississippi argued that any money spent on the education of Negroes was wasted and a "robbery of the white man. . . . You take it from the toiling white men and women, you rob the white child of the advantages it would afford him, and you spend it upon the negro in an effort to make of the negro what God Almighty never intended should be made, and which men cannot accomplish. . . ."

In the drive to economize on the education of Negroes, and to evade constitutional provisions concerning equal education of the races, states developed "certification" laws which enable them to pay Negro teachers half as much as white. Another way to save money was to have large classes: for example, the average class size in southern Negro schools in 1912–13, was sixty-seven. As Booker T. Washington lamented, standards for selecting teachers for Negro schools were abysmal; as late as 1930 more than one-third of the Negro teachers in fifteen southern states had not completed high school. The majority of school buildings were miserable shacks, the books and equipment ante-diluvian. In 1931 in the South as a whole the average figures spent on white students in the public schools were $45.63 in comparison with $14.95 for Negro. And besides having poor teachers and squalid classrooms, the Negro child bore the yoke of inferiority which Richard Wright has described in his vivid account of his school days in *Black Boy*.

The Negro was the man farthest down. White supremacists were determined to keep him there. In many counties of the Georgia and Mississippi black belts not more than one Negro in one hundred owned the land he worked. In the South as a whole three-fourths of Negro farmers were sharecroppers or tenants. In a relatively good year for cotton prices —1881—*monthly* farm wages ran from $4 to $15. Increasingly Negroes were barred from the crafts and trades they had learned as slaves and were relegated to the hardest and dirtiest work in cities and towns.

One would suppose that the "free labor" of the share cropper or road crew was the economic mudsill, but such was not the case: below even the poorest worker lay the horror of the convict labor gang. For trivial offenses or trumped-up charges a Negro might be sentenced to work for five years under the lash. Contractors turned convict labor into private profit in a system whose closest parallel is the Nazi or Soviet labor camp. Crowded beyond endurance at night in filthy rolling pens or log stockades, infested with vermin, bereft of medical care, whipped into working at a frenzied pace in mines and in turpentine camps, on roads and construction jobs, the convicts died at rates sometimes reaching 25 per cent annually.

Even after white Southerners had regained control of their governments, many conservatives believed that the disenfranchisement of the Negro was "a political impossibility under any circumstances short of revolution." As late as 1890 the Superintendent of Public Instruction in Mississippi declared that Southerners "have no fears of serious or general trouble growing out of the act of negro suffrage, if not interfered with by a low class of political agitators." But by the end of the century disenfranchisement of the Negro was in sight in almost all the South. Although the South had never welcomed the Negro as a voter—and had tried to exclude him by the persuasion of groups like the Ku Klux Klan and the Pale Faces—only when the Negro became a pawn in party struggles between whites did both Populists and Bourbons conclude that the Negro must lose the vote. In a series of state constitutional conventions Southerners passed regulations which struck at Negro suffrage: the poll tax, requiring voters to "understand" the constitution (as interpreted by discriminating registrars); and the "grandfather clause," exempting from property and literacy tests those citizens—and their sons and grandsons—who were entitled to vote on January 1, 1867 (a new version of the divine right of kings, complained one Negro). The provisions effectively excluded most Negroes. In 1897, 130,344 Negroes were registered in Louisiana; under the New Constitution only 5,320 were registered in 1900.

In the southern constitutional conventions delegates revealed a depth of hatred and fear toward the Negro which alarmed moderates. Ex-Governor Oates declared in the Alabama convention that "now, when the negro is doing no harm, why, people want to kill him and wipe him from the face of the earth." A Negrophobic fever swept the South and other parts of the nation. In the decade from 1889 to 1899 there was an average of 187 lynchings a year. Race riots raged through both northern and southern cities in the first decade of the twentieth century. In Springfield, Illinois, mobs seized control of the city, terrorizing and killing Negroes, crying "Lincoln freed you, we'll show you where you belong." The rankest form of anti-Negro literature—books like *The Clansman* and *The Negro a Beast*—found a ready audience. The older paternalistic stereotype was sometimes expressed—paeans to the happy "little fellow coming down the street . . . with a piece of watermelon in one hand and a set of cane quills from the swamp tied together with a string, in the other, blowing 'Boogoo Eyes' "—but distrust came to replace the intimacy which the old plantation system sometimes afforded. Moderates in the South bowed to the white supremacists; the North, having largely abandoned the Negro in the Compromise of 1877 which concluded Reconstruction, was embarked with the South on imperialistic adventures in the Spanish-American war, with its own jargon of Anglo-Saxon superiority. Thus racism had an open field.

One result was the legal codification of the social caste system, a movement partially underway when ratified by the United States Supreme Court in 1896 in the case of *Plessy v. Ferguson*. Homer Plessy, one-eighth Negro, protested that the Fourteenth Amendment forbad legislation of the state of Louisiana requiring racial segregation on railroad cars. The Court replied that the Amendment "in the nature of things . . . could not have been intended to abolish distinctions based on color . . . or a commingling of the two races upon terms unsatisfactory to either." Fortified by the Court's "separate but equal" doctrine, southern states passed a plethora of detailed caste laws.   In 1898 a South Carolina newspaper tried to stem the Jim Crow tide by ridicule: "If there must be Jim Crow cars on the railroads, there should be Jim Crow cars on the street railways.   Also on all passenger boats. . . .   If there are to be Jim Crow cars, moreover, there should be Jim Crow waiting saloons at all stations, and Jim Crow eating houses. . . .   There should be Jim Crow sections of the jury box, and a separate Jim Crow dock and witness stand in every court—and a Jim Crow Bible for colored witnesses to kiss."   The tragedy was that this *reductio ad absurdum*, with the exception of the witness stand, became cold fact.

During this nadir of Negro rights in the United States an ex-slave, Booker T. Washington, became the chief spokeman for his people. Thwarted on every hand, his early hopes to rise through education dashed, the southern Negro learned from Washington a gospel of industrial education, of patient endurance of wrong, of thrift and cleanliness.   In a famous speech to white Southerners in 1895, later labeled "the Atlanta Compromise," Washington declared that "the agitation of questions of social equality is the extremist folly."   "In all things that are purely social we can be as separate as the five fingers," he said, "yet one as the hand in all things essential to mutual progress."   Negroes needed farms and wages, not opera tickets.

Washington believed that social equality was an impractical goal—however desirable it might be in the long run—and he was a pragmatist above all.   Recognizing that the Negro needed just about everything, he believed it wisest to start with the improvements least threatening to the dominant whites: the training of the hand and heart.   It is perhaps not coincidental that the white supremacist James Vardaman was also fond of talking about educating the Negro's hand and heart.   So permeated was Washington's school, Tuskeegee Institute, with the ethic of manual work that a faculty member was rebuked for carrying too many books under his arm —it might give wealthy visitors the wrong idea, he was told.   Actually, many of the trades taught at Tuskeegee were anachronistic in an industrial age.   Washington's emphasis on middle-class virtues made him a parent-surrogate and patron of the black bourgeoisie.   Without irony Washington could announce: "I have watched carefully the influence of the tooth-brush, and I am convinced that there are few single agencies of civilization that are more far-reaching."

As a moderate, Washington pleased neither the white supremacists nor the integrationists. An Alabamian foe of Washington's portrayed him as "a rattler with his mouth open and his fangs ready, a rattler who has control of nearly all the other snakes, especially of his color and of his pedigree." Some Negroes, like W. E. B. duBois, on the other hand, blamed him for accepting the caste system, for neglecting the Negro's intellect, and for being the puppet of the white power structure. Washington was neither rattler nor puppet, of course. But he was indeed a compromiser. In a reply to a man who claimed that education could not solve the race problem because Negroes were inherently inferior, Washington could actually commend his opponent's "sincere and kindly spirit." In the ugly racist climate of the turn of the century, in the midst of lynchings and rigid Jim Crowism, when white liberals had all but abandoned the Negro, Washington's compromising stance was perhaps the most rational and effective one. A self-made man if anyone was—for he went from a slave's cabin to a meal in the White House with President Theodore Roosevelt —he worshipped success and was a Philistine. But set in his time and place, he deserves to be recognized as a man of limited though beneficent vision and great energy and good will, neither lionized as in his day nor vilified as in recent years by those who see him as an Uncle Tom.

One answer which Washington might have given to the Mississippian who claimed that education could not solve the race problem was that the southern Negro, in the mass, had never really been educated. Denied political power, economically and socially suppressed, the Negro was entitled, said a candid educator, only to "have the crumbs that fall from the white man's table." What this policy meant in practice was explained by a Negro boy in Chicago who was six years behind his grade level. His teacher in the South had been the town iceman: "He didn't come to school until he was through totin' ice around. Then if anyone wanted ice they comed after him. He wasn't learning me anything so I quit."

From such schools as these came the Negroes who emigrated to the cities of the North in the great internal migrations of the twentieth century. To the promised land they went, to North Philadelphia, to South Chicago, to Harlem. Within the decade 1910–1920 the Negro population of Chicago doubled, reaching 109,000. The labor shortages of World War I brought similar growth elsewhere. In the northern cities Negroes escaped legalized Jim Crowism but entered a world in many ways as trying as the one they had left. Locked into ghettoes by residential segregation, they often paid exorbitant rents for hovels or single tenement rooms furnished with a light bulb, sink, and bed. In these crowded communities malnutrition, disease, crime, and vice abounded. Mutual fear and hatred of white and Negro did not stop at the Mason-Dixon line. In 1919 in city after city of the North and West racial violence broke out. On July 27, 1919, in Chicago a Negro swam offshore near a beach the whites had reserved for themselves, was stoned, and drowned, touching off a riot which lasted for thirteen days and resulted in 38 killed, 537 wounded, and over 1,000 people homeless.

In a study of *The Negro in Chicago*, probing the causes of the 1919 riot, the Commission on Race Relations found that the public school was one of the few places where white and Negro children could come to know one another. Despite some prejudice on the part of teachers and students, the school seemed to offer hope of bridging the chasm of racism. But as the influx of Negroes grew and northern attitudes hardened, contacts between the races in most schools declined, either through isolation by housing, by gerrymandering of school boundaries, or by state or local policy requiring segregation. A reporter studying race relations in the North in 1907 wrote that the white "people one ordinarily meets don't know anything about the Negro, don't discuss him, and don't care about him." The Negro seemed invisible and nameless.

Foreign immigrants in urban ghettoes often had a social cohesiveness and pride created by strong family, church and ethnic ties. They could see members of their group succeed in moving up the American economic and social ladder. Negroes, on the other hand, inherited from slavery a weak, matriarchical family structure which further disintegrated under the impact of urban life. They saw that economic opportunities in white America were restricted for Negroes. The white child saw all around him models for emulation, in his textbooks, in newspapers, in his everyday life. In a society which coveted success the Negro child bore the scar of knowing that even if he acquired skill and knowledge he might have to dig ditches and carry trays. A New York school principal said early in the century that "the saddest thing that faces me in my work is the small opportunity for a coloured boy or girl to find proper employment." He told of talking with a typical bright student asking for his working papers:

> 'Well, my boy, you want to work, do you? What are you going to do?' 'I'm going to be a door-boy, sir.' 'Well, you will get $2.50 or $3 a week, but after a while that will not be enough; what then?' After a moment's pause he will reply: 'I should like to be an office boy.' 'Well, what next?' A moment's silence, and 'I should try to get a position as bell-boy.' 'Well, then, what next?' A rather contemplative mood, and then, 'I should like to climb to the position of head bell-boy.' He has now arrived at the top; further than this he sees no hope. He must face the bald fact that he must enter business as a boy and wind up as a boy.

While economic opportunities improved as Negro communities developed their own business and professional class, and new jobs opened in the white world considerably during World War II, school segregation continued to belie the basic premises of the common school. As late as 1951 twenty-one states and the District of Columbia either compelled or permitted by law the separate education of the races. In that year, Linda Brown, an eight-year-old Negro girl in Topeka, Kansas, had to cross the railroad tracks and take a bus twenty-one blocks to a segregated school because she could not attend the white school five blocks away. Her father instituted a case which found its way to the Supreme Court and transformed American history.

In the years immediately preceding the 1954 *Brown* decision the Supreme Court had slowly whittled down the doctrine of "separate but equal" enshrined since 1896. In a series of cases involving graduate education the Court had denied that admitting Negroes to segregated law schools or giving them out-of-state scholarships granted them equal education. In the Brown case, however, the Court went well beyond these precedents by ruling that separate education was "inherently unequal." Employing psychological and sociological evidence on the effects of segregation and pointing to the crucial role of the school in modern society, the Court concluded that "segregation is a denial of the equal protection of the laws." In a subsequent opinion the following year the Court, recognizing the formidable difficulties in implementing the decision, left with the District Courts the duty of enforcing compliance "with all deliberate speed."

Though most communities of the border states and the District of Columbia readily obeyed the decision, the deep South resisted bitterly. Whether in open defiance—as at Little Rock, Arkansas, and the University of Mississippi—or through tactics of evasion and delay, the old Confederate States slowed integration to a snail's pace. But gradually through court orders and the denial of federal funds to discriminatory school systems the will of the highest court in the land and the federal government have begun to be felt.

In the 1960's national attention in the Negro revolution has also focused on the school systems of northern cities. In the 1961 case of *Taylor v. Board of Education of New Rochelle* the New York Federal Court of Appeals upheld a lower court decision that the New Rochelle School Board had unconstitutionally gerrymandered school district boundaries to perpetuate a segregated school. In other communities, in which no intent to segregate was apparent, schools in the North were often entirely Negro because of a residential segregation which isolated both the Negro neighborhood schools of the inner city and the white neighborhood schools of the periphery.

Unavoidably, much of the burden of bringing the Negro more fully into the mainstream of American society, of providing him with genuine equality of opportunity, has fallen on the public schools. In concert with other social agencies the schools are being asked to alleviate racial isolation and distrust created by residential segregation and mutual stereotypes and antipathies; to provide the basic intellectual and emotional background lacking in many disadvantaged children; and to give white and Negro children alike a sense of their intertwined history and destiny. Only as it makes progress in this arduous task can the *common* school fulfil its promise.

8.1   "Up from Slavery": The Story of Booker T. Washington.

Of my ancestry I know almost nothing. In the slave quarters, and even later, I heard whispered conversations among the coloured people of the tortures which the slaves, including, no doubt, my ancestors on my mother's side, suffered in the middle passage of the slave ship while being conveyed from Africa to America. I have been unsuccessful in securing any information that would throw any accurate light upon the history of my family beyond my mother. She, I remember, had a half-brother and a half-sister. In the days of slavery not very much attention was given to family history and family records—that is, black family records. My mother, I suppose, attracted the attention of a purchaser who was afterward my owner and hers. Her addition to the slave family attracted about as much attention as the purchase of a new horse or cow. Of my father I know even less than of my mother. I do not even know his name. I have heard reports to the effect that he was a white man who lived on one of the near-by plantations. Whoever he was, I never heard of his taking the least interest in me or providing in any way for my rearing. But I do not find especial fault with him. He was simply another unfortunate victim of the institution which the Nation unhappily had engrafted upon it at that time. . . .

After the coming of freedom there were two points upon which practically all the people on our place were agreed, and I find that this was generally true throughout the South: that they must change their names, and that they must leave the old plantation for at least a few days or weeks in order that they might really feel sure that they were free. . . .

In the midst of my struggles and longing for an education, a young coloured boy who had learned to read in the state of Ohio came to Malden. As soon as the coloured people found out that he could read, a newspaper

Booker T. Washington, *Up from Slavery* (Garden City, New York: Doubleday & Company, Inc., 1901), pp. 2–3, 23, 28–29, 51–53, 80–81.

was secured, and at the close of nearly every day's work this young man would be surrounded by a group of men and women who were anxious to hear him read the news contained in the papers. How I used to envy this man! He seemed to me to be the one young man in all the world who ought to be satisfied with his attainments.

About this time the question of having some kind of a school opened for the coloured children in the village began to be discussed by members of the race. As it would be the first school for Negro children that had ever been opened in that part of Virginia, it was, of course, to be a great event, and the discussion excited the widest interest. The most perplexing question was where to find a teacher. The young man from Ohio who had learned to read the papers was considered, but his age was against him. In the midst of the discussion about a teacher, another young coloured man from Ohio, who had been a soldier, in some way found his way into town. It was soon learned that he possessed considerable education, and he was engaged by the coloured people to teach their first school. As yet no free schools had been started for coloured people in that section, hence each family agreed to pay a certain amount per month, with the understanding that the teacher was to "board 'round"—that is, spend a day with each family. This was not bad for the teacher, for each family tried to provide the very best on the day the teacher was to be its guest. I recall that I looked forward with an anxious appetite to the "teacher's day" at our little cabin.

This experience of a whole race beginning to go to school for the first time, presents one of the most interesting studies that has ever occurred in connection with the development of any race. . . .

As soon as possible after reaching the grounds of the Hampton Institute, I presented myself before the head teacher for assignment to a class. Having been so long without proper food, a bath, and change of clothing, I did not, of course, make a very favourable impression upon her, and I could see at once that there were doubts in her mind about the wisdom of admitting me as a student. I felt that I could hardly blame her if she got the idea that I was a worthless loafer or tramp. For some time she did not refuse to admit me, neither did she decide in my favour, and I continued to linger about her, and to impress her in all the ways I could with my worthiness. In the meantime I saw her admitting other students, and that added greatly to my discomfort, for I felt, deep down in my heart, that I could do as well as they, if I could only get a chance to show what was in me.

After some hours had passed, the head teacher said to me: "The adjoining recitation-room needs sweeping. Take the broom and sweep it."

It occurred to me at once that here was my chance. Never did I receive an order with more delight. I knew that I could sweep, for Mrs. Ruffner had thoroughly taught me how to do that when I lived with her.

I swept the recitation-room three times. Then I got a dusting-cloth and I dusted it four times. All the woodwork around the walls, every bench, table, and desk, I went over four times with my dusting-cloth. Besides, every piece of furniture had been moved and every closet and corner in the room had been thoroughly cleaned. I had the feeling that in a large measure my future depended upon the impression I made upon the teacher in the cleaning of that room. When I was through, I reported to the head teacher. She was a "Yankee" woman who knew just where to look for dirt. She went into the room and inspected the floor and closets; then she took her handkerchief and rubbed it on the woodwork about the walls, and over the table and benches. When she was unable to find one bit of dirt on the floor, or a particle of dust on any of the furniture, she quietly remarked, "I guess you will do to enter this institution." . . .

The years from 1867 to 1878 I think may be called the period of Reconstruction. This included the time that I spent as a student at Hampton and as a teacher in West Virginia. During the whole of the Reconstruction period two ideas were constantly agitating the minds of the coloured people, or, at least, the minds of a large part of the race. One of these was the craze for Greek and Latin learning, and the other was a desire to hold office.

It could not have been expected that a people who had spent generations in slavery, and before that generations in the darkest heathenism, could at first form any proper conception of what an education meant. In every part of the South, during the Reconstruction period, schools, both day and night, were filled to overflowing with people of all ages and conditions, some being as far along in age as sixty and seventy years. The ambition to secure an education was most praiseworthy and encouraging. The idea, however, was too prevalent that, as soon as one secured a little education, in some unexplainable way he would be free from most of the hardships of the world, and, at any rate, could live without manual labour. There was a further feeling that a knowledge, however little, of the Greek and Latin languages would make one a very superior human being something bordering almost on the supernatural. I remember that the first coloured man whom I saw who knew something about foreign languages impressed me at that time as being a man of all others to be envied.

Naturally, most of our people who received some little education became teachers or preachers. While among these two classes there were many capable, earnest, godly men and women, still a large proportion took up teaching or preaching as an easy way to make a living. Many became teachers who could do little more than write their names. I remember there came into our neighbourhood one of this class, who was in search of a school to teach, and the question arose while he was there as to the shape of the earth and how he would teach the children concerning this subject. He explained his position in the matter by saying that he was prepared to teach that the earth was either flat or round, according to the preference of a majority of his patrons.

8.2   A Northerner Discusses Education in the Conquered South, 1865.

What can education do for the slaveholders? The great majority of those who formerly held slaves are now just what they were before and during the war; and I am extremely doubtful whether there are any means by which they can be made, as a class, good and loyal citizens. . . . Events seem to show that nearly all are at heart still opposed to free governments, and to the crowning excellencies of free governments—free men, free thought, free speech and free schools. If pardoned, and permitted to retain their property and the privileges of citizens, they will soon attempt to regain their lost power in the State and National Governments, and to revive the aristocratic forms of Southern society. If pardoned, but not permitted to retain their property, or the privileges of citizens, a few may quietly submit to what they will consider their hard condition; some will leave the country—the more the better—while others will remain, to trouble every community in which they live with their ill-concealed treason. They have been already sadly mis-educated, and they would scornfully reject all proffers of education at our hands. They are the thorns around which, and in spite of which, the wounds of the body politic must heal. We must treat them as Western farmers do the stumps in their clearings; work around them, and let them rot out. . . .

What can education do for the non-slaveholding whites of the South? . . . The great majority are deplorably ignorant—more ignorant, . . . than the slaves themselves. They were described by travelers in the South, before the war, not only as ignorant, but as idle and debased. Those who have seen much of the rebel armies or of the rebel prisoners during the war, can well believe that those accounts are not exaggerations. At Point Lookout, only about one out of twenty of the rebel prisoners could read and write; and these prisoners were equally intelligent with those confined elsewhere.

It was this ignorance that enabled the rebel leaders to create a prejudice in the minds of this class of persons against the North, and to induce them to enlist in their armies. . . . As long as they are ignorant, they will re-

Walter L. Fleming, ed., *Documentary History of Reconstruction* (Cleveland: Arthur H. Clark Company, 1907), II, pp. 172–173.

main the tools of political demagogues, and therefore be incapable of self-government. . . .

What can education do for the freedmen? . . . It still depends upon the North—upon us—whether the freedmen are to survive the "struggle for life" which they must now confront, or whether, like the native red men, they are to perish. . . . To set the slaves free will be a doubtful blessing to them, if we do no more. American society has little patience with the weak and the thriftless. . . .

8.3 New England Freedmen's Aid Society Reports on the Education of the Negro.

Their belief that reading and writing are to bring with them inestimable advantages, seems, in its universality and intensity, like a mysterious instinct. All who have been among them bear witness to this fact. As respects aptitude to learn, there is similar unanimity of testimony. It cannot be expected that a man or woman whose only school-training heretofore has been that of the plantation-school, or that children whose ancestors have been slaves for generations back, should show the same quickness that the children of New-England parents manifest. The negro adult or child, before he enters the Freedmen's school, has been at a very bad preparatory school. Slave-masters are not good schoolmasters: still,—due allowance made for parentage and training—it is not too much to say, that the aptitude at acquiring the elements of knowledge is, by the testimony of all our teachers, marvelous under the circumstances. They do not write as if they found calls for more patience than is demanded in our ordinary Northern schools. And it is a most significant fact, that the most enthusiastic are not the new teachers, but those who have been at their posts from the beginning. It may be of interest to some, to know that they do not find any difference, in respect to intellect, between those of pure blood and those of mixed blood.

Walter L. Fleming, ed., *Ibid.*, p. 174.

8.4 A Northern Teacher Corresponds with a Southern Editor.

Charlottesville, Va., Feb. 9, 1867.

Mr. J. C. Southall.

Not knowing any Southerners personally, I have always sent to the North for everything indispensable in the prosecution of my work here;

Walter L. Fleming, ed., *Ibid.*, pp. 183–184.

but having heard colored people speaking of you as a true friend to the cause of education among them, I take the liberty, on their behalf, of requesting you to make a donation to the Jefferson School, in the form of printed diplomas, stating that the graduate is qualified to commence teaching the rudiments of an English education, &c.

If you are sufficiently favorable to the work to aid it in this way, I will send you a manuscript to be printed. Six or eight copies will suffice. . . .

Yours respectfully,
ANNA GARDNER.

Chronicle Office, Charlottesville, Va.
Feb. 12, 1867.

MISS GARDNER, I take as deep an interest in the welfare of the negro race as any one. I am anxious to see them educated and elevated, and am prepared to give my aid to further those objects. The impression among the white residents of Charlottesville is, that your instruction of the colored people who attend your school contemplates something more than the communication of the ordinary knowledge implied to teaching them to read, write cypher, &c. The idea prevails that you instruct them in politics and sociology; that you come among us not merely as an ordinary school teacher, but as a political missionary; that you communicate to the colored people ideas of social equality with the whites. With your first object we sympathize; the second we regard as mischievous, and as only tending to disturb the good feeling between the two races.

If I am mistaken in supposing that you do not confine your teachings to the topics usually covered by school instruction, I will cheerfully furnish without charge the circulars you applied for.

Respectfully,
JAMES C. SOUTHALL.

MR. J. C. SOUTHALL, I teach *in school* and *out*, so far as my political influence extends, the fundamental principles of "politics" and "sociology," viz.:—

"Whatsoever ye would that men should do to you, do ye even so unto them."

Yours in behalf of truth and justice,
ANNA GARDNER.

8.5 A Frenchman Reports on Negro Education.

It was in Washington that the first schools for the children of freedmen were established. The schools are of all grades, and the general [Howard] is even constructing large, beautiful edifices for a college and a university. I was full of the memories of the most flourishing schools in the East, and I was well qualified to judge for myself of the differences in intellectual aptitudes of the two races. I must say that I have been unable to discover any. All the teachers . . . that I have consulted on that point are of the same opinion.

My opinion of the intellectual aptitudes of colored children is shared by men of good faith who have, like me, visited the schools of the South. An English traveler, Dr. Zincke, in an account of his travels in America, says: "I must confess my astonishment at the intellectual acuteness displayed by a class of colored pupils. They had acquired, in a short space of time, an amount of knowledge truly remarkable: never in any school in England, and I have visited many, have I found the pupils able to comprehend so readily the sense of their lessons, never have I heard pupils ask questions which showed a clearer comprehension of the subjects they were studying."

What I saw at Oberlin confirmed entirely the opinion I had formed. . . . This remarkable institution is educating a large number of colored students. I found fourteen young colored girls in the most advanced class, and they appeared in no way inferior to their white companions. In 1868 the degree of A.B. was conferred upon fifteen young men and ten young women. The principal of the institution, in an address to the students, stated that in literary taste and philological ability these colored pupils were unexcelled by any of their white fellow graduates. The opinion of the professors at Oberlin is that there is no difference in intelligence manifested by the two races. In a Greek class of twenty-seven pupils of both races, instructed by a young lady of twenty-five years, daughter of one of the professors of the college, a young colored girl translated with exactitude, a chapter of the first book of Thucydides. The negro race constitutes nearly a fifth part of the population of Oberlin, and one of the professors assured me that the most peaceable, well-behaved, and studious citizens of that place belonged to the colored race. They are associated with the whites in all business and social relations, and no animosity is exhibited by either. The white man there is no more disturbed at sitting beside a colored man in the municipal council or on the committee of education than in an omnibus or at a restaurant

Walter L. Fleming, ed., *Ibid.*, pp. 184–185.

table. This fair treatment of the blacks, however, is by no means universal; but every day weakens the repugnance which has hitherto constituted an insuperable barrier between the two races.

8.6   A White "Scalawag" and a Negro Debate Integrated Education in the South Carolina Constitutional Convention.

Southern White

The subject of education is, under the peculiar conditions of our State, probably the most important one we have had to consider in this body. . . . Our success as a party, and our success as a people, depends entirely upon our being able to educate the masses of the people. Of this, no one is more convinced than I am, and no one is more earnest in the desire than I am, to see every man, woman and child in our State educated without regard to the complexion of their skins. . . .

If we begin by educating the masses, we end by overcoming their prejudices. But if we begin by attempting to overcome the prejudices by force and educating them afterwards, I am convinced that the whole plan will result in a failure.

Now, what is likely to be the result of . . . opening the public schools to all? Simply that they would be attended only by the colored children. If the attempt is made to enforce a mixture in this way, I have no idea that fifty white children in the State would attend the public schools. The freedmen's [Bureau] schools are now . . . opened to all; and yet I believe not one white pupil in the State attends them. The result would be exactly the same with our public schools. This is the state of affairs that we should certainly desire to avoid. In the first place, the poor white children would be deprived of any chance of education. They would continue ignorant and degraded and prejudiced. The whites who have means could send their children to private schools, but the poor whites would be as heretofore, unable to do so. You would also have the strange condition of affairs of the whites paying probably nine-tenths of the expense of institutions, which . . . they would regard themselves as shut out from using. This would be a continual barrier in the way of peaceful and friendly relations existing between the two races all over the country. . . .

The report [is] fraught with danger to the peace and harmony of the State, and to the friendly relations between the two races. They attempt to force upon South Carolina measures even in advance of Massachusetts, though they know that we are in every respect, at least one hundred years

Walter L. Fleming, ed., *Ibid., pp.* 187–189.

behind that much favored State. They do not reflect that civilization is is a plant of slow growth; that we can only arrive at it gradually, and after long years of toil. . . .

Southern Negro

His first point is, that this provision [for mixed schools] runs counter to the prejudices of the people. To my mind, it is inconsistent that such an argument should come from a member of the Convention. . . . The whole measure of reconstruction is antagonistic to the wishes of the people of the State, and this section is a legitimate portion of that scheme. It secures to every man in this State full political and civil equality. . . .

The gentleman from Newberry said he was afraid we were taking a wrong course to remove these prejudices. The most natural method to effect this object would be to allow children, when five or six years of age, to mingle in schools together, and associate generally. Under such training, prejudice must eventually die out; but if we postpone it until they become men and women, prejudice will be so established that no mortal can obliterate it. This, I think, is a sufficient reply to the argument of the gentleman under this head.

8.7   An Educational Missionary Becomes Discouraged, 1875.

While . . . the children of freedmen are still zealous in acquiring knowledge, this desire, which was once full-orbed, is fast waning with the masses of those who have passed their childhood. There was a time during the war and shortly after, when groups of colored men in middle life, and even in life's decline, could have been seen gathered about field stumps on which pine knots were blazing, trying thus to acquire the rudiments of an education. The enthusiasm was then at fever-heat. But this sight is at present rarely, if ever, witnessed. Said one of the speakers at the last anniversary of Fiske University, Nashville: "At the close of the war the people rushed into the schools—old gray-headed men and almost helpless children. There was an impulse that carried everything before it. Our own institution numbered at one time (1866) twelve hundred students. Then it dropped down to less than three hundred." There are ample data upon which to establish on general grounds these deductions. We need, perhaps, refer to but a single instance, inasmuch as it is one that furnishes an illustration which is almost an exact parallel to the case before us. When the blacks of the British West Indies were emancipated they manifested a

Walter L. Fleming, ed., *Ibid.*, p. 207.

zeal for education only second to that shown by the freedmen of America; but to-day, especially in Jamaica, "the liberated slaves," says Colonel Baylor, "have relaxed into degrading sloth, if not also into barbarism." No one who has investigated this case questions but it might have been otherwise. The fatal mistakes were in diminishing their wages to such a pittance as required all their energies to eke out a mere subsistence; also, the withdrawal of all government aid by way of educational provisions; likewise the absence of personal encouragement to people so much needing it, and without which the emancipated will seldom, if ever, do otherwise than lapse gradually from their first ambitions and aims into idleness and indifference.

8.8   J. A. B. Lovett. School Administrator in Alabama, Discusses "The Education of the Negro in the South," 1890.

It is a matter to be deeply regretted that the great sections of the United States are so meagerly acquainted with each other socially, religiously, politically, and educationally. If the North and the South only knew each other better there would be a greater unanimity of feeling between them, and they would cherish that fraternal spirit which should hold them in one great national brotherhood. . . .

Feeling that this Department is the most important branch of the National Educational Association, and believing in its readiness to sympathize with, and its willingness to render all possible aid for the educational advancement of every race and section of the Union, I am here to present, for its thoughtful consideration, the subject of "Negro Education in the South."

In this presentation I have but one aim in view—the improvement of the negro's condition as a man and citizen, and the welfare of those who are directly confronted with the abstruse problem of negro civilization. It will be my steadfast purpose to deal with the facts, as I understand them, carefully avoiding the fulsome gush and patronizing sentimentality so frequently intermixed with discussions on this subject. I would prefer the condemnation of my countrymen for uttering the truth in this discussion, than to receive at their hands the sickly panegyrics which follow in the wake of a more sickly sentimentalism.

In the first place, the Southern people deserve the sympathy and aid of the people at the North concerning the education of the colored people. One of the prime hindrances to negro education at the South to-day, is a

National Education Association, *Journal of Proceedings and Addresses* (Topeka, Kansas: Kansas Publishing House, 1890), pp. 497–505.

want of confidence in Southern philanthropy and patriotism, and an absence of sympathy from those who know so little of the struggles experienced by a people upon whose shoulders has been placed the burden of
eight millions of enfranchised slaves.

Generally speaking, the fortunes, as well as the misfortunes of life, are
shared in common by the various sections of the country. The crops are
grown, the manufactories are operated, the nation's commerce is transported, health is enjoyed, schools and churches are fostered, all contributing to our national wealth, dignity, and prosperity. These are among the
fortunes that we have in common. On the other hand, no section can
claim entire exemption from the ravages of crime and the devastations of
unavoidable disasters. New England, the North, the South, and the West,
all have their epidemics, pestilence, floods, fires, forgeries, embezzlements,
drunkenness, robberies, suicides, murders, and a thousand other disturbing
elements. These are endured by our people in common.

But the South stands alone under the burden of a vast colored population whose rapidly increasing illiteracy bids defiance to her best efforts at
educating them to intelligent citizenship. This condition of things is without a parallel, possibly, in the history of nations. The enormous influx of
foreign immigration at the North would seem to approach the Southern
situation; but when we remember that the North is so well equipped with
public schools, the great Americanizing institutions of our country, the
seeming parallelism vanishes, and the South stands alone. . . .

I have intimated that the South is entitled to the sympathy of the Northern people on the question of negro education. But, before this sympathy
is likely to come in copious showers, the people of the North must largely
increase their confidence in the Southern white population on the race
question.

It will be admitted that there are about three types of Northern sentiment concerning the race question in the South:

1. There are those who have something of a vague idea of the whole
question, connecting the present condition of the negro with the highly
exaggerated stories of his *ante-bellum* sufferings as a slave.

2. There are those who, for political reasons, keep up an unjust and
hurtful agitation of the race question in the South: unjust, because such
agitations are generally not well founded; hurtful, because they tend to
stimulate race prejudices between the white and colored population, with
a proportionate detriment to negro civilization and prosperity.

3. Still there are others in the North who are very decided in their opinions concerning the various relationships of the races at the South. They
hold that there should be a reasonable public commingling of the decent,
well-behaved colored people with the same class of white people, thus ele-

vating and strengthening the blacks, and educating them to the level of modern civilization. Without the fear of successful contradiction, I here remark that there exists in the South to-day, and has existed for many years past, between the whites and blacks, substantially such a commingling. But this commingling is not of the character that comes under the head of social equality. The truth is, as intelligence increases among the colored people they are led to see, and they do generally recognize the fact, that there is a line drawn between them and the whites which no human agency can set aside. I prefer not to call this a "color line," for the color of the negro constitutes only a part of his distinctive race qualities. Give to the negro the fairest Caucasian skin, and still there would remain race distinctions. Those who are at all familiar with ethnological study, must confess, willingly or unwillingly, that there exist peculiarities between the races which reach far beneath the skin. Every intelligent negro knows this, and he knows, too, not only that these differences exist, but he understands that the peculiar, distinctive features of his own race naturally forbid close social relations with the whites.

Then let us be content to speak of the dividing-line, not as a "color line," but as a race line. This being true, it is worse than nonsense for any section of this great and free country to undertake, by agitation or otherwise, to modify what is known as the "social problem" of the race question. And permit me to say here that the constant agitation of this social-equality question has done much to retard the negro's educational and material progress. For it must be known to you that the best element of our Southern citizenship bears the burden of taxation for the support of negro education. Not only so, but those in the South who lend their moral influence to the institutions which are accomplishing much for negro civilization, represent the highest type of Southern patriotism. It can readily be seen, therefore, that when this question is uselessly agitated, and that in a manner which puts the negro on the offensive, the white man naturally falls upon the defensive, and so an unnecessary feeling of race prejudice is engendered. This always damages the cause of negro education.

The South, for the past twenty-five years, has certainly had her trials and tribulations. History furnishes no parallel to the dark ordeal through which she has passed. Emerging from the bloody conflict of the civil war, she lay limp and languid, bleeding from a thousand gaping wounds. Instead of being visited by angels of mercy, her fair breast was made the stamping-grounds for a set of thieving ghouls who had deluded the Government with their pretensions to loyalty. Though too feeble to speak in tones to be heard by the conquering power, in her heart of hearts she entertained a spirit of patriotism that towered high above the heads of her *post-bellum* plunderers. It was a ray of sunshine that penetrated the dense darkness, when the Government began to appreciate the situation, and when she relegated these tormentors to their legitimate social and moral level.

The light has continued to shine, and reason, coupled with a calm and deliberate judgment, is rapidly dispelling the deeply-rooted prejudices which have so long existed between the best elements of both the North and the South. These sections are better acquainted with each other, and this acquaintance is ripening into a fraternal sympathy and union that will finally demolish every vestige of sectional discord. The negro problem seems to be the only lingering discordant element between these sections, and it is a matter for congratulation that, although a satisfactory solution of the question is not clearly in sight, all true patriots of the whole country are giving their best thoughts to its proper adjustment.

I desire here to state that the people at the North are becoming better and more thoroughly informed concerning the question of negro civilization, and the peculiar environments of the Southern white people, in their efforts to educate him for good-citizenship. Ninety-nine out of every hundred of the intelligent Northern people, regardless of political faith and practice, who visit the South for any length of time, or who have made the South their home, testify with no uncertain emphasis on this question. Their usual expression is, "My eyes are opened—I am converted." It is unnecessary for me to state here that life is too short, and traveling expenses are too great for the entire Northern population to visit the South for the purpose of receiving an object lesson on this subject. However, were such a thing expedient, there would be no bounds to Southern hospitality in entertaining our friends from the North, for the consummation of an undertaking that would forever banish from the minds of all people those lingering prejudices and stinging criticisms which have operated so powerfully against the peace and happiness of our Southern population. Regarding the education of the negro, together with all the perplexing questions growing out of his citizenship in the South, I believe the Southern people would be willing, without the least hesitation, for a hundred thousand intelligent Northern voters, promiscuously gathered from various States, to come South and spend one year in experience and observation, and then settle the whole affair at the ballot-box. The only objection the Southern people, white and colored, would likely raise to such a procedure, would be in the fact that the verdict of these Northern voters would doubtless be to the negro's disfavor; for it cannot be denied that our best Southern people have a tender regard and kindly feeling toward the negro, and in return the colored man respects and honors his white friends.

But, I am asked here: What of the "race riots" in the South? My answer is given in one sentence: What are known as "race difficulties" in the South, are mostly confined to localities wherein a peculiar state of affairs exists; they are generally conceived in the minds of the lawless and ignorant of both races, carried into effect under the influence of bad whisky, and receive the condemnation of the intelligent, law-abiding citizens of both races.

When the intelligent Southern negro reads the highly-colored descriptions of the "race riots," as they find their way into Northern newspapers from the hands of unscrupulous correspondents, wherein the whole South is condemned and slandered on account of the dastardly deeds of a few miscreants, he casts his eyes heavenward, heaves a sigh, and gives utterance to the unique Americanism, "*Rodentes!*"

In the foregoing remarks I have presented this question as it is connected with Northern sentiments and views, with the hope of dispelling some erroneous ideas concerning the attitude of the South toward the colored people. The sentiments and purposes of our Southern white population, on the subject of negro education, will now be considered.

The following propositions may be relied upon by all who are interested in this discussion as reflecting the views of the intelligent, law-abiding citizens, of Anglo-Saxon blood, in the South:

1. This class of Southern citizens would not, under any circumstances, favor the reënslavement of the colored people. Six millions of slaves at an average of six hundred dollars each, aggregates the enormous sum of three billions six hundred millions of dollars. This was all swept away by the emancipation proclamation, and should the Government propose to return this great loss of property to the Southern people in the persons of the negro population, as slaves, there would be a unanimous Southern voice against the resumption of such a burden.

2. They entertain the kindliest feelings toward the colored population: and, with their counsel and aid, they are ever ready to assist them in the acquisition of property, and to deal fairly with him all along the line of his political, legal, and natural rights.

3. They have no fears of any serious or general trouble growing out of the fact of negro suffrage, if not interfered with by a low class of political agitators.

4. Were the question submitted to a vote, I feel quite sure that the representative Southern people would elect the negro to remain on his native heath, if he desired to do so.

With regard to the education of the negro, there is a variety of sentiment among our people. We have those among us who do not warmly favor the education of the masses of either race. This sentiment is shown in the fact that we suffer some opposition to popular education. A class similar to this may be found in all educating countries. We have also those who do not advocate negro education, because they have never become reconciled to negro citizenship. Their neutrality on the subject is about all the opposition that comes from this source; and, if their passiveness is an indication of doubt on the subject, it is plain that the negro gets the benefit of the doubt. But the most formidable opposition we have to negro education, is the positive declaration made by a large and respectable class of citizens that education is a decided detriment to the negro's best interest. It is claimed by these opponents that just as soon as the negro obtains a little learning, he is disposed to abandon manual labor, and seeks to engage in politics, preaching, or teaching. It is also claimed that the educated negro often becomes a firebrand among the more ignorant of his race, and uses his acquired talents in stirring up and perpetuating hatred and strife between the races.

Despite all these various phases of opposition to negro education in the South, their schools are generally well filled with enthusiastic learners, and they are making as fair a headway as their limited facilities will admit. And this very fact shows that the majority of the Southern white people are strongly favorable to negro civilization; for it must be known to those who are familiar with the statistics of Southern education, that our legislators make, substantially, the same provision for the education of the colored children as they do for the whites. Nor do we ever hear of our representatives being arraigned by their constituents for supporting measures which give equal advantages to our colored youth. When this is fairly considered, in connection with the fact that the negro population contributes a very diminutive per centum of the State appropriations for public education, it will be seen that the white people of the South richly deserve the gratitude of the negro, as well as the commendation of all who are interested in his cause.

Having reviewed the opinions of the white people, North and South, on this question, it is proper that something should be said from the negro's point of view.

For the past several years my official relations in the field of education have been of such a character as to enable me to learn something of the purposes and ambitions of the representative negroes of the South. From various conversations with the most intelligent persons of this race, I have gleaned the following facts:

They believe that the intelligent white people of the South are their best friends. They know they are at liberty to leave the South, but thy prefer to remain. They take but little stock in the exodus agitations.

They think the time for such a movement is not yet. When the Good Father shall arrange his program of final destiny for the negro, possibly there shall be a great emigration of the race to the land of their fathers. At present the burning bush, the presence of a Moses, the inviting Canaan, are not in sight. However, when this day shall come, if ever it shall, there will be no wicked Southern Pharaoh that will detain the colored man from a brighter inheritance; and there will be no infuriated Southern host to be swallowed up in the angry seas, in the wake of his departure. But there will be, should such an event ever occur, a mighty host of friends to the colored man in the South who would raise their prayers to Almighty God to protect and defend the negro, and make of his race a strong and mighty people.

The intelligent Southern negroes do not think that social equality with the whites is either practicable or desirable; not practicable, because it would be unnatural; not desirable, even on their part, because those who undertake to practice it with them inflict upon them a positive injury. In conversation with a highly-cultivated colored man, not long since, I asked him to give me his views on this subject. His answer was replete with wisdom, and full of good common-sense. He said: "The whites who put themselves on an equal social basis with us come to us in white skins, but their hearts are black—they always lower us in the moral scale."

The intelligent Southern negroes are also opposed to the co-education of the races. They generally have a natural parental feeling toward their children, and they would be unwilling to have their offspring to undergo the unavoidable embarrassments that would surely attend the presence of their children among those of the white race. The negroes in the South, as a rule, are eager to receive enlightenment on all subjects which tend to elevate their race; and, while the great mass of them still remain in gross ignorance for want of better educational facilities, very many of them have achieved phenomenal success in the acquisition of knowledge and culture. Wherever the means of education have been placed before them by conscientious, able and faithful teachers, the colored youth have always been improved thereby. And I am fully persuaded that, while a little learning has a tendency to turn the heads of some, the only philosophical, safe and just course to pursue is to educate the colored people. The citizenship of the negro has been settled by governmental action, and this is not likely to be reversed. He should therefore be given a fair and patient trial on the line of civilization. We should remember that it took the colored man several years to fully comprehend the nature of his freedom from slavery. For a number of years immediately succeeding his emancipation, many thought that their freedom meant entire exemption from all kinds of labor; but their natural wants soon taught them differently, and they returned to the abandoned cotton-fields to earn a liveli-hood. So in their education; many of them are slow to understand the grand end of civilization which the schools have in view. We must learn to labor and to wait. Those who have closely observed the slow but steady improvement of the negro, where good schools have been in their reach, freely confess that education is elevating them not only intellectu-ally, but morally and civilly.

8.9   A Georgia Professor Asks "Will Education Solve the Race Problem?"

The race problem is again occupying a large place in the public attention. The renewed focusing of interest on it arises from two causes—first, the conditions in the South growing out of the rape and lynching evils; sec-ond, the disquisitions of Professor Booker T. Washington and other thinkers on the problem, maintaining that education will solve it. The educational argument opens an interesting field for thought and investiga-tion. Let us consider it briefly under the following heads:

I. Will education solve the race problem? That is, will it bring about such an advance on the part of the negro as will adapt him fully to his environments and make him a worthy integer in our national life, if he is allowed fully to enter that life, by the breaking down of the race preju-dice and antipathy against him?

II. If education will not accomplish the desired advance, what are the causes which prevent such a result?

There are reasons for fearing that the hope for the solution of the race problem through education is based upon inadequate grounds. One of the most vital factors in the problem is the negro's tendency to immorality and crime. This tendency in the colored race is of fundamental impor-tance in any consideration of the problem, because, if it continues, it means, instead of the hoped-for growth, permanent decay and degeneracy in every particular. No race can make a true advance which has not be-neath its feet the firm foundation of the moral idea. The tendency is of fundamental importance, further, because, if it continues to develop, the gulf between the races will grow ever wider and the friction ever more intense, thereby rendering the proposed solution more difficult.

How is the tendency being affected by education?

It is necessary to use the *ante-bellum* conditions as an aid in tracing ten-dencies among the colored race. Two things are reasonably certain about

John Roach Straton, "Will Education Solve the Race Problem?" *North American Review*, CLXX (June 1900), pp. 785–791.

those conditions. The first is that, previous to the war, the negro was not educated. In most of the Southern States there were laws prohibiting education among the slaves. Such occurrences as the Nat Turner rebellion, in 1831, tended to the rigid enforcement of the laws, and it is safe to say that practically the entire negro race was illiterate. The second is that, previous to the war, the negro was not more criminal than other men. The slaves were noted for their docile and peaceable natures. Petty misdemeanors were usually their worst offenses. There were surprisingly few crimes against the person among them. So far as the writer can ascertain, there was only one case of the negro's crime against womanhood during all the days of slavery, while his fidelity and simple discharge of duty during the Civil War, when the whites were away fighting against his liberty, have challenged the admiration of the world.

Starting with these conditions, the changes which have come about may be traced. After the war, the education of the negro began and advanced rapidly; but side by side with it has gone his increase in crime and immorality in even greater ratio. Measured by the proportion of negro criminals to the entire negro population, the race grew more criminal between 1870 and 1880 by as much as twenty-five per cent.; this despite the fact that illiteracy decreased by over ten per cent. During the decade from 1880 to 1890, the negroes grew more criminal by thirty-three and a third per cent.; yet illiteracy decreased during that decade by over eighteen per cent. So by the census of 1890, twenty-five years from their emancipation in the South, we are confronted with the fact that the race, though constituting less than twelve per cent. of the population of this country, furnished thirty per cent. of all the crime of the country, including thirty-seven per cent. of all homicides, fifty-seven per cent. of all female homicides, and forty per cent. of all assaults. This in the face of the fact that over $100,000,000 had been spent on their education in twenty-five years, and that illiteracy among them had decreased by forty-two per cent. Though there are as yet no census reports covering the period, any one who has been observant of criminal records in recent years must conclude that the increase in the proportion of negro criminals has gone on from 1890 to the present time. Especially has this been true of the negro's horrible crime against female virtue. When Henry Smith was burned at Paris, Texas, in 1893, for mutilating and murdering a little white girl of four years old, it was predicted by Bishop Haygood, of Georgia, and other observers, that the restraining influence of that terrible example, coupled with the efforts of the good negroes to prevent them, would stop these shocking crimes. Since then, however, despite all that has been done, they have increased with alarming rapidity, until, during the few weeks following the Sam Hose burning in Georgia recently, it is not extreme to say that there were more outrages and attempts at outrage than in the two preceding years combined. The papers were laden almost daily with accounts of one, two, and sometimes three of these crimes, within or near the borders of Georgia, followed by the swift and awful vengeance of the whites; and some are committed, followed by the usual punishment, news of which never reaches the papers. . . .

The negro's growth in sexual immorality goes on like his growth in crime. The report of the health office of the District of Columbia shows that, while the percentage of illegitimate to the total number of births decreased among the whites during the decade, 1884 to 1894, from 3.60 per cent. to 2.56 per cent. (28.8 per cent. decrease), it increased among the negroes from 19.02 per cent. to 26.46 per cent. (39 per cent. increase), and stood in 1894 at over ten times that of the whites. Like conditions prevail in other localities. And even these figures, it is thought, do not adequately indicate the extent of the sexual sin of the negro, for it is the common belief among the whites, especially in the South, that the idea of chastity is scarcely known to the vast lower strata of the race. . . .

Going a step further in the investigation, we will find, not only that the negro is more criminal in the North than in the South, but that, dividing the South into groups of States, he is most criminal in the States where he is best educated. . . .

The consideration in this article, however, is not how much blame is to be attached to the negro for these things, but what effect our remedies are having. Though the foregoing statistics, like all other statistics, are liable to the criticism of a lack of absolute finality as indicators of conditions and tendencies, still there must be some strong element of truth in them when they are so decisive; and, judging from them, the educational work for the negroes does not seem to be realizing the expectations based upon it. Education may not be the cause of these evils, as some go so far as to claim; but the facts seem to warrant the conclusion that it is not checking them and therefore is not solving the problem.

8.10 Booker T. Washington Replies That "Education Will Solve the Race Problem."

"Will Education Solve the Race Problem?" is the title of an interesting article in the June number of the *North American Review*, by Professor John Roach Straton, of Macon, Georgia. My own belief is that education will finally solve the race problem. In giving some reasons for this faith,

Booker T. Washington, "Education Will Solve the Race Problem: A Reply," *North American Review*, CLXXI (August 1900), pp. 221–229.

I wish to express my appreciation of the sincere and kindly spirit in which Professor Straton's article is written. I grant that much that he emphasizes as to present conditions is true. When we recall the past, these conditions could not be expected to be otherwise; but I see no reason for discouragement or loss of faith. When I speak of education as a solution for the race problem, I do not mean education in the narrow sense, but education which begins in the home and includes training in industry and in habits of thrift, as well as mental, moral and religious discipline, and the broader education which comes from contact with the public sentiment of the community in which one lives. Nor do I confine myself to the education of the negro. Many persons, in discussing the effect that education will have in working out the negro question, overlook the helpful influence that will ultimately come through the broader and more generous education of all the race elements of the South. As all classes of whites in the South become more generally educated in the broader sense, race prejudice will be tempered and they will assist in lifting up the black man.

In our desire to see a better condition of affairs, we are too often inclined to grow impatient because a whole race is not elevated in a short time, very much as a house is built. In all the history of mankind there have been few such radical, social and economic changes in the policy of a nation as have been effected within thirty-five years in this country, with respect to the change of four million and a half of slaves into four million and a half of freemen (now nearly ten million). When all the conditions of the past are considered, and compared with the present, I think the White South, the North and the Negro are to be congratulated on the fact that conditions are no worse, but are as encouraging as they are. The sudden change from slavery to freedom, from restraint to liberty, was a tremendous one; and the wonder is, not that the negro has not done better, but that he has done as well as he has. Every thoughtful student of the subject expected that the first two or three generations of freedom would lead to excesses and mistakes on the part of the negro, which would in many cases cause moral and physical degeneration, such as would seem to the superficial observer to indicate conditions that could not be overcome. It was to be anticipated that, in the first generation at least, the tendency would be, among a large number, to seek the shadow instead of the substance; to grasp after the mere signs of the highest civilization instead of the reality; to be led into the temptation of believing that they could secure, in a few years, that which it has taken other races thousands of years to obtain. Any one who has the daily opportunity of studying the negro at first hand cannot but gain the impression that there are indisputable evidences that the negro throughout the country is settling down to a hard, common sense view of life; that he is fast learning that a race, like

an individual, must pay for everything it gets—the price of beginning at
the bottom of the social scale and gradually working up by natural processes to the highest civilization.   The exaggerated impressions that the
first years of freedom naturally brought are giving way to an earnest,
practical view of life and its responsibilities.

Let us take a broad, generous survey of the negro race as it came into
the country, represented by twenty savages, in 1619, and trace its progress through slavery, through the Civil War period, and through freedom
to the present moment.   Who will be brave enough to say that the negro
race, as a whole, has not increased in numbers and grown stronger mentally, morally, religiously, industrially, and in the accumulation of property?   In a word, has not the negro, at every stage, shown a tendency to
grow into harmony with the best type of American civilization?

Professor Straton lays special stress upon the moral weakness of the
race.   Perhaps the worst feature of slavery was that it prevented the development of a family life, with all of its far-reaching significance.   Except
in rare cases, the uncertainties of domicile made family life, during two
hundred and fifty years of slavery, an impossibility.   There is no institution so conducive to right and high habits of physical and moral life as the
home.   No race starting in absolute poverty could be expected, in the
brief period of thirty-five years, to purchase homes and build up a family
life and influence that would have a very marked impression upon the life
of the masses.   The negro has not had time enough to collect the broken
and scattered members of his family.   For the sake of illustration, and to
employ a personal reference, I do not know who my own father was; I
have no idea who my grandmother was; I have or had uncles, aunts and
cousins, but I have no knowledge as to where most of them now are.   My
case will illustrate that of hundreds of thousands of black people in every
part of our country.   Perhaps those who direct attention to the negro's
moral weakness, and compare his moral progress with that of the whites,
do not consider the influence of the memories which cling about the old
family homestead upon the character and aspirations of individuals.   The
very fact that the white boy is conscious that, if he fails in life, he will disgrace the whole family record, extending back through many generations,
is of tremendous value in helping him to resist temptations.   On the other
hand, the fact that the individual has behind him and surrounding him
proud family history and connections serves as a stimulus to make him
overcome obstacles, when striving for success.   All this should be taken
into consideration, to say nothing of the physical, mental and moral training which individuals of the white race receive in their homes.   We must
not pass judgment upon the negro too soon.   It requires centuries for the
influence of home, school, church and public contact to permeate the

mass of millions of people, so that the upward tendency may be apparent to the casual observer. It is too soon to decide what effect general education will have upon the rank and file of the negro race, because the masses have not been educated.

Throughout the South, especially in the Gulf States, the great bulk of the black population lives in the country districts. In these districts the schools are rarely in session more than three months of the year. When this is considered, in connection with poor teachers, poor school-houses, and an almost entire lack of apparatus, it is obvious that we must wait longer before we can judge, even approximately, of the effect that general education will have upon the whole population. Most writers and speakers upon the subject of the negro's non-progressiveness base their arguments upon alleged facts and statistics of the life of negroes in the large cities. This is hardly fair. Before the Civil War the negro was not, to any considerable extent, a denizen of the large cities. Most of them lived on the plantations. The negro living in the cities has undergone two marked changes: (1.) the change from slavery to freedom; (2.) the change from country life to city life. At first the tendency of both these changes was, naturally, to unsettle, to intoxicate and to lead the negro to wrong ideas of life. The change from country life to city life, in the case of the white man, is about as marked as in the case of the negro. The average negro in the city, with all of its excitements and temptations, has not lived there more than half a generation. It is, therefore, too soon to reach a definite conclusion as to what the permanent effect of this life upon him will be. This, I think, explains the difference between the moral condition of the negro, to which Professor Straton refers, in the States where there has been little change in the old plantation life, as compared with that in the more northern of the Atlantic States, where the change from country to city life is more marked.

Judging from close observation, my belief is that, after the negro has overcome the false idea which city life emphasizes, two or three generations will bring about an earnestness and steadiness of purpose which do not now generally obtain. As the negro secures a home in the city, learns the lessons of industry and thrift and becomes a taxpayer, his moral life improves. The influence of home surroundings, of the school, the church and public sentiment will be more marked and have a more potent effect in causing him to withstand temptations. But, notwithstanding the shortness of the time which the negro has had in which to get schooled to his new life, any one who has visited the large cities of Europe will readily testify that the visible signs of immorality in those cities are far greater than among the colored people of America. Prostitution for gain is far more prevalent in the cities of Europe than among the colored people of our cities.

Professor Straton says that the negro has degenerated in morals since he became free; in other words, that his condition in this respect is not as hopeful as it was during the early period of slavery. I do not think it wise to place too much reliance upon such a view of the matter, because there are too few facts upon which to base a comparison. The bald statement that the negro was not given to crime during slavery proves little. Slavery represented an unnatural condition of life, in which certain physical checks were kept constantly upon the individual. To say that the negro was at his best, morally, during the period of slavery is about the same as to say that the two thousand prisoners in the State prison and the city penal institutions in the city of Boston are the most righteous two thousand people in Boston. . . .

In the matter of assault upon white women, the negro is placed in a peculiar attitude. While this vile crime is always to be condemned in the strongest language, and should be followed by the severest legal punishment, yet the custom of lynching a negro when he is accused of committing such a crime calls the attention of the whole country to it, in such a way as is not always true in the case of a white man, North or South. Any one who reads the daily papers carefully knows that such assaults are constantly charged against white men in the North and in the South; but, because the white man, in most cases, is punished by the regular machinery of the courts, attention is seldom attracted to his crime outside of the immediate neighborhood where the offense is committed. This, to say nothing of the cases where the victim of lynch law could prove his innocence, if he were given a hearing before a cool, level-headed set of jurors in open court, makes the apparent contrast unfavorable to the black man. It is hardly proper, in summing up the value of any race, to dwell almost continually upon its weaker element. As other men are judged, so should the negro be judged, by the best that the race can produce, rather than by the worst. Keep the searchlight constantly focused upon the criminal and worthless element of any people, and few among all the races and nations of the world can be accounted successful. More attention should be directed to individuals who have succeeded, and less to those who have failed. And negroes who have succeeded grandly can be found in every corner of the South.

I doubt that much reliance can safely be placed upon mere ability to read and write a little as a means of saving any race. Education should go further. One of the weaknesses in the negro's present condition grows out of failure, in the early years of his freedom, to teach him, in connection with thorough academic and religious branches, the dignity and beauty of labor, and to give him a working knowledge of the industries by which he must earn a subsistence. But the main question is: What is the present tendency of the race, where it has been given a fair opportunity, and where there has been thorough education of hand, head and heart? This question I answer from my own experience of nineteen years in the heart of the South, and from my daily contact with whites and blacks. In the first place, the social barrier prevents most white people from coming into real contact with the higher and better side of the negro's social life. The negro loafer, drunkard and gambler can be seen without social contact. The higher life cannot be seen without social contact. As I write these lines, I am in the home of a negro friend, where in the matter of cleanliness, sweetness, attractiveness, modern conveniences and other evidences of intelligence, morality and culture the home would compare favorably with that of any white family in the neighborhood; and yet, this negro home is unknown outside of the little town where it exists. . . .

As to the effect of industrial education in the solution of the race problem, we should not expect too much from it in a short time. To the late General S. C. Armstrong, of Hampton Institute, in Virginia, should be given the credit, mainly, for inaugurating this system of education. When the Hampton Institute began the systematic, industrial training of the negro, such training was unpopular among a large class of colored people. Later, when the same system was started by me at the Tuskegee Normal and Industrial Institute, in Alabama, it was still unpopular, especially in that part of the South. But the feeling against it has now almost completely disappeared in all parts of the country; so much so, that I do not consider the opposition of a few people here and there as of material consequence. Where there is one who opposes it there are thousands who indorse it. So far as the colored people are concerned, I consider that the battle for this principle has been fought and the victory won. What the colored people are anxious about is that, with industrial education, they shall have thorough mental and religious training; and in this they are right. For bringing about this change in the attitude of the colored people, much credit should be given to the John F. Slater Fund, under the wise guidance of such men as Mr. Morris K. Jesup and Dr. J. L. M. Curry, as well as to Dr. H. B. Frissell, of the Hampton Institute. That such institutions for industrial training as the Hampton Institute and the Tuskegee Institute are always crowded with the best class of negro students from nearly every State in the Union, and that every year they are compelled to refuse admission to hundreds of others, for lack of room and means, is sufficient evidence that the black race has come to appreciate the value of industrial education. The almost pathetic demand of the colored people for industrial education in every corner of the South is added evidence of the growing intelligence of the race. In saying what I do in regard to industrial education, I do not wish to be understood as meaning that the education of the negro should be confined to that kind alone, because we need men and women well educated in other directions; but, for the masses, industrial education is the supreme need.   I repeat that we must not expect too much from this training, in the redemption of a race, in the space of a few years.

There are few institutions in the South where industrial training is given upon a large and systematic scale, and the graduates from these institutions have not had time to make themselves felt to any very large extent upon the life of the rank and file of the people.   But what are the indications? As I write, I have before me a record of graduates, which is carefully compiled each year.   Of the hundreds who have been trained at the Tuskegee Institute, less than ten per cent. have failed, and less than five per cent. have failed because of any moral weakness.   These graduates, as well as hundreds of other students who could not remain to finish the course, are now at work in the school-room, in the field, in the shop, in the home, or as teachers of industry, or in some way they are making their education felt in the lifting up of the colored people.   Wherever these graduates go, they not only help their own race, but, in nearly every case, they win the respect and confidence of the white people.

8.11   The Chicago Commission on Race Relations Takes a Look at Racial Contacts in the Public Schools.

The public schools furnish one of the most important points of contact between the white and Negro races, because of the actual number of contacts in the daily school life of thousands of Negro and white children, and also because the reactions of young children should indicate whether or not there is instinctive race prejudice.

The Chicago Board of Education makes no distinction between Negro and white children.   There are no separate schools for Negroes.   None of the records of any teacher or principal shows which children are Negroes and which white.   The board does not know how many Negro children there are in any school or in the city at large, nor how many of the teachers are Negroes.   It was impossible to obtain from the board, for example, a list of the schools having a large Negro enrolment with which to begin the investigation.   An unfortunate but unavoidable incidental effect of the investigation was the focusing of attention of principals and teachers on the Negroes in their schools.

Chicago Commission on Race Relations, *The Negro in Chicago: A Study of Race Relations and a Race Riot* (Chicago: University of Chicago Press, 1922), pp. 238–241, 246–248.   Reprinted by permission of the University of Chicago Press.

Frequently white teachers in charge of classes with Negro pupils are race conscious and accept the conduct of white children as normal and pay disproportionate attention to the conduct of Negro children as exceptional and distinctive. As a result of the focusing of attention on Negro children, the inquiry, which was intended to get balanced information, developed a disproportionate amount of information concerning their conduct as compared with that of whites. Teachers who considered both races were inclined to believe that Negro children as a group had no special weaknesses that white children as a group did not also exhibit; that some Negro children, like any other children, were good, some were bad, and some indifferent, and that no generalizations about the race could be made from the characteristics or attitude of a few.

It became evident as soon as the investigation started that it was necessary to distinguish between the northern and the southern Negro. The southern Negro is conspicuous the moment one enters the elementary schools. Over-age or retarded children are found in all the lower grades, special classes, and ungraded rooms, and are noticeable all the way to the eighth grade, where seventeen- and nineteen-year-old children are sometimes found. In some schools these children are found in the regular classes; in others there are special rooms for retarded children, and as these groups are often composed almost entirely of Negro children, there is an appearance of segregation which made necessary a study of these retarded children from the South.

The southern child is hampered first of all by lack of educational opportunity in the South. He is usually retarded by two or more years when he enters the northern school because he has never been able to attend school regularly, due to the short term in southern rural schools, distance from school, and inadequacy of teaching force and school equipment. According to a report by the United States Bureau of Education on *Negro Education* 90 per cent of the Negro children between fifteen and twenty years of age attending school in the South are over-age. Says this report:

> The inadequacy of the elementary school system for colored children is indicated both by the comparisons of public appropriations and by the fact that the attendance in both public and private schools is only 58.1 per cent of the children six to fourteen years of age. The average length of the public school term is less than five months in practically all of the states. Most of the school buildings, especially those in the rural districts, are in wretched condition. There is little supervision and little effort to improve the schools or adapt their efforts to the needs of the community. The reports of the state departments of Georgia and Alabama indicate that 70 per cent of the colored teachers have third grade or temporary certificates, representing a preparation less than that usually given in the first eight elementary grades. Investigations made by supervisors of colored schools in

other states indicate that the percentage of poorly prepared colored teachers is almost as high in the other southern states. . . .

Another difficulty was suggested by the principal of a Chicago school
(Webster) where 30 per cent of the children are Negroes, who said:
"We base our educational ideas on certain backgrounds. The curriculum
in Chicago was planned for children who come from families who are
educated. It doesn't take children coming from uneducated families into
consideration. That isn't fair either to the white or colored children."

The problem of readjustment to life in a northern city also affects the
child's school life, and he is self-conscious and inclined to be either too
timid or too self-assertive. A Negro teacher in speaking of the difficulties
confronting the southern Negro, as well as the whole Negro group, said:

> The southern Negro has pushed the Chicago Negro out of his home, and
> the Chicago Negro in seeking a new home is opposed by the whites. What
> is to happen? The whites are prejudiced against the whole Negro group.
> The Chicago Negro is prejudiced against the southern Negro. Surely it
> makes a difficult situation for the southern Negro. No wonder he meets a
> word with a blow. And all this comes into the school more or less.

Another Negro teacher thus analyzes further the adjustment problems
which tend to make the Negro newly come from the South unpopular
with the Chicago Negro, as well as with the whites:

> These families from the South usually come from the country where
> there are no close neighbors. . . . Then the family is transplanted to Chi-
> cago to an apartment house, and even in with another family. The whole
> environment is changed and the trouble begins. No sense of property
> rights, no idea of how to use conveniences, no idea of how to live in the
> new home, to keep it up, to live with everybody else so near. On top of
> that, the father does not fit into his work, and therefore cannot support the
> family; the mother goes out to work, and what is the result? Poorly kept
> houses and poorly kept children. . . . A normal home shows itself in the
> school, and poor home conditions show up still more.

The Negro child born in the North is not found to an unusual extent
among the retarded children. He has been able to enter school on time
and to attend the full term of nine months; his teachers compare favorably
with those in white American and foreign neighborhoods, and his parents as a rule have a better background. Many teachers say that the progress of northern-born Negroes compares very favorably with that of
whites. . . . Most kindergarten teachers found the most natural relationship existing between the young Negro and white children. "Neither
colored nor whites have any feeling in our kindergarten," said one principal in a school 30 per cent Negro (Webster); "they don't understand the
difference between colored and white children." In visiting one school

the investigator noticed that the white children who objected to holding hands with the Negro children in the kindergarten and first and second grades were the better-dressed children who undoubtedly reflected the economic class and race consciousness of their parents. The Armour Mission near the school had excluded Negroes from its kindergarten, thereby fostering this spirit among the whites. A teacher in Doolittle (85 per cent) told of a little white girl in another school who cried because she was afraid the color from the Negro children's hands would rub off on hers; in her present school she has known no such instances in the kindergarten. This conduct is paralleled in instances in which Negro children who have never had any contact with white children in the South are afraid of them when they first come North.

Most of the teachers in the higher grades reported that there were no signs of race prejudice in the room. A teacher at Oakland (26 per cent) said that white girls sometimes asked to be moved to another seat when near a very dirty Negro child, but that this often happened when the dirty child was white. This teacher said it was the white mothers from the South, not the children, who wanted their children to be kept away from the Negroes. "The white children don't seem to mind the colored," she said. "I have had three or four mothers come in and ask that their children be kept away from the colored, but they were women from the South and felt race prejudice strongly. But they are the only ones who have complained."

A teacher in a school 90 per cent Negro said that when doubling up in the seats was necessary whites and Negroes frequently chose each other. A teacher at Moseley (70 per cent), when the investigator was present, called upon a white girl to act as hostess to a Negro girl who had just come from the South, and the request was met with pride and pleasure by the white girl. On the same occasion a white boy was asked to help a Negro boy with his arithmetic, and the two doubled up and worked together quite naturally.

"Race makes no difference," declared the principal of a school 92 per cent Negro (Colman). "The other day I had them all digging in the garden, and when they were all ready to go in I kept out one colored boy to help me plant seeds. We could use another boy, so I told Henry to choose anyone out of two rooms and he returned with an Italian. The color makes no difference."

A few instances of jealousy are cited. In one of them resentment ran high because when a loving cup was presented in McKinley (70 per cent) for the best composition, it was awarded by a neutral outside jury to a white girl. The principal of this 70 per cent Negro school, in addition to finding the Negro children jealous, considered their parents insolent and resentful.   On the investigator's first visit she said that military discipline was the only kind for children, and that absolute segregation was necessary.   At the next interview she said she preferred her school to any other; that there was never any disciplinary difficulty, and that white children who had moved from the district were paying car fare to finish their course at her school.

Discipline

There was considerable variety of opinion among the teachers as to whether Negro children presented any special problems of discipline. The principal of a school 20 per cent Negro (Felsenthal), for example, said that discipline was more difficult in this school than in the branch where 90 per cent were Negroes (Fuller).   This principal is an advocate of separate schools.   She was contradicted by a teacher in her school who said she had never used different discipline for the Negroes.   In schools where the principals were sympathetic and the interracial spirit good the teachers reported that Negro children were much like other children and could be disciplined in the same way.   One or two teachers reported that Negro children could not be scolded but must be "jollied along" and the work presented as play.   This is interesting in view of the frequent complaint of the children from the South that the teachers in Chicago played with them all the time and did not teach them anything.

Attitude toward Negro teachers

Few Negro teachers were found in the schools investigated.

At Doolittle (85 per cent) there were thirty-three teachers, of whom two were Negroes.   There was also a Negro cadet.   At Raymond (93 per cent) there were six Negro teachers and a Negro cadet in a staff of forty. At Keith (90 per cent) there were six Negro teachers in a staff of twelve. Two of these principals said that their Negro teachers compared favorably with their white teachers and that some of them were excellent.   Asked whether there was much antagonism if a Negro teacher was assigned where all the children were white, the principal of a 93 per cent school (Raymond) said there had been one or two such cases.   "They are most successful in the foreign districts on the West Side.   The European people do not seem to resent the presence of a colored teacher."

Another principal said that this was especially true where the foreign element was Jewish.   A Negro teacher in a West Side school, largely Italian, is considered one of the ablest teachers in the school and proved herself highly competent during the war, when she assisted with the work of the draft board in the district.

One or two principals said that they would not have Negro teachers in their schools because the white teachers "could not be intimate with colored teachers," or because Negro teachers were "cocky," or because "the *Defender* preaches propaganda for colored teachers to seek positions in white schools." Sometimes an effort was made to explain the principal's objection to Negro teachers by saying that Negro children had no respect for Negro teachers. One principal whose white teachers were rather below the accepted standard said that the one colored teacher who had been there was obliged to leave because of the children's protest against her. A Negro teacher in a 20 per cent school (Haven) was valued highly by the principal, who advised with her as to what measures could be taken to prevent the appearance of race feeling.

8.12   A New Law of the Land in School Desegregation: "Brown *et al.* v. Board of Education of Topeka *et al.*"

Argued December 9, 1952–Reargued December 8, 1953–Decided May 17, 1954

Mr. Chief Justice Warren delivered the opinion of the Court. These cases come to us from the States of Kansas, South Carolina, Virginia, and Delaware. They are premised on different facts and different local conditions, but a common legal question justifies their consideration together in this consolidated opinion.

In each of the cases, minors of the Negro race, through their legal representatives, seek the aid of the courts in obtaining admission to the public schools of their community on a nonsegregated basis. In each instance, they have been denied admission to schools attended by white children under laws requiring or permitting segregation according to race. This segregation was alleged to deprive the plaintiffs of the equal protection of the laws under the Fourteenth Amendment. In each of the cases other than the Delaware case, a three-judge federal district court denied relief to the plaintiffs on the so-called "separate but equal" doctrine announced by this Court in Plessy v. Ferguson, 163 U.S. 537, 16 S.Ct. 1138, 41 L.Ed. 256. Under that doctrine, equality of treatment is accorded when the races are provided substantially equal facilities, even though these facilities be separate. In the Delaware case, the Supreme Court of Delaware adhered to that doctrine, but ordered that the plaintiffs be admitted to the white schools because of their superiority to the Negro schools.

The plaintiffs contend that segregated public schools are not "equal"

347 U.S. 483 (1954): The U.S. Supreme Court's decision, written by Mr. Chief Justice Warren.

and cannot be made "equal," and that hence they are deprived of the equal protection of the laws. Because of the obvious importance of the question presented, the Court took jurisdiction. Argument was heard in the 1952 Term, and reargument was heard this Term on certain questions propounded by the Court.

Reargument was largely devoted to the circumstances surrounding the adoption of the Fourteenth Amendment in 1868. It covered exhaustively consideration of the Amendment in Congress, ratification by the states, then existing practices in racial segregation, and the views of proponents and opponents of the Amendment. This discussion and our own investigation convince us that, although these sources cast some light, it is not enough to resolve the problem with which we are faced. At best, they are inconclusive. The most avid proponents of the post-War Amendments undoubtedly intended them to remove all legal distinctions among "all persons born or naturalized in the United States." Their opponents, just as certainly, were antagonistic to both the letter and the spirit of the Amendments and wished them to have the most limited effect. What others in Congress and the state legislatures had in mind cannot be determined with any degree of certainty.

An additional reason for the inconclusive nature of the Amendment's history, with respect to segregated schools, is the status of public education at that time. In the South, the movement toward free common schools, supported by general taxation, had not yet taken hold. Education of white children was largely in the hands of private groups. Education of Negroes was almost nonexistent, and practically all of the race were illiterate. In fact, any education of Negroes was forbidden by law in some states. Today, in contrast, many Negroes have achieved outstanding success in the arts and sciences as well as in the business and professional world. It is true that public school education at the time of the Amendment had advanced further in the North, but the effect of the Amendment on Northern States was generally ignored in the congressional debates. Even in the North, the conditions of public education did not approximate those existing today. The curriculum was usually rudimentary; ungraded schools were common in rural areas; the school term was but three months a year in many states; and compulsory school attendance was virtually unknown. As a consequence, it is not surprising that there should be so little in the history of the Fourteenth Amendment relating to its intended effect on public education.

In the first cases in this Court construing the Fourteenth Amendment, decided shortly after its adoption, the Court interpreted it as proscribing all state-imposed discriminations against the Negro race. The doctrine of "separate but equal" did not make its appearance in this Court until 1896 in the case of Plessy v. Ferguson, supra, involving not education but transportation. American courts have since labored with the doctrine for over half a century. In this Court, there have been six cases involving the "separate but equal" doctrine in the field of public education. In Cumming v. Board of Education of Richmond County, 175 U.S. 528, 20 S.Ct. 197, 44 L.Ed. 262, and Gong Lum v. Rice, 275 U.S. 78, 48 S.Ct. 91, 72 L.Ed. 172, the validity of the doctrine itself was not challenged. In more recent cases, all on the graduate school level, inequality was found in that specific benefits enjoyed by white students were denied to Negro students of the same educational qualifications. State of Missouri ex rel. Gaines v. Canada, 305 U.S. 337, 59 S.Ct. 232, 83 L.Ed. 208; Sipuel v. Board of Regents of University of Oklahoma, 332 U.S. 631, 68 S.Ct. 299, 92 L.Ed. 247; Sweatt v. Painter, 339 U.S. 629, 70 S.Ct. 848, 94 L.Ed. 1114; McLaurin v. Oklahoma State Regents, 339 U.S. 637, 70 S.Ct. 851, 94 L.Ed. 1149. In none of these cases was it necessary to re-examine the doctrine to grant relief to the Negro plaintiff. And in Sweatt v. Painter, supra, the Court expressly reserved decision on the question whether Plessy v. Ferguson should be held inapplicable to public education.

In the instant cases, that question is directly presented. Here, unlike Sweatt v. Painter, there are findings below that the Negro and white schools involved have been equalized, or are being equalized, with respect to buildings, curricula, qualifications and salaries of teachers, and other "tangible" factors. Our decision, therefore, cannot turn on merely a comparison of these tangible factors in the Negro and white schools involved in each of the cases. We must look instead to the effect of segregation itself on public education.

In approaching this problem, we cannot turn the clock back to 1868 when the Amendment was adopted, or even to 1896 when Plessy v. Ferguson was written. We must consider public education in the light of its full development and its present place in American life throughout the Nation. Only in this way can it be determined if segregation in public schools deprives these plaintiffs of the equal protection of the laws.

Today, education is perhaps the most important function of state and local governments. Compulsory school attendance laws and the great expenditures for education both demonstrate our recognition of the importance of education to our democratic society. It is required in the performance of our most basic public responsibilities, even service in the armed forces. It is the very foundation of good citizenship. Today it is a principal instrument in awakening the child to cultural values, in preparing him for later professional training, and in helping him to adjust normally to his environment. In these days, it is doubtful that any child may reasonable be expected to succeed in life if he is denied the opportunity of an education. Such an opportunity, where the state has undertaken to provide it, is a right which must be made available to all on equal terms.

We come then to the question presented: Does segregation of children in public schools solely on the basis of race, even though the physical facilities and other "tangible" factors may be equal, deprive the children of the minority group of equal educational opportunities? We believe that it does.

In Sweatt v. Painter, supra [339 U.S. 629, 70 S.Ct. 850], in finding that a segregated law school for Negroes could not provide them equal educational opportunities, this Court relied in large part on "those qualities which are incapable of objective measurement but which make for greatness in a law school." In McLaurin v. Oklahoma State Regents, supra [339 U.S. 637, 70 S.Ct. 853], the Court, in requiring that a Negro admitted to a white graduate school be treated like all other students, again resorted to intangible considerations: "* * * his ability to study, to engage in discussions and exchange views with other students, and, in general, to learn his profession." Such considerations apply with added force to children in grade and high schools. To separate them from others of similar age and qualifications solely because of their race generates a feeling of inferiority as to their status in the community that may affect their hearts and minds in a way unlikely ever to be undone. The effect of this separation on their educational opportunities was well stated by a finding in the Kansas case by a court which nevertheless felt compelled to rule against the Negro plaintiffs:

> Segregation of white and colored children in public schools has a detrimental effect upon the colored children. The impact is greater when it has the sanction of the law; for the policy of separating the races is usually interpreted as denoting the inferiority of the negro group. A sense of inferiority affects the motivation of the child to learn. Segregation with the sanction of law, therefore, has a tendency to [retard] the educational and mental development of Negro children and to deprive them of some of the benefits they would receive in a racial[ly] integrated school system.

Whatever may have been the extent of psychological knowledge at the time of Plessy v. Ferguson, this finding is amply supported by modern authority. Any language in Plessy v. Ferguson contrary to this finding is rejected.

We conclude that in the field of public education the doctrine of "separate but equal" has no place. Separate educational facilities are inherently unequal. Therefore, we hold that the plaintiffs and others similarly situated for whom the actions have been brought are, by reason of the segregation complained of, deprived of the equal protection of the laws guaranteed by the Fourteenth Amendment. This disposition makes unnecessary any discussion whether such segregation also violates the Due Process Clause of the Fourteenth Amendment.

Because these are class actions, because of the wide applicability of this decision, and because of the great variety of local conditions, the formulation of decrees in these cases presents problems of considerable complexity. On reargument, the consideration of appropriate relief was necessarily subordinated to the primary question—the constitutionality of segregation in public education. We have now announced that such segregation is a denial of the equal protection of the laws. In order that we may have the full assistance of the parties in formulating decrees, the cases will be restored to the docket, and the parties are requested to present further argument on Questions 4 and 5 previously propounded by the Court for the reargument this Term. The Attorney General of the United States is again invited to participate. The Attorneys General of the states requiring or permitting segregation in public education will also be permitted to appear as *amici curiae* upon request to do so by September 15, 1954, and submission of briefs by October 1, 1954.

It is so ordered.

8.13 The Committee on Race and Education of the Portland, Oregon, School Board Discusses Racial Isolation and Compensatory Education.

Certain words have become headlines in the present social upheaval involving the public schools in the United States. "Segregation" (both de jure and de facto), "discrimination" (both obvious and subtle), "racial imbalance" or "concentration," and "integration" are words which invoke a troubled and sometimes passionate response. They reflect concepts which are central to the problems which concern society, yet their usage is not yet settled and is frequently ambiguous. "Desegregation" and "integration" are often used interchangeably. Likewise, "de facto segregation" and "racial imbalance" and "racial concentration" are frequently used interchangeably.

Segregation, De Facto and De Jure

In the *Brown* decision of May, 1954, the United States Supreme Court held that a state law which required that children be assigned to certain

Committee on Race and Education, *Race and Equal Educational Opportunity in Portland's Public Schools* (Portland: Portland Public Schools, 1964), pp. 181–189. Reprinted by permission of the Portland Public Schools.

schools solely upon the ground of their race was invalid. The Court thus overruled the earlier long established doctrine that legal or de jure segregation upon the ground of race was valid provided that equal school facilities were in fact provided. The Court premised its conclusion upon a finding that legally segregated facilities for education were inherently inferior by reason of the effect of segregation and its aura of inferiority upon the minority so segregated.

The term "de facto segregation" is used in different ways. Sometimes it is applied to segregated situations which are brought about by extralegal means, or by law or practice not phrased in terms of race. So defined, de facto segregation does not really differ from de jure segregation in terms of result or intention. Both types of segregation share a common element —the conscious purpose to produce or maintain segregation.

However, segregation in the sense of separation, regardless of intent to cause it, can exist for other reasons. Hence, even when there is no deliberate intent to segregate, a school is sometimes also described as de facto segregated when it is almost entirely white or almost entirely Negro as a result of residential patterns, or when it is composed predominantly of ethnic or economic groups, such as white Appalachian children in Detroit or Puerto Ricans in New York, again as a result of residential patterns. Such concentrations in schools, sometimes racial, sometimes religious, are frequently produced by a series of complex human actions, many of them individual choices. In urban communities population shifts can alter housing patterns with astonishing rapidity, and the resulting impact upon the school may be wholly unintended.

Racial Imbalance

Where, as in Portland, any intent by the school system to segregate on the basis of race is lacking, those schools in which a concentration of any race appears by reason of changing neighborhood housing patterns, have also been called "racially imbalanced" as well as "de facto segregated." These concepts lead necessarily to the question of what is balance, because imbalance is essentially a negative term which can be understood only in relation to its positive counterpart, balance.

In Portland, with roughly a 7% Negro component in our public school population, is an ideal balance 7% Negro and 93% white in any given school? In this context is a Portland school with 93% Negroes considered imbalanced, while another school with 93% whites is considered balanced? Totally different equations are posed by Detroit with 51% Negroes in public schools, St. Louis with 57% Negroes in public schools, and on Manhattan with 75% Negroes in public schools. Does racial balance also mean equal distribution of races throughout all levels of society and all institutions in society? As applied to schools, does it mean that ideally in each school in a particular district all races must be represented in proportion to their numbers?

To pose these questions is to pose the difficulty inherent in trying to answer them.

There is, insofar as we can see, no basis or formula by which one may determine when racial balance is achieved. A statistical image of a racially balanced society is not necessarily a well integrated society, nor is it one which must or perhaps even can exist. We do not believe therefore, that the introduction of the quantitative concepts of "balance" or "imbalance" into the question is of any help in suggesting possible solutions or even in clarifying the problem.

Integration, Desegregation

We believe that it is in the consideration of these two concepts that the racial problems which are our concern will be most clearly delineated and the direction of solution indicated.

It is commonly agreed as we noted in our Introduction that racial integration will have been achieved when citizens of all races shall have been assimilated into the educational, cultural, social, political and economic spheres of American life. Such integration, which for the Negro generally remains a goal yet to be attained, parallels ethnic integration which has been virtually accomplished, at least in the Portland community.

Integration therefore is a goal, an end, an objective. How is it to be achieved?

As we have seen above, conscious efforts to separate, segregate members of a particular race from the rest of society render impossible a racially integrated society. Further, as we noted, a similar result occurs when the members of a particular race themselves deliberately choose to separate themselves from the rest of society. Consequently, if racial integration is to be achieved, it must be by a process of desegregation—that is the removal of all contrived barriers to social movement which are based upon race and the development of conditions, particularly of the intellect, which will allow individuals to make reasonable choices from an entire spectrum of choices.

In the light of this concept of desegregation, the following principles are suggested:

1) Proposals for desegregation should not contain demands that choices be exercised in only one way.

Not all human decisions which are thought to be desirable can or should necessarily be required. In a free society, we attempt to leave to the individual many areas of individual choice. Striking the balance between that which is required or prohibited as a matter of public policy and that which is left to the sum of individual choices is a difficult problem and nowhere more so than in the area we are discussing.

To be more specific, our society ideally seeks to leave to the individual the right to make an individual choice as to where he shall live, leaving to him the selection of a state, city, locality and neighborhood. Our practice has fallen greatly short of this, and particularly in the case of minorities. But once artificial barriers—whether legal or customary—are removed, we believe that the limit of public policy as expressed in terms of compulsion has been reached. Thus when individuals, in the absence of such barriers, freely make choices which result in forming or continuing racial, religious or nationality concentrations in the places where they live, they remain within the bounds of public policy whether or not we consider their choice a happy one.

To demand that choices be exercised in only one way in order to achieve desegregation is to nullify the very freedom which is sought.

2) Proposals to further the process of integration should contain provisions to:

a. Remove contrived barriers to freedom of choice.

b. Create opportunities for individual choice.

c. Develop awareness of value of individual choice and social responsibilities consequent to freedom of choice. . . .

The Social Role of the School

The public school system in the United States has long been recognized as a social agency whose role transcends the mere transmission of academic skill and technical knowledge. It has been consciously employed as a means of producing the sort of political climate and the sort of ideal of citizenship which we have felt necessary to maintain our system of government. The schools have helped to transform generations of immigrants from many foreign lands speaking many different languages into a people which conceives itself as having a common heritage, speaking a common tongue, and aspiring to a common future.

It is a fact beyond controversy that today the largest single remaining unassimilated minority in American life is the American Negro. It is fortunate that the Negro wants to participate more fully in the mainstream of American life, rather than maintain a relatively separate existence in opposition to the values and goals of that greater society. Because the public school has been successful in this role before, because the school reaches substantially every person in our land, because it reaches us when we are forming our first impressions of the world about us, the schools have a vital role to play in the assimilation process. By the same token, we must recognize that this task of assimilation and reconciliation will require imagination, energy, and, above all, wisdom.

The good of the individual child of whatever talent or whatever handicap must be given prime consideration by the school system. Any steps that it takes to further the process of integration must be educationally valid.

Hence, racial considerations must not be the sole criterion for educational decisions, or desegregation efforts.

The School and Equality of Opportunity

The assumption has been made in the past, not without strong justification, that equal opportunities were being provided when essentially comparable facilities and services were made equally available. Generally, it has been felt that recognition of the principle of human equality requires uniformity of treatment as evidence of the school's equality of concern for all students irrespective of race, creed or color. It has been recognized, however, that the unique qualities possessed by some individuals as classes of people must be met by qualitatively different kinds of resources and programs and/or instructional methods and devices; thus, both the mentally deficient and the gifted are segregated for special purposes which are designed to accomplish maximum benefits for each. The fact of cultural deprivation would now seem to suggest yet another classification wherein equality of concern and the equalization of educational opportunity requires the energetic and imaginative use of unequal resources in order to achieve essentially equal results.

The School and Desegregation

The foregoing discussion of the school permits us to draw these summary conclusions:

1) While the neighborhood school concept is essential as a basis for planning an initial pupil assignment, some modification of the neighborhood school and its attendance district should be possible and in specific cases may be desirable and necessary.

2) The public school system in the United States has in the past successfully aided in the assimilation of racial and ethnic groups into American life; it should perform a similar task today for the American Negro.

3) The school will aid in the assimilation of the Negro by:
    a) Removing contrived barriers to freedom of choice.
    b) Determining that each child, irrespective of race, shall have full access and opportunity to profit from those educational programs which the schools provide.
    c) Developing an awareness in the child of the value of individual choice and the social responsibilities consequent upon such choice.

4) An integrated school therefore is one in which all children are ac-

cepted as of essentially equal human worth, in which all children are judged in terms of their individual characteristics, and in which all children are taught to feel capable of freedom of movement and choice in developing their natural talents.

5) In addition to special programs for the mentally deficient, the gifted and the physically handicapped, the schools should also provide special programs in order to achieve essentially equal results for culturally deprived students.

The Portland Situation

Our study suggests that the primary cause of low achievement in those schools located in neighborhoods which are depressed in a socio-economic sense, is the background which the child brings to school when he arrives at the age of five or six, and the environment in which he lives.

This observation is applicable to both white and Negro schools. Racial concentrations of Negroes add problems of motivation and feelings of alienation to the problems of socio-economic deprivation.

Likewise racial isolation has deprived both Negro and white children of opportunities to learn, to know and respect each other as individuals with common interests rather than as races with different or hostile interests.

Democracy, Bureaucracy, and Education: 9
John Dewey and the Redefinition
of the Common School

The school reformers of Horace Mann's generation hoped to create system where they saw chaos. To unify the people public education must itself be unified and efficient. Hence most reformers wished to standardize textbooks and curriculum, to grade classes, to train teachers in approved methods, and to improve regulation and supervision of the schools. To a large degree the schoolmen succeeded in standardizing public education during the latter half of the nineteenth century, at least in the larger towns and cities of the North and West.

Their success became an affliction, often the fate of reforms when they become institutionalized. The quest for educational uniformity began as individual agitation, gained momentum as others joined the cause, and finally became fixed by law or institutional custom—thus becoming a self-perpetuating pattern of institutional behavior. What was originally a means to an end—a healthy regularity to aid the common school in training upright citizens—become an end in itself. An original hope that the school could be a centripetal force in a centrifugal society degenerated into a program to fill children's minds with certified thoughts and to enforce stereotyped behavior. The large city schools became increasingly mechanized and structured like the large bureaucracies of industry, commerce, and the military that were arising in this age of consolidation.

A case in point is *A Statement of the Theory of Education in the United States* signed by dozens of college presidents and state and city superintendents of schools and issued by the U. S. Office of Education in 1874. "The commercial tone prevalent in the city," said the report, "tends to develop, in its schools, quick, alert habits and readiness to combine with others in their tasks. Military precision is required in the maneuvering of classes. Great stress is laid upon (1) punctuality, (2) regularity, (3) attention, and (4) silence, as habits necessary through life for successful combination with one's fellow-men in an industrial and commercial civilization." Since in America "the peculiarities of civil society and the political organization draw the child out of the influence of the family-nurture" at an early age, the school must compensate by laying stress on discipline and by making "far more prominent the moral phase of education. It is obliged to train the student into habits of prompt obedience to his teachers. . . ." The curriculum was familiar: reading and writing; arithmetic (especially valued for cultivating "the habit of attention and accuracy"); grammar ("to discern the categories of the mind" and to introduce the child "to pure thought"); and geography. The purpose of the common school was "to give the pupil the great arts of receiving and communicating knowledge."

What this often meant in practice Joseph Rice discovered when he visited 1,200 classrooms in thirty-six cities in 1892. Rice, a pediatrician who had studied education in German universities, was appalled by what he saw in American urban schools. In New York he talked with a principal who believed, Rice said, that "when a child enters upon school life his vocabulary is so small that it is practically worthless, and his power to think so feeble that his thoughts are worthless." Consequently, the pupil "should be supplied with ready-made thoughts as given in a ready-made vocabulary." The children had no excuse to move their heads during recitations: " 'Why should they look behind when the teacher is in front of them?' " asked the principal. Bobbing up and down and rapidly screaming their pat definitions, the children were perfect automata. While this school was more regimented than the average, Rice visited other schools in New York similar in kind if not in degree, for almost everywhere he went he found the children silent and passive, the teachers engaged in drilling them in the city syllabus, powerless to change the system. In St. Louis and several other cities he found substantially the same conditions. The supervisors in St. Louis judged the effectiveness of the teachers by how closely they followed the curriculum and by how well they stuffed facts into the students. The result was a grim, factory-like routine: "The unkindly spirit of the teacher is strikingly apparent; the pupils, being completely subjugated to her will, are silent and motionless; the spiritual atmosphere of the classroom is damp and chilly." During recitation students lined up, standing stiffly, their toes touching the edge of a floorboard. Rice heard one teacher say " 'How can you learn anything with your knees and toes out of order?' "

As irate muckraker and reformer, Rice published the results of his investigations in an influential series of articles in *The Forum*. The arbitrary cult of uniformity, Rice angrily wrote, converted childhood "into years of slavery." Although his reports precipitated a cloudburst of controversy, many urban systems continued their grim miseducation. An assistant superintendent told Charles W. Eliot, President of Harvard, that teachers saw no reason to treat students as individuals. "They wanted all the pupils in a given room to be in one grade," Eliot snapped, "to move together like soldiers on parade, and to arrive on examination-day having all performed precisely the same tasks. . . ." To Eliot, uniformity was false democracy.

In Portland, Oregon, decades of effort had produced what Ellwood P. Cubberley called in 1913 "a uniformity in the schools that is almost appalling"—and Cubberley, an administrator himself, was no muckraker. The curriculum of grades three through nine in Portland was neatly divided into fifty-four parts, each section further subdivided into topics indicated by pages in the textbook. Not content with this, the superintendent met regularly with teachers to tell them what questions they should ask. He gave preference in hiring teachers to graduates of the normal program conducted for high school students in his system. At any time of the school day he could confidently say on what page of the text in what subject all third graders were reciting. Even the principals did not escape: they had to pay fines of $5 for failing to hold a fire drill, $2 for not opening the school doors at 8:30, and $1 for missing any meeting called by the superintendent.

Four pages of the book of Portland school rules and regulations dealt with the details of the examination system, the ordeal through which all students passed twice a year and which determined their promotion to the next treadmill. Every child—even the students in the class for the deaf—took exactly the same tests in every subject at the same level. In grammar in the seventh grade the student might be asked to define "attribute complements," "independent elements," and "appositives." In geography he was expected to regurgitate the sentences of the textbook carefully stuffed in by his anxious teacher (whose own employment depended in part on how well the students did on the tests). The system as a whole was a caricature of education, a vast percolation of words, an imposition of a culture which bore little relation to the experience of the child.

Convinced that the nature of the child and service to society should be the controlling factors in schooling, reformers at the turn of the century launched a massive campaign to redefine education. They joined the "revolt against formalism" characteristic of American thought at the time. In common with progressives in politics and in other social reforms they set out to recast institutions to meet the challenges of the period. They shared a common vision of the promise of American life and a common abhorrence of the social evils they saw around them.

Two works by educational reformers—John Dewey's *School and Society* (1899) and Ellwood Cubberley's *Changing Conceptions of Education* (1909)—reveal much about the concerns, the tone and temper, of the larger political and social movement called Progressivism, as well as the diverse directions which the new education would take. The educators discussing the *Theory of Education in the United States* in 1874 had observed the lack of "family-nurture" and the weakening moral influence of both the nuclear and extended family; their response had been to stress discipline more severely in the school. For Dewey and Cubberley the transformation of the family as a result of industrialism and urbanization had far broader educational implications. The family had given the child of the pioneer period more than moral imperatives: it had provided a rounded education which the schools must now attempt to imitate. It had taught the child to build a house, make candles, fix a wagon, make clothing, sow and reap crops. Consequently, the child learned not only skills but also social cooperation. "In all this," wrote Dewey, "there was continual training of observation, of ingenuity, constructive imagination, of logical thought, and of the sense of reality acquired through first-hand contact with actualities." But the consolidation of industry and the division of labor had nearly wiped out household industries and neighborhood trades.

The child was deprived of this informal education afforded by the old system; the adult worker could not see the social meaning of his labor. "How many of the employed are today mere appendages to the machines they operate!" Dewey exclaimed. Cubberley commented that economic opportunities were narrowing for most citizens: "Increasing specialization . . . has divided the people into dozens of more or less clearly defined classes, and the increasing centralization of trade and industry has concentrated business in the hands of a relatively small number. . . . No longer can a man save up a thousand dollars and start in business for himself with much chance of success. The employee tends to remain an employee; the wage earner tends to remain a wage earner . . . . the worker tends more and more to become a cog in the machine. . . ." From the middle-class perspective characteristic of most progressives, Cubberley observed that "success is higher up the ladder now than it was a generation ago, while the crowd about the bottom increases every year."

As rural Americans moved to the cities, Cubberley wrote, much of the old communal feeling and restraints disappeared. In small and homogeneous communities the church and public opinion, as well as the family, had enforced a common code of conduct. In the city these customs and traditions broke down, new "amusements and temptations" appeared, and home and community, formerly allied in training children to be righteous, now seemed to have abdicated and "turned over to the public school the whole matter of the training and education of the young." Despite a nostalgia for the rural past—an agrarian tradition often exaggerated to mythic proportions at the turn of the century—Cubberley did not flinch from the new task thrust on the schools:

> Our state governments are weak and inefficient, we say; the school must then teach, and teach in some effective manner, the principles of strong and effective government. Our city governments are corrupt, we hear; fundamental moral and economic principles must then be taught to the masses, so that they may realize the importance of civic righteousness, and understand as well who ultimately pays the bills for all mismanagement. Our people waste their money and their leisure in profligate ways, we say; a knowledge of values and of how to utilize leisure time must then be taught.

Indeed, progressives in politics and in other social reform movements— shocked by corruption, pinched by constricted opportunities in a world of large organizations, outraged by slums and foul working conditions in a land of plenty, concerned about swarms of immigrants crowding the ghettoes—turned to education, broadly construed, to restore morality and justice to American life. Many progressive politicians themselves looked on their task as essentially an educational one; one progressive spokesman, Herbert Croly, suggested that all public life might be a vast educative community. In 1912 Theodore Roosevelt told the Ohio Constitutional Convention, "it is impossible to invent constitutional devices which will prevent the popular will from being effective for wrong without also preventing it from being effective for right. The only safe course to follow . . . is to provide for making the popular judgment really effective." Someone once commented to Roosevelt that he was a clever politician because he could predict what the people were going to think. Roosevelt replied that this was not true: "I did not divine how the people were going to think; I simply made up my mind what they ought to think and then did my best to get them to think it." Roosevelt acted the role of schoolmaster to the nation, Woodrow Wilson the role of professor. In Wisconsin Governor Robert LaFollette assembled a brain trust of University experts and sent the extension service of the University as a band of progressive circuit riders to arouse and educate the populace.

Underlying most progressive thought and action was a trust in formal schooling as a lever of reform. Jacob Riis, who had aroused the conscience of the nation in his study of *How the Other Half Lives*, wrote in 1902: "Do you see how the whole battle with the slum is fought out in and around the public school?" When the school is reformed, he said, "the battle with the slum will be over." Progressives had a generalized belief in moderate social reform *through* education; as Lawrence Cremin has observed, their full program demanded as well a reform *of* education (though "progressives" by no means agreed on what educational reforms were needed). Jane Addams, founder of Hull House in Chicago and friend of Dewey, declared that "we are impatient with the schools which lay all stress on reading and writing, suspecting them to rest on the assumption that all knowledge and interest must be brought to the children through the medium of books. Such an assumption fails to give the child any clew to the life about him, or any power to usefully or intelligently connect himself with it." To make the common school socially efficient, progressive educators had to tear down the wall between school and society.

To break down the wall between school and society—a proposition easy to state but difficult to interpret. The progressives agreed that new social conditions called for new methods, new subjects, new organization of schools. They agreed that public education would need to take over training previously performed by other social agencies. But what was to be the model for the transaction of school and society? Should the urban school become a carbon copy of the world of large bureaucratic organizations of industrial America, fitting each child to take his place in society as it was? Or should the school become a means of changing and regenerating that society, a prototype of the ideal community?

Believing that democracy was action, not litany, Dewey argued that the school should be "a miniature community, an embryonic society" which would produce "a larger society which is worthy, lovely, and harmonious." One social model for the school was the family: "What the best and wisest parent wants for his own child, that must the community want for all its children." To Dewey the traditional school, where students sat in rows, passively receiving and transmitting information, belied both sound learning theory and sound social policy. Dewey thought that mind and body, thought and action, were inseparable. To learn, a student must sense a real problem or question, must be free to form hypotheses and test them in practice. And mind itself, Dewey believed, grew through meanings acquired in social exchange; thus students must be allowed to work together, not penalized for helping one another—as in "cheating" in the authoritarian atmosphere of the traditional school—but praised for cooperation.

For Dewey the *methods* of scientific investigation and social cooperation were the constants in curriculum, *subject matter* the variable. This is not to suggest that he thought logically organized knowledge unimportant

—far from it. The teacher, he urged, must not abdicate her role as intellectual guide, but rather she "can direct the child's activities, giving them exercise along certain lines, and thus can lead up to the goal which logically lies at the end of the path followed." But Dewey opposed the percolator version of education, in which proper beliefs and behavior were predetermined at the top of the educational system. "The school system," he said, "upon the whole, has grown from the top down." This resulted in disregard for the experience of the child and the way he learns. In such a school, Dewey complained, the pupil "has to leave his mind behind, because there is no way to use it. . . ."

Dewey based the curriculum at the University of Chicago Laboratory School upon activities like weaving, cooking, and woodworking. This shopwork was not an antiquarian throwback to idyllic pioneer days, nor clearly was it vocational training. In the hands of skillful teachers in the School these activities served as points of departure for studying geography, history, science, and literature. The investigation of flax, wool, and cotton led the students to rediscover ways of turning these materials into cloth and the applications of science in industrial life. A visit to a farm led students to inquire into modern ways of preparing and marketing produce. Dewey's teachers tried to arouse and exploit the interests of the children, regarding their curiosity as the origin of real learning. Scholars helped to shape the school's curriculum. Albert Michelson, the eminent physicist who calculated the speed of light, often visited Dewey's school and found the work of the students fascinating.

Under Dewey's direction the Laboratory School gave children a fine introduction to natural and social science but may have slighted the humanities. Reacting against abstract linguistic study and the certified "culture" of the traditional school, Dewey sometimes went to an opposite extreme, as in his statement that Penelope in the Odyssey was "a classic in literature because the character is an adequate embodiment of a certain industrial phase of social life." And parents sometimes complained that students failed to learn the three R's systematically, leading Dewey to give an elaborate explanation of why Johnny in the Lab School might not read very well.

Dewey abhorred "fixed ends"—or absolute values—in education, since these were alien to his naturalistic view of ethics. But his writings on education are suffused with value judgments, and clearly he had a social ideal. He complained that the traditional school could not be "a natural social unit" because the "element of common and productive activity is absent." To him the only "natural" association was a "democratic" group, one in which "common needs and aims demand a growing interchange of thought and growing unity of sympathetic feeling." Smuggled into an apparently neutral word such as "natural" was ethical commitment to a *cooperative* commonwealth.

But the *actual* social world a child would enter—whether it was "natural" or not—exhibited many of the same characteristics as the bureaucratic school: the urban landscape of factory and commercial establishment was large and impersonal, the relation of employer to employee authoritarian, the tasks a worker performed were often dull and repetitious, and the struggle to survive often overcame the impulse to help. Dewey did not wish the school to adapt the child to such a society; he wished to humanize industry rather than industrialize humanity. He shared a hope common at the time that the worker might be taught the human significance of his job, and he feared that segregated vocational education would simply supply cogs for an industrial machine. He wanted the school to open a door into the business community, not in order to teach commercial geography and accounting but to "liberalize" business. He believed that in the social world as in the biological, variation was essential for the evolution of new and improved forms. He cast his ballot for change: education he defined as "that reconstruction or reorganization of experience which adds to the meaning of experience, and which increases ability to direct the course of future experience." The true teacher, he wrote in *My Pedagogic Creed*, "is the prophet of the true God and the usherer in of the true kingdom of God."

Not particularly cast for the role of prophet himself, with his bushy moustache and quiet manner, his lumbering prose and massive erudition, Dewey did help to transform American education—though he is not responsible for much of the credit or blame accorded him by friends and foes. Small private or wealthy public schools could readily adopt the tenets of "progressive education," often with flourishes borrowed from Freudian theory, but changing public education in the large was another matter. It is always easier to change rhetoric than substance, simpler to modify subjects than methods; and such was the case with much of the "new education" in the common school. Dewey's ideas were easy enough to distort. Witness the comment of the Los Angeles Superintendent in 1913: "The principal business of the child is to play and to grow—not to read, write, spell, and cipher. These are incidental in importance. If they can be made a part of the play, it is well to use them; if not, they should be handled sparingly."

A gifted teacher in a one-room country schoolhouse might turn her class into a model of progressive teaching. But changing a large city system was more difficult, for Dewey's ideas of democratic education were subtle and anti-bureaucratic in tendency. To put into effect Dewey's conception of teaching and learning as inquiry required of teachers great skill and knowledge; to carry out his vision of a cooperative school community demanded great social insight and flexibility from administrators. Ironically, the call for a "new education" in an urban school system sometimes brought more, not less bureaucracy—more forms to fill out, more supervisors to tell teachers what to do, new (and often more rigid) ways of testing and classifying pupils—which could, but usually didn't, stimulate more imaginative teaching. Or the call for reform might simply result in pasting new labels on the same old courses, or in employing the same old methods in courses with new labels. It was difficult, indeed, to capture the spirit of progressive education in a crowded slum school, to transform a class of sixty polyglot children into the sort of family at work which Dewey described as the ideal school.

A number of educational leaders, like Cubberley, agreed with Dewey that the school was out of touch with society, that its curriculum was bookish and unreal, that the school must be more efficient. But often breaking down the wall between school and society to them, unlike to Dewey, meant conforming better to the status quo. Thus in the years after 1910 school executives widely copied the techniques and ideology of businessmen, sometimes wisely, as in efficient purchasing of supplies, and sometimes inappropriately, as in attempting to judge the value of subjects solely by cost-accounting techniques. The factory rather than the family suggested itself to Cubberley as an apt analogy for the school:

> Our schools are, in a sense, factories in which the raw materials (children) are to be shaped and fashioned into products to meet the various demands of life. The specifications for manufacturing come from the demands of the twentieth-century civilization, and it is the business of the school to build its pupils to the specifications laid down. This demands good tools, specialized machinery, continuous measurement of production to see if it is, according to specifications, the elimination of waste in manufacture, and a large variety in output.

Cubberley thought this "large variety in output" essential, for one of the key faults of the traditional school was its undifferentiated curriculum. The old school "establishment was not equipped with enough pieces of special type machinery, located in special shops or units of the manufacturing plant, to enable it to meet modern manufacturing conditions." He believed that urban schools should "give up the exceedingly democratic idea that all are equal, and that our society is devoid of classes," and adapt the school to the social classes. Vocational schools for the lower classes would nicely round out the public schools—a point of view anathema to Dewey, who feared a freezing of the class structure. An education professor at the University of Wisconsin praised a variant of this class education: "There are three races in San Antonio, the Americans, the Mexicans, and the negroes.   Supt. Meek now proposes to develop an educational program which will be adapted to the abilities, traits and needs of each race."

The common school greatly enlarged its aim and curriculum as it expanded its enrollments during the progressive era.   To fulfil the promises of the crusaders of Horace Mann's generation, schoolmen believed that they must do far more than produce basic literacy.   In language reminiscent of Benjamin Rush's statement that "the pupil is public property," Cubberley declared in 1909 that "each year the child is coming to belong more and more to the state, and less and less to the parent."   In 1919 Utah made the school a moral policeman.   It passed a law requiring every boy and girl up to the age of eighteen either to go to school or to work, and demanding three sets of reports from the authorities on health, work, and out-of-school activities, including details about "the use of narcotics, care of person, sleeping habits, and kind and amount of recreation."   Now supervising youth for the three thousand waking hours they spent out of school as well as the thousand hours in, superintendents praised this "call to civic and moral righteousness for all the youth."   This was social uplift with a vengeance.

What has been the legacy of the progressive movement in American education?   It is difficult indeed to say precisely what difference it made in actual classrooms, though changes have clearly come.   Even the most cantankerous critics of Dewey and his disciples do not urge a return to the regimented common schools of the 1890's; few would deny that the elementary school has become a more humane and flexible institution.   It may be argued that schoolmen and scholars are just now beginning to implement the full extent of Dewey's program, as in the new curricula stressing the "discovery approach" (surely nothing new to those who have read Dewey's *Democracy and Education*).   The rhetoric of progressive education soon became orthodox in professional meetings, journals, textbooks.   In many programs of teacher education prospective teachers were indoctrinated with progressive tenets, spurring Dewey to observe, wryly, that "it may perhaps be said that to train teachers in the right principles the wrong way is an improvement over teacher-training that is wrong in both respects.   But it is not much of an improvement."   As Dewey himself saw, the new conceptions of education he helped to develop often became institutionalized by people who half understood them.   Dewey redefined the role of the common school to rescue it from the dessication of a reform movement gone stale, and he knew that his own reformulation had to be constantly tested lest it in turn become a tired orthodoxy.

9.1   Selection from "A Statement of the Theory of Education in the United States of America as Approved by Many Leading Educators" —Signed in 1874 by Seventy-Seven College Presidents and City and State Superintendents of Schools.

The idea of the state and the idea of civil society—the former the idea of the actualization of justice and the latter that of the supply of human wants and necessities through the creation and distribution of wealth—conspire, by general consent, in the production of the American system of public education; and, to its maintenance and support, the property of the community is made to contribute by taxation. Both the preservation of property by the actualization of justice and the increase of property by productive industry are directly conditioned, in a republic, upon the educated intelligence of the people. This is so, especially in that species of incorporeal property of the nature of franchises, such as constitute the basis of those corporate combinations formed for the promotion of manufactures and commerce, the creation of transit-facilities, and the diffusion of information, (patent-rights, charters for railroads, canals, telegraphs, banks of issue, insurance-companies, &c.). These franchises, vested in corporations, incite to the production of wealth to an extraordinary degree, and at the same time make such a demand upon the community for directive intelligence that it may be said that the modern industrial community cannot exist without free popular education carried out in a system of schools ascending from the primary grade to the university. And without a free development of productive industry, enabling the individual to accumulate the wealth necessary for the supply of the necessities of life faster than he consumes them, there is not left the leisure requisite to that cultivation of intelligence needed in the theoretical discussion and comprehension of public affairs; and without such occupation of the individual with public affairs, a democracy could exist only in name.

VIII

The past and present history of the United States exhibits a process of development comprising three stages:

(*a*) The settlement of new territory by pioneers and the reduction of the wilderness to an agricultural country.

(*b*) The rise of commercial towns and the creation of transit-facilities in the new regions.

Written by Duane Doty, Superintendent of Detroit Schools, and William T. Harris, Superintendent of St. Louis Schools (Washington: Government Printing Office, 1874), pp. 12–16.

(*c*) The development of manufacturing centers and the ascendency of domestic commerce.

In consequence of this constant spectacle of the entire process of founding a civilization and developing it from the rudimentary stages up to the completed type, there is produced a peculiar phase of character in the American people. There is always unlimited opportunity for the individual to build anew his fortunes when disaster has overtaken him in one locality.

As a consequence of the perpetual migration from the older sections of the country to the unoccupied Territories, there are new States in all degrees of formation, and their institutions present earlier phases of realization of the distinctive type than are presented in the mature growth of the system as it exists in the thickly-settled and older States. Thus States are to be found with little or no provision for education, but they are rudimentary forms of the American State, and are adopting, as rapidly as immigration enables them to do so, the type of educational institutions already defined as the result of the American political and social ideas.

IX

The education of the people in schools is a phase of education lying between the earliest period of family-nurture, which is still a concomitant and powerful auxiliary, on the one hand, and the necessary initiation into the specialties of a vocation in practical life on the other. In America, the peculiarities of civil society and the political organization draw the child out of the influence of family-nurture earlier than is common in other countries. The frequent separation of the younger branches of the family from the old stock renders family-influence less powerful in molding character. The consequence of this is the increased importance of the school in an ethical point of view.

X

In order to compensate for lack of family-nurture, the school is obliged to lay more stress upon discipline and to make far more prominent the moral phase of education. It is obliged to train the pupil into habits of prompt obedience to his teachers and the practice of self-control in its various forms, in order that he may be prepared for a life wherein there is little police-restraint on the part of the constituted authorities.

XI

The school-discipline, in its phase of substitute for the family, uses *corrective* punishment, which presupposes a feeble development of the sense of honor in the child. It is mostly corporal punishment. But in the phase wherein the school performs the function of preparing the pupil for the formal government of the state, it uses *retributive* punishment and suspends the pupil from some or all the privileges of the school. In this phase of discipline, a sense of honor is presupposed and strengthened.

XII

In commercial cities and towns, the tendency preponderates towards forms of punishment founded on the sense of honor and towards the entire disuse of corporal punishment. This object has been successfully accomplished in New York, Chicago, Syracuse, and some other cities. In the schools of the country, where the agricultural interest prevails, the tendency to the family-form of government is marked.

XIII

A further difference between the discipline of city-schools and that of country-schools is founded partly on the fact that the former schools are usually quite large, assembling from three hundred to fifteen hundred pupils in one building, while the latter have commonly less than fifty pupils. In the former, the large numbers admit of good classification; in the latter, classes are quite small, sometimes containing only a single pupil, and the discipline of combination is consequently feebly developed. The commercial tone prevalent in the city tends to develop, in its schools, quick, alert habits and readiness to combine with others in their tasks. Military precision is required in the maneuvering of classes. Great stress is laid upon (1) punctuality, (2) regularity, (3) attention, and (4) silence, as habits necessary through life for successful combination with one's fellow-men in an industrial and commercial civilization.

XIV

The course of study is laid down with a view to giving the pupil the readiest and most thorough practical command of those conventionalities of intelligence, those arts and acquirements which are the means of directive power and of further self-education. These preliminary educational accomplishments open at once to the mind of the pupil two opposite directions: (*a*) the immediate mastery over the material world, for the purposes of obtaining food, clothing, and shelter directly; (*b*) the initiation into the means of association with one's fellow-men, the world of humanity.

XV

(*a*) The first theoretical study necessary for the mastery over the material world is arithmetic—the quantification of objects as regards numbers.

In American schools, this is looked upon as of so much importance that more time is given to it than to any other study of the course. Its cultivation of the habit of attention and accuracy is especially valued.

After arithmetic follows geography, in a parallel direction, looking towards natural history. Arithmetic is taught from the first entrance into school, while geography is begun as soon as the pupil can read well.

XVI

(*b*) The first theoretical study necessary to facilitate combination of man with his fellow-men is reading the printed page. Accordingly, the prevailing custom in American schools is to place a book in the hands of the child when he first enters school and to begin his instruction with teaching him how to read. As soon as he can read, he is able to begin to learn to study books for himself, and thus to acquire stores of knowledge by his own efforts. The art of writing is learned in connection with reading. This culture, in the direction of knowing the feelings, sentiments, and ideas of mankind, is continued throughout the course by a graded series of readers, containing selection of the gems from the literature of the language, both prose and verse. This culture is re-enforced about the fifth year of the course by the study of English grammar, in which, under a thin veil, the pupil learns to discern the categories of the mind and to separate them analytically from modifying surroundings and define them. The common forms of thought and of its expression are thus mastered, and in this way the pupil is to some extent initiated into pure thought and acquires the ability to resolve problems of the material world and of his own life into their radical elements. The study of the history of the United States (and, in most instances, of the national Constitution) carries on this culture by the contemplation of the peculiarities of his nation as exhibited in its historic relations.

XVII

The cardinal studies of the "common school" are: (1) reading and writing, (2) grammar, (3) arithmetic, (4) geography; the first two look towards mastery over spiritual combination; the latter two, over material combination. The common school aims to give the pupil the great arts of receiving and communicating intelligence. Drawing and vocal music are taught quite generally and the rudiments of natural science are taught orally in most city-schools. Declamation of oratorical selections is a favorite exercise and is supposed to fit the youth for public and political life. Debating societies are formed for the same purpose.

9.2   Dr. Joseph M. Rice Describes Regimented City Schools in the 1890's.

Now, what is the character of the instruction that will be passed as satisfactory by the superintendents of the public schools of New York city? Surely no one can call me unjust when I answer this question by describing the work of a school whose principal has been marked uniformly "excellent" during the twenty-five years or more that she has held her present position. I cannot say that this school is a typical New York primary school; I shall describe typical work later. But I do most positively assert that the mere fact that a superintendent is permitted to give a school of this nature his warmest indorsement is sufficient to prove that the school system of New York is not conducted for the benefit of the child alone.

The principal of this school has pedagogical views and a maxim peculiarly her own. She believes that when a child enters upon school life his vocabulary is so small that it is practically worthless, and his power to think so feeble that his thoughts are worthless. She is consequently of the opinion that what the child knows and is able to do on coming to school should be entirely disregarded, that he should not be allowed to waste time, either in thinking or in finding his own words to express his thoughts, but that he should be supplied with ready-made thoughts as given in a ready-made vocabulary. She has therefore prepared sets of questions and answers, so that the child may be given in concise form most of the facts prescribed in the course of study for the three years of primary instruction. The instruction throughout the school consists principally of grinding these answers *verbatim* into the minds of the children. The principal's ideal lies in giving each child the ability to answer without hesitation, upon leaving her school, every one of the questions formulated by her. In order to reach the desired end, the school has been converted into the most dehumanizing institution that I have ever laid eyes upon, each child being treated as if he possessed a memory and the faculty of speech, but no individuality, no sensibilities, no soul.

So much concerning the pedagogical views on which this school is conducted; now as to the maxim. This maxim consists of three short words—"Save the minutes." The spirit of the school is, "Do what you like with

Joseph M. Rice, *The Public School System of the United States* (New York: The Century Co., 1893), pp. 30–33, 36–37, 38–39, 93–95, 98.

the child, immobilize him, automatize him, dehumanize him, but save, save the minutes." In many ways the minutes are saved. By giving the child ready-made thoughts, the minutes required in thinking are saved. By giving the child ready-made definitions, the minutes required in formulating them are saved. Everything is prohibited that is of no measurable advantage to the child, such as the movement of the head or a limb, when there is no logical reason why it should be moved at the time. I asked the principal whether the children were not allowed to move their heads. She answered, "Why should they look behind when the teacher is in front of them?"—words too logical to be refuted.

During the recitations many minutes are saved. The principal has indeed solved the problem of how the greatest number of answers may be given in the smallest number of minutes. In the first place, no time is spent in selecting pupils to answer questions, every recitation being started by the first pupil in the class, the children then answering in turn, until all have recited. Secondly, time is economized in the act of rising and sitting during the recitations, the children being so drilled that the child who recites begins to fall back into his seat while uttering the last word of a definition, the next succeeding child beginning his ascent while the one before him is in the act of descending. Indeed, things appear as if the two children occupying adjoining seats were sitting upon the opposite poles of an invisible see-saw, so that the descending child necessarily raises the pupil next to him to his feet. Then, again, the minutes are saved by compelling the children to unload their answers as rapidly as possible, distinctness of utterance being sacrificed to speed, and to scream their answers at the tops of their voices, so that no time may be wasted in repeating words inaudibly uttered. For example, the principal's definition of a note—"A note is a sign representing to the eye the length or duration of time"—is ideally delivered, when it sounds something like "Notsinrepti length d'ration time."

Another way in which time is saved is by compelling the children to stare fixedly at the source whence the wisdom flows. When the teacher is the source of wisdom, all the children in the room stare fixedly in the direction of the teacher; when a word on the blackboard is the source of wisdom, all eyes stare fixedly at a point on the blackboard. There is one more peculiarity. When material, of whatever nature, is handed to the children, enough to supply a whole row is given to the end child. The material is then passed along sideways until each child in the row has been supplied. During this procedure the children are compelled to look straight in front of them, and to place their hands sidewise in order to receive the material, without looking whence it comes. The pupils are thus obliged to grope, as if they were blind, for the things passed to them. The principal assured me, however, that to drill the children in this groping is not attended with much difficulty, the pupils in the lowest primary grade—the little five-year-olds—learning to take and pass things like blind people during the first week or two of their school life. . . .

In the third lesson in form the teacher played the "star" part. This lesson was carried on as follows: The automatized teacher stood before the blackboard and began the exercise by drawing upon the board, with a rapid stroke, a straight line. When this stroke had been made, the following words were spoken:

Teacher: "What is this?"
First pupil: "It is a line."
Teacher: "What kind of a line?"
Second pupil: "It is a straight line."

The teacher now drew a crooked line upon the blackboard, and asked: "What is this?"

Third pupil: "It is a crooked line."
Teacher (to third pupil): "Wrong." (To fourth pupil): "Why don't you get up when the child before you makes a mistake?"
Fourth pupil: "It is a line."
Teacher: "What kind of a line?"
Fifth pupil: "It is a crooked line."

The teacher here said to me that the third child was a new pupil, and had not yet learned the methods of the school; but she assured me that the new pupils come round all right in a few days.

The reason why the third pupil's answer was considered wrong was not because it was wrong, but because each stroke of the chalk was intended to bring forth two questions and two answers, so that when the first question was answered in such a manner as to leave no occasion to ask the second question, the charm was broken, and the answer could not be accepted. . . .

The typical New York city primary school, although less barbarous and absurd than the one just described, is nevertheless a hard, unsympathetic, mechanical-drudgery school, a school into which the light of science has not yet entered. Its characteristic feature lies in the severity of its discipline, a discipline of enforced silence, immobility, and mental passivity. The differences found in going from room to room and from school to school—I have seen many of them—are differences in degree only, and not in kind. One teacher will allow her pupils to move their heads a little more freely than the standard, another will allow a little more freedom to the shoulder-joints, but less freedom in moving the head, and a third will require the children to keep their hands in their laps, instead of behind their backs.

The character of the instruction is identical with that found wherever this false system of discipline prevails, being of that form which appeals to the memory alone. The aim of the teacher is simply to secure results by drilling the pupils in the facts prescribed for the grade. The public-school system of New York city offers, therefore, a striking example of how, under unwise management, a trained teacher may be reduced to the level of one who has had no training. Many New York school-teachers have told me that the New-York school gave them no opportunity to put their knowledge of psychology and pedagogy to practical use, and that they consequently felt the normal-school influence vanish soon after beginning to teach. . . .

In St. Louis the superintendent does little if anything beyond observing that the teachers succeed in putting the child through the studies prescribed for the grade. He visits each school from time to time in order to examine classes, which examination is intended as an examination of the teachers, and the teachers are judged by the results. The important factor to be noted is that the results alone are considered, the manner in which they are reached being left entirely out of consideration. What follows? The teacher strives beyond all else to secure such results as will tell in her favor. Since nothing, as a rule, tells so well at an examination as a knowledge of facts,—mental power and moral strength being incapable of exact measurement,—it becomes the sole aim of the teacher to load the memory of her pupils with facts. An ideal teacher, even when judged by results alone, will endeavor to secure the desired results without converting her pupils into automatons or robbing them of their happiness. But when, under these conditions, a teacher is wanting in professional skill or sympathy, or both, her teaching will be likely to present a picture of a pure, unadulterated, old-fashioned grind. Her ability is judged by the number of facts which her pupils retain, and she therefore spends all her time in crowding the memory of her pupils with facts. To introduce into a lesson an illustrative story which contains no food for the examination, to allow the child to study an object when the facts relating to that object can be learned so much more quickly by words alone, to allow the pupils time to think or time to move, are things which simply waste the time of the teacher; and why should she waste her time at her own peril?

Reading now becomes the art of recognizing printed or written words at sight without regard to the thought expressed; arithmetic, the art of computing numbers without regard to the relation of things; geography and history, physics and physiology simply represent so many words to be memorized by the pupils. If compelling pupils to memorize words be teaching, then indeed is all training superfluous, as any one equipped with a knowledge of the three R's, a sound pair of lungs, and a stout ratan is able to compel children to memorize words. And as long as words alone

are taught and the teacher can read words, she is able to secure results regardless of what the subject may be.   To her a page consists of a collection
of words and a book a collection of pages, and with her views upon education there is no reason why she should not teach Spinoza's "Ethics" as well
as "Mother Goose's Melodies," "Physiological Chemistry" as well as "Mrs.
Caudles Curtain Lectures," "Kant's Critique of Pure Reason" as well as
"What I Know About Farming."

When the aim of the supervision is limited to securing results, though
the children be rendered motionless and the room as silent as a grave, the
school is entirely lawless, because the only laws which the school should
obey—the laws of mental development—are entirely ignored.   The superintendent here reigns supreme; his rulings are arbitrary; his word is law.
But in exercising his license he deprives the child of his liberty.   The child
is twisted and turned or made immobile to suit the pleasure of the teacher,
and the fact that the child is a frail and tender human being is entirely
disregarded.   The innocent child is thrust into bondage, the years of childhood are converted into years of slavery. . . .

In one regard the treatment of the children cannot be considered otherwise than barbarous.   During several daily recitation periods, each of
which is from twenty to twenty-five minutes in duration, the children are
obliged to stand on the line, perfectly motionless, their bodies erect, their
knees and feet together, the tips of their shoes touching the edge of a
board in the floor.   The slightest movement on the part of a child attracts
the attention of the teacher.   The recitation is repeatedly interrupted with
cries of "Stand straight," "Don't bend the knees," "Don't lean against the
wall," and so on.   I heard one teacher ask a little boy: "How can you
learn anything with your knees and toes out of order?"   The toes appear
to play a more important part than the reasoning faculties.   The teacher
never forgets the toes; every few moments she casts her eyes "toe-ward."

9.3   A Description of the Portland, Oregon, Public Schools in 1913 by Superintendent Frank E. Spaulding of the Newton Public Schools.

The most fundamental principle observed in the present conduct of the
Portland school system is the maintenance unchanged of a rigidly prescribed, mechanical system, poorly adapted to the needs either of the children or of the community.   The universal practice—whether approved or
disapproved by those participating in it—is enlisted in the maintenance of a

Ellwood P. Cubberley, *The Portland Survey: A Textbook on City School Administration Based on a Concrete Study* (Yonkers-on Hudson, New York: World Book
Company, 1916), pp. 125, 130, 134–135.

rigid, minutely and mechanically prescribed system of instruction, organization, administration, supervision, examination, and inspection. Any change in this elaborate mechanism meets with resistance, positive as well as negative. So far as this system is adapted at any point to the actual needs of the individual children and youth that come under it, so far as it is adapted to the needs of the community for adequately trained recruits to serve the community, the adaptation is accidental—not the result of intelligence now operative at that point.

School board and superintendent, as well as principals, teachers, and pupils, are victims of the system for which no one is primarily responsible. So far as we have been able to learn, the spirit and fundamental outlines of this rigid, mechanical system antedate the beginnings of the services of those now longest connected with the schools. No single individual, no single group or class of individuals, at present within or without the school system, can fairly be held responsible, either primarily or chiefly, for the system as it today exists. . . .

A dead curriculum—Portland's dead curriculum—is the standard by which the living child is measured and to which he must conform; if the fifteen, sixteen, seventeen, or even eighteen-year old child has not yet transferred to his memory parts thirty-seven to fifty-four inclusive of the dead and comminuted curriculum, the chief constituents of which, in these parts, are abstract arithmetic and technical grammar, then he must begin with part thirty-seven and appropriate that and each of the succeeding seventeen parts in order, before he can even be associated with youth of approximately his own age,—an important matter educationally,—before he can engage in studies suited to his age and condition, studies and exercises that will be of immediate and practical value to him in the effort that he must shortly make to serve society for the sake of his own livelihood. . . .

The only recognition accorded the individualities of pupils, no matter how much they differ through peculiar strength, weakness, or defects, is the recognition that the school mechanism compels; their treatment varies only in so far as it is necessary to vary it temporarily that everyone may learn exactly the same things and in the same way—from part one to part fifty-four inclusive—that everyone else must learn. All must be made just as nearly alike as possible. To this mechanical end every phase of the elementary curriculum and its administration seems to be adjusted—and very nicely and thoughtfully adjusted. This adjustment can best be revealed through a brief analysis and examination of the several chief aspects of the curriculum and of its administration.

The Mechanical Form and Prescriptions of the Elementary Course of Study

The form in which the elementary course of study is outlined and prescribed is characteristic of the universal mechanism. Following is a sample:

Seventh B Grade—Part Forty

Reading. Cyr's Fifth Reader, pages 97 to 142.

Arithmetic. Smith's Practical Arithmetic, pages 202 to 216. (For forms of analysis, read parts 21 and 22.)

Language. (1) Buehler's Grammar, pages 81 to 95 inclusive. (2) and (3) See part 31.

Geography. Natural School Geography, pages 124 to 137, to end of "China." (Pages 40, 41, and 42.) Map Drawing—The Humboldt Geographical Note Book, part 4 (No. 51), pages 15 to 32 inclusive.

Spelling. (Parts 40, 41, and 42.) Reed's Word Lessons, pages 115 to 127 inclusive.

Writing. Outlook Writing System No. 6.

Drawing. Prang's Text Book of Art Education, Book VI.

Music. New Educational Third Music Reader.

Physiology. Krohn's Graded Lessons in Physiology and Hygiene, Chapters X, XI, and XII.

9.4   Aaron Gove, Superintendent of Schools, Denver, Colorado, Speaks on the "Limitations of the Superintendent's Authority and of the Teacher's Independence."

In school administration a definite partition, positive and evident, must lie between the functions of the legislative and of the executive departments.

While the superintendent of schools is permitted, and it is his duty, to participate in the councils of the legislative department, his evident duty lies in the execution of the plans which have been made as well by others as by himself. That part of the executive department of a school system which relates to the teaching of pupils is vested primarily in the superintendent; the responsibility is his, and theoretically the knowledge of the

Aaron Gove, "Limitations of the Superintendent's Authority and of the Teacher's Independence," National Education Association, *Journal of Proceedings and Addresses* (Winona, Minnesota: National Education Association, 1904), pp. 152–157.

best method lies with him.   He obtains that knowledge not only by personal investigation, study, and observation, but quite as much by contact and by the advice of his associates.   No man undertakes alone to frame a course of study, but seeks counsel, and urges his associates in all grades and departments to give to him the sum of their knowledges and experiences obtained in the active performance of their duties.

The limitations of the superintendent's authority are, or ought to be, definitely stated in the formal rules and regulations of the board of education.   An inspection of the many rules now in print, from all sorts and conditions of school corporations, demonstrates a notable unity of legislation in this respect.   While the appellate privilege lies to the board in the instance of all cases concerning the adjustment of difficulties between schools and home, or teachers and principals, it is the superintendent's duty to decide so far as to prevent, if possible, the necessity for an appeal to the legislative body.

The independence of a teacher is limited to that part of his official life which depends upon ethical relations.   No independence can be, with regard to the performance of an assigned duty.   It is comparable to the turning out of work by an industrial establishment, the performance of a task assigned by the chief of police of a city, or communicated to a soldier while on duty.   While a polite remonstrance must always be the privilege of a teacher, it is understood that the decision lies only with that authority which is responsible for the accomplishment of the assignment.

The personal characteristics of the superintendent and his method of dealing with subordinates largely modify the character of the output. One has a right to conclude that only polite conduct shall be, but what is polite on the part of one authority is despotic on the part of another. The autocracy of the office of the superintendent of a public-school system is necessary for the accomplishment of his purposes, but that despotism can be wielded with a gloved hand.   A dangerous tendency exists toward usurpation by teachers, thru organization, of powers which should be retained by the superintendent.   An apparently growing feeling seems to exist—in truth it does exist, especially in one of the large cities of the country—that the public-school system should be a democratic institution, and that the body of teachers constitute the democratic government. This is a false conception of true democracy.   The truth is that the boards of education are the representative bodies of the democracy—the people —for whom they are making laws, and to whom they are responsible for their acts.   A democracy of teachers for the purpose of controlling authoritatively the many hundred lines of activity connected with the administration of schools is as fatal to accomplishment as would be that of the patrolmen of the police department of a great city to organize and give directions, according to their own will, to the department in which they are placing their services.

It seems to be along the line of action whereby, in the industrial interests of our country, trades unions are so active, and either helpful or harmful according to the temper of the organizations and the wisdom of the chiefs of these organizations. Concerning neither administrative nor educational policies can the teaching body be intrusted with final decision.

People can be found who believe and speak and write that, as trades unions, in their authority over the membership, modify the kind of work put out, the amount of work done, saying to its members only so much effort shall be made each day, controlling the organization as to the manner of the work and the amount of wages paid, the number and kind of appointments, the tenure of position; so ought the teachers of a school district similarly to organize and act.

Is it possible that the members of the National Educational Association, or a respectable minority, believe that a similar organization will be helpful to the great interests for which they are spending their lives? Can it be possible that there are in the ranks of our profession—four hundred thousand of us today—men and women who are willing to be bound by rules and regulations and promises whereby they shall officially determine upon the merits one of the other; that no teacher can be employed unless he belongs to the organization; that he shall have just the wages that the organization directs; and that, when necessary, he shall stop the machinery of public education in return for some real or fancied grievance?

The people are represented in the administration of a school system by a body of men and women whom they elect for that purpose. In that body rests necessarily all effective power and direction. That body selects an officer whose sole business is to execute the plans prepared by the people thru their representatives, the board of education. The instruments used for that execution, namely the teachers, are furnished to this executive officer, who is instructed to use them in the performance of his duties, he having the knowledge and skill and ability to select given instruments for given purposes in order to obtain the results.

An organization of teachers for legislative purposes or for directive purposes is comparable to an organization on the line of the younger part of a large family for the control of the parents' efforts. I know such conditions do sometimes exist in domestic affairs. It is not rare to find the sons and daughters directing the affairs of the household in opposition to the opinion of the parents. The fact of the existence of this condition occasionally, however, will scarcely justify us in commending it.

On the other hand, one cannot forget that the amount of technical ability and intelligence embodied in the teachers of a city school system is of a scope far exceeding that of any one or group of ones. This effective knowledge must be used; the schools will never be at their best while their policy represents only executive power, or even while they represent the power of the legislative and executive department. But this counsel, this giving of advice which is essential, is not to be given in a formal way thru the orders and directions and laws and rules of an organized body like that of a trades union; but, on the other hand, it is to be given as the good daughter talks with the father and mother; as the kindly son participates in the counsels of the home. Practically it is to be given by frequent convocations, experience meetings, advice, the result of personal study and investigation; not by dictatorial law. The dictation must come from the other end.

The superintendent of schools is given a route along which to travel. At the various stations he finds his associates doing an allotted duty. His limitations require him to demand the result; that is to say, the ultimate performance of the task. He cannot and must not presume to interfere with the manner of that performance; he asks that when he reaches the end of the route his inspection shall have demonstrated that all the machinery is working, and expects to discover that the methods of that work have been materially modified according to the instrumentalities of the performance.

No two minds approach a given subject along the same trail, altho both reach the objective. No instructors train their charges in identical ways; and yet the results of that training are similar; never, however, identical.

The personal characteristics of the superintendent long associated with a school system are bound to be largely infused, injected, into that system; and they ought to be. In the same way the positive characteristics of the teacher are bound to be infused into the little character which he has in his training; and it ought to be; for it is because of the excellencies of these characteristics that superintendent and teachers are engaged for the work.

It is wicked to work at cross-purposes. Both superintendent and teacher have abundant limitations. Complete confidence is an essential; contest, conflict, suspicion, and strife are fatal.

The teacher's independence, as mentioned in the title of this paper, is the independence of the free American citizen who has entered upon the performance of a duty definitely and positively outlined at the outset. The purpose is defined at the commencement; the demand is that it be accomplished. The teacher has independence and can have independence like that of the man in the shoe factory who is told tomorrow morning to make a pair of No. 6 boots. The independence of that workman consists in the fact that he can sew four stitches in a minute or forty, can work rapidly or slowly, as he chooses or as he is able; but his dependence is that the boots must be made and made exactly, according to the order both in size and quality and execution.

Under the present typical school organizations of the country, the limitations of the superintendent's authority are necessarily loosely defined. A system has grown up of superintendents of schools with a corps of assistant superintendents of schools. Not only the title of the office of "assistant superintendent" is unfortunate, but it is quite out of place for an efficient organization. The better plan is that but one superintendent of any enterprise be appointed to office and intrusted with its duties. No one official can do all the work which falls upon the duties of his office; he must have assistance. In older and well-organized institutions but one head exists. As many men and women as are needed should be appointed and nominated school inspectors. A great part of the actual labor connected with the superintendent's office is in the department of inspection. The superintendent of large interests cannot be also an effective inspecting officer. He must call about him a corps of inspectors whose duties should be to inspect and to report.

A notable illustration of what I am trying to say is in the War Department of the nation. Those who are fairly familiar with that department of our government understand how emphatic and essential is regarded the inspection of garrisons, posts, divisions, battalions, and regiments. The commanding officer at headquarters keeps in touch with all stations in his department by occasional personal inspection, but frequent and detailed inspection is necessary, and is performed by officers of the inspector-general's department.

The time never was nor can be when a superintendent of schools can efficiently perform his duties from his desk; but in every school district comes the time when, owing to the increasing size, hours at his desk are increased, and the superintendent's opportunities to inspect grow less. He substitutes for his original personal inspection that of a lieutenant sent out. While we have grown to call this office that of "assistant superintendent," I suggest that that name be omitted hereafter in the titles of school officials, and that one responsible directive power called the superintendent's office be, as it is sometimes now, practically the ultimatum in school affairs. Some local and political embarrassments would not exist as they do now, were the office of assistant superintendent unknown.

Then, again, the most valuable power, that which deserves and must receive more compensation than any other, is the directive power—the superintendent—whether it be of a transportation company, or of a great industrial enterprise, or of schools.

The expense of the office can be reduced by appointing school inspectors—young men, growing men, men in training for the office of superintendent; but who can afford, while learning that business and growing up, to receive a part of their remuneration in the value of the training.

The executive department of a school system of thirty thousand pupils would be ideal with one superintendent and four school inspectors who shall spend their entire time, as does the inspecting officer of the army, in reviewing and examining in detail every part of the enterprise and reporting promptly and often, in a very careful way, what he finds; and in recommending, if the superintendent asks for recommendation; if not, avoiding comment altogether.

Such an organization would remove too, beyond cavil, any possible envies, jealousies, or discords that occasionally rise to the surface in some of our cities.

We realize fully the general tendency of our country to organize men and women for the purpose of self-defense, self-protection, and frequently for offensive operation. In general terms, we call it the conflict between labor and capital; in particular terms, we name on the one side "trusts," on the other "unions." So general is this agitation, this inclination, this tendency, that, as has been intimated, it has reached the teachers of the country; and in no pessimistic humor I am compelled to view this tendency with alarm. It is fraught with danger. Some effort has been made in this paper to condemn teacher's trade unions. I am unable to approach this subject on a common plane of action; if it be industrial, it concerns artisans laboring under working contracts; if it be spiritual, it concerns the training of intellects and souls in the love of patriotism and devotion to family and country, as well as for immortal life. If sordidness of our personal life, whereby most effort is gauged by the dollar to be returned for the effort, who can feel secure for the future of our nation? The schools themselves are modifying the courses of study, while the character of the teacher and the purpose intended are those which shall bring the greatest financial returns. The boys and girls in the high school are surrounded by the environment of an idealism which is represented by the accumulation of great fortunes. An organization of teachers is intended to increase rather than diminish that tendency.

I place the subject before you, and would that I could portray as upon canvas the inevitable outcome, should the school world descend to a lower plane of social life, where the measurements of life's work cease to be honor, integrity, patriotism, and love, and become that which represents acquisitiveness, selfishness and financial success at the expense of the neighbor; striving chiefly for a superiority of wealth over everybody, regardless of the truths of ideal manhood.

9.5   John Dewey Sketches a New Type of School: The Principles and Practices of the Laboratory School at the University of Chicago.

The School and Social Progress

We are apt to look at the school from an individualistic standpoint, as something between teacher and pupil, or between teacher and parent. That which interests us most is naturally the progress made by the individual child of our acquaintance, his normal physical development, his advance in ability to read, write, and figure, his growth in the knowledge of geography and history, improvement in manners, habits of promptness, order, and industry—it is from such standards as these that we judge the work of the school. And rightly so. Yet the range of the outlook needs to be enlarged. What the best and wisest parent wants for his own child, that must the community want for all of its children. Any other ideal for our schools is narrow and unlovely; acted upon, it destroys our democracy. All that society has accomplished for itself is put, through the agency of the school, at the disposal of its future members. All its better thoughts of itself it hopes to realize through the new possibilities thus opened to its future self. Here individualism and socialism are at one. Only by being true to the full growth of all the individuals who make it up, can society by any chance be true to itself. And in the self-direction thus given, nothing counts as much as the school, for, as Horace Mann said, "Where anything is growing, one former is worth a thousand reformers."

Whenever we have in mind the discussion of a new movement in education, it is especially necessary to take the broader, or social view. Otherwise, changes in the school institution and tradition will be looked at as the arbitrary inventions of particular teachers; at the worst transitory fads, and at the best merely improvements in certain details—and this is the plane upon which it is too customary to consider school changes. It is as rational to conceive of the locomotive or the telegraph as personal devices. The modification going on in the method and curriculum of education is as much a product of the changed social situation, and as much an effort to meet the needs of the new society that is forming, as are changes in modes of industry and commerce.

It is to this, then, that I especially ask your attention: the effort to conceive what roughly may be termed the "New Education" in the light of larger changes in society. Can we connect this "New Education" with

John Dewey, *The School and Society* (Chicago: University of Chicago Press, 1899; Copyright 1900 by John Dewey), Ch. I.

the general march of events? If we can, it will lose its isolated character, and will cease to be an affair which proceeds only from the over-ingenious minds of pedagogues dealing with particular pupils. It will appear as part and parcel of the whole social evolution, and, in its more general features at least, as inevitable. Let us then ask after the main aspects of the social movement; and afterwards turn to the school to find what witness it gives of effort to put itself in line. And since it is quite impossible to cover the whole ground, I shall for the most part confine myself to one typical thing in the modern school movement—that which passes under the name of manual training, hoping if the relation of that to changed social conditions appears, we shall be ready to concede the point as well regarding other educational innovations.

I make no apology for not dwelling at length upon the social changes in question. Those I shall mention are writ so large that he who runs may read. The change that comes first to mind, the one that overshadows and even controls all others, is the industrial one—the application of science resulting in the great inventions that have utilized the forces of nature on a vast and inexpensive scale: the growth of a world-wide market as the object of production, of vast manufacturing centers to supply this market, of cheap and rapid means of communication and distribution between all its parts. Even as to its feebler beginnings, this change is not much more than a century old; in many of its most important aspects it falls within the short span of those now living. One can hardly believe there has been a revolution in all history so rapid, so extensive, so complete. Through it the face of the earth is making over, even as to its physical forms; political boundaries are wiped out and moved about, as if they were indeed only lines on a paper map; population is hurriedly gathered into cities from the ends of the earth; habits of living are altered with startling abruptness and thoroughness; the search for the truths of nature is infinitely stimulated and facilitated and their application to life made not only practicable, but commercially necessary. Even our moral and religious ideas and interests, the most conservative because the deepest-lying things in our nature, are profoundly affected. That this revolution should not affect education in other than formal and superficial fashion is inconceivable.

Back of the factory system lies the household and neighborhood system. Those of us who are here today need go back only one, two, or at most three generations, to find a time when the household was practically the center in which were carried on, or about which were clustered, all the typical forms of industrial occupation. The clothing worn was for the most part not only made in the house, but the members of the household were usually familiar with the shearing of the sheep, the carding and spinning of the wool, and the plying of the loom.   Instead of pressing a button and flooding the house with electric light, the whole process of getting illumination was followed in its toilsome length, from the killing of the animal and the trying of fat, to the making of wicks and dipping of candles.   The supply of flour, of lumber, of foods, of building materials, of household furniture, even of metal ware, of nails, hinges, hammers, etc., was in the immediate neighborhood, in shops which were constantly open to inspection and often centers of neighborhood congregation.   The entire industrial process stood revealed, from the production on the farm of the raw materials, till the finished article was actually put to use.   Not only this, but practically every member of the household had his own share in the work.   The children, as they gained in strength and capacity, were gradually initiated into the mysteries of the several processes.   It was a matter of immediate and personal concern, even to the point of actual participation.

We cannot overlook the factors of discipline and of character-building involved in this: training in habits of order and of industry, and in the idea of responsibility, of obligation to do something, to produce something, in the world.   There was always something which really needed to be done, and a real necessity that each member of the household should do his own part faithfully and in coöperation with others.   Personalities which became effective in action were bred and tested in the medium of action. Again, we cannot overlook the importance for educational purposes of the close and intimate acquaintance got with nature at first hand, with real things and materials, with the actual processes of their manipulation, and the knowledge of their social necessities and uses.   In all this there was continual training of observation, of ingenuity, constructive imagination, of logical thought, and of the sense of reality acquired through first-hand contact with actualities.   The educative forces of the domestic spinning and weaving, of the saw-mill, the grist-mill, the cooper shop, and the blacksmith forge, were continuously operative.

No number of object-lessons, got up *as* object-lessons for the sake of giving information, can afford even the shadow of a substitute for acquaintance with the plants and animals of the farm and garden, acquired through actual living among them and caring for them.   No training of sense-organs in school, introduced for the sake of training, can begin to compete with the alertness and fullness of sense-life that comes through daily intimacy and interest in familiar occupations.   Verbal memory can be trained in committing tasks, a certain discipline of the reasoning powers can be acquired through lessons in science and mathematics; but, after all, this is somewhat remote and shadowy compared with the training of attention and of judgment that is acquired in having to do things with a real motive behind and a real outcome ahead. At present, concentration of industry and division of labor have practically eliminated household and neighborhood occupations—at least for educational purposes. But it is useless to bemoan the departure of the good old days of children's modesty, reverence, and implicit obedience, if we expect merely by bemoaning and by exhortation to bring them back. It is radical conditions which have changed, and only an equally radical change in education suffices. We must recognize our compensations—the increase in toleration, in breadth of social judgment, the larger acquaintance with human nature, the sharpened alertness in reading signs of character and interpreting social situations, greater accuracy of adaptation to differing personalities, contact with greater commercial activities. These considerations mean much to the city-bred child of today. Yet there is a real problem: how shall we retain these advantages, and yet introduce into the school something representing the other side of life—occupations which exact personal responsibilities and which train the child with relation to the physical realities of life?

When we turn to the school, we find that one of the most striking tendencies at present is toward the introduction of so-called manual training, shop-work, and the household arts—sewing and cooking.

This has not been done "on purpose," with a full consciousness that the school must now supply that factor of training formerly taken care of in the home, but rather by instinct, by experimenting and finding that such work takes a vital hold of pupils and gives them something which was not to be got in any other way. Consciousness of its real import is still so weak that the work is often done in a half-hearted, confused, and unrelated way. The reasons assigned to justify it are painfully inadequate or sometimes even positively wrong.

If we were to cross-examine even those who are most favorably disposed to the introduction of this work into our school system, we should, I imagine, generally find the main reasons to be that such work engages the full spontaneous interest and attention of the children. It keeps them alert and active, instead of passive and receptive; it makes them more useful, more capable, and hence more inclined to be helpful at home; it prepares them to some extent for.the practical duties of later life—the girls to be more efficient house managers, if not actually cooks and sempstresses; the boys (were our educational system only adequately rounded out into trade schools) for their future vocations. I do not underestimate the worth of these reasons. Of those indicated by the changed attitude of the children I shall indeed have something to say in my next talk, when speaking directly of the relationship of the school to the child. But the point of view is, upon the whole, unnecessarily narrow. We must conceive of work in wood and metal, of weaving, sewing, and cooking, as methods of life not as distinct studies.

We must conceive of them in their social significance, as types of the processes by which society keeps itself going, as agencies for bringing home to the child some of the primal necessities of community life, and as ways in which these needs have been met by the growing insight and ingenuity of man; in short, as instrumentalities through which the school itself shall be made a genuine form of active community life, instead of a place set apart in which to learn lessons.

A society is a number of people held together because they are working along common lines, in a common spirit, and with reference to common aims.   The common needs and aims demand a growing interchange of thought and growing unity of sympathetic feeling.   The radical reason that the present school cannot organize itself as a natural social unit is because just this element of common and productive activity is absent. Upon the playground, in game and sport, social organization takes place spontaneously and inevitably.   There is something to do, some activity to be carried on, requiring natural divisions of labor, selection of leaders and followers, mutual coöperation and emulation.   In the schoolroom the motive and the cement of social organization are alike wanting.   Upon the ethical side, the tragic weakness of the present school is that it endeavors to prepare future members of the social order in a medium in which the conditions of the social spirit are eminently wanting.

The difference that appears when occupations are made the articulating centers of school life is not easy to describe in words; it is a difference in motive, of spirit and atmosphere.   As one enters a busy kitchen in which a group of children are actively engaged in the preparation of food, the psychological difference, the change from more or less passive and inert recipiency and restraint to one of buoyant outgoing energy, is so obvious as fairly to strike one in the face.   Indeed, to those whose image of the school is rigidly set the change is sure to give a shock.   But the change in the social attitude is equally marked.   The mere absorption of facts and truths is so exclusively individual an affair that it tends very naturally to pass into selfishness.   There is no obvious social motive for the acquirement of mere learning, there is no clear social gain in success thereat.   Indeed, almost the only measure for success is a competitive one, in the bad sense of that term—a comparison of results in the recitation or in the examination to see which child has succeeded in getting ahead of others in storing up, in accumulating the maximum of information.   So thoroughly is this the prevalent atmosphere that for one child to help another in his task has become a school crime.   Where the school work consists in simply learning lessons, mutual assistance, instead of being the most natural form of coöperation and association, becomes a clandestine effort to relieve one's neighbor of his proper duties. Where active work is going on all this is changed. Helping others, instead of being a form of charity which impoverishes the recipient, is simply an aid in setting free the powers and furthering the impulse of the one helped. A spirit of free communication, of interchange of ideas, suggestions, results, both successes and failures of previous experiences, becomes the dominating note of the recitation. So far as emulation enters in, it is in the comparison of individuals, not with regard to the quantity of information personally absorbed, but with reference to the quality of work done—the genuine community standard of value. In an informal but all the more pervasive way, the school life organizes itself on a social basis.

Within this organization is found the principle of school discipline or order. Of course, order is simply a thing which is relative to an end. If you have the end in view of forty or fifty children learning certain set lessons, to be recited to a teacher, your discipline must be devoted to securing that result. But if the end in view is the development of a spirit of social coöperation and community life, discipline must grow out of and be relative to this. There is little order of one sort where things are in process of construction; there is a certain disorder in any busy workshop; there is not silence; persons are not engaged in maintaining certain fixed physical postures; their arms are not folded; they are not holding their books thus and so. They are doing a variety of things, and there is the confusion, the bustle, that results from activity. But out of occupation, out of doing things that are to produce results, and out of doing these in a social and coöperative way, there is born a discipline of its own kind and type. Our whole conception of school discipline changes when we get this point of view. In critical moments we all realize that the only discipline that stands by us, the only training that becomes intuition, is that got through life itself. That we learn from experience, and from books or the sayings of others *only* as they are related to experience, are not mere phrases. But the school has been so set apart, so isolated from the ordinary conditions and motives of life, that the place where children are sent for discipline is the one place in the world where it is most difficult to get experience—the mother of all discipline worth the name. It is only where a narrow and fixed image of traditional school discipline dominates, that one is in any danger of overlooking that deeper and infinitely wider discipline that comes from having a part to do in constructive work, in contributing to a result which, social in spirit, is none the less obvious and tangible in form—and hence in a form with reference to which responsibility may be exacted and accurate judgment passed.

The great thing to keep in mind, then, regarding the introduction into the school of various forms of active occupation, is that through them the entire spirit of the school is renewed. It has a chance to affiliate itself with life, to become the child's habitat, where he learns through directed living; instead of being only a place to learn lessons having an abstract and remote reference to some possible living to be done in the future. It gets a chance to be a miniature community, an embryonic society. This is the fundamental fact, and from this arise continuous and orderly sources of instruction. Under the industrial *régime* described, the child, after all, shared in the work, not for the sake of the sharing, but for the sake of the product. The educational results secured were real, yet incidental and dependent. But in the school the typical occupations followed are freed from all economic stress. The aim is not the economic value of the products, but the development of social power and insight. It is this liberation from narrow utilities, this openness to the possibilities of the human spirit that makes these practical activities in the school allies of art and centers of science and history.

The unity of all the sciences is found in geography. The significance of geography is that it presents the earth as the enduring home of the occupations of man. The world without its relationship to human activity is less than a world. Human industry and achievement, apart from their roots in the earth, are not even a sentiment, hardly a name. The earth is the final source of all man's food. It is his continual shelter and protection, the raw material of all his activities, and the home to whose humanizing and idealizing all his achievement returns. It is the great field, the great mine, the great source of the energies of heat, light, and electricity; the great scene of ocean, stream, mountain, and plain, of which all our agriculture and mining and lumbering, all our manufacturing and distributing agencies, are but the partial elements and factors. It is through occupations determined by this environment that mankind has made its historical and political progress. It is through these occupations that the intellectual and emotional interpretation of nature has been developed. It is through what we do in and with the world that we read its meaning and measure its value.

In educational terms, this means that these occupations in the school shall not be mere practical devices or modes of routine employment, the gaining of better technical skill as cooks, sempstresses, or carpenters, but active centers of scientific insight into natural materials and processes, points of departure whence children shall be led out into a realization of the historic development of man.

9.6 "The Principles of Progressive Education" as Stated by the Progressive Education Association in 1924.

I. Freedom to Develop Naturally

The conduct of the pupil should be governed by himself according to the social needs of his community, rather than by arbitrary laws. Full opportunity for initiative and self-expression should be provided, together with an environment rich in interesting material that is available for the free use of every pupil.

II. Interest, the Motive of All Work

Interest should be satisfied and developed through: (1) Direct and indirect contact with the world and its activities, and use of the experience thus gained. (2) Application of knowledge gained, and correlation between different subjects. (3) The consciousness of achievement.

III. The Teacher a Guide, Not a Task-Master

It is essential that teachers should believe in the aims and general principles of Progressive Education and that they should have latitude for the development of initiative and originality.

Progressive teachers will encourage the use of all the senses, training the pupils in both observation and judgment; and instead of hearing recitations only, will spend most of the time teaching how to use various sources of information, including life activities as well as books; how to reason about the information thus acquired; and how to express forcefully and logically the conclusions reached.

Ideal teaching conditions demand that classes be small, especially in the elementary school years.

IV. Scientific Study of Pupil Development

School records should not be confined to the marks given by the teachers to show the advancement of the pupils in their study of subjects, but should also include both objective and subjective reports on those physical, mental, moral and social characteristics which affect both school and adult life, and which can be influenced by the school and the home. Such rec-

Progressive Education: *A Quarterly Review of the Newer Tendencies in Education*, I (April 1924), p. 1.

ords should be used as a guide for the treatment of each pupil, and should also serve to focus the attention of the teacher on the all-important work of development rather than on simply teaching subject matter.

V. Greater Attention to All that Affects the Child's Physical Development

One of the first considerations of Progressive Education is the health of the pupils. Much more room in which to move about, better light and air, clean and well ventilated buildings, easier access to the out-of-doors and greater use of it, are all necessary. There should be frequent use of adequate playgrounds. The teachers should observe closely the physical condition of each pupil and, in co-operation with the home, make abounding health the first objective of childhood.

VI. Co-operation Between School and Home to Meet the Needs of Child-Life

The school should provide, with the home, as much as is possible of all that the natural interests and activities of the child demand, especially during the elementary school years. These conditions can come about only through intelligent co-operation between parents and teachers.

VII. The Progressive School a Leader in Educational Movements

The Progressive School should be a leader in educational movements. It should be a laboratory where new ideas, if worthy, meet encouragement; where tradition alone does not rule, but the best of the past is leavened with the discoveries of today, and the result is freely added to the sum of educational knowledge.

9.7   John Dewey Discusses the Difficulty of Putting the Principles of the "New Education" into Practice and Chastizes Extreme Progressives.

The general principles of the new education do not of themselves solve any of the problems of the actual or practical conduct and management of progressive schools. Rather, they set new problems which have to be worked out on the basis of a new philosophy of experience. The problems are not even recognized, to say nothing of being solved, when it is assumed that it suffices to reject the ideas and practices of the old education and then go to the opposite extreme. Yet I am sure that you will

John Dewey, *Experience and Education* (New York: The Macmillan Company, 1938), pp. 9–11, 68, 92–96. Reprinted by permission of The Macmillan Company.

appreciate what is meant when I say that many of the newer schools tend to make little or nothing of organized subject-matter of study; to proceed as if any form of direction and guidance by adults were an invasion of individual freedom, and as if the idea that education should be concerned with the present and future meant that acquaintance with the past has little or no role to play in education. Without pressing these defects to the point of exaggeration, they at least illustrate what is meant by a theory and practice of education which proceeds negatively or by reaction against what has been current in education rather than by a positive and constructive development of purposes, methods, and subject-matter on the foundation of a theory of experience and its educational potentialities.

It is not too much to say that an educational philosophy which professes to be based on the idea of freedom may become as dogmatic as ever was the traditional education which is reacted against. For any theory and set of practices is dogmatic which is not based upon critical examination of its own underlying principles. Let us say that the new education emphasizes the freedom of the learner. Very well. A problem is now set. What does freedom mean and what are the conditions under which it is capable of realization? Let us say that the kind of external imposition which was so common in the traditional school limited rather than promoted the intellectual and moral development of the young. Again, very well. Recognition of this serious defect sets a problem. Just what is the role of the teacher and of books in promoting the educational development of the immature? Admit that traditional education employed as the subject-matter for study facts and ideas so bound up with the past as to give little help in dealing with the issues of the present and future. Very well. Now we have the problem of discovering the connection which actually exists *within* experience between the achievements of the past and the issues of the present. We have the problem of ascertaining how acquaintance with the past may be translated into a potent instrumentality for dealing effectively with the future. We may reject knowledge of the past as the *end* of education and thereby only emphasize its importance as a *means*. When we do that we have a problem that is new in the story of education: How shall the young become acquainted with the past in such a way that the acquaintance is a potent agent in appreciation of the living present? . . .

Visitors to some progressive schools are shocked by the lack of manners they come across. One who knows the situation better is aware that to some extent their absence is due to the eager interest of children to go on with what they are doing. In their eagerness they may, for example, bump into each other and into visitors with no word of apology. One might say that this condition is better than a display of merely external punctilio accompanying intellectual and emotional lack of interest in school work. But it also represents a failure in education, a failure to learn one of the most important lessons of life, that of mutual accommodation and adaptation. Education is going on in a one-sided way, for attitudes and habits are in process of formation that stand in the way of the future learning that springs from easy and ready contact and communication with others. . . .

Because the studies of the traditional school consisted of subject-matter that was selected and arranged on the basis of the judgment of adults as to what would be useful for the young sometime in the future, the material to be learned was settled upon outside the present life-experience of the learner. In consequence, it had to do with the past; it was such as had proved useful to men in past ages. By reaction to an opposite extreme, as unfortunate as it was probably natural under the circumstances, the sound idea that education should derive its materials from present experience and should enable the learner to cope with the problems of the present and future has often been converted into the idea that progressive schools can to a very large extent ignore the past. If the present could be cut off from the past, this conclusion would be sound. But the achievements of the past provide the only means at command for understanding the present. Just as the individual has to draw in memory upon his own past to understand the conditions in which he individually finds himself, so the issues and problems of present *social* life are in such intimate and direct connection with the past that students cannot be prepared to understand either these problems or the best way of dealing with them without delving into their roots in the past. In other words, the sound principle that the objectives of learning are in the future and its immediate materials are in present experience can be carried into effect only in the degree that present experience is stretched, as it were, backward. It can expand into the future only as it is also enlarged to take in the past.

If time permitted, discussion of the political and economic issues which the present generation will be compelled to face in the future would render this general statement definite and concrete. The nature of the issues cannot be understood save as we know how they came about. The institutions and customs that exist in the present and that give rise to present social ills and dislocations did not arise overnight. They have a long history behind them. Attempt to deal with them simply on the basis of what is obvious in the present is bound to result in adoption of superficial measures which in the end will only render existing problems more acute and more difficult to solve. Policies framed simply upon the ground of knowledge of the present cut off from the past is the counterpart of heedless carelessness in individual conduct. The way out of scholastic systems that made the past an end in itself is to make acquaintance with the past a *means* of understanding the present. Until this problem is worked out, the present clash of educational ideas and practices will continue. On the one hand, there will be reactionaries that claim that the main, if not the sole, business of education is transmission of the cultural heritage. On the other hand, there will be those who hold that we should ignore the past and deal only with the present and future.

That up to the present time the weakest point in progressive schools is in the matter of selection and organization of intellectual subject-matter is, I think, inevitable under the circumstances. It is as inevitable as it is right and proper that they should break loose from the cut and dried material which formed the staple of the old education. In addition, the field of experience is very wide and it varies in its contents from place to place and from time to time. A single course of studies for all progressive schools is out of the question; it would mean abandoning the fundamental principle of connection with life-experiences. Moreover, progressive schools are new. They have had hardly more than a generation in which to develop. A certain amount of uncertainty and of laxity in choice and organization of subject-matter is, therefore, what was to be expected. It is no ground for fundamental criticism or complaint.

It is a ground for legitimate criticism, however, when the ongoing movement of progressive education fails to recognize that the problem of selection and organization of subject-matter for study and learning is fundamental. Improvisation that takes advantage of special occasions prevents teaching and learning from being stereotyped and dead. But the basic material of study cannot be picked up in a cursory manner. Occasions which are not and cannot be foreseen are bound to arise wherever there is intellectual freedom. They should be utilized. But there is a decided difference between using them in the development of a continuing line of activity and trusting to them to provide the chief material of learning.

The People's College:

The Emergence of the High School

10

During much of its history the American high school has been an institution in search of an identity. "The term high school is the vaguest in the school vocabulary," observed a schoolman in 1892. "It covers an endless variety of schools with an infinite variety of courses of study, aims, ideals, and methods." Seen from the college, ignominiously, as a "gap" between elementary and higher education, but viewed with different perspective from the elementary school, the public high school has come into its own only in the twentieth century. Report after report has recorded the soul-searching of those concerned with the character of the high school and its function in society: the Committee of Ten's response in 1893, the *Cardinal Principles* enunciated in 1918, the writings of the life adjustment group in the 1940's and 1950's, and James B. Conant's report to the nation on *The American High School Today* in 1959. Was the high school to prepare students for "life," and if so, what sort of life? Or was it to prepare students for college (in itself a rapidly changing institution)? While schoolmen have, of course, also debated about elementary and higher education, the secondary school has elicited greater controversy and anxiety, greater pendulum swings of philosophical position and classroom practice.

This was not always so. There was little confusion in the purpose or curriculum of the Boston Latin School when it was founded in 1635, nor of other town grammar schools in seventeenth-century New England. Their curriculum was a compound of Latin, Greek, and mathematics, as evolved by tradition in England since the thirteenth century. Their purpose was to prepare youth to enter Harvard, which, in turn, would train them to serve church and state. As demonstrated in Benjamin Franklin's career, however, by the eighteenth century people began to want a different sort of education beyond the dame school. A host of private schools met this demand for utilitarian training, whether in the form of night schools for craftsmen or ambitious academies similar in intent to Franklin's.

During most of the nineteenth century the academy dominated secondary education. The old Latin grammar schools persisted in a few communities, and a new institution called a "high school" appeared in Boston in 1821. But probably not until the 1880's did students enrolled in high schools begin to outnumber those in academies. The academy defies simple characterization. Though private boards of trustees controlled them, the schools often received grants of land or funds from the state. Students came to "academies" from a broad gamut of social classes, sons and daughters of the business elite who attended finishing schools and expensive prep schools, rustic farm boys who attended the local one-room school on a tuition scholarship. An astounding range of subjects appeared, from embroidery to Hebrew, surveying to ethics. Usually the subjects were grouped into patterns appropriate to the aspirations of the students; at Gould's Academy in Bethel, Maine, for example, different courses of study were arranged for "those fitting for College, Teaching, or the Counting Room."

Both a generalized American faith in education and local pride multiplied these academies. Boosters and land speculators thought it good for the town's image to have an academy. Public-spirited men and women and parents eager for further education for their children founded schools with the entrepreneurial zeal and optimism characteristic of mid-century America. The endowment of one academy in Indiana for one year was "one day's work, one horse collar, one steel trap, five pounds of coffee, six pounds of sugar, fifty pounds of flour and four bushels of wheat." In many cases the students studied "the common branches" with a little window dressing of more advanced study of rhetoric, history, and literature. In some, however, like the Phillips Academies in Andover, Massachusetts, and Exeter, New Hampshire, students could find the best preparation for college then available. The majority of the academies were more responsive to the academic and vocational interests of students than were the high schools of the time. Classes were often small, individual tutorial common. More for commercial than for theoretical reasons, academies allowed election of studies long before it became a topic of discussion in meetings of the National Education Association.

Academies provided educational opportunities otherwise unavailable in a period when the population was widely dispersed and the tax base in most communities was barely sufficient to support elementary schools.

Indeed, as boarding academies began to die out in the latter half of the nineteenth century, rural youth may have had less chance for obtaining secondary education than earlier in the century. Charles W. Eliot said in 1890 that "the mass of the rural population—that is to say, three-quarters of the American people—is unprovided with secondary schools."

The fate of individual academies shows how varied the institutions had been. Some became colleges, some elementary schools, some public high schools; some continued as elite college preparatory schools, some as sectarian schools; some simply died.

Unlike the academy, the public high school in the nineteenth century was mainly an urban invention. When the Boston School Committee decided in 1821 to build a high school to complement its Latin school, it persuaded the citizens that Yankee common sense dictated rounding out the educational system that had served them so well. "A parent who wishes to give a child an education that shall fit him for active life, and shall serve as a foundation for eminence in his profession, whether mercantile or mechanical," was forced to send him away to an academy, said the Committee. If the town should fit boys for college, then it should equally well fit them for the mercantile and mechanical "professions."

Under the prodding of the pioneer reformer James Carter, who feared that private academies would undermine the public schools by attracting the wealthy, Massachusetts passed a law in 1827 requiring towns of 500 families or more to maintain a high school which would offer United States history, surveying, algebra, bookkeeping, and geometry; cities of 4,000 inhabitants or more needed to add the classics. For over a half century Massachusetts was the only state to require towns to establish high schools, and even there this law was often ignored.

In contrast with the Latin grammar school, which was a ladder leading to college, the first Boston High School was a projection upward from the common school, ornamented by detail copied from academies. In many communities the so-called "high school" was simply a room or two of the regular common school reserved for the older children. Tennessee passed a law in 1891 defining "secondary education" as grades six, seven, and eight. In Illinois 220 of the 258 high schools in 1896 were housed in elementary school quarters. Washington Territory refused to grant funds for schools teaching "languages other than English and mathematics higher than algebra." An individual teacher in such a "high school" annexed to the common school would generally be expected to teach all subjects. In rural communities the name *high school* was customarily an honorific label attached to the upper grades, just as the term *college* in the nineteenth century often signified high aspirations but low achievement.

A number of cities, however, supported high schools of high caliber. In Cincinnati, St. Louis, San Francisco, and Portland, Oregon, for example, the high school was one of the grandest buildings in town, a palace which held its own with the fanciest private academy. The Woodward High School in Cincinnati, endowed by a private gift, soared in Tudor splendor, buttresses capped with ornamented pinnacles, windows surrounded by rich tracery, a Gothic wrought iron fence enclosing the grounds. Inside were two "philosophical rooms"—or laboratories—a grand lecture hall, library, and classrooms. Particularly in these western cities which had no tradition of Latin grammar schools, high schools tended to base their curriculum on the college preparatory subjects, perhaps in part to persuade leading citizens to enroll their children.

The high school was not, however, a rich man's school. It is probable that individual students came from a wide social spectrum, but most emerging from the upper range of the middle class. One study of several cities in Massachusetts revealed that the parents of 25 per cent of the students paid no tax, or only a poll tax; 12.9 per cent paid taxes on over $10,000 of assessed real estate. Similar reports came from Lake View Township, Illinois, and Erie, Pennsylvania. In 1890 there were about 200,000 children in public high schools, about 360,000 in all secondary schools (these statistics are quite inaccurate because of poor returns from local and state officials, different ways of classifying schools from state to state, and shifting ways of grouping these returns). The latter figure represented about 6.7 per cent of the population aged 14–17. And even these schools had a very high drop-out rate; in most states only 10–20 per cent reached graduation during the 1890's.

Though only a small proportion of high school graduates went on to college, higher education exerted a powerful influence on secondary education. The college men vociferously complained about the caliber of instruction their students had received in high schools and elementary schools. In turn, schoolmen bitterly objected to the detailed and diverse admission requirements of colleges. In consternation one principal reported in 1891 that admission standards "are found to range from the merest rudiments of arithmetic, reading, and writing, up to the highest mathematics, Greek, moral philosophy, and the history of art. It is hardly an exaggeration to say that the histories of all states and all times are included, from Babylonian and Assyrian history, specially designated, in the requirements of one college, and of Persian history, in those of another, down to the history of Texas and North Carolina, the former required by three, the latter by two colleges."

When colleges drew students from a small group of local schools, the problem of admission requirements had not been so serious: the colleges laid down the law, and the preparatory schools obeyed. But as colleges drew students from wider and wider areas, with the advent of the railroad and the nationalizing of public life, colleges searched for other controls over the character of secondary preparation. Some states attempted to accredit high schools, using either the faculty of the state university or special state boards to visit high schools; accreditation, once granted, allowed principals to recommend students for admission to the state university without examination. Regional associations of colleges and secondary schools, like the North Central, founded in 1895, further broadened the scope of accreditation. The College Entrance Examination Board, the brainchild of President Charles W. Eliot of Harvard, gave its first tests in 1901 as another means of standardizing college admissions. But before any of these plans could be carried out efficiently, a blueprint was needed to bring order out of the chaos that was the American high school.

To make such a blueprint was the task of the Committee of Ten. The Committee was a group appointed in 1892 by the National Council of Education, the inner braintrust of the National Education Association. The chairman was Eliot, a master at arousing discussion. Six of the ten were college presidents; one was the United States Commissioner of Education, the brilliant William T. Harris; two were public high school principals; and one a private school headmaster. Carrying authority in both university and school circles, the Committee hoped that its report would cause the colleges to modify their admission requirements and the high schools to change their programs. They took an Olympian view of their task: to provide a model of excellence. Not a word about East Overshoe with its ten students and one teacher, or West Sinkhole with its corrupt school board annually holding a "family night" when members hired indigent relatives.

The Committee's definition of its task was classically simple in comparison with the view of curriculum design which emerged later in the *Cardinal Principles*. The job of the Committee of Ten and their subcommittees was to select and arrange academic content. They did not talk about the "needs of youth" or "social efficiency." They considered themselves experts in education, which meant the imparting of knowledge and the development of intellectual power. And in their report they fulfilled, in clear prose, the limited mandate given them by the National Council of Education: to develop secondary school programs by considering "the proper limits of . . . [each] subject, the best methods of instruction, the most desirable allotment of time for the subject, and the best methods of testing the pupils' attainments therein. . . ."

Eliot wrote the report, abstracting the sub-committee recommendations on the traditional subjects of Latin, Greek, and mathematics, and the "moderns": English, social science, and natural science. Sharing a belief all but universal among educated men at the time, Eliot stressed "mental discipline," the view that intensive study led to increased power of observation, reasoning, memory, and expression. In subsequent attacks on the report—especially by educational psychologists in the twentieth century—critics assumed that Eliot and his colleagues were victims of the fallacy that training acquired in one field could automatically be transferred to another. Edward L. Thorndike undermined naive trust in "transfer of training" through his psychological research. But Eliot did not subscribe to a simplistic "muscles of the mind" theory (that a subject was good for you only if it was difficult and you didn't like it). Actually Eliot was an early advocate of the spirit of scientific inquiry in teaching and learning, and his comments on mental training seem not far from the view of psychologists today who assert that a child can "learn how to learn." The Committee of Ten was also broad-minded for its day in giving equal time to the "moderns."

Eliot thought it wise to postpone critical educational and vocational decisions to the latest moment, since only thus could students discover their true interests and talents. This conviction helps to explain what some have interpreted as a devious smokescreen in the *Report*, the implication that preparation for college was the best preparation for life—or that what was good for Harvard was good for the country. Eliot knew that preparing students for college was not the main function of the high school. But he believed that the door to college should be open for everyone to the end of high school and thought that the mental discipline acquired through the academic program would prove valuable whatever the graduate's career. In observing that high school was designed for those few students of high intellectual ability "whose parents are able to support them" while they attended school, he was simply stating a fact of life. It was not as observers but as predictors that he and the Committee failed: within a generation the student population and the social role of the high school were to undergo radical changes.

However liberal Eliot and his colleagues may have seemed to their traditionalist opponents, the curriculum they recommended was abstract and verbal. The city high school of the 1890's was usually a world removed from everyday life, often housed in fortress-like buildings, with corridors lined with mezzotint pictures of the Appian Way, the Forum, or characters from Sir Walter Scott. Even for highly verbal students the experience of secondary school was often dismal. "We went to school for facts and got them," wrote Henry S. Canby, a Yale professor, about his schooldays in the 1890's. "Facts about Latin, facts about history, facts about algebra, which gave us valuable experience in taking intellectual punishment without a quaver. But of education there was very little because, with one exception, none of our teachers were educated. They had knowledge but, not knowing what to do with it, passed it on to us in its raw condition of fact. . . . They believed in their subjects with the absolute conviction of the baker that his bread is the staff of life, but there was no passion in their belief, and, to tell the truth, not much reason." Self-expression the school knew "only as a form of naughtiness." Canby recalled "how little Miss Brown, with her watery voice, reduced the campaigns of Caesar to a pulp of grammar, . . . how all art was compressed into drawing the outlines of a dirty bust." As one teacher at the time said, teaching became too often mere "stereotyped incompetence."

In the 1890's a majority of schoolmen seem to have approved in principle the report of the Committee of Ten. One superintendent described it as "the cloud by day and the pillar of fire by night that is to lead us into the promised land." Then, changing the metaphor significantly, he called the report "the superintendents' armor, offensive and defensive." This was the key to the impact of the report: the great prestige of the Committee and their clear outline of an institution then in chaotic condition gave harried superintendents their armor. Although one investigator found ten years after the report that many of the specific recommendations had been violated more than followed, the report still shaped the high school in this transitional period. The United States Office of Education had distributed 30,000 free copies to educational leaders and used its curriculum tables as a basis for its own yearly statistical reports on the high school. High schools generally seem to have followed the suggestion that students should take only a few subjects and study them thoroughly.

An evolving system of academic bookkeeping was capped in 1909 by a definition of a "standard unit," given the nickname "Carnegie unit." The Board of the Carnegie Foundation for the Advancement of Teaching defined a "unit" as a course offered five periods weekly during the academic year. State and regional accrediting bodies increasingly enacted this suggestion into administrative law by requiring schools to adopt this system of accounting. At the time this was perhaps a desirable step toward uniformity amid chaotic practice, but it rapidly became a straight jacket, all the more serious because not recognized as such by most educators. Only in the 1960's did schools across the country begin to examine the possibilities inherent in flexible scheduling.

In the years between 1890 and 1920 the secondary school population mushroomed from 360,000 to 2,500,000, in the latter year including almost one-third of the population from 14 to 17 years old. Although the majority of *students* attended urban schools, the majority of *high schools* were small and rural; in 1904, for example, only 1,356 of the 7,199 high schools had five or more teachers.   Accordingly it is hard to find any typical school, yet probably the high schools which Sara Burstall, an English headmistress, visited in 1908 were representative of the best city school systems.   While these schools had programs reminiscent of the courses of study proposed by the Committee of Ten, they mostly resembled the eclectic ideal sketched by W. R. Garrett in 1891 in his address on "The Future High School."   In these schools college preparatory, commercial, and vocational courses were often given side by side in the fashion characteristic of American comprehensive secondary education.   Miss Burstall found a few eastern cities which established separate academic and vocational schools.   She remarked on the free mixing of students from different social classes, though this seemed undermined somewhat by the informal cliques and social clubs associated with the schools.

In a movement which accelerated in the second decade of the twentieth century, the larger spirit of social reform called progressivism entered the high school, culminating in a new N.E.A. report, *The Cardinal Principles of Secondary Education,* published in 1918, two years after Dewey's *Democracy and Education.*   The slogan of these reformers—"social efficiency"—indicated a profound shift in the burden of proof in decisions about the high school curriculum.   If schoolmen could once take academic tradition for granted, not so any longer.   Not only were the old liberal arts disciplines—the classics and mathematics—under siege, but by 1910 the "moderns," which had been shoehorned into the college preparatory curriculum a generation before, were now considered outmoded.   Now deciding what to teach required assessment of individual and social needs.   The new science of education would then determine what schooling could do to meet these needs.

One by one the old disciplines were put on the witness stand—or the rack.   "Latin, justify thy presence in a twentieth-century American high school curriculum!" said one principal.   History and the social sciences were to be replaced by social studies, defined as investigation "of social efforts to improve mankind."   Algebra faced assault; one man said that it had "injured the mind, destroyed the health, and wrecked the lives of thousands of children" (another added mysteriously that it had also caused many girls to lose their souls).   Even biology had to do its part to uplift humanity.   A teacher in New York said that children should study the living bee and ant to raise the "moral tone" of society by examples of "efficiency in the concrete."   The search for ulterior motives went grimly on.   When Otto Jespersen spoke to some teachers of English in 1910, he said that he disagreed with those who thought grammar utilitarian but boring. "I really think that grammar is really more or less useless, but that it is extremely fascinating." Jespersen was clearly out of step.

Some of the advocates of social control, intoxicated by the possibilities they saw in normative sociology, spoke of a Brave New World. David Snedden, Massachusetts' Commissioner of Education, said that science was everywhere gaining sway. In mating of couples "reason, understanding, and even science play an increasing part." As men gain control of their environment, "why should the world again miss the desires and strivings that formerly in the ages of faith produced a Homer, a Phidias, an Angelo, a Wren, a Palestrina, a Shakespeare?" Another sociologist, worried about misuse of leisure, said that sociologists should discover the best forms of recreation and then persuade the people to enjoy themselves properly. John Dewey heard a "hard and metallic" ring in the pronouncements of these social engineers, and was, in turn, criticized by one of them for being too individualistic. "While it is true," his critic said, "that citizens of a democracy should be taught to think, it is even more important . . . that they be trained to revere and obey."

Of the members-at-large of the committee which wrote *The Cardinal Principles,* three were education professors, one a university president who had recently been an education professor, one the United States Commissioner of Education, one a normal school principal, two were state high school supervisors, one a high school principal, one a representative of a private school, and one a Y.M.C.A. secretary. Few university professors of academic disciplines sat on sub-committees treating individual subjects. The committee discussed the nature of the students, the social role of the school, the transformation of society, new theories of education—all issues important in the 1890's as well, but almost totally neglected by the Committee of Ten. The 3 R's wormed into the seven cardinal principles disguised as "command of fundamental processes" (this was added in a later revision, having been omitted entirely in earlier drafts!). Now the rhetoric stressed "efficiency," "democracy," "activities," and seemed to relegate traditional knowledge to the scrap heap. Subjects ignored in 1893 thrust themselves forward in the sub-committee reports: business education, household arts, agriculture, art education, industrial arts, music, and physical education. The report made explicit and dramatic how the new education should shape the high school.

Under the spur of child labor legislation, the Depression, and changing social values, as the century progressed the high school did become "the people's college," clearly influenced in its ideology and practice by the common school from which it grew. By 1929–30, about 4,804,000 students were enrolled in secondary schools, 51.3 per cent of the age group from 14 to 17 years old; by 1939–40 the percentage had grown to 73.3 per cent, by 1959–60 to 83.2 per cent.

The Cardinal Principles was widely praised as a plan for reorganizing secondary schooling to meet these new conditions, but often those who applauded it admitted that few schools really put it into practice. Ten years after the report was issued 1,228 high school principals were asked if they had implemented the report. Of this group 689 said they had, 255 said they had never heard of the report, and 9 said they didn't believe in the report. Thousands of prospective teachers memorized the seven *Cardinal Principles*, hundreds of administrators analyzed them in curriculum classes. While it is difficult to judge the importance of such a report, it seems clear that it both reflected and shaped a growing consensus among schoolmen on the broad purposes of secondary education.

During the generation following the first World War most new statements on the aims of the high school echoed *The Cardinal Principles*. Eliot's name became synonymous with "traditional education" and the Committee of Ten with the domination of the high schools by the colleges; few recalled that Eliot had changed his views as the high school itself had changed, and in accepting the honorary presidency of the Progressive Education Association (preceding John Dewey in that position) in 1924, he had predicted that progressive schools "are to be the schools of the future." Eliot was right: the reforms of one period had become the stereotypes of the next.

During World War II the Educational Policies Commission of the National Education Association issued a new study on *Education for ALL American Youth* which incorporated many of the ideas of *The Cardinal Principles* and foreshadowed the "life-adjustment" philosophy of the 1940's and 1950's. In the "common learnings" part of this program the lines between academic and vocational fields, already blurred, became well-nigh indistinguishable. Once fresh and challenging in the early days of progressive education, terms like "zestful, purposeful learning" and the "needs of youth" were beginning to strike many thoughtful observers as cliches, the departure from logically organized knowledge a hazardous venture in a society sorely in need of experts.

In 1951 and 1954 the two Commissions on Life Adjustment Education for Youth issued reports which carried to Alexandrinian excess the non-intellectual accents of the progressive movement in the secondary school. These documents exemplified a prophetic comment of John Dewey in 1929: "Anybody can notice today," he said, "that the effect of an original and powerful teacher is not all to the good. Those influenced by him often show a one-sided interest; they tend to form schools, and to become impervious to other problems and truths; they incline to swear by the words of their master and to go on repeating his thoughts after him, and often without the spirit and insight which originally made them significant."

Partly in response to these reports, a chorus of angry criticism shattered the calm of the groves of academe in the 1950's as men like Arthur Bestor and Admiral Rickover attacked life-adjustment education and called for a return to traditional disciplines. Most critics urged the schools to narrow their concern to intellectual training, to what Bestor called "the deliberate cultivation of the ability to think." The swarm of unsolicited advisers included conscientious academicians like Bestor himself, members of ultra-right claques, political and religious conservatives, and a host of citizens of all persuasions who sensed that the time had come for a change in the schools. The appearance of Russian satellites overhead and the fizzling of American rockets on the pads alarmed average citizens and gave new force to the criticisms. Harried by shortages of funds, buildings, and teachers, confronted with a great surge of school-age children, schoolmen still had to face the practical problem of somehow teaching the children of all the people.

It was a period of crisis in American education, and it is not surprising that tempers on both sides of the controversy were often short. In this context James Bryant Conant issued his report in 1959 to the American people on *The American High School Today*. Calmly, Conant said that the comprehensive high school was a basically sound and democratic institution in need of minor repair, especially in its failure to challenge talented youth. Like another Harvard President's report—Eliot's in 1893—Conant's book became a coat of armor for many a besieged superintendent, for it contained practical criteria for evaluating and improving high schools—an inventory aimed as much for an audience of school board members and other laymen as for professionals themselves.

In some respects there has been a pendulum swing in the late 1950's and 1960's back towards the approach of the 1890's. Scholars in the universities have again joined their colleagues in the schools to create new academic curricula to replace the anachronistic or watery studies frequently taught. The Educational Policies Commission of the N.E.A. published in 1961 a statement of *The Central Purpose of American Education* which reaffirmed the basic importance of developing the "rational powers" of each citizen: "the processes of recalling and imagining, classifying and generalizing, comparing and evaluation, analyzing and synthesizing, and deducing and inferring"—a statement strikingly similar to Eliot's in 1893. And in declaring the development of these powers to be the *central* purpose of the schools the Educational Policies Commission seemed to accept the basic premise of Arthur Bestor's earlier criticism—though not his tone, his narrow view of liberal education, or his hostility to the field of education. Together, the new cooperation of scholars and schoolmen and the new emphasis on intellectual training as a prime function of the high school have constituted a silent revolution. This silent revolution in secondary education has accomplished far more practical good than the angry tirades of the 1950's and the panic accompanying Sputnik. It promises to bring into better balance the conflicting demands on the people's college.

10.1 Boston Founds a High School in 1821: The Report of the Boston School Committee.

Though the present system of public education, and the munificence with which it is supported, are highly beneficial and honorable to the Town; yet in the opinion of the Committee, it is susceptible of a greater degree of perfection and usefulness, without materially augmenting the weight of the public burdens. Till recently, our system occupied a middle station: it neither commenced with the rudiments of Education, nor extended to the higher branches of knowledge. This system was supported by the Town at a very great expense, and to be admitted to its advantages, certain preliminary qualifications were required at individual cost, which have the effect of excluding many children of the poor and unfortunate classes of the community from the benefits of a public education. The Town saw and felt this inconsistency in the plan, and have removed the defect by providing Schools in which the children of the poor can be fitted for admission into the public seminaries.

The present system, in the opinion of the Committee, requires still farther amendment. The studies that are pursued at the English grammar schools are merely elementary, and more time than is necessary is devoted to their acquisition. A scholar is admitted at seven, and is dismissed at fourteen years of age; thus, seven years are expended in the acquisition of a degree of knowledge, which with ordinary diligence and a common capacity, may be easily and perfectly acquired in five. If then, a boy remain the usual term, a large portion of the time will have been idly or uselessly expended, as he may have learned all that he may have been taught long before its expiration. This loss of time occurs at that interesting and critical period of life, when the habits and inclinations are forming by which the future character will be fixed and determined. This evil, therefore, should be removed, by enlarging the present system, not merely that

As quoted in Elmer E. Brown, *The Making of Our Middle Schools* (New York: Longmans, Green and Co., 1903), pp. 298–301.

the time now lost may be saved, but that those early habits of industry and application may be acquired, which are so essential in leading to a future life of virtue and usefulness.

Nor are these the only existing evils. The mode of education now adopted, and the branches of knowledge that are taught at our English grammar schools, are not sufficiently extensive nor otherwise calculated to bring the powers of the mind into operation nor to qualify a youth to fill usefully and respectably many of those stations, both public and private, in which he may be placed. A parent who wishes to give a child an education that shall fit him for active life, and shall serve as a foundation for eminence in his profession, whether Mercantile or Mechanical, is under the necessity of giving him a different education from any which our public schools can now furnish. Hence, many children are separated from their parents and sent to private academies in this vicinity, to acquire that instruction which cannot be obtained at the public seminaries. Thus, many parents, who contribute largely to the support of these institutions, are subjected to heavy expense for the same object, in other towns.

The Committee, for these and many other weighty considerations that might be offered, and in order to render the present system of public education more nearly perfect, are of the opinion that an additional School is required. They therefore, recommend the founding of a seminary which shall be called the English Classical School, and submit the following as a general outline of a plan for its organization and of the course of studies to be pursued.

1st. That the term of time for pursuing the course of studies proposed, be three years.

2ndly. That the School be divided into three classes, and one year be assigned to the studies of each class.

3rdly. That the age of admission be not less than twelve years.

4thly. That the School be for Boys exclusively.

5thly. That candidates for admission be proposed on a given day annually; but scholars with suitable qualifications may be admitted at any intermediate time to an advanced standing.

6thly. That candidates for admission shall be subject to a strict examination, in such manner as the School Committee may direct, to ascertain their qualifications according to these rules.

7thly. That it be required of every candidate, to qualify him for admission, that he be well acquainted with reading, writing, English grammar in all its branches, and arithmetic as far as simple proportion.

8thly. That it be required of the Masters and Ushers, as a necessary qualification, that they shall have been regularly educated at some University.

The Studies of the First Class to be as follows:

Composition.
Reading from the most approved authors.
Exercises in Criticism; comprising critical analyses of the language, grammar, and style of the best English authors, their errors & beauties.
Declamation.
Geography.
Arithmetic continued.

The Studies of the Second Class.

Composition.
Exercises in Criticism.
Reading.   } [continued]
Declamation.
Algebra:
Ancient and Modern History and Chronology.
Logic.
Geometry.
Plane Trigonometry; and its application to mensuration of Heights and Distances.
Navigation.
Surveying.
Mensuration of Superficies & Solids.
Forensic Discussions.

The Studies of the Third Class.

Composition;
Exercises in Criticism;
Declamation;
Mathematics;   } continued
Logic;
History; particularly that of the United States;
Natural Philosophy, including Astronomy;
Moral and Political Philosophy.

10.2   James Carter, Massachusetts Educational Reformer, Comments on "Academies and Their Influence on Free Schools."

The academies were unknown in Massachusetts before the revolution. The oldest of these institutions is Phillips' Academy at Andover, the date of whose charter is 1780. Before this time, all public schools, it should seem, were also free. The number of these seminaries or high schools did

James G. Carter, *Essays on Popular Education, Containing a Particular Examination of the Schools of Massachusetts, and an Outline of an Institution for the Education of Teachers* (Boston: Bowles and Dearborn, 1826), pp. 27–32.

not much increase for many years after the close of the revolutionary war. But, during a short period, about ten or fifteen years since, they were multiplied to a very great extent. The people of Massachusetts, always desirous of following the policy of the pilgrims of Plymouth in regard to schools, seemed for a time absurdly to suppose, that they had but to get an academy incorporated and established in their neighbourhood, and that their children would be educated without farther trouble. But in this too sanguine expectation, they have been most of them somewhat disappointed. An act of incorporation has not been found, on experiment, to be quite so efficacious as was, at first, anticipated. And many of these institutions, which, in the imagination of their projectors, rose at once almost to the dignity of colleges, are now found in a very inefficient, indeed, in a most wretched condition.

The legislature of the State, then willing and anxious to encourage "learning and good morals" among the people,—a duty, which the constitution solemnly enjoins upon them,—by all means in their power, granted as many acts of incorporation as were petitioned for; and to many of these corporations, in token of their good will, they appropriated townships of land in the interiour and northerly part of Maine, which then formed a part of Massachusetts. Some of these townships of land, by the way, it is to be feared may be found on the wrong side of the boundary line to be drawn between Maine and the British Provinces. So far as this policy evinced a desire to encourage the diffusion of knowledge, it should receive the commendation, which good intentions always deserve; but, for all practical purposes for perhaps fifty years from the date of these charters and appropriations, the legislature might about as well have assigned to the petitioners for them a tract of the Moon.

When these hungry corporate beings had been created by the legislature, and their first cries for sustenance had been soothed by the unsavoury dish of eastern lands, they were then abandoned to the charity of their friends; or, if they proved cold, to a lingering death by starvation. The eastern lands, which constituted the patrimony of the State, were in most cases utterly unavailable. The benevolence of friends was, generally, exhausted in accumulating the means to erect suitable buildings. And the corporation were left to rely upon their own sagacity for procuring other resources to put their institution in operation. The more essential, indeed, almost the only essential part of a good academy, viz: a good instructer, was left unprovided for. The only expedient which remained, was, to support the teacher by a tax upon the scholars. It seemed but reasonable that those, who enjoyed the exclusive benefit of the institution, should pay for their own instruction. But this condition, though perhaps but a small sum was required of each pupil in order to produce an adequate salary for an instructer, removed the advantages of the academies, at once, beyond the reach of a large proportion of the inhabitants. The appropriations of the State, therefore, for the support of these schools, if they benefitted any body in particular, surely benefitted not the poor, but the rich and middling classes of the community. At least, these enjoyed the chief advantage of them, the direct rays of the State's favour; while the poor could feel only a dim reflection of them.

That the academies, at least, those of them which have been put and sustained in a tolerably respectable condition, have been a great accommodation to a few of our inhabitants, cannot be doubted. And how few are those, who have received any advantages from them, may be easily estimated by comparing the small number of children instructed in them, with the whole number in the Commonwealth. Still these are, or may be, useful institutions. I have certainly no desire to lessen the high repute, in which they seem to be held. On the contrary, I wish they were in higher estimation than they really are. And, what is more, I wish they were more worthy of that estimation. But they should be appreciated for the character which they possess, and never for that which they do not possess. And they are not establishments for the instruction of the poor. Neither can they be relied upon as efficient means for the education of the mass or even a majority of the people; because as has been before intimated, their conditions exclude nineteen twentieths of the whole population of the State from a participation of their advantages. If they are sustained, therefore, it must be upon some other ground. What that ground is, it is not my purpose now to inquire. But what has been their influence upon the free or town schools?

One influence, which they undoubtedly have had, has been to prepare young instructers *some* better than they could be prepared in the town schools themselves. This is a good influence. And if the same object could not be attained much better by other means, it would deserve great consideration in estimating the utility, which we are to expect from those establishments for the future. But the preparation of instructers for the free schools, never formed a part of the original design of the academies. They were intended to afford instruction in other and higher branches of education, than those usually taught in the free schools; and not merely to give better instruction in the same branches. Much less did it come within the wide scope of their purposes to give instruction in the science of teaching generally. So that the little good derived from them in this respect is only incidental.

The preparation of instructers for free schools is a subject of such moment to this community, that it will hardly be thought expedient, on reflection, to trust it to chance or to incidents. Experience and observation have convinced those, who have attended to the subject, that adequate instructers for the free schools are not prepared by these incidental means. In order to be efficient and effectual in attaining that desirable object, means must be applied directly to it. But of the education of instructers, more by and by. I wish merely now to say, and I trust I have shown, that the academies cannot be relied upon for accomplishing that object, so as in any good degree to meet the demands and answer the reasonable expectations of the community.

But the academies have had another influence upon the public town schools, which has much impaired their usefulness, and, if not soon checked, it will ultimately destroy them. This influence, operating for a series of years, has led, already, to the abandonment of a part of the free school system, and to a depreciation in the character and prospects of the remaining part. And it is working, not slowly, the destruction of the vital principle of the institution, more valuable to us than any other, for the preservation of enlightened freedom. The pernicious influence, to which I allude, will be better understood, by taking an example of its operation on a small scale; and then extending the same principle of examination to the whole State, or to New England.

Take any ten contiguous towns in the interiour of this Commonwealth, and suppose an academy to be placed in the centre of them. An academy, as I have before observed, commonly means a corporation, with a township of land in Maine, given them by the State, and a pretty convenient house, built generally by the patriotic subscriptions of those who expect to use it; the instructer being supported, chiefly or altogether, by a separate tax on the scholars. In each of these ten towns, select the six individuals, who have families to educate, who set the highest value on early education, and who are able to defray the expenses of the best which can be had, either in a private school among themselves, or at the academy, which, by the supposition, is in their neighbourhood. Now of what immediate consequence can it be to the six families of each town, or to the sixty families of the ten towns, whether there be such a thing as a free school in the Commonwealth or not! They have a general interest in them, to be sure, because they have themselves been there instructed, and the early associations of childhood and youth are strong; and they have a sort of speculative belief, if it be not rather an innate sentiment, that free schools make a free people. But how are their own particular, personal, and immediate interests affected? Without any libel upon good nature, these are the main springs to human actions. These are the motives, which find their way soonest to the human heart, and influence most powerfully and steadily the opinions of men, and the conduct founded upon and resulting from them.

As soon as difficulties and disagreements, in regard to the free schools, arise, as they necessarily must, upon various topics; such as, the amount of money to be raised, the distribution of it among the several districts, the manner of appropriation, whether it be to the "summer schools" or to the "winter schools," to pay an instructer from this family or from that family, of higher qualifications or of lower qualifications, of this or that political or religious creed, or a thousand other questions which are constantly occurring; if any of our six families happen to be dissatisfied or disgusted with any course which may be adopted, they will, immediately, abandon the free schools, and provide for the education of their children in their own way. They may organize a private school, for their own convenience, upon such principles as they most approve. Or, they may send their scholars, at an expense trifling to them, to the academy in their neighbourhood. Well, what if they do? The free schools remain, all taxes are paid, cheerfully, for their support, and the number of scholars is lessened. What is the evil of their sending their children somewhere else to be educated? We should, at first, suppose that it would be an advantage; inasmuch as the amount of money to be expended would be left the same, and the number of pupils to receive the benefit of it would be considerably diminished.

But the evils of this course, and of the general policy of the State government, which has led to it, are very serious ones. When the six individuals of any country town, who are, by the supposition, first in point of wealth and interest in the subject, and who will generally be also first in point of intelligence and influence in town affairs, withdraw their children from the common schools; there are, at the same time, withdrawn a portion of intelligence from their direction and heartfelt interest from their support. This intelligence is needed, to manage the delicate and important concerns of the schools. And this heartfelt interest is needed, to lead the way to improvements, to stimulate and encourage larger and larger appropriations, and to ensure vigilance in their expenditure. Patriotism and philanthropy are dull motives to exertions for the improvement of common schools compared with parental affection. And this quickening power has gone off to the academies or somewhere else with the children, who are the objects of it.

Look at the operation of this influence of the academies upon the free schools, on a still smaller scale. Examine the condition of the latter in the very towns, where academies are placed; and where, if their influence be a happy one, we should expect to find the common schools in the best condition. What is the fact? From observation and from information collected from authentic sources, the assertion may be hazarded that the condition of the free schools will be found, on examination, to be worse, far worse, in those towns than in any others. And it is for this plain reason: because those, who can barely afford the expense of tuition, will send their children to the academy, which the state or benevolent individuals have built up for their accommodation, and give themselves no farther trouble about the free schools, but to pay the tax-bill for their support when it is presented.

Thus the men, who would have the most interest in the subject, the most intelligence and the most leisure to conduct the concerns of the town schools, secede from them, and join themselves to other institutions. Abolish the academy and leave these six families of each town to the free schools alone, and you would find all their powers assiduously employed to put them in the best condition possible. Or rather put the free schools in a state to afford as good instruction as the academies now do, and you would supersede in a great degree the necessity of them. And it is apprehended, that it would be quite easy to place them upon a footing to give even better instruction, at least, in all the elementary branches of a common education, than the academies now give or ever have given. If the principles suggested above for the examination of our means of popular education be correct, and if the influence of the private establishments upon the academies, and of the academies upon the free schools be really such as it has been described to be, my readers, by following out the inquiries which those principles lead to, in all their relations and bearings, cannot fail to convince themselves, that something may be done, as well as much said upon this subject.

10.3 Henry Barnard Describes the Woodward High School in Cincinnati in 1867.

The System of Common Schools in Cincinnati was established in 1828–29 under a special act of the Legislature, by which a tax of $7,000 was annually imposed for the building of school-houses, and a like amount, in addition to the state appropriation, for the support of the schools. Under this act, school-houses were erected, in point of location, size and internal convenience, greatly in advance of the generally received notions of school architecture.

In 1834 the system was greatly extended, and, in 1845, the trustees were authorized to establish schools of different grades, and in 1850 to appoint a superintendent.

Henry Barnard, "Woodward High School in Cincinnati," *American Journal of Education,* XI (December 1857), pp. 520–521.

In 1847 a central high school was organized, under the charge of Prof. H. H. Barney, and in 1852 the Woodward Fund and the Hughes Fund, amounting to $300,000, and yielding over $5,000, (the Woodward estate in 1856 yielded $4,510,) were united for the purpose of sustaining two schools of this grade.

In 1853 a building was erected for the accommodation of the Hughes High School, at an expense, including lot, of about $40,000, and in 1856, in an opposite section of the city, another building, at a cost of $50,000, for the Woodward High School. Before giving the plan of this last structure, we will give the course of study, text-books, &c., from the "*Twenty-Eighth Annual Report of the Board of Trustees and Visitors of Common Schools,*" for the school year ending July 7, 1857.

The system of public instruction in Cincinnati in 1856–57 embraced—

I. 9 district night schools, and 1 night high school, with 23 teachers and 1,143 pupils.

II. 20 district, sub-district and special district schools, with 201 teachers, and an average daily attendance of 9,983 pupils, distributed in each school into four sections or grades.

III. 4 intermediate schools, with 22 teachers and 943 pupils.

IV. 2 high schools, with 12 teachers and 295 pupils.

V. 1 normal school, with 1 teacher and 31 pupils.

VI. A central school library, with an aggregate of 12,000 volumes.

The current expense of the public schools, for 1856–7, apart from buildings, was $143,088.11, or about $12.75 per pupil.

The following is the Course of Study, Text-Books, &c., prescribed for the Public High Schools of Cincinnati, January, 1856.

FIRST YEAR.

First Session.

English Grammar, *Brown or Pinneo,* completed.
English History, *Goodrich or Markham,* completed.
Algebra, *Ray's,* to Section 172.
Five lessons in each of the above weekly.

Second Session.

Latin Lessons, *Weld's,* to Part Second.
Physical Geography, *Fitch,* completed.
Latin Grammar, *Andrews' and Stoddard's.*
Algebra, Ray's, to Section 305.
Five lessons each week in Latin and Algebra.
Three lessons in Physical Georgraphy, and two in Reading.
Once a week during the year—
    Lectures by the Principal, on Morals, Manners, &c.
    Aids to Composition, completed.
    Composition and Declamation, by Sections, once in three weeks.
    Reading and Vocal Music. Penmanship, if needed.

SECOND YEAR.

First Session.

Latin Lessons, *Weld's*, to History.
Latin Grammar, *Andrews' and Stoddard's*.
Geometry, *Davies' Legendre, to Book* V.
Natural Philosophy, *Gray's*, to Pneumatics.
Five lessons per week during the year.

Second Session.

Latin Lessons, *Weld's* completed.
Latin Grammar, *Andrews' and Stoddard's*.
Geometry, *Davies' Legendre, to Book* IX.
Natural Philosophy, *Gray's, completed.*
Five lessons a week, in each of the above.
One exercise per week—
    Reading, Elemental Sounds.
    Rhetoric and Vocal Music.
    Composition and Declamation, by Sections, once in three weeks.

THIRD YEAR.

First Session.

Chemistry, *Silliman's, to Section* 282, five lessons a week.
Cæsar or Sallust, *Andrews', fifty Sections*, three lessons a week.
German or French, three lessons a week.
Algebra and Spherics, *Ray's and Davies' Legendre*, completed, five lessons a week.

Second Session.

Virgil's Æneid, *Cooper's three books*, three lessons.
German or French, three lessons.
Chemistry, *Silliman's, to Vegetable Chemistry*, five lessons.
Trigonometry, *Davies'*, completed, five lessons.
Once a week—
    Constitution of the United States, completed.
    Logic, *Hedge's*, completed.
    Reading, Rhetoric and Vocal Music.
    Composition and Declamation, by Sections once in three weeks.

FOURTH YEAR.

First Session.

Physiology and Hygiene, *Cutter*, completed, five lessons.
Cicero, *Folsom's*, three Orations, three lessons.
German or French, three lessons.
Astronomy, *McIntire's*, completed, five lessons.
Geology, *Gray and Adams'*, completed, five lessons.
Moral Philosophy, once a week.

Second Session.

German or French, three lessons.
Mental Philosophy, *Wayland's*, completed, five lessons.
General History, *Weber's*, completed, five lessons.
Navigation and Surveying, *Davies'*, completed.
Evidences of Christianity, once a week.
Once a week during the year—
    Critical Readings. Vocal Music once a week.
    Compositions, by Sections, once in three weeks.
    Original Addresses, once in three weeks.

COLLEGE CLASS.

In view of preparation to enter college, this class is permitted to substitute the following studies for the regular ones, in the fourth year:

Crosby's Greek Grammar, completed.
Felton's Greek Reader, completed.
Cicero's Orations, six in number.

Virgil's Æneid, six books.
Cæsar or Sallust, completed.

10.4   President Charles W. Eliot of Harvard Discusses "The Gap Between the Elementary Schools and the Colleges."

No State in the American Union possesses anything which can be properly called a *system* of secondary education. The elementary school system, both in city and country, is tolerably organized in many States; but between the elementary schools and the colleges is a wide gap very imperfectly bridged by a few public high schools, endowed academies, college preparatory departments, and private schools, which conform to no common standards and are under no unifying control. The mass of the rural population—that is to say, three-quarters of the American people—is unprovided with secondary schools. The town and city high schools are, on the one hand, independent of each other and of any superior educational authority; and, on the other, are entirely in the power of local committees or boards which can but rarely look beyond the immediate interests of the particular region which supports each school. Many States have adopted permissive legislation with regard to the maintenance of high schools; but for the most part this legislation has produced no fruits. Only one State in the Union—namely, Massachusetts—has mandatory legislation on this subject; but in that State a large proportion of the 230 so-called high schools are not secondary schools in any proper sense. Because of the lack of secondary schools competent to prepare their pupils for college, five-sixths of the colleges and universities in the United States maintained preparatory departments, against their will, and in disregard of the interests of the higher instruction.

One would infer from Professor Canfield's report that with regard to secondary education the condition of things in Massachusetts—a little old State in which 60 per cent. of the population may fairly be called urban—is better than anywhere else in the United States. Perhaps it is; but how wide is the gap between the common schools in Massachusetts and her colleges may be inferred from a few facts about the supply of students to

Charles W. Eliot, "The Gap Between the Elementary Schools and the Colleges," National Education Association, *Journals of Proceedings and Addresses* (Topeka: Kansas Publishing House, 1890), pp. 522–523, 525–527, 530–533.

Harvard College. Only nine Massachusetts high schools send pupils to Harvard College every year. In 1889, out of 352 persons who were admitted to Harvard College as candidates for the degree of bachelor of arts, 97 (or $27\frac{1}{2}$ per cent.) were prepared at free public schools; but these schools were only 30 in number from the whole country, 23 of them being New England schools. The plain fact is that not one-tenth of the schools called high in Massachusetts habitually maintain a course of study which enables the pupil to prepare himself for admission to Harvard College, or to any other college in the State which enforces its requirements for admission as stated in its catalogue.

If this is the condition of things in what may be called an urban State, what must it be in a rural? If a patriot were compelled to choose between two alternatives, one, that the less intelligent half of his countrymen should be completely illiterate, the other, that half of the select children capable of receiving the highest instruction should be cut off from that instruction, which would he choose? He would find the decision a dreadful one to make; for either alternative would entail an incalculable loss upon his country. Yet in the present condition of secondary education one-half of the most capable children in the United States, at a moderate estimate, have really no open road to colleges and universities. I rehearse these well-known facts, that we may appreciate the gravity of the problems presented by the subject assigned me, and may see in them the problems now most worthy of the attention of American educationists. . . .

To improve secondary education in the United States two things are necessary: (1) More schools are needed, and (2) the existing schools need to be brought to common and higher standards, so that the colleges may find in the school courses a firm, broad, and reasonably homogeneous foundation for their higher work.

   1. *More Schools.* Secondary schools are either day-schools or boarding-schools, the urban school being primarily a day-school, and the rural a boarding-school. The public secondary school is now urban almost exclusively; and it must be admitted that it is likely to continue so, for no promising suggestion has as yet been made of a rural area of support for a highly-organized secondary school. It is admitted that neither a rural township, nor a union of contiguous rural districts, can support such a school. The county has been suggested as a possible area of support; but there is no sufficient evidence that a rural county, apart from its town or towns of dense population, could support a good high school. To increase the present number of secondary schools which can really fit pupils for college, what are the most hopeful lines of action? In the first place, every effort should be made by school authorities, the press, and all leaders of public opinion, to promote the establishment of secondary urban

day-schools, both public and private, and to adapt the programs of existing schools to the admission requirements of some college course which leads to a degree. It is noticeable that in the older cities, and to some extent in the younger also, the best private schools exist right beside the best public schools. The causes which produce one class of schools simultaneously produce the other. Secondly, rural communities ought to be authorized by suitable legislation to contribute to the establishment (including in that term the provision of buildings) and annual support of urban secondary schools which are conveniently situated for their use. Thirdly, there should be created by law special secondary school districts much larger than the areas which support primary and grammar schools, and taking account of railroad communications. It is much easier for a boy or girl to go to school fifteen miles by rail than to walk to school in all weathers two miles by country lanes. The rural population has something to hope from legislative recognition of railroads as chief features in secondary school districts. The Massachusetts normal schools illustrate this principle; for they are really high schools, partly boarding-schools, and partly local and railroad day-schools. Fourthly, every effort should be made to stimulate private benevolence to endow rural secondary boarding-schools, or academies, under corporate management. A boarding-school ought always to be in the country; and a rural secondary school would almost necessarily be, in part at least, a boarding-school.

2. *Common Standards.* The existing means of elevating and regulating secondary school instruction may be conveniently considered under two heads—(*a*) State aid and supervision, and (*b*) college admission requirements. Both agencies are already useful, but both may be greatly improved and extended.

(*a*) *State Aid and Supervision.* It seems to have been the object of high-school legislation in some States, as for example in Massachusetts and in Maine, to encourage the creation of a large number of low-grade high schools without really expecting them to effect any junction with colleges. Such at any rate has been the effect of the mandatory legislation of Massachusetts, and such must be the general result of the aid offered to free high schools by Maine. This unprosperous State now offers to give any free high school as much money per year as its supporting area annually appropriates for instruction in the school, provided the State grant shall not exceed $250 in any case. No inspection or examination of aided schools is provided for. Such legislation encourages the establishment of numerous weak schools, without helping appreciably the schools already strong.

Much wiser is the legislation of Minnesota, which established twelve years ago a State High School Board and offered $400 a year to any high school which was found by the board after competent inspection to fulfill the following conditions: the aided school must receive both sexes free, and non-resident pupils also without fees, provided such pupils can pass examinations in all common-school subjects below algebra and geometry, and must maintain "regular and orderly courses of study, embracing all the branches prescribed as prerequisite for admission to the collegiate department of the University of Minnesota not lower than the sub-freshman class." The board can appoint any competent persons to visit the high schools and may pay them, but not more than $3 a day. Not more than five schools can be aided in any one county, and any school once accepted by the board, and continuing to comply with all the regulations, must be aided for not less than three years. The State appropriated in 1878 only $9,000 for the use of the board; but this amount was raised the next year to $20,000 and in 1883 to $23,000. The board consists of the Governor, the State Superintendent of Public Instruction, and the President of the University of Minnesota. By careful inspections the board has classified the high schools of the State, the nine high schools of the first rank preparing pupils for the freshman class of the University. This high-school legislation seems to me the wisest which has been adopted in the United States. It encourages only schools which are already well organized; insists that aided schools shall connect directly with the University; avoids expensive examinations; provides any needed amount of inspection; grades schools by their programs and general efficiency, not by individual examination-results; gives no pecuniary advantage to a large school over one equally well conducted but smaller; requires aided schools to take non-resident pupils without charge; and applies almost the whole of the State's grant to the direct development of instruction, which is by far the most productive application of any money intended to benefit schools. Minnesota is a new and sparsely-settled State, and its High School Board acts as yet upon a modest scale; but the principles of its high-school legislation may be advantageously copied in any State of the Union, however old, or rich, or densely populated. . . .

(*b*) Let us turn now to the consideration of college-admission requirements as means of raising and controlling secondary school instruction.

College requirements for admission act effectively only on those secondary schools which prepare some of their pupils for college; upon that large proportion of high schools and academies which do not, they have only an indirect although a sensible effect. For the broad purposes of the State, the influence of colleges, even if they were associated together, could not be so immediate and potent as the influence of the State, whether the latter were exerted by inspection or by examination. It is in a narrower field, therefore, that the higher institutions of education can act on the lower. At present they act in three ways.

The feeblest way is by prescribing for admission a knowledge of certain books, or of certain well-defined subjects, and then admitting candidates on the certificate of any schoolmaster that they have gone over all the prescribed books or subjects. If the prescriptions of the college are judicious, they are not without some favorable effect on the curricula of the certifying schools; but it may be reasonably objected to this method that it gives the college very inadequate protection against incompetent students, and the public no means of forming a just estimate of different schools. Certificates are apt to be accepted from good and bad schools alike, the anxiety to secure students in a struggling college over-riding every other consideration. Particularly is this apt to be the case in a small college in which the president has succeeded in getting the subject of admissions out of the hands of the faculty and into his own. Under this system a really good school has no means of proving itself good, and a bad school is not promptly exposed. Within a few years this feeblest of all methods has come into use, without any safeguards whatever, in the large majority of New England colleges, no system of State inspection or examination existing there, and no pretense being made that the certifying schools are examined, or even occasionally visited, by the colleges. A more demoralizing method of establishing a close connection between secondary schools and colleges it would be hard to imagine. Nevertheless, even under this loose and unguarded method, which only the two largest New England colleges have completely resisted, some good has resulted from coöperative action between preparatory schools and colleges to make admission requirements, on paper at least, uniform for the same subjects. The uniform requirements in English, which prevail all over New England except at Yale University, and have lately been adopted by some institutions in the Middle States, supply a noteworthy case in point.

The method just described is a corruption, or degradation, of a somewhat safer method of securing close connection between secondary schools and colleges which was first adopted twenty years ago by the University of Michigan. This safer method, as developed by that University, amounts to this: The University admits candidates on the diplomas given by any schools, near or remote, within the State or without, which are visited once in three years by a committee of the Faculty, or by other persons designated by the University. The visit may be repeated if any important changes take place in a school within the three years. The diplomas must specify that the candidates have sustained examinations at school in all the studies prescribed for admission to one or other of the University courses leading to a degree. There were in 1889 seventy schools holding this "diploma relation" to the University of Michigan. It cannot be doubted that this method is well adapted for recruiting rapidly a single dominant State university; but its value as a method for general adoption obviously depends on the thoroughness, impartiality, and publicity of the inspection which it provides. To me the inspection seems to fail on all three points. Considering the rapidity with which teachers are changed in American schools, an inspection once in three years seems too infrequent. I am wholly at a loss to understand how a busy college faculty can get time to inspect properly any considerable number of secondary schools, or how it can furnish a sufficient number of inspectors competent in all secondary school subjects. The Michigan Faculty of arts and sciences is not so large as the corresponding Harvard Faculty; but I am sure that the Harvard Faculty would say at once that they could not inspect twenty secondary schools a year with sufficient thoroughness to warrant them in expressing a public judgment on the merits of the several schools—unless indeed they neglected their own proper work of collegiate instruction. Moreover, I am clear that there is not a single member of the Harvard Faculty who would feel himself competent, without a good deal of special preparation, to examine a well-organized secondary school in all its departments. To examine thoroughly such a school a committee of at least three members of the Harvard Faculty would be required, and these teachers would have to be withdrawn from their college work for three or four days in the case of a neighboring school, and for a longer time in the case of a distant school. As to procuring competent inspectors —not of the Faculty—in numerous remote localities, it seems quite impossible when we consider how much knowledge, experience, and good judgment are required for examining all the work of any school. The moment we come down to such details as these, we inevitably begin to think that the inspection of secondary schools provided by the University of Michigan, single-handed, must be rather cursory. It is also obvious that the method is not public enough in its processes to demonstrate its fairness and sufficiency, and therefore to command general confidence. The single acting authority obviously has interests of its own to serve. I am not maintaining that this diploma method, as conducted in Michigan, has not worked well, or even that it has not worked so well as the method of admission by examination, as conducted in Michigan. It is some gain to establish friendly relations between seventy secondary schools and any university. I am urging that it lacks adequate securities, and is therefore not fit for general adoption. The Minnesota method, which provides in the State High School Board an independent inspecting authority, is in my opinion greatly to be preferred.

There remains the most effective mode in which colleges act on the superior sort of secondary schools, namely, the method of conducting careful examinations in all the subjects acceptable for admission. These examinations have a fair degree of publicity; for most colleges circulate freely their question-papers. Harvard College also publishes in detail the results of its examinations for admission. Such examinations are no longer, as formerly, held only at the seat of the college conducting them; but may be held simultaneously at as many places as the convenience of candidates may require. Several Eastern colleges now conduct examinations at numerous places widely distributed over the country. Yale University distinctly announces that it will hold an admission examination "in any city or at any school where the number of candidates and the distance from other places of examination may warrant it." The method can easily be given a national application by any institution which has prestige and a numerous staff. In the long run, it grades schools fairly, and it is very stimulating to the older classes of secondary schools. Like all examinations conducted by an authority independent of the schools, it also protects the masters of schools, both public and private, against the unwarrantable importunities of parents, trustees, and committeemen. Nevertheless it is open to some serious objections. In the first place, it is not sufficiently public. The question-papers may look well; but the standard for passing may be unreasonably low, the public having no means of estimating the degree of strictness with which the answer-papers are marked. Secondly, the colleges have, until lately, acted singly—each for itself without consultation or concert. Each college or university is, therefore, naturally supposed to be seeking its own interest rather than the common welfare. Thirdly, in a small college a few men, who perhaps have peculiarities or whims, may control all the admission examinations for many years, to the disadvantage of the college and the annoyance of schools. All these evils would be removed, or reduced, by a system of coöperation among several colleges.

At the conclusion of this rapid survey I venture to suggest that there are three directions in which patriots who desire to see American secondary schools improved and connected more closely with colleges may look for progress:

1. We may expect State examining and inspecting systems to improve and extend, for they have demonstrated their utility; and remembering the extremes to which examination-methods have been carried in England, we may reasonably hope that State boards will inspect institutions more and more thoroughly, as well as examine individuals. In this connection we may expect that the profession of school inspector will become well recognized as a separate and honorable calling.

2. We may hope to see formed a combination of four, five, or six of the universities which have large departments of arts and sciences to conduct simultaneously, at well-selected points all over the country, examinations in all the subjects anywhere acceptable for admission to colleges or professional schools, the answer-papers to be marked by persons annually selected by the combined universities, and announced to the public, all results to be published but without the names of candidates, and certificates to be good anywhere for the subjects mentioned in them. We see reason to believe that such a coöperative system would be simple though extensive; that it would present no serious difficulties, mechanical or other; that it would be very convenient and economical for candidates, and self-supporting at a moderate fee; and finally, that it would be authoritative, flexible, stimulating, unifying, and just.

3. We may expect to see a great extension of the scholarship system, whereby promising youth are helped through secondary schools and colleges. States, cities, towns, and endowments provided by private benevolence will all contribute to the development of this well-proved system.

10.5 Tables and Excerpt on College Admission Requirements from the Report of the Committee of Ten, 1893.

One of the subjects which the Committee of Ten were directed to consider was requirements for admission to college; and particularly they were expected to report on uniform requirements for admission to colleges, as well as on a uniform secondary school programme. Almost all the Conferences have something to say about the best mode of testing the attainments of candidates at college admission examinations; and some of them, notably the Conferences on History and Geography, make very explicit declarations concerning the nature of college examinations. The improvements desired in the mode of testing the attainments of pupils who have pursued in the secondary schools the various subjects which enter into the course will be found clearly described under each subject in the several Conference reports; but there is a general principle concerning the relation of the secondary schools to colleges which the Committee of Ten, inspired and guided by the Conferences, feel it their duty to set forth with all possible distinctness.

Committee of Ten on Secondary School Studies, *Report* (New York: Published for the National Education Association by the American Book Company, 1894), pp. 41, 46–47, 51–55.

The secondary schools of the United States, taken as a whole, do not exist for the purpose of preparing boys and girls for colleges. Only an insignificant percentage of the graduates of these schools go to colleges or scientific schools. Their main function is to prepare for the duties of life that small proportion of all the children in the country—a proportion small in number, but very important to the welfare of the nation—who show themselves able to profit by an education prolonged to the eighteenth year, and whose parents are able to support them while they remain so long at school. There are, to be sure, a few private or endowed secondary schools in the country, which make it their principal object to prepare students for the colleges and universities; but the number of these schools is relatively small. A secondary school programme intended for national use must therefore be made for those children whose education is not to be pursued beyond the secondary school. The preparation of a few pupils for college or scientific school should in the ordinary secondary school be the incidental, and not the principal object. At the same time, it is obviously desirable that the colleges and scientific schools should be accessible to all boys or girls who have completed creditably the secondary school course. Their parents often do not decide for them, four years before the college age, that they shall go to college, and they themselves may not, perhaps, feel the desire to continue their education until near the end of their school course. In order that any successful graduate of a good secondary school should be free to present himself at the gates of the college or scientific school of his choice, it is necessary that the colleges and scientific schools of the country should accept for admission to appropriate courses of their instruction the attainments of any youth who has passed creditably through a good secondary school course, no matter to what group of subjects he may have mainly devoted himself in the secondary school. As secondary school courses are now too often arranged, this is not a reasonable request to prefer to the colleges and scientific schools; because the pupil may now go through a secondary school course of a very feeble and scrappy nature—studying a little of many subjects and not much of any one, getting, perhaps, a little information in a variety of fields, but nothing which can be called a thorough training. Now the recommendations of the nine Conferences, if well carried out, might fairly be held to make all the main subjects taught in the secondary schools of equal rank for the purposes of admission to college or scientific school. They would all be taught consecutively and thoroughly, and would all be carried on in the same spirit; they would all be used for training the powers of observation, memory, expression, and reasoning; and they would all be good to that end, although differing among themselves in quality and substance. In preparing the programmes of Table IV., the

TABLE III.

1ST SECONDARY SCHOOL YEAR.	
Latin	5 p.
English Literature, 2 p. ⎫ " Composition, 2 p. ⎭ . . .	4 p.
German [or French]	5 p.
Algebra	4 p.
History of Italy, Spain, and France	3 p.
Applied Geography (European political—continental and oceanic flora and fauna)	4 p.
	25 p.

2ND SECONDARY SCHOOL YEAR.	
Latin	4 p.
Greek	5 p.
English Literature, 2 p. ⎫ " Composition, 2 p. ⎭ . . .	4 p.
German, continued	4 p.
French, begun	5 p.
Algebra,* 2 p. ⎫ Geometry, 2 p. ⎭	4 p.
Botany or Zoölogy	4 p.
English History to 1688	3 p.
	33 p.

* Option of book-keeping and commercial arithmetic.

3RD SECONDARY SCHOOL YEAR.	
Latin	4 p.
Greek	4 p.
English Literature, 2 p. ⎫ " Composition, 1 p. ⎬ . . . Rhetoric, 1 p. ⎭	4 p.
German	4 p.
French.	4 p.
Algebra,* 2 p. ⎫ Geometry, 2 p. ⎭	4 p.
Physics	4 p.
History, English and American . .	3 p.
Astronomy, 3 p. 1st ½ yr. ⎫ Meteorology, 3 p. 2nd ½ yr. ⎭ . . .	3 p.
	34 p.

* Option of book-keeping and commercial arithmetic.

4TH SECONDARY SCHOOL YEAR.	
Latin	4 p.
Greek	4 p.

English Literature,   2 p. ⎫
    "   Composition, 1 p. ⎬ . . .
    "   Grammar,   1 p. ⎭
	4 p.

German	4 p.
French.	4 p.
Trigonometry, ⎫ Higher Algebra, ⎭	2 p.
Chemistry	4 p.
History (intensive) and Civil Government	3 p.
Geology or Physiography, 4 p. 1st ½ yr. ⎫ Anatomy, Physiology, and Hygiene, ⎬ 4 p. 2nd ½ yr. ⎭	4 p.
	33 p.

Committee had in mind that the requirements for admission to colleges might, for schools which adopted a programme derived from that table, be simplified to a considerable extent, though not reduced. A college might say,—We will accept for admission any groups of studies taken from the secondary school programme, provided that the sum of the studies in each of the four years amounts to sixteen, or eighteen, or twenty periods a week,—as may be thought best,—and provided, further, that in each year at least four of the subjects presented shall have been pursued at least three periods a week, and that at least three of the subjects shall

Table IV.

CLASSICAL. Three foreign languages (one modern).		LATIN-SCIENTIFIC. Two foreign languages (one modern).	
I.	Latin . . . . 5 p. English . . . . 4 p. Algebra . . . . 4 p. History . . . . 4 p. Physical Geography . . . . . 3 p. ———— 20 p.		Latin . . . . 5 p. English . . . . 4 p. Algebra . . . . 4 p. History . . . . 4 p. Physical Geography . . . . . 3 p. ———— 20 p.
II.	Latin . . . . 5 p. English . . . . 2 p. *German [or French] begun . . . 4 p. Geometry . . . . 3 p. Physics . . . . 3 p. History . . . . 3 p. ———— 20 p.		Latin . . . . 5 p. English . . . . 2 p. German [or French] begun . . . . 4 p. Geometry . . . . 3 p. Physics . . . . 3 p. Botany or Zoölogy . . . . . . 3 p. ———— 20 p.
III.	Latin . . . . 4 p. *Greek . . . . 5 p. English . . . . 3 p. German [or French] . . . . . 4 p. Mathematics {Algebra 2 / Geometry 2} . . . 4 p. ———— 20 p.		Latin . . . . 4 p. English . . . . 3 p. German [or French] . . . . . 4 p. Mathematics {Algebra 2 / Geometry 2} . . . 4 p. Astronomy $\frac{1}{2}$ yr. & Meteoroloy $\frac{1}{2}$ yr. 3 p. History . . . . 2 p. ———— 20 p.
IV.	Latin . . . . 4 p. Greek . . . . 5 p. English . . . . 2 p. German [or French] . . . . . 3 p. Chemistry . . . . 3 p. Trigonometry & Higher Algebra or }. 3 p. History ———— 20 p.		Latin . . . . 4 p. English {as in Classical 2 / additional 2} . . . 4 p. German [or French] . . . . . 3 p. Chemistry . . . . 3 p. Trigonometry & Higher Algebra or }. 3 p. History Geology or Physiography $\frac{1}{2}$ yr. and }3 p. Anatomy, Physiology, & Hygiene $\frac{1}{2}$ yr. ———— 20 p.

TABLE IV. (*continued*)

	MODERN LANGUAGES. Two foreign languages (both modern).		ENGLISH. One foreign language (ancient or modern).	
I.	French [*or* German] begun.	5 p.	Latin, or German, or French	5 p.
	English	4 p.	English	4 p.
	Algebra	4 p.	Algebra	4 p.
	History	4 p.	History	4 p.
	Physical Geography	3 p.	Physical Geography	3 p.
		20 p.		20 p.
II.	Frency [*or* German]	4 p.	Latin, or German, or French.	5 or 4 p.
	English	2 p.	English	3 or 4 p.
	German [*or* French] begun.	5 p.	Geometry	3 p.
	Geometry	3 p.	Physics	3 p.
	Physics	3 p.	History	3 p.
	Botany or Zoölogy	3 p.	Botany or Zoölogy	3 p.
		20 p.		20 p.
III.	French [*or* German]	4 p.	Latin, or German, or French	4 p.
	English	3 p.	English { as in others 3 / additional 2 }	5 p.
	German [*or* French]	4 p.		
	Mathematics { Algebra 2 / Geometry 2 }	4 p.	Mathematics { Algebra 2 / Geometry 2 }	4 p.
	Astronomy ½ yr. & Meteorology ½ yr.	3 p.	Astronomy ½ yr. & Meteorology ½ yr.	3 p.
	History	2 p.	History { as in the Latin-Scientific 2 / additional 2 }	4 p.
		20 p.		20 p.
IV.	French [*or* German]	3 p.	Latin, or German, or French	4 p
	English { as in Classical 2 / additional 2 }	4 p.	English { as in Classical 2 / additional 2 }	4 p.
	German [*or* French]	4 p.	Chemistry	3 p.
	Chemistry	3 p.	Trigonometry & Higher Algebra.	3 p.
	Trigonometry & Higher Algebra 3 / *or* / History	3 p.	History	3 p.
	Geology or Physiography ½ yr. / and / Anatomy, Physiology, & Hygiene ½ yr.	3 p.	Geology or Physiography ½ yr. / and / Anatomy, Physiology, & Hygiene ½ yr.	3 p.
		20 p.		20 p.

have been pursued three years or more. For the purposes of this reckoning, natural history, geography, meteorology, and astronomy might be grouped together as one subject. Every youth who entered college would have spent four years in studying a few subjects thoroughly; and, on the theory that all the subjects are to be considered equivalent in educational rank for the purposes of admission to college, it would make no difference which subjects he had chosen from the programme—he would have had four years of strong and effective mental training. The Conferences on Geography and Modern Languages make the most explicit statement to the effect that college requirements for admission should coincide with high-school requirements for graduation. The Conference on English is of opinion "that no student should be admitted to college who shows in his English examination and his other examinations that he is very deficient in ability to write good English." This recommendation suggests that an ample English course in the secondary school should be required of all persons who intend to enter college. It would of course be possible for any college to require for admission any one subject, or any group of subjects, in the table, and the requirements of different colleges, while all kept within the table, might differ in many respects; but the Committee are of opinion that the satisfactory completion of any one of the four years' courses of study embodied in the foregoing programmes should admit to corresponding courses in colleges and scientific schools. They believe that this close articulation between the secondary schools and the higher institutions would be advantageous alike for the schools, the colleges, and the country.

Every reader of this report and of the reports of the nine Conferences will be satisfied that to carry out the improvements proposed more highly trained teachers will be needed than are now ordinarily to be found for the service of the elementary and secondary schools. The Committee of Ten desire to point out some of the means of procuring these better trained teachers. For the further instruction of teachers in actual service, three agencies already in existence may be much better utilized than they now are. The Summer Schools which many universities now maintain might be resorted to by much larger numbers of teachers, particularly if some aid, such as the payment of tuition fees and travelling expenses, should be given to teachers who are willing to devote half of their vacations to study, by the cities and towns which these teachers serve. Secondly, in all the towns and cities in which colleges and universities are planted, these colleges or universities may usefully give stated courses of instruction in the main subjects used in the elementary and secondary schools to teachers employed in those towns and cities. This is a reasonable service which the colleges and universities may render to their own communities.

Thirdly, a superintendent who has himself become familiar with the best mode of teaching any one of the subjects which enter into the school course can always be a very useful instructor for the whole body of teachers under his charge. A real master of any one subject will always have many suggestions to make to teachers of other subjects. The same is true of the principal of a high school, or other leading teacher in a town or city. In every considerable city school system the best teacher in each department of instruction should be enabled to give part of his time to helping the other teachers by inspecting and criticising their work, and showing them, both by precept and example, how to do it better.

In regard to preparing young men and women for the business of teaching, the country has a right to expect much more than it has yet obtained from the colleges and normal schools. The common expectation of attainment for pupils of the normal schools has been altogether too low the country over. The normal schools, as a class, themselves need better apparatus, libraries, programmes, and teachers. As to the colleges, it is quite as much an enlargement of sympathies as an improvement of apparatus or of teaching that they need. They ought to take more interest than they have heretofore done, not only in the secondary, but in the elementary schools; and they ought to take pains to fit men well for the duties of a school superintendent. They already train a considerable number of the best principals of high schools and academies; but this is not sufficient. They should take an active interest, through their presidents, professors, and other teachers, in improving the schools in their respective localities, and in contributing to the thorough discussion of all questions affecting the welfare of both the elementary and the secondary schools.

10.6   A School Administrator, W. R. Garrett, Describes A Vision of "The Future High School" Which Contrasts with the Blueprint of the Committee of Ten.

Historical

During the first quarter of the present century there prevailed a diversity of opinions on social, political, and commercial matters, but upon the great principle that citizenship in a free government is practicable as the masses are educated, all were agreed. Men in public and private walks of life alike cherished these elevated views. The academies of the day were reaching but a favored few. Tuition fees and boarding expense shut out

W. R. Garrett, "The Future High School," National Education Association, *Journal of Addresses and Proceedings* (New York: National Education Association, 1891), pp. 620–630.

the many. This fact, together with the further one that school officers preferred to spend the public money on schools whose management they themselves could control, soon led to the organization of the free public high school. These high schools were modelled after the academies and were like them in the courses of study and work done, but they were free in the fullest sense and public in the broadest meaning of the term. Such they have ever continued to be, such they will ever remain.

Object

Thus we see that the mission of the high school is to make education free, far-reaching, and fully adequate to the wants of the people. Though its functions are twofold, its main object is to prepare boys and girls for the duties of active, useful, happy lives. It takes the pupils at about the age of fourteen, after nine years of drill and discipline in the elementary schools, and for four years seeks to fix more firmly their knowledge already acquired, to extend their lines of research, and to develop other powers, till at the age of eighteen or nineteen, in the full bloom of youthful womanhood and manhood, the pupils are sent forth to exercise what the schools have given them that they may aid themselves and their fellowmen.

Generous Maintenance

The American people will always give generous maintenance to the high school, for they hold it to be both just and wise. They will be still more liberal when they discern more clearly the fact that elementary schools do not supply learning, but only the instruments by which learning may be secured; when they come to fully realize the influence the high schools exert upon the elementary schools in determining the work of the lower grades, and in being a constant intellectual stimulus to the pupils by the standards they set and the opportunities they offer; when they learn accurately how well suited the school work is to the pupil's life-work, and finally, and best of all, when they note that it awakens a desire in the pupils to be "participants in the higher living of humanity." Here is the ultimate aim of the high school, as it is the ultimate aim of toil. The State should not be content to rear children for bread-getting and money-getting only. As Ray Green Huling has so beautifully and so aptly put it, "In public education there must be a nobler aim—nothing less than to endow every worker with aspiration for a broad outlook into life, to raise every boy and girl, if they will, into some degree of companionship with the best and wisest of mankind. The high school it is which brings this boon to the hearts and homes of the people. With one hand it lifts the pupil's downcast face till his eyes behold the broad horizon of human knowledge; with the other it offers the golden key by which he may unlock every closed door upon his life's journey, to bring forth treasures new and old, for himself and for his community. From its portals a few climb to higher schools, offering larger opportunities and ampler returns; but many more turn at once to their tasks in the world's great workshop, carrying with them in their newly-developed powers and freshly-kindled aspirations—even more surely than in their actual attainments—the seeds of countless blessings to ripen as need shall arise."

The Laboring Man's Pride

The intellectual part of our country's population will govern the ignorant part not only in politics, but in social and business affairs as well. This condition will obtain so long as our present form of government exists. The laboring man is coming to know this, and in order to have his boy stand alongside of the rich man's son he makes great sacrifice, that his child may be kept in the high school. He knows that knowledge is the only thing that will enable his boy, when he becomes a man, to stand among men. He knows that unless his boy secures such a training as the "people's college" can give he will be some one's slave. Thus it is that the high school is the laboring man's friend, and should and will be his pride, for he is coming to know that this is the institution which shall level the distinction between the rich and the poor, as far as power and place are concerned.

The People's College

The high school is the people's college. It draws its pupils from all classes of society. Here come the sons and daughters of the farmer, the mechanic, the laborer, the miner, the merchant, the professional man, the capitalist. The education secured must be of such a character as to be serviceable where sound the hammer, anvil, and loom; where struggle men for mastery in the avenues of trade; where is exerted the power of logic, rhetoric, and eloquence; where are seen and felt the grace, culture, and conduct of educated men and women. If our high school is to do for all classes, and furnish finished products exhibiting such varied qualifications, then it must present a variety of subjects and branches. Its sphere must be enlarged so as to put it into closer touch with the activities of daily life.

A Change Needed

Alterations and additions must be made, for the high school, as it now is, cannot meet the wondrous demands of this marvellous age. . . . Hence we must listen to the demand for that in our schools which will meet the wants of the public. The high school, being the servant of the public, must be kept near the people and must answer the needs of the people.

No one surpasses me in enthusiastic confidence in the American high school. Yet I do not believe it has fulfilled its mission. That the high school of the present does not secure proper and sufficient results in its efforts to develop the typical American citizen is evidenced by the growing and widespread feeling which has settled into a determination to effect radical changes in certain directions. No one alive to what is passing in this changing, formative age can be oblivious to the situation and the demands of the times. *Education* for June, in its leading editorial, boldly sets forth the faulty condition of affairs and briefly suggests the remedy. In speaking of the boy after he has completed the work of the elementary grades the periodical adds:

> If he looks forward to the high school, he finds himself contemplating a four-years' course in an institution modelled on the plan of the university-fitting school of a generation ago—four years of cramming in Latin and mathematics, with a little dabbling in science and mild flirtation with English Literature, under a faithful group of teachers who honestly believe the present educational methods a mischievous falling away from 'the good old times' . . . This is neither a fancy sketch nor a portrait of a solitary place. It represents a condition of affairs that exists today in the majority of towns and cities of five thousand population and upward in the United States. And the one receipt for the arrest of the American small boy on his flight from the school-room is making the school-room, to the age of twelve, as attractive, effective, and thoroughly educational as it is now the reverse, and placing in the upper story a corps of teachers competent to reconstruct the little paradise of pedantry which the high school so often becomes into a broad-gauge seminary, competent to the needs of American citizenship.

It is not necessary for me to endorse or disprove these sweeping assertions. They serve their purpose fully, as far as this paper is concerned, when they mirror the feeling of unrest which seems to pervade the general public—an unrest which calls, loudly and imperatively, for a readjustment of the high school, that the needs of the present and the future may be more fully conserved.

The Ideal High School

The question which here arises is as difficult as it is important. What will constitute an ideal high school of the immediate future?

To lift the curtain that hides the future and attempt to fathom its mystic depths, or to predict what should obtain, is ever and always a delicate and dangerous task. I attempt it, however, with many misgivings.

The Course of Study

It is true that the varying interests of communities demand different courses in different places, but the natures and desires of pupils in each educational centre are so various that the course of study, in order to satisfy all, must be comprehensive. The various studies which seem necessary to develop a liberal education follow three lines:
1. A knowledge of nature, or those branches which acquaint the student with man's abode—geography, geology, botany, zoology, physics, chemistry, and astronomy.
2. A knowledge of man, or those branches which set forth the achievements of the race—language, literature, history, civics, arts, and psychology.
3. A knowledge of fixed relations, or mathematics—arithmetic, algebra, and geometry—studies which enable man to determine the relations of number and space. . . .

Manual Training and Domestic Economy

But we must grant the great and growing demand for a so-called practical education, a demand for manual training and domestic economy. For those who desire or who seem to need this work the schools must provide it. Aside from the practical knowledge afforded by a course in manual training, it seems to be a valuable avenue through which to reach the boys, both in inducing them to enter the high school and in holding them to the course when there, and in awakening an interest in them for education. It should be remembered that many grow tired of books when held to them for nine long years, and if, when they complete the grade work, the pupils can look forward to an attractive course, which combines manual labor with intellectual effort, they are induced to take it. . . .

If the high-school course is to serve all classes it must prepare some for college, some for business, some for artisanism, and all for citizenship. In doing all this work it performs the twofold function of the "fitting" and the "finishing" school. It is obvious, then, that the future high school, in order to meet these extended demands, must provide instruction in all the various fields of thought. It is equally obvious, too, that for the sake of the best discipline and the most thorough work the number of studies which each pupil takes shall be reduced, and that more time and toil be placed on the balance.

To suit the varying needs of those who seek admission to the high school, the carefully-selected classical course and English course will fit for college; the business course, with electives from either of the other courses, for active business life; the manual-training and domestic-economy courses for the industrial phase of human activities.

Civics and Patriotism

From none of these courses should be omitted lessons in civics and patriotism. Wherever the sentiment in any lesson of any study touches the important field of civics, the mind of the pupil should be imbued with its nobility. The teacher should remember that all studies at some time touch the field of civics, and should develop these lessons. . . .

Music and Physical Culture

That high school falls far short of its province and opportunities which neglects to give training in music and physical culture. . . .

Textbooks

High-school text-books should be illustrated with cuts suitable for reproductions, and the pupils should be required to sketch these in the preparation of the lesson. . . .

The Typewriter

The use of the typewriter in high schools will be not only common but universal. There is no doubt but that this machine will fulfil an important educational mission. . . .

Obedience

The future high school must teach obedience. Without the pupil practises self-control and self-denial everything is lost. Obedience secured by proper school discipline is the foundation stone of law and order, of governments and civilizations. For the incalculable good sure to come to the individual, society, and the government, school discipline must be of that sort that will secure willing obedience on the part of the pupil. When this is complete, loyalty to country and obedience to her laws are sure to follow.

Industry

The future high school should teach boys and girls to be industrious. Industry is God's universal law. . . .

The High School Teacher

The future high-school teacher will be characterized by high scholarship, mental leadership, moral responsibility, and a thorough understanding of the art of teaching. They will possess these high qualifications because the public will demand them and colleges will furnish them. The teacher will be so well paid, so fully appreciated, and so nicely situated that, as the Toronto *Educational Journal* puts it, "No one will desire to leave the profession of teaching for trade, law, or medicine," and thus our work will reach the dignity of a profession. . . .

10.7   Sara Burstall, an English Headmistress, Describes a Typical Day in the Life of a High School Student in 1908.

Let us try to imagine a typical day in an American high school and contrast it with what is so familiar to some of us in England. There is no assembly of the whole school, first thing in the morning every day, for prayers. The school law of many places does not allow of any religious observance, and as we have seen it would not always be possible to get the whole school into the hall or auditorium; but the principle of an assembly at least once a week for different parts of the school is, so far as we know, universal; some have it twice a week. In the McKinley High School, at St. Louis, numbering 1,500, they assemble first thing on Friday morning for one hour, and music is performed by visitors and pupils; speakers from the city or the university or visitors may deliver addresses, or lantern lectures may be given. In Philadelphia and New York the old custom of the reading of a passage from the Bible by the headmaster continues. A hymn of a simple character, such as one of Whittier's, is sung by the pupils, and at Philadelphia the Lord's Prayer is repeated. This represents, we

Sara A. Burstall, *Impressions of American Education in 1908* (New York: Longmans, Green and Co., 1909), pp. 60–67.

think, the maximum of religious observance allowed anywhere in the public high school. The writer had the privilege of addressing several assemblies. The order and attention were perfect, and the marching out to music at the close is as fine as anything she had ever seen in England. The way in which the thousands of girls in the Philadelphia High School and the Wadleigh High School, in New York, marched out in under two minutes was wonderful. It was a triumph of discipline and organisation. The wide passages and skilful arrangement of seats make possible what would need much more care and time in the average English school hall.

The hours are from 8.30 to 1.30, or 9 to 2, or 9 to 2.30; roughly, a five hours' session with six or seven periods of forty, forty-five or fifty minutes each and a recess or break of twenty minutes to half an hour, rarely longer, for food and rest. One sees pupils hurrying the first thing in the morning in the familiar way, but they do not wear a school cap or a school-hat ribbon. This is quite contrary to American sentiment and would be resented. The girls do not change their shoes, but they wear rubbers in bad weather, which are slipped off quickly with the other outdoor garments, and the girls proceed at once to the room where they have the first recitation of the day. Here one comes at once upon a difference; the teacher keeps the room and the pupils move about. This has the advantage that the room is arranged for mathematics, for history, for classics, but it is of course impossible to combine this with the Form system. After three-quarters of an hour electric bells ring and the recitation or lesson ends. The pupils gather up their books and go on somewhere else, just as they please. We did not see any general marching about; everything is done quite freely, but quickly, neatly and in perfect order, and though conversation is allowed at the change of lessons, without any loitering and noise; and this we must remember with 1,500 to 2,000 young people from fourteen to eighteen years of age and no teachers or prefects on duty up and down the stairs and on the corridors. One could only wonder how it is done, and wish all our young people were as quiet and orderly. There will generally be four lesson periods before recess. One may be spent in the gymnasium and one may be a study period, when a pupil is free to go to the library or to a large study hall and work alone. A teacher was always to be found seated on duty in these rooms, which would contain from 40 to 100 or more students—boys and girls. If a pupil has his or her own desk it will be in a study hall. The recitation-rooms often have chairs with a flap to rest a notebook, if they are used for literary subjects. Silence is, of course, observed in periods of private study. There seem to be in some cases the beginnings of a Form system—when a master or a mistress is specially responsible for pupils belonging to one study hall.

An experienced teacher cannot, of course, help noticing boys and girls and formulating opinions about them. The American schoolgirl is very much neater and carries herself much better than the average English one. She wears, in winter, a short, well-made woollen skirt and a white shirt waist or blouse, often daintily trimmed with embroidery. She is, of course, exquisitely shod. Short sleeves were in fashion in the winter of 1907–8, and the arms and hands were obviously very well cared for. A good deal of jewellery is worn, and apparently it would not be possible to make a rule against it, as is the custom in some schools in England. We are speaking, it is understood, of a public high school, attended by all sections of the community, not only by the well-to-do. A private school might forbid jewellery as do some. The hair is always beautifully dressed, and girls seem to put it up at the earliest possible age; the flowing tresses which often have to be tied back according to rule in England do not appear in general. The girls in the first year, at fourteen or fifteen, wear large ribbon-bows and plaits somewhat after the French style. Obviously the ensemble is very different from that one sees in England, where there is a very much greater variety of appearance, unless it should happen that all our girls are wearing gymnastic costume with coloured ribbons.

One is not entitled to form an opinion on the boys; but they are much less noisy; one understands, too, why some Americans buy their clothes from English tailors. But when American boys are in uniform, as in the cadet corps in the Washington High Schools, they look exceedingly well; the dark blue and gold, with the brown leather belts, is most effective. The type of countenance is quite different; paler, more intellectual, often more resolute than our youths. . . .

After lunch work goes on again, two more recitations, or possibly three, filling up the time till 1.30 P.M. or 2 P.M. or later. Then the girls and boys go home. There is no "seeing out" by teachers in any formal way. In a very large school one staircase will be used for ascending and one for descending. Organised games in the afternoon are rare; more study out of school is done than with us, and in the afternoon one sees pupils (students they are called) of the high schools working in public libraries. Teachers complain of the distractions of parties, theatres, bazaars, and amusements generally, which exhaust the strength of the girls in particular and take the energy and time that ought to be given to school work. The boys are affected also.

The good discipline of American schools is always noticed by English observers; the most remarkable thing about it is that it seems to come of itself. It is not maintained by artificial sanctions. Corporal punishment, the inalienable right of the English public school boy, is all but obsolete. There appear to be no small penalties, bad marks, impositions or the like.

Detention is rare, and, if it does happen, seems to be unsystematised. As far as one could understand, their school discipline depends on two natural sanctions, the spirit of the nation and the teacher's personal force. When teachers do not possess this, even in good schools the discipline goes to pieces. With members of the other sex present, girls or boys, there is not the same positive disorder in the classroom we should get in such a case, but there is considerable slackness and inattention. A teacher who has not this personal force has before long to leave. There is, however, with difficult pupils, reference to the headmaster, or principal. Boys and girls are sent for, and talked to, and, if the worst comes to the worst, expelled. The personal force of the principal counts for a great deal, as with us, in the maintenance of discipline. While in some ways the work of a teacher is easier in America than here, in others it is more difficult. We have a traditional authority and, in a public school, a reasonable security of tenure and some dignity of status. A weak teacher can get along better here with the strong framework of customary order to help him or her. Apparently in America it would never do for a teacher to assume the official superiority of status, which our young people take as in the natural order of things, and to act as a master or mistress. The very words are unknown in their school terminology.

Social life in an American public high school among the pupils themselves takes forms somewhat different from ours. There is a good deal more of the "party" element, acting, dances, "socials," etc., managed by the boys and girls themselves. They have debating and literary societies, and school magazines managed by committees; glee and mandoline clubs are also very popular. The pupils of a particular year or "class" choose and wear a class pin. Philanthropic school societies for charitable work seem less common than with us. Games exist; in some schools the authorities say they are too popular and cause too much excitement. Girls are prohibited in some cases from playing matches with other schools; they would be so keen on winning that they would do no work. There is much less regular playing of games as a matter of course just as one eats or bathes; a Rhodes scholar says that in England brainworkers *must* play games to keep in health (what we say of India), but that in America it is not necessary. One difference in the American public high school is obvious: that teachers are not so much *in* things, games and societies as with us; the pupils run their societies themselves. A curious example of this separation is the existence of secret fraternities and sororities, imitated from the Greek-letter secret fraternities that are so important, so influential, and, it is said, so valuable an element in American college life. The National Education Association made an inquiry into the question in 1904. Nearly all the headmasters and others consulted condemned these societies as undemocratic, snobbish, detrimental to good school work and to the student's own character, and subversive of discipline. In Chicago this winter the question was a burning one, the City Superintendent having forbidden fraternities in the city high schools. In Kansas City, where the same action was taken, parents took the case into the courts, denying the right of the high school principal to penalise students who belonged to fraternities. The courts supported the school.

10.8   Excerpt from the "Cardinal Principles of Secondary Education," 1918.

Secondary education should be determined by the needs of the society to be served, the character of the individuals to be educated, and the knowledge of educational theory and practice available. These factors are by no means static. Society is always in process of development; the character of the secondary-school population undergoes modification; and the sciences on which educational theory and practice depend constantly furnish new information. Secondary education, however, like any other established agency of society, is conservative and tends to resist modification. Failure to make adjustments when the need arises leads to the necessity for extensive reorganization at irregular intervals. The evidence is strong that such a comprehensive reorganization of secondary education is imperative at the present time.

1. *Changes in Society*

Within the past few decades changes have taken place in American life profoundly affecting the activities of the individual. As a citizen, he must to a greater extent and in a more direct way cope with problems of community life, State and National Governments, and international relationships. As a worker, he must adjust himself to a more complex economic order. As a relatively independent personality, he has more leisure. The problems arising from these three dominant phases of life are closely interrelated and call for a degree of intelligence and efficiency on the part of every citizen that can not be secured through elementary education alone, or even through secondary education unless the scope of that education is broadened.

The responsibility of the secondary school is still further increased because many social agencies other than the school afford less stimulus for

Commission on the Reorganization of Secondary Education, *Cardinal Principles of Secondary Education* (U.S. Bureau of Education, Bulletin, No. 35, 1918; Washington: Government Printing Office, 1918), pp. 7–11.

education than heretofore. In many vocations there have come such significant changes as the substitution of the factory system for the domestic system of industry; the use of machinery in place of manual labor; the high specialization of processes with a corresponding subdivision of labor; and the breakdown of the apprentice system. In connection with home and family life have frequently come lessened responsibility on the part of the children; the withdrawal of the father and sometimes the mother from home occupations to the factory or store; and increased urbanization, resulting in less unified family life. Similarly, many important changes have taken place in community life, in the church, in the State, and in other institutions. These changes in American life call for extensive modifications in secondary education.

2. *Changes in the Secondary-School Population*

In the past 25 years there have been marked changes in the secondary-school population of the United States. The number of pupils has increased, according to Federal returns, from one for every 210 of the total population in 1889–90, to one for every 121 in 1899–1900, to one for every 89 in 1909–10, and to one for every 73 of the estimated total population in 1914–15. The character of the secondary-school population has been modified by the entrance of large numbers of pupils of widely varying capacities, aptitudes, social heredity, and destinies in life. Further, the broadening of the scope of secondary education has brought to the school many pupils who do not complete the full course but leave at various stages of advancement. The needs of these pupils can not be neglected, nor can we expect in the near future that all pupils will be able to complete the secondary school as full-time students.

At present only about one-third of the pupils who enter the first year of the elementary school reach the four-year high school, and only about one in nine is graduated. Of those who enter the seventh school year, only one-half to two-thirds reach the first year of the four-year high school. Of those who enter the four-year high school about one-third leave before the beginning of the second year, about one-half are gone before the beginning of the third year, and fewer than one-third are graduated. These facts can no longer be safely ignored.

3. *Changes in Educational Theory*

The sciences on which educational theory depends have within recent years made significant contributions. In particular, educational psychology emphasizes the following factors:

(*a*) *Individual differences in capacities and aptitudes among secondary-school pupils.* Already recognized to some extent, this factor merits fuller attention.

(*b*) *The reexamination and reinterpretation of subject values and the teaching methods with reference to "general discipline."* While the final verdict of modern psychology has not as yet been rendered, it is clear that former conceptions of "general values" must be thoroughly revised.

(*c*) *Importance of applying knowledge.* Subject values and teaching methods must be tested in terms of the laws of learning and the application of knowledge to the activities of life, rather than primarily in terms of the demands of any subject as a logically organized science.

(*d*) *Continuity in the development of children.* It has long been held that psychological changes at certain stages are so pronounced as to over-shadow the continuity of development. On this basis secondary education has been sharply separated from elementary education. Modern psychology, however, goes to show that the development of the individual is in most respects a continuous process and that, therefore, any sudden or abrupt break between the elementary and the secondary school or between any two successive stages of education is undesirable.

The foregoing changes in society, in the character of the secondary-school population, and in educational theory, together with many other considerations, call for extensive modifications of secondary education. Such modifications have already begun in part. The present need is for the formulation of a comprehensive program of reorganization, and its adoption, with suitable adjustments, in all the secondary schools of the Nation. Hence it is appropriate for a representative body like the National Education Association to outline such a program. This is the task entrusted by that association to the Commission on the Reorganization of Secondary Education.

II. The Goal of Education in a Democracy

Education in the United States should be guided by a clear conception of the meaning of democracy. It is the ideal of democracy that the individual and society may find fulfillment each in the other. Democracy sanctions neither the exploitation of the individual by society, nor the disregard of the interests of society by the individual. More explicitly—

The purpose of democracy is so to organize society that each member may develop his personality primarily through activities designed for the well-being of his fellow members and of society as a whole.

This ideal demands that human activities be placed upon a high level of efficiency; that to this efficiency be added an appreciation of the significance of these activities and loyalty to the best ideals involved; and that the individual choose that vocation and those forms of social service in which his personality may develop and become most effective. For the achievement of these ends democracy must place chief reliance upon education.

Consequently, education in a democracy, both within and without the school, should develop in each individual the knowledge, interests, ideals, habits, and powers whereby he will find his place and use that place to shape both himself and society toward ever nobler ends.

III. The Main Objectives of Education

In order to determine the main objectives that should guide education in a democracy it is necessary to analyze the activities of the individual. Normally he is a member of a family, of a vocational group, and of various civic groups, and by virtue of these relationships he is called upon to engage in activities that enrich the family life, to render important vocational services to his fellows, and to promote the common welfare. It follows, therefore, that worthy home-membership, vocation, and citizenship, demand attention as three of the leading objectives.

Aside from the immediate discharge of these specific duties, every individual should have a margin of time for the cultivation of personal and social interests. This leisure, if worthily used, will recreate his powers and enlarge and enrich life, thereby making him better able to meet his responsibilities. The unworthy use of leisure impairs health, disrupts home life, lessens vocational efficiency, and destroys civic-mindedness. The tendency in industrial life, aided by legislation, is to decrease the working hours of large groups of people. While shortened hours tend to lessen the harmful reactions that arise from prolonged strain, they increase, if possible, the importance of preparation for leisure. In view of these considerations, education for the worthy use of leisure is of increasing importance as an objective.

To discharge the duties of life and to benefit from leisure, one must have good health. The health of the individual is essential also to the vitality of the race and to the defense of the Nation. Health education is, therefore, fundamental.

There are various processes, such as reading, writing, arithmetical computations, and oral and written expression, that are needed as tools in the affairs of life. Consequently, command of these fundamental processes, while not an end in itself, is nevertheless an indispensable objective.

And, finally, the realization of the objectives already named is dependent upon ethical character, that is, upon conduct founded upon right principles, clearly perceived and loyally adhered to. Good citizenship, vocational excellence, and the worthy use of leisure go hand in hand with ethical character; they are at once the fruits of sterling character and the channels through which such character is developed and made manifest. On the one hand, character is meaningless apart from the will to discharge the duties of life, and, on the other hand, there is no guarantee that these duties will be rightly discharged unless principles are substituted for impulses, however well-intentioned such impulses may be. Consequently ethical character is at once involved in all the other objectives and at the same time requires specific consideration in any program of national education.

This commission, therefore, regards the following as the main objectives of education: 1. Health.   2. Command of fundamental processes. 3. Worthy home-membership. 4. Vocation. 5. Citizenship. 6. Worthy use of leisure.   7. Ethical character.

The naming of the above objectives is not intended to imply that the process of education can be divided into separated fields. This can not be, since the pupil is indivisible. Nor is the analysis all-inclusive. Nevertheless, we believe that distinguishing and naming these objectives will aid in directing efforts; and we hold that they should constitute the principal aims in education.

10.9   Harold Rugg of Teachers College, Columbia, Discusses Curriculum-Making by Scholars in the Academic Disciplines.

The Personnel and Procedure of National Committees (1892–1926)

We are now in a position to evaluate contemporary American practice in curriculum-making via national committees. From the Committee of Ten to date, national committees have been dominated by specialists in subject matter and by a faith in mental discipline. Their personnel, even to the present time, has only rarely included professional students of the curriculum, that is of child abilities, interests, and capacities, rates of learning, grade-placement, experimentation, and social analysis.

Lacking interest and training in the professional field of curriculum-making, the members of these national committees have used subjective and *a priori* methods in arriving at their recommendations and, with the two recent exceptions, have ignored the results of curricular research. The basis of recommendations throughout has been individual judgment.

National Society for the Study of Education, *Twenty-Sixth Yearbook* (Bloomington, Illinois: Public School Publishing Company, 1926), pp. 62–65. Reprinted by permission of the National Society for the Study of Education.

In the early days there was a great need through roundtable conferences for exchange of views among those who were organizing the curricula of our schools—there is still great need—and because the college men constituted the only group trained to do the job, it fell to their lot to undertake it. Great praise should be given to the hundreds of university men and school administrators who gave freely of their time and energy in those formative years of the national school curriculum.

However, the conclusion can not be escaped that, as the years went on, the technique was not modified to take advantage of progress in the technique of curriculum-making. Once in print, the pronouncements of national committees were quite generally followed, both in major outline and much in detail, by town and city schools throughout the United States. Special academic points of view became entrenched. The curriculum crystallized, became difficult to change. One committee supported another and acquiesced in the elimination of particularly obnoxious elements from the curriculum only after prolonged and reiterated demand from curriculum reformers.

It was curriculum-making by accretion and elimination. New topics were added slowly within the school 'subjects,' but the total reconstruction of the curriculum scheme was never considered by these subject committees.

Until after 1919 there was almost no utilization of objective methods of investigation by these national committees. Careful search of their reports (prior to the report of the National Committee on Mathematical Requirements, 1923) fails to reveal a single instance in which the committee set up experimental and scientific studies to aid them in their choice of recommended content, grade-placement, and organization of the materials of the curriculum.

The case is worse than that, however, for the indictment of the armchair methods of these 'subject-matter' committees. The search reveals practically no use of the conclusions of *available* scientific studies. Not until 1920, with the financing on a large scale of national committees in mathematics, classics, modern languages, and history, did the committee set aside executive investigators actually to make use of quantitative studies of curriculum-making.

The Influence of the Committees Through Courses of Study and Textbooks

In spite of the opinionated basis of the recommendations of the national committees, they have exerted a tremendous influence in shaping the school curriculum. The prestige of their reports was so great that, once published, their recommendations were copied into entrance requirements of universities and they constituted the outline to which textbooks had to correspond if the authors and publishers expected widespread adoption. Both state and local, town and city systems came to base their syllabi definitely upon the recommendations of the committees.

Authors and publishers of entrenched textbooks played an important rôle in this *a priori* committee work. Frequently, they served on the committees and wrote the recommendations. I have before me as I write the report of one national committee representing a great association, in which the outline of topics recommended by the member who wrote the report follows almost exactly—indeed almost verbatim—the order and treatment in his own textbook. According to the statements of members of another committee (one of the most influential of recent national committees), its procedure and recommendations were dominated by the author of the most widely used series of textbooks in that subject.

Naturally, progress in curriculum-making was slow, and will continue to be slow, if such influences are permitted to play an important rôle. It is clear that the curriculum of American schools will be based upon reading materials. It appears to be evident, furthermore, that in carrying on the huge task of preparing and distributing textbooks to 23,000,000 young people, we should make use of the machinery which the great publishing houses have built up.

As matters have stood during the past three decades, however, the 'scissors and paste method' has been used by new authors and publishers desiring to secure widespread adoption of their books and who fear to deviate widely from current practice. New books are made, therefore, from old ones. Since 1895, textbook companies, with an eye to sales, have tended more to form partnerships of 'professors' and public-school workers—superintendents, principals, or teachers. Few schoolbooks get wide adoption that are not prepared by such a partnership of subject-matter authority and practical school administration. The maintenance of the *status quo* is the *desideratum;* innovation is not favored—accepted only grudgingly when new proposals gradually secure a widespread hearing from progressive school people, themselves trained in the new educational teachings.

There is a great need that the publishers of textbooks support programs of more thorough and scientific curriculum-making. Indeed, in their own defense they can well afford to do so. A well-grounded program will make eventually for more stability in the curriculum.

10.10   The Educational Policies Commission of the National Education Association Describes the "Common Learnings."

These were the two major questions: What are the learning experiences which all boys and girls should have in common? And how may these be organized so as to be most effective? There were many discussions of these questions, which we shall not attempt to recount. In the end, most of the staff accepted the statement of "imperative educational needs of youth" as the basis for defining the "common studies" of secondary education and were ready to move to the problem of organization.

Here several possibilities were considered. One was to set up one or more separate required courses for each of the "common studies"—citizenship, family life, health, consumer economics, science, English, literature, and the arts. Another was to have a single course covering all the experiences deemed necessary for all pupils, which would be continuous throughout the years of high school and community institute for two or more periods daily. A third possibility was some combination of the first two—a basic course to include most of the "common learnings," supplemented by special courses in certain fields.

The first plan had the advantage of simplicity of scheduling, because courses would be set up in single period units for either a semester or a year. It followed the traditional pattern with which pupils and teachers alike were acquainted. In effect, it would simply substitute, for some of the currently required semester and year courses, other courses with a somewhat different and more useful content. The range of knowledge required of individual teachers would be somewhat wider than in conventional courses, but not greatly so. . . .

The second plan—a continuous course using two or more hours daily throughout the upper secondary schools—was advocated on the ground that people's daily work, their civic interests, their family life, their leisure-time activities, the things they think about, and their ways of thinking are all bound up together, each influencing the other. Therefore, it was said, learning in these fields will be more effective and more closely tied to the imperative needs of life if teachers and students are able to deal with all aspects of a given subject, to study problems as they are found in life outside the school, and to keep aware of interrelations which cut across conventional subjectmatter lines.

Educational Policies Commission, *Education for ALL American Youth* (Washington: National Education Association, 1944), pp. 234–238. Reprinted by permission of the National Education Association.

Someone cited housing as an example. In home economics, he said, pupils study about planning and furnishing their own homes. Questions relating to public planning of housing developments, government subsidies, and low-cost credit appear in "American Problems" courses. Courses in physics and chemistry frequently include units on science applied to houses and their equipment. History classes often study the types of houses characteristic of various periods in national development. Courses on health have their units on "building homes for health." In mathematics, one finds lessons on computing interest charges and amortization of home loans. In art—but why go on? For nowhere—so ran the argument—*nowhere,* under the conventional organization of courses, is it possible to study the subject of housing in its *entirety.* Yet today the paramount problem for fully one-fifth of the families in American City is that of getting a home to live in, within the family means, which will serve all the members of the family in all the ways a home can and should serve them. And within five years, the same problem will rank among those at the top for the majority of the boys and girls in classes today. Why not make it possible, this advocate of the new-type course concluded, for a teacher and a class to turn all their time and all their energies to an all-round study of housing? Why not develop the habit of attacking large problems and using information drawn from a number of subjectmatter fields?

Some of the most persuasive arguments came from teachers who had already been doing some experimenting in this field—combining two, or occasionally three, classes, usually literature and social studies, with science or art added now and then. They and others pointed out these advantages:

Under the proposed comprehensive course, students can better understand the relations between the different things they are learning. For example, the impact of science on industry and urban life can be better understood when science and social studies are part of the same course. In like manner, literature is better understood in relation to the life of the times in which it was written and which it portrays, and in turn it throws light upon the history of those times.

Within the broad areas planned for the year, classes can begin their work in any year with the problems and purposes of which students are most keenly aware at the time. This gets the class off to an active start at zestful, purposeful learning. The skilful teacher will not be worried if these beginnings deal with the relatively simple and sometimes transient affairs of everyday life. For he knows that when once the processes of interested, purposeful learning are under way, they can be guided toward the more complex and enduring needs of youth.

Learning experiences which are important, but which do not require a large amount of time, can be included in the proposed course more readily than in a curriculum organized along the conventional semester-unit lines; for example, brief, intensive work on the improvement of study habits, or on the budgeting of time, or on the recreational resources of the neighborhood.

The proposed course would permit the adaptation of learning experiences in some fields to changing interests and outlooks as students become more mature. For example, during the three years from fifteen to eighteen there are marked shifts in the attitudes of students toward family relationships as boys and girls become less conscious of themselves as children, more concious of themselves as potential husbands, wives, and parents. So also with interest in occupations. The tenth-grade student is interested in the choice of a possible occupational field and in planning a course to get him ready for a job that is still faraway. Three years later, he is likely to be concerned about the job that is just ahead—how to get it and hold it, requirements and conditions of work, industrial and labor relations, and the like. Given the comprehensive course, the learnings about family life and occupations could be distributed throughout the three years and matched to the changing interests of learners.

Greater flexibility in use of time would be possible and with it types of learning experiences that were impracticable under the system of single-period courses. When any problem or project required special attention for a week or a month, nearly the full triple or double period could be used for that purpose. Field trips and firsthand studies of the community would be feasible because of the longer blocks of time.

Most important of all, each teacher in the proposed course would have fewer *different* pupils and more time to work with and observe each pupil in a wider variety of situations. Therefore, it was said, let the teachers of these new "Common Learnings" courses serve also as counselors to their students. Such an arrangement would dovetail exactly with the recommendations already made that more adequate provision should be made for guidance and that most student counseling should be done by teachers.

The proposal was widely discussed before any action was taken. Some feared, as they said, a "soft pedagogy"—an aimless shifting from one point of transient interest to the next without sustained intellectual effort. In reply it was pointed out that the needs to be met would be clearly defined by the staff for each year of the course. There, to be sure, the planning-in-advance-for-everybody would end. Within the broad outlines of each year's work, each teacher and class would be free to plan and organize their own learning. But planning and organizing, in itself, is an act which requires no mean intellectual effort.

Some feared the danger of superficiality. Classes, they said, would "gallop off in all directions at once" and fail to learn anything thoroughly. The reply was made that here, as everywhere, the quality of learning would depend upon skilful teaching. Orderly sequences of learning might be expected in this course, quite as much as in single-subject courses. But there would be various types of sequences, each deliberately chosen by teacher and class because it seemed best suited to the task at hand. Sometimes the class would follow the method of scientific inquiry to conduct an experiment or solve a problem. Sometimes it would trace the relations of cause and effect through the events of history. Sometimes it would follow the logic of organized bodies of knowledge. And sometimes the order of learning would be that appropriate to growth in appreciations. To be able to choose a sequence of learning appropriate to one's aim is again an intellectual achievement.

Finally, there were some who feared—quite mistakenly, as it turned out —that this course would put an end to the systematic study of bodies of knowledge, such as the sciences, mathematics, history, and languages. This objection was withdrawn, however, when it was shown that there would be ample time in the total school program for any student who wished to do so, to complete all the courses in subject fields required for admission to college or university, even by those institutions which still held to their prewar requirements. Moreover, it was asserted, the conventionally required subjects would appear in the new course, insofar as they were needed to meet the common needs of all youth. English language, literature, history, and science would certainly be found among the "Common Learnings," though possibly in unaccustomed settings.

10.11   Arthur Bestor, Professor of History at the University of Illinois, Criticizes "Life-Adjustment" Education.

"Life-adjustment" education took its rise from a resolution—now hailed as "historic"—which was adopted at a conference of educators in 1945:

> It is the belief of this conference that, with the aid of this report in final form, the vocational school of a community will be able better to prepare 20 percent of the youth of secondary-school age for entrance upon desirable skilled occupations; and that the high school will continue to prepare another 20 percent for entrance to college. We do not believe that the remaining 60 percent of our youth of secondary school age will receive the life-adjustment training they need and to which they are entitled as Ameri-

Arthur Bestor, *Educational Wastelands* (Urbana: University of Illinois Press, 1953), pp. 81–84. Reprinted by permission of the University of Illinois Press.

can citizens—unless and until the administrators of public education with the assistance of the vocational education leaders formulate a similar program for this group.

Consider for a moment the extraordinary implications of this statement. Sixty percent—three-fifths—of the future citizens of the United States, it asserts without qualification, are incapable of being benefited by intellectual training or even training for skilled and desirable occupations. If this is true, it is a fact of the most shattering significance, for it declares invalid most of the assumptions that have underlain American democracy. It enthrones once again the ancient doctrine that a clear majority of the people are destined from birth to be hewers of wood and drawers of water for a select and superior few. The "mud-sill" theory of society has come back with a vengeance, and likewise the good old argument that schooling for the ordinary man must teach him to know his place, to keep it, and to be content with it.

So eager were these educational leaders to proclaim their distrust of the abilities of the American people that they seem to have drawn their actual figures out of a hat. At any rate, their percentages differ markedly from the conclusions of another educational commission which found, almost contemporaneously, that "at least 49 percent of our population has the mental ability to complete 14 years of schooling" and "at least 32 percent . . . the mental ability to complete an advanced liberal or specialized professional education." The discrepancy is not of particular moment, for "life-adjustment" training is not a matter of statistics, it is a philosophy of education. It is the philosophy which asserts that the public schools must "adjust" a majority of our children—three-fifths or some other proportion—to the bitter fact that they are good for nothing but undesirable, unskilled occupations, and that intellectual effort is far beyond their feeble grasp. . . .

The National Commission on Life Adjustment Education for Youth sized up with considerable realism the difficulties it would have to overcome in eliminating intellectual training from the schools. "Traditional subjects are logically organized," it had to admit, and the contrast with what it was proposing was all too obvious. "Effective teachers are enthusiastic about the subjects they teach," the Commission lamented, and such enthusiasm was going to be hard to stamp out. The public, too, presented a problem, for the Commission regretfully observed that "there are enormous continuing pressures for teachers and principals to continue doing the things they do well"—a hopelessly old-fashioned attitude that would require a good deal of propaganda to eradicate. "The Commission," according to its own modest statement, "recognizes these difficulties and it has no panacea for overcoming them." Refreshing as it is to encounter a group of educationists without a panacea, one cannot escape the feeling that under such circumstances the Commission desperately needed one.

It is well that the Commission refused to recognize as an additional difficulty what others might regard as such. The curriculum, it asserted, should be planned "to meet the imperative needs of all youth," but the Commission did not believe it should give first consideration to the needs of pupils now in school. "Even more, it is concerned with the types of education needed by the adolescent youth who drop out of school because their needs are not being met realistically." Apparently the Commission felt justified in sacrificing the interests of the students who were already attending school with the intention of studying, if it could thereby lure back into the classroom those who never wanted to be there in the first place.

10.12   The Educational Policies Commission Issues a New Statement on the Aims of Education.

Education in the American Society

In any democracy education is closely bound to the wishes of the people, but the strength of this bond in America has been unique. The American people have traditionally regarded education as a means for improving themselves and their society. Whenever an objective has been judged desirable for the individual or the society, it has tended to be accepted as a valid concern of the school. The American commitment to the free society—to individual dignity, to personal liberty, to equality of opportunity—has set the frame in which the American school grew. The basic American value, respect for the individual, has led to one of the major charges which the American people have placed on their schools: to foster that development of individual capacities which will enable each human being to become the best person he is capable of becoming.

The schools have been designed also to serve society's needs. The political order depends on responsible participation of individual citizens; hence the schools have been concerned with good citizenship. The economic order depends on ability and willingness to work; hence the schools have taught vocational skills. The general morality depends on choices made by individuals; hence the schools have cultivated moral habits and upright character.

Educational Policies Commission, *The Central Purpose of American Education* (Washington: National Education Association, 1961), pp. 1–5. Reprinted by permission of the National Education Association.

Educational authorities have tended to share and support these broad concepts of educational purposes. Two of the best-known definitions of purposes were formulated by educators in 1918 and 1938. The first definition, by the Commission on the Reorganization of Secondary Education, proposed for the school a set of seven cardinal objectives: health, command of fundamental processes, worthy home membership, vocational competence, effective citizenship, worthy use of leisure, and ethical character. The second definition, by the Educational Policies Commission, developed a number of objectives under four headings: self-realization, human relationship, economic efficiency, and civic responsibility.

The American school must be concerned with all these objectives if it is to serve all of American life. That these are desirable objectives is clear. Yet they place before the school a problem of immense scope, for neither the schools nor the pupils have the time or energy to engage in all the activities which will fully achieve all these goals. Choices among possible activities are inevitable and are constantly being made in and for every school. But there is no consensus regarding a basis for making these choices. The need, therefore, is for a principle which will enable the school to identify its necessary and appropriate contributions to individual development and the needs of society.

Furthermore, education does not cease when the pupil leaves the school. No school fully achieves any pupil's goals in the relatively short time he spends in the classroom. The school seeks rather to equip the pupil to achieve them for himself. Thus the search for a definition of the school's necessary contribution entails an understanding of the ways individuals and societies choose and achieve their goals. Because the school must serve both individuals and the society at large in achieving their goals, and because the principal goal of the American society remains freedom, the requirements of freedom set the frame within which the school can discover the central focus of its own efforts.

The freedom which exalts the individual, and by which the worth of the society is judged, has many dimensions. It means freedom from undue governmental restraints; it means equality in political participation. It means the right to earn and own property and decide its disposition. It means equal access to just processes of law. It means the right to worship according to one's conscience.

Institutional safeguards are a necessary condition for freedom. They are not, however, sufficient to make men free. Freedom requires that citizens act responsibly in all ways. It cannot be preserved in a society whose citizens do not value freedom. Thus belief in freedom is essential to maintenance of freedom. The basis of this belief cannot be laid by mere indoctrination in principles of freedom. The ability to recite the values of a free society does not guarantee commitment to those values. Active belief in those values depends on awareness of them and of their role in life. The person who best supports these values is one who has examined them, who understands their function in his life and in the society at large, and who accepts them as worthy of his own support. For such a person these values are consciously held and consciously approved.

The conditions necessary for freedom include the social institutions which protect freedom and the personal commitment which gives it force. Both of these conditions rest on one condition within the individuals who compose a free society. This is freedom of the mind.

Freedom of the mind is a condition which each individual must develop for himself. In this sense, no man is born free. A free society has the obligation to create circumstances in which all individuals may have opportunity and encouragement to attain freedom of the mind. If this goal is to be achieved, its requirements must be specified.

To be free, a man must be capable of basing his choices and actions on understandings which he himself achieves and on values which he examines for himself. He must be aware of the bases on which he accepts propositions as true. He must understand the values by which he lives, the assumptions on which they rest, and the consequences to which they lead. He must recognize that others may have different values. He must be capable of analyzing the situation in which he finds himself and of developing solutions to the problems before him. He must be able to perceive and understand the events of his life and time and the forces that influence and shape those events. He must recognize and accept the practical limitations which time and circumstance place on his choices. The free man, in short, has a rational grasp of himself, his surroundings, and the relation between them.

He has the freedom to think and choose, and that freedom must have its roots in conditions both within and around the individual. Society's dual role is to guarantee the necessary environment and to develop the necessary individual strength. That individual strength springs from a thinking, aware mind, a mind that possesses the capacity to achieve aesthetic sensitivity and moral responsibility, an enlightened mind. These qualities occur in a wide diversity of patterns in different individuals. It is the contention of this essay that central to all of them, nurturing them and being nurtured by them, are the rational powers of man.

The cultivated powers of the free mind have always been basic in achieving freedom. The powers of the free mind are many. In addition to the rational powers, there are those which relate to the aesthetic, the moral, and the religious. There is a unique, central role for the rational powers of an individual, however, for upon them depends his ability to achieve his personal goals and to fulfill his obligations to society.

These powers involve the processes of recalling and imagining, classifying and generalizing, comparing and evaluating, analyzing and synthesizing, and deducing and inferring. These processes enable one to apply logic and the available evidence to his ideas, attitudes, and actions, and to pursue better whatever goals he may have.

This is not to say that the rational powers are all of life or all of the mind, but they are the essence of the ability to think. A thinking person is aware that all persons, himself included, are both rational and nonrational, that each person perceives events through the screen of his own personality, and that he must take account of his personality in evaluating his perceptions. The rational processes, moreover, make intelligent choices possible. Through them a person can become aware of the bases of choice in his values and of the circumstances of choice in his environment. Thus they are broadly applicable in life, and they provide a solid basis for competence in all the areas with which the school has traditionally been concerned.

The Education of Teachers
and the Teaching of Education

11

"To be a teacher, one must first of all be a scholar. So much stress is now placed on method, and on the theory of teaching, that there is great danger of forgetting the supreme importance of scholarship and culture." So spoke not a liberal arts professor in the 1950's but one of the first American educationists, David Page, in 1847. His cautionary remark foreshadowed a conflict which would agitate the academic world for more than a century. What does a teacher need to know? Fierce battles have been waged over the answer to this apparently innocent question, struggles which all too often have resembled the battles of the ancient Chinese warlords, who summoned their troops to an imaginary line, hurled insults at each other, and departed, leaving tempers riled but bodies intact and the landscape unchanged.

The question of how to educate teachers is debatable, to be sure, and it involves in the most intimate way the campus politics of higher education as well as the welfare of elementary and secondary education. But the violence of the controversy in recent years has obscured the fact that *any* adequate education of teachers is a recent adventure. Before the twentieth century a majority of teachers probably had no more than elementary schooling (if indeed they had graduated from the eighth grade); in 1931 only about 10 percent of all elementary teachers had a bachelor's degree; and as late as 1952 not even a majority of elementary teachers had graduated from college. Furthermore, the developing education of teachers should be compared with their social and economic status. Although America has had poorly prepared teachers during most of its history, it probably had better teachers than it had any right to expect when one considers their pay and conditions of work.

412

At no time in American history have there been greater disparities in the status of teachers than during the colonial period. On one end of the spectrum were Latin grammar school teachers, almost always college-trained (in the liberal arts), fairly well paid, and often ranking close to the minister or magistrate in social esteem. In Boston, for example, grammar school teachers were practically all Harvard graduates, and several served long and honored careers as schoolmasters. In smaller communities recent college graduates often taught school while awaiting a call to the ministry, or local clergymen prepared a handful of boys for college. As Phillip Fithian learned in Virginia, tutors in planters' families were often well accepted socially (in fact, Fithian's successor in the Carter family married the planter's daughter). In the middle of the spectrum of teachers were the goodwomen who taught young children to read in their homes, the farmers' daughters who ran summer schools for little children, and young men who taught the older scholars in winter district schools when they were not needed on the farm and when other work was slack. Normally teaching was a casual and part-time occupation which sometimes attracted the transported convict, the drunkard, and the "low bred clown" about whom Noah Webster complained so bitterly.

Although sometimes a master teacher advertised that he would teach the "art and mysteries" of his craft to an apprentice, few Americans looked on teaching as a bona fide craft, much less a profession. After the American Revolution such haphazard employment of teachers continued. The period before the Civil War was a time when career patterns were fluid, when men were apt to sample many occupations. This lack of precise standards and training meant that caricatures of teachers like Ichabod Crane wandered into schoolrooms, yet it also allowed men like John Adams, Ralph Waldo Emerson, Henry David Thoreau, and Walt Whitman to try their hand at teaching.

Commonly the local school committee or private school trustees had free rein in certifying their own teachers. While some laymen took this responsibility seriously, and tried to find literate, experienced, and moral teachers, others were apt to introduce irrelevant considerations: the sectarian or political opinions of the applicant, pity for his poverty or infirmity, or a desire to employ a relative. One teacher commented that a sure way to get a job was to be in debt to a board member. In any case, committeemen scrutinized the muscles and tested the grit of the prospect, for ability to discipline children was paramount; in 1837 in Massachusetts alone 300 schools were closed because unruly pupils had ejected their teachers. And a patient willingness to endure poverty recommended any teacher. In 1841 the average weekly pay of men in rural schools was $4.15, of women, $2.51; by 1861 this had increased to only $6.30 and $4.05

respectively. Such salaries were below the wages paid to artisans in most communities, and often below even the earnings of scrubwomen and day laborers.

Not only were teachers paid starvation wages but they were also bereft of the usual immunities of American citizenship. Under constant scrutiny by the community, they were usually expected to abhor drink and tobacco, to be pillars of the church, to keep decorous hours, to be models of neutrality in all public questions, and even to deny the attractions of the opposite sex. One teacher, furious at public criticism because he escorted his female assistant home from school, snorted, "I do not intend, for $35.00 a month, to resign all the privileges guaranteed to me by the social compact." The hero of Edward Eggleston's perceptive novel, *The Hoosier Schoolmaster,* learned what a tightrope the country teacher needed to walk.

The practice of "boarding 'round" further subjugated the teacher to the community. Under this system, teachers in rural areas lived with the parents of the children they taught—an arrangement which was a sort of primitive PTA. Sometimes, when the parents wished to impress a favored teacher, the experience could be pleasant for all concerned: the best dishes trotted out, the choicest beef cooked, and pies baked every night. But often parents and teachers alike resented the intrusion, and householders tried to make the master's stay economical. More often than not the practice was barbaric. It was widespread in rural communities; in Vermont, for example, 68 percent of the teachers in 1862 boarded 'round. One of these victims left a vivid—though perhaps apocryphal—account of his misery:

> Monday. Went to board at Mr. B's; had baked gander for dinner; suppose from its size, the thickness of the skin and other venerable appearances it must have been one of the first settlers of Vermont; made a slight impression on the patriarch's breast. Supper—cold gander and potatoes. Family consists of the man, good wife, daughter Peggy, four boys, Pompey the dog, and a brace of cats. Fire built in the square room about nine o'clock, and a pile of wood lay by the fireplace; saw Peggy scratch her fingers, and couldn't take the hint; felt squeamish about the stomach, and talked of going to bed; Peggy looked sullen, and put out the fire in the square room; went to bed and dreamed of having eaten a quantity of stone wall.

The gander pursued the poor man at breakfast, dinner, and supper; Peggy angled for him continually; and bad dreams stole his rest.

Most Americans took more care in selecting blacksmiths to shoe their horses—and paid them better—than teachers to instruct their children. It is little wonder, then, that most teachers were young, untrained, inexperienced, and uncommitted to their calling. This disgrace troubled the common school reformers. They sought to raise professional morale and prowess by organizing "teachers' institutes," which today would be called conventions, and teachers' associations. But they realized that such intermittent instruction was no substitute for professional training; hence they created normal schools.

Some private academies had introduced "normal courses" for prospective teachers, but before the common school crusade no state had taken responsibility for preparing teachers. In Prussia the reformers found a model of state teacher education. The early state normal schools—the first began at Lexington, Massachusetts in 1839—borrowed features of both the American academy and the Prussian and French schools for teachers. They admitted students directly from the elementary schools and taught them largely a review of the "common branches" (the subjects taught in the lower schools), a smattering of natural and moral philosophy, and the theory and practice of instruction. Books on teaching, like those by Jacob Abbott and David Page, began to appear, and were widely used as texts. Usually the state normal schools were understaffed; Cyrus Pierce, the talented principal of Lexington Normal School, for example, had to teach seventeen subjects. Instruction in many normal schools was inferior to that available in the better high schools and academies of the day. Normal schools did call public attention to the need for careful preparation of teachers and did create a sense of professional dedication and skill among the new prospective teachers who entered their doors. But they could not claim to have fulfilled Horace Mann's hope that they would display "a vigor whose uncoiling may wheel the spheres." By 1898 the number of public normal schools had grown to 127, with about the same number of private ones. But all the normal schools together graduated that year no more than one-quarter of the new teachers.

After the Civil War formal study of education entered the college and university curriculum. As knowledge mushroomed, and as an increasingly technical and interdependent economy demanded experts, society came to expect that higher education should train workers in a host of new fields such as engineering, business, agriculture, and education. During the middle third of the nineteenth century a number of state universities had "normal departments," but these really gave secondary rather than collegiate instruction. In 1873 the University of Iowa established the first permanent chair of pedagogy to prepare teachers "for *advanced schools*." "Didactics, in the higher sense, is a liberal study," stated the catalogue that year. The department admitted only university seniors and comparable special students. The University of Michigan followed Iowa's precedent in 1879, aiming to give instruction in the "Science and Art of

Teaching"; to advance educational research; to prepare university students for positions of leadership in the public schools (thereby bringing better coordination between secondary and higher education); "to teach the history of education and of educational systems and doctrines"; and to professionalize the vocation of teaching. By the end of the century most of the major universities and colleges had established departments or schools of education.

No one was quite sure what a department of education should do or be. Early educationists turned to German universities for guidance. In Germany pedagogy was often subsumed under some other discipline such as philosophy, psychology, or history, and eminent scholars such as Kant and Herbart had concerned themselves with the problems of education. The German universities also had special pedagogical seminaries to prepare teachers for *gymnasia* (or secondary schools). These models proved useful to pioneer American educationists. Most of them believed that normal schools should prepare elementary teachers while universities should concentrate on training high school teachers, administrators, and educational specialists.

When universities introduced new subjects into the curriculum, they often could not find trained professors. President Eliot of Harvard invited Henry Adams to teach history, but Adams complained that he hardly knew enough history to profess. Eliot replied that if Adams knew anyone who knew more, he would hire him. (Adams accepted the job.) The same difficulty plagued education departments. All sorts of people were hired to teach pedagogy: school superintendents and principals, philosophers, historians, scientists, ministers, psychologists. Often universities founded departments of education from expediency, to meet competition from other institutions.

In 1903 an education professor complained about cavalier appointments:

> It is not an uncommon occurrence for a president of a university to call to the professorship of education a man who has had absolutely no scientific training for the field over which he is given control. These calls have resulted, no doubt, as a reward of merit, but too often it has been for merit in some other than pedagogical lines, and in some cases it seems that the call has been the result of an effort to find a place for a man who is thought to be able to do less harm in a department of education than elsewhere.

Another education professor, explaining why many prospective teachers avoided education courses, said that sometimes "the pedagogical work is so namby-pamby and stupid that an active brain gets too weary to stand it." Professors of education found themselves under attack from their colleagues in the liberal arts and from instructors in normal schools whose work they challenged. One educationist hopefully stated in 1903 that the academic critics gave "an honest and wholesome opposition, which will give way in time to better judgment and wiser counsel."

Perhaps the very amorphousness and newness of the field was one of the reasons for the great intellectual ferment in education at the turn of the century. Scholars in diverse disciplines found in the study of education questions which went to the center of their own research, and they refused to look on education as a pre-empted field: witness the work of William James, G. Stanley Hall, Edward L. Thorndike in psychology; John Dewey in philosophy; Herbert Baxter Adams in history; and Albion Small and Thorstein Veblen in sociology. In any case, most of the early professors of education turned to the disciplines of history, psychology, philosophy, and the social sciences for the intellectual structure of their research on educational questions.

Schoolmen commonly believed that preparing high school teachers was the proper province of colleges and universities, rather than normal schools. In a survey at the turn of the century 84 per cent of over 100 city school superintendents indicated that they preferred to hire college graduates with professional training for high school positions; 10 per cent said they preferred college graduates without work in education, while only 6 per cent would have chosen normal school graduates. The accreditation requirements for high schools helped to shape teacher education. Accrediting agencies ordinarily demanded that high school teachers have B.A. degrees. Partly in response to this demand many normal schools in the twentieth century transformed themselves into four-year, degree-granting teachers' colleges. During the period from 1911 to 1930 there were eighty-eight such conversions. In 1930–31 over seventy-eight per cent of senior high school teachers had four or more years of college education.

Yet in 1900 the great mass of elementary school teachers had studied neither in normal schools nor in universities. The standards for admission to teaching were little short of scandalous. In a number of states the local school district had power to certify teachers it selected; thus, in effect, certification and employment became indistinguishable, without any outside control of eligibility for positions. Such absolute power was likely to corrupt absolutely. Teachers might not be hired because they were Congregationalists in Baptist territory, or vice-versa. Politics often entered teachers' examinations. A girl might be hired in the South only if she said that states' rights caused the Civil War, and in the North only if she blamed slavery. And many urban politicians regarded the schools as a part of their patronage system. 1,189 answers from schoolmen to a questionnaire circulated in 1896 by the *Atlantic Monthly*, revealed corruption in teacher appointment and tenure all over the nation. In summarizing these replies G. Stanley Hall concluded that "it is impossible to resist the conclusion that civil service reform is greatly needed for teachers."

The movement to improve certification of teachers owed a good deal of its ideology and methods to civil service reform in government. In place of capricious, corrupt, or politically determined ways of choosing public servants—in this case teachers—the advocates of civil service reform in education sought uniform standards for screening applicants, criteria which could be bureaucratically defined and enforced.

In the late nineteenth century the customary agent for certifying teachers was the county superintendent or examiner, the usual device a written examination. In 1898 only three *states* issued all certificates; elsewhere the county and state shared the responsibility (the state prescribing general rules but the county administering them with some discretionary power). Examinations covered the rudiments taught in the common school and were often anachronistic in content. Only seventeen states in 1898 tested candidates' knowledge of pedagogy. In some states the foes of strong drink and tobacco managed to insert questions to test the orthodoxy of teachers: example—"What effect has alcohol on the circulation?" (answer: it causes almost immediate arteriosclerosis). In certain communities teachers had hanging over their heads the Damocles sword of annual examinations for renewing their certificates, sometimes inflicted by laymen eager to wreak vengeance on all pedagogues. A San Francisco teacher described one such ordeal in 1860 when the examiner asked the applicants to name all the major bodies of water, cities, and countries on earth—in one hour. That teacher, John Swett, later spearheaded the drive for uniform teacher certification in California when he became state superintendent.

At best the local examinations were apt to be trials by trivia, at worst a farcical way to salve consciences while providing a mudsill entry to teaching. Not until the twentieth century did most states begin to exert effective control over the qualifications of teachers. Authority which had previously been splintered among autonomous local districts or counties became increasingly centralized in state boards of education. As schools became bureaucratized, like government itself, it became easier to classify positions, to set salaries, to determine qualifications, and to fix relatively impartial and uniform rules of eligibility for employment. The state codified these standards into law and enforced them. To harrassed superintendents, beset by political pressures to hire unqualified instructors, and to teachers, victims of capricious certification and employment, such civil service safeguards provided by the state were welcome indeed.

In the twentieth century the state requirements for certification shifted from examinations to professional courses and college degrees. In 1900 no states required graduation from high school and professional training for certification; by 1925 twenty-one states required both. By the latter date all certificates demanded a knowledge of pedagogy. Whereas in the nineteenth century teaching certificates did not specify levels or subjects, increasingly the states separated certificates for elementary and secondary teachers and added a number of other special credentials (such as administrative certificates).

The rapid growth of departments and schools of education, as well as the expansion of normal schools and teachers colleges, made it feasible for the first time to meet the demand for professionally prepared teachers. Educationists helped to set state certification requirements and then found it necessary to establish college programs which conformed to these regulations. The pattern of teacher education thus became crystallized into legally fixed courses which differed from state to state but which were fairly uniform within the state. The subjects most frequently required were educational psychology, methods of teaching, social foundations of education, and student teaching; customarily elementary teachers took more hours in professional courses than did secondary teachers. While statewide certification gave teachers greater mobility than local or county certificates, they still inhibited interstate migration (during the teacher surplus of the 1930's many states even enacted tariff barriers in the form of required courses in state history or school law to prevent immigration of out-of-state teachers).

For decades professors of the liberal arts and sciences had neglected their responsibility for forming policy in the education of teachers. But in the years following World War II many of them became bitterly critical of educationists. The most articulate and persistent of these critics was Arthur Bestor, whose *Educational Wastelands* in 1953 severely indicted what he called "an interlocking public school directorate." According to Bestor a clique of education professors, school administrators, and state and federal education officials, hostile to scholarly values, conspired to control the preparation and employment of teachers. Creating by state laws a monopoly over teacher education, they multiplied professional courses and requirements. Bestor believed that education, once a promising field in the days of John Dewey, had become a pretentious and ingrown establishment. Only a strong infusion of the liberal arts—coupled with the barest modicum of professional training—could redeem teacher education. Other critics, like Albert Lynd in *Quackery in the Public Schools* (1953) and James Koerner in *The Miseducation of American Teachers* (1963), joined the attack. As in the assault on progressive education, the polemicists often gave a distorted picture of both the aims and practice of teacher education, and educationists frequently reacted defensively and in an equally emotional tone. Indeed, it sometimes seemed that both critics and defenders were only pouring burning oil on troubled waters. Disguised beneath self-righteous rhetoric were self-interested concerns of professors over who should determine the teacher education curriculum; religious and political opinions not infrequently thrust their way into the argument. Sometimes the persons most directly concerned —the teachers and the children they taught—seemed to disappear from view.

But in the long run this resurgence of interest in teacher education and in pre-college schooling directed the attention of the entire academic community to forgotten responsibilities. As professors of the liberal arts learned more about the schools, they discovered the intellectual challenge and the practical difficulties of deciding what and how to teach; many of them turned to the task of preparing teachers with new awareness of their own role in teacher education. And under the stimulus of criticism many education professors realized that the time had come to raise the intellectual level of their own enterprise, to change certification practices which had once been reforms but which had calcified, and to seek to rebuild a sense of intellectual community within the university and between the schools and higher education.

Controversy makes more headlines than constructive dialogue. In recent years, on campuses and in meetings such as those sponsored by the Teacher Education and Professional Standards Commission of the N.E.A., professors of education and liberal arts have hammered out areas of agreement and have begun to subordinate their remaining disagreements to the task at hand: preparing good teachers. There is increasing consensus today that the proper education of teachers must include three carefully planned elements: a sound general education, thorough training in the subject taught, and intellectually challenging and practically efficient professional instruction. Many problems remain: how to attract outstanding individuals into teaching and to compensate them according to their ability and training; how to replace the regimentation of many certification laws with better guarantees of competence; and how to fight the continuing battle against obsolescence in teacher education in a society undergoing several revolutions simultaneously. Retrospect suggests that the very terms of the present controversies offer more reason for hope than despair. Obscured sometimes in the internecine warfare in the university is an assumption which has become widely held only since the middle of the twentieth century: that all teachers need a superior education and should receive commensurate rewards.

11.1   The Hiring of a Schoolmaster: A Cautionary Tale in a School Reader.

Dialogue between a School-Master, and School-Committee

[N.B. *The Author is happy in believing, that the following Dialogue is applicable to but few towns and few teachers in this country; but, so long as there are any remaining to whom it may apply, he thinks a sufficient apology exists for its publication.*]

SCENE, *a Public House in the Town of* ——.
Enter School-Master, with a pack on his back.

Schoolmaster. How fare you, landlord? what have you got that's good to drink?

Landlord. I have gin, West-India, genuine New-England, whiskey, and cider brandy.

Schoolm. Make us a stiff mug of sling. Put in a gill and a half of your New-England; and sweeten it well with lasses.

Land. It shall be done, Sir, to your liking.

Schoolm. Do you know of any vacancy in a school in your part of the country, landlord?

Land. There is a vacancy in our district; and I expect the parson, with our three school-committee men, will be at my house directly, to consult upon matters relative to the school.

Schoolm. Well, here's the lad that will serve them as *cheap* as any man in America; and I believe I may venture to say as *well* too; for I profess no small share of skill in that business. I have kept school eleven winters, and have often had matter of fifty scholars at a time. I have teach'd a child its letters in a day, and to read in the Psalter in a fortnight: and I always feel very much ashamed, if I use more than one quire of paper in larnin a boy to write as well as his master. As for government, I'll turn my back to no man. I never flog my scholars; for that monstrous doctrine of whippin children, which has been so long preached and practised by our rigid and superstitious forefathers, I have long since exploded. I have a rare knack of *flattering* them into their duty. And this according to a celebrated Doctor at Philadelphia, whose works I have heard of, though I never read them, is the grand criterion of school government. It is landlord, it is the very philosopher's stone. I am told, likewise, that this same great Doctor does not believe that Solomon and others really meant *licken*, in the proper sense of the word, when they talked so much

Caleb Bingham, *The Columbian Orator* . . . (Hartford: Lincoln and Gleason, 1807), pp. 158–165.

about using the rod, &c. He supposes that they meant confining them in
dungeons; starving them for three of four days at a time; and then giving
them a portion of tatromattucks, and such kinds of mild punishment.
And, zounds, landlord, I believe he's above half right.

Land. [*Giving the cup to the master.*]   Master —— What may I call
your name, Sir, if I may be so bold?

Schoolm. Ignoramus, at your service, Sir.

Land. Master Ignoramus, I am glad to see you. You are the very man
we wish for. Our committee won't hesitate a moment to employ you,
when they become acquainted with your talents. Your sentiments on
government I know will suit our people to a nicety. Our last master was
a tyrant of a fellow, and very extravagant in his price. He grew so important, the latter part of his time, that he had the frontery to demand
ten dollars a month and his board. And he might truly be said to rule
with a rod of iron; for he kept an *ironwood* cudgel in his school, four feet
long; and it was enough to chill one's blood to hear the shrieks of the little innocents, which were caused by his barbarity. I have heard my wife
say, that Sue Gossip told her, that she has seen the marks of his lashes on
the back of her neighbour Rymple's son Darling, for twelve hours after
the drubbing. At least, the boy told her with his own mouth, that they
might be seen, if they would only take the trouble to strip his shirt off.
And, besides, Master Ignoramus, he was the most niggardly of all the human race. I don't suppose that my bar-room was one dollar the richer
for him, in the course of the whole time which he tarried with us. While
the young people of the town were recreating themselves, and taking a
social glass, of an evening, at my house, the stupid blockhead was eternally
in his chamber, poring over his musty books. But finally he did the job
for himself, and I am rejoiced. The wretch had the dacity to box little
Sammy Puney's ears at such an intolerable rate, that his parents fear the
poor child will be an idiot all the days of his life. And all this, for nothing
more, than partly by design, and partly through mere accident, he happened to spit in his master's face. The child being nephew to the 'squire,
you may well suppose, that the whole neighbourhood was soon in an up-
roar. The indignation of the mother, father, aunts, uncles, cousins, and
indeed the whole circle of acquaintance, was roused; and the poor fellow
was hooted out of town in less than twenty-four hours.

Schoolm. [*Drinking off his liquor.*]   This is a rare dose. Believe me,
landlord, I have not tasted a drop before, since six o'clock this morning.
[*Enter Parson and Committee Men.*]   Your humble sarvant, gentlemen. I
understand you are in want of a school-master.

Parson. Yes Sir; that is the occasion of our present meeting. We have
been so unfortunate as to lose one good man; and we should be very glad
to find another.

1st Committee Man. Pray don't say *unfortunate*, Parson. I think we may consider ourselves as very *fortunate*, in having rid the town of an extravagant coxcomb, who was draining us of all the money we could earn, to fill his purse, and rig himself out with fine clothes.

2d Com. Ten dollars a month, and board, for a man whose task is so easy, is no small sum.

3d Com. I am bold to affirm, that we can procure a better man for half the money.

Schoolm. That I believe, friend; for, though I esteem myself as good as the best; that is to say, in the common way; yet I never ax'd but five dollars a month in all my life.

Par. For my own part, whatever these gentlemen's opinion may be, I must tell you, that I am much less concerned about the wages we are to give, than I am about the character and abilities of the man with whom we intrust the education of our children. I had much rather you had said you had received forty dollars a month, than five.

1st Com. Dear Sir, you are beside yourself. You will encourage the man to *rise* in his price; whereas I was in hopes he would have *fallen*, at least one dollar.

Par. Before we talk any further about the price, it is necessary that we examine the gentleman according to law, in order to satisfy ourselves of his capability to serve us. Friend, will you be so obliging as to inform us where you received your education, and what your pretensions are, with respect to your profession?

Schoolm. Law, Sir! I never went to college in my life.

Par. I did not ask you whether you had been to college or not. We wish to know what education you have had; and whether your abilities are such, as that you can do yourself honor in taking the charge of a common English school.

Schoolm. Gentlemen, I will give you a short history of my life. From seven, to fifteen years of age, I went to school perhaps as much as one year. In which time, I went through Dilworth's Spelling-Book, the Psalter, the New-Testament; and could read the newspaper without spelling more than half the words. By this time, feeling a little above the common level, I enlisted a soldier in the army, where I continued six years; and made such proficiency in the military art, that I was frequently talked of for a corporal. I had likewise learn'd to write considerably, and to cypher as fur as Division. The multiplication table I had at my tongue's end, and have not forgot it to this day. At length, receiving a severe flogging for nothing at all, I am not ashamed to own that I deserted, and went into one of the back settlements, and offered myself as a teacher. I was immediately employed in that service; and, though I am obliged to say it myself, I do assure you I soon became very famous. Since that time, which is eleven years, I have followed the business constantly; at least, every winter; for in the summer, it is not customary in the towns in general, to continue a man's school. One thing I would not forget to mention; and that is, I have travelled about the country so much, and been in the army so long (which is allowed to be the best school in the world) that I consider myself as being thoroughly acquainted with mankind. You will not be insensible, gentlemen, of what great importance this last acquisition is, to one who has the care of youth.

3d Com. I admire his conversation. I imagine, by this time, you have cyphered *clear through;* have you not, Sir?

Schoolm. Why, as to that, I have gone so fur that I thought I could *see through.* I can tell how many minutes old my great grandfather was when his first son was born; how many barley corns it would take to measure round the world; and how old the world will be at the end of six thousand years from the creation.

1st Com. It is very strange! You must have studied hard, to learn all these things, and that without a master too.

Schoolm. Indeed I have, Sir; and if I had time, I could tell you things stranger still.

Par. Can you tell in what part of the world you were born; whether in the torrid, frigid, or temperate zone?

Schoolm. I was not born in the *zoon,* Sir, nor in any other of the West-India Islands; but I was born in New-England, in the state of New-Jersey, and Commonwealth of the United States of America.

Par. Do you know how many parts of speech there are in the English language?

Schoolm. How many speeches! Why as many as there are "stars in the sky, leaves on the trees, or sands on the sea shore."

1st Com. Please to let *me* ask him a question, Parson, How many commandments are there?

Schoolm. Ten, Sir; and I knew them all before I went into the army.

2d Com. Can you tell when the moon changes, by the almanac?

Schoolm. No! but I'll warrant you, I could soon tell by cyphering.

3d Com. How many varses are there in the 119th Psalm?

Schoolm. Ah! excuse me there, if you please, Sir; I never meddle with psalmody, or metaphysics.

Par. Will you tell me, my friend, what is the difference between the circumference and the diameter of the globe?

Schoolm. There you are to hard for me again. I never larn'd the rule of circumstance nor geometry. I'll tell you what, gentlemen, I make no pretensions to minister larnin, lawyer larnin, or doctor larnin; but put me upon your clear schoolmaster larnin, and there I am even with you.

1st Com. I am satisfied with the gentleman. He has missed but one question, and that was such a metatisical one, that it would have puzzled a Jesuit himself to have answered it. Gentlemen, shall the master withdraw a few minutes, for our further consultation? [*Exit Master.*

2d Com. I am much pleased with the stranger. He appears to be a man of wonderful parts; and I shall cheerfully agree to employ him.

3d Com. For my part, I don't think we shall find a *cheaper* master; and I move for engaging him at once.

Par. Gentlemen, how long will you be blind to your own interest? I can say with you, that I am perfectly satisfied—that the man is, in his profession, emphatically what he calls himself by name, an *ignoramus;* and totally incapable of instructing our children. You know not who he is, or what he is; whether he be a thief, a liar, or a drunkard. The very terms, on which he offers himself, ought to operate as a sufficient objection against him. I am sensible that my vote will now be of no avail, since you are all agreed. I have been for years striving to procure a man of abilities and morals, suitable for the employment; and such a one I had obtained; but, alas! we were unworthy of him. We aspersed his character; invented a multitude of falsehoods; magnified every trifling error in his conduct; and even converted his virtues into vices. We refused to give him that pecuniary reward which his services demanded; and he knowing his own worth, and our unworthiness, has left us forever.

1st Com. Come, come, Parson, it is easy for salary men to talk of *liberality*, and to vote away money which they never earned; but it won't do. The new master I dare engage, will do as well or better than the old one. Landlord, call him in for his answer.

Par. I protest against your proceedings, and withdraw myself forever from the committee. But I must tell you, your children will reap the bitter consequences of such injudicious measures. It has always been surprising to me, that people in general are more willing to pay their money for any thing else, than for "the one thing needful," that is, for the education of their children. Their tailor must be a workman, their carpenter, a workman, their hairdresser, a workman, their hostler, a workman; but the instructor of their children must——work *cheap!* [*Exit Parson.*

Re-enter School-Master.

1st Com. We have agreed to employ you, Sir; and have only to recommend to you, not to follow the steps of your predecessor. This is an "age of reason"; and we do not imagine our children so stupid, as to need the rod to quicken their ideas, or so vicious, as to require a moral lesson from the ferule. Be gentle and accommodating, and you have nothing to fear.

Land. I'll answer for him. He's as generous and merry a lad as I've had in my house this many a day.

11.2 James Carter Proposes a School to Prepare Teachers in 1824.

It will do but little good for the Legislature of the State to make large appropriations directly for the support of schools, till a judicious expenditure of them can be insured. And in order to this, we must have skillful teachers at hand. It will do but little good to class the children till we have instructors properly prepared to take charge of the classes. It will do absolutely no good to constitute an independent tribunal to decide on the qualifications of teachers, while they have not had the opportunities necessary for coming up to the proper standard. And it will do no good to overlook and report upon their success, when we know beforehand that they have not the means of success. It would be beginning wrong, too, to build houses and to tell your young and inexperienced instructors to teach this or to teach that subject, however desirable a knowledge of such subjects might be, while it is obvious that they cannot know how, properly, to teach any subject. The *science of teaching*—for it must be made a science—is first, in the order of nature, to be inculcated. And it is to this point that the public attention must first be turned, to effect any essential improvement.

And here let me remark upon a distinction in the qualifications of teachers, which has never been practically made; though it seems astonishing that it has so long escaped notice. I allude to the distinction between the possession of knowledge, and the ability to communicate it to other minds. When we are looking for a teacher, we inquire how much he *knows*, not how much he can *communicate;* as if the latter qualification were of no consequence to us. Now it seems to me that parents and children, to say the least, are as much interested in the latter qualification of their instructor as in the former.

Though a teacher cannot communicate more knowledge than he possesses, yet he may possess much, and still be able to impart but little. And the knowledge of Sir Isaac Newton could be of but trifling use to a school, while it was locked up safely in the head of a country schoolmaster. So far as the object of a school or of instruction, therefore, is the acquisition of knowledge, novel as the opinion may seem, it does appear to me that both parents and pupils are even more interested in the part of their teacher's knowledge which they will be likely to get, than in the part which they certainly cannot get.

One great object in the education of teachers which it is so desirable on every account to attain, is to establish an intelligible language of com-

James G. Carter, *Outline of an Institution for the Education of Teachers,* as reprinted in *American Journal of Education,* XVI (1866), pp. 77–79.

munication between the instructor and his pupil, and enable the former to open his head and his heart, and infuse into the other some of the thoughts and feelings which lie hid there. *Instructors and pupils do not understand each other.* They do not speak the same language. They may use the same words; but this can hardly be called the same language, while they attach to them such very different meanings. We must either, by some magic or supernatural power, bring children at once to comprehend all our abstract and difficult terms, or our teachers must unlearn themselves, and come down to the comprehension of children. One of these alternatives is only difficult, while the other is impossible.

The direct, careful preparation of instructors for the profession of teaching, must surmount this difficulty; and I doubt if there be any other way in which it can be surmounted. When instructors understand their profession, that is, in a word, when they understand the philosophy of the infant mind, what powers are earliest developed, and what studies are best adapted to their development, then it will be time to lay out and subdivide their work into an energetic system of public instruction. Till this step toward a reform, which is preliminary in its very nature, be taken, every other measure must be adopted in the dark; and, therefore, be liable to fail utterly of its intended result. Houses, and funds, and books are all, indeed, important; but they are only the means of enabling the minds of the teachers to act upon the minds of the pupils. And they must, inevitably, fail of their happiest effects, till the minds of the teachers have been prepared to act upon those of their pupils to the greatest advantage.

If, then, the first step toward a reform in our system of popular education be the scientific preparation of teachers for the free schools, our next inquiry becomes, How can we soonest and most perfectly achieve an object on every account so desirable? The ready and obvious answer is, establish an institution for the very purpose. To my mind, this seems to be the only measure which will insure to the public the attainment of the object. It will be called a new project. Be it so. The concession does not prove that the project is a bad one, or a visionary, or an impracticable one. Our ancestors ventured to do what the world had never done before, in so perfect a manner, when they established the free schools. Let us also do what they have never so well done yet, and establish an institution for the exclusive purpose of preparing instructors for them. This is only a second part, a development or consummation of the plan of our fathers. They foresaw the effect of universal intelligence upon national virtue and happiness; and they projected the means of securing to themselves and to us universal education. They wisely did a new thing under the sun. It has proved to be a good thing. We now enjoy the results of their labors, and we are sensible of the enjoyment. Their posterity have praised them, loudly praised them, for the wisdom of their efforts. Let us, then, with hints from them, project and accomplish another new thing, and confer as great a blessing on those who may come after us. Let us finish the work of our fathers, in regard to popular education, and give to it its full effect. Let us double, for we easily may, the happy influences of an institution which has already attracted so much notice from every part of our country, and drawn after it so many imitations, and send it, thus improved, down to posterity for their admiration.

If a seminary for the purpose of educating teachers scientifically be essential in order to give the greatest efficacy to our system of popular education, then, in the progress of the discussion, the three following questions arise in the order in which they are stated. By whom should the proposed institution be established? What would be its leading features? And what would be some of the peculiar advantages to the public which would result from it? To answer these several questions at length would require a book; while I have, at present, only leisure to prepare one or two newspaper essays. A few hints, therefore, upon the above three topics are all that I dare profess to give, and more than I fear I can give, either to my own satisfaction or that of those readers who may have become interested in the subject.

The institution, from its peculiar purpose, must necessarily be both literary and scientific in its character. And although, with its design constantly in view, we could not reasonably expect it to add, directly, much to the stock of what is now called literature, or to enlarge much the boundaries of what is now called science, yet, from the very nature of the subject to which it would be devoted, and upon which it would be employed, it must in its progress create a kind of literature of its own, and open a new science somewhat peculiar to itself—the science of the development of the infant mind, and the science of communicating knowledge from one mind to another while in a different stage of maturity. The tendency of the inquiries which must be carried on, and the discoveries which would be constantly made, in a seminary for this new purpose, would be to give efficacy to the pursuits of other literary and scientific institutions. Its influence, therefore, though indirect, would be not the less powerful upon the cause of literature and the sciences generally. These remarks may seem to anticipate another part of my subject; but they are introduced here to show that a seminary for the education of teachers would stand, at least, on as favorable a footing in relation to the public, as other literary and scientific institutions. It seems now to be believed that the Legislature of the State are the rightful proprietors of all public institutions for the diffusion of knowledge. And if they are of any, they certainly ought to be of one for such a purpose. Because there are none in which the public would be more deeply interested. There are none which would tend so much to diffuse knowledge among the whole mass of the people. And this, as has been before remarked, is a solemn duty enjoined upon our government by the constitution under which they are organized, and from which they derive their authority. Besides, it is the first impulse of every government, operating as quickly and steadily as instinct, to provide for its own preservation. And it seems to be conceded on all hands, by the friends as well as the enemies of freedom, that a government like our own can only exist among a people generally enlightened; the only question as to the permanency of free institutions being, whether it be possible to make and to keep the whole population of a nation so well educated as the existence of such institutions supposes and requires.

11.3 David Page, Principal of the State Normal School of Albany, New York, Makes "Some Very Plain Remarks on . . . the Habits of the Teacher."

1. Neatness

This implies cleanliness of the person. If some who assume to teach were not proverbial for their slovenliness, I would not dwell on this point. On this point, however, I must be allowed great plainness of speech, even at the expense of incurring the charge of excessive nicety; for it is by attending to a *few little things* that one becomes a strictly neat person. The morning ablution, then, should never be omitted, and the comb for the hair and brush for the clothes should always be called into requisition before the teacher presents himself to the family, or to his school. Every teacher would very much promote his own health by washing the whole surface of the body every morning in cold water. This is now done by very many of the most enlightened teachers, as well as others. When physiology is better understood, this practice will be far more general. To no class of persons is it more essential than to the teacher; for on account of his confinement, often in an unventilated room, with half a hundred children during the day, very much more is demanded of the exhalents in him than in others. His only safety is in a healthy action of the skin.

The *teeth* should be attended to. A brush and clean water have saved many a set of teeth. It is bad enough to witness the deplorable neglect

David Page, *Theory and Practice of Teaching: Or, the Motives and Methods of Good School-Keeping* (New York: A. S. Barnes Co., 1849), pp. 40–43.

of these important organs so prevalent in the community; but it is extremely mortifying to see a filthy set of teeth in the mouth of the teacher of our youth.   The *nails*, too, I am sorry to say, are often neglected by some of our teachers, till their *ebony tips* are any thing but ornamental. This matter is made worse, when, in the presence of the family or of the school, the penknife is brought into requisition to remove that which should have received attention at the time of washing in the morning. The *teacher* should remember that it is a *vulgar* habit to pare or clean the nails while in the presence of others, and especially during conversation with them.

The teacher should be neat in his *dress*.   I do not urge that his dress should be expensive.   His income ordinarily will not admit of this.   He may wear a very plain dress; nor should it be any way singular in its fashion.   All I ask is, that his clothing should be in good taste, and *always clean*.   A slovenly dress, covered with dust, or spotted with grease, is never so much out of its proper place, as when it clothes the teacher.

While upon this subject I may be indulged in a word or two upon the use of tobacco by the teacher.   It is quite a puzzle to me to tell why any man but a Turk, who may lawfully dream away half his existence over the fumes of this filthy narcotic, should ever use it.   Even if there were nothing wrong in the use of unnatural stimulants themselves, the filthiness of tobacco is enough to condemn it among teachers, especially in the form of chewing.   It is certainly worth while to ask whether there is not some moral delinquency in teaching this practice to the young, while it is admitted, by nearly all who have fallen into the habit, to be an evil, and one from which they would desire to be delivered.   At any rate, I hope the time is coming, when the good taste of teachers, and a regard for personal neatness and the comfort of others, shall present motives sufficiently strong to induce them to break away from a practice at once so unreasonable and so disgusting.

2. Order

In this place I refer to that *system* and regularity so desirable in every teacher.   He should practise it in his room at his boarding-house.   Every thing should have its place.   His books, his clothing, should all be arranged with regard to this principle.   The same habit should go with him to the schoolroom.   His desk there should be a pattern of orderly arrangement.   Practising this himself, he may with propriety insist upon it in his pupils.   It is of great moment to the teacher, that, when he demands order and arrangement among his pupils, they cannot appeal to any breach of it in his own practice.

3. Courtesy

The teacher should ever be courteous, both in his language and in his manners. *Courtesy of language* may imply a freedom from all *coarseness*. There is a kind of communication, used among boatmen and hangers-on at bar-rooms, which should find no place in the teacher's vocabulary. All vulgar jesting, all double-entendres, all low allusions, should be forever excluded from his mouth. And profanity!—can it be necessary that I should speak of this as among the habits of the teacher? Yes, it is even so. Such is the want of moral sense in the community, that men are still employed in some districts, whose ordinary conversation is poisoned with the breath of blasphemy; ay, and even the walls of the schoolroom re-sound to undisguised oaths! I cannot find words to express my astonish-ment at the indifference of parents, or at the recklessness of teachers, wherever I know such cases to exist.

Speaking of the *language* of the teacher, I might urge also that it should be both *pure* and *accurate*. Pure as distinguished from all those cant phrases and provincialisms which amuse the vulgar in certain localities; and accurate as to the terms used to express his meaning. As the *teacher teaches* in this, as in every thing, by example as well as by precept, he should be very careful to acquire an unexceptionable use of our language, and never deviate from it in the hearing of his pupils or elsewhere.

11.4 Cyrus Pierce, Principal of the First Public Normal School, at Lexing-ton, Massachusetts, Describes His Teaching.

You ask for a full account of my manner of instruction in the *art of Teaching*. This it is not easy to give. From what I say, you may get some idea of what I *attempt*, and of the *manner* of it. Two things I have aimed at, especially in this school. 1. To teach *thoroughly* the principles of the several branches studied, so that the pupils may have a *clear* and *full un-derstanding* of them. 2. To teach the pupils, by my own *example*, as well as by *precepts*, the *best way of teaching the same things* effectually to others. I have four different methods of recitation. 1st, by question and answer; 2d, by conversations; 3d, by calling on one, two, three, more or less, to give an analysis of the whole subject contained in the lesson; and 4th, by requiring written analyses, in which the *ideas* of the author are stated in the *language* of the pupil. I do not mean that these are all prac-

Arthur O. Norton, ed., *The First State Normal School in America: The Journals of Cyrus Pierce and Mary Swift* (Cambridge: Harvard University Press, 1926), pp. 1–liii. Reprinted by permission of the Harvard University Press.

tised at the same exercise. The students understand that, at all the recitation, they are at perfect liberty to suggest queries, doubts, opinions. At all the recitations we have more or less of discussion. Much attention is paid to the *manner* in which the pupils *set forth, or state* their positions. I am ever mingling, or attempting to mingle, at these exercises, theory and example; frequently putting the inquiry to them, not only, "How do you understand such and such a statement?" but, "How would you express such and such a sentiment, or explain such a principle, or illustrate such a position to a class, which you may be teaching?" "Let me," I say to them, "hear your statements, or witness your modes of illustrating and explaining." In this connection, I frequently call them to the blackboard for visible representation. They make the attempt; I remark upon their manner of doing it, and endeavor to show them in what respect it may be improved. Sometimes, instead of reciting the lesson directly to me, I ask them to imagine themselves, for the time, acting in the *capacity* of *teachers*, to a class of young pupils, and to adopt a style suitable for such a purpose. At many of our recitations, more than half the time is spent with reference to teaching *"the art of teaching."* Besides delivering to the school a written *Formal Lecture* once a week, in which I speak of the qualifications, motives, and duties of teachers, the discipline, management, and instruction of schools, and the *manner* in which the various branches should be taught, I am every day, in conversations, or a familiar sort of lectures, taking up and discussing more *particularly* and *minutely*, some point or points suggested by the exercises or occurrences, it may be, of the day, relating to the *internal operations* of the schoolroom, or to physical, moral, or intellectual education:—I say much about the views and motives of teachers, and the motives by which they should attempt to stimulate their pupils. And here I would state, that my theory goes to the entire exclusion of the *premium and emulation system*, and of corporal punishment. My confidence in it is sustained and strengthened by a full and fair experiment for more than one year in a public school composed of seventy scholars of both sexes. I am constantly calling-up real or supposed cases, and either asking the pupils what they would do, in such case, or stating to them what I would do myself, or both. As a specimen of such questions, take the following, viz: On going into a school as teacher, what is the first thing you would do? How will you proceed to bring to order, and arrange your school? Will you have many rules, or few? Will you announce beforehand a code of laws, or make special rules as they may be needed? What *motives* do you purpose to appeal to, and what *means* will you adopt to make your pupils interested in their studies? What method will you adopt to teach spelling, reading, arithmetic? What will you do with the perseveringly idle and troublesome? What will you do if your scholars quarrel? lie? swear? What will you do if a scholar tells you he *won't* do as he is directed? If a question in any ordinary lesson, say arithmetic, comes up, which you cannot solve readily, what will be your resort? Should you be chiefly ambitious to teach *much*, or to teach thoroughly? How would you satisfy yourself that your teaching is thorough, effectual? To what branches shall you attach most importance, and why? Will you aim chiefly to exercise the *faculties*, or communicate instruction? Besides these daily discussions or conversations, we have a *regular debate* every Saturday, in which the principles involved in these and similar questions are discussed.

11.5 Sophia Blake, an English Traveler, Describes the Salem Normal School in the 1860's.

The Normal Schools in Massachusetts are four in number, two of them being devoted to the education of female teachers only, and two to that of both sexes. This fact illustrates the preponderance in number of female teachers throughout the States, though it is rare for a woman to be at the head of any of the High or Normal Schools.

Believing it better to master thoroughly the working of one Normal school than to see something of them all, I attended the one at Salem for more than a week continuously, meeting with the most courteous welcome from all the teachers, and seeing more and more to interest me each day, till at length my one regret was that I could not transplant the whole affair bodily to England, that other teachers might share my pleasure in seeing any school so thoroughly well worked as this was by its excellent Head Master and a first-rate staff of most earnest lady teachers, whose actual erudition was almost overwhelming.

Indeed, the amount of sheer learning acquired by really good teachers in America has often surprised me, and it is, as I have before remarked, the more striking when, as is so often the case, it co-exists with a very imperfect knowledge of English.

Each of the teachers at Salem has her own especial class of subjects, and to each is moreover assigned more or less charge of some one of the classes.

The number of pupils at Salem is about 120, and of teachers (besides the Head Master) 8. The pupils are divided into four classes, respectively lettered A, B, C, D, of which "A" is the most advanced, and "D" the least so. At the completion of the two years of study represented by these classes, such students as desire still further instruction may enter an "Ad-

Sophia Jex Blake, *A Visit to Some American Schools and Colleges* (London: Macmillan and Co., 1867), pp. 201–208, 211–212.

vanced Class," which, generally speaking, receives only the *crême de la crême*.

Students are not admitted to the Normal School under the age of sixteen, and spend their first term in Class D.

The studies of this class comprise grammar, including analysis and syntax, the geography of the Western Continent, history of the United States, arithmetic and algebra, with some study of chemistry and physiology. In grammar and analysis the teaching is chiefly on a system devised by a late head-master, not altogether unlike that of Morell, but not, I think, equal to his. In geography and physiology a plan is pursued which I understand to be borrowed from the Westfield Normal School. While any state or country, or any portion of the structure of the body, is described by one pupil, the whole class draws the same with chalk on black boards which surround the room. This system was entirely new to me, and seemed very efficacious in securing thorough understanding of the subject by all. Its adoption at Salem was an instance of wise and liberal variation from old custom, the teacher whose duty it was to teach the subjects above-named being a graduate of Westfield, and being allowed to teach according to her own idea.

Arithmetic and algebra are very thoroughly taught at Salem; in the several classes almost daily, and also in general *vivâ voce* examinations of the whole school, which latter take place very frequently for a few minutes at a time.

In these examinations the teacher, or sometimes a senior pupil of the advanced class, will rapidly enunciate such a question as the following, and as her voice ceases some pupil will generally be ready with the answer:— "Take two; add one; cube; take away two; square; take away one; divide by two; subtract twelve; divide by fifteen; divide by ten; square; square; square.—Miss Smith?" "Two hundred and fifty-six." "Right." And so on, just as quickly as voice can speak. Of course, splendid rapidity of calculation will follow such training, unless with a few unfortunates who may get hopelessly confused.

Class C studies arithmetic, algebra, geometry, the "geography of the Eastern Continent" (not, we will hope, excluding England), grammatical analysis, parsing, and history.

One of the plans by which history is taught struck me as curious. One pupil has specially to get up a given subject or era, and then by memory to teach it to the whole class, and at the next lesson to examine them in it, the teacher in charge listening meanwhile to correct errors on either side. Such devices certainly break the monotony of study, and help to give life and spirit to the pupils. Each history class will generally include one such examination and one such lesson.

In geometry, also, there is a plan of mutual instruction. On one occasion I saw the whole of Class C divided into pairs round the great hall, which is surrounded with black boards, and then one of each pair would from memory repeat the problem in question, while the other from memory corrected errors, the figure being drawn by the scholar *pro tem.* who, having finished her recitation, forthwith became teacher in turn; and so on till the problems are all recited, the teacher in charge moving round from one to the other, criticising or approving each. Of course, such a plan would not answer with any class of students less earnest, thorough, and conscientious than the Salem girls, but with them it seemed excellent.

Class B continue the study of arithmetic and algebra, and enter on that of natural and mental philosophy, as well as of English language and literature. The lessons in both natural and mental philosophy seemed calculated to develop much thought. I noticed here, as well as elsewhere throughout the school, that when a pupil made an error, or was in doubt as to a fact, the teacher rarely, if ever, gave her the required information, but simply noted the fact of its being wanted, and passed on to other subjects for that lesson; but on the next meeting of the class made it a point to ask the said girl a question directly bearing on the subject, thus ensuring that what was not known should be *searched out*. This plan, and the success it met with, seemed to me almost the perfection of teaching, and brought into strong light the earnest and ready co-operation between teachers and scholars,—both eager to ensure the acquisition of knowledge.

Class A take some lessons in book-keeping and in perspective drawing, and devote much of their time to the study of the theory and practice of teaching and school government. They are also required to make themselves acquainted with the school laws of Massachusetts, and the constitution of the United States. Mental philosophy is further pursued into the region of logic, and also with relation to questions of the will; and physical geography, astronomy, and geology, each have some share of attention.

Those pupils who have passed successfully through these four classes, and also through written examinations, are given diplomas of proficiency, and said to be graduates of the school.

A small number of pupils remain after completing their studies in Class A, and form the Advanced Class. The subjects pursued in this division are geometry, algebra, plane and spherical trigonometry, the Latin and French languages, natural philosophy, chemistry, botany, and general history.

That Latin and French should be postponed for study in the Advanced Class seems a little curious, as both languages are usually taught at the High Schools, the standard of which should hardly be supposed to be equal to that of Normal Schools. It is, however, probable that the resolution to aim at thoroughness before all things is the true explanation of deferring these studies, as parts, at least, of the regular course.

I think, however, that the weak point in the American Normal School system is, that these schools are neither made to run parallel with the High Schools, nor to form a sequence to them; but I have heard this explained to be the consequence of the demand for "common school" (*i.e.* primary and grammar) teachers, who are not required to know all the subjects taught in the High Schools.

The Normal School certificate given at "graduation" only guarantees fitness for teaching in these lower schools. Practically, many of the pupils do enter *after* going through the High Schools, and they, of course, are able to take a much better position. The Normal School itself professes less to give instruction in *what* is to be taught, than to teach (after the knowledge has been acquired) *how* it should be imparted. . . .

I heard some spirited compositions read at Salem, and the plan on which the subjects were given was novel to me, and I think excellent, at least for occasional use. The teachers took a number of small papers or cards, and, dividing them in pairs, wrote on each pair the "attack" and "defence" of some subject. For instance: on one card would be inscribed (as was, I remember, the case on one occasion), "Attack the conduct of England during the late war"; and on the other, "Defend the conduct of England," &c. Or, again, "Attack the character of Queen Elizabeth;" "Defend the character," &c. These cards were then mixed together, and assigned by chance to the pupils, who were, however, allowed to exchange by mutual consent. Sometimes the attack and defence were written independently of each other; sometimes the two writers would combine their essays in the form of a dialogue, and argue out the question fiercely enough, with more or less competent special pleading.

Sometimes abstract subjects would be treated in the same manner; as, for instance, "attack" and "defence" of the "Normal School System" furnished a pair of very amusing essays.

11.6   B. A. Hinsdale, an Education Professor at the University of Michigan, Justifies "Pedagogical Chairs in Colleges and Universities."

By common consent the university has two great functions. One of these is research, the discovery of truth; the other is instruction, the practice of the art of teaching—that is, the university first finds out truth, and then

B. A. Hinsdale, "Pedagogical Chairs in Colleges and Universities," National Education Association, *Journal of Addresses and Proceedings* (Topeka, Kansas: Kansas Publishing House, 1889), pp. 560–564.

gives it forth. The two interact. Furthermore, the university not only practices research, but it makes research itself the object of study and investigation. Science becomes reflective, and lays bare all her processes and methods. Why, then, should it not investigate and teach its other function, viz., that of teaching? Why should an institution that exists for the sake of investigating the arts and sciences, leave its own peculiar art neglected and despised?

But education is much more than a great and difficult art: it is a noble science. Back of its methods, processes, and systems, are facts, ideas, principles, and theories—in fact, whole systems of philosophy. As Rosenkranz remarks, pedagogy cannot be deduced from a single principle with such strictness as logic and ethics, but is a mixed science, like medicine, deriving its presuppositions from other sciences, as physiology, psychology, logic, æsthetics, ethics, and sociology. It is therefore conditioned upon some of the noblest of the sciences, especially those of the moral group. The very fact that it is a mixed science adds to its difficulty, and emphasizes the demand for its cultivation. It is hard to see how the university, whose admitted function is education, can pass by the science of education without discrediting its own work and virtually denying its own name. To practice the art and refuse to cultivate or teach the science of teaching, is little better than rank empiricism.

The last argument derives additional strength from the peculiar stage of education upon which the foremost nations and countries have now entered. Education has at last reached the reflective or scientific stage. Throwing off the clutch of the empiricist, she has ascended to her long-vacant seat in the family of sciences. Evidences of this are the increased attention paid to education by text-writers on psychology and ethics, the later pedagogical literature, and the more systematic and rational methods of instruction in schools, and the rapidly-increasing facilities for teaching educational science. Thus the very existence of the chair is a proof of its usefulness and its necessity. On this ground alone—indeed, on the narrower ground of endowing research alone—the chair can be fully vindicated.

Again, education has a history. In the very broadest sense, the field of educational history is the field of human culture; and even when limited, as before, to the conscious work of teachers in schools, it still presents whole series of facts, problems and lessons of the greatest interest and importance. Before the pedagogist lies the whole field of school-life, from the simple prophets' and priests' schools of early times to the highly-developed schools and school systems of Europe and America. While education belongs to general history, the study of which is pursued for its culture value, it has been almost wholly neglected. The writer and lecturer on general history do indeed touch the education of the ancients, and make mention of the mediæval universities; they pay some small attention to the marvelous educational developments of modern times; but they lay much more emphasis on subjects of far inferior interest. But education should be made the subject of special historical study as much as religion, art, or politics. Were it as thoroughly investigated as the Polytechnic School of Münich investigates engineering (maintaining forty-five distinct courses of lectures in that science), the history of education alone would tax the resources of the most learned and laborious professor. It is not contended that the chair of pedagogy can at present cultivate this field as carefully as this allusion may imply; but certainly here are topics of the greatest interest and importance, that demand admission to the university list on an equal footing with other subjects of historical investigation. So long as the history of education is a means of education, so long will it continue a proper university study.

Thus far the argument has been theoretical, resting on the need of investigating the science, art and history of teaching, and on their educational value. But the practical phases of the subject must also be presented.

1. Even if the work done by the pedagogical chair should pay no immediate attention to the preparation of teachers, it could not fail to be of much practical value. The scientific study and teaching of a science and an art in their purely theoretical aspects always promote the practice of the art; and the presence in every university in the land of a pedagogical professor, thoroughly devoted to his chair, could not fail to quicken interest in the subject, and to promote the teaching art.

2. While it is a serious error to hold the university merely as a place of instruction and to overlook research—an error that is only too common in the United States—instruction is still one of its grand functions. It is engaged in teaching the highest branches of knowledge. Its professors hold their chairs by reason of their professional ability, as well as by reason of their learning. Where, then, may the science, the history, and the art of teaching be so properly taught as where the art flourishes in its highest forms?

3. The conditions of pedagogical study existing in the university are the best that can be imagined. First, the university offers the student a varied curriculum from which to choose collateral studies. Secondly, it illustrates teaching in all the branches of liberal, and in many branches of technical study. Thirdly, the library, which furnishes an extensive apparatus for general as well as special study, is an invaluable facility. Fourthly, the university is the home of liberal studies; its traditions and associations are conducive to cultivation,

and the student in residence finds himself in the midst of a learned and cultivated society.

The last of these points is deserving of a more elaborate statement. It is well known that special schools tend at once to depth and narrowness: intension is secured at the expense of extension. This is necessary to a degree; but if the process is carried too far, mischievous results follow. Hence the advantage of uniting the professional school with the school of liberal studies; an advantage greater now than ever before, because scholars, men of science and teachers are pushing specialization to its extreme limits. We should not be surprised, therefore, to find all the writers who have touched the topic laying much stress on the advantage to the student of receiving his pedagogical instruction in unacademical institutions. Professor Laurie insists that the teachers of the secondary schools of Scotland need professional preparation as well as university training. "Where shall they get this?" he asks. "They might be required to combine attendance at a training college with attendance at the university for a degree; but this, though it might serve as a provisional arrangement, would not secure the end we seek. And why should not this arrangement secure the end we seek? For this reason, and for no other, that a specialist training college does not answer the same purpose as a university. The broader culture, the purer air, the higher aims of the latter give to it an educational influence which specialist colleges can never exercise."

Whether academical teaching should be furnished in a normal school, is a question often discussed. That question does not come within the range of this paper; but the observation may be made that such instruction must be defended theoretically, if at all, on the ground of its liberalizing and strengthening tendencies.

4. It is a function of the university to furnish society with teachers. Research, teaching, and the preparation of teachers, are the three great duties that it owes society. The preparation of teachers for primary and grammar schools, and possibly for the lower classes of high schools, may be left to normal and training schools. But high schools and other secondary schools must receive their character from teachers of a higher grade of scholarship. It is the favorite conceit of some public-school men that the public schools are fully adequate to create their own teachers, unless it be in some of the more special lines of high-school study and instruction; even the superintendents, they hold, should "come up from the ranks"; but no man who understands the tendencies and effects of specialization, particularly the results of breeding in-and-in, will for a moment favor such

a narrow policy. The public schools have done an invaluable work in furnishing teachers to society; but it is a weighty fact that no schools more need to be kept in vital relation with the schools of higher instruction.

5. The chair of pedagogy and the teaching profession need the strength and dignity that university recognition will give them. Such recognition will be the strongest testimony that the university can bear to the public of the estimate in which it holds the art that it exists to practice. In that way, too, it will most strongly impress its students with the estimate in which it holds the teacher's calling. When our aspiring young men and women see accomplished professors of the science, history and art of teaching in the colleges and universities of the land, vying with the professors of philosophy, ethics, jurisprudence, political economy, and history, in the exposition of their favorite subjects, they will form a higher conception of the teacher's work. This argument also has been urged with much force by writers on education. Professor Laurie, for example, says that the teaching profession of Scotland, almost with one voice, hailed the action of the trustees of the Bell fund, who established the Bell chairs at St. Andrews and Edinburgh. The feeling was, they "have conferred honor on a department of work that Dr. Bell delighted to honor. They have unquestionably done very much to promote education in Scotland, not only by raising the work of the school-master in public estimation, but also by attracting public attention to education as being not merely a question of machinery for the institution of schools (essential though this undoubtedly is), but a question of principles and methods—in brief, of philosophy." He says, further, that the institution of the Edinburgh chair increased the importance of the teaching body, gave it academical standing, and made it possible for the first time to institute in the universities a faculty of education, like the faculties of law, medicine, and theology.

11.7 A School Superintendent Discloses Favoritism in the Appointment of Teachers.

So far as the appointment and retention of teachers are concerned, the whole foundation of evil is broadly covered by this unblushing declaration of a San Francisco school director:

Anonymous, "Confessions of Three School Superintendents," *Atlantic Monthly*, LXXXII (November 1898), pp. 645–646.

I was brought up in this town, and of course have a certain number of friends who want and expect positions. Each director appoints his own friends and relatives, and their names are never questioned by the elementary committee, nor by the full board when it meets to elect candidates. That is a courtesy which is extended by every director to each of his fellow directors,—the minority, of course, excepted.

My own experience is that school committee men act upon the same principle in New England as in California, though they are less outspoken about it.

The appointment of teachers is as well managed as are other city appointments. The poor get relief, the streets are laid out, the police are selected, not on the sole basis of the best service to the public, but, in many cases, on the plan of every man getting as much for his neighborhood or his friends as possible. An alderman who cannot get work on the streets or in the parks for his constituents, who has small influence in securing places on the police force or in the fire department, will have small chance of reëlection, in many wards.

A remedy for the evils connected with appointments must be found in a change of public sentiment. "Public office is a public trust," and not a "private snap." A generation of schoolchildren must be trained to right views on such questions. The schools must share in the general moral uplift; yea, more, they must stand apart from ordinary municipal departments as something to be managed on a higher moral plane.

The evil influence of the appointment of teachers by means of "pulls" does not appear so much in the character of the persons appointed as it does in the demoralization of the body of teachers. It removes a strong incentive to personal improvement. If appointments depend on "pulls," so may promotions and transfers. Each teacher feels secure in her position as long as she has a friend who has influence, or who is on friendly terms with some one who has it. It has several times happened to me that teachers who have been admonished of some neglect, mistake, or inefficiency have gone to their friends for protection, instead of avoiding danger by trying to do better.

I would not, however, leave the false impression that dealing with teachers who fail in their work and depend upon influence to keep their positions is one of the chief troubles of a superintendent. His greatest difficulty with teachers is with those—and their name is legion—who are conscientious and painstaking, anxious to do well, always doing their best, and yet from lack of vigor and adaptation failing to become efficient. A superintendent, even if he have the heart to dismiss such teachers, will rarely find either his committee or the public supporting his action; for no one but himself realizes how schools suffer from such teachers.

11.8 A Teacher Discusses Hiring, Firing, and Administrators.

During the period of my preliminary service as teacher in the public schools, my name was reported for a permanent place, and was "on the slate" when it left the teachers' committee. My father was at that time a voter with the party in power; but the teacher who was number five on the list had a kinsman on the board, who saw that unless she was appointed during his term she might never be. One of the trustees, therefore, brought in a charge of "cruelty to a boy" against me, and, without an investigation, my name was taken off, and number five was elected. To fail of appointment when it was my right was astonishing; but to have any one believe that I pulled a boy's ears till he could not put his head on a pillow hurt me deeply. I began an investigation on my own account, and I discovered that number five's sister was the guilty teacher. The boy's father appeared before the board and explained. The teacher was not even censured; but I had lost the permanent position.

For a year I went from one school to another, teaching for six weeks in the high school. When not busy in a schoolroom, I was visiting, studying, or reading. I attended the teachers' meetings, and was surprised to find so many who had no opinion to express on important subjects. When the year had passed, I was put on the permanent list. I was assigned to a first-year school of fifty-four scholars. Most of them were beginners, and some "left-overs." I felt ready for my work. But my greatest trial was when Superintendent Goodenough selected my room as his place to doze, or really to sleep, while my little people were doing their work. He was never known to praise a teacher's work while she was in service. The only consolation was that he praised teachers who died, or regretted that it was always the "bright teachers who married." I might never marry, and therefore I could with confidence look forward to his praise only at my funeral.

A change in the political control of the city took place, and the party long in power was defeated. The other party decided to do without a supervisor for a year. Superintendent Goodenough, therefore, was dropped. It was a momentous year. But I had now a chance to throw away the old and to use the new. I made all kinds of word and number games; I bought new readers for my supplementary work; I learned new songs, and I looked up kindergarten games.

The next August the board elected a superintendent, and there was no politics in this election. But there was much anxiety as to what kind of

Anonymous, "Confessions of Public School Teachers," *Atlantic Monthly*, LXXVIII (July 1896), pp. 106–109.

man he would turn out to be. Superintendent Quincy, a live New Englander, came, and he brought a breeze. At first he said little. He asked me what I had read. The next time he brought Mr. Michael Brannigan, chairman of the teachers' committee. He said, "Miss Allison is doing the kind of work I want. Has she your permission to carry it on?" Mr. Michael Brannigan was kind enough to abstain from any action that affected me. Superintendent Quincy rid us of many harmful practices. He held grade meetings; he required the schoolrooms to be empty fifteen minutes after the close of school; and no corporal punishment could be inflicted and not reported.

My scholars liked to come to school, and now they numbered eighty-seven. They sat on the edge of the platform, and even on the floor against the wall. I suggested that some come in the morning, and the others in the afternoon. This was done, and one little girl said, "Miss Allison is the best teacher, for we have to go only a half day, and we learn as much as they learn all day at the other schools." I found the work easier, and just as many were promoted to the next class as before.

This year I obtained my state certificate, and I felt that I could now be called a teacher. But a great misfortune threatened me just as I began to feel secure. My father had left the "party without an issue," and had become a member of the "party with a principle." Election time came, and the "party without an issue" thought that they saw a chance to win. As our district was likely to have a close contest, it was suggested that my father be "whipped into line." The only lash that he could be made to feel, they thought, was a threat to remove me. They sent their candidate for school trustee to our home, and he knocked timidly at the back door and made known his errand. In a very few minutes he walked rapidly away. His party was defeated,—luckily for me, no doubt, for a local politician was asked how a teacher whose work was good could be dismissed without "charges." He replied, "We always have charges when we need them." This is the only time that I ever heard of danger to a teacher in our city because of her father's political faith. The rule has been, once a teacher, always a fixture, even when glaring deficiencies could not be hidden, and complaints were "too numerous to mention."

But Superintendent Quincy was too progressive, and his church was on the wrong street. Perhaps he might have been kept if one of the teachers had not wanted the salary. This teacher always reminded us of the line of a hymn:

I can tarry, I can tarry but a term.

He never sat down; but he stood by the door with his coat and hat in his hands, as if something were urging him on.

About this time there was a vacancy in the grammar school, and the superintendent asked me if I would take the place. I liked my work, and declined the empty honor. It meant longer hours for no greater salary; for we are paid according to length of service, and there is no strife for promotion. Of course principals of the higher schools get more pay, but not principals of buildings, unless there are grammar schools in them.

In the middle of the year the superintendent left to study a profession, and a man who had "taught his way through" one of our best normal schools became his successor. At last this superintendent fell a victim to church influences, and he gave place to a young teacher whose church was right, but whose political party was wrong. "He had no principles to hinder," as one of our legislators said, so he turned his back on the party which claimed his first vote, and the position was his. He was younger than most of the teachers, but see how wise he was! He would come into the classroom and say, "Go to page 73 this month." He delivered extempore speeches at the teachers' meetings, and we wondered what it had all been about. In the three years that he was in service he never listened to one recitation in my room. He generally came to gather statistics or to dole out pages of textbooks. I did what I could to keep pace with the other schools, but I felt that there was nothing done thoroughly. At last came his turn to be decapitated, and his successor, who now holds the office, is the best of the long succession of superintendents. They say that he may not be here next year. It is time for a change.

For two years I have had a real grievance. Miss Wellpaid has a school of the same grade as mine, but mine requires more personal work. Yet Miss Wellpaid receives $260 a year more than I am paid, and my salary is the same as that of her assistants, who have no responsibility. Every one admits the justice of my claim, and the board promises to equalize the salary. Children who, by school district lines, ought to attend Miss Wellpaid's school ask six months ahead if I will save them seats if there be room for outsiders. I will not take one of these pupils, even when they bring a demand from two trustees. Once, however, I was obliged to take two of them. They had an order from the president of the board, and a doctor's certificate which said, "It is bad for the health of these girls to attend Miss Wellpaid's school." I must be a "natural healer" of the woes of school life.

Is there nothing to make up that missing $260? Yes, many things. The ambition of every child in the building is "to go to school to Miss Amelia Allison." Ask a kindergarten child who will be his next teacher, and he will generally say, "Miss Allison." One of the ways of inciting good behavior and perfect lessons is to promise a visit to my school. Then I have once more my little people grown tall, sitting in my classes, glad to anticipate my desires about their work and play. Half of my present school have been in my first-year grades. When they argue that it is not late enough in the week to be Friday, one girl says, "We have only two days in our room, and they are Monday and Friday; nothing between." I have also notes of appreciation from parents, and I think with Whittier:

> And when the world shall link your names
> With gracious lives and manners fine,
> The teacher shall assert her claims,
> And proudly whisper, 'These are mine!'

11.9 A High School Principal Analyzes "The Teacher's Social and Intellectual Position."

A careful examination of the answers to the inquiries sent by The Atlantic Monthly to superintendents and teachers of the public schools has put me in closest touch with my fellow-teachers in every part of the country, and has given me a clear insight into the varied conditions under which they have to work. . . . To point out just what the defects are in the status of the teacher, and what we teachers must do to remedy these defects, is the purpose of what follows.

The comments upon the American public school teacher made by visiting French and German educators have usually been favorable. Notwithstanding these comments, were his case to be tried before a jury of foreign educational experts, on the basis of the evidence furnished by the confessions in the letters we have been examining, he would be found guilty on the three following counts: (1) lack of general culture, (2) lack of scholarship, and (3) lack of professional preparation.

Although morally the status of the teacher is high socially it is found to be lower than the status of the average lawyer, the physician, or the theologian. Teachers do not give proper time and thought to the social side of life. To begin with, they are thought to be like the old-fashioned scholar in matters of personal appearance. Fortunately, there is no special style of dress by which they are known, but there is a carelessness that characterizes the rank and file of them. They do not feel the desirability of meeting people in a social way. The fault, however, is not in the occupation, but in the persons who take it up. Whenever teachers meet other men and women on equal terms, they get all the esteem their character and personality deserve. Undoubtedly, as many complain, they are overworked, and have not strength left for society; often the drudgery

F. W. Atkinson, "The Teacher's Social and Intellectual Position," *Atlantic Monthly,* LXXVII (April 1896), pp. 534–538.

of the school robs them of time for social duties, and tends to quench any social desire. Moreover, many are not paid enough to dress properly. In school we teachers are associated with less mature minds, and it is easy to become self-satisfied. Unless we come in contact with men and women of equal or higher intellectual attainments, we fail to realize our littleness.

The general testimony of the replies is that in the larger villages and smaller cities the social position is higher than in the larger cities and smaller villages. From Maine the statement comes that there has been no advance for the last twenty years in the respect with which the public regards the teacher. Of the older States, Pennsylvania also is represented in an unfavorable light: "A teacher is apparently of little account." "He is regarded as an inferior of humanity." "He has no influence in the community outside of the schoolroom." It is evident that in all parts of the country where the educational sentiment is strong, because of the presence of colleges, normal schools, or large private schools, more consideration is shown to teachers as a class. One man in the West gives his opinion that the teacher is a "great big cipher." One from the South writes: "The teachers are expected to help the church, subscribe to the political fund, take all the papers, be helpers for everybody and everything, and carry the burden of humanity generally, and *never assert their own views*, but patiently serve." From all over the Union comes the testimony from teachers that, if they wish to keep their positions, they must not express their opinions on local and national questions. This subserviency of itself would tend to make the calling an inferior one. A few of the New England States furnish evidence of a respectful recognition of the teacher in society; Georgia, Colorado, Minnesota, and Illinois leave with me the impression that they are the hopeful States. The reports from some of the States, especially from New York, are very conflicting. There is hardly a State from which there is not the opinion expressed that the chief lack among our teachers is "general culture, and the refinement of manner that comes with it."

Intellectually, the teacher, whether in city or in country, has not attained a high status. Overcrowded as the profession is, because it is the best stepping-stone to other callings, the average teacher has not deliberately qualified himself either in scholarship or in professional knowledge. This testimony goes to corroborate the statements on this point made annually by the National Commissioner of Education. As the public school teacher is not scholarly, it follows that his interests are not broad, and that intellectually he is not a power in the community. In the schoolroom itself, it often happens that the teacher has no greater knowledge of his subjects than an acquaintance with the facts required for the recitation. A superintendent in Illinois writes: "The criticism I have to offer upon teachers as a class is their limited literary qualifications. They do not know their subjects sufficiently to make instruction definite and logical." A teacher in a neighboring State notes chiefly the teachers' lack of "an accurate and broad knowledge. Our elementary schools are taught by young persons who are not always graduates of grammar schools, and hardly ever of high schools. Further, our high school faculties are not, as a rule, made up of college graduates."

The standard of professional equipment of the American teacher is, as would be expected, even lower than his social status. Throughout the Union the idea prevails that any one who knows schoolroom subjects can teach, and that any one with sufficient muscle can discipline. The public is satisfied with a low standard of scholarship, and makes little demand for professional skill. Until quite recently the normal schools have furnished what professional preparation there has been. Nothing struck me more forcibly, in studying these opinions, which came straight out of the experience of those who wrote them, than the note of dissatisfaction with the normal schools. Several teachers ask, Why require a normal school training when our normal school graduates are not successful teachers? The majority of the students of the normal schools enter with little more than an elementary education. For this reason the normal schools tend to lose their peculiar function of preparing young men and women to teach the elementary branches. As a superintendent in Illinois well expressed it, "Most of our normal schools try to give an average of academic with an equal amount of professional training, all at once." The result is an apology for both. The normal schools tend also to "deify method, and to lose sight of the supreme importance of the teacher's individuality and personal force." The kindliness of the American heart rather than professional responsibility characterizes those in charge of these schools, and those candidates not fitted by qualities of temper and manner for teaching are not weeded out. One educator from a small State observes, "A teacher is born, not made," and then continues, "We need a few more teachers born."

A person can become a successful member of none of the professions who is not naturally fitted for it. It is not sufficiently understood, however, that a good teacher cannot be made out of a person who lacks all the qualities of a teacher. A second or third rate man cannot begin to do the harm in one of the so-called "learned" professions that he can do in a school where he has the sole charge of forty or fifty boys and girls for five or six hours a day, five days in the week, seven or eight months in the year. The school age is the impressionable age. In the formation of habits, lines of thought, and rules of action, unconsciously the pupils adopt their teachers as models. A South Dakota teacher makes an utterance from that new

State which has a genuine ring in it when he says: "The lack of professional training prevents the teacher from holding that standing in the community which other professionally trained persons have. The low status of the profession has not made the teacher the adviser of the Board of Education and of the parent to the same extent to which the physician and lawyer are advisers in their professions." It is to be acknowledged that the lack of confidence in teachers is well grounded.

If it has been a question in the past whether teaching should be considered a profession, the data hereby furnished leave no further doubt that it is yet a makeshift, a "procession" rather than a profession. Only a very few choose the work deliberately as a permanent vocation because they think it best for them. A few take it up because they cannot get anything else to do, and remain in it for life. Teaching has the reputation of being a "berry-picking roadside, where spare change is to be picked up before jumping into the field and going to work," and of being a "hospital for the blind, the halt, and the lame of every other craft." From a New England State a teacher reports: "Many in the community think teachers must have failed in some other business before being willing to take up teaching." Among the teachers employed in the country schools are many young girls. Often an American girl, after she leaves school, "keeps school" until she has the opportunity to keep house, and this fact alone shows that teaching is not a life-work with the majority who take it up. Men, also, frequently regard teaching as an incident in their career; it is a step to their professions, or else a temporary means of support to the doctor while waiting for patients, to the lawyer while waiting for clients, and to the preacher while waiting for a pulpit. Successful professional men are apt to look upon men who remain in teaching with a sort of compassion. If a teacher's purpose in taking up the calling is of a temporary or trivial kind, it will be to the detriment of the pupils; for the teacher's purpose is reflected in the schoolroom. Instability of the teacher's purpose accounts directly for much of the inefficiency of our schools. If a person is in the work because of a lack of brains or force to succeed in something else, his presence will tend to keep out better persons. Among other reasons, the status of the teacher is low because the ablest men and women are not attracted to it in very great numbers, and because such persons of ability as are drawn into it are not retained; and thus the system tends to the survival of the unfittest.

This instability of purpose leads to a great deal of moving about within the calling. . . .

One weakness of the occupation as compared with the legal and medical professions is that persons outside of the calling determine who shall enter it. As letter after letter shows, school committees do not know how to estimate the qualifications of a teacher. They elect, in many cases, those who will bid the lowest, or else those of a particular religious sect or political party. Further, that there is a lack of stability because of improper outside influences the massing of the testimony by President Hall shows conclusively. That insecurity from this source is harmful in keeping out or removing good teachers, and appointing poor teachers, no one can deny. In some States legislation attempts to reach this evil. Tenure of office is extended to the teacher during good behavior. It results in electing for life teachers who will do better work because of the greater security, but it makes stable also those teachers who, although not decidedly incompetent, are willing to drift along in the old currents.

11.10   The U.S. Office of Education Reports on the Education of Teachers in Service in 1930–1931.

Approximately 1 out of every 20 elementary teachers in the United States in 1930–31 had no schooling beyond the high school. This is the surprising answer to the first of the questions just asked. The rural schools had the largest percentage of their teachers in this group, but on the other hand, the cities, and even the largest cities, had 3 or more percent of their teachers with this inexcusably meager preparation—inexcusable because, even though many of them were older teachers who entered teaching 20 or more years ago when standards were lower, they should not have been permitted to remain in teaching during that time without adding to their educational preparation.

The answer to the second question is equally disquieting. One-fifth of the elementary teachers of the United States who had completed high school reported 1 year or less in college as the highest level of their training. This group and those with 4 years of high school or less make a total of more than a fourth of America's elementary teachers who in 1930–31 had not had the minimum of 2 years of education beyond the completion of a 4-year high-school course. One out of four elementary teachers had less education than is represented by the completion of the junior college which, according to many estimates, represents about the same level of intellectual maturity as the completion of the secondary schools of Europe.

From an inspection of the percentages in table 1 it is clear that most of these undereducated teachers were teaching in the rural schools, the consolidated schools, and the villages—the locations in which the work of teaching is most difficult and where the need for the highest type of teach-

Edward S. Evenden, *National Survey of the Education of Teachers: Summary and Evaluation* (U.S. Office of Education, Bulletin No. 10, Vol. VI; Washington: Government Printing Office, 1933), pp. 37, 39, 42.

ing service is probably greatest. The selection of the most poorly qualified teachers in the rural and small village schools is an unfortunate continuation of one element in the vicious circle of inadequately prepared teachers, poor teaching, ineffective schools, low educational standards, resulting in the selection of inadequately prepared teachers and the beginning of another circle. Thus it continues from school generation to school generation in circles of ever-narrowing educational opportunities.

TABLE 2.

Highest levels of training reported by elementary, junior high school, and senior high school teachers in the United States distributed according to the percent at each level, 1930–31.

Highest levels of training	Elementary teachers	Junior high school teachers	Senior high school teachers
1	2	3	4
Nongraduate of elementary school	0.1—	0.1—	0.1—
Graduate of elementary school only.	.3	.2	.1
1 year of high school	.2	.1	.1
2 years of high school	.5	.2	.1
3 years of high school	.7	.3	.1
4 years of high school	4.0	1.1	.5
6 to 12 weeks of college	3.6	.6	.2
Half year of college	2.4	.4	.2
1 year of college	14.5	3.2	1.1
2 years of college	46.2	17.5	4.4
3 years of college	15.5	16.0	6.1
4 years of college	10.2	43.7	58.1
1 year of graduate work.	1.3	12.1	20.2
2 years of graduate work	.4	3.1	5.9
3 years of graduate work	.1	.8	1.5
More than 3 years of graduate work	.1	.7	1.4
Number of cases involved	248,593	36,186	84,767

11.11   George S. Counts, Professor at Teachers College, Columbia, Calls in 1935 for Reformers to "Break the Teacher Training Lockstep."

From state to state over the entire land the curricula of the public normal schools and teachers colleges are as like as peas in a pod. Only with extreme rarity does a state or city educational administrator display real

George S. Counts, "Break the Teacher Training Lockstep." *The Social Frontier,* I (June 1935), pp. 6–7.

statesmanship by looking the teacher training problem in the face and proposing a program at variance with tradition. So-called reforms there have been; they pass in waves from region to region—patchwork tinkerings with the familiar curricular pattern. The American Association of Teachers Colleges appears to be using its newly attained prestige to put the final stamp of approval upon well-established and vested methods of preparing teachers for the public schools. Various "standardizing" agencies are hard at work ironing out the few remaining sectional variations in policy and technique among professional schools of education.

The most radical thing that has happened in recent years in this field has been the practically universal extension of the training period for elementary school teachers from two years to three or four years beyond the high school. This time extension, which has considerably increased state educational expenditures in a period of economic stress, obviously cannot be depended upon markedly to raise the qualitative level of teaching. It has, however, been hailed by many educators as the final answer to all the criticisms levelled at the inadequacy of the teaching in American public schools. The strenuous agitation to have every public school teacher bear a degree after her name exemplifies a common tendency among educators to prefer appearance to reality. It was easily assumed that the main fault with the traditional teacher training program was its briefness. Thus the cause for the reported poor quality of teaching was shifted from the *nature* of the training which candidates received to the *shortness* of the training period. The remedy which naturally enough suggested itself was more years of the same kind of training. An examination of the recently revised courses of study in the state teachers colleges shows quite clearly that the new ones are mere padded versions of the old.

Rapid advance in the social sciences together with the remarkable changes wrought in the professional education of young men and women for medical, engineering, and law careers renders demonstrably false any belief that the education of teachers now approaches a stage of perfection. Standardization of practice, no matter how worthy in conception, has no place in a field which seems so obviously to have reached only the early stages of experimentation.

What a setting for experimental teacher training programs our state-controlled public school systems provide! State educational leaders with vision should glory in the experimenter's paradise which is theirs. Many different types of state teacher training programs are imaginable. The possibilities for determining the major outlines of a stable American policy in the professional education of teachers are illimitable, if only vision and daring combine to replace outworn practices. Already the private and semi-public universities are experimenting with fresh programs of teacher preparation and the fundamental background for intelligently guided departures from tradition has been explored. Some of the major variables in teacher training are well known. Others will be discovered. But as yet even the willingness to vary factors like selective admissions, the curriculum, and the utilization of master teachers, has been lacking.

Constructive efforts to set up adequate selective machinery for candidates have been instituted in most training centers, public and private. But only the surface of this problem has been scratched. A few of the utterly unlikely candidates are being eliminated. The real need is to construct selective machinery in terms solely of the high cultural quality and professional aptness desired in the young men and women to whom the basic education of American boys and girls is to be entrusted. The present over-supply of so-called trained teachers is a golden opportunity to cut the number of young people entering teacher training institutions to a relatively drastic minimum. Psychological science, personnel service, the experience of other professions upon this problem cry out to be applied.

The familiar curricular pattern of orientation courses, subject matter courses, theory courses, observation courses, and practice-teaching assignments is but a conglomeration of precepts and practices inherited from the more limited environment of a former day. No matter how much science in the way of statistical summaries, surveys by experts, and correlational studies is applied to this type of curriculum, the best result obtainable can be only a minor refinement added to something fundamentally inadequate. It is necessary to get completely outside the present teacher training picture and from a new vantage point to consider modern educational needs and modern teaching opportunities. The buildings and grounds now available can be used as well for new techniques, new purposes, new attitudes, as for old. It is conceivable for instance that if the selection of trainees be properly made, the advanced academic education provided for prospective teachers can consist entirely of cultural material, especially selected and communicated, to promote mellow wisdom, imaginative vision, and a driving educative zeal—qualities sadly lacking in the average school teacher today. It is also possible that the theoretic professional background so necessary in the teaching art may be provided in the highest degree by a carefully planned and extended internship service under master teachers in particular studies or at particular educational levels.

Perhaps the most neglected opportunity in the field today is the universal failure to make use of those teachers now practicing in the public schools who have proved highly capable in stimulating the learning powers of pupils. These artists of the profession exercise almost no influence upon teacher training at present. An appalling waste is involved in thus denying to apprentices constant intimate give and take with masters. It may be said with impunity that until master teachers are placed in a key position in teacher training programs, no real progress in raising qualitative standards in the profession will be recorded.

Those of us who are interested in making the educational profession function adequately in realizing a new American society equal to modern economic and cultural opportunities, must appreciate the necessity for breaking the present lockstep in teacher training. It will be necessary boldly to establish experimental procedures of far-reaching scope in different states as a means to reliable, efficient, and stable programs for attaining broad professional objectives. The stakes are a teaching profession capable of weighting public opinion in the direction of increased reliance upon experimental intelligence.

11.12   Arthur Bestor Attacks "The Interlocking Directorate of Professional Educationists."

The school administrator requires, and has always required, guidance in curriculum-making from those who are in a better position than he to judge of the intellectual skills that are needed by mature men in a complex society and that must therefore be developed in the lower schools. Until forty or fifty years ago that guidance was furnished by the men professionally engaged in the higher branches of science and scholarship. Much of this guidance was taken for granted. School administrators received their training in the recognized academic disciplines and accepted the postulates common to all the learned professions. The aims of education could be considered settled by common consent. Training in the basic intellectual skills and disciplines formed the unquestioned foundation. The arrangement and grading of subjects was more or less fixed by tradition. And at the top the known entrance requirements of the colleges provided a kind of ultimate directive. Under such circumstances the school administrator had clear standards to guide him in exercising his responsibility with respect to the curriculum.

With the rise of the new American university in the last quarter of the nineteenth century, this guidance was placed on a more formal basis. University scholars served on commissions which, in co-operation with educational administrators, labored thoughtfully and effectively to work out, for each school subject, a course of study that would meet the cri-

Arthur Bestor, *Educational Wastelands: The Retreat from Learning in Our Public Schools* (Urbana: University of Illinois Press, 1953), pp. 104–114, 120–121. Reprinted by permission of the University of Illinois Press.

teria both of scholarly soundness and of pedagogical fitness. In 1894 appeared the *Report* of the Committee of Ten on Secondary School Studies, appointed by the National Education Association. Its chairman was President Charles W. Eliot of Harvard, and its membership included five college presidents, one college professor, one high school principal, the heads of two private preparatory schools, and the United States Commissioner of Education. Its recommendations on history, civil government, and political economy were drawn up by a group which comprised six college professors, one college president, two high school principals, and one private school headmaster. The same responsible scholarly participation characterized a long series of subsequent studies in the field, up to and including the report on *The Study of History in Secondary Schools*, published in 1911 by the Committee of Five of the American Historical Association.

This promising form of co-operation petered out in the second decade of the twentieth century. In 1916 appeared a report of the Committee on Social Studies of the Commission on the Reorganization of Secondary Education of the National Education Association. The composition of this committee of twenty-one stood in the sharpest possible contrast with that of the Committee of Ten two decades earlier. Only four university professors were among its members, plus one teacher from Hampton Institute, and there were no representatives of preparatory schools. But there were ten high school teachers and principals, two superintendents of schools, one state high school inspector, two officials from the United States Bureau of Education, and one member of the faculty of a School of Pedagogy. This established a completely new pattern in curriculum making, and a pattern which has persisted. The old pattern of co-operation, indeed, has been emphatically repudiated by most present-day educationists. "Until about 1910," says a recent textbook, with obvious condescension to the backward past, "curriculum-making was largely in the hands of subject-matter specialists who were dominated by a philosophy of formal discipline, the sacredness of subject matter, and a worship of the past and the status quo."

For this rejection of academic co-operation, scholars themselves were partly to blame. Their responsibilities within their own fields—in graduate instruction, in research, and in public service—grew heavier, and the content of each field grew increasingly more complex. University professors tended to turn their backs upon elementary and secondary education. They are reaping today the whirlwind which their indifference helped to sow.

In the long run, however, the negligence of scholars was less significant than another development, which promised to make co-operation even more effective but which actually impeded and destroyed it. This was the rise of pedagogy as an independent subject in the university curriculum, with offerings even on the graduate level. At the outset, this was a promising development. Research in pedagogical methods was to be conducted under university auspices by scientists and scholars educated in the recognized disciplines applicable to the problems involved. Many thoroughly trained psychologists, philosophers, historians, statisticians, linguists, and others accepted the title of professor of education, and shouldered the new responsibilities that went with it. These responsibilities were clear. Professors of education were to be mediators between the more advanced and the more elementary sectors of the educational world. As members of a university community they were supposed to grasp the growing complexity of intellectual life and to see its implications for secondary education. As teachers of teachers they were expected to translate these developments in science and scholarship into the language of the classroom. They were expected to make clear to school administrators the increasingly heavy intellectual requirements of modern life, and thus to encourage the development of public school curricula more thorough and rigorous than those of the slipshod past. The great responsibility of professors of education was to stimulate and encourage rising standards of disciplined intellectual training throughout the school system, using the prestige of their university position to advance the ideals of liberal education to which the university is dedicated.

The men who undertook to deal with pedagogical problems at the university level in the late nineteenth and early twentieth centuries took these responsibilities seriously and acquitted themselves well. They have their true successors at the present day—men bred in the liberal arts, trained at the advanced level in one of the basic disciplines, and imbued with faith in the value of intellectual endeavor. These men I honor, and I am gratified that many of them have written me approving both the positive affirmations and the negative criticisms set forth in preceding chapters of this book. Such men, however, form but a small minority among professors of education at the present day. The pedagogical departments at most universities have developed in quite a different direction during the past half century. The change was the result of certain factors which were neither recognized nor foreseen at the outset.

University and graduate departments of education began as agencies of genuine interdisciplinary investigation and teaching. When, however, they began to recruit their faculties from young men trained by themselves, they gradually lost their original character. Several academic generations have now passed, and the overwhelming majority of present-day professors of education have received virtually all their advanced training in departments of education. Their knowledge of the disciplines that are required to solve pedagogical problems is for the most part elementary and secondhand. And this knowledge is being passed on, increasingly diluted and increasingly out-of-date, to new generations of professional educationists. John Dewey was himself a philosopher, and he brought philosophy to bear upon educational problems. Today, however, the so-called "philosophy of education" offered in most departments of pedagogy has lost touch with living philosophical thought, for it is taught mainly by men trained not in philosophy itself but merely in their predecessors' courses in the philosophy of education. What began as the free and creative speculation of philosophic minds upon educational questions has congealed into educational dogma passed on from generation to generation by men who no longer speculate but merely expound.

This has happened to each of the great disciplines that ought to be contributing to vital educational thinking. Educational psychologists maintain closer connections with the parent discipline than other educationists, perhaps, but the gap is wide and growing wider. The history of education and educational sociology are rarely taught by men trained as historians or sociologists. Professors of educational administration have practically nothing to do with the experts who study and teach public administration in general in departments of political science. Even the courses in the teaching of specific subjects—mathematics, history, English, and the like—are mainly in the hands of educationists, not mathematicians or historians or scholars in the field of English language and literature.

Cross-fertilization, the original purpose of departments of education, has ceased, and we are up against the fact that the products of cross-fertilization—the hybrids—are frequently sterile.

The quality of purpose has declined with the decline in the quality of staff. University and graduate departments of education were founded with the idea of raising school-teaching from a vocation to a profession. This was to be accomplished—it could only be accomplished—by requiring a thorough training in the liberal arts before permitting a student to embark upon specialized training in pedagogy. But the founders of advanced departments of education failed to reckon with the fact that a large number of institutions and instructors had a vested interest in a lower and narrower type of pedagogical training. Normal schools were reluctant to give up what they had been doing. They expanded into colleges, but rarely sloughed off completely their narrow vocational approach to the problem of training teachers. The old-time specialists in normal-school pedagogy were insistent that they be recognized as full-fledged professors of education, and they began to migrate to the new university departments. As a result there occurred a rapid debasement of the original ideal. Instead of a new and genuinely professional approach to education there was a mere upgrading in the numbering of the old courses in pedagogical method. For most students these courses were apt to be piled, layers thick, upon an undergraduate major in pedagogy, not upon a major in one of the liberal arts. In the end, so-called graduate work in education tended to become merely a prolonged and attenuated program of vocational training.

Another unforeseen factor leading to the deterioration of university departments of education was the tremendous influence that came to be exerted upon them by the administrative bureaucracy of the public schools. It was peculiarly necessary for professors of education to maintain their independence from such pressures, since one of their major responsibilities was to examine, criticize, and judge with scholarly impartiality the programs that school administrators were carrying out. Their duty was to transmit to superintendents, principals, and teachers in the field the considered judgment on educational matters of the academic world. Such a pattern, however, never came into being. Instead, public school administrators and university departments of education drew together in a community of interest that was far stronger than any which developed between the department of education and the other faculties of the university. The direct consequence was that professors of education abandoned any pretence of being independent, academic critics of public school development, and became hard-and-fast partners of the administrative bureaucracy in the making of public school policy. Their role thereafter could only be that of apologists, and rather indiscriminate apologists, for every new program introduced into the public schools.

To the scholar from an established discipline, one of the most shocking facts about the field of education is the almost complete absence of rigorous criticism from within. Among scientists and scholars, criticism of one another's findings is regarded as a normal and necessary part of the process of advancing knowledge. But full and frank criticism of new educational proposals rarely comes from other professional educationists. The educational journals are almost devoid of critical reviews, which form an essential part of similar publications in other fields. The paean of praise that greets every novel program, the closing of ranks that occurs whenever a word of criticism is spoken from outside, is a symptom of the fact that independence of thought has ceased to be a virtue among professional educationists. This monolithic resistance to criticism reveals the existence and influence of what can only be described as an educational party-line—a party-line that protects the vested interests of both school administrators and professors of education. Even in Parent-Teacher Associations—admirable bodies in many respects—free discussion of the basic educational philosophy of the public schools is tightly controlled through frequent invocation and strict interpretation of a national by-law which provides that the organization "shall not seek to direct the administrative activities of the schools or to control their policies." Communication thus becomes a one-way affair. The theories of professional educationists may be freely expounded in P.T.A. meetings. But program committees are often given to understand that they may not schedule speakers of opposite views, for this would constitute an attempt to interfere with the policies of the schools.

The extreme unwillingness of professional educationists to submit their proposals to free public discussion and honest criticism frequently assumes the even uglier form of showering critics, no matter how upright and well-informed, with vituperation and personal abuse. A scientist or scholar who publishes a criticism of educational trends, even in a scientific journal, is liable to be denounced by professional educationists in responsible positions who do not think it beneath their dignity to hurl at him such epithets as these: "a peripatetic hatchet man," "a demagogue rather than a scholar," and "a master of the pointed phrase rather than the finished thought." Other educationists shamelessly employ the doctrine of "guilt by association" and try to show that because certain criticisms made by responsible scholars have been utilized in the propaganda of reactionary opponents of public education, all alike are to be regarded as "enemies" of the public schools.

Implicit in this kind of statement is the idea that no person can have an informed opinion on school matters save one who has been trained in pedagogy. A lifetime of teaching apparently cannot make a scholar or scientist anything but a meddlesome amateur when public educational policy is up for discussion. Such notions tend to inspire among the lesser lights of the educationist world an arrogance such as one meets in no other profession and which occasionally erupts in an attempt even to suppress freedom of discussion on public educational questions.

This hushing up of criticism is an attitude that belongs, not to a company of independent scholars, but to a bureaucracy, a party, a body united in defense of a vested interest. Professors of education are too deeply involved in the current public school situation to be reliable and fearless critics of it. They have aided the educational administrators in freeing the schools from their rightful responsibility to science and scholarship. In return, the educational bureaucracy has aided the professors of education in gaining within the universities a position of power which has enabled them to defy the academic standards of other departments of the institution. The structure of power within the educationist profession has much more to do with the present state of the public schools and the teaching profession in America than citizens are apt to realize.

The existence of what amounts to an interlocking directorate involving professors of education and school administrators is most clearly revealed in the policies governing the training of teachers. State educational officials exert control over such programs by the requirements they lay down for the certification of teachers, and these universally include substantial course work in pedagogy. Public school superintendents and principals reinforce this emphasis by the criteria they use in employing and promoting teachers. The beneficiaries are the professors of education, who are thus assured of a steady flow of students through their courses. This elaborate and rigorous prescription of pedagogical courses is rather curiously at variance with the principles which educationists profess in other matters. They wish as little as possible of the secondary school curriculum to be prescribed by outside authorities, and they vehemently assert that the colleges need not and should not insist upon any particular set of courses as a prerequisite for admission. But educationists are quite ready to invoke the coercive power of the state to compel every prospective teacher to take a specified number of courses in pedagogy.

Another inconsistency is involved. If an historian asserts that a knowledge of history can contribute to intelligent citizenship, the educationist is apt to condemn him for believing in "transfer of training" and to insist that history must prove its right to a place in the curriculum by incontrovertible experimental evidence that its study does produce better citizens. But the educationist demands a state-imposed requirement in pedagogy without presenting any experimental evidence whatsoever that such course work produces better teachers. A professor of education informs me that nowhere in the literature of the "science" of education "can be found a single study, or controlled experiment, that establishes that a person is any better teacher by virtue of professional courses in Education. Surely this is a primary question into which their research organizations ought to inquire, and the worth of courses in Education could be established easily by the use of control and experimental groups equated as to initial ability, if there is any worth there. Is it not a little curious that such elemental research has been avoided by them?" I have called the statement to the attention of a number of educationists, and none has been able to point out to me a single study that would invalidate the generalization.

Justifiable or not, the state-enforced requirement in pedagogy is the taproot of the great educationist upas tree. The one inescapable prerequisite to a career in public school teaching and administration is course work in a department of education. Consequently this is the one department in which every student must enroll who wishes to teach or to be eligible to teach. The typical department of education knows very well how to extort every possible advantage from this strategic position. In most institutions it has managed to seize effective control over the placement of teachers. It frequently undertakes to plan all teachers' programs for them, regardless of their academic interests. It institutes programs of its own leading to a major or even a separate degree in education. It encourages its students to pile up course work in pedagogy far beyond the legal minimum. It frequently creates among its students the impression that they will be suitably rewarded for strict adherence in class to the educationist party line, and that too-vocal dissent will hurt their chances of future employment.

Protected behind state requirements which no department but itself can satisfy, the department is able to defy, or even to wage aggressive warfare against, the academic standards of the university. It exerts almost continuous pressure to break down admissions requirements, particularly those that might affect the work of the high schools. It frequently works to eliminate general graduation requirements that specify work in foreign languages and mathematics. The department of education typically refuses to look upon the university as a community of scholars working to a common end, and attempts to arrogate to itself control over all course offerings relating to educational problems. It sets up courses of its own in the teaching of the various school subjects, and gradually withdraws all future teachers from courses of this kind offered by the subject-matter departments. It generally refuses to entrust the teaching of educational psychology to independent departments of psychology, or the philosophy of education to departments of philosophy. In its relationship with the university of which it is a part, the typical department of education shows no real interest in interdisciplinary co-operation and no sense of academic partnership. Instead its faculty manifest a desire to insulate the schools and their teachers from every possible contact with recognized academic disciplines.

The abuse is even more appalling at the graduate level. The argument that pedagogical courses are necessary to prepare a novice for an unfamiliar vocation no longer has the slightest relevance, for graduate students in education are, as a rule, teachers with considerable experience. But administrators and teachers have been so thoroughly indoctrinated with the view that course work in pedagogy is the one thing of supreme importance, that experienced teachers return year after year, or summer session after summer session, to thresh old straw in departments of education, completely overlooking the glaring inadequacies of their training in the disciplines they profess to teach. Such inadequacies are unavoidable in a beginning teacher, for he cannot well know in advance what courses he may be assigned to handle outside the field of his major interest. If teacher certification requirements were designed for the benefit of the schools, however, instead of the benefit of professors of education, they would be phrased in such a way as to compel a teacher to bring his training in every subject he teaches up to a respectable minimum before embarking on additional courses in mere pedagogy.

On every hand there is evidence of the debasement which the teaching profession is undergoing at the hands of the interlocking directorate of professional educationists. Forced to undergo the humiliation of piling up credits in sterile courses in pedagogy, virtually forbidden to align himself with scholars and scientists in his chosen field, ceaselessly indoctrinated in an "official" educational philosophy, subjected to minute control and supervision by a professional educational hierarchy, the public school teacher cannot hope to resist administrative dictation or to secure a real voice in the formulation of educational policy. Though large numbers of able teachers oppose the anti-intellectual trend in education that is so obvious today, they are powerless to do anything about it. The educational directorate has seen to that. It does the hiring and firing, and it knows how to check thereby the expression of critical opinions. The organs by which teachers might bring their views to public attention—the educational associations and the journals—are under the throttling control of the directorate. The public has been led to believe that the educational philosophy now guiding the public schools is a philosophy to which the teachers and the scholars of the nation willingly subscribe. Actually, however, the voice which the citizen hears in favor of programs like "life-adjustment" education is the voice neither of the classroom teacher nor of the scholar. It is the voice of the professor of education or one of his allies in the public school directorate.

Across the educational world today stretches an iron curtain which the professional educationists are busily fashioning. Behind it, in slave-labor camps, are the classroom teachers, whose only hope of rescue is from without. On the hither side lies the free world of science and learning, menaced but not yet conquered. A division into two educational worlds is the great danger that faces us today. American intellectual life is threatened because the first twelve years of formal schooling in the United States are falling more and more completely under the policy-making control of a new breed of educator who has no real place in—who does not respect and who is not respected by—the world of scientists, scholars, and professional men.

11.13   An Educationist Replies to Bestor.

The first flaw in Mr. Bestor's analysis seems to me to be the narrowness of his idea as to what the task of the school and the teacher should be in our country today. For him that task is intellectual training alone. He is aware, of course, that children have other than intellectual interests, needs, and problems; but when he does not consider these trivial—a word frequent in his writings—he insists that they are none of the teacher's business. He knows, too, that young people differ in their ability to handle ideas; but he is convinced that developing that ability as far as possible is the only legitimate task of the schools.

Now I do not think I underestimate the value of the intellect. Man's mind is his glory, and his intellectual powers distinguish him from the rest of creation. But he is not only mind. He has a body; he has emotions; he has social relations. Education dare not ignore his growth in these respects. This is all the more true since his capacity to grow intellectually depends in part on factors of bodily, emotional, and social development. When Henry Murray and his associates in the Harvard Psychological Clinic made their intensive psychological studies of Harvard graduate students a few years ago they found not a single one whose intellectual progress was not being hampered by emotional problems. . . .

This brings me to my second fundamental criticism of Mr. Bestor's position. He grossly underestimates the quantity and quality of special knowledge and skill that good teaching requires. A teacher as such must have a clear idea of educational purpose, a considerable understanding of children, a grasp of social realities and their implications for the schools, resources of scholarship, and ability to use those resources to facilitate the growth of children according to guiding purpose.

It will not do for Professor Bestor to lump all of these requisites except scholarship under the heading "know-how" and then dispose of them by references to bedside manner, sharpness in the courtroom, and their easiness compared to the skills essential in many crafts. The ends of education have been the subject of argument for centuries and the prospective teacher ought to think his way through to a position on these matters. He cannot read and digest the views of Aristotle, Comenius, Rousseau, Dewey, Whitehead—and Bestor—on some odd afternoon!

Nor can it be allowed that the nature and potentialities of a child can be plumbed in short order. Nor that skill in establishing contact with a child—in inspiring, stimulating, encouraging, and relieving—is a small mat-

Karl Bigelow, "How Should America's Teachers Be Educated?" *Teachers College Record*, LVI (October 1954), pp. 20–24.

ter. A. N. Whitehead—a mathematician and philosopher of the first rank, a master of the fundamental disciplines—knew better when he wrote forty years ago: "We are only just realizing that the art and science of education require a genius and a study of their own; and that this genius and this study are more than a bare knowledge of some branch of science or of literature. . . . When you analyse in the light of experience the central task of education," he continued, "you find that its successful accomplishment depends on a delicate adjustment of many variable factors. The reason is that we are dealing with human minds, and not with dead matter. The evocation of curiosity, of judgment, of the power of mastering a complicated tangle of circumstances, the use of theory in giving foresight in special cases—all these powers are not to be imparted by a set rule embodied in one schedule of examination subjects. . . ."

What, then, should the education of America's teachers be like? It should include a general education that relates the findings and the tools of scholarship to the insistent present. Professor Bestor believes this can only be done by teaching the liberal disciplines separately and systematically. But this is by no means evident. He himself would agree that this time-hallowed procedure has fallen far short of having the educational consequences that he desires: the development of disciplined minds that deal easily and skilfully with the problems of human existence. Many who are experimenting with newer methods of general education are not at all anti-intellectuals: they are rather seeking more effective ways of developing intellectual powers.

Nor are these persons always educationists—if I may use what Professor Bestor evidently considers a dirty word! Let me cite another historian, James Harvey Robinson. Over thirty years ago this eminent scholar, prolific textbook writer, and great teacher had this to say: "Teaching," he wrote, "aims to be logical; learning is strangely illogical, or rather, has its own logic and its own effective methods which have hitherto been almost completely disregarded. The 'principles' or 'elements' of a branch of science are really the ultimate outcome of a knowledge of it, not the thin edge of the wedge which insinuates it into our minds . . . Personally," he added, "I have reached the conclusion, after many years of teaching, that one should choose for instruction, whether one be dealing with young or old, some phase of human interest rather than some field of scientific investigation."

Robinson's conclusion is only one of many findings that justify us in encouraging experimentation in programs of education. Let us insist on careful evaluation of the consequences of these experiments—as we should of older procedures—not damn them in advance on highly theoretical grounds. Let us do the same with the second essential element in the education of a teacher—a deeper study of those scholarly resources required by a given teaching specialty. (Incidentally, I should like to say that I find considerable merit in one of Professor Bestor's ideas regarding this matter. I should like to see teachers permitted to broaden their depth of knowledge in graduate school, not forced into greater narrowness. I do not, however, accept his recommendation that five undergraduate majors should serve as the basis for the award of a Doctor's degree.

So much for general education and a deeper study of certain subjects. But the preparatory program must also take education, and children, and teaching, and learning seriously. It must concern itself with emotion as well as science, with flesh and blood as well as theoretical constructs. These are matters that involve knowledge and thought and discipline, too. There is more than "know-how" here.

Now how should these elements be proportioned, combined, and ordered? This is an issue of practical judgment, complicated by the fact that there is not time enough in four or five years, and would not be in six or seven, to accomplish everything that could be desired. After long study the Commission on Teacher Education recommended that "the primary objectives of at least three-eighths of the undergraduate work of prospective teachers should be those properly ascribable to general education," that "strictly professional elements should be allocated from one-eighth to one-sixth of the time available in a four- or five-year program," leaving one-half—or perhaps a little less—for advanced instruction in the nonprofessional subjects. This seems to me a modest proposal, scarcely indicative of that megalomaniac imperialism that Professor Bestor declares in his writings to be the educationists' chronic characteristic.

All these elements in a program of teacher education should, I believe, be related as vitally as possible to one another—as well as to Whitehead's "insistent present." This requires concern by all the members of the faculty with all the purposes—including the purpose of teaching—that animate their students. Hence I am profoundly sympathetic with Mr. Bestor's campaign to get professors of arts and sciences more concerned with the schools and with the problems of teacher education—although I hope they will enter into converse with the educationists about these matters in a somewhat less intransigent mood than he seems to recommend. . . .

Let me now sum up the views I have been expressing. Teachers for today should be educated to work in today's schools—and to be able to contribute to their improvement tomorrow. They must become sensitive to the insistent demands of today's complex society and to the nature and needs of today's children. They must have learning and the ability to think. They must be habituated to the use of thought in the guidance of behavior and to the correction of thought in the light of experience.

This requires a vital general education for teachers. It calls for advanced study in their teaching fields that inspires enthusiasm, ensures mastery, and reveals significances for children and the social order. And it demands as well professional studies that clarify purpose, create an understanding of children, and equip the teacher with basic methodological skills. These elements are all essential.

Let them be well and organically combined through the cooperative labors of all of us who share in the privilege of educating America's teachers today.

APPENDIX

Statistics on American Education

Elementary and Secondary Schools, Enrollment and Attendance, and High School Graduates: 1870 to 1956 *

School year ending—	Total [1]	School enrollment				Public school attendance			High school graduates [3]	
		Public day schools			Nonpublic schools [2]	Average daily attendance (all grades)	Average length of school term (days)	Average number of days attended per enrolled pupil	Number	Percent of population 17 years old
		Total		Kindergarten and grades 1 to 8	Grades 9 to 12 and post-graduates					
		Number	Percent of population 5 to 17 years old							
	223	224	225	226	227	228	229	230	231	232	233
1956	35,872,203	31,162,843	83.6	24,290,257	6,872,586	4,709,360	27,740,149	178.0	158.5	1,414,800	62.3
1954	33,175,215	28,836,052	83.5	22,545,807	6,290,245	4,339,163	25,643,871	178.6	158.9	1,276,100	60.0
1952	30,372,028	26,562,664	84.7	20,680,867	5,881,797	3,809,364	23,256,523	178.2	156.0	1,196,500	58.6
1950	28,491,566	25,111,427	81.6	19,386,806	5,724,621	3,380,139	22,284,000	177.9	157.9	1,199,700	59.0
1948	26,998,446	23,944,532	79.4	18,291,227	5,653,305	3,053,914	20,910,000	177.6	155.1	1,189,909	54.0
1946	26,124,441	23,299,941	80.5	17,677,744	5,622,197	2,824,500	19,848,507	176.8	150.6	1,080,033	47.9
1944	25,757,907	23,266,616	80.4	17,713,096	5,553,520	2,491,291	19,602,772	175.5	147.9	1,019,233	42.3
1942	27,179,002	24,562,473	84.2	18,174,668	6,387,805	2,616,529	21,031,322	174.7	149.6	1,242,375	51.2
1940	28,044,589	25,433,542	85.3	18,832,098	6,601,444	2,611,047	22,042,151	175.0	151.7	1,221,475	50.8
1938	28,662,591	25,975,108	84.4	19,748,174	6,226,934	2,687,483	22,298,200	173.9	149.3	1,120,079	45.6
1936	29,005,873	26,367,098	83.4	20,392,561	5,974,537	2,638,775	22,298,767	173.0	146.3	1,015,345	....
1934	29,162,732	26,434,193	81.6	20,765,037	5,669,156	2,728,539	22,458,190	171.6	145.8	914,853	....
1932	29,061,403	26,275,441	82.0	21,135,420	5,140,021	2,785,962	22,245,344	171.2	144.9	826,991	....
1930	28,329,059	25,678,015	81.3	21,278,593	4,399,422	2,651,044	21,264,886	172.7	143.0	666,904	29.0
1928	27,810,309	25,179,696	81.5	21,268,417	3,911,279	2,630,613	20,608,353	171.5	140.4	596,655	....
1926	27,180,193	24,741,468	82.3	20,984,002	3,757,466	2,438,725	19,855,881	169.3	135.9	561,469	....
1924	26,016,072	24,288,808	82.8	20,898,930	3,389,878	1,727,264	19,132,451	168.3	132.5	494,006	....
1922	24,820,100	23,239,227	81.2	20,366,218	2,873,009	1,580,873	18,432,213	164.0	130.6	357,000	....
1920	23,277,797	21,578,316	77.8	19,377,927	2,200,389	1,699,481	16,150,035	161.9	121.2	311,266	16.8
1918	22,515,917	20,853,516	75.3	18,919,695	1,933,821	1,662,401	15,548,914	160.7	119.8	285,047	....
1916	22,171,897	20,351,687	75.8	18,895,626	1,456,061	1,820,210	15,358,927	160.3	120.9	259,396	....
1915	21,474,344	19,704,209	74.6	18,375,225	1,328,984	1,770,135	14,985,900	159.4	121.2	239,728	....
1914	20,934,953	19,153,786	73.7	17,934,982	1,218,804	1,781,167	14,216,459	158.7	117.8	218,784	....
1913	20,347,796	18,609,040	72.7	17,474,269	1,134,771	1,738,756	13,613,656	158.1	115.6	199,783	....
1912	19,830,041	18,182,937	72.2	17,077,577	1,105,360	1,647,104	13,302,303	158.0	115.6	180,574	....
1911	19,636,348	18,035,118	72.5	17,050,441	984,677	1,601,230	12,871,980	156.8	111.8	167,918	....

* Statistics on education taken from *U.S. Bureau of the Census, Historical Statistics of the United States, Colonial Times to 1957* (Washington, D.C., U.S. Government Printing Office, 1960), pp. 207–210, 214.

Year											
1910	19,372,289	17,813,852	73.5	16,898,791	915,061	1,558,437	12,827,307	157.5	113.0	156,429	8.8
1909	18,994,876	17,506,175	72.2	16,664,902	841,273	1,488,701	12,684,837	155.3	112.6	141,574	
1908	18,608,023	17,061,962	69.3	16,291,506	770,456	1,547,061	12,154,172	154.1	109.8	128,654	
1907	18,200,182	16,890,818	69.6	16,139,737	751,081	1,309,364	11,925,672	151.8	107.3	127,194	
1906	18,055,625	16,641,970	70.4	15,919,278	722,692	1,413,655	11,712,300	150.6	106.0	125,860	
1905	17,806,168	16,468,300	70.3	15,788,598	679,702	1,337,868	11,481,531	150.9	105.2	119,329	
1904	17,560,258	16,256,038	70.6	15,620,230	635,808	1,304,220	11,318,256	146.7	102.1	111,736	
1903	17,205,084	16,009,361	70.1	15,417,148	592,213	1,195,723	11,054,502	147.2	101.7	105,231	
1902	17,125,976	15,917,385	71.5	15,366,774	550,611	1,208,591	11,064,164	144.7	100.6	99,277	
1901	17,072,410	15,702,517	71.7	15,160,787	541,730	1,369,893	10,716,094	143.7	98.0	97,221	
1900	16,854,832	15,503,110	72.4	14,983,859	519,251	1,351,722	10,632,772	144.3	99.0	94,883	6.4
1899	16,473,939	15,176,219	72.0	14,699,992	476,227	1,297,720	10,389,407	143.0	97.9	89,528	
1898	16,458,764	15,103,874	72.7	14,654,274	449,600	1,354,890	10,356,458	143.0	98.0	84,173	
1897	16,140,059	14,823,059	72.4	14,413,626	409,433	1,317,000	10,052,554	142.0	96.3	79,758	
1896	15,833,756	14,498,956	71.8	14,118,463	380,493	1,334,800	9,781,475	140.5	94.8	75,813	
1895	15,454,985	14,243,765	71.5	13,893,666	350,099	1,211,220	9,548,722	139.5	93.5	72,019	
1894	15,314,157	13,995,357	71.3	13,706,083	289,274	1,318,800	9,187,505	139.5	91.6	65,320	
1893	14,826,168	13,483,340	69.7	13,229,317	254,023	1,342,828	8,855,717	136.3	89.6	59,178	
1892	14,555,521	13,255,921	69.5	13,016,365	239,556	1,299,600	8,560,603	136.9	88.4	53,039	
1891	14,540,732	13,050,132	69.4	12,838,536	211,596	1,490,600	8,329,234	135.7	86.6	48,380	
1890	14,479,409	12,722,581	68.6	12,519,618	202,963	1,756,828	8,153,635	134.7	86.3	43,731	3.5
1889	13,660,821	12,392,260	68.2			1,268,561	8,005,969	133.7	86.4	38,516	
1888		12,182,600	68.3				7,906,986	132.3	85.9	33,301	
1887		11,884,944	68.0				7,681,806	131.3	84.9	32,146	
1886		11,664,460	68.1				7,526,351	130.4	84.1	32,997	
1885		11,398,024	68.0				7,297,529	130.7	83.6	32,468	
1884		10,982,364	67.0				7,055,696	129.1	82.9	30,962	
1883		10,651,828	66.4				6,652,392	129.8	81.1	28,348	
1882		10,211,578	65.0				6,331,242	131.2	81.3	27,151	
1881		10,000,896	65.0				6,145,932	130.1	80.0	24,954	
1880	9,867,505		65.5	9,757,228	110,277		6,144,143	130.3	81.1	23,634	2.5
1879	9,504,458		64.6				5,876,077	130.2	80.5	23,128	
1878	9,438,883		65.7				5,783,065	132.0	80.9	21,939	
1877	8,965,006		63.9				5,426,595	132.1	80.0	20,693	
1876	8,869,115		64.7				5,291,376	133.1	79.4	20,448	
1875	8,785,678		65.5				5,248,114	130.4	77.9	19,707	
1874	8,444,251		64.4				5,050,840	128.8	77.0	18,966	
1873	8,003,614		62.4				4,745,459	129.1	76.5	18,225	
1872	7,815,306		62.2				4,658,844	133.4	79.5	17,483	
1871	7,561,582		61.5				4,545,317	132.1	79.4	16,741	
1870	6,871,522	7,481,355	57.0		80,227		4,077,347	132.2	78.4	16,000	2.0

¹ Partially estimated. Includes enrollment in regular public and nonpublic day schools. Excludes pupils enrolled in residential schools for exceptional children, sub-collegiate departments of institutions of higher education, and Federal schools.

² Partially estimated.

³ Includes graduates from public and nonpublic schools. Nonpublic graduates are partially estimated.

Public Elementary and Secondary Day Schools' Instructional Staff, School Districts, and Schools: 1870 to 1956

School year ending—	Total	Average annual salary [1]	Instructional staff			Principals	Other supervisors or consultants	School districts	Schools			One-teacher public schools
			Classroom teachers and other nonsupervisory staff [2]						Total	Public	Private	
			Total	Male	Female							
	234	235	236	237	238	239	240	241	242	243	244	245
1956	1,213,459	4,156	1,149,223	[3]294,170	[3]838,923	50,973	13,263	54,773	146,782	130,478	16,259	34,964
1954	1,098,820	3,825	1,042,313	[3]253,518	[3]778,620	45,729	10,278	62,969	152,164	136,512	15,652	42,825
1952	1,012,884	3,450	962,864	234,942	727,922	39,695	9,825	70,993	161,497	147,509	13,988	50,742
1950	962,174	3,010	913,671	194,968	718,703	39,314	9,189	83,614	166,473	152,767	13,706	59,652
1948	907,013	2,639	860,678	161,913	698,765	37,144	9,191	94,817	185,607	172,244	13,363	75,096
1946	867,248	1,995	831,026	138,209	692,817	29,416	6,806	[4]101,273	197,698	184,541	13,157	86,563
1944	865,038	1,728	827,990	126,672	701,318	31,569	5,479	111,274	212,174	198,878	13,296	96,302
1942	898,001	1,507	858,888	183,194	675,694	33,057	6,056	115,384	221,531	208,235	13,296	107,692
1940	911,835	1,441	875,477	194,725	680,752	31,521	4,837	116,999	238,169	223,295	14,874	113,600
1938	918,715	1,374	877,266	185,103	692,163	36,484	4,965	118,892	260,446	247,127	13,319	121,178
1936	906,376	1,283	870,963	179,073	691,890	29,570	5,843	....	271,145	257,826	13,319	131,101
1934	880,226	1,227	847,120	161,949	685,171	28,068	5,038	....	274,269	260,950	13,319	139,166
1932	901,204	1,417	871,607	153,861	717,746	23,910	5,687	127,422	272,182	259,159	13,023	143,391
1930	892,027	1,420	854,263	141,771	712,492	30,876	6,888	....	274,769	262,236	12,533	149,282
1928	868,422	1,364	831,934	138,193	693,741	28,829	7,659	....	....	....	....	156,066
1926	849,502	1,277	814,169	138,810	675,359	26,933	8,400	....	....	....	....	162,756
1924	787,113	1,227	761,808	128,731	632,577	17,881	7,924	....	....	....	....	169,718
1922	755,698	1,166	722,976	118,085	604,891	18,616	14,106	....	....	....	....	180,762
1920	699,754	871	[5]679,533	95,654	563,648	13,638	6,583	....	....	....	....	190,655
1918	....	635	650,709	105,194	545,515	....	....	....	....	....	....	196,037
1916	....	563	622,371	123,038	499,333	....	....	....	....	....	....	[6]200,094

470

Instructional staff

School year ending	Average annual salary [1] (235)	Classroom teachers and other nonsupervisory staff [2]		
		Total (236)	Male (237)	Female (238)
1915	543	604,301	118,449	485,852
1914	525	580,058	114,662	465,396
1913	512	565,483	113,213	452,270
1912	492	547,289	114,559	432,730
1911	466	533,606	110,328	423,278
1910	485	523,210	110,481	412,729
1909	....	506,453	108,300	398,153
1908	....	495,463	104,495	390,968
1907	....	481,316	104,414	376,902
1906	....	466,063	109,179	356,884
1905	386	460,269	110,532	349,737
1904	....	455,242	113,744	341,498
1903	....	449,287	117,035	332,252
1902	....	441,819	120,883	320,936
1901	....	431,918	125,838	306,080
1900	325	423,062	126,588	296,474
1899	....	414,272	131,207	283,065
1898	....	410,813	132,257	278,556
1897	....	404,958	131,221	273,737
1896	....	400,296	130,373	269,923
1895	286	398,042	129,706	268,336
1894	....	388,949	125,402	263,547
1893	....	383,010	122,056	260,954

Instructional staff

School year ending	Average annual salary [1] (235)	Classroom teachers and other nonsupervisory staff [2]		
		Total (236)	Male (237)	Female (238)
1892	....	374,226	121,573	252,653
1891	....	368,388	128,360	245,028
1890	252	363,922	125,525	238,897
1889	....	356,577	124,467	232,110
1888	....	347,134	126,240	220,894
1887	....	339,460	127,093	212,367
1886	....	331,393	123,792	207,601
1885	224	325,916	121,762	204,154
1884	....	314,015	118,905	195,110
1883	....	304,389	116,388	188,001
1882	....	299,079	118,892	180,187
1881	....	293,860	122,511	171,349
1880	195	286,593	122,795	163,798
1879	....	280,330	121,490	158,840
1878	....	277,147	119,404	157,743
1877	....	267,050	114,312	152,738
1876	....	259,618	109,780	149,838
1875	....	257,865	108,791	149,074
1874	....	248,447	103,465	144,982
1873	....	237,513	97,790	139,723
1872	....	229,921	94,992	134,929
1871	....	220,225	90,293	129,932
1870	189	200,515	77,529	122,986

[1] Computed for teaching positions only, prior to 1920; beginning 1920, also includes supervisors and principals.
[2] Prior to 1938, number of different persons employed rather than number of positions. Includes librarians and guidance and psychological personnel.
[3] Classroom teachers only. Excludes other nonsupervisory instructional staff.
[4] Excludes 1,840 districts in Texas "in legal existence" which do not operate schools.
[5] Includes 231 part-time teachers not classified by sex.
[6] Partially estimated.

Public Elementary and Secondary Schools' Receipts, by Source: 1890 to 1956

[In thousands of dollars]

School year ending—	Total (revenue and non-revenue)	Sources of revenue receipts				
		Total[1]	Federal	State[2]	Local[3]	Other
	246	247	248	249	250	251
1956	12,042,866	9,686,677	441,442	8,828,886	5,894,059	22,291
1954	9,690,856	7,866,852	355,237	2,944,103	4,547,254	20,258
1952	7,636,884	6,423,816	227,711	2,478,596	3,716,421	1,086
1950	6,401,022	5,437,004	155,849	2,165,689	3,115,386	121
1948	4,869,431	4,811,534	120,270	1,676,362	2,514,572	330
1946	3,318,173	3,059,845	41,378	1,062,057	1,956,156	254
1944	2,699,076	2,604,322	35,886	859,183	1,708,980	274
1942	2,593,959	2,416,580	34,305	759,993	1,622,035	246
1940	2,521,470	2,260,527	39,810	684,354	1,536,069	294
1938	2,492,598	2,222,885	26,535	655,996	1,540,053	300
1936	[4]2,178,106	[4]1,971,402	[4]9,850	578,369	1,382,889	294
1934	1,940,251	1,810,652	21,548	423,178	1,365,554	372
1932	2,229,423	2,068,029	8,262	410,550	1,648,687	530
1930	2,469,311	2,088,557	7,334	353,670	1,726,709	844
1928	2,324,708	2,025,750	6,174	333,279	1,685,330	967
1926	2,171,845	1,830,017	5,552	284,569	1,539,896	....
1924	1,958,529	1,618,438	3,986	261,997	1,290,239	....
1922	1,743,192	1,444,242	2,891	230,517	1,184,530	....
1920	1,155,507	970,120	2,475	160,085	807,561	....
1918	802,613	736,876	1,669	122,256	612,951	....
1916	....	633,901	....	95,278	488,120	....
1915	....	589,652	....	91,104	456,956	....
1914	....	561,743	....	87,895	425,457	....
1913	....	507,227	....	78,376	375,582	....

472

Year						
1912	....	....	469,111	....	75,814	346,898
1911	....	....	451,151	....	69,071	333,832
1910	....	....	433,064	....	64,605	312,222
1909	....	....	403,647	....	63,547	288,643
1908	....	....	381,920	....	58,097	259,341
1907	....	....	355,016	....	44,706	231,738
1906	....	....	322,106	....	47,948	228,491
1905	....	....	301,819	....	44,349	210,168
1904	....	....	279,134	....	42,558	193,216
1903	....	....	251,637	....	40,456	173,731
1902	....	....	245,498	....	39,216	173,151
1901	....	....	235,839	....	36,281	163,897
1900	....	....	219,766	....	37,887	149,487
1899	....	....	203,337	....	35,341	144,893
1898	....	....	199,833	....	35,122	185,516
1897	....	....	191,959	....	33,942	180,318
1896	....	....	182,480	....	35,082	124,880
1895	....	....	176,565	....	34,638	118,915
1894	....	....	170,404	....	32,750	112,785
1893	....	....	165,023	....	38,695	108,425
1892	....	....	157,175	....	29,908	105,630
1891	....	....	147,915	....	27,682	100,359
1890	....	....	143,195	....	26,345	97,222

[1] For 1922, 1924, and years prior to 1918, includes receipts undistributed by source.

[2] Prior to 1913, excludes receipts from sources other than State taxes and appropriations.

[3] Includes county and other intermediate sources of income. Prior to 1918, excludes receipts from sources other than local taxes and appropriations.

[4] Includes only Federal aid for vocational education.

Public Elementary and Secondary Schools' Expenditures by Purpose: 1870 to 1956

[In thousands of dollars, except as noted]

School year ending —	Total expenditures for all schools	Current expenditures for day schools						Capital outlay	Interest	Other expenditures [5]
		Total [1]		Administration	Instruction [3]	Plant operation and maintenance	Other [4]			
		Amount	Per pupil in average daily attendance [2]							
	252	253	254	255	256	257	258	259	260	261
1956	10,955,047	8,251,420	294.22	372,956	5,501,921	1,072,299	1,304,244	2,387,187	215,699	100,743
1954	9,092,449	6,790,923	264.76	310,995	4,552,349	907,542	1,020,037	2,055,178	153,884	92,464
1952	7,344,237	5,722,162	244.24	265,636	3,781,837	757,249	917,440	1,477,332	114,310	30,432
1950	5,837,643	4,687,274	208.83	220,050	3,112,340	641,751	713,132	1,014,176	100,578	35,614
1948	4,311,176	3,794,702	179.43	169,999	2,571,539	526,164	526,999	412,467	76,331	27,676
1946	2,906,886	2,707,441	136.41	132,899	1,853,911	371,535	349,097	111,046	76,923	11,477
1944	2,452,581	2,293,337	116.99	110,631	1,590,634	316,098	275,975	53,856	96,805	8,583
1942	2,322,698	2,067,660	98.31	101,463	1,457,877	288,651	219,670	137,552	108,781	8,704
1940	2,344,049	1,941,799	88.09	91,571	1,403,285	267,687	179,257	257,974	130,909	13,367
1938	2,233,110	1,870,090	83.87	86,441	1,359,704	260,168	163,777	238,853	114,102	10,065
1936	1,968,898	1,656,799	74.30	67,436	1,214,363	233,264	141,736	171,322	132,983	7,794
1934	1,720,105	1,515,530	67.48	64,093	1,120,874	203,477	127,086	59,277	137,037	8,262
1932	2,174,651	1,809,939	81.36	74,910	1,333,332	257,424	144,273	210,996	140,235	13,480
1930	2,316,790	1,843,552	86.70	78,680	1,317,727	294,882	152,263	370,878	92,536	9,825
1928	2,184,337	1,705,538	82.76	77,266	1,219,820	278,367	130,085	382,996	92,025	3,778
1926	2,026,308	1,537,874	77.45	68,426	1,127,009	243,510	98,929	411,038	71,901	5,495
1924	1,820,744	1,368,584	71.53	54,753	1,001,356	220,951	91,523	388,469	58,963	4,729
1922	1,580,671	1,234,669	66.98	51,327	903,474	202,785	69,266	305,941	35,788	4,273
1920	1,036,151	861,120	53.52	36,752	632,555	146,139	45,673	153,543	18,212	3,277
1918	763,678	629,441	40.48	25,179	444,138	132,958	27,165	119,083	15,155	....
1916	640,717	537,210	34.98	15,483	377,841	....	143,886	103,507	....	....
1915	605,461	502,704	33.55	13,499	358,210	....	130,995	102,756	....	....
1914	555,077	463,471	32.60	12,428	335,489	....	115,554	91,606	....	....
1913	521,546	437,941	32.17	9,948	315,909	....	112,083	83,606	....	....
1912	482,887	404,868	30.44	8,577	294,857	....	101,434	78,019	....	....
1911	446,727	371,171	28.84	6,266	273,483	....	91,422	75,556	....	....
1910	426,250	356,272	27.85	6,827	260,179	....	89,265	69,978	....	....
1909	401,398	319,519	25.19	....	237,014	....	82,505	81,879	....	....
1908	371,344	297,704	24.49	....	219,780	....	77,924	73,640	....	....
1907	336,898	271,565	22.77	....	202,048	....	69,517	65,333	....	....
1906	307,766	247,158	21.10	....	186,483	....	60,674	60,608	....	....

474

Year						
1905	291,617	235,201	20.49	177,463	57,738	56,416
1904	273,216	223,763	19.77	167,825	55,938	49,453
1903	251,458	205,169	18.56	157,110	48,058	46,289
1902	238,262	198,299	17.92	151,444	46,856	39,963
1901	227,523	187,651	17.51	143,379	44,272	39,872
1900	214,965	179,514	16.67	137,688	41,826	35,451
1899	200,155	168,926	16.26	129,346	39,579	31,229
1898	194,293	162,878	15.73	124,192	38,685	31,415
1897	187,682	155,306	15.45	119,311	35,995	32,376
1896	183,499	150,909	15.43	117,140	33,769	32,590
1895	175,809	146,372	15.33	113,872	32,500	29,437
1894	172,503	142,495	15.51	109,202	33,293	30,008
1893	164,171	133,877	15.12	104,560	29,317	30,294
1892	155,817	126,472	14.77	100,298	26,174	29,345
1891	147,495	121,047	14.53	96,303	24,744	26,448
1890	140,507	114,300	13.99	91,836	22,463	26,207
1889	132,540	109,144	13.63	87,568	21,576	23,396
1888	124,245			83,023		
1887	115,784			78,640		
1886	113,323			76,270		
1885	110,328			72,879		
1884	103,213			68,384		
1883	96,750			64,799		
1882	88,990			60,595		
1881	83,643			58,012		
1880	78,095			55,943		
1879	76,192			54,640		
1878	79,083			56,155		
1877	79,440			54,974		
1876	83,083			55,358		
1875	83,504			54,722		
1874	80,054			50,786		
1873	76,238			47,932		
1872	74,234			45,936		
1871	69,108			42,581		
1870	63,397			37,833		

[1] Prior to 1918, includes expenditures for interest.

[2] In dollars. For 1948–1956, excludes expenditures not allocated to pupil costs.

[3] Prior to 1910, includes only expenditures for salaries of teachers and superintendents.

[4] Prior to 1918, includes plant operation and maintenance; prior to 1910, includes all current expenditures except salaries of teachers and superintendents.

[5] Beginning 1954, includes expenditures for community services, previously included in "current expenditures for day schools."

Public Secondary Day School Pupils Enrolled in Specified Subjects: 1890 to 1949

[In percents. Figures cover enrollment in last 4 years of school. For school years ending in year indicated]

Series No.	Specified subject	1949	1934	1928	1922	1915	1910	1900	1890
262	Total enrollment	5,399,452	4,496,514	2,896,630	2,155,460	1,165,495	739,143	519,251	202,963
263	English	92.9	90.5	93.1	76.7	58.4	57.1	88.5	
264	Journalism	1.9	0.7	0.2	0.1				
265	Radio speaking and broadcasting	0.1							
266	United States history	22.8	17.3	17.9	15.3	[2] 50.5	[2] 55.0	[2] 38.2	[2] 27.3
267	English history	(1)	0.5	0.9	2.9				
268	World history	16.2	11.9	6.1					
269	Civil government	8.0	6.0	6.6	19.3	15.7	15.6	21.7	
270	Community government	(3)	10.4	13.4					
271	Geography	5.6	2.1	0.3					
272	Problems of democracy	5.2	3.5	1.0					
273	Economics	4.7	4.9	5.1	4.8				
274	Sociology	3.4	2.5	2.7	2.4				
275	Psychology	0.9	0.3	1.0	0.9				
276	Consumer education	0.7				1.2	1.0	2.4	
277	General science	20.8	17.8	17.5	18.3		1.1		
278	Biology	18.4	14.6	13.6	8.8	6.9			
279	Botany	0.1	0.9	1.6	3.8	9.1	15.8		
280	Physiology	1.0	1.8	2.7	5.1	9.5	15.3	27.4	
281	Zoology	0.1	0.6	0.8	1.5	3.2	6.9		
282	Earth science	0.4	1.7	2.8	4.5	15.3	21.0	29.8	
283	Chemistry	7.6	7.6	7.1	7.4	7.4	6.9	7.7	10.1
284	Physics	5.4	6.3	6.8	8.9	14.2	14.6	19.0	22.8

No.	Subject								
285	Algebra	26.8	30.4	35.2	40.2	48.8	56.9	56.3	45.4
286	General mathematics	13.1	7.4	7.9	12.4				
287	Geometry	12.8	17.1	19.8	22.7	26.5	30.9	27.4	21.3
288	Trigonometry	2.0	1.3	1.3	1.5	1.5	1.9	1.9	
289	Spanish	8.2	6.2	9.4	11.3	2.7	0.7		
290	Latin	7.8	16.0	22.0	27.5	37.3	49.0	50.6	34.7
291	French	4.7	10.9	14.0	15.5	8.8	9.9	7.8	5.8
292	German	0.8	2.4	1.8	0.6	24.4	23.7	14.3	10.5
293	Italian	0.3	0.2	0.1					
294	Portuguese	(¹)			(¹)				
295	Russian	(¹)							
296	Industrial subjects	26.6	21.0	13.5	13.7	11.2			
297	General business training	5.2	6.2	3.0					
298	Business arithmetic	4.6	4.9	6.9	1.5				
299	Bookkeeping	8.7	9.9	10.7	12.6	3.4			
300	Typewriting	22.5	16.7	15.2	13.1				
301	Shorthand	7.8	9.0	8.7	8.9				
302	Business law	2.4	3.2	2.6	0.9				
303	Business English	1.0	0.9	0.5					
304	Economic geography	1.7	4.0	4.8	1.7				
305	Office practice	2.0	1.8	1.5	0.4				
306	Retailing	0.5							
307	Salesmanship and advertising	1.0	0.7	0.4	0.8				
308	Cooperative office training	0.4							
309	Cooperative store training	0.3							
310	Home economics	24.2	16.7	16.5	14.3	12.9	3.8		
311	Agriculture	6.7	3.6	3.7	5.1	7.2	4.7		
312	Physical education	69.4	50.7	15.0	5.7				
313	Music	30.1	25.5	26.0	25.3	31.5			
314	Art	9.0	8.7	11.7	14.7	22.9			
315	Teacher training	(¹)	0.1	1.8	1.0				

¹ Less than 0.05 percent, or fewer than 1 pupil in 2,000.   ² Includes ancient history and medieval and modern history.   ³ Comparable data for 1949 not available.

Institutions of Higher Education—Number, Faculty, and Enrollment: 1922 to 1956

School year ending—	Number of institutions	All institutions										Junior colleges	
		Faculty			Resident instructional staff	Enrollment (1,000)					Number	Enrollment (1,000)
		Total				Total		Under-graduate	Graduate			
		Both sexes	Male	Female		Number	Percent of population 18 to 21 years old					
	316	317	318	319	320	321	322	323	324		325	326
1956	1,850	298,910	230,342	68,568	228,188	2,637	....	2,387	250		....	....
1954	1,863	265,911	204,871	61,040	207,365	2,200	29.90	1,977	223		495	325
1952	1,832	244,488	187,136	57,352	183,758	2,302	26.78	2,069	233		480	230
1950	1,851	246,722	186,189	60,533	190,353	2,659	29.88	2,422	237		483	243
1948	1,788	223,660	164,616	59,044	174,204	2,616	28.87	2,442	174		472	240
1946	1,768	165,324	116,134	49,190	125,811	1,677	20.84	1,556	121		464	156
1944	1,650	150,980	106,254	44,726	105,841	1,155	12.78	1,100	59		413	89
1942	1,720	151,066	109,309	41,757	114,693	1,404	14.68	1,819	85		461	141
1940	1,708	146,929	106,328	40,601	110,885	1,494	15.68	1,388	106		456	150
1938	1,690	135,989	97,362	38,627	102,895	1,351	13.96	1,270	91		453	122
1936	1,628	121,036	86,567	34,469	92,580	1,208	12.60	1,129	79		415	102
1934	1,418	108,873	78,369	30,504	86,914	1,055	11.20	964	71		322	78
1932	1,460	100,789	71,680	29,109	88,172	1,154	12.62	1,028	78		342	85
1930	1,409	82,386	60,017	22,369	82,386	1,101	12.42	1,054	47		277	56
1928	1,415	....	....	....	76,080	1,054	12.13	....	....		248	45
1926	1,377	....	....	....	70,674	941	11.27	....	....		153	27
1924	....	....	....	....	63,999	823	10.27	....	....		132	21
1922	....	....	....	....	56,486	681	8.87	....	....		80	12

School Enrollment, by Age: 1910 to 1957

[Number in thousands. Figures for 1945–1957 are estimates based on Current Population Survey sample, except for 1950 Census data which are based on 20-percent sample]

Year	Total, 5 to 19 years			5 to 13 years			14 to 17 years			18 and 19 years		
	Population	Enrolled		Population	Enrolled		Population	Enrolled		Population	Enrolled	
		Number	Percent		Number	Percent		Number	Percent		Number	Percent
	383	384	385	386	387	388	389	390	391	392	393	394
CURRENT POPULATION SURVEY												
1957	44,407	39,010	87.8	30,231	28,534	94.4	10,134	9,067	89.5	4,042	1,409	34.9
1956	42,832	37,863	87.2	29,314	27,543	94.0	9,540	8,413	88.2	3,978	1,407	35.4
1955	41,342	35,750	86.5	28,268	26,548	93.9	9,169	7,970	86.9	3,905	1,282	31.5
1954	39,972	34,448	86.2	27,118	25,396	93.6	8,936	7,784	87.1	3,918	1,268	32.4
1953	38,445	32,934	85.7	25,885	24,216	93.6	8,775	7,538	85.9	3,785	1,180	31.2
1952	36,972	31,158	84.3	24,643	22,756	92.3	8,631	7,341	85.1	3,698	1,061	28.7
1951	35,398	29,705	83.9	23,171	21,513	92.8	8,458	7,201	85.1	3,769	991	26.3
1950	34,722	28,859	83.1	22,330	20,716	92.8	8,351	6,953	83.3	4,041	1,190	29.4
1949	34,850	28,659	82.2	22,486	20,853	92.7	8,302	6,778	81.6	4,062	1,028	25.8
1948	34,320	27,969	81.5	21,769	20,011	91.9	8,342	6,824	81.8	4,209	1,134	26.9
1947	33,446	26,950	80.6	20,817	19,206	92.3	8,492	6,737	79.8	4,137	1,007	24.3
1946	32,705	25,780	78.8	20,117	17,996	89.5	8,666	6,900	79.6	3,922	884	22.5
1945	31,835	25,204	79.2	19,725	17,580	89.1	8,878	6,956	78.4	3,232	668	20.7
DECENNIAL CENSUS												
1950	35,092	27,605	78.7	22,305	19,136	85.8	8,443	7,068	83.7	4,344	1,401	32.3
1940	34,764	25,998	74.8	20,025	16,840	84.1	9,720	7,709	79.3	5,019	1,449	28.9
1930	36,165	26,558	73.4	22,230	18,567	83.5	9,341	6,826	73.1	4,593	1,165	25.4
1920	31,470	21,226	67.4	19,993	15,791	79.0	7,736	4,768	61.6	3,741	666	17.8
1910	27,931	17,491	62.6	17,020	12,552	73.7	7,220	4,250	58.9	3,691	689	18.7

Median Years of School Completed, by Age, Sex, and Color: 1940 and 1950

[Statistics for 1950 are estimates based on 20-percent sample; 1940 from a complete count]

Series No.	Age	Total		Male						Female					
				All classes		White		Nonwhite		All classes		White		Nonwhite	
		1950	1940	1950	1940	1950	1940	1950	1940	1950	1940	1950	1940	1950	1940
395	Total, 25 and over	9.3	8.6	9.0	8.6	9.3	8.7	6.4	5.4	9.6	8.7	10.0	8.8	7.2	6.1
396	25 to 29 years......	12.1	10.3	12.0	10.1	12.4	10.5	8.4	6.5	12.1	10.5	12.2	10.9	8.9	7.5
397	30 to 34 years......	11.6	9.5	11.4	9.2	11.9	9.7	7.8	6.2	11.8	9.9	12.1	10.3	8.4	7.0
398	35 to 39 years......	10.7	8.8	10.3	8.7	10.7	8.8	7.1	5.8	10.7	8.9	11.2	9.1	7.8	6.5
399	40 to 44 years......	9.8	8.6	9.4	8.6	9.9	8.7	6.5	5.5	10.1	8.7	10.5	8.8	7.2	6.1
400	45 to 49 years......	8.9	8.5	8.9	8.4	8.9	8.5	6.0	5.2	9.0	8.5	9.5	8.6	6.7	5.7
401	50 to 54 years......	8.7	8.4	8.6	8.3	8.7	8.4	5.6	4.8	8.8	8.4	8.9	8.5	6.1	5.2
402	55 to 59 years......	8.5	8.3	8.4	8.2	8.5	8.3	5.1	4.6	8.6	8.4	8.7	8.5	5.8	4.9
403	60 to 64 years......	8.4	8.3	8.3	8.2	8.3	8.3	4.7	4.3	8.4	8.3	8.5	8.4	5.3	4.5
404	65 to 69 years......	8.2	8.2	8.1	8.1	8.2	8.2	4.0	3.7	8.3	8.2	8.4	8.3	4.5	3.8
405	70 to 74 years......	8.2	8.1	8.0	8.0	8.1	8.1	3.9	2.9	8.3	8.2	8.4	8.3	4.2	2.8
406	75 years and over	8.1	8.0	7.9	7.7	8.1	8.0	3.1	1.5	8.2	8.1	8.3	8.2	3.4	1.0

Percent Illiterate in the Population, by Color and Nativity: 1870 to 1952

[Data for 1870 to 1940 are for population 10 years old and over; data for 1947, 1950, and 1952 are for population 14 years old and over]

Year	Total	White			Non-white
		Total	Native	Foreign born	
	407	408	409	410	411
1952	2.5	1.8	(¹)	(¹)	10.2
1950	²3.2	(¹)	(¹)	(¹)	(¹)
1947	2.7	1.8	(¹)	(¹)	11.0
1940	2.9	2.0	1.1	9.0	11.5
1930	4.3	3.0	1.6	10.8	16.4
1920	6.0	4.0	2.0	13.1	23.0
1910	7.7	5.0	3.0	12.7	30.5
1900	10.7	6.2	4.6	12.9	44.5
1890	13.3	7.7	6.2	13.1	56.8
1880	17.0	9.4	8.7	12.0	70.0
1870	20.0	11.5	(¹)	(¹)	79.9

¹ Not available.
² See source, pp. 6 and 7, for an explanation of the estimating procedure used to obtain this figure and a possible explanation as to why it is somewhat higher than others in recent years.

INDEX

C D E F G H I J   5 4 3 2 1 7 0 6 9 8

ABOUT THE AUTHOR

David Tyack is Associate Professor of History of Education at the University of Illinois. After receiving his A.B., A.M.T., and Ph.D. from Harvard University, he served there as Instructor in education and history from 1958 to 1959. During 1959 to 1966 he taught history of education and American intellectual history at Reed College and directed Reed's Master of Arts in Teaching program. He is the author of *George Ticknor and the Boston Brahmins* (Harvard University Press, 1967) as well as several articles on the history of education and on the education of teachers.

THIS BOOK WAS SET IN

JANSON TYPEFACE BY THE

PLIMPTON PRESS.

IT WAS DESIGNED BY THE STAFF OF

BLAISDELL PUBLISHING COMPANY.